THE ANNOTATED LUTHER

Volume 1

The Roots of Reform

Additional Praise for *The Roots of Reform*

"The advent of The Annotated Luther series should be cause for celebration among scholars, pastors, students, and others eager to have easy access to so many of Martin Luther's key writings. If the appealing layout, rich images, and erudite editorials featured in Volume 1 are an indication of what's to come, then The Annotated Luther will quickly become *the* go-to resource for learning about Luther's work and context."

> **—Hans Wiersma** | Augsburg College

"As congregations and members of congregations face an increasingly more diverse and chaotic world, their struggle for what it means to be Christian in their context increases, not unlike Christians in Luther's day. I am thrilled that Fortress Press is publishing The Annotated Luther, Volume I: *The Roots of Reform*. The individual works included in this volume are central to the particular witness Lutherans can share for a life of faith in the world and how it can be a witness of hope in the midst of pluralism and change. The essays and study tools, included alongside the original texts, bring these works to life for us today. I encourage you to include this series in your congregation's library and use it for group or personal study."

> **—The Rev. Gordon J. Straw** | Program Director
> for Lay Schools for Ministry,
> Congregational and Synodical Mission Unit, ELCA

THE ANNOTATED LUTHER

Volume 1
The Roots of Reform

VOLUME EDITOR
Timothy J. Wengert

GENERAL EDITORS
Hans J. Hillerbrand
Kirsi I. Stjerna
Timothy J. Wengert

Fortress Press
Minneapolis

THE ANNOTATED LUTHER, Volume 1
The Roots of Reform

Fortress Press Publication Staff: Scott Tunseth, Project Editor; Marissa Wold Uhrina, Production Manager; Laurie Ingram, Cover Design; Esther Diley, Permissions.

Copyeditor: David Lott
Series design and typesetting: Ann Delgehausen, Trio Bookworks
Proofreader: Laura Weller

Library of Congress Cataloging-in-Publication Data
Luther, Martin, 1483-1546.
 [Works. Selections. English (Wengert)]
 The roots of reform / volume editor, Timothy J. Wengert ; general editors, Hans J. Hillerbrand, Kirsi I. Stjerna, Timothy J. Wengert.
    pages cm.—(The annotated Luther ; Volume 1)
 Includes bibliographical references and index.
 ISBN 978-1-4514-6269-2 (alk. paper)—ISBN 978-1-4514-6535-8
 1. Reformation. 2. Theology—Early works to 1800. I. Wengert, Timothy J., editor. II. Title.
 BR331.E5 2015
 230'.41—dc23

                                                              2015021161

Print ISBN: 978-1-4514-6269-2
eISBN: 978-1-4514-6535-8

Contents

Series Introduction

Engaging the Essential Luther

Even after five hundred years Martin Luther continues to engage and challenge each new generation of scholars and believers alike. With 2017 marking the five-hundredth anniversary of Luther's *95 Theses*, Luther's theology and legacy are being explored around the world with new questions and methods and by diverse voices. His thought invites ongoing examination, his writings are a staple in classrooms and pulpits, and he speaks to an expanding assortment of conversation partners who use different languages and hale from different geographical and social contexts.

The six volumes of The Annotated Luther edition offer a flexible tool for the global reader of Luther, making many of his most important writings available in the *lingua franca* of our times as one way of facilitating interest in the Wittenberg reformer. They feature new introductions, annotations, revised translations, and textual notes, as well as visual enhancements (illustrations, art, photos, maps, and timelines). The Annotated Luther edition embodies Luther's own cherished principles of communication. Theological writing, like preaching, needs to reflect human beings' lived experience, benefits from up-to-date scholarship, and should be easily accessible to all. These volumes are designed to help teachers and students, pastors and laypersons, and other professionals in ministry understand the context in which the documents were written, recognize how the documents have shaped Protestant and Lutheran thinking, and interpret the meaning of these documents for faith and life today.

The Rationale for This Edition

For any reader of Luther, the sheer number of his works presents a challenge. Well over one hundred volumes comprise the scholarly edition of Luther's works, the so-called Weimar Ausgabe (WA), a publishing enterprise begun in 1883 and only completed in the twenty-first century. From 1955 to 1986, fifty-five volumes came to make up *Luther's Works* (American Edition) (LW), to which Concordia Publishing House, St. Louis, is adding still more. This English-language contribution to Luther studies, matched by similar translation projects for Erasmus of Rotterdam and John Calvin, provides a theological and historical gold mine for those interested in studying Luther's thought. But even these volumes are not always easy to use and are hardly portable. Electronic forms have increased availability, but preserving Luther in book form and providing readers with manageable selections are also important goals.

Moreover, since the publication of the WA and the first fifty-five volumes of the LW, research on the Reformation in general and on Martin Luther in particular has broken new ground and evolved, as has knowledge regarding the languages in which Luther wrote. Up-to-date information from a variety of sources is brought together in The Annotated Luther, building on the work done by previous generations of scholars. The language and phrasing of the translations have also been updated to reflect modern English usage. While the WA and, in a derivative way, LW remain the central source for Luther scholarship, the present critical and annotated English translation facilitates research internationally and invites a new generation of readers for whom Latin and German might prove an unsurpassable obstacle to accessing Luther. The WA provides the basic Luther texts (with some exceptions); the LW provides the basis for almost all translations.

Defining the "Essential Luther"

Deciding which works to include in this collection was not easy. Criteria included giving attention to Luther's initial key works; considering which publications had the most impact in his day and later; and taking account of Luther's own favorites, texts addressing specific issues of continued importance for today, and Luther's exegetical works. Taken as a whole, these works present the many sides of Luther, as reformer, pastor, biblical interpreter, and theologian. To serve today's readers and by using categories similar to those found in volumes 31–47 of Luther's works (published by Fortress Press), the volumes offer in the main a thematic rather than strictly chronological approach to Luther's writings. The volumes in the series include:

Volume 1: *The Roots of Reform* (Timothy J. Wengert, editor)
Volume 2: *Word and Faith* (Kirsi I. Stjerna, editor)
Volume 3: *Church and Sacraments* (Paul W. Robinson, editor)
Volume 4: *Pastoral Writings* (Mary Jane Haemig, editor)
Volume 5: *Christian Life in the World* (Hans J. Hillerbrand, editor)
Volume 6: *The Interpretation of Scripture* (Euan K. Cameron, editor)

The History of the Project

In 2011 Fortress Press convened an advisory board to explore the promise and parameters of a new English edition of Luther's essential works. Board members Denis Janz, Robert Kolb, Peter Matheson, Christine Helmer, and Kirsi Stjerna deliberated with Fortress Press publisher Will Bergkamp to develop a concept and identify contributors. After a review with scholars in the field, college and seminary professors, and pastors, it was concluded that a single-language edition was more desirable than dual-language volumes.

In August 2012, Hans Hillerbrand, Kirsi Stjerna, and Timothy Wengert were appointed as general editors of the series with Scott Tunseth from Fortress Press as the project editor. The general editors were tasked with determining the contents of the volumes and developing the working principles of the series. They also helped with the identification and recruitment of additional volume editors, who in turn worked with the general editors to identify volume contributors. Mastery of the languages and unique knowledge of the subject matter were key factors in identifying contributors. Most contributors are North American scholars and native English speakers, but The Annotated Luther includes among its contributors a circle of international scholars. Likewise, the series is offered for a global network of teachers and students in seminary, university, and college classes, as well as pastors, lay teachers, and adult students in congregations seeking background and depth in Lutheran theology, biblical interpretation, and Reformation history.

Editorial Principles

The volume editors and contributors have, with few exceptions, used the translations of LW as the basis of their work, retranslating from the WA for the sake of clarity and contemporary usage. Where the LW translations have been substantively altered, explanatory notes have often been provided. More importantly, contributors have provided marginal notes to help readers understand theological and historical references. Introductions have been expanded and sharpened to reflect the very latest historical and theological research. In citing the Bible, care has been taken to reflect the German and Latin texts commonly used in the sixteenth century rather than modern editions, which often employ textual sources that were unavailable to Luther and his contemporaries.

Finally, all pieces in The Annotated Luther have been revised in the light of modern principles of inclusive language. This is not always an easy task with a historical author, but an intentional effort has been made to revise language throughout, with creativity and editorial liberties, to allow Luther's theology to speak free from unnecessary and unintended gender-exclusive language. This important principle provides an opportunity to translate accurately certain gender-neutral German and Latin expressions that Luther employed—for example, the Latin word *homo* and the German *Mensch* mean "human being," not simply "males." Using the words *man* and *men* to translate such terms would create an ambiguity not present in the original texts. The focus is on linguistic accuracy and Luther's intent. Regarding creedal formulations and trinitarian language, Luther's own expressions have been preserved, without entering the complex and important contemporary debates over language for God and the Trinity.

The 2017 anniversary of the publication of the *95 Theses* is providing an opportunity to assess the substance of Luther's role and influence in the Protestant Reformation. Revisiting Luther's essential writings not only allows reassessment of Luther's rationale and goals but also provides a new look at what Martin Luther was about and why new generations would still wish to engage him. We hope these six volumes offer a compelling invitation.

Hans J. Hillerbrand
Kirsi I. Stjerna
Timothy J. Wengert
General Editors

Abbreviations

BC	*The Book of Concord*, ed. Robert Kolb and Timothy J. Wengert (Minneapolis: Fortress Press, 2000).
Brecht 1	Martin Brecht, *Martin Luther: His Road to Reformation, 1483–1521*, trans. James L. Schaaf (Minneapolis: Fortress Press, 1985).
CA	*Augsburg Confession*
CR	*Corpus Reformatorum: Philippi Melanthonis opera quae supersunt omnia*, ed. Karl Brettschneider and Heinrich Bindseil, 28 vols. (Braunschweig: Schwetchke, 1834–1860).
DWB	*Deutsches Wörterbuch*, ed. Jakob and Wilhelm Grimm, 16 vols. in 32 parts (Leipzig, 1854–1960).
Friedberg	*Corpus iuris canonici*, ed. Emil Friedberg, 2 vols. (Leipzig: Tauchnitz, 1879–1881).
LC	*Large Catechism*
LW	*Luther's Works* (American edition), ed. Helmut Lehmann and Jaroslav Pelikan, 55 vols. (Philadelphia: Fortress Press/St. Louis: Concordia Publishing House, 1955–1986).
MLStA	*Martin Luther: Studienausgabe*, ed. Hans-Ulrich Delius, 6 vols. (Berlin/Leipzig: Evangelische Verlagsanstalt, 1979–1999).
MPL	*Patrologiae cursus completus, series Latina*, ed. Jacques-Paul Migne, 217 vols. (Paris, 1815–1875).
NPNF	*Nicene and Post-Nicene Fathers*, ed. Philip Schaaf and Henry Wace, series 1, 14 vols.; series 2, 14 vols. (London/New York: T&T Clark, 1886–1900).
RTA	Adolf Wrede et al., eds., *Deutsche Reichstagsakten, jüngere Reihe*, 20 vols. (Gotha: Perthes, 1893–2009).
WA	*Luthers Werke: Kritische Gesamtausgabe [Schriften]*, 73 vols. (Weimar: H. Böhlau, 1883–2009).
WA Br	*Luthers Werke: Kritische Gesamtausgabe: Briefwechsel*, 18 vols. (Weimar: H. Böhlau, 1930–1985).
WA DB	*Luthers Werke: Kritische Gesamtausgabe: Deutsche Bibel*, 12 vols. (Weimar: H. Böhlau, 1906–1961).
WA TR	*Luthers Werke: Kritische Gesamtausgabe: Tischreden*, 6 vols. (Weimar: H. Böhlau, 1912–1921).
Wander	Karl F. W. Wander, ed., *Deutsches Sprichwörterlexikon: Ein Hausschatz für das deutsche Volk*, 5 vols. (Leipzig: Brockhaus, 1867–1880; reprint Aalen: Scientia, 1963).

REFORMATION EUROPE
in the 16th century

— - Holy Roman Empire
boundary

---- Provincial boundary

ATLANTIC OCEAN

NORWAY

• Stockholm

ESTONIA
LIVONIA
KURLAND

SCOTLAND

• Edinburgh

North Sea

SWEDEN

DENMARK

Baltic Sea

• Copenhagen

• Königsberg

PRUSSIA

IRELAND

• York

ENGLAND

London •

Ghent •

Hamburg •

POMERANIA

BRANDENBURG

POLAND

ARTOIS

NETHERLANDS

FLANDERS

HESSE

COLOGNE

LUXEMBOURG

SAXONY

SILESIA

Paris •

Mainz •

BOHEMIA

Nantes •

• Orleans

LOWER PALITANATE

UPPER PALITANATE

MORAVIA

FRANCE

FRENCH COMTE

BAVARIA

Augsburg •

AUSTRIA

Vienna •

IMPERIAL HUNGARY

Budapest •

HUNGARY

BOURBON LANDS

SWISS CONFEDERATION

TYROL

CARINTHIA

CARNIOLA

• Mohacs

Valladolid •

Toulouse •

SAVOY

Milan •

Pavia •

Trent •

Venice •

Avignon •

PORTUGAL

NAVARRE

SPAIN

Madrid •

Barcelona •

Genoa •

VENETIAN REPUBLIC

Florence •

PAPAL STATES

OTTOMAN EMPIRE

Lisbon •

CASTILE

Toledo •

ARAGON

BALERIC ISLANDS

CORSICA (TO GENOA)

Rome •

ITALY

Seville •

Granada •

GRANADA

SARDINIA (TO SPAIN)

Naples •

NAPLES

Tangier •

Algiers •

Mediterranean Sea

SICILY (TO SPAIN)

Bizerte •

Tunis •

Lucidity Information Design, LLC

0   300 Miles

LUTHER'S GERMANY

- - - - Major political subdivisions

N

Baltic Sea

DENMARK

Wolgast
Hamburg
POMERANIA
Stettin
Bremen
Elbe
Amsterdam
NETHERLANDS
Magdeburg
Wittenberg
POLAND
Brussels
Cologne
Eisenach
Eisleben
Torgau
Marburg
Erfurt
Leipzig
Breslau
Schmalkalden
Oder
LUXEMBURG
Mansfeld
Prague
Worms
Nuremberg
Metz
Rhine
Regansburg
Strasbourg
Danube
Augsburg
AUSTRIA
FRANCE
Zürich
Salzburg
Vienna
SWISS
CONFEDERATION
HUNGARY
Milan
Venice
VENETIAN
DOMINION
Adriatic Sea
Florence

0   200 Miles

A woodcarving of Wittenberg Castle Church
by Lucas Cranach the Elder (1472–1553), as it appeared in 1518.

Introduction to Volume 1

TIMOTHY J. WENGERT

On 31 October 1517 a little-known professor of theology at an out-of-the-way, relatively new university in the town of Wittenberg, Saxony, enclosed a copy of ninety-five statements concerning indulgences in a letter to Archbishop Albrecht of Mainz, primate of the Catholic churches in the Holy Roman Empire of the German Nation.[1] By 1520 that same professor, an Augustinian friar named Martin Luther, had become the world's first living best-selling author while, at the same time, was threatened with excommunication by Pope Leo X (1475–1521). The documents in this first volume of The Annotated Luther contain some of the most important documents from this period, beginning with the *95 Theses* of 1517 and concluding with the tract *The Freedom of a Christian* from 1520. These writings outline Luther's development from those early days to within six months of his dramatic appearance before the imperial diet meeting in Worms in 1521, where he gave his defense for many of the writings contained in this volume.[a] Whatever other differences between Luther and his opponents emerged in later stages of what came to be called the Reformation, these documents,

1. For the most thorough account of Luther's life during this period, see Martin Brecht, *Martin Luther: His Road to Reformation, 1483–1521*, trans. James L. Schaaf (Minneapolis: Fortress Press, 1985).

a   See *Luther at the Diet of Worms* (1521), in LW 32:101–31.

and others that he wrote during this time, surely provided the initial sparks of that remarkable conflagration within the late medieval Western church.

The *95 Theses* quickly became a central icon for the Reformation and the split between Roman Catholicism and Protestantism: an angry friar nailing theses to a church door in Wittenberg (or, in the earliest depiction [see p. 3], writing on the door with a quill, the end of which tickles the pope's nose in Rome). Yet, their origins had nothing to do with their eventual effect on church unity in the West. Instead, if they were indeed posted, they simply represented an attempt by this obscure Augustinian friar, Martin Luther, to gain clarity on a theological issue using the tools appropriate to a professor of theology: provocative theses, posted on church doors (the equivalent of the university bulletin board) in compliance with university regulations and coupled with an invitation to a university debate. Moreover, sending a copy to his archbishop, Albrecht of Mainz (and also to his immediate bishop, Jerome Scultetus [c. 1460–1522], bishop of Brandenburg), also possibly fell within the realm of what a professor was expected to do—especially when commenting on such a volatile topic as indulgences.

Because of modern uncertainty about whether and on what day the *95 Theses* may have been posted, the second document in this volume is of equal importance. The letter to Archbishop Albrecht of Mainz (1490–1545) not only survives in a Swedish archive but also bears the date of 31 October 1517 (the eve of All Saints' Day)—reason enough that ten years later Luther would remember All Saints' Day as the beginning of the affair. More importantly, the letter reveals both what Luther thought were his most important theological arguments and his pastoral heart, as he appeals for indulgence preachers and his archbishop to consider the effect of such preaching on their flocks. Archbishop Albrecht, suspecting heresy, submitted the theses in December to his theological faculty in Mainz and to the papal court. With this, the *processus inhibitorius* (ban on teaching) commenced, meaning that from December 1517 charges of heresy were being formalized.

Elector Frederick III of Saxony's dream in Schweinitz of Luther writing the *95 Theses*
on the church door in Wittenberg and knocking off the pope's crown in Rome,
from a 100th anniversary publication of the *95 Theses* printed in 1617.

Given what later happened, it is easy to forget just how much of an unknown Luther was. His early attempts at publication were modest: a preface to an incomplete version of the mystical tract *Theologia Deutsch* (*German Theology*) and a German translation and exposition of the seven penitential psalms. Other writings from this time, as well as reprints of these works, occurred only *after* he had become a literary star. Yet, what made him a household name was not so much the *95 Theses*—published in Latin in Leipzig, Nuremberg, and Basel (and probably Wittenberg)—but the German-language equivalent, the *Sermon on Indulgences and Grace*, published in place of any translation of the *95 Theses* into German for a German audience. This tract, republished over twenty times in the coming months, spread Luther's message and fame far and wide. It also lacked any direct reference to the limits of papal authority, an important aspect of the *Theses* themselves. Instead, Luther showed here his ability to communicate directly and plainly to a German-speaking audience (which included not only readers but also illiterate listeners as well), reducing complicated theological concepts, such as penance or indulgences, to their simplest terms. Because Luther was already familiar with the first attacks on his theses from the indulgence preacher Johann Tetzel (c. 1460–1519) and Konrad Wimpina (1460–1531), professor at the University of Frankfurt (Oder), this sermon also provides Luther's earliest responses to his critics.

If the *Sermon* catapulted Luther to celebrity, a document written nearly simultaneously caused barely a ripple at the time but has in the last one hundred years become synonymous with Luther's theology. At a gathering of German Augustinian friars, meeting in Heidelberg in 1518, Luther defended another set of theological and philosophical theses, in what has become known as the *Heidelberg Disputation*. While the theses themselves were reprinted immediately (copies from Paris and Leiden survive), the explanations to the theological theses were not published until 1530, with a fuller form first appearing in 1545 in the first volume of Luther's Latin works. (Another portion of these explanations first saw the light of day in 1703, and the explanations to the philosophical theses, not included here, were not published until 1979.) Nevertheless, these terse antithetical statements outline such quintessential, Luther-esque teachings as the distinction between law and gospel, the bondage of the will, justification by faith not works, and, most celebrated today, the theology of the cross. Of course, these themes hardly disappeared from Luther's later thought, and many of them also appear in Luther's *Explanations of the 95*

Theses, written at the same time but published in the summer of 1518.[b]

Six months later, in October 1518, Luther appeared in Augsburg before the papal legate, Tommaso de Vio (Cardinal Cajetan [1469–1534]). By this time, Luther's *Theses* had become a full-blown case in Rome. The papal court theologian, Sylvester Prierias (Sylvester Mazzolini [c. 1456–1523]), because of his official position as Master of the Sacred Palace and with some reservations, had just published a thoroughgoing refutation, accusing Luther of attacking papal authority. As more of Luther's publications, especially the *Sermon on Indulgences and Grace* and his *Explanations of the 95 Theses*, became available, the authorities in Rome grew more concerned and deputized Cajetan, already in Augsburg for an imperial diet,[2] to bring Luther to Rome for trial. Through the intervention of Luther's prince, Elector Frederick of Saxony (1463–1525), Cajetan agreed instead to meet with Luther and explain Rome's case against him. Luther's account of this encounter, which lasted from 12 to 14 October, one of the few if only face-to-face meetings between Luther and a direct representative of the pope, forms a crucial source for measuring the growing gap between Luther's theology and his opponents' appraisal of it. Two issues particularly—the authority of the pope and the certainty of forgiveness—came up for debate but resulted in little or no movement on either side. Fearing arrest, Luther left hastily for Wittenberg, but not before having a direct appeal to Pope Leo X posted on the door of the Augsburg Cathedral.[c]

In 1519, the tensions between Luther and his opponents increased—fueled in part by the Leipzig Debate of that summer, where Johann Eck (1486–1543) faced off against both Luther's colleague Andreas Bodenstein from Karlstadt (1486–1541) and Luther himself.[3] But Luther also pursued both his exegetical interests, with the publication of his first commentary on Galatians,[d] and his pastoral goals,

2. An assembly of imperial leaders of the Holy Roman Empire (secular and clerical), convoked by the emperor, which concerned itself with legislation, taxation, and military defense, as well as the airing of grievances, especially against the papacy, in the form of *gravamina*.

3. LW 31:307–25. It seems that the disputants were still treating this as a university debate, somewhat separate from Luther's case in Rome.

---

b   LW 31:77–252.

c   WA 2:27–33.

d   LW 27:151–410.

A view of sixteenth-century Augsburg, Germany

publishing popular sermons in German on, among other things, confession, penance, marriage, Christ's passion, the Lord's Prayer, the Ten Commandments, dying, the Lord's Supper, baptism, and usury.*e* Luther viewed three of these— on penance, the Supper, and baptism—as a series; indeed, they contain many of the arguments that he would include in the one important Latin tract of 1520 not included in this volume but scheduled for inclusion in volume 3: *The*

e   In addition to the four sermons in this volume, see *An Exposition of the Lord's Prayer for Simple Laymen* (LW 43:15–81); *On Rogationtide Prayer and Procession* (LW 43:83–93); *A Sermon on Preparing to Die*

Babylonian Captivity of the Church.[f] Along with the sermon on Christ's passion, which later became a part of his oft-republished *Church Postil* (German: *Kirchenpostil*—interpretation of the appointed Sunday Gospels and Epistles),[g] these four sermons show Luther's deep pastoral concern for proper instruction of the German-speaking public and his ability to wed word and sacrament in his theology.

By 1520, what had begun as a university debate threatened to divide the Western church. Luther's appeal to Pope Leo resulted in the pope's restatement of the very approach to indulgences that Luther had questioned. His consequent appeals to a general council of the church[h] were viewed in Rome, especially by supporters of papal supremacy in all matters of doctrine, as *prima facie* evidence of heresy. Moreover, Luther's opponent in Leipzig, Johann Eck, journeyed to Rome to assist in the preparation of an official bull of excommunication. Meanwhile, Luther himself continued to address charges against him and to provide new fuel for the fire by writing on other church teachings and practice, for which he provided interpretations based on the central premises of his theology. Thus, early in 1520 another interpretation of the Ten Commandments, the *Treatise on Good Works*, appeared in German. It insisted that the commandments embraced all Christians, both attacking the popular medieval notion that those under a vow (monks, nuns, friars, and bishops) were subject to a higher law that included the so-called evangelical counsels of Christ and insisting that the commandments are all fulfilled through faith alone.

(LW 43:95–115); *A Sermon on the Estate of Marriage* (LW 44:3–14); *Two Kinds of Righteousness* (LW 31:293–306); *Eine kurze Unterweisung wie man beichten soll* (*A Short Instruction on How One Should Confess*, WA 2:57–65); *Kleiner Sermon von dem Wucher* (*A Short Sermon on Usury*, WA 6:1–8, cf. *Trade and Usury* [1524], 6:231–310); and, from 1518, *Decem praecepta Wittenbergensi praedicata populo* (*The Ten Commandments Preached to the People of Wittenberg*, WA 1:394–521).

f   LW 36:3–126.

g   John Lenker, ed., *The Sermons of Martin Luther*, 8 vols. (Reprint: Grand Rapids: Baker, 1989).

h   WA 2:34–40 (1518); WA 7:74–90 (1520).

Bulla contra errores
Martini Lutheri
z sequacium.

The title page of *Exsurge Domini*, the papal bull
threatening Luther with excommunication,
promulgated in Rome in 1520.

As hopes for a settlement of the conflict dimmed, Luther appealed in his German *Address to the Christian Nobility* for the Christian nobility of the empire to take action. This tract, imitating the style of official imperial *gravamina* (grievances) against Rome, called upon the princes to exercise their authority as Christians to correct abuses in the church and society. This early foray into the political realm demonstrated how Luther now imagined a political scene in which the pope no longer held sway over both church and empire.

Then, in late August 1520, a final attempt was made to prevent Luther's condemnation in Rome. Another papal legate, Karl von Miltitz (c. 1490–1529), persuaded the leaders of Luther's Augustinian order in Germany, Johann von Staupitz (c. 1460–1524) and Wenzeslaus Linck (1483–1547), to convince Luther to write an appeal to Leo X as a demonstration of Luther's respect for and obedience to the pope. At the same time, Luther penned a tract that summarized the heart of his teaching, titled *The Freedom of a Christian*, published in both German and Latin versions and prefaced (at least in all the Latin and some German versions) by the letter to Leo. As these were appearing, however, the official bull of excommunication, *Exsurge Domini*, was being posted throughout German lands, giving Luther sixty days to recant. Instead, on 10 December 1520 Luther burned the bull (and a copy of canon law) outside the Elster Gate in Wittenberg in protest.[4]

4. See *Why the Books of the Pope and His Disciples Were Burned by Doctor Martin Luther* (1520), in LW 31:379–95; and *Defense and Explanation of All the Articles Condemned by the Most Recent Bull of Leo X* (1521), in LW 32:3–99. *Canon law* is a term designating various published collections of church law, the earliest coming from the twelfth century.

THEOLOGICAL ROOTS
OF THE REFORMATION

Over the past century in Luther research, particular attention has been paid to Luther's early lectures and marginal notations in an attempt to reconstruct the development of his theology and, often, to search for his Reformation "breakthrough."[i] In fact, however, Luther's contemporaries knew nothing about this earliest work and learned of him and his ideas only through what he published beginning in 1517. Thus, the tracts, sermons, and theses contained in this volume reflect best the first impressions of Luther's theology gained not only by his initial readers but also readers down through the nineteenth century.[5]

These documents display a Luther grounded in late medieval theology and its peculiar issues, trained in the latest techniques of Renaissance, humanist method, and, most especially, showing sensitivity toward the pastoral consequences for theological positions. Luther was trained at the University of Erfurt in late medieval Nominalism.[6] In preparation for his ordination, he worked through Gabriel Biel's (c. 1420–1495) tome on the sacrament and doubtless used Biel's commentary on the *Sentences* during his own lectures on the same in 1509.[7] Luther's writings reflect a deep familiarity with this tradition, by far the most dominant in late medieval central Europe, especially in the *95 Theses*, the

---

i See, among others, Karl Holl, "Die Rechtfertigungslehre in Luthers Vorlesung über den Römerbrief mit besonderer Rücksicht auf die Frage der Heilsgewißheit," in *Gesammelte Aufsätze zur Kirchengeschichte*, vol. 1: *Luther* (Tübingen: Mohr Siebeck, 1921), 91–130; Gerhard Ebeling, *Luther: An Introduction to His Thought*, trans. R. A. Wilson (Philadelphia: Fortress Press, 1970); Helmar Junghans, *Der junge Luther und die Humanisten* (Weimar: Böhlaus Nachfolger, 1984); Berndt Hamm, *The Early Luther: Stages in a Reformation Reorientation*, trans. Martin Lohrmann (Grand Rapids: Eerdmans, 2014). Even the Roman Catholic scholar, Heinrich Denifle, *Luther and Lutherdom from Original Sources*, trans. Raymond Volz (Somerset, Ohio: Torch Press, 1917), used the newly discovered Romans lectures of 1515–1516 extensively.

5. Luther's earliest lectures on the Bible (Psalms, Romans, Galatians, and Hebrews), delivered from 1513 to 1518, were not published until the end of the nineteenth century into the twentieth. In fact, of the documents in this volume, all but the *Address to Christian Nobility*, which was never translated into Latin, and the *Treatise on Good Works* are contained in the first two volumes of Luther's Latin works, published in Wittenberg in 1545 and 1546. The *Address* and *Treatise* were printed in the first volume of Luther's German works published in Jena in 1555.

6. Nominalism or the *via moderna* (modern way), the name for the second major philosophical and theological school of medieval Scholasticism and associated with William of Occam (c. 1287–1347), argued (against the "Realists" or *via antiqua*, associated with Thomas Aquinas [1225–1274]) that each entity was associated with its own individual essence. Thus, categories that grouped things together were simply "names" (Latin: *nomina*) and not realities in themselves. Thinkers like Occam or, later, Gabriel Biel, also held to an understanding of justification before God that depended far more on meritorious works performed by individuals and given reward out of the goodness of God's heart.

7. The *Sentences* of Peter Lombard (c. 1096–1160) were a collation of sayings of the church fathers structured into four books. To receive the doctorate in theology, late medieval candidates had to lecture on this book. As a result, we have commentaries on the *Sentences* by

Thomas Aquinas, Duns Scotus (c. 1266–1308), William of Occam, and Gabriel Biel, among others. Luther's marginal notes in his copy of the *Sentences* are printed in WA 9:28–94.

Sermon on Indulgences and Grace and the *Heidelberg Disputation*, where he directly attacks several aspects of medieval Scholasticism and its dependence on Aristotelian philosophy. For example, in the Heidelberg Disputation Luther attacks the common slogan, "To those who do what is in them, God will not deny grace," replacing it with a far stricter, Augustinian approach to the bondage of the will. For Luther, grace can never be earned but only bestowed as pure gift.

Luther's common cause with Renaissance humanism also appears in several aspects of his work from this period. Both the *95 Theses* and *The Freedom of a Christian* demonstrate his familiarity with and use of a variety of rhetorical techniques and organizational patterns. The first four theses of the *95 Theses* demonstrate a close reading of Erasmus of Rotterdam's (1466–1536) *Annotations on the New Testament*, published the preceding year. His early publication on the penitential psalms showed his indebtedness to the first great Christian Hebraist of the Renaissance, Johannes Reuchlin (1455–1522). Even Luther's employment of a variety of literary genres—from theses to sermons to *gravamina* to persuasive tracts—shows a sensitivity held in common with many of his contemporaries. His willingness to return to the early sources (*ad fontes!*) and to attribute to them higher authority than to later, especially Scholastic, arguments is a further mark of humanism's influence and is especially pronounced in the *Proceedings at Augsburg*. What Luther discovered in the Scriptures and the church fathers, however, was not the Christian moral philosophy that a thinker like Erasmus found there but, quite to the contrary, a single-minded trust in God's creative and redeeming Word. This afforded Luther a certain freedom of argumentation that allowed him to reject much of late medieval theology in favor of what he understood as the central message of Scripture, witnessed to not only by the early church but also by later thinkers (such as Bernard of Clairvaux [1090–1153], Johannes Tauler [c. 1300–1361], and the anonymous *German Theology*).

But running through all of these works from this period was also Luther's particular pastoral passion. His complaints about bad preaching and the effect on the listeners find clear expression in the *95 Theses*, the *Address to Christian Nobility*, and *The Freedom of a Christian*. His sermons from 1519 offer Luther's own counterpoint, as he attempted to wean his hearers away from much of late medieval theology and piety and to express what he viewed as a radically biblical perspective of the Christian life and faith. The same pastoral perspective dominated his *Treatise on Good Works*, where he reframes the Christian life of all the baptized under the Ten Commandments and within faith in God's mercy. In all the tracts from 1520, Luther worked to erase the late medieval distinction between secular Christians (who in a "state of grace" may fulfill the commandments) and Christians under a vow (who in a "state of perfection" may fulfill also the counsels of Christ, especially vowing perpetual poverty, chastity, and obedience to their superiors). Faith in the gospel of God's unconditional mercy frees Christians to love their neighbor in all of life's callings—a love that includes special care for and concern about the poor, a note already struck in the *95 Theses* and reiterated throughout Luther's career, but here especially in the *Treatise on Good Works*, the *Address to Christian Nobility*, and *The Freedom of a Christian*.

[The 95 Theses or]

Disputation for Clarifying the Power of Indulgences[1]

1517

TIMOTHY J. WENGERT

INTRODUCTION

The *95 Theses* of Martin Luther may constitute one of the best known and yet least understood of his writings. Given the terseness of individual theses, the technical nature of many of the arguments, and the debates over the history of the document, this is hardly surprising. For a twenty-first-century reader to understand them more fully, one must consider certain theological, historical, and literary aspects of the document.

Theological Background

Already St. Jerome (c. 347–420) had argued that after the shipwreck of sin, Christians had at their disposal two planks: first, baptism, which forgave the guilt and punishment for all sin; and then, for mortal sins committed after baptism, penance. Medieval theology defined a mortal sin as a grave act of commission or omission involving willful disregard for God's clear commands.[2] Such a sin put a person in a state of mortal sin (that is, dead to God and liable to punishment in hell) and included two consequences: guilt and

1. This title (Latin: *Disputatio . . . pro declaratione virtutis indulgentiarum*) is taken from the 1517 reprint of Luther's theses, which in all other printings bore no title at all.

2. Venial sins, which involved minor infractions, ignorance of the consequences, or lack of intention, were forgiven anytime one prayed the Fifth Petition of the Lord's Prayer.

3. The others being baptism, the Lord's Supper, confirmation, ordination, marriage, and last rites (extreme unction). In *The Babylonian Captivity of the Church* (1520; LW 36:3–126), Luther reduced the number to three (baptism, Lord's Supper, and, as a daily use of baptism, confession and absolution [= penance]).

4. This contrasted with attrition, defined as a sorrow for sin out of fear of punishment.

punishment (Latin: *culpa et poena*).[a] According to Peter Lombard (c. 1096–1164), the early Scholastic theologian from Paris whose *Sentences* (collected statements of the church fathers interspersed with his brief comments) became the basic theological textbook at universities for the next four hundred years, penance was one of the seven sacraments of the church.[3] The sacrament of penance consisted of three parts: contrition, confession, and satisfaction. While baptism contained stronger grace and remitted the guilt and punishment for all sin, it could only be performed once. As a result, the sacrament of penance, to which one had continual access because it was repeatable, became in the Middle Ages the crucial means of moving the sinner from a state of sin into a state of grace. While repeatable, the grace of this sacrament differed in that, although it fully removed the guilt of sin, it only reduced the penalty or punishment (Latin: *poena*) from an eternal punishment to a temporal one.

Contrition, or sorrow for sin out of love of God,[4] was the first part of the process. By the late Middle Ages, some teachers, including Gabriel Biel (c. 1420–1495) a professor in Tübingen and author of several textbooks that Luther used while in Erfurt, insisted that with such sorrow for sin a person already moved from a state of sin to a state of grace. Most other theologians, such as Thomas Aquinas (1225–1274), argued that the transfer took place during the second part of the sacrament, when one went to confession and, upon a thorough confession of all sins committed since the previous confession, heard the priest's absolution. (By contrast, for Biel the person went to the priest for confession for the same reason cleansed lepers in the Old Testament went to the Levitical priests—to guarantee that the contrition was genuine and, thus, that the leprosy of sin was gone.)[b] Whenever it took place, the move from a state of sin to a state of grace was brought about by an infusion into the soul of a disposition of love (Latin: *habitus charitatis*), that is,

a   Luther uses this distinction in theses 5 and 6, for example.
b   See below, *Sermon on Penance*, p. 197 n. 29.

the grace that makes one acceptable to God (Latin: *gratia gratum faciens*). The guilt of sin was completely removed, and the punishment reduced from eternal to temporal.

The third part, satisfaction, took place after private confession, when the forgiven Christian, now in a state of grace, did good works to *satisfy* the temporal punishment remaining for his or her sin. In addition to the traditional good works of prayer, fasting, and almsgiving, other things like participating in a crusade for religious reasons, founding a monastery, contributing to the construction of churches, going on pilgrimages, and the like were also included. For each mortal sin, penitential books used by the priests specified certain penalties. Because most persons committed so many mortal sins over their lifetimes as to accumulate more works of satisfaction than could be done while alive, and because the Bible insisted that only the pure in heart would "see God" (that is, participate in the heavenly, beatific vision), God mercifully established a place of purgation (Latin: *purgatorium*) where the remaining temporal punishments could be satisfied under the overarching assumption that, for the sake of divine righteousness, punishment had to be exacted for every sin. There was some debate over whether the soul in purgatory could then make progress or whether the suffering there was experienced only passively. While the suffering in purgatory was far worse than human suffering on earth, there was only one exit, so to speak, namely, heaven (see theses 16–19). When the power of indulgences came to include purgatory, a few theologians also raised questions over the mode of papal authority over such souls, since the souls had passed from this life (see theses 25–26).

Indulgences came into play precisely in this third part of the sacrament of penance, in that the church could be "indulgent" and reduce or eliminate the temporal penalty demanded for particular mortal sins far beyond the value of an individual work. Certain actions, including donations of money, insofar as they were connected to honoring Christ, Mary, or other saints, could result in obtaining such an indulgence. There were basically two kinds of indulgences, both under the ultimate authority of the pope as Peter's

Portrait by Raphael (1483–1520) of Pope Leo X and his cousins, cardinals Giulio de' Medici and Luigi de' Rossi.

successor (based on Matt. 16:19), who granted to local bishops authority over the first kind. This kind was a partial indulgence, wherein the church lessened by a fixed amount the temporal penalty for sin for anyone who performed a certain act of piety. The viewing of relics (such as those assembled by Luther's prince, Elector Frederick III of Saxony [1463–1525] and displayed twice a year in the Castle Church in Wittenberg), making a pilgrimage to a saint's shrine, being in attendance at the annual celebration of a church's dedication, and many other activities had indulgences attached to them.

The other kind of indulgence was a full, or plenary indulgence, attached especially to the apostles and their holy sites, and offering the remission of all one's temporal punishment for all sins committed up until the time the indulgence was received. It was under the exclusive aegis of the pope. Pope Urban II (c. 1042–1099) offered the first such indulgence in 1095 for those who participated in the Crusades for religious reasons (namely, to wrest the holy sites in Jerusalem from the control of the "infidel"). In 1300 Pope Boniface VIII (c. 1235–1303) offered a "Jubilee Indulgence" for those who made a pilgrimage to the shrines of the apostles in Rome. Although these were originally to be offered every century, this indulgence soon became available every twenty-five years. In time, other such plenary indulgences came to be offered not just for religious acts but also for the financial support of such acts. In 1476 Pope Sixtus IV (1414–1484) first allowed indulgences to be applied to souls in purgatory.

Indeed, the practice often outran the theological arguments, so that the source of such churchly indulgence—given the widespread belief that for the sake of divine justice satisfaction for every sin must be made—finally came to rest in a "treasury of merits" accumulated by Christ and saints. The pope, by virtue of having been given the keys to heaven by Christ (Matt. 16:19), could open this "treasury" to the faithful purchaser of an indulgence. Pope Clement VI (1291–1352) formally attached this treasury to indulgences.[c]

The History of the 95 Theses

By the late Middle Ages, indulgences had become a central part of piety for many people in the Western church. It was also a useful means of financial support for a cash-strapped papacy, so that indulgence preaching was labeled a *sacrum negotium* (holy business). When Leo X (1475–1521) proclaimed a plenary "Peter's Indulgence" in 1515, the stated reason was to raise money to rebuild the Basilica of Sts. Peter and Paul in Rome—the Renaissance result of which may still be seen today. It is true that half of the money raised was to go to the Augsburg banking family, the Fuggers, in order to pay a debt owed by the archbishop of Mainz, Albrecht von Brandenburg (1490–1545), who had used the loan to pay Rome for the right to hold multiple sees (including archbishop of Magdeburg and administrator of the diocese of Halberstadt) upon his accession to the see in Mainz.[5] But this would have been considered serving the same religious purpose, namely, to support the building of St. Peter's, and thus should not be construed as the unscrupulous act of a secularized religious leader who had no conscience and was only interested in servicing a debt. The religious benefits

Jacob Fugger, head of the Augsburg banking family.

5. Canon (ecclesiastical) law forbade the holding of multiple offices (in this case, three bishoprics), for which an exemption needed to be purchased.

---

c Already in his *Commentary on the Sentences* IV, d. 20, q. 1, a. 3, qc. 1 co (also found in the supplement to the *Summa Theologica* q. 25, art. 1, compiled by Rainaldo da Piperno [d. 1290]), Thomas Aquinas provided theological grounding for the doctrine.

IOHANNES TETZELIUS, LIPSIENSIS
MISNICUS, MONACHUS ORDINIS SANCTI DOMINICI
FRANCOFURTI AD ODERAM PRÆCO, FORNICARIUS ET
NUNDINATOR BULLARUM PAPALIUM
INDULGENTIARUM Anno 1517.
Senatus d 7 August Anno 1519.

A 1717 depiction of Johann Tetzel (1465–1519) giving a
blessing. Pope Leo X and indulgences appear above him on
either side; his hand is on the money chest, and the papal bull
authorizing indulgence sales is in the lower righthand corner.

attached to the indulgence were surely also part of Albrecht's concern. In any case, at the time of writing the *95 Theses*, Luther knew nothing of such backroom dealings. His concerns as expressed in the *95 Theses* and his letter to Albrecht were purely theological and pastoral.

Albrecht first turned to the Franciscans to proclaim this indulgence but finally settled on the well-known Dominican, Johann Tetzel (1465–1519), an indulgence commissioner who then worked with other functionaries in selling the individual letters. In preparation for preaching of this indulgence, Albrecht's court theologians prepared a booklet, the *Instructio Summaria* [*Summary Instruction*], which described the limits and benefits of this indulgence for potential preachers.[6] Some of Luther's objections in the *95 Theses* arose from this source. Tetzel's preaching, some of which likely overstepped the boundaries of the *Summary Instruction*, began in earnest in early 1517. According to contemporary accounts and pictures, he would have been met at a town's gates by all the important government and church officials, who would have processed to the town's main church, where the papal coat of arms and the papal bull[d] decreeing this indulgence would be prominently displayed, while all the organs and bells in the town's churches sounded. All other preaching would be halted so that the citizenry had opportunity to give full attention to Tetzel and the indulgences he had to offer.

6. This included threats to any who impeded preaching this indulgence, the invalidation of previous indulgences, the necessity for building St. Peter's in Rome, the promise of complete remission of all temporal penalties here and in purgatory, the sliding scale of payment depending on one's station

d   A technical term for an official papal bulletin or message.

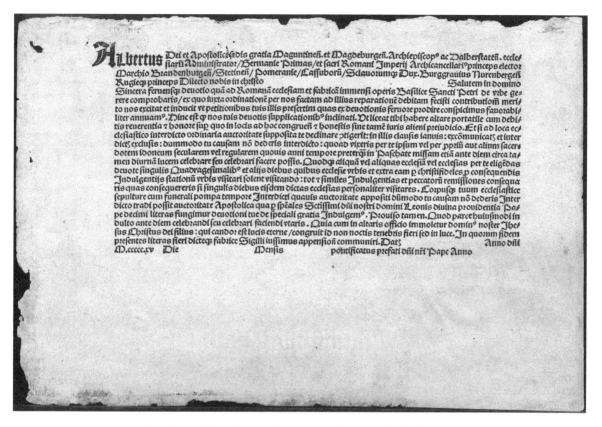

Indulgence for priests and other clergy, issued at the insistence
of Johann Tetzel, to support the rebuilding of St. Peter's Basilica
in Rome and to repay the loan with which Albert of Brandenburg
obtained his office for the pallium, which was the sign of his office.

Elector Frederick banned Tetzel from electoral Saxony because he wanted to protect the indulgences of over 100,000 years that were available to the viewer of his collection of relics and because he also feared the drain of gold from his lands. Therefore, Tetzel set up shop around the edges of electoral Saxony, preaching in towns not controlled by Saxon's elector: Eisleben, Halle, Zerbst, and finally Jüterbog (like Halle, a town directly under the control of Albrecht). Wittenberg's citizens, however, could undertake the daylong journey to in life, a confessional letter instructing the confessor to forgive all sins (which could be used twice—including at the time of death), participation of oneself and one's dead relatives in the "goods" of the church (especially its prayers and other good works), and remission of penalties for souls in purgatory.

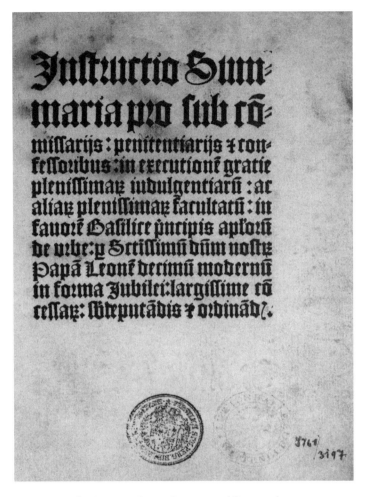

The *Summary Instruction* prepared for preachers
of the so-called Peter's Indulgence by the
court theologians to Archbishop Albrecht of Mainz.

purchase this religiously valuable blessing. Those who purchased such certificates began describing Tetzel's preaching and showing their certificates of indulgence to their priests at home, including to Martin Luther, Augustinian friar and preacher at St. Mary's, the city church in Wittenberg.

Although many focus Luther's discomfort with indulgences on Tetzel and the "Peter's Indulgence," we can see in Luther's own surviving sermons from early 1517 that he had serious theological questions regarding indulgences from the very moment Tetzel showed up on Saxony's doorstep. For example, Luther delivered a sermon probably on 16 or 17 January 1517, at the anniversary of the Castle Church's dedication and just as Tetzel was beginning to preach in Eisleben.[e] Martin Luther was thus preaching a dedication indulgence on which occasion Frederick the Wise may have even been in the congregation (given Luther's later recollections about the elector's anger at his questioning indulgences).[7] Not only did Luther warn about confusing the dedication of churches with the dedication of one's heart

7. See LW 41:232. Luther directed his comments not at the prince's relics but at the entire "foundation," which was connected to the church's dedication. These were not Luther's only critical comments about indulgences from sermons delivered during this time.

e   The text of the sermon is in WA 1:95–99 and WA 4:670–74. For arguments about dating and a translation of the relevant passages, see Timothy J. Wengert, "Martin Luther's Preaching an Indulgence in January 1517," *Lutheran Quarterly* 29, no. 1 (2015): 62–75.

to God, but also, near the end of the sermon, he observed: "Indulgences . . . may only be useful or exist . . . to support the truth of contrition; they take away nothing other than the personal imposition of satisfaction. And it must be feared that frequently they work against interior penitence. For interior penitence is true contrition, true confession, and true satisfaction in the spirit." He then reflected on his own preaching: "You see, therefore, just how dangerous a thing the preaching of indulgences is, which teaches by cutting short grace, that is, it teaches avoiding satisfaction and punishment."[f] These arguments will also appear in the *Theses* themselves.

On top of his own uncertainty, Luther encountered uncertainty and complaints about indulgences from lay-persons and rumors about exaggerations in Tetzel's indulgence preaching (perhaps in the confessional from his parishioners).[g] Then, having obtained a copy of the *Summary Instruction*, he began serious investigation concerning the nature of indulgences in the summer of 1517, researching the books of canon law[8] and asking experts for their assistance. His approach to the problem betrayed a method of investigation, shared with other humanist scholars of the day, which insisted that to understand a topic fully, one had to return *ad fontes* (to the sources), where the earliest sources were more reliable than later ones.[h] What this study revealed to Luther was that the ancient church had understood the satisfaction owed for temporal punishment of sin quite differently than the church of his day. In Luther's studied opinion, the pope had authority to grant indulgences but could offer them

8. A collection of binding church decrees from councils and popes assembled by Gratian (active c. 1150) beginning in the twelfth century and commented upon by professors of church law in the centuries following.

---

f   WA 1:96, 9–10, 27–28; 98, 37–99, 2; 99, 20–22.

g   See LW 51:26–31, a sermon preached on 24 February 1517 at the city church. For an analysis of earlier criticism of indulgences, see Wilhelm Ernst Winterhager, "Ablaßkritik als Indikator historischen Wandels vor 1517: Ein Beitrag zu Voraussetzungen und Einordnung der Reformation," *Archive for Reformation History* 90 (1999): 6–71.

h   That Luther was doing this consciously becomes clear in his letter to Bishop Jerome from 13 or 20 February 1518 (WA Br 1:135–41, esp. 138, 17–23).

only for ecclesiastical punishment established in canon law, which had nothing to do with divine punishment.

As for the publication history of the *95 Theses* themselves, scholars are divided on exactly what happened in late October and early November 1517.[i] This much is certain. On 31 October 1517, Martin Luther wrote a letter to Archbishop Albrecht in which he warned the young prelate about the dangers of unchecked preaching of indulgences (given how uncertain the theology was) and, to prove his point, attached to the letter a copy of the *95 Theses*.[j] The original letter in Luther's hand still exists in the royal archives in Stockholm, Sweden. At approximately the same time, he also wrote a letter to his immediate bishop, Jerome Schultz (c. 1460–1522) of Brandenburg, with whom he also corresponded in late February 1518.[k] This bishop apparently simply warned Luther to be careful about the new ideas contained in the *Theses*. It is also certain that on 11 November 1517 Luther sent a copy of the *Theses* to his friend in Erfurt, Johannes Lang (c. 1487–1548), asking for his opinion.[l]

But, despite what movies about Luther and countless pictures have portrayed, did Luther actually post the theses on the door of the Castle Church on 31 October 1517? Here scholars have been divided since the 1960s, when several first called into question some details of the story.[m] For one thing, the first time anyone directly stated in print that Luther posted the *Theses* came in June 1546, shortly after Luther's death, in a preface to the second volume of his Latin works, written by Philip Melanchthon (1497–1560), who

---

i   See Volker Leppin and Timothy J. Wengert, "A Critical Analysis of the Sources for the Posting of the *95 Theses*," *Lutheran Quarterly* (forthcoming).

j   See below, p. 55. He also attached a copy of what is now called the *Tract on Indulgences* (WA Br 12:2–9; WA 1:65–69).

k   WA Br 1:135–41. Bishop Jerome also gave Luther permission to publish his defense of the *95 Theses*, the *Explanations* (LW 31:77–252).

l   WA Br 1:121–23.

m   For recent contributions to the debate, see Joachim Ott and Martin Treu, eds., *Luthers Thesenanschlag—Faktum oder Fiktion* (Leipzig: Evangelische Verlagsanstalt, 2008).

first arrived in Wittenberg in August 1518 and thus was not an eyewitness to the event.[9] The historical details that Melanchthon provided throughout the preface are at best mixed, where some "factual errors" are included with descriptions of events that historians have since discovered to be completely accurate. Melanchthon and Luther had countless conversations not recorded elsewhere, so that Melanchthon could well have simply been reporting what Luther had told him, namely, that on 31 October 1517, Luther posted a copy of the *95 Theses* on the Castle Church door.[n]

Melanchthon could, however, simply have *assumed* that Luther acted in line with university statutes and posted these theses the way he had posted others for regular disputations.[o] The door of the Castle Church functioned as a kind of University of Wittenberg bulletin board; it was such an important source of information that printers in the 1540s and beyond began publishing collections of the notices and poems that regularly appeared there. Moreover, in the early statutes of the university, notices for disputations along with their theses were to be posted on all of the church doors in the city—a small detail that may either substantiate Melanchthon's story or, since Melanchthon mentioned only the Castle Church, call it into question. A handwritten note recorded before Luther's death in a book owned by Georg Rörer (1492–1557), Luther's faithful scribe who preserved many of his later lectures and sermons, mentions how the *Theses* were published on all the church doors. In any case, Melanchthon could hardly have anticipated the future use of his offhand remark, which turned the posting into an icon. Instead, he was simply mentioning what Luther had told him or describing the normal turn of events: Luther wrote and posted the theses because of Tetzel's preaching.

9. One of Melanchthon's students, Georg Major (1502–1574), was indeed a choir boy in the Castle Church at the time and also referred in later letters to the posting, but the language in these letters is too closely related to Melanchthon's own account to provide indisputable proof for the posting. Some criticism of Melanchthon arises from long-held views of his reliability as a Lutheran theologian, an issue that the most recent scholarship has rejected. Besides Major, Johann Agricola (1494–1566) and Nicholas von Amsdorf (1483–1565) also lived in Wittenberg in 1517. Neither is known to have objected.

n In a lecture from the 1550s, Melanchthon mentioned that this happened at Vespers. See CR 25:777.

o Some of these disputations are mentioned in the *Liber Decanorum: Das Dekanatsbuch der Theologische Fakultät zu Wittenberg*, ed. Johannes Ficker (Halle: Niemeyer, 1923), records kept by the deans of the theology faculty from the university's founding in 1502.

Luther's later recollections of these times occasionally single out 31 October but make no mention of an actual posting of the *Theses*. In the November letter to Lang, Luther simply passed along the theses as to a friend (apologizing for not having sent them sooner), which reflects the fact that even in his introduction to the *95 Theses* he expected people from a distance to respond by letter—a somewhat unique request regarding theses for disputation. Scholars agree that no public disputation ever took place, as Luther later admitted, although the faculty of the University of Mainz, to which the archbishop gave responsibility to judge Luther's theses, assumed in their judgment of December 1517 that such a disputation must have taken place, as would normally have occurred in such cases.

A related question regarding the posting is whether Luther had the theses printed. The only press in Wittenberg at the time was, after all, in the basement of the Augustinian friary where Luther lived and worked. That the printer Johann Grünenberg (d. c. 1525) had typeset Luther's *97 Theses against Scholastic Theology* from September 1517 indicates that printing such theses was a normal part of the press's work.[10] But a scholar such as Luther was also accustomed to making multiple handwritten copies, which he could then have sent to the prelates and friends mentioned above and which he may have posted. The fact that no copy from Wittenberg's press has yet been discovered may mean that not Luther but his friends, who lived in the publishing centers of Leipzig and Nuremberg (from which we have extant printed copies), first had it printed in the well-known placard form.[11]

The debate over these questions contributes very little to understanding the *Theses* themselves, especially since their most important recipient was Archbishop Albrecht, to whom the theses were sent on 31 October. It was Albrecht's subsequent actions—asking both his own theologians in Mainz and Rome for an opinion of the *Theses*—that turned a serious disputation into a legal case before the pope. One can also see why such matters may have some relevance, especially in clarifying Luther's motives for writing the

10. See LW 31:3–16. The Wittenberg printing was discovered in the Duke August Library in Wolfenbüttel, Germany. Whether Luther also had the *95 Theses* printed does not affect the arguments about posting one way or the other.

11. A third printing in booklet form and dated 1518 comes from Basel, probably the most famous printing center north of the Alps. In a letter to Christoph Scheurl (1481-1542) in Nuremberg, dated 5 March 1518 (WA Br 1:151–53), Luther thanked him for copies of the Latin and German text, where the former at least must have been printed copies. No copy of a German translation is extant.

Theses in the first place. First and foremost, if Luther did not post and, subsequently, did not print his theses, the famous image of an angry young man with hammer and nails in hand, striding to the Castle Church door and destroying the papacy and the unity of the church is shown for what it is (even if he did post them)—a legend. Yet, even if Luther did print and post the *Theses* for debate, he had no notion what the results of such a debate would be and certainly did not have in mind attacking the papacy or splitting the church—something he never claimed to have done in any case. Indeed, in letters from early 1518, Luther seemed rather surprised at how widely the *Theses* had been disseminated. Moreover, if Luther only "posted" the *Theses* in the mail as an attachment to letters addressed to his superiors, this would underscore further Luther's clear adherence to the rules governing theological debate at the time, although it is not entirely clear that all theses had first to be approved by one's ordinary bishop, as later was the case. In any event, the posting of theses was part of the normal life of every late medieval European university and not the defiant act of a dissatisfied monk. Thus, Luther wrote and distributed the *95 Theses* as a matter of pastoral and theological concern, showing every respect for his ecclesiastical superiors by informing and warning them of the *Theses'* content.

The single-sheet printing of the *95 Theses* by Michael Lotter in Leipzig. Now in the National Library in Berlin.

In some ways, the notoriety of the *95 Theses* has been exaggerated because of later events. Although we have three separate printings in Latin, the number of actual copies in circulation would have been relatively small. Although someone in Nuremberg translated the *Theses* into German, it is uncertain whether this translation was ever published (given that no printed copies of such a translation now exist). Moreover, in a letter to a colleague in Nuremberg, Luther voiced skepticism about whether laypersons would understand them—a skepticism that led him to publish the *Sermon on Indulgences and Grace*, designed to explain the matter in German to the laity.[p] Not the *95 Theses* but this second publication, which appeared in early 1518, made Luther into a household name and best-selling author.

Literary Considerations

Luther clearly composed the *95 Theses* as theses for debate. Yet, when compared to other theses that he and other professors were composing at around the same time, the *95 Theses* contain some aspects that were decidedly not intended for classroom debate using logic and syllogisms. They have a far more rhetorical flare than one finds in other university theses, both before and after 1517. Indeed, it may help to consider this document as a mixture of logical argument and impassioned speech, as Luther addresses what he viewed as a looming pastoral and theological problem in the church. His defense of the *Theses* published in the summer of 1518 contains lengthy arguments gleaned from Scripture, the church fathers, papal decrees, and canon law, and thus takes the form of an academic debate.[q] But the *Theses* themselves, the letter to Albrecht, and the *Sermon on Indulgences and Grace* aim at both the head and the heart of the reader

---

p   See below, pp. 60–65. See also Luther's response to Johann Eck, *Luther's Asterisks against the Obelisks of Eck* (1518; WA 1:311, 19–25, here 19–20): "For since I had not had them published in the people's language nor had I sent them out more widely than to those around us."

q   LW 31:77–252.

(although Luther would hardly have made the same distinction between the two that today's readers do).

As an example of a tightly constructed logical argument, there are the first four theses, which briefly outline Luther's assumptions about the nature of penitence.[12] Similarly, theses 5–20 provide a focused argument about the limits of papal authority in giving indulgence. Again, theses 56–68 address the single question of the nature of the "treasury of merits," which, Luther argued, had not been well understood in the church. Yet, even these sections of the *95 Theses* contain certain rhetorical turns of phrase that are unusual and thus worth noting.

As a student at the University of Erfurt in the early 1500s, Luther would have learned the basics of constructing and ornamenting writings according to the rhetorical rules current in his day.^r One began with an *exordium*, designed to get the reader's attention and favor. Then a narration of the accepted facts or presuppositions followed. A succinct *description* of the subject under discussion (sometimes labeled the "state of the controversy" or simply "theme") was followed by what was always the longest part of any speech or writing, the *confirmation*, which sought to prove the various parts of the author's argument. A so-called *confutation*, which anticipated opponents' objections and rebutted them, was followed by the *peroration*, a conclusion that either summarized the author's point or once again appealed to the reader's goodwill in taking the arguments to heart.[13] One hint that Luther was also thinking rhetorically comes from the *Explanations of the 95 Theses*, where Luther labels theses 81–91 a confutation. The theses that follow (92–95) are clearly an open appeal to the readers and form an obvious peroration. They have such a high rhetorical tone that several of Luther's opponents ignored them altogether.

12. Throughout Luther's works, in both Latin and German, a single word (*poenitentia* and *Buße*), may be best rendered penance, penitence, or repentance, depending on the context.

13. The Latin terms, some already found in Cicero (106 BCE–43 BCE) and Quintilian (c. 35–c. 100), were *exordium, narratio, status controversiae, confirmatio, confutatio,* and *peroratio.*

---

r   For Luther's use of rhetoric, see Birgit Stolt, *Martin Luthers Rhetorik des Herzens* (Tübingen: Mohr Siebeck, 2000); Neil R. Leroux, *Luther's Rhetoric: Strategies and Style from the Invocavit Sermons* (St. Louis: Concordia, 2002); Helmar Junghans, *Martin Luther und die Rhetorik* (Leipzig: Hirzel, 1998).

Based on the presence of these more explicitly rhetorical parts, one can also notice a rhetorical structure in other sections of the *Theses*. The announcement of the debate, far from being an unimportant historical vestige, functions as a simple exordium, asking for the reader's attention and response for the sake of the truth and invoking Christ's blessing. The first four theses, as Luther later insists in his *Explanations*, were not up for debate but represented the underlying assumptions on which the entire writing rested, and thus functioned as a narration. The fifth thesis, by contrast, states precisely the heart of the debate: "The pope neither desires nor is able to remit any penalties except those imposed by his own authority or that of the canons." That Luther includes the word *desires* here is a further indication of the rhetorical, emotive side to these *Theses*. The determination of papal desires was hardly a matter of syllogisms and logical arguments. In the *Explanations*, Luther insists that this thesis is up for debate.

What follows in theses 6–80 is the heart of the piece, rhetorically speaking. Here Luther addresses the central topic of the limits of papal authority to remove the penalty (though not the guilt) of a person's sin (theses 6–20). Thesis 20, introduced by "therefore," summarizes the foregoing arguments in language echoing thesis 5. In thesis 21 he mentions for the first time the indulgence preachers and begins the first of three corollaries to his main point: 21–40 reject bad preaching and its false claims;[14] theses 41–55 discuss how Christians ought to be taught given the tension between preaching indulgences and encouraging truly Christian works and the gospel;[15] and theses 56–68 define the treasures of the church again over against the claims of indulgence preachers. A final section (69–80) outlines the proper response church leaders should take to restrain such preachers.

What Luther himself later labels the confutation (81–91) possesses its own rhetorical cleverness. Instead of providing objections to his *own* argument (that indulgences only lifted ecclesiastical penalties), Luther introduces the questions of an "informed layperson." Such objections to the reign-

14. This first corollary has three parts: preaching release from all penalties is wrong (21–24); the papal relation to the souls in purgatory (25–29); the relation of contrition to indulgence preaching (30–40).

15. This corollary explores proper preaching and employs the rhetorically charged phrase "Christians are to be taught." After introducing the theme (40), a first section deals with wealth, almsgiving, and the problem of false trust (42–52), and a second, smaller section contrasts indulgences to the gospel (53–55).

ing view of indulgences had (in Luther's mind) no answers except by returning to Luther's simple solution (thesis 91), which (like thesis 5) is connected to "the spirit and intention of the pope." Many of these objections may be found in the writings of others before 1517. Luther's conclusion, or peroration (92–95), contains some of the most rhetorically charged language of the entire piece, associating the sharp condemnation of the prophet Jeremiah with the indulgence preachers, who falsely imagine they are offering peace, and contrasting it to the proper preaching of the cross. The final two theses match the argument at the very beginning of the tract, that the entire life of the Christian is one of penitence.

Themes

Because of the form of Luther's argument, using tightly worded theses to express his point, and because of the foreign nature of the debate itself, it is often hard to understand the *Theses* and the effect they had on their first readers. Paying attention to the structure of the *Theses* helps to identify several different important points. First and foremost, Luther had indulgence preachers in mind while writing, as the cover letter to Archbishop Albrecht also makes clear. References to their abuses appear throughout the *Theses*. At the same time, Luther's research into the nature of indulgences had driven him to the conclusion that their original usage had become obscured by later practices, especially by the confusion of penalties imposed by the church for the sake of discipline with punishments ordained by God (thesis 5). But his research also led him to Erasmus's commentary on the New Testament, where the Dutch humanist argues against using Matt. 4:17 as a proof text for the sacrament of penance, given that the Greek word *metanoia* should not be translated (as had Jerome in the Latin Vulgate) "Do penance" (*poenitentiam agite*). Luther thus argues, in line with his developing theology, that the entire life of the Christian is one of penitence (theses 1–4).

On this basis, he also argues that the present practice surrounding indulgences, which gave the pope authority over God's punishment of sinners on earth and in purgatory, actually harmed the Christian life of dying to sin and rising to faith in God's promises. (See thesis 5 and the proofs in 6–7 on the removal of guilt and 8–20 on the nature of punishment in this life and in purgatory.) He then attacks what he sees as the exaggerated claims of the indulgence preachers, who promised forgiveness to those who purchased the letters for themselves and, for those who purchased them for their deceased loved ones, release from purgatory (thesis 21ff.). After providing the content of proper preaching (theses 41–51, with their refrain, "Christians are to be taught"), which includes a plea to give to the poor, Luther summarizes what he sees as other exaggerations by these preachers (theses 52–55) and then examines a related problem of the "treasury of the church," from which, it had been claimed, the pope could apply the merits of Christ and the saints to sinners by means of indulgences. Having rejected other definitions, Luther insists that this treasury was none other than the gospel itself (theses 56–67) and concludes with a plea to bishops and others to rein in these preachers (theses 68–80). After listing the sharp objections of the laity, Luther ends with an emotion-laden conclusion, contrasting the false peace offered Christians through indulgences to the cross of Christ and, hence, the Christian life of continual penitence.

Reactions

The *95 Theses* elicited immediate reactions from several groups and individuals. First, Luther's friends in Nuremberg and elsewhere saw to its wider distribution through printings spread throughout the Holy Roman Empire. Individuals, especially people associated with Renaissance humanism, regarded this as a further step in the renewal of good theology on the basis of ancient sources.[5] Those in

---

5 See the classic arguments by Lewis Spitz, *The Protestant Reformation: 1517–1559* (New York: Harper & Row, 1985), 88–101.

natus in pago Eck.13.Nov.1486. Obiit 10 Febr.1543 æt.57.
Procancellarius Acad. Ingolstad.

Johann Eck (1486–1543).

Wittenberg also supported Luther's position, and Luther's colleague Andreas Bodenstein from Karlstadt (1486–1541), soon entered the lists in attacking Johann Eck (1486–1543).[16]

But Luther's appeal to Archbishop Albrecht resulted in the cardinal sending the *Theses* to his own theological faculty in Mainz and to the papal court for judgment. Near the end of 1517, the former published a mild rejection of Luther's

16. Johann Eck, whose family name was Maier, was born in the town of Eck in southwestern Germany. After schooling at the universities of Heidelberg, Tübingen, and Freiburg im Breisgau, he became professor of theology at the University of Ingolstadt. He was one of Wittenberg's most intractable opponents, debating Luther in Leipzig in 1519, writing countless refutations of Evangelical positions, opposing Lutherans at the Diet of Augsburg in 1530, and holding conversations with Philipp Melanchthon in Worms and Regensburg in 1540–41.

claims. The much harsher response from Rome, which was entrusted to Sylvester Prierias (c. 1456–1527), the papal court theologian, was published by the summer of 1518.[t] Meanwhile, in January 1518 Johann Tetzel received his doctorate at the University of Frankfurt/Oder defending theses composed by Konrad Wimpina (1465–1531), all of which attacked Luther's theses. A few months later, in March or April, Tetzel published another fifty theses, each one using Luther's own pointed phrase ("Christians must be taught") to refute him.[u] Luther responded in part to Tetzel in his German *Sermon on Indulgences and Grace*, going into even more detail in his *Explanations*.[v] Meanwhile, Johann Eck, from the University of Ingolstadt, had also gotten ahold of a copy of the *95 Theses* and wrote a response that he shared only in manuscript form with some friends. When Luther received a copy of these *Obelisks* (so-called because Eck had marked each objection to Luther's theses with an obelisk [†]), he felt betrayed, since just the year before he had attempted to begin a correspondence with Eck. He published a response, called the *Asterisks*, in which he answered line for line Eck's objections, using an asterisk (*) to mark his own arguments. By October 1518, when Luther traveled to Augsburg for an interview with Cardinal Cajetan, the arguments had begun to move beyond the original issue of indulgences and their preaching and on to other topics, especially the authority of the pope, which all of Luther's opponents believed Luther's *Theses* had attacked as well.[w] Nevertheless, several later judgments by the Universities of Louvain and Paris, and an extensive refutation by the French theologian Jacobus Latomus (c. 1475–1544) also formed part of the initial reaction

---

t   Luther replied in his *Response to the Dialogue of Silvester Prierias concerning the Power of the Pope* (1518), in WA 1:644–86, with 9:782–86.

u   Both are contained in Peter Fabisch and Erwin Iserloh, eds., *Dokumente zur Causa Lutheri (1517–1521)*, vol. 1: *Das Gutachten des Prierias und weitere Schriften gegen Luthers Ablaßthesen (1517–1518)* (Münster: Aschendorff, 1988), 310–37 (*Frankfurter Thesen*), and 363–75 (*Fünfzig Positiones*).

v   See below, pp. 60–65, and, for the *Explanations*, LW 31:77–252.

w   For the interview with Cajetan, see below, pp. 128–65.

to the *Theses*.[x] By the time Eck squared off with Karlstadt and Luther for the Leipzig Debates in the summer of 1519, the central issue in Luther's case had become the authority of the papacy and church councils in relation to the word of God.

Despite what Luther may have expected to result from the *Theses*, things had taken an unexpected (and, perhaps, unwanted) turn, one that was light-years from the original debate. Nevertheless, when Eck arrived in Rome in 1520, bent on writing a papal bull of excommunication for Luther, at least some of the "heretical" doctrines came from the *95 Theses* and its defense.[y] At the same time, Luther continued to find a variety of supporters throughout the Holy Roman Empire. While Erasmus of Rotterdam (1466–1536) and others remained somewhat distant and finally antagonistic and some only praised Luther for his courage to stand up to the authorities of the day, still others found his thought quite convincing. Thus, when in the spring of 1518 he appeared before a meeting of representatives of the German Augustinian chapter houses and held the Heidelberg Disputation, several, including the future reformers of Strasbourg, Martin Bucer (1491–1551), and of Schwäbisch Hall and later Württemberg, Johannes Brenz (1499–1570), marked this encounter as the beginning of their support for Luther and his theology.[z]

---

x See Hannegreth Grundmann, *Gratia Christi: Die theologische Begründung des Ablasses durch Jacobus Latomus in der Kontroverse mit Martin Luther* (Berlin: LIT, 2012) and Luther's response, *Against Latomus* (1521), in LW 32:133–260.

y See Luther's *Defense and Explanation of All the Articles Condemned by the Most Recent Bull of Leo X* (1521) in LW 32:3–99.

z For the *Heidelberg Disputation*, see below, pp. 80–120.

17. This translation is based upon that of Charles M. Jacobs, revised by Harold J. Grimm in LW 31:17–33, as well as upon WA 1:233–38, with reference to the helpful notes in MLStA 1:171–85. The title is taken from the 1518 Basel reprint.

18. There is no evidence that such a public debate took place in Wittenberg. Their publication and subsequent distribution led to vigorous reactions. This functions as a kind of exordium to the entire document. See the introduction, p. 28.

19. Luther is quoting the standard Vulgate rendering of Matt. 4:17 (*Poenitentiam agite*, translated "Repent!" in most English versions). In Latin and German, however, the phrase may be rendered "Do penance," "Be penitent," or "Repent." These first four theses represent the basic narration of what Luther considered generally accepted facts.

20. As the *Explanations of the 95 Theses* (1518), LW 31:83f., made clear, Luther was relying here on Erasmus's annotations to the Greek text, first published in 1516, which pointed out that the Greek verb *metanoeite* did not mean "do penance" but "come to one's senses" and thus did not refer to the sacrament of penance.

21. For the parts of the sacrament of penance (contrition, confession, and satisfaction) and the distinction between guilt and punishment, see the introduction, p. 14f. Luther touched on contrition in thesis 3 and punishment (*poena*) in thesis 4.

[THE NINETY-FIVE THESES OR]

DISPUTATION FOR CLARIFYING THE POWER OF INDULGENCES[17]

OUT OF LOVE AND ZEAL for bringing the truth to light, what is written below will be debated in Wittenberg with the Reverend Father Martin Luther,[a] Master of Arts and Sacred Theology and regularly appointed lecturer on these subjects at that place, presiding. Therefore, he requests that those who cannot be present to discuss orally with us will in their absence do so by letter.[18] In the name of our Lord Jesus Christ. Amen.

1.   Our Lord and Master Jesus Christ, in saying "Do penance . . . ,"[19] wanted the entire life of the faithful to be one of penitence.
2.   This phrase cannot be understood as referring to sacramental Penance,[20] that is, confession and satisfaction as administered by the clergy.[21]

a   Or, in two printings, Lutther. Around this time, he began spelling his name "Luther" in his letters, in part as a play on the Greek word *eleutherius* ("the free one"). See WA Br 1:122 (letter to Johannes Lang [c. 1487–1548], dated 11 November 1517) and LW 48:55 (letter to Georg Spalatin [1484–1545], dated 18 January 1518).

3. Yet it does not mean solely inner penitence—indeed such inner penitence is nothing unless it outwardly produces various mortifications of the flesh.[22]

4. And thus,[23] penalty[b] remains as long as hatred of self[c] (that is, true inner penitence) remains, namely, until our entrance into the kingdom of heaven.[d]

5. The pope neither desires nor is able to remit[e] any penalties except those imposed by his own discretion or that of the canons.[24]

6. The pope cannot remit any guilt except by declaring and confirming its remission by God or, of course, by remitting guilt in [legal] cases reserved to himself.[25] In showing contempt regarding such cases, the guilt would certainly remain.

22. Inward penitence is contrition. External putting to death of the flesh was part of satisfaction. For the medieval debate over when God's grace was infused in the penitent (at the moment of contrition or in confessional), see the introduction, p. 14.

23. Latin: *itaque*. These theses consisted in a series of logical arguments, so that this concludes the underlying narrative for the actual disputation.

24. Thesis 5 states Luther's central premise. Old church law had specified that penalties (*poena*) for sin be imposed before absolution was administered (see thesis 12) and were part of church discipline. Hence, Luther argues that the church could show leniency, or indulgence, only in regard to these ecclesiastical penalties, not God's punishment. See the introduction, p. 21f. The phrase "by his discretion or that of the canons" was a technical term describing how a priest in the confessional would first see if the sin in question had a penalty prescribed in the penitential canons and, if not, could use his discretion.

25. In terms of divine grace and the removal of guilt (*culpa*), priests simply announced God's forgiveness. Regarding especially heinous sins, ecclesiastical absolution was restricted to the papal see.

---

b Latin: *poena*, the root of *poeni-tentia*. The linguistic and theological connection between penalty and penance is hard to capture in English.

c See John 12:25.

d See Matt. 7:21-23. That is, until after death.

e That is, set aside or forgive.

26. In the *Explanations* (1518) of this thesis, LW 31:99, Luther emphasizes how God moves the penitent from condemnation (law) to absolution (gospel). In October 1518, Cardinal Cajetan rejected Luther's position about certainty, as expressed in the *Explanations* (31:100), that "the person who is to be absolved must guard himself very carefully from any doubt that God has remitted his sins, in order that he may find peace of heart." On Luther's encounter with Cajetan, see below, pp. 132f., 141–47.

27. These rules, contained in medieval penitential books, were derived from the practices of the ancient church for imposing ecclesiastical penalties on flagrant sinners, in order to reconcile them to the church.

28. Luther is referring to the parable of the wheat and tares (sown by the evil one while the owner slept) from Matt. 13:25. Already John Chrysostom (c. 347–407) in his homilies on Matthew (XLVI) had connected those who sleep with ecclesiastic rulers. Throughout the *Theses*, Luther distinguished between canonical (ecclesiastical) penalties and penalties imposed by God during life and in purgatory.

29. This association of terror with the punishment of purgatory, already found among German mystics like Johannes Tauler (c. 1300–1361), is central to Luther's experience of the cross and attacks on his faith. See the *Explanations* (1518), LW 31:125–30.

30. Latin: *securitas*. Security often had a negative connotation in the Middle Ages, but here Luther uses it to describe the complete assurance of the soul in heaven.

7. God remits the guilt of absolutely no one unless at the same time God subjects in all things the one humbled to God's vicar, the priest.[26]

8. The penitential canons[27] were imposed only on the living, and, according to the canons themselves, nothing should be imposed on those about to die.[f]

9. Accordingly, the Holy Spirit through the pope acts in a kindly manner toward us in papal decrees by always exempting the moment of death and the case of necessity.[g]

10. Those priests act ignorantly and wickedly who, in the case of the dying, reserve canonical penalties for one's time in purgatory.

11. Those "tares" about changing the canonical penalty into the penalty of purgatory certainly seem to have been "sown" while the bishops "were sleeping."[28]

12. Formerly, canonical penalties were imposed not after, but before absolution, as tests of true contrition.[h]

13. Through death, those about to die are absolved of all [such penalties] and are already dead as far as canon laws are concerned, in that by right they have release from them.[i]

14. Imperfect purity or love on the part of the dying person necessarily brings with it great fear. The smaller the love, the greater the fear.

15. This fear or horror is enough by itself alone (to say nothing of other things) to constitute the penalty of purgatory, since it is very near the horror of despair.[29]

16. It seems that hell, purgatory, and heaven differ from each other as much as despair, near despair, and assurance.[30]

f   Given that the church's juridical authority ended at death. See also thesis 13.

g   These two exceptions may be found throughout canon law. See MLStA 1:177, nn. 20–21.

h   See above, n. 21.

17. It seems necessary that, for souls in purgatory, as the horror decreases so love increases.[31]

18. It neither seems proved—either by any logical arguments or by Scripture—that souls in purgatory are outside a state of merit,[32] that is, unable to grow in love;

19. nor does it seem to be proved that these souls, at least not all of them, are certain and assured of their own salvation—even though we ourselves are completely certain about [their destiny].

20. Therefore,[33] the pope understands by the phrase "plenary[j] remission of all penalties" not actually "all penalties" but only "penalties imposed by himself."

21. And so,[34] those indulgence preachers err who say that through the pope's indulgences a person is released[k] and saved from every penalty.

22. On the contrary, to souls in purgatory he remits no penalty that they should have paid[l] in this life according to canon law.

23. If any remission of all penalties whatsoever could be granted to anyone, it would certainly be granted only to the most perfect, that is, to the very fewest.

24. Because of this, most people are inevitably deceived by means of this indiscriminate and high-sounding promise of release from penalty.

25. The kind of power that a pope has over purgatory in general corresponds to the power that any bishop or local priest[m] has in particular in his diocese or parish.[35]

26. The pope does best in that he grants remission to souls [in purgatory] not by "the power of the keys," which he does not possess [here], but "by way of intercession."[36]

---

i   See theses 8–10.

j   I.e., "full."

k   Latin: *solvere*.

l   Latin: *solvere*.

m   Latin: *curatus*, the particular priest serving a parish.

---

31. Luther had stated a similar view in his lectures on Romans (1515–1516), LW 25:381f. For earlier discussions over whether a soul is active or passive in purgatory, see Thomas Aquinas (*Commentary on the Sentences*, bk. IV d. 45, q. 2, a. 1), who came to the opposite conclusion.

32. That is, a state of grace as opposed to a state of sin.

33. Latin: *igitur*. This concludes the argument in the previous theses (6–19) and reiterates the point in thesis 5.

34. Latin: *itaque*. This introduces a first corollary (theses 21–40) to Luther's just-concluded main argument and begins an attack on indulgence preachers, focusing on preaching release from all penalties, the limits of papal authority, and the nature of contrition.

35. Luther's second argument against the indulgence preachers (theses 25–29) aims at their exaggerated claims about releasing souls from purgatory.

36. Luther was arguing that the "power of the keys," given to Peter (Matt. 16:19) and, by extension, to all priests and bishops to forgive sin, did not extend to purgatory but that only intercession did. *Per modum suffragii* ("by way of intercession"), a technical term, denotes when one intercedes with prayers and in other ways especially for souls in purgatory (e.g., through Masses for their souls). Some medieval theologians, including Bonaventure (1221–1274), had suggested that this was the basis for the papal authority to grant indulgences. In the summer of 1517, however, Luther came into possession of tracts by Johann Eck, who argued that by virtue of the papal "plenitude of power," the pope also had direct authority to release souls, a position that Luther rejected here. Luther discussed this more fully in the other document enclosed with Albrecht's letter, the so-called *Tractate on Indulgences*.

37. Perhaps a phrase used by Johann Tetzel (see Luther's *Letter to Archbishop Albrecht*, p. 52), as he admitted in his attack on the 95 Theses. The German ditty "As soon as money in the chest rings, a soul from purgatory springs," predated Tetzel and was used commonly to sell indulgences.

38. Severinus, archbishop of Cologne (late fourth century), and Paschasius, deacon of Rome (fifth century), preferred to remain longer in purgatory to gain greater glory in heaven, according to Luther's source, Johann von Paltz (1445–1511), a theologian at the University of Erfurt when Luther studied there, who mentioned both saints in his *Supplementum Coelifodinae* (Erfurt, 1504), E 6v, and made the same misspelling. Paltz based his comments about Paschasius on Pope Gregory I (c. 540–604), *Dialogues*, bk. 4, ch. 40, and about Severinus on Peter Damian (c. 1007–1072/73), *De variis miraculosis narrationibus*, ch. 5 (MPL 145:578).

39. This begins a third argument against bad preaching, foreshadowed in the saying in thesis 27. Luther connects assurance to God's promise. See above, n. 26. Luther quotes a technical term used in the *Summary Instruction*, which connects the Peter's Indulgence to *complete* forgiveness of

27. They "preach human opinions"[n] who say that, as soon as a coin thrown into the money chest clinks, a soul flies out [of purgatory].[37]

28. It is certain that when a coin clinks in the money chest profits and avarice may well be increased, but the intercession of the church rests on God's choice alone.

29. Who knows whether all the souls in purgatory want to be redeemed, given what is recounted about St. Severinus and St. Paschasius?[38,o]

30. No one is secure in the genuineness of one's own contrition—much less in having attained "plenary remission."[39]

31. As rare as a person who is truly penitent, just so rare is someone who truly acquires indulgences; indeed, the latter is the rarest of all.[p]

32. Those who believe that they can be secure in their salvation through indulgence letters will be eternally damned along with their teachers.

33. One must especially beware of those who say that those indulgences of the pope are "God's inestimable gift" by which a person is reconciled to God.[40]

34. For these indulgent graces are only based on the penalties of sacramental satisfaction instituted by human beings.[q]

---

n   Plato (c. 428–c. 347 BCE), *Theaetetus*, 170.

o   Latin: *Paschalius*. Luther also referred to such legends somewhat skeptically in the *Explanations* (1518), LW 31:178.

p   Here "penitence" is understood as contrition and "indulgences" as lenience. See n. 19.

q   See above, thesis 5.

35. Those who teach that contrition is not necessary on the part of those who would rescue souls [from purgatory] or who would buy confessional privileges[41] do not preach Christian views.

36. Any truly remorseful Christian has a right to full remission of guilt and penalty,[r] even without indulgence letters.

37. Any true Christian, living or dead, possesses a God-given share in all the benefits[s] of Christ and the church, even without indulgence letters.

38. Nevertheless, remission and participation [in these benefits] from the pope must by no means be despised, because—as I said[t]—they are the declaration of divine remission.

39. It is extremely difficult, even for the most learned theologians, to lift up before the people the liberality of indulgences and the truth about contrition at one and the same time.[42]

40. The "truth about contrition" seeks and loves penalties [for sins]; the "liberality of indulgences" relaxes penalties and at very least gives occasion for hating them.[43]

41. Apostolic indulgences[44] are to be preached with caution, so that the people do not mistakenly think that they are to be preferred to other good works of love.

sin (i.e., guilt and punishment). In the *Explanations* (1518), LW 31:178f., Luther claims to be using the language of the indulgence preachers, who insisted that the benefits of indulgences were tied to genuine contrition.

40. This addresses another claim of indulgence preachers (see theses 21, 27), also found in the *Summary Instruction*.

41. Latin: *confessionalia*. Such letters allowed penitents to choose their own confessors and were specifically mentioned in the *Summary Instruction* that defined the Peter's Indulgence. See above, p. 30. Luther again touches on this in thesis 84.

42. Here and in thesis 40, Luther summarizes the problem of contrition and indulgence preaching, something he himself had also referred to in preaching the anniversary indulgence for the Castle Church in January 1517. Luther also explains this in the so-called *Tract on Indulgences*, attached to the letter to Albrecht. See the introduction, p. 18, and below, p. 50.

43. See Luther's comments in a sermon from 24 February 1517, in LW 51:31: "Would that I were a liar when I say that indulgences are rightly so called, for to indulge means to permit, and indulgence is equivalent to impunity, permission to sin, and license to nullify the cross of Christ."

44. That is, indulgences granted by the successor to the apostles, the pope, in this case the so-called Peter's Indulgence. Luther now introduces a second corollary and explores the possibility of good preaching of indulgences and their relation to good

---

r See the introduction, p. 13f. In Advent sermons of 1516 and Lenten sermons in 1517 (published in early 1517), Johann von Staupitz (c. 1460–1524), the head of Luther's order in Germany, had made a similar point.

s Latin: *participatio omnium bonorum Christi et Ecclesie*, literally, "a share in all the goods of Christ and the church." This common technical term (used, e.g., by Thomas Aquinas, *Summa Theologica* II/II, d. 63, a. 2, ad 1) encompassed all manner of spiritual blessings.

t See above, thesis 6.

works and the gospel. See also the *Sermon on Indulgences and Grace*, below, p. 64.

45. This striking phrase, used to introduce theses 42–51, was then borrowed by Tetzel to begin a set of countertheses.

46. The Peter's Indulgence was, however, priced on a sliding scale, depending on one's station in life.

47. In his letter to Pope Eugene III (d. 1153), bk. 5, Bernard of Clairvaux (1090–1153) describes the importance of the prayers of the faithful in aiding the pope to fulfill his office.

42. Christians are to be taught[45] that the pope does not intend the acquiring of indulgences to be compared in any way with works of mercy.

43. Christians are to be taught that the one who gives to a poor person or lends to the needy[u] does a better deed than if a person acquires indulgences,

44. because love grows through works of love and a person is made better; but through indulgences one is not made better but only freer from penalty [for sin].[v]

45. Christians are to be taught that anyone who sees a destitute person and, while passing such a one by, gives money for indulgences does not buy [gracious] indulgence of the pope but God's wrath.

46. Christians are to be taught that, unless they have more than they need, they must set aside enough for their household and by no means squander it on indulgences.[46]

47. Christians are to be taught that buying indulgences is a matter of free choice, not commanded.[w]

48. Christians are to be taught that the pope, while granting indulgences, needs and thus desires their devout prayer for him more than their money.[47]

49. Christians are to be taught that papal indulgences are useful [for them] only if they do not put their trust in them but extremely harmful if they lose their fear of God because of them.

50. Christians are to be taught that if the pope knew the demands made by the indulgence preachers, he would rather that the Basilica of St. Peter were burned to ashes than that it be constructed using the skin, flesh, and bones of his sheep.[x]

---

u   See Matt. 5:42.

v   Theses 43 and 44 are, grammatically speaking, one sentence.

w   See below, *Sermon on Indulgences and Grace*, p. 64f.

x   For the connection of this papal indulgence to St. Peter's in Rome, see the introduction, p. 17.

51. Christians are to be taught that the pope ought to give and would want to give of his own wealth—even selling the Basilica of St. Peter if necessary—to those from whom certain declaimers[48] of indulgences are wheedling money.

52. It is vain to trust in salvation by means of indulgence letters, even if the [indulgence] agent—or even the pope himself—were to offer his own soul as security for them.[49]

53. People who forbid the preaching of the Word of God in some churches altogether in order that indulgences may be preached in others are enemies of Christ and the pope.[50]

54. An injustice is done to the Word of God when, in the very same sermon, equal or more time is spent on indulgences than on the Word.[y]

55. It is necessarily the pope's intent that if indulgences, which are a completely insignificant thing, are celebrated with one bell, one procession, and one ceremony, then the gospel, which is the greatest thing of all, should be preached with a hundred bells, a hundred processions, and a hundred ceremonies.[z]

56. The treasures of the church, from which the pope distributes indulgences, are not sufficiently discussed or known among Christ's people.[51]

57. That [these treasures] are not transient worldly[a] riches is certainly clear, because many of the [indulgence] declaimers do not so much freely distribute such riches as only collect them.

48. *Concionatores*: a word for preacher favored by Renaissance humanists and connoting a higher level of oratory, sometimes (as here and in theses 57, 67, and 72) used derogatorily.

49. This summarizes themes brought up in theses 27, 32, and 33 before contrasting preaching of indulgences and the gospel in theses 53–55. The agent (*commisarius*), is the highest authority under whose supervision the indulgence preachers operated.

50. The *Summary Instruction* orders that something like this be done.

51. Theses 56–68 introduce a third corollary dealing with the unsettled question about the treasury of merits. See the introduction, pp. 17, 27, and 30.

---

y   One version reads: "on the gospel Word."

z   For a description of the ceremonies surrounding indulgence sales, see the introduction, p. 18.

a   Latin: *temporales*.

58. Nor are they the merits of Christ and the saints, because, even without the pope, these merits always work grace for the inner person and cross, death, and hell for the outer person.[52]

59. St. Laurence said that the poor of the church were the treasures of the church, but he spoke according to the usage of the word "treasure" in his own time.[53]

60. Not without cause, we say that the keys of the church[b] (given by the merits of Christ) are that treasure.

61. For it is clear that the pope's power only suffices for the remission of [ecclesiastical] penalties and for [legal] actions.[c]

62. The true treasure of the church is the most holy gospel of the glory and grace of God.

63. But this treasure is deservedly the most hated, because it makes "the first last."[d]

64. In contrast, the treasure of indulgences is deservedly the most acceptable, because it makes "the last first."

65. Therefore, the treasures of the gospel are nets with which they[e] formerly fished for men of wealth.

66. The treasures of indulgences are nets with which they now fish for the wealth of men.

67. Indulgences, which the declaimers shout about as the greatest "graces," are indeed understood as such—insofar as they promote profits.[f]

68. Yet they are in truth the least of all when compared to the grace of God and the goodness of the cross.

52. See Luther's lengthy defense in the *Explanations* (1518), LW 31:212–28, which includes reference to the theology of the cross. In the Augsburg interview with Luther in October 1518, Cardinal Cajetan especially objected to this thesis as contradicting the clear teaching of Pope Clement VI (1291–1352). See below, pp. 127f. and 131f. Luther points out that by attaching another's merit to indulgences, they cease being truly an indulgence of the church but only another way of paying the same penalty, and that such merits work death and life even without papal indulgences.

53. From the *Legenda aurea* [*Golden Legends*] (Strasbourg, 1492): "During these three days Laurence gathered together the poor, lame and blind and carried them into the palace . . . saying, 'Look! These are the eternal treasure.'"

b   See above, n. 36. Here "the keys" is now a synonym for the gospel of forgiveness.

c   See theses 5–6. In the medieval church, the papal Curia was the court of last resort.

d   Matt. 19:30 and 20:16.

e   It is not clear who "they" are—perhaps preachers.

f   A play on the word "graces" (*gratiae*), which can also mean "recompense."

69. Bishops and parish priests are bound to admit agents[g] of the Apostolic indulgences with all reverence.[54]

70. But all of them are much more bound to strain eyes and ears intently, so that these [agents] do not preach their own daydreams in place of the pope's commission.

71. Let the one who speaks against the truth of the Apostolic indulgences be anathema and accursed,

72. but let the one who guards against the arbitrary and unbridled words used by declaimers of indulgences be blessed.

73. Just as the pope justly thunders against those who, in whatever way they can, contrive to harm the sale of indulgences,[55]

74. much more so does he intend to thunder against those who, under the pretext of indulgences, contrive to harm holy love and the truth.

75. To imagine that papal indulgences are so great that they could absolve a person even for doing the impossible by violating the mother of God is insanity.[56]

76. On the contrary, we have said[h] that papal indulgences cannot take away the very least of venial sins, as far as guilt is concerned.[57]

77. That it is said that even St. Peter, if he were now pope, could not grant greater graces is blasphemy against St. Peter and the pope.

78. On the contrary, we say that even the present pope, or any pope whatsoever, possesses greater graces—namely, the gospel, "deeds of power, gifts of healing . . ."—as in 1 Cor. 12[:28].

54. Theses 69–80 introduce a final corollary dealing with the question of proper episcopal oversight for indulgence preachers. See also Luther's *Letter to Albrecht*, pp. 52-54.

55. A reference to threats contained in the *Summary Instruction*.

56. In later writings, Luther attributes the statements in theses 75, 77, and 79 directly to Johann Tetzel, who categorically denied ever saying these things. See *Against Hanswurst* (1541), LW 41:231–35.

57. For the distinction between penalty and guilt and between venial and mortal sins, see the introduction, p. 13f.

g   See above, n. 49.

h   Especially in theses 5–20. Other versions read: "we say."

58. This was already the argument of Johann von Paltz, *Supplementum*, A 3v, supporting the early sixteenth-century indulgence preacher in Germany, Cardinal Raimund Peraudi (1435–1505), who even preached a plenary indulgence in Erfurt while Luther was a student there.

59. In theses 81–91, Luther examines the consequences of such preaching (see thesis 72) by means of a refutation of objections (*confutatio*), typical in the classical structuring of a speech or writing. See the introduction, p. 26f.

60. The problem of papal avarice was often mentioned in the official complaints (*gravamina*) lodged at imperial diets. See also Luther's *Sermon on Indulgences and Grace*, p. 64f.

61. The medieval theologian Gabriel Biel had dealt with this question in relation to Masses for baptized children (who were not subject to purgatory). Canon law did not allow prayers for the souls of saints or for the damned.

62. This objection cannot be found before Luther.

63. Here Luther touches on the question of whether a person could continue to suffer in purgatory for an infraction of canon law now no longer enforced.

79. To say that the cross, emblazoned with the papal coat-of-arms and erected [in the church where indulgences are preached], is of equal worth to the cross of Christ is blasphemy.[58]

80. The bishops, parish priests, and theologians who allow such sermons free course among the people will have to answer for this.

81. This unbridled preaching makes it difficult even for learned men to defend the reverence due the pope from slander or from the truly sharp questions of the laity:[59]

82. Namely, "Why does the pope not empty purgatory for the sake of the holiest love and the direst need of souls[i] as a matter of the highest justice, given that he redeems countless souls for filthy lucre to build the Basilica [of St. Peter] as a completely trivial matter?"[60]

83. Again, "Why continue funeral and anniversary Masses for the dead instead of returning or permitting the withdrawal of the endowments founded for them, since it is against the law to pray for those already redeemed?"[61]

84. Again, "What is this new piety of God and the pope that, for the sake of money, they permit someone who is impious and an enemy to redeem [from purgatory] a pious, God-pleasing soul and yet do not, for the sake of the need of that very pious and beloved soul, redeem it purely out of love?"[62]

85. Again, "Why are the penitential canons—long since abrogated and dead in actual fact and through disuse—nevertheless now bought off with money through granting indulgences, as if they were very much alive?"[63]

---

i   See thesis 9.

86. Again, "Why does the pope, whose riches today are more substantial than the richest Crassus,[64] not simply construct the Basilica of St. Peter with his own money rather than with the money of the poor faithful?"

87. Again, "What exactly does the pope 'remit' or 'allow participation in' when it comes to those who through perfect contrition have a right to full remission and a share [in the church's benefits]?"[65]

88. Again, "Could any greater good come to the church than if the pope were to bestow these remissions and participation to each of the faithful a hundred times a day, as he now does but once?"[66]

89. "Since, rather than money, the pope seeks the salvation of souls through indulgences, why does he now suspend the documents and indulgences previously granted, although they have equal efficacy?"[67]

90. To suppress these very pointed arguments of the laity by force alone and not to resolve them by providing reasons is to expose the church and the pope to ridicule by their enemies and to make Christians miserable.

91. Therefore, if indulgences were preached according to the spirit and intention of the pope, all of these [objections] would be easily resolved—indeed, they would not exist.[68]

64. Latin: *opulentissimis crassis crassiores*, literally, "crasser than the richest Crassus," a play on words. Marcus Licinius Crassus (d. 53 BCE) was said at one point in life to have owned most of Rome. Luther again is echoing contemporary suspicions about papal wealth.

65. For Luther's sharp layperson, the saints, who through perfect contrition merited complete forgiveness, would not have need for indulgences. This reflected especially the Nominalist emphasis on human ability to love God in a state of sin completely and thus to bring forth sorrow for sin out of love of God according to the substance of the deed. See theses 37 and 38, which discuss participation in the church's benefactions.

66. Plenary indulgences allowed one application during one's lifetime and at the approach of death, and they were sometimes declared null and void for a certain period of time with the promulgation of a new indulgence. See thesis 89.

67. This objection was already in the imperial complaints (*gravamina*) of 1511. Both Leo X's bull proclaiming the Peter's Indulgence (31 May 1515) and the *Summary Instruction* did this very thing.

68. By applying his basic premise from the earlier theses (especially thesis 5), which limited papal authority to issuing indulgences only for ecclesiastical penalties, Luther thought to solve all of these sharp objections.

69. Latin: *itaque*, introducing theses 92–95, as a kind of conclusion or peroration. See the introduction, p. 29.

70. In a letter from 23 June 1516, addressed to the deposed Augustinian prior in Neustadt an der Orle, Michael Dressel (d. after 1523) (WA Br 1:27, 38–46), Luther writes: "Are you ignorant, most honorable father, that God . . . places his peace in the midst of no peace, that is, in the midst of all trials? . . . Therefore, that person whom no one disturbs does not have peace—on the contrary, this is the peace of the world. Instead, that person whom everyone and everything disturbs has peace and bears all of these things with quiet joy. You are saying with Israel, 'Peace, peace, and there is no peace'; instead say with Christ, 'Cross, cross, and there is no cross.' For as quickly as the cross ceases to be cross so quickly you would say joyfully [with the hymn], 'Blessed cross, among the trees there is none such [as you].'"

92. And thus,[69] away with all those prophets who say to Christ's people, "Peace, peace," and there is no peace![j]

93. May it go well for all of those prophets who say to Christ's people, "Cross, cross," and there is no cross![70]

94. Christians must be encouraged diligently to follow Christ, their head,[k] through penalties, death, and hell,

95. and in this way they may be confident of "entering heaven through many tribulations"[l] rather than through the [false] security of peace.

1517

---

j   See Jer. 6:14; 8:11; and Ezek. 13:10, 16. Peace with God comes through the promise of absolution, not the purchase of indulgences. See also thesis 39 for this difficulty.

k   See, e.g., Col. 1:18.

l   Acts 14:22.

Letter from Martin Luther

to Albrecht, Archbishop of Mainz

31 October 1517

TIMOTHY J. WENGERT

INTRODUCTION

On 31 October 1517, Martin Luther wrote the following letter to the highest ecclesiastical authority in the Holy Roman Empire of the German Nation, Albrecht of Brandenburg (1490–1545).[a] He was the younger son of Margrave Johann II (1455–1499), elector of Brandenburg.[1] Upon Johann's death in 1499, his older brother, Joachim I (1484–1535), succeeded their father as elector. Together in 1506, Joachim and Albrecht founded the University of Frankfurt/Oder, which Albrecht also attended. As the scion of the powerful Hohenzollern family, he became archbishop of Magdeburg in 1513 and administrator of the diocese of Halberstadt, both just west of the lands of the Saxon elector, Frederick III ("the Wise" [1463–1525]). The next year he was named archbishop of Mainz, one of three ecclesiastical electors in the empire, but he ruled from Halle, a city near Magdeburg directly under

1. The term *elector* designates the seven highest princes in the Holy Roman Empire, who were constitutionally responsible for the election of the emperor. In the early sixteenth century, this included four secular princes (the margrave of Brandenburg, the duke of Saxony, the count of the Palatinate [with his central castle in Heidelberg], and the king of Bohemia [who was also the archduke of Austria]), and three ecclesiastical princes (the archbishops of Trier, Cologne, and Mainz).

---

a   For the facts in this introduction, see Bodo Nischan, "Albert of Brandenburg," in *The Oxford Encyclopedia of the Reformation*, ed. Hans J. Hillerbrand, 4 vols. (New York: Oxford University Press, 1996), 1:15–16, and Gottfried Krodel's introduction to the letter in LW 48:43–45.

SIC·OCVLOS·SIC·ILLE·GENAS·SIC·
ORA·FEREBAT
ANNO·ETATIS·SVE·XXIX·
·M·D·XIX·

Cardinal Albrecht of Brandenburg.
Engraving by Dürer, 1519.

2. Luther knew nothing of these arrangements when he wrote the *95 Theses*.

3. By the time Luther was writing this letter, Tetzel had already in the spring preached in Eisleben, Halle, Zerbst, and Jüterbog, all in lands bordering Saxony (Thuringia). Halle and Jüterbog were directly controlled by Albrecht.

4. In 1530, the imperial diet met in Augsburg where, on 25 June 1530, the Evangelical princes and cities presented their confession of faith and defense of changes in practice made since the Reformation began, drafted in large part by Philipp Melanchthon. It came to be known as the *Augsburg Confession* (BC, 27–105).

the control of the archdiocese of Mainz. For the privilege of holding more than one ecclesiastical position (normally forbidden in canon law) and of receiving such a prestigious appointment, Albrecht paid 24,000 ducats (14,000 for the position and another 10,000 for the exemption).

To finance this enormous fee, he received a loan from the powerful Fugger banking family of Augsburg, which he planned to pay off using half the proceeds from the so-called Peter's Indulgence.[2] Already in 1506, Pope Julius II (1443–1513) had proclaimed a plenary indulgence[b] to support building the Church of St. Peter and Paul in Rome. Pope Leo X (1475–1521) renewed this indulgence and in 1515 permitted Albrecht to sell this indulgence in his territories. Albrecht entrusted Johann Tetzel (1465–1519) with the promotion of this indulgence and ordered his court theologians to write the *Summary Instruction*, which explained the benefits of this indulgence and the limits of the preaching that accompanied its sale.[3]

Although Albrecht did not answer Luther's letter directly for at least two years, he did turn over the *95 Theses* enclosed with Luther's letter both to his theology faculty in Mainz and to Rome for their judgment, because he suspected the *Theses* were heretical. A patron of the arts and music, of architecture and humanist scholarship, Albrecht continued to function as Germany's ecclesiastical leader even after the Reformation began but under very different circumstances. He was involved in conversations with the Saxon theologians, especially Philipp Melanchthon (1497–1560), at the Diet of Augsburg in 1530.[4] During the same period, however, especially in the face of the Peasants' War of 1525, he more and more actively supported Luther's opponents.[5] When Albrecht's nephew, Elector Joachim II (1505–1571), introduced the Reformation into Brandenburg in 1539, he abandoned Halle (in 1541), and soon thereafter both Halle and Magdeburg introduced the Reformation. He died in Mainz in 1545.

b For this kind of indulgence, see above, p. 16.

DISEGNO DELA BENEDITIONE DEL PONTEFICE NELA PIAZA DE SANTO PIETRO

View of Rome's uncompleted St. Peter's in 1549 from Sebastian Münster's *Cosmographia universalis*.

Luther's letter reflects the high Renaissance style that was expected in any direct appeal to such a powerful ecclesiastical and political figure.[c] What may strike modern readers as false humility simply reflects the customs of the day. As friar and obscure teacher, Luther was expected to show such deference. But Luther's deference to the person of Albrecht did not prevent him in harshly criticizing practices (namely, the

5. The Peasants' War took place in 1524 and 1525 throughout German-speaking lands, beginning with farmers and day laborers in Swabia and spreading to Alsace in the west, Salzburg in the east, and as far north as Thuringia, where it involved poor artisans and townspeople. It was suppressed by the secular and ecclesiastical princes, who exacted stiff penalties from their rebellious subjects and put many to death.

c   For more on this style, see below, the letter to Leo, p. 469f.

sale of indulgences and especially the misleading preaching accompanying them) he doubtless knew were going on with Albrecht's full knowledge. To give Albrecht a "way out," so to speak, Luther opined that the *Summary Instruction* went out without Albrecht's knowledge (which could hardly have been the case).

In any case, the letter reflects many of the issues in the *95 Theses* themselves. The letter also reflects Luther's deep pastoral concern. The current preaching of the Peter's Indulgence was misleading people and confusing them. True sorrow for sin (contrition) was being undermined, and the theology undergirding the preachers' claims was unsupported by any church authority, or was at least uncertain.

Luther appended two documents to the letter, not to gain the archbishop's permission to disseminate them but to lay bare the questionable theology and practice surrounding indulgences.[6] The first, the *95 Theses*, would be distributed and published in the coming months and became the focus of Luther's case with Rome. The other was a brief essay on indulgences (in some later versions mistaken for a sermon). It raised some of the same questions but was never published.[d]

The original letter is in the royal archives (*Riksarkivet*) in Stockholm, Sweden. According to a note made on the back of the letter by a secretary to Archbishop Albrecht, the letter was opened by Albrecht's advisers in Magdeburg on 17 November 1517 and sent on to the archbishop, who was at the time in Aschaffenburg (a city belonging to the archbishopric of Mainz). On 13 December 1517, the archbishop began a process against Luther to prevent further dissemination of his arguments (by which time he had sent the documents to the University of Mainz and Rome), instructing the advisers in Magdeburg to charge Johann Tetzel with the

6. At around the same time Luther seems also to have sent a letter warning about Tetzel's preaching to his ordinary bishop, Jerome of Brandenburg (c. 1460–1522), in which he included a copy of the *95 Theses*.

---

d   See WA Br 12:2–10; WA 1:65–69; WA 9:764. Some of the arguments of this second enclosure were then taken up by Luther in the *Sermon on Indulgences and Grace* (1518), below, pp. 60–65.

task of informing Luther of this. On 17 December, Albrecht received a mildly negative judgment against Luther's arguments from Mainz's theological faculty.

LETTER FROM MARTIN LUTHER

TO ALBRECHT, ARCHBISHOP OF MAINZ

31 OCTOBER 1517[7]

TO THE MOST REVEREND FATHER in Christ, the Most Illustrious Lord, Lord Albrecht, archbishop of the churches of Magdeburg and Mainz, Primate [of German Lands], Margrave of Brandenburg, etc., to his venerably revered and most beloved lord and shepherd in Christ,

Jesus!

God's grace and mercy[8] and whatever may be and is![9] Forgive me, most Reverend Father in Christ and Most Illustrious Sovereign, that I, the dregs of humanity, have the temerity even to dare to conceive of a letter to Your Sublime Highness. The Lord Jesus is my witness, that, aware of my insignificance and unworthiness, I have up until the present put off what I am doing now "with a bold face,"[e] motivated completely by the duty of my loyalty, which I know I owe to you, Reverend Father in Christ. Therefore, may Your Highness deign in the meantime to turn your eye toward this grain of dust and, for the sake of your episcopal clemency, look into my request.

7. This is a revision of LW 48:43–49, a translation by Gottfried Krodel, based upon WA Br 1:108–15.

8. See 1 Tim. 1:2 and 2 Tim. 1:2, Paul's greetings to his associate. Here Luther combines his early epistolary greetings ("Jesus!"), perhaps taken from monastic practice, with a Pauline style that by 1522 he would exclusively employ in all of his letters.

9. This unusual greeting (instead of "my complete devotion" or some other demonstration of humility) occurs only one other time in Luther's correspondence, as a greeting to Frederick the Wise, elector of Saxony (WA Br 1:236, 1–5): "To the most illustrious . . . Frederick, Elector . . .

e   Erasmus, *Adages*, I, 8, 47, citing Seneca and others; or it could be translated "shamelessly."

Brother Martin Luther Augustinian [wishes] felicity and whatever else the prayer of a sinner can." For a discussion of the style of this letter, see the introduction, p. 49.

10. Due to the fact that Elector Frederick of Saxony had forbade the selling of this indulgence in his territories, fearing a drain of gold and less appeal for the indulgences received by viewing the relics housed in the Castle Church in Wittenberg.

11. A technical term for the grace received through the sacrament of penance. See the introduction, p. 14f. Medieval theology and practice, relying on Augustine's (354–430) definition of pride as the chief sin, insisted that security regarding salvation was a sign of pride. Luther, by contrast, would come to argue that assurance of forgiveness rested in God's word. See thesis 7, p. 36, with n. 26.

Under your most distinguished [name and] title, papal indulgences are being disseminated among the people for the construction of St. Peter's [in Rome]. In these matters, I do not so much find fault with the cries of the preachers, which I have not heard,[10] but I do bewail the people's completely false understanding, gleaned from these fellows, which they spread everywhere among the common folk. For example, these poor souls believe: that if they were to purchase these letters of indulgence they would then be assured of their salvation;[f] likewise, that souls immediately leap from purgatory when they have thrown a contribution into the chest;[g] and then that the graces [of indulgences] are so great that no sin is of such magnitude that it cannot be forgiven—even if (as they say) someone should rape the Mother of God, were this possible;[h] likewise, that through theses indulgences a person is freed from every penalty and guilt.[i]

O great God! In this way, excellent Father, souls committed to your care are being directed to death. A most severe reckoning has fallen on you above all others and is indeed growing.[j] For that reason I could no longer keep silent about these things. For a human being does not attain security about salvation through any episcopal function, since a person does not even become secure through the infused grace of God.[11] But instead the Apostle [Paul] orders us constantly to "work out our salvation in fear and trembling."[k] "It is [even] hard for the righteous to be saved."[l] Furthermore, "the way is [so] narrow that leads to life,"[m] that the Lord

f   See thesis 32, p. 38.

g   See thesis 27, p. 38.

h   See thesis 75, p. 43, an exaggeration Tetzel denied having made. Christians in the sixteenth century held to the perpetual virginity of Mary.

i   See theses 21 and 76, pp. 37 and 43, respectively.

j   See thesis 80, p. 44.

k   Phil. 2:12.

l   1 Pet. 4:18.

m   Matt. 7:14 (following a literal translation of the Greek and the Latin).

through the prophets Amos and Zechariah calls those who will be saved "a brand plucked from the fire."[n] The Lord, too, announces the difficulty of salvation everywhere. How then can the [indulgence preachers] make the people secure and unafraid through those false tales and promises linked to indulgences, given that indulgences confer upon souls nothing of benefit for salvation or holiness but only remove external penalty, once customarily imposed by the [penitential] canons?[o]

Furthermore, works of godliness and love are infinitely better than indulgences, and yet [the indulgence preachers] do not preach such things with the same kind of pomp and effort.[p] On the contrary, they remain silent about those works for the sake of preaching indulgences, even though it is the first and sole office of all bishops that the people learn the gospel and the love of Christ. For Christ nowhere commanded indulgences to be preached, but he strongly commanded the gospel to be preached.[q] Therefore, what a horror, what a danger to a bishop if—while the gospel is being silenced—he only permits the clamoring of indulgences among his people and is more concerned with them than the gospel! Did not Christ say to them, "You strain out a gnat but swallow a camel"?[r]

Added to this, my Reverend Father in the Lord, is the fact that in that [*Summary*] *Instruction* for the indulgence commissioners,[s] published under Your Fatherly name, it is stated (surely without the consent or knowledge of your Reverend Father) that one of the principal graces [of this Peter's Indulgence] is that inestimable gift of God by which a human being is reconciled to God and all the penalties of

---

n   Amos 4:11 and Zech. 3:2.

o   See thesis 5, p. 35, the heart of Luther's argument in the *95 Theses*, and thesis 8, p. 36).

p   See theses 41 and 55, pp. 39 and 41, respectively.

q   Mark 16:15. See theses 53–54, p. 41.

r   Matt. 23:24.

s   For more on this booklet, see the introduction, p. 48.

12. See theses 11 and 32, pp. 36 and 38, respectively. The *Summary Instruction* states: "The first grace [of this indulgence] is the complete remission of all sins; and nothing greater than this can be named, since the sinner, deprived of God's grace, obtains complete remission by these means and once more enjoys God's grace; moreover through this remission of sins the punishment that one is obliged to suffer in purgatory on account of the affront to the Divine Majesty is all remitted and the pains of purgatory completely blotted out." This revised translation is from Henry Bettenson and Chris Maunder, eds., *Documents of the Christian Church*, 4th ed. (Oxford: Oxford University Press, 2011), 195.

13. See thesis 35, p. 39. The *Summary Instruction* (Bettenson and Maunder, *Documents*, 196f.) states: "The fourth important grace is for those souls in purgatory, and it is the complete remission of all sins. . . . It is furthermore not necessary that the persons who place their contributions in the chest for the dead should be contrite in heart and have orally confessed."

purgatory are blotted out.[12] Likewise, [it stated] that contrition is not necessary for those who purchase souls [from purgatory][13] or acquire confessional privileges.[14]

But what can I do, Most Excellent Prelate and Most Illustrious Sovereign, except beseech you, Most Reverend Father, through our Lord Jesus Christ that you may deign to turn your fatherly eye toward [this matter] and completely withdraw this little book and impose upon the preachers of indulgences another form of preaching? Otherwise, perhaps someone may arise who by publishing pamphlets may refute those [preachers] and that booklet [the *Summary Instruction*]—to the greatest disgrace of Your Most Illustrious Highness—something that I indeed would strongly hate to have happen, and yet I fear that it may happen in the future unless things are quickly remedied.[15]

I beg Your Most Illustrious Grace to deign to accept in a princely and episcopal, that is, in the kindest way this faithful service of my humble self, just as I, too, with a most faithful and devoted heart am presenting these things to you, Reverend Father. For I, too, am a part of your flock. May the Lord Jesus protect you forever, Most Reverend Father! Amen.

From Wittenberg, 1517, on the Eve of All Saints' Day.[16]

If it pleases the Reverend Father, he could examine my disputation [theses],[17] so that he may understand how dubious a thing this opinion about indulgences is, an opinion that those [preachers] disseminate with such complete certainty.

Your unworthy son,
Martin Luther
Augustinian, called as Doctor of Sacred Theology[18]

14. See thesis 35, p. 39, with n. 41. The *Summary Instruction* (Bettenson and Maunder, *Documents*, 196) states: "The second principal grace is a 'confessional' [confessional letter] replete with the greatest, most important, and hitherto unheard of privileges." These included choosing one's own confessor and forgiving sins usually reserved to the pope.

15. See theses 81–90, p. 41. Whether Luther had himself in mind here is uncertain. However, the publication of the *95 Theses* and the German *Sermon on Indulgences and Grace* certainly caused this very thing.

16. 31 October.

17. The *95 Theses*. See above, pp. 34–46.

18. Luther justified his attacks on indulgences in part on the basis of his responsibility as an officially called Doctor of Sacred Theology. The oath of loyalty to the church and its Scriptures that he took upon receiving his doctorate, he argued, compelled him to speak out.

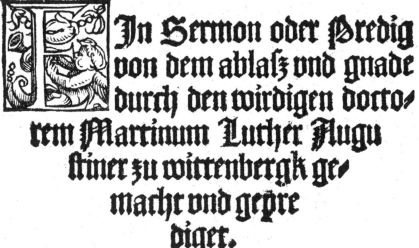

Ein Sermon oder Predig von dem ablasz vnd gnade durch den wirdigen doctorem Martinum Luther Augustiner zu wittenbergk gemacht vnd geprediget.

✠

Title page woodcut for Luther's *Sermon on Indulgences and Grace*,
showing a man approaching a church building with a rosary
in his left hand and perhaps a slip of paper in his right.

A Sermon[1] on Indulgences[a] and Grace

1518

TIMOTHY J. WENGERT

INTRODUCTION

In the months after the distribution and publication of the *95 Theses*, reactions came from both friend and foe. Suspecting they contained heresy, the cardinal archbishop of Mainz, Albrecht von Brandenburg (1490–1545),[b] sent copies to his theological faculty for their judgment (they responded on 13 December 1517) and to Rome for its opinion.

By the summer of 1518 the papal court's theologian, Sylvester Prierias (c. 1456–1523),[2] had published a lengthy refutation. But even earlier, on 20 January 1518, at the University of Frankfurt an der Oder (only a little over one hundred miles [177 km] east of Wittenberg and founded by Albrecht), Johann Tetzel (1465–1519) defended 106 theses, composed under the direction of Konrad Wimpina (1460–1531), a professor of theology, that refuted Luther's position and earned

1. The German word for "sermon" was *Predigt*, although in the sixteenth century people also used the Latin, *sermo* [German: *sermon*], but often with the broader Latin meaning of "essay" or "reflections." It is a matter of debate whether this "*Sermon*" was ever preached.

2. Sylvester Prierias, a Dominican theologian, active at the court of Pope Leo X.

a Here and throughout the singular in the German (the indulgence) is rendered as plural (indulgences) and the word *indulgence* (without an article) is rendered "an indulgence."

b For more on Albrecht, see "Letter to Albrecht, Archbishop of Mainz," pp. 47–49 of this volume.

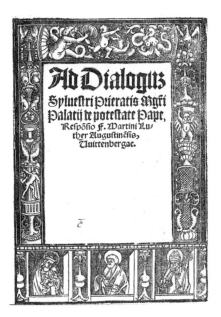

Ad dialogum Sylvestri Prieratis Magistri Palatii de potestate Pape Responsio. When Luther received Prierias's *Dialogue on the 95 Theses*, he published a refutation, printing Prierias's text next to his own replies.

---

3. Christopher Scheurl was a some-time professor of law at the University of Wittenberg and legal adviser to and oft-time resident of the imperial city of Nuremberg.

4. Luther's *Explanations* (LW 31:77–252) were published with dedications to Johann von Staupitz (LW 48:64–70) and Pope Leo X. Luther had been working on them at least since March of that year, but they were first published in May after successful negotiations concerning publication with Luther's immediate bishop, Jerome Scultetus (c. 1460–1522), bishop of Brandenburg.

him a doctorate. By March, a printed version of these theses had come into Luther's hands.[c]

At the same time, Luther had also learned about the publication of the *95 Theses* in Nuremberg through his contact there, Christoph Scheurl (1481–1542).[3] We know from Scheurl's correspondence with others earlier in January 1518 that he and others in Nuremberg intended to translate them into German; something that another Nuremberger, Caspar Nützel (1471–1529), then proceeded to do. By March, Luther had received copies of the Latin and German versions and wrote back on 5 March 1518, not simply thanking Scheurl for copies but also complaining that a bare translation of the *95 Theses* into German was "not fitting for educating the common folk."[d] Indeed, it is not at all clear (given that *no* printed copies of a German translation of the *95 Theses* from this period exist) whether Scheurl sent Luther a *printed* translation or, as seems more likely, simply a manuscript of Nützel's translation. In any case, Luther made it clear that he wanted to provide something more fitting for the German reader. The result was the *Sermon on Indulgences and Grace.*[e]

The *Sermon* uses more basic language and categories to talk about the nature of the sacrament of penance and indulgences than does the *95 Theses*. It summarizes points contained there (while omitting all references to the pope), and, because it was written at the same time as Luther was working on the *Explanations of the 95 Theses*,[4] it also reflects the language and arguments found in that document. But at several points it also responds directly to Tetzel's theses (for specifics, see below). Its popularity far surpassed that of the *95 Theses*, with at least twenty-four printings between 1518 and 1520. Indeed, this tract more than any other catapulted Luther into the public eye and made him a best-

c   For details, see *Die 106 Frankfurter Thesen*, in *Dokumente zur Causa Lutheri (1517–1521)*, pt. 1: *Das Gutachten des Prierias und weitere Schriften gegen Luthers Ablaßthesen (1517–1518)*, ed. Peter Fabisch and Erwin Iserloh (Münster: Aschendorff, 1988), 310–20.

d   WA Br 1:152, 12–13.

e   This reconstruction disagrees slightly with WA 1:239. See Brecht 1:208 for corrections.

selling author overnight. Here Luther's clear explanations of complicated theological arguments and his edgy style, in which he repeatedly attacked Scholastic theologians and their "opinions," made a splash with the German reading public. Whatever may have been known about the dispute before March 1518, the publication of this *Sermon* transformed Luther into a new, popular writer throughout Germany, one who very likely was saying publicly what at least some of his contemporaries may well have been thinking and sharing privately: that the bases for certain aspects of the sale of indulgences were theologically shaky. Moreover, his criticisms of Scholastic theology[5] had much in common with similar attacks by other popular humanists, such as Erasmus of Rotterdam (c. 1466–1536) and Johannes Reuchlin (1455–1522),[6] and would have endeared him to his Renaissance-minded readers.[7]

With Luther having now crossed over into the vernacular, Tetzel also felt constrained to respond in German, publishing in April his *Refutation Made by Brother Johann Tetzel, Dominican and Inquisitor of Heretics against an Impudent Sermon of Twenty Erring Articles concerning the Papal Indulgence and Grace: For All Christian Believers to Know and Note.*[f] He labored to show just how heretical Luther's statements were and warned Christians not to be seduced by what Luther wrote. In contrast to Luther's bestseller, no reprints of Tetzel's work occurred. Luther responded to Tetzel's refutation in *The Freedom of the "Sermon on Papal Indulgences and Grace" of Doctor Martin Luther against the "Refutation," Being Completely Fabricated to Insult That Very Sermon* (WA 1:380–93). Also a best seller, this defense was printed eleven times between 1518 and 1520.

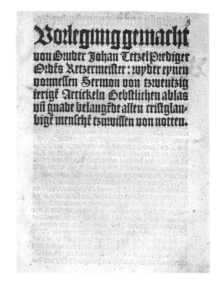

Johann Tetzel's *Rebuttal against Luther's Sermon on Indulgences and Grace,* published in 1518 in Leipzig by Melchior Lotter Jr.

5. Scholastic theology denotes medieval and late medieval approaches to theology especially wedded to logical argumentation and the division of topics using certain aspects of Aristotelian thought.

6. Erasmus of Rotterdam, the Dutch humanist whose works in moral philosophy and his editions of the church fathers and Greek New Testament made him famous throughout Europe. Johannes Reuchlin was a relative by marriage to Philip Melanchthon, whom he nominated for the Greek professorship at the University of Wittenberg.

7. As Helmar Junghans, *Der junge Luther und die Humanisten* (Weimar: Böhlau, 1984), 319–25, has demonstrated, Luther was himself a humanist,

---

f   *Dokumente zur Causa Lutheri,* 1:337–63; English: *Johann Tetzel's Rebuttal against Luther's Sermon on Indulgences and Grace,* trans. Dewey Weiss Kramer (Atlanta: Pitts Theology Library, 2012).

in that he showed profound interest in the original sources (using both Erasmus's Greek New Testament as soon as it appeared in 1516 and Reuchlin's Hebrew commentary on the penitential psalms) and in good letters, especially in his use of rhetoric. In this tract, as in his *Disputation on Scholastic Theology* of 1517 (LW 31:5–16), Luther also joined with humanists in criticizing the scholastic method of doing theology.

8. The following translation of *Ein Sermon von Ablaß und Gnade* is based upon WA 1:239–46.

9. Peter Lombard (c. 1096–1160), and Thomas Aquinas (c. 1225–1274), a Dominican Scholastic theologian. At this time, Luther understood his struggle to be against Dominicans who overwhelmingly favored papal authority.

10. See Peter Lombard, *Sentences*, IV d. 16, q. 1, and all medieval teachers after him: "In the perfection of penance three things must be observed, namely, compunction of the heart, confession of the mouth and satisfaction of works." Lombard claimed to derive this from John Chrysostom, *De poenitentia*, dist. 1, ch. "Perfecta." Lombard's medieval commentators defined contrition as sorrow for sin out of love of God (as opposed to attrition, which was sorrow for sin out of fear of punishment) and confession as the recitation of all of one's mortal sins to a priest. Depending on the medieval school of thought, at the moment of either contrition or confession a person had the guilt of his or her sins forgiven, was moved from a state of sin to a state of grace, and had

A SERMON ON INDULGENCES AND GRACE[8]

FIRST, you should know that some new teachers, such as the Master of Sentences, St. Thomas [Aquinas], and their disciples,[9] divide [the Sacrament of] Penance[g] into three parts: contrition, confession, and satisfaction.[10] And, although this distinction and opinion of theirs is scarcely or not at all to be found based in Holy Scripture or in the ancient holy Christian teachers,[11] nevertheless we will pass over this for now and speak using their categories.

Second, they say that indulgences do not involve the first or the second part, that is, contrition or confession, but rather satisfaction.

Third, satisfaction is further divided into three parts, that is, prayer, fasting, and almsgiving.[12] Thus, prayer includes all kinds of works proper to the soul, such as reading, meditation, hearing God's word, preaching, teaching, and the like. Fasting includes all kinds of work that mortify the flesh, such as vigils, working,[13] [sleeping on a] hard bed, [wearing rough] clothes, etc. Almsgiving includes all kinds of good works of the body and mercy toward the neighbor.

Fourth, all of these [teachers] hold for a certainty that indulgences take away these very works of satisfaction that ought to be done for sin or are required[14] to be done. For an indulgence is supposed to take away all these works so that nothing good remains for us to do.

Fifth, among many [teachers] it is an open and unresolved debate whether indulgences also take away even more than such good works as are required, namely, whether they

---

g   *Buß* or *poenitentia* has three meanings in English: the sacrament of penance, penitence, and repentance.

A so-called Peter's Indulgence purchased on 15 April 1517.

his or her punishment reduced from eternal punishment (hell) to temporal punishment. Satisfaction, imposed by the confessor, was thus a matter of satisfying the remaining temporal punishment by doing good works.

11. Alongside Scripture, Luther maintained throughout his career that ancient church teachers also had authority in the church, albeit under God's Word. See also Luther's point 20 below, p. 65.

12. See the Sermon on the Mount in Matt. 6:1-18, from which these categories arose.

13. The monastic vow of the Benedictines was often summarized as *ora et labora* (prayer and work).

14. The confessor or penitential books determined certain temporal penalties for each mortal sin as part of the sacrament of penance. See above, p. 15.

15. Here Luther may be referring to differences among such teachers as Thomas Aquinas, Bonaventure (c. 1221–1274) and Gabriel Biel (c. 1420–1495), where the latter two argued that normal works of satisfaction were better than indulgences.

16. At this point in the dispute, Luther does not see himself attacking church doctrine but, rather, the "opinions" of Scholastic theologians, opinions that he views as unfounded in Scripture or tradition. From this point on, his arguments reflect the *95 Theses*, here theses 1–4 and 39–40.

17. The traditional medieval understanding of these texts was that Mary Magdalene anointed Jesus.

also remove the punishment for sin that God's righteousness demands.[15]

Sixth, for the moment I will put their opinions aside without refuting them.[16] This is what I say: No one can defend the position with any passage from Scripture that God's righteousness desires or demands any punishment or satisfaction from sinners except for their heartfelt and true contrition or conversion alone—with the condition that from that moment on they bear the cross of Christ[h] and practice the aforementioned works (but not as imposed by anyone). For this is what God said through Ezekiel [18:21 with 33:14-16, paraphrase]: "If the wicked turn away from all their sins . . . and do . . . right, so will I no longer think on their sins."[i] Thus, in the same way he himself absolved Mary Magdalene [Luke 7:36–50],[17] the paralytic [Mark 2:1–12],

h See Matt. 16:24.

i Luther again used this passage in his *Explanations of the 95 Theses*, on thesis 5 (LW 31:96). The traditional medieval understanding of these texts was that Mary Magdalene anointed Jesus.

18. See statement 5 above, p. 61, n. 15.

19. This is the only place in this tract where Luther employs Latin terms meaning "for medication" or "for satisfaction." He is citing terms employed by Johann Tetzel and Konrad Wimpina ("new preachers," as Luther labels them here) in their attack on the *95 Theses*: *Die 106 Frankfurter Thesen*, in *Dokumente zur Causa Lutheri*, 323 and 331 (theses 14 and 72). Thomas Aquinas uses a similar distinction in *Quodlibet* II, q. 8, a. 2, ad 3, but to a different end: "It must be said that satisfaction is both punitive (insofar as it is an act of vindictive justice) and also medicative (insofar as it is something sacramental). Thus, indulgences complete the role of satisfaction insofar as it is punitive because indeed the punishment, which someone else underwent, is imputed to another person as if that one had undergone it, and therefore it takes away the actual punishment. But it does not take the place of satisfaction insofar as it is medicative, because there remain the inclinations toward sinning that are left behind from the previous sin, for the cleansing of which there is necessarily the work of satisfaction."

the woman taken in adultery [John 8:1–11], etc.*j* I would like to hear who would prove the opposite—besides the fact that some doctors have made this up.

Seventh, in point of fact one finds that God punishes some according to his righteousness or through punishment impels them to contrition as in Psalm 89 [:30–33]: "If his [David's] children forsake my law . . . then I will punish their transgressions with the rod . . . but I will not remove my steadfast love from them."*k* But this punishment is in no one's power to lessen, except God's alone. Indeed, God will not relax such punishment but instead promises to impose it.

Eighth, for this reason, because no one has a name for this made-up punishment [of Scholastic teachers] and does not know what it is, therefore if this penalty is nothing, then the above-mentioned good work [of procuring indulgences] is nothing.

Ninth, I say that even if this very day the Christian church decided and decreed that indulgences took away more than the works of satisfaction did,[18] nevertheless it would still be a thousand times better that no Christian buy or desire indulgences but instead that they would rather do works and suffer punishment. For indulgences are and may continue to be nothing other than the neglect of good works and salutary suffering, which a person should rather choose than omit—even though some of the new preachers have invented two kinds of sufferings: *Medicativae, Satisfactoriae*,[19] that is, some suffering is for satisfaction and some for improvement. But, praise God, we have more freedom to disdain this kind of prattle than they have freedom to dream it up. For all suffering, indeed, everything God lays upon Christians is for their betterment and benefit.

---

j   Luther employed these and other examples in his *Explanations of the 95 Theses*, to thesis 7 (LW 31:101f.).

k   Luther also referred to this text in his *Explanations* to thesis 5 (LW 31:89–97) and in his *Asterisks* against Johann Eck (WA 1:285, 2f.), which were both being composed in the spring of 1518.

Tenth, nothing is being said [by arguing] that the punishment and works may be too much, that the individual may not complete them because of the shortness of life, and therefore there is need for indulgences for such a person.[20] I respond that this has no basis in fact and is pure fiction. For God and the holy church impose on no one more than they are able to carry, as St. Paul also says [1 Cor. 10:13, paraphrase]: "God will not let [anyone] be tested beyond [what that person can endure]." And this heaps no small insult upon Christianity when someone accuses it of imposing heavier burdens than we can bear.

Eleventh, although the satisfaction set in canon law is still on the books—that for each mortal sin seven years of satisfaction is imposed—nevertheless Christianity must let these very laws go and impose nothing more than what they allow each to bear. Much more, given that this [rule] is not in force, should one take care not to impose more than any one person will be able to bear.[21]

Twelfth, it is fine to say that the sinner with residual punishment should be directed to purgatory or to indulgences. But more must be said about the basis and underpinnings for this.

Thirteenth, it is a tremendous error when people imagine that they can make satisfaction for their sins, which God instead always forgives gratis out of immeasurable grace while desiring nothing for this [grace] except that one live well from then on.[22] Whenever Christianity demands something further, it may and should set such a thing aside and not impose anything heavy or unbearable.

Fourteenth, indulgences are tolerated for the sake of the imperfect and lazy Christians, who either do not want to practice good works in a lively way or want to avoid suffering. For indulgences do not demand improvement but tolerate and accept such people as imperfect. For this reason, one should not speak against indulgences, but one must also not speak in favor of using them.

Fifteenth, a person who gives to build St. Peter's [in Rome], or whatever else is mentioned [in indulgence preaching], purely for God's sake is acting in a far better and more

20. This is another direct attack on Tetzel and Wimpina's *Die 106 Frankfurter Thesen*, in *Dokumente zur Causa Lutheri*, 336.

21. Canon law, a medieval compilation of papal and conciliar decrees and statements of the church fathers first made by Gratian (twelfth century), reflected in its section on penance the earlier practice of public punishment for members of the church who committed serious crimes and could only be reconciled to the church after seven years of penitence. These punishments were then applied to all mortal sins (serious misdeeds, the immorality of which the perpetrator understands and to which he or she consents). Luther already makes this objection in the *Tractatus de Indulgentiis* (WA 1:65–69, here 65, 25–31; and WA Br 12:2–10, here lines 19–25), which was appended to his letter to Albrecht.

22. This point (that forgiveness arises from God's grace alone) and the next, also made in the *95 Theses*, thesis 36, will become increasingly important for Luther.

23. See theses 42–46 in the *95 Theses*.

24. This is one place where a more homiletical style appears, pointing to this piece's sermonic origin.

25. The greed of indulgence preachers, a common trope at the time, is also reflected in the *95 Theses*.

26. Here, as in the *95 Theses*, Luther is instructing preachers. By insisting that he is not hindering purchase of indulgences, Luther was attempting to stay within the strictures of canon law and the decrees surrounding the Peter's Indulgence.

27. Purgatory (a place of purgation) was understood to be an interim state between death and the beatific vision (heaven), designed to purge a soul of any remaining impurities and thereby satisfying the remaining punishment for mortal sins. Although the suffering in purgatory was understood to be worse than any on earth, the souls could only leave purgatory for heaven. Souls that died in a state of sin went directly to hell. Luther here is referring to a relatively new doctrine that applied indulgences to souls in purgatory, first decreed by Pope Sixtus IV (1414–1484) in a 1476 papal bull.

certain way than those who take an indulgence for it. For it is dangerous when they give such a gift for the sake of an indulgence and not for God's sake.

Sixteenth, a work shown to the poor is much better than one given toward [constructing] a building, and it is also much better than when an indulgence is given for such a work.[23] For, as stated above, a good deed done is much better than many avoided. Indulgences, however, mean avoiding many good works, or else nothing is avoided.

Furthermore, so that I may instruct you correctly,[24] please note the following. If you want to give something, you ought above all else (without considering St. Peter's building or indulgences) give to your poor neighbor. When it comes to the point that there is no one in your city who needs help (unless God deigns it, this will never happen!), then you ought to give where you want: to churches, altars, decorations, or chalices that are for your own city. And when that, too, is no longer necessary, then first off—if you wish—you may give to the building of St. Peter's or anywhere else. Moreover, you should not do this for the sake of an indulgence, for St. Paul says [1 Tim. 5:8], "And whoever does not provide for . . . family members, is no Christian and is worse than an unbeliever."[1] And avoid those who tell you differently, who deceive you or who search for your soul in a moneybag. And when they find a penny in the purse, it is dearer to them than any soul whatsoever.[25]

Suppose you say, "Then I will never again buy an indulgence." I respond, "That is what I already said above. My will, desire, plea, and counsel are that no one buy an indulgence. Let the lazy and sleepy Christians buy indulgences. You run from them."

Seventeenth, indulgences are neither commanded nor recommended. Instead, they count among the things that are permitted and allowed. Therefore, it is not a work of

---

1   The NRSV has "has denied the faith." Luther also used this text in his *Explanations of the 95 Theses* to thesis 47 (LW 31:204).

obedience and also not meritorious but instead a departure from obedience. Therefore, although one should not hinder someone from buying them, nevertheless, one should draw Christians away from them and arouse and encourage them to do those works and [suffer those] punishments that indulgences avoid.[26]

Eighteenth, whether souls are rescued from purgatory through indulgences, I do not know and I also do not believe it, although some new doctors [of the church] say it.[27] But it is impossible for them to prove it, and the church has not yet decided the matter.[28] Therefore, for the sake of greater certainty, it is much better that each of you prays and works for these souls. For this has more value and is certain.

Nineteenth, in these points I have no doubt, and they are sufficiently grounded in the Scripture. Therefore, all of you should have no doubts about it and let the scholastic doctors alone. Taken altogether, they do not have enough with their opinions to put together a single sermon.

Twentieth, although some (for whom such truth really damages their treasure chests)[29] now want to call me a heretic, nevertheless, I consider such blathering no big deal,[30] especially since the only ones doing this are some darkened minds, who have never even smelled a Bible, who have never read a Christian teacher, and who do not even understand their own teachers but instead remain stuck with their shaky and close-minded opinions. For if they had understood them, they would have known that they should not defame anyone without a hearing and without refuting them. Still, may God give them and us a right understanding! Amen.

28. Luther invokes the standard defense of the teacher's freedom to debate matters not yet decided by a church council. At the Leipzig Debates in the summer of 1519, he would be forced to admit that councils, too, can err. His position here is similar to that of Bonaventure (c. 1221–1274), who argued in his *Commentary on the Sentences of Peter Lombard* that the pope had authority over purgatory only *per modum suffragii* (in the mode of one begging [God] for another). This will become one of the points debated between Luther and Cardinal Cajetan (1469–1534) in the interview in Augsburg in October 1518. See below, p. 131f.

29. Luther was thinking specifically of Johann Tetzel and Konrad Wimpina, the first to attack the *95 Theses* in print.

30. At the time the *Sermon* was published, Luther had not yet received the equally strong reactions from others, including Johann Eck (1486–1543) and Silvester Prierias.

Heidelberg Disputation

1518

DENNIS BIELFELDT

INTRODUCTION

Paradigm Shift

Some view Luther's 1518 *Heidelberg Disputation*[1] as offering a new beginning for theology. In the words of Robert Kolb, "Luther cut to the quick and talked about the nature of God and the nature of the human creature trapped in sin. His assertions on these topics constituted a paradigm shift within Western Christian thought in the understanding of God's revelation of himself, God's way of dealing with evil, and what it means to be human."[a] There is indeed much in the disputation that supports Kolb's assertion.[2]

Luther had inherited a set of theological assumptions, methods, and theoretical formulations that had proven to be a rich resource over the centuries. This established theological paradigm used logical and semantic analysis to clarify a whole host of theological issues, including the nature of

1. Latin: *disputatio.* A disputation was a formalized method of debate seeking truth in theology and the sciences. Traditional authorities were to be referenced, and debaters were expected to understand the classic arguments related to the theological points under debate.

2. Classical theological texts determine new paradigms as with Augustine's (354–430) *De civitate Dei* [*On the City of God*] or Anselm's (c. 1033–1109) *Cur Deus Homo* [*Why God Became a Human Being*].

---

a   Robert Kolb, "Luther on the Theology of the Cross," *Lutheran Quarterly* 16 (2002): 443–66.

3. The paradigm on grace and its mechanics is grounded in Augustine's rejection of the human will being able to effect the beginning of faith. Augustine held that human beings, while possessing some free choice (*liberum arbitrium*), have no freedom vis-à-vis God's grace, which moves the sinner from captivity to freedom. Human beings are justified when their will is brought back into its proper relationship with God's will. See Alister McGrath, *Iustitia Dei: A History of the Christian Doctrine of Justification, The Beginnings to the Reformation* (Cambridge: Cambridge University Press, 1986), 17–36.

4. Late medieval schools on justification included the Dominican School (the *via antiqua*, e.g., Thomas Aquinas [1225–1274]), the early Franciscan School (e.g., Bonaventure [1221–1274]), the later Franciscan School, the *via moderna*, e.g., William of Occam [c. 1287–1347] or Gabriel Biel [c. 1420–1495]), and various forms of medieval Augustinianism. See ibid., 155–79.

5. The terms "Scholastic method" or "Scholastic theology" are difficult to define. While Scholastic theology is "not a uniform structure," it was generally accepted that it proceeds by commenting on an authoritative text through *lectio, disputatio,* and *praedicatio* (reading, disputation, and preaching) the text. See Ulrich G. Leinsle, *Introduction to Scholastic Theology*, trans. Michael Miller (Washington, DC: Catholic University of America Press, 2010), 15.

grace and the mechanics of salvation.[3] While there were different understandings of justification in Luther's time, there was general agreement on how theologians should proceed in adjudicating among the various opinions.[4] The Scholastic method demanded that theologians know the differing opinions of theologians on the disputed points so that they could defend their own views by showing how theologians holding contrary opinions had erred.[5] The study of Aristotle (384–322 BCE) was particularly important in Luther's era because his *Organon* provided the logical, semantic, and rhetorical tools to accomplish the theological task.[b]

By the time of the *Heidelberg Disputation*, however, Luther was convinced that the established theological paradigm could not adequately deal with a number of burning theological issues and concerns. These concerns displayed themselves as what might be called "anomalies" over against the inherited paradigm.[c] For Luther, neither his *experience* before God nor his understanding of the gospel fit the dominant paradigm and its central assumption that noble, but fallen, human beings need transformation in order to return to their true home with God, that is, to enjoy the beatific vision.[d]

Solutions to such theological anomalies could not occur, given the assumptions of "normal theology" as it had been practiced. For instance, the late medieval believer's experience of brokenness and helplessness before a wrathful God did not square well with the means of acquiring salvation offered by a late medieval tradition that insisted "to those who do what is in them, God will not deny grace."[e] Moreover,

---

b Aristotle's *Organon* includes *The Categories, On Interpretation, The Prior Analytics, The Posterior Analytics, The Topics,* and *The Sophistical Refutations.*

c Within the philosophy of science, "anomaly" means a violation of expectations arising from an accepted scientific method and theory.

d See Gerhard Forde, *On Being a Theologian of the Cross: Reflections on Luther's Heidelberg Disputation, 1518* (Grand Rapids: Eerdmans, 1997), 6.

e See Berndt Hamm, *The Early Luther: Stages in Reformation Reorientation*, trans. Martin Lohrmann (Grand Rapids: Eerdmans, 2014), 9.

while the tradition assumed that clues to God's true nature could be discerned in creation, this seemed to run contrary to the overarching centrality of Christ's suffering and death upon the cross and the consequence of the believer's salvific identification with this suffering.[f] Finally, many theological statements grounded in the biblical and patristic tradition as rediscovered by Christian humanists seemed in tension with the central principles and assumptions of the regnant theology.

In many ways, Luther in this disputation sets out on a path discontinuous with the tradition. Here and elsewhere Luther discards the Scholastic philosophical categories in favor of a biblical proclamation of the *theology of the cross*. He argues that human grasping after God is spiritual hubris supported by Aristotle's philosophical categories. With his critique of a *theology of glory*, he criticizes the way in which traditional theology had been understood and practiced. Nevertheless, while Luther describes his Scholastic opponents as theologians of glory and employs

A Roman marble copy of an original Greek bust of the philosopher Aristotle.

paradox to advance his theses concerning the *theologian of the cross*, one should not overstate Luther's discontinuity with the tradition. There is much in this disputation that is consonant with "normal theology." Like most late medieval theologians, Luther did not reject reason or philosophy

---

f   See Ronald Rittgers, *The Reformation of Suffering: Pastoral Theology and Lay Piety in Late Medieval and Early Modern Germany* (New York: Oxford University Press, 2012).

in toto but, rather, a particular and limited employment and understanding of it that supposed reason, through its own resources, could provide access to God's nature and actions. Similarly, Luther did not reject morality and good works, but clarified how particular notions of human action fail to conform to a proper notion of God's relationship to creation. One must avoid reading the disputation in a way that identifies philosophy itself with a theology of glory.[g] Luther does not reject philosophy wholesale in the disputation but, rather, theologically and philosophically criticizes a particular kind of philosophical orientation and method he associates with Aristotle. Indeed, in his rejection of Aristotle and the late medieval reception of Aristotle, Luther shows himself to be a competent philosophical thinker.

Text, Context, and the Theological Theses

The general chapter of the German Augustinians convened in Heidelberg on 25 April 1518. While Luther's *95 Theses* had already stirred controversy, Luther avoided discussion of indulgences and penance altogether in the *Heidelberg Disputation*, articulating instead a number of theological points he believed important for proper gospel proclamation.[h] Luther's attempt in the disputation to be faithful to Paul and his interpreter, Augustine, constituted a sustained attack on the Aristotelian assumptions of Scholastic theology.

g   See Graham White, *Luther as Nominalist: A Study of the Logical Methods Used in Martin Luther's Disputations in the Light of Their Medieval Background* (Helsinki: Luther-Agricola-Society, 1994), 26–27.

h   See, among others, K. Bauer, "Die Heidelberger Disputation Luthers," *Zeitschrift für Kirchengeschichte* 21 (1901): 233–68, 299–329; Walter Delius, "Die Augustiner Eremitenorden im Prozess Luthers," *Archiv für Reformation Geschichte* 63 (1972): 22–42; Heinz Scheible, "Die Universität Heidelberg and Luthers Disputation," *Zeitschrift für die Geschichte Oberrheins* 131 (1983): 309–29; Gottfried Seebass, "Die Heidelberger Disputation," *Heidelberger Jahrbücher* 28 (1983): 77–88; and Karl-Heinz zur Mühlen, "Die Heidelberger Disputation Martin Luthers vom 26. April 1518: Programm und Wirkung," in *Semper Apertus: Sechshundert Jahre Ruprecht-Karls-Universität Heidelberg 1386–1986*, vol. 1, ed. Wilhelm Dörr (Berlin: Springer, 1985),

It was sometime after 9 April when Luther departed on foot toward Heidelberg with fellow Augustinian Leonhard Beier (c. 1495–c. 1552). After stopping in Weissenfels and Judenbach, he arrived in Coburg on 15 April. After spending the night at the Augustinian monastery in Würzburg on 18 April, Luther's party continued in the company of Erfurt brethren Johannes Lang (c. 1487–1548) and Bartholomew Arnoldi of Usingen (c. 1465–1532), arriving in Heidelberg about 21 April.[i] Johann von Staupitz (c. 1460–1524), the vicar of the German congregation of the order, had asked Luther to prepare theses on the topics of sin, free will, and grace in order to acquaint the brothers with the new theological accents at Wittenberg. The disputation began on 26 April in the philosophical faculty building with Luther presiding and Beier debating.[6] Students, citizens, and representatives of the Palatine court were present. The Heidelberg theology professors must have participated as well, because their lowest ranking member, Georg Niger (d. c. 1560), reportedly declared at one point to Luther, "If the peasants hear this, they will stone you."[j]

Luther prepared twenty-eight theological and twelve philosophical theses prior to the debate and wrote short proofs for the theological disputations and a longer explanation of the sixth thesis. He also penned *probationes* (demonstrations)

University of Heidelberg, a woodcut in a book authored by Sebastian Münster, 1544.

6. It was previously thought to have occurred in the Augustinian cloister. See Bernard Lohse, *Martin Luther's Theology: Its Historical and Systematic Development*, trans. Roy Harrisville (Minneapolis: Fortress Press, 1999), 106.

198–212. Earlier in 1518, Johann Tetzel (1465–1519) had defended theses composed by Konrad Wimpina (1460–1531) to refute the *95 Theses* at the University of Frankfurt (Oder) as part of a meeting of the Saxon province of the Dominican order. This was the Augustinian order's response. See MLStA 1:186.

i   Brecht 1:214–16.

j   Brecht 1:215.

7. Brecht 1:233–34 points out that Luther used *theologia gloriae* and *theologia crucis* a few times in 1518 but without establishing a strict theological principle. Justification is not based on what one sees, but, rather, comes through the cross of Christ.

8. The Heidelberg theses are paradoxical in that one would not reasonably expect God to be found in weakness.

9. Luther understood the standard moves of late medieval humility theology but connected faith and humility together in a deeper way. Humility and hope were "no longer understood as qualities of love which mold from within, but are now purely relational concepts which express that the heart is passively stirred by the address of divine truth and loving-kindness." See Berndt Hamm, *The Reformation of Faith in the Context of Late Medieval Theology and Piety: Essays by Berndt Hamm,* ed. Robert J. Bast (Leiden: Brill, 2004), 167–72.

for the first nine philosophical theses.[k] Joseph Vercruysse gives an overview of the disputation's structure.[l] The first eighteen theses are anthropological, with theses 1 through 12 treating good works and the next six, free will. The very next six (19–24) concern "true wisdom" as it pertains to Luther's "theology of the cross."[7, m] The final four relate to the righteousness of faith. Throughout the disputation's explicitly theological section, Luther appeals to both Paul and Augustine in order to show that human beings cannot properly claim righteousness on their own. Faith in Christ is necessary.

Luther's theses are carefully crafted and paradoxical.[8] For instance, while the first thesis claims that the law cannot advance a person in righteousness, the second adds that advance is even less likely by doing good works. The notion that human beings naturally drive toward the good is rejected: what appears attractive and good in human beings is nonetheless mortal sin. What seems to be good is actually evil, and what appears to be evil is actually good. Luther offers a radical inversion of perspective; the human moral standpoint itself shares in fallen human hubris. True humility demands that the believer fear God's eternal judgment in every human work.[9]

Luther also rejects free will, declaring "after the fall it exists in name only." At issue was the well-known late

k   The latter were first published in 1979 and are in WA 59:405–26.

l   See Joseph E. Vercruysse, "Gesetz und Liebe: die Struktur der 'Heidelberger Disputation' Luthers (1518)," *Lutherjahrbuch* 68 (1981): 7–43.

m   Many studies locate the theology of the cross at the center of Luther's theology. See Forde, *On Being a Theologian of the Cross*; Walther von Loewenich, *Luther's Theology of the Cross,* trans. Herbert J. A. Bouman (Minneapolis: Augsburg, 1976); Dennis Ngien, *The Suffering God according to Martin Luther's 'Theologia Crucis'* (New York: Lang, 1995); Hans Joachim Iwand, "Theologia Crucis," in *Nachgelassene Werke II* (Münich: Kaiser, 1966), 381–98; and Robert Kolb, "Luther's Theology of the Cross Fifteen Years after Heidelberg: Lectures on the Psalms of Ascent," *The Journal of Ecclesiastical History* 61 (2010): 69–85. For a contrary view, see David S. Yeago, "The Catholic Luther," in Carl Braaten and Robert Jenson, *The Catholicity of the Reformation* (Grand Rapids: Eerdmans, 1996), 27.

medieval notion that "God will not deny grace to those who do what is within them." Standard theology of the time assumed that human beings must make some autonomous movement toward God in order that through God's grace this intrinsically nonmeritorious movement could be extrinsically regarded by God as meriting salvation. Luther denies that human beings can make this movement. In fact, their true hope lies in despairing that they have the ability to make *any* such movement.

In discerning their true standing before God, believers realize that they cannot see God's naked glory but can glimpse only the "backside" of God in Christ's suffering and death. Because the eternal, impassible God is incarnate in "ungodly" suffering and death, one glimpses God in that which is seemingly not of God. The theology of the cross recognizes that human beings cannot approach God through their own rational and moral resources—though God nonetheless remains the standard by which rationality and morality are measured. While a theology of glory falsely claims to know God from God's works in creation, a theology of the cross actually knows God from the sufferings of the cross of Christ.

The Philosophical Theses

While generations of the disputation's readers have been exposed to Luther's theological critique of the tradition, the philosophical theses have often seemed to be extraneous. But a close reading of these theses and their *probationes* displays that Kolb's statement of a paradigm shift applies to the entire disputation, including the explicitly philosophical material. Both the theological and philosophical theses concern the sinner's inability to effect reconciliation with God: just as human doing does not place a demand upon the *actions* of God, so, too, human gazing on the visible objects of creation and history does not deliver a right *conception* of the divine." This cross clearly exposes our natural, human

---

n Kolb, "Luther on the Theology of the Cross," 446–48.

10. Epistemology is the branch of philosophy concerned with the nature and scope of knowledge. Applied to knowledge of God, a theology of glory claims that true belief about God is justified and that a theory of knowledge about God can be founded upon *sources* available in principle to all thinkers.

presuppositions in both *epistemology* and *ethics*, presuppositions resting upon a fundamental commitment to a theology of glory.[10]

In the time since the first English translation of the *Heidelberg Disputation* by Harold Grimm in 1957, much has been learned about the philosophical theses. Most of the *probationes* accompanying the philosophical theses were unpublished until 1979, when Helmar Junghans published them.[o] Research over the past five decades on Luther's concerns in the philosophical theses has remained largely unknown to English-speaking audiences.[p] Indeed, no English translation of the *probationes* is yet available.[q] Yet understanding the entire disputation demands making a connection between these theses and the first twenty-eight. Looking back on the *Heidelberg Disputation*, Luther acknowledged the importance of the philosophical theses: "For what could be gained with respect to the understanding of material things if you could quibble and trifle with matter, form, motion, measure, and time—words taken over and copied from Aristotle?"[r] Luther maintained that Aristotle had been *misunderstood* by theolo-

----

o   Helmar Junghans, "Disputatio Heidelbergae habita 1518," MLStA 1:186–218; idem, "Die Probationes zu den Philosophischen Thesen der Heidelberger Disputation im Jahre 1518," *Lutherjahrbuch* 46 (1979): 10–59; and especially WA 59:405–26. The first two *probationes* were known since the early eighteenth century. See Gerhard Ebeling, *Lutherstudien*, vol. 2: *Disputatio de Homine*, pt. 2: *Die Philosophische Definition des Menschen. Kommentar zu These 1-19* (Tübingen: Mohr Siebeck, 1982), 71. See Junghans, "Disputatio," 212–13; and Theodor Dieter, *Der junge Luther und Aristoteles: Eine historisch-sytematische Untersuchung zum Verhältnis von Theologie und Philosophie* (Berlin: de Gruyter, 2001). Dieter argues that Luther believed that late medieval Scholastic interpretation of Aristotle was a *misunderstanding* of the authentic Aristotle.

p   Some of the work includes a German translation of the *probationes* by Ebeling, *Lutherstudien*, 472–89; Helmar Junghans, *Der junge Luther und die Humanisten* (Göttingen: Vandenhoeck & Ruprecht, 1985), 143–71; 293–301; Karl-Heinz zur Mühlen, "Luthers Kritik am scholastischen Aristotelismus in 25. These der 'Heidelberger Disputation' von 1518," *Lutherjahrbuch* (1981): 54–79; and esp. Dieter, *Der junge Luther und Aristoteles*, 431–631.

q   A translation by Eric Phillips will appear in LW 72.

r   WA 9:170. That this may have been written down first in 1528, see Dieter, *Der junge Luther und Aristoteles*, 433.

gians of his time, that this misunderstanding had eventuated in much theological and philosophical mischief, and that theologians must understand Aristotle correctly if they are to avoid being misled with regard to the possibilities of human goodness and knowledge.[s]

While Luther engages in overt philosophical argumentation in the *probationes*, he does so to theological ends. Aristotle's metaphysical misunderstandings are of profound theological concern for Luther. He argues that just as Aristotle failed to grasp that there are no resources within the fallen created order to make moral progress in pleasing God through keeping the law, so, too, he did not recognize that created reality lacks *in se* the requisite metaphysical conditions for intelligibility. Apart from divine aid, fallen creation is profoundly unknowable and moral progress within it wholly impossible.

Luther carefully avoids a blanket condemnation of philosophy in the disputation but asserts instead its value if properly used: just as the erotic dimension of sexual love should be employed only in marriage, so the attractions of philosophy must be saved for faith. Luther delivers a stinging critique of a particular *kind* of philosophy, that is, the philosophy of Aristotle, a philosophy that he thinks the late medieval Scholastic tradition had wholly misunderstood. Consistent with his claims in his 1517 *Disputation against Scholastic Theology*, Luther aims to show that Aristotle's philosophy, rightly understood, is inimical to theology.[t] According to Luther, since Aristotle holds that form is realized only materially, his philosophy prioritizes the principle of matter over form. But this materialistic emphasis lacks the metaphysical resources of Plato's incorporeal forms to know, understand, and explain created reality. Moreover, Luther contends that on purely Aristotelian grounds the soul is *mortal*, and thus talk of its "eternity" can only be understood as an activity of a temporal, mortal being.

s   This is argued conclusively in Dieter's *Die Junge Luther und Aristoteles*, 431–631.

t   LW 31:3–16.

11. Luther's rejection of the theology of glory in the theological theses is consistent with his denial in the philosophical theses that spatial or temporal objects have intrinsic intelligibility. The theological assertion that one cannot know God on the basis of natural experience of the world is consonant with the metaphysical assertion that finite worldly objects lack intrinsic intelligibility.

12. The Pythagorean school is associated with a great many assertions including that "all things are made of number." Parmenides authored a very difficult poem that suggests he held that all things are one thing and that there is no becoming. Anaxagoras is famous for his view of mind (*nous*) as an explanatory hypothesis for the mixing and separating of things that eventuates in the world. All of these philosophers are criticized in Aristotle's *Metaphysics*, bk. I.

Plato's philosophy is superior to Aristotle's because it allows for a region of infinity and immateriality that Aristotle's metaphysics precludes, a region necessary to account for human knowledge of the created order and for the profound human transcendence of that order.[11] In making his point, Luther goes so far as to praise the Pythagoreans, Parmenides (late fifth century BCE), and even Anaxagoras (500–428 BCE) over Aristotle.[12]

Excursus: Luther's Proof of Thesis 31

One of the hardest-to-understand philosophical theses is thesis 31. In his *Probatio*, Luther states that Aristotle held that the world's eternity is incompatible with the immortality of the soul, for were the world eternal and the human soul immortal, there would exist an infinite number of human souls. But Aristotle famously denies that the actual infinite exists. Aristotle treats the topic of infinity in both his *Physics* and his *Metaphysics*. While he allows potentially infinite series formed by successive addition or division, he denies that there could be an actual *collection* or *set* of an infinite number of objects. In the accompanying *probatio*, Luther gives Aristotle's arguments for why the world is eternal and the soul mortal. The argument for the eternity of the world is this: it is evident that motion is perpetual and everlasting. But if a motion is perpetual, it is continuous, and if it is continuous, it is one. But if a motion is one, then it is moved by one mover. Thus, there is a perpetual being moving for an infinite time.

Luther then gives eight reasons why Aristotle thought that the soul is mortal: (1) If the soul is the actuality of a body having a potentiality to live, and humans share this constitution with the other animals, then the human soul is mortal, like animal souls. (2) Just as matter and form comprise a corruptible composite, so do soul and body. (3) While Aristotle grants that the soul is "something divine" and participates in immortality, he is referring to the *act* of the soul and not the soul itself, which is neither "perpetual, immortal nor a God." (4) Alexander Aphrodisias claimed that his teacher Aristotle held that the soul was mortal. (5) Aristotle is committed to the view that matter, form, and their composite comprise one single thing. Since a human being is a corruptible composite, the soul, which is part of the corruptible composite, is itself corruptible. (6) Aristotle maintains that there is no mover if there is nothing to move. But since the soul is the mover of the body, and if there is no body, there can be no mover and thus no immortal soul. (7) Aristotle speaks a great deal about things he knows, but he says "no more than ten words" in any one place about the soul being immortal. Thus, Aristotle does not know it is immortal. (8) Aristotle hides his ignorance about the immortality of the *human* soul by treating the notion of soul in general. After providing evidence based upon Aristotelian principles for claiming that Aristotle's soul must be mortal, Luther offers direct quotations.

Luther's reading of Aristotle's classic treatment in *On the Soul* convinces him that the philosopher is clearly applying "perpetual" to the agent or active intellect, not the entire intellect. Aristotle holds that the agent intellect "forms" the passive intellect by abstracting the form from external objects and impressing it upon the potential intellect. Luther points out that the form is a *habitus* or dispositional state, and that when this *habitus* exists in matter, the operation of abstraction ceases. Because the active intellect is the form of the potential intellect—just like a "figure of bronze"—it might be said to be separable and a substance. Luther attacks Aristotle: "Observe that most slippery eel! He does not say that the soul is separable and unmixed and without passion, but that the *active intellect* is separable."[u] Aristotle, accordingly, is not talking about a separate soul but, rather, the form that is in the soul, namely the active intellect. Luther argues that the "composite" about which Aristotle speaks is not the composite of mind and body, but the composite of active

---

u WA 59:416, 16–17.

and potential intellect in one act of intellection or knowledge. Luther explains that the form of the active intellect cannot be defined but is that by which "the other things" are defined, and thus it gives "being to the thing." Just because the form of the active intellect "is what it is," this does not entail that it is separable as soul to body. What alone is immortal and perpetual is this active intellect separable from the composite of *knowing* itself. Luther believes that Aristotle occludes his belief that the soul is mortal by engaging in intentional ambiguity about the ontological status of the active intellect. Without the potential intellect upon which form is impressed, the active intellect really has no *being* and thus "we cannot remember"—though there is a sense in which the active intellect nonetheless remains separable in itself.

The overall point that Luther makes here is that any "immortality" or "perpetuity" that can be claimed for the soul cannot be claimed *substantially* of the soul in the composite of soul/body, but can only be claimed *operationally* of the active intellect in the composite of active intellect/potential intellect. The active intellect, however, can never be a *substance* in Aristotle's sense of that which exists on its own, because its very being depends upon the impression of its form on the potential intellect.

Luther discerns the culprit in the theology of glory to be the Aristotelian "turn towards the phantasm," a move that philosophically legitimates the ubiquitous human proclivity to grasp the infinite on the basis of the finite, to reach heaven by building a tower on the earth. He recognizes that such human vanity must fail. After all, what could be a surer philosophical assertion of God's *grace* than that the finite has intelligibility only upon the basis of the infinite? Just as grace is requisite in order for human beings to approach God on the basis of their actions, so, too, the divine is required to understand, however dimly, God and God's creation. To begin with God as the locus of intelligibility lucidly displays that just as in the moral sphere, so, too, in the epistemological, there is no way for finite human beings to build a bridge to the infinite.[v] Just as, despite appearances to the contrary, God's love and concern are manifest on the dereliction of the cross, so, too, despite contrary appearances, human knowledge of higher things is only displayed upon the horizon of those higher things. The heavenly has its own logic of grace that illuminates human standing before God—both in the moral and epistemological orders.

The Aftermath

While Luther may have failed to convince his seniors, he was nonetheless both inspiring and persuasive in the encounter, and his theses were accordingly well received by some younger theologians. Martin Bucer (1491–1551) was impressed by Luther's knowledge of the Bible, the church fathers, and his courtesy and courage in answering questions.[13] He writes, "[Luther's] sweetness in answering is remarkable, his patience in listening is incomparable, in his explanations you will recognize the acumen of Paul."[w] Although Luther continued to hold his Erfurt teachers Jodocus Trutfetter (c. 1460–1519) and Bartholomew Arnoldi of Usingen (c. 1465–1521) in high respect, he ultimately failed to gain the theological confidence of either. Luther's letter written to Trutfetter immediately after the disputation displays what had been at issue during the debate: "I simply believe it is impossible to reform the church, unless the canons, decretals, scholastic theology, philosophy, logic, as we now have them, be eradicated completely and other studies substituted; and I proceed accordingly in that conviction, when I pray that this may happen immediately, and the purest study of the Bible and the holy fathers be recalled. You think I am no logician, and perhaps I am not, but this I know, that I fear no one's logic in defending this conviction."[x]

13. See the letter of Martin Bucer (1491–1551) to Beatus Rhenanus (1485–1547) from May 1, 1518, in *Luther's Correspondence and other Contemporary Letters,* 2 vols., trans. and ed. Preserved Smith et al. (Philadelphia: The Lutheran Publication Society, 1913–1918), 1:82 (WA 9:162, 1–5): "Although our chief men refuted him with all their might, their wiles were not able to make him move an inch from his propositions. His sweetness in answering is remarkable, his patience in listening is incomparable, in his explanations you will recognize the acumen of Paul, not of Scotus; his answers, so brief, were drawn from Holy Scriptures, easily made all his hearers his admirers." Also in attendance was Johannes Brenz (1499–1570), later the reformer in the imperial city of Schwäbisch Hall (where he also was also adviser for the margraviate of Brandenburg-Ansbach and for Nuremberg) and in the duchy of Württemberg.

v   Cf. Paul Althaus, *The Theology of Martin Luther,* trans. Robert Schultz (Philadelphia: Fortress Press, 1966), 27.

w   James Kittelson, *Luther the Reformer: The Story of the Man and His Career* (Minneapolis: Augsburg, 1986), 112.

x   WA Br 1:170, 33–40.

The publication of these theses and their explanations is quite convoluted. The original theses have not come down to us in any form, although they were reprinted around 1520 in Paris and Leiden and in 1530 in Wittenberg as part of a larger collection of Luther's theses for disputations.[y] The explanations to the theological theses were first published in 1545 as part of the first volume of Luther's Latin works, and they may well have come from Luther's original manuscript, since he also provided the preface to that volume.[z] An incomplete version of arguments on thesis 6 also found a separate place in the same volume, titled simply "Against the Opinion of the Scholastics." Another version, without the final material, was published in 1720. A manuscript for the explanations to the philosophical theses was first published in 1979. Thus, this version of Luther's theology of the cross was not readily accessible to sixteenth-century readers. Luther did, however, use these same categories elsewhere. For example, in his *Explanations of the 95 Theses*, written at the same time but published in August 1518, he also defines the theology of the cross.[a]

THE DISPUTATION[14, 15]

BROTHER MARTIN LUTHER, Master of Sacred Theology, will preside, and Brother Leonhard Beier, Master of Arts and Philosophy, will defend the following theses before the Augustinians of this

14. The theological theses, with this caption, were perhaps printed for the disputation itself, although they could have been distributed only in handwritten copies. Contemporary reprints, probably from 1520 and published in Paris and Leiden, have survived.

15. The English translation here, based upon the Latin in WA 1:353–74, was originally done by Harold Grimm and published in volume 31 of *Luther's Works*.

y   *Proposiciones [sic!] a M. Luthero subinde disputatae* (Wittenberg: Klug, 1530). For a reconstruction of the order in which this material arose, see MLStA 1:188–89, where it is argued that the proofs of the theological theses were prepared before the disputation but not delivered there.

z   LW 34:323–38. It contains no mention of the *Heidelberg Disputation*.

a   See LW 31:125–30; 212–28.

renowned city of Heidelberg in the customary place. In the month of May, 1518.[16]

Theological Theses

Distrusting completely our own wisdom, according to that counsel of the Holy Spirit, "Do not rely on your own insight" [Prov. 3:5], we humbly present these theological paradoxes to the judgment of all those who wish to attend, so that it may become clear whether they have been deduced well or poorly from St. Paul, the especially chosen vessel and instrument of Christ, and also from St. Augustine, his most trustworthy interpreter.

1. The law of God, the most salutary doctrine of life, cannot advance human beings on their way to righteousness, but rather hinders them.[b]

2. Much less can human works, done over and over again with the aid of a "natural principle" (as it is called),[17] lead to that end.

16. The disputation actually took place on April 26. Leonhard Beier (aka Reiff) was an Augustinian monk from Munich who matriculated at the University of Wittenberg in May 1514. See the *Album Academiae Vitebergensis*, vol. 1: *Ab A. Ch. MDII usque ad A. MDLX*, ed. Karl Förstemann (Leipzig: Tauchnitz, 1841), 51. He received his bachelor of arts in 1516 and his master's in 1518 and accompanied Luther to Augsburg in October of that year.

17. Latin: *naturale dictamen*, literally, "a natural precept." Luther is referring to Gabriel Biel's argument that a person in a state of sin merits grace *ex puris naturalibus* (by pure natural [powers]).

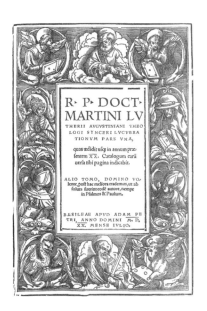

This historiated title page border, based on the design of Hans Holbein the Younger, features the symbols of the four Gospels in the corners (angel for Matthew, ox for Luke, lion for Mark, and eagle for John); the apostles Peter and Paul at the top and bottom; and the four doctors of the Western church along the edges (Pope Gregory I; St. Jerome; St. Ambrose, bishop of Milan; and St. Augustine, bishop of Hippo).

---

b   Throughout, the Latin word *homo* in all its declensions is translated as "human being," "person," or "man or woman."

18. According to medieval Scholastic theology, mortal sins kill the soul completely, while venial sins make one's spiritual life sick, but not irreparably so. A venial sin is immediately pardonable while a mortal sin is not, because God's gift of love has been withdrawn from the soul. Thomas Aquinas points out, for example, that although one cannot recover from a mortal sin on one's own, divine power is able to overcome any affliction of mind or body. See Thomas Aquinas, *Summa Theologica* II, q. 88, a. 1: "Mortal sin utterly destroys the order which directs the soul by reason and God's law; it inflicts on the soul damage that is naturally irreparable. Venial sin is a disorder, but not a destructive one." Thomas goes on to argue (in q. 86, a. 6) that before reaching an age where reason is properly used, no one can commit a mortal sin. Luther, on the contrary, argues that all sins are mortal.

19. Latin: *facit quod in se est*, a technical term in late medieval theology, championed by Gabriel Biel, with whose writings Luther was intimately familiar. The longer version was: "To those who do what is in them, God will not deny grace." This was for Biel an important part of the defense of the free will. Luther would return to this and the following theses in his final arguments below, pp. 116–19. This is the only thesis explicitly condemned in 1520 by the papal bull *Exsurge Domini*. See MLStA 1:214, n. 633.

3. Although the works of human beings always seem attractive and good, it is nevertheless probable that they are mortal sins.[18]

4. Although the works of God always seem unattractive and evil, they are nevertheless really immortal[c] merits.

5. The works of human beings—we speak of works which appear to be good—are thus not mortal sins as if they were crimes.

6. The works of God—we speak of those that are done through human beings—are thus not merits as if they were sinless.

7. The works of the righteous would be mortal sins were they not feared as mortal sins by the righteous themselves out of pious fear of God.

8. All the more are human works mortal sins when they are done without fear and in unadulterated, evil self-security.

9. To say that works without Christ are indeed dead but not mortal sins[d] seems a perilous rejection of the fear of God.

10. Indeed, it is very difficult to see how a work can be dead and at the same time not a culpable,[e] or mortal, sin.

11. Arrogance cannot be avoided nor can true hope be present, unless the judgment of damnation is feared in every work.

12. As a consequence, in the sight of God sins are truly venial when human beings fear them as mortal.

13. Free will, after [the fall into] sin, exists in name only, and when "it does what is within it," it commits a mortal sin.[19]

---

c   Latin: *immortalia*, in direct contrast to mortal sins.

d   Luther is making a play on words between *mortua* (dead) and *mortalia* (a technical term for mortal sins).

e   Latin: *noxium*, rendered "culpable" rather than "harmful" to display more clearly Luther's point as to the sinner's extrinsic culpability before God.

Gabriel Biel (c. 1420–1495), a late-medieval
scholastic theologian who taught in Tübingen.

14. Free will, after [the fall into] sin, has the power to do good only passively but always has the power to do evil actively.[20]

15. Nor in the state of innocence could free will remain an active power, much less make progress in the good, but remains in innocence only a passive power.[21]

16. The person who believes that one can obtain grace "by doing what is in oneself" adds sin to sin and thus becomes doubly guilty.

17. Nor does speaking in this manner give cause for despair, but rather for humility,[f] for it arouses the desire to seek the grace of Christ.

18. It is certain that one must utterly despair of oneself in order to be made fit to receive the grace of Christ.

19. That person does not deserve to be called a theologian who perceives the invisible things of God as understandable on the basis of those things which have been made [Rom. 1:20].[22]

20. Latin: *potentia subiectiva*. The late medieval dictionary of theological terms, *Vocabularius Theologie*, comp. Johannes Altenstaig (Haguenau: Rynman, 1517), 196r, defines three modes of *potentia* (potential): objective, active, and subjective. The first is the potential to exist, the second a potential to act, and the third a potential to be acted upon. Luther says that while human beings actively do evil, they can only passively do good.

21. Any good done by human beings before the fall is by *potentia subiectiva*, having been moved by God. Thus, even the state of innocence results from being moved by God.

22. The terse, precise wording of theses 19 and 20 asserts that a theologian should not perceive (*conspicit*) the invisible things of God as understood (*intellecta*) by things that have been made but, rather, should understand (*intelligit*) the visible things of God as perceived (*conspecta*) through Christ's passion and cross. The theologian of glory thus attempts to *see* on the basis of understanding, while the theologian of the cross *understands* on the basis of what is seen. The distinction is between perceiving God on the basis of understanding the world and understanding God on the basis of perceiving the cross of Christ.

---

f   Latin: *desperandi* and *humiliandi*, passive participles: "to be driven to despair" and "to be made humble."

23. The Latin here cannot be properly translated literally. At issue here is a traditional group of theological distinctions, normally employed in describing grace in the sacraments. One must contrast the *opus operatum* (literally, "the work which has been worked"), the *opus operans* (literally, "the work working"), and (not used here) the *opus operantis* (the work of the one doing the work). Luther claims that Christ is the one working (*operans*), that our work has been worked by God (*operatum*), and is thus pleasing in God's sight by the grace of the working work (*gratia operis operantis*), that is, by the work of Christ who is actually doing the work.

24. The philosophical theses were first published with the theological theses in 1530.

25. This thesis bears marked similarity to theses 43, 44, and 50 of Luther's *Disputation concerning Scholastic Theology* (LW 31:14). For Luther's extensive proof of this thesis, see the excursus in the introduction, pp. 76–78. Luther demonstrates this thesis by citing 1 Corinthians 1, concerning the dangers of pursuing knowledge for knowledge's sake, declaring that to know things outside Christ is "to know that I know nothing." Luther counsels that the only way rightly to have knowledge beyond Christ is to possess it "as if it were not possessed," that is, by not taking pleasure in it.

26. If one philosophizes using Aristotle, *necessarily* one must become foolish in Christ. The *probatio* for this thesis adds *ad salutem* (409:9), making apparent that the danger relates to

20. The person deserves to be called a theologian, however, who understands the visible and the "backside" of God [Exod. 33:23] seen through suffering and the cross.[g]

21. A theologian of glory calls evil good and good evil. A theologian of the cross calls a thing what it actually is.

22. That wisdom which sees the invisible things of God in works as understood by human beings is puffed up, blinded, and hardened.[h]

23. The law works the wrath of God, kills, reviles, accuses, judges, and condemns everything that is not in Christ [Rom. 4:15].

24. Yet that wisdom is not of itself evil, nor is the law to be evaded; but without the theology of the cross a person misuses the best things in the worst way.

25. That person is not righteous who does many works but who, without works, believes much in Christ.[i]

26. The law says, "Do this," and it is never done. Grace says, "Believe in this One," and everything has already been done.

27. Properly speaking, one should call Christ's work an active work and our work a passive work, and thus the passive work is pleasing to God by the grace of the active work.[23]

---

g   Latin: *posteriora Dei* refers to Exod. 33:23 and translates "backside" or "back end."

h   The interplay between *conspicit* and *intelligit* continues. Human wisdom perceives (*conspicit*) what it understands and thus becomes blind (*excaecat*).

i   Luther plays on the words *operatur* (to work or to do), opposed to the one who believes *sine opera* (without works).

28. God's love does not find, but creates, that which is pleasing to it. Human love comes into being through that which is pleasing to it.

Philosophical Theses[24]

29. Whoever wishes without danger to philosophize using Aristotle must beforehand become thoroughly foolish in Christ.[25, 26]

30. Just as no one uses the evil of lust properly unless married, so nobody philosophizes well unless a fool, that is, a Christian.[27, 28]

31. It was easy for Aristotle to believe that the world was eternal since he believed that the human soul was mortal.*j*

32. After it was held [by Aristotle] that there are just as many substantial forms as composite ones, it was necessary to hold also that there are just as many material ones.[29]

salvation. Read in light of the second thesis and the corresponding *probatio*. Here "Aristotle" refers to speculative philosophy in general.

27. Just as lust is the perverse desire for pleasure outside marriage, so philosophy outside the grace of Christ is the perverse love of knowing (*perversus amor sciendi*) (WA 59:410, 2–3). Luther explains that philosophy and pleasure are not bad in themselves, but that, without Christ, sinful human beings can desire them only in a perverse way. Of all the parts of the body that desire their objects perversely, the intellect does so most egregiously because its end is truth, and the intellect desires truth for its own glory (*in gloriam suam*) (410, 7). "To philosophize outside of Christ is the same as fornicating outside of marriage" (410, 10–11).

28. The two theses together connect to the central themes of the disputation. Theses 19–24 associate the theology of glory with knowledge and contemplation and the theology of the cross with salvation and the light of the cross of Christ. The second thesis draws the parallel between a perverse love of pleasure with a perverse love of knowledge.

29. Luther tries to show on Aristotelian grounds that a particular composite must be comprised of a particular form and a particular matter being formed. By citing several passages from Aristotle, Luther sketches a philosophical argument against the notion of prime matter, that is, the existence of a potentiality-in-general awaiting the impression of form. Luther believes that the identity conditions of matter in Aristotle must

---

j This curious thesis and its demonstration (WA 59:410, 24–420, 3) concern an issue that Augustine discusses in the *City of God* 12:17–20. For a detailed look at Luther's refutation, see the introduction, pp. 76–78 above.

be related to the composite substance formed. It is not matter-as-such that receives a form constituting substance, but matter having a *particular potentiality* that receives it (WA 59:420, 11ff.). How could there be prime matter if the earth has generable matter and the heavens do not? Luther is saying that just as Aristotle holds that there are as many substantial forms as composite ones, so must he hold that there are just as many material forms as composite ones. The result is that substantial forms are correlated one to one with material ones. Luther thus holds that Aristotle, unlike Plato (c. 427–c. 348 BCE), is forced to identify form and matter.

30. The modality here is important: While particular beings do not necessarily emerge from other particular beings, all entities emerging naturally necessarily emerge from matter. The second part of the statement forms a conceptual truth, so that Luther argues in the *probatio* that the definition of "matter" is "that from which something comes to be in such a way so as not to involve an accident." Luther points out that a chicken comes into being not necessarily from an egg but, rather, from that which is "chickable" (*pullabili*), that is, necessarily, "from the potential chicken comes the actual chicken" (WA 59:422, 6–7).

31. Latin: *de potentia Dei absoluta*, a technical term especially in Gabriel Biel's Nominalist theology. Luther explains that matter and form are inseparable because one cannot have an act without the potential for the act. Luther does not allude in this demonstration to the issue raised

33. Nothing comes about necessarily from any particular reality in the world; nevertheless, necessarily whatever comes about naturally, comes about from matter.[30]

34. If Aristotle had recognized "the absolute power of God," he would have maintained that it is impossible for matter to exist unformed (*nudam*).[31]

Portrait bust of the
ancient philosopher Plato.

35. According to Aristotle, there is no actual infinite, yet with respect to potentiality and form there are as many infinites as there are composite things.[32]

36. Aristotle wrongly rebukes and lampoons the philosophy of "Platonic ideas," a philosophy that is better than his own.[k]

37. The "imitation of numbers" in things is cleverly asserted by Pythagoras, but cleverer still is the participation of ideas asserted by Plato.[33]

k   Theses 36–39 directly attack Aristotle's *Metaphysics* I, which outlines previous attempts to understand reality. Here Luther takes exception to Aristotle's criticism of Plato beginning in *Metaphysics* I.6. Luther prefers the Platonic forms over Aristotle's metaphysics because, in the words of the *probatio* (WA 59:424, 8–425, 8), "the philosophy of Plato is better than the philosophy of Aristotle is clear from the fact that Plato always strives for the divine and immortal, separate and eternal, insensible and intelligible, from whence he also recommends that singulars, individuals, and sensible things be abandoned because they cannot be known on account of their instability. Aristotle, being opposed to this in every way, derides the separable and intelligible and carries in sensible things and singulars and thoroughly human and natural things. It is true that he does this most cunningly: Firstly, because he cannot deny that the individual is transient [*fluxa*], he invents a form and a different matter, so the thing is not knowable as matter, but as form. Therefore, he says that the form is the cause of knowing [*causam sciendi*], and he calls this 'divine, good, desirable [*appetibile*]' and he assigns the intellect to this. In this way he frustrates every mind, while he examines the same thing in two ways. Secondly, this 'form' is a quiddity and the sum of his *Metaphysics*. So, he destroys all the ideas, putting in their place his own forms and quiddities conjoined to matter, ridiculing and denying [the existence of] the ideas separable from matter, as appears in many places, especially *Metaphysics* 1 and [*Nicomachean*] *Ethics* 1. But, it is well known through Augustine, Iamblichus [245–325], and all the Platonic disputants that the ideas of Plato are separate. And so it appears that the philosophy of Aristotle crawls in the dregs of corporeal and sensible things, whereas Plato moves among things separable and spiritual."

in the thesis: divine omnipotence makes problematic the existence of unformed matter. Presumably, it is conceptually impossible for God to will an incomplete potentiality. If God wills a thing, it must be actual, and if God wills that it not be, it is not possible. Later in the Reformation, the debate would revolve around whether the concupiscence that remains in the person after baptism (the "tinder of sin") is simply the "matter" of sin and thus not truly sin without the addition of its "form." Luther would argue that concupiscence itself is sin (in Aristotle's language, fully "formed").

32. Luther works here with a technical philosophical vocabulary; e.g., *infinitum actu* refers to Aristotle's actual infinite, an actual collection of infinite things. This must be distinguished from the potential infinite, which is an infinite formed in mathematical operations but never completed (actual). The Scholastic tradition followed Aristotle in claiming there is no *infinitum actu*. Luther points out that a magnitude cannot be actually infinite, but since it can always be divided again, it nonetheless is potentially infinite. Dividing something into composites does not, however, entail that these composites are actualized.

33. Luther is directly criticizing Aristotle's *Metaphysics* I.5-6, which describes how Pythagoreans are arguing that things exist by "imitation of numbers" and how Plato talked of participation, which Aristotle dismissed as not much better. Plato believed that individuals *participate* in the forms of which they are instances. The greater the participation, the more perfect or complete the individual.

Luther also argues that odd numbers symbolize form and even numbers symbolize matter. Since matter is infinitely divisible, even numbers also symbolize infinity while odd numbers connote the finite. The Pythagorean School flourished during and after the life of Pythagoras (570–490 BCE). It is associated with a great many assertions, including that "all things are made of number." This was interpreted by the tradition to mean that there are an infinite number of unities comprising any magnitude.

34. Again Luther takes issue with Aristotle's criticisms of Parmenides in *Metaphysics* I.3-5. Parmenides authored a very difficult poem suggesting that all things are one thing and there is no becoming. The One is both form and finite, yet there lies within it all things, something which is potentially infinite. In this way the One is "beyond all things and nevertheless in all things" (WA 59:426, 7).

35. Luther again takes issue with Aristotle's criticism of Anaxagoras in *Metaphysics* I.8. Anaxagoras claimed that nothing actually comes into being or passes away, but that a separating and mixing accounts for the world as we experience it. Additionally, he held that everything is made of everything

38. The disputation of Aristotle (if a Christian will pardon this) "fights against" Parmenides' idea of oneness "by beating the air" [1 Cor. 9:26].[34]

39. If Anaxagoras posited the infinite before form [of things], as it seems he did, he was the best of the philosophers, even if Aristotle was unwilling to acknowledge this.[35]

40. To Aristotle, privation, matter, form, mobility, immobility, actuality, potentiality, etc. seem to be the same thing.

Proofs of the Thesis Debated in the Chapter at Heidelberg, May, AD 1518[1]

1

The law of God, the most salutary doctrine of life,
cannot advance human beings on their way to righteousness,
but rather hinders them.

This is made clear by the Apostle in his letter to the Romans 3[:21]: "But now, apart from law, the righteousness of God has been disclosed," St. Augustine explains this in his book, *On the Spirit and the Letter*: "Without the law, that is, without its support."[m] In Rom. 5[:20] the Apostle states, "the law came in, with the result that the trespass multiplied," and in Rom. 7[:9] he adds, "but when the commandment came, sin revived." For this reason, he calls the law a "law of death" and "a law of sin" in Rom. 8[:2]. Indeed, in 2 Cor. 3[:6] he says, "the letter kills," which St. Augustine throughout his book, *The Spirit and the Letter*, understands as applying to every law, even the holiest law of God.[36]

---

l These "proofs" were first published in the first volume of Luther's Latin works in 1545. Given that Luther provided the preface to that volume, it is possible that he also provided the original text still in his possession. MLStA 1:187–89 includes all the material that was part of Luther's preparation for the disputation.

m Augustine, *On the Spirit and the Letter (De Spiritu et Litera)*, I.9 (15) in NPNF, ser. 1, 5: 89.

2

Much less can human works, done over and over again
with the aid of a "natural principle" (as it is called),
lead to that end.

Since the law of God, which is holy and unstained, true, just, etc., is given to human beings by God as an aid [above and] beyond human natural powers so as to enlighten the person and move that person to do the good, and nevertheless the opposite takes place, namely, that one becomes more wicked, how can one, left to one's own power and without such aid, be moved to do good?[37] If persons do not do good with help from without, they will do even less by their own strength. Therefore the Apostle, in Rom. 3[:10-12], calls all persons corrupt and impotent who neither understand nor seek God, for all, he says, have gone astray.

3

Although the works of human beings always seem
attractive and good, it is nevertheless probable
that they are mortal sins.

Human works appear attractive outwardly, but within they are filthy, as Christ says concerning the Pharisees in Matt. 23[:27]. They appear to the doer and to others good and beautiful, yet God does not judge according to appearances but searches "the minds and hearts" [Ps. 7:9]. For without grace and faith it is impossible to have a pure heart. Acts 15[:9]: "cleansing their hearts by faith."

The thesis is proven in the following way: If the works of the righteous are sins, as thesis 7 of this disputation states, this is much more the case concerning the works of those who are not righteous. But the righteous speak in behalf of their works in the following way: "Do not enter into judgment with your servant, for no one living is righteous before you" [Ps. 143:2]. Second,*n* the Apostle speaks in Gal. 3[:10], "For all who rely on the works of the law are under a curse." But the works of human beings are works of the law, and the

and that there is no smallest or largest. Anaxagoras is famous for his view of mind (*nous*) as an explanatory hypothesis for the mixing and separating of things that eventuates in the world. Although criticized by both Plato and Aristotle, he did hold that *nous* neither mixes with nor partakes of other elements, an assertion consistent with the mind's incorporeality. It would seem that Luther prefers these thinkers over Aristotle because of the latter's criticisms in the *Metaphysics*. In the *probatio* he approves Parmenides's notion of the One as an indivisible unity that is "beyond all things, yet nevertheless within all things," just as Augustine had claimed in *On True Religion* (WA 59:426, 7-8).

36. There were two strains of interpretation of what Paul meant by "law" in Romans and Galatians: as ceremonial law (c. Jerome [347–420] and Erasmus [1466–1536]) or as all law (Augustine and Luther). Luther would attack Jerome (and Erasmus) specifically in his Galatians commentary of 1519.

37. The law about which Luther thus speaks is not merely an external yardstick of how things should be, but it possesses causal power through the Holy Spirit in bringing things about.

---

n Latin: *Item*, literally, "likewise."

curse will not be placed upon venial sins. Therefore they are mortal sins.

In the third place, Rom. 2[:21] states, "While you preach against stealing, do you steal?" St. Augustine interprets this to mean that people are thieves according to their guilty consciences even if they publicly judge or reprimand other thieves.°

4

Although the works of God always seem unattractive and evil, they are nevertheless really immortal merits.

That the works of God are unattractive is clear from what is said in Isa. 53[:2], "He had no form of majesty," and in 1 Sam. 2[:6], "The Lord kills and brings to life; he brings down to Sheol and raises up." This is understood to mean that the Lord humbles and frightens us by means of the law and the sight of our sins so that we seem in human eyes, including in our own, as nothing, foolish, and wicked, for we are in truth that. Insofar as we acknowledge and confess this, there is no form or beauty in us, but our life is hidden in God (i.e., in the bare confidence in his mercy), finding in ourselves nothing but sin, foolishness, death, and hell, according to that verse of the Apostle in 2 Cor. 6[:9-10], "As sorrowful, yet always rejoicing; as dying, and see—we are alive." And that it is what Isa. 28[:21] calls the alien work of God so that he may do his own work (that is, he humbles us thoroughly, making us despair, so that he may exalt us in his mercy, giving us hope), just as Hab. 3[:2] states, "In wrath may you remember mercy."[38] Such persons therefore are displeased with all their works; they see no beauty, but only their own ugliness. Indeed, they also do those things publicly that appear foolish and disgusting to others.[39]

This ugliness, however, comes into being in us either when God punishes us or when we accuse ourselves, as 1 Cor. 11[:31] says, "If we judged ourselves truly, we should not be judged" by the Lord. Deut. 32[:36] also states, "The Lord will vindicate his people and have compassion on his

38. Luther develops the distinction between the alien and proper work of God particularly in his sermon on *Two Kinds of Righteousness* (LW 31:297–300). God's work of wrath is alien to God's own nature and God's work of mercy proper to it. Through suffering, tribulation, temptation, and despair God drives sinners to abandon themselves and flee to God's mercy.

39. The works of God that seem unattractive are works that unmask human pretensions of being attractive in the sight of God. The works of God are thus not unattractive in themselves but, rather, unattractive to the sinner.

o   This reference to Augustine cannot be determined.

servants." In this way, consequently, the unattractive works which God does in us, that is, those which are humble and devout, are really eternal, for humility and fear of God are our entire merit.

5

The works of human beings—we speak of works which appear
to be good—are thus not mortal sins as if they were crimes.

For crimes are such acts that can also be condemned before humankind, such as adultery, theft, homicide, slander, etc. Mortal sins, on the other hand, are those which seem good yet are essentially fruits of a bad root and a bad tree. Augustine states this in the fourth book of *Against Julian.*[p]

6

The works of God—we speak of those that are done
through human beings—are thus not merits
as if they were sinless.

In Ecclesiastes 7[:20], we read, "Surely there is no one on earth so righteous as to do good without ever sinning." In this connection, however, some people say that the righteous person indeed sins, but not when doing good.[40] They may be refuted in the following manner: "If that is what this verse wants to say, why waste so many words? Or does the Holy Spirit like to indulge in loquacious and foolish babble?" For this meaning would then be adequately expressed by the following: "There is not a righteous person on earth who does not sin." Why does [the Holy Spirit] add "Who does good," as if another person were righteous who did evil? For no one except a righteous person does good. Where, however, he speaks of sins outside the realm of good works he speaks thus [Prov. 24:16], "for though they [the righteous] fall seven times, they will rise again." Here he does not say, "A righteous

40. This expresses Luther's idea of *simul iustus et peccator* (at the same time righteous and sinner) and a criticism of the idea that a person is either in a state of sin or a state of grace.

p   Augustine is concerned in Book IV to refute the suggestion of the young Italian bishop Julian of Eclanum that concupiscence is a natural good. See *The Fathers of the Church,* vol. 35: *St. Augustine against Julian,* trans. Matthew A. Schumacher (New York: Fathers of the Church, 1957), 167–240.

person falls seven times a day when doing good." There is a comparison: If someone cuts with a rusty and rough hatchet, even though the worker is a good craftsman, the hatchet leaves bad, jagged, and ugly gashes. So it is when God works through us, etc.[q]

7

The works of the righteous would be mortal sins
were they not feared as mortal sins by the righteous themselves
out of pious fear of God.

This is clear from thesis 4. To trust in a work, which one ought to do in fear, is equivalent to giving oneself the honor and taking it from God, to whom fear is due in connection with every work. But this is completely perverse, namely, to please and enjoy oneself in one's works, and to worship oneself as an idol. Persons who are self-confident and without fear of God, however, act entirely in this manner. For if they had fear they would not be self-confident, and for this reason they would not be pleased with themselves but would be pleased with God.

In the second place, it is clear from the words of the Psalmist [Ps. 143:2], "Do not enter into judgment with your servant," and Ps. 32[:5], "I said, 'I will confess my transgressions to the Lord,'" etc. But that these are not venial sins is clear because those people[r] say that confession and repentance are not necessary for venial sins. If, therefore, they are mortal sins and all the saints intercede for them, as it is stated in the same place [Ps. 32:6], then the works of the saints are mortal sins. But the works of the saints are good works, wherefore they are not meritorious except through the fear of humble confession.

In the third place, it is clear from the Lord's Prayer, "Forgive us our trespasses" [Matt. 6:12]. This is a prayer of the saints; therefore those trespasses for which they pray are

---

q   For the same metaphor, see the *Bondage of the Will* (1525), LW 33:176.
r   I.e., Scholastic theologians.

good works. But that these are mortal sins is clear from the following verse, "but if you do not forgive others, neither will your Father forgive your trespasses" [Matt. 6:15]. Note that these trespasses are such that, if unforgiven, such sins would condemn them, unless they pray this prayer sincerely and forgive others.

In the fourth place, it is clear from Rev. 21[:27], "But nothing unclean will enter [the kingdom of heaven]." But everything that hinders entrance into the kingdom of heaven is mortal sin (or else it would be necessary to interpret the concept of mortal sin in another way). Venial sin, however, impedes [such entry] because it makes the soul unclean and has no place in the kingdom of heaven. Consequently, etc.

8

All the more are human works mortal sins when they
are done without fear and in unadulterated, evil self-security.

The inevitable deduction from the preceding thesis is clear. For where there is no fear there is no humility. Where there is no humility there is pride, and where there is pride there are the wrath and judgment of God, for God opposes the haughty. Indeed, if pride would cease there would be no sin anywhere.[41]

9

To say that works without Christ are indeed dead
but not mortal sins seems a perilous rejection of the fear of God.

For in this way people become secure and therefore proud, which is perilous. For in such a way God is constantly deprived of the glory which is due him and which is transferred to other things, since one should strive with all diligence to give him the glory—the sooner the better. For this reason, the Bible advises, "Do not delay being converted to the Lord" [Sir. 5:7]. For if that person who withdraws glory from him offends God, how much more does that person offend him who continues to withdraw glory from him and does this in complete security! But whoever is not in Christ or who withdraws from him withdraws glory from him, as is well known.

41. Here Luther uses the central principle of Augustine, that the heart of sin is pride over against true humility.

10

*Indeed, it is very difficult to see how a work can be dead
and at the same time not a culpable, or mortal, sin.*

This I prove in the following way: Scripture does not speak of dead things in such a manner, stating that something is not mortal which is nevertheless dead. Indeed, neither does grammar, which says that "dead" is a stronger term than "mortal."[s] For, as the grammarians say, a mortal work is one that kills, a dead work not one that has been killed but one that is not alive. But God despises what is not alive, as is written in Prov. 15[:8], "The sacrifice of the wicked is an abomination to the Lord."[42]

Second, the will must certainly do something regarding such a dead work, namely, either love or hate it. Because the will is evil, it cannot hate a dead work. Consequently, the will loves a dead work, and therefore it loves something dead. In that act itself it thus brings forth an evil work of the will against God, whom it should love and honor in this and in every deed.

11

*Arrogance cannot be avoided nor can true hope be present,
unless the judgment of damnation is feared in every work.*

This is clear from thesis 4. For it is impossible to hope in God unless one has despaired regarding all creatures and knows that nothing can profit oneself without God. Since there is no person who has this pure hope, as we said above, and since we still place some confidence in the creature, it is clear that we must, because of impurity in all things, fear the judgment of God. Thus arrogance may be avoided, not [just] in acts but in disposition, that is, it must displease us still to have confidence in the creature.

42. Luther interprets this verse to be speaking of those in a state of sin, who thus do "dead works," which (he argues) are nevertheless an abomination.

---

s Unlike English, in Latin the words *dead* (*mortuum*) and *mortal* (*mortale*) are etymologically related.

12
As a consequence, in the sight of God sins are truly venial when human beings fear them as mortal.

This becomes sufficiently clear from what has been said. For as much as we accuse ourselves, so much God pardons us, according to the verse, "Confess your misdeed so that you will be justified" [Cf. Isa. 43:26],*t* and according to another [Ps. 141:4], "Do not turn my heart to any evil, to busy myself with wicked deeds."

13
Free will, after [the fall into] sin, exists in name only, and when "it does what is within it," it commits a mortal sin.

The first part is clear, for the will is captive and subject to sin. Not that it is nothing but that it is not free except to do evil.[43] According to John 8[:34, 36], "Everyone who commits sin is a slave to sin. . . . So if the Son makes you free, you will be free indeed." Hence St. Augustine says in his book *The Spirit and the Letter*, "Free will without grace has the power to do nothing but sin";*u* and in the second book of *Against Julian*, "You call the will free, but in fact it is an enslaved will," and in many other places.*v*

The second part is clear from what has been said above and from the verse in Hos. 13[:9], "Israel, you are bringing misfortune upon yourself, for your salvation is alone with me etc."*w*

14
Free will, after [the fall into] sin, has the power to do good only passively, but always has the power to do evil actively.

Just as a dead person can do something vis-à-vis life only passively, but, while living, a person can also do something

43. Latin: *liberum arbitrium* (free choice). In late medieval theology, the "free choice" was a faculty of the will (*voluntas*). For Luther, human beings have such a faculty, but it can only choose to do evil—what is best for itself.

---

t   Luther alludes to Isa. 43:26, which reads in Latin: "Declare what you have, so that you may be justified."

u   Augustine, *On the Spirit and the Letter*, 5 (3) writes (NPNF, ser. 1, 5:84): "A human being's free will indeed avails for nothing except to sin."

v   Augustine, *Against Julian*, II.8.23, in *St. Augustine against Julian*, 83.

w   Cited according to the Vulgate.

44. While a dead person has only a *potentia subiectiva* (passive power) to live (i.e., the property "alive" can be predicated of a dead person, but such a person cannot bring it about that it is so predicated), one has an active power to bring about one's own death while living. Free will (*liberum arbitrium*) is signified by "dead" (*mortuum*), as are the dead whom God has raised up (*suscitivat*) also signified (*signifactum*). The notion of *significatio* has a causal connotation within late medieval semantic theory, meaning, "that of which it makes the mind think."

45. Luther is thinking of the traditional allegorical interpretation of miracle stories as applied to the dead or diseased soul.

46. Pelagius (c. 354–c. 420), a British monk, argued against Augusine's understanding of grace and insisted that God's grace consisted of giving both the commandments that revealed God's will and the human powers needed to fulfill them. Luther is arguing that free will can no longer causally produce the good but can causally bring about evil. If human beings are to be good, something must causally produce goodness in them.

47. Luther suggests that this passive capacity is hypothetical. Humans have free will in that *if* they will x, then they can bring about x. But they have no freedom to do good because they have no ability to will it.

actively toward death.[44] Free will, however, is dead, as demonstrated by the dead whom the Lord has raised up, as the holy teachers of the church say.[45] St. Augustine, moreover, proves this same thesis in his various writings against the Pelagians.[46]

15

Nor in the state of innocence could free will remain an active power, much less make progress in the good, but remains in innocence only a passive power.

The Master of the *Sentences* in book 2, distinction 24, chapter 1, after quoting Augustine, states in the end, "By these testimonies [of Augustine] it is obviously demonstrated that human beings received a righteous nature and a good will when they were created, and also the help by means of which they could prevail. Otherwise it would appear as though they had not fallen because of their own fault."[x] He speaks of the active capacity, which is obviously contrary to Augustine's opinion in his book, *Treatise on Rebuke and Grace*, where the latter puts it in this way: "He received the ability to act, if he so willed, but he did not have the will by means of which he could act."[y] By "ability to act" he understands the passive capacity, and by "will by means of which he could," the active capacity.[47]

The second part (about making progress), however, is sufficiently clarified by the Master in the same distinction.

16

The person who believes that one can obtain grace "by doing what is in oneself" adds sin to sin and thus becomes doubly guilty.

On the basis of what has been said, the following is clear: People "doing what is in them" sin and seek their own things

---

x   Peter Lombard (c. 1096–1160), *The Sentences*, bk. 2, d. 24, ch. 1 (MPL 192:702), based upon Hugh of St. Victor (1096–1141), *Summa Sententiarum Septem Tractatibus Distincta*, tr. III, ch. 7 (MPL 176:98–99), and citing Augustine in *Treatise on Rebuke and Grace*, ch. 12.

y   See Augustine, *Treatise on Rebuke and Grace*, ch. 12 (33) (NPNF, ser. 1, 5:485; MPL 44:936).

in everything.*z* But if they should suppose that through sin they become worthy of, or apt for, grace, they would add haughty arrogance to their sin and not believe that sin is sin and evil is evil, which is an exceedingly great sin. As Jer. 2[:13] says, "For my people have committed two evils: they have forsaken me, the fountain of living water, and dug out cisterns for themselves, cracked cisterns that can hold no water," that is, through sin they are far from me and yet they presume to do good by their own ability.

Now you ask, "What then shall we do? Shall we be idle because we can do nothing but sin?" I would reply, By no means. But, having heard this, fall down and pray for grace and place your hope in Christ in whom is our salvation, life, and resurrection. For this reason, we are so instructed—for this reason the law makes us aware of sin so that, having recognized our sin, we may seek and obtain grace. Thus, God "gives grace to the humble" [1 Pet. 5:5], and "all who humble themselves will be exalted" [Matt. 23:12]. The law humbles, grace exalts. The law effects fear and wrath, grace effects hope and mercy. "Through the law comes knowledge of sin" [Rom. 3:20]; through knowledge of sin, however, comes humility, and through humility grace is acquired. Thus an action which is alien to God's nature results in a deed proper to his very nature: God makes a person a sinner so that he may make him righteous.[48]

17

Nor does speaking in this manner give cause for despair, but rather for humility, for it arouses the desire to seek the grace of Christ.

This is clear from what has been said, for, according to the gospel, the kingdom of heaven is given to children and the humble [Mark 10:14, 16], and Christ loves them. They cannot be humble who do not recognize that they are damnable and stinking sinners. Sin is recognized only through the law. It is apparent that not despair but rather hope is

48. The work alien to God's true nature (*opus alienum*) brings about his proper work (*opus proprium*).

z   Singular ("a person") in the original.

preached when we are told that we are sinners. Such preaching concerning sin is a "preparation for grace," or rather the recognition of sin and faith in such preaching.[49] Yearning for grace wells up when recognition of sin has arisen. A sick person seeks treatment when that person recognizes the seriousness of the illness. Therefore one does not give cause for despair or death by telling a sick person about the danger of his or her illness, but, in effect, one urges that one to seek a medical cure. To say that we are nothing and constantly sin when we do what is within us does not mean that we make people desperate (unless they are fools), but rather that we make them concerned about the grace of our Lord Jesus Christ.

18

It is certain that one must utterly despair of oneself
in order to be made fit to receive the grace of Christ.

The law wills that people[a] despair of their own ability, for it leads them into hell and makes them poor and shows that they are sinners in all their works, as the Apostle does in Rom. 2 and 3[:9], where he says, "We have already charged that all . . . are under the power of sin." However, those who "do what is in them" and believe themselves to be doing something good neither seem worthless to themselves nor despair of their own strength. Indeed, they presume to strive toward grace by their own strength.

19

That person does not deserve to be called a theologian
who perceives the invisible things of God as understandable
on the basis of those things which have been made [Rom. 1:20].

This is apparent in the example of those who were "theologians" and still were called fools by the Apostle in Rom. 1[:22]. Furthermore, the invisible things of God are virtue, godliness, wisdom, justice, goodness, and so forth. The recognition of all these things does not make one worthy or wise.

---

a   Singular in the original.

49. In this period, Luther still uses the scholastic phrase "preparation for grace" (*praeparatio ad gratiam*) occasionally.

20

The person deserves to be called a theologian, however,
who understands the visible and the "back side" of God
[Exod. 33:23] seen through suffering and the cross.

The "back" and visible things of God are placed in opposition
to the invisible, namely, humanity, infirmity, foolishness,
etc. The Apostle in 1 Cor. 1[:25] calls them the weakness and
folly of God. Because human beings misused the knowledge
of God through works, God wished again to be recognized
in suffering, and to condemn wisdom concerning invisible things by means of wisdom concerning visible things,
so that those who did not honor God as manifested in his
works should honor him as he is hidden in his suffering. As
the Apostle says in 1 Cor. 1[:21], "For since, in the wisdom
of God, the world did not know God through wisdom, God
decided, through the foolishness of our proclamation, to
save those who believe." Now it is not sufficient for any, and
it does them no good to recognize God in his glory and majesty, unless they recognize him in the humility and shame
of the cross. Thus God destroys the wisdom of the wise, as
Isa. [45:15] says, "Truly, you are the hidden God."

So also in John 14[:8], where Philip spoke according to the
theology of glory: "Show us the Father." Christ immediately
set aside Philip's flighty thoughts about seeking God elsewhere and led him to back himself (Christ), saying, "Philip,
whoever has seen me has seen the Father" [John 14:9]. For
this reason, true theology and knowledge of God are in the
crucified Christ, as it is also stated in John 10 [John 14:6]:
"No one comes to the Father, except through me." "I am the
gate, etc." [John 10:9].

21

A theologian of glory calls evil good and good evil.
A theologian of the cross calls a thing what it actually is.

This is clear: The person who does not know Christ does not
know God hidden in suffering. Therefore, this person prefers works to suffering, glory to the cross, strength to weakness, wisdom to folly, and, in general, good to evil. These are
the people whom the Apostle calls "enemies of the cross of

Christ" [Phil. 3:18]. To be sure, because they hate the cross and suffering, they love works and the glory of works. Thus, they call the good of the cross evil and the evil of a deed good. However, God can be found only in suffering and the cross, as has already been said. Therefore the friends of the cross say that the cross is good and works are evil, for through the cross works are dethroned and [the old] Adam, who is especially edified by works, is crucified. For those who have not first been deflated and destroyed by suffering and evil, it is impossible not to be puffed up by their own good works, until they know that they are nothing and that their works are not their own but God's.[b]

22

That wisdom which sees the invisible things of God
in works as understood by human beings
is puffed up, blinded, and hardened.

This has already been said. Because people do not know the cross and hate it, they necessarily love the opposite, namely, wisdom, glory, power, and so on. Therefore they become increasingly blinded and hardened by such love, for desire cannot be satisfied by the acquisition of those things which it desires. Just as the love of money grows in proportion to the increase of the money itself, so the dropsy of the soul becomes thirstier the more it drinks, as the poet says: "The more water they drink, the more they thirst for it."[c] The same thought is expressed in Eccles. 1[:8]: "The eye is not satisfied with seeing, nor the ear filled with hearing." This holds true of all desires.[50]

Thus also the desire for knowledge is not satisfied by the acquisition of wisdom but is stimulated that much more. Likewise the desire for glory is not satisfied by the acquisition of glory, nor is the desire to rule satisfied by power and authority, nor is the desire for praise satisfied by praise, and so on, as Christ shows in John 4[:13], where he says, "Everyone who drinks of this water will be thirsty again."

50. The *probatio* of this thesis expresses an opinion similar to thesis 30. Philosophy that seeks after wisdom and glory, that is, a philosophy unbridled by the cross of Christ, is oriented toward what is attractive and perishable. In this it functions like the human libido.

b   Singular in the original.
c   Ovid (43 BCE–CE 17/18), *Fasti*, I.216.

Therefore the remedy opposes desire, for it is cured not by satisfying it but by extinguishing it. In other words, the person who wishes to become wise does not seek wisdom by progressing toward it but becomes a fool by regressing into seeking folly. Likewise one who wishes to have much power, honor, pleasure, satisfaction in all things must flee rather than seek power, honor, pleasure, and satisfaction in all things. This is the wisdom which is folly to the world.[d]

23
The law works the wrath of God, kills, reviles, accuses, judges, and condemns everything that is not in Christ [Rom. 4:15].

Thus Gal. 3[:13] states, "Christ redeemed us from the curse of the law"; and: "For all who rely on works of the law are under the curse" [Gal. 3:10]; and Rom. 4 [15]: "For the law brings wrath"; and Rom. 7[:10]: "The very commandment that promised life proved to be the death of me"; Rom. 2[:12]: "All who have sinned in the law will also be judged through the law." Therefore whoever boasts of being wise and learned in the law boasts in one's own confusion and damnation, in the wrath of God and in death. As Rom. 2[:23] puts it: "Why do you boast in the law?"

24
Yet that wisdom is not of itself evil, nor is the law to be evaded; but without the theology of the cross a person misuses the best things in the worst way.

Indeed the law is holy [Rom. 7:12], every gift of God good [1 Tim. 4:4], and everything that is created exceedingly good, as in Gen. 1[:31]. But, as stated above, the person who has not been brought low, reduced to nothing through the cross and suffering, takes credit for works and wisdom and does not give credit to God. That person thus misuses and defiles the gifts of God.

---

d   Throughout the proofs for theses 20–22, Luther refers the terms "sufferings" and "works" to God (20 and 22) and to human beings (21).

Those,[e] however, who have been emptied through suffering [cf. Phil. 2:7] no longer do works but know that God works and does all things in them. For this reason, whether they work or not, it is all the same: They neither boast if they do works nor are disturbed if God does not work through them. They know that it is sufficient if they suffer and are brought low by the cross in order to be annihilated all the more. It is this that Christ says in John 3[:7], "You must be born anew."[f] To be born anew, one must consequently first die and then be raised up with the Son of Man. To die, I say, is to feel death at hand.

25

That person is not righteous who works much,
but who without work believes much in Christ.

For the righteousness of God is not acquired by means of acts frequently repeated, as Aristotle taught,[51] but it is imparted by faith, for "the one who is righteous will live by faith" (Rom. 1[:17]), and "for one believes with the heart and so is justified" (Rom. 10[:10]). Therefore I wish to have the words "without work" understood in the following manner: Not that the righteous person does nothing, but that one's works do not do righteousness and instead that one's righteousness does works.[52] For grace and faith are infused without our works.[53] After they have been infused, works follow. Thus, Rom. 3[:20] states, "No human being will be justified in His sight by deeds prescribed by the law," and, "For we hold that a person is justified by faith apart from works prescribed by the law" (Rom. 3[:28]), that is, works contribute nothing to justification. Thus, because people[g]

51. This is one of Luther's chief objections to Aristotle's ethical belief that one becomes good by doing good. Luther insisted that one is first good and therefore does good.

52. Good works can be necessary for righteousness without thereby causing such righteousness or otherwise being sufficient for it.

53. First in 1521 will Luther stop defining grace as an infused quality, taking up Erasmus's argument that in the New Testament Greek *charis* (grace) means God's favor, not a disposition in the soul.

---

e   Singular in the original.

f   Luther is using the Vulgate, which reads, "You ought to be born again."

g   Singular in the original.

know that works done by such faith are not their own, but God's, therefore they do not seek to become justified or glorified through such works but seek God. Their justification by faith in Christ suffices for them, that is, Christ is their wisdom, righteousness, etc., as 1 Cor. 1[:30] has it, but they may be Christ's action and instrument.

26

The law says, "Do this," and it is never done. Grace says, "Believe in this One," and everything has already been done.

The first part is clear from what has been stated by the Apostle and his interpreter, St. Augustine, in many places.[h] And it has been stated often enough above that the law works wrath and keeps all people under the curse. The second part is clear from the same sources, for faith justifies. "And the law (says St. Augustine) commands what faith obtains."[i] For through faith Christ is in us, indeed, one with us. Christ is righteous, fulfilling all the commands of God, wherefore we also fulfill everything through him as long as he has been made ours through faith.[54]

27

Properly speaking, one should call Christ's work an active work and our work a passive work, and thus the passive work is pleasing to God by the grace of the active work.[j]

[This is so] because while Christ lives in us through faith, he now moves us to do good works through that living faith in his works. For the works that he does are for us the fulfillment, given through faith, of God's commands. When we look at them, we are moved to imitate them. For this reason, the Apostle says [Eph. 5:1], "Therefore be imitators of God, as beloved children." Thus, works of mercy are called forth by his works, through which he has saved us, as St. Gregory says: "Every action of Christ is instruction for us," indeed,

54. Here Luther introduces the idea of union with Christ, understood as accomplished through faith.

---

h   See *On the Spirit and the Letter*, NPNF, ser. 1, 5:80–114.

i   Augustine, *On Nature and Grace*, XVI.17, NPNF, ser. 1, 5:126.

j   See above, p. 84, n. 23.

55. As in the entire medieval tradition, Luther interpreted the Song of Solomon as a paean to the relation between the soul and Christ.

56. Luther's criticism of Aristotle arises from the (Augustinian) notion of love of self.

57. In Luther's view, Aristotle makes the human agent passive in its reception of what comes from outside of it but must share the "form" of the thing. In the moral sphere, anything that loves another thing presupposes a similar sharing of form. Luther rejects this Aristotelian way of looking at things because it obscures the actual causation between creature and creator. It is *God* who creates love in human beings; it is *God* who makes possible human knowing and loving.

an incitement.[k] If his action is in us, it lives through faith, for it is exceedingly alluring according to the verse [Song of Sol. 1:4, 3], "Draw me after you; we hasten toward the fragrance of your anointing oils," that is, "of your works."[55]

28

God's love does not find, but creates, that which is pleasing to it.
Human love comes into being through that which is pleasing to it.

The second part is clear and is accepted by all philosophers and theologians, for the object of love is its cause, assuming, according to Aristotle, that each power of the soul is passive and material and active only in receiving something.[l] Thus, it is also demonstrated that Aristotle's philosophy is contrary to theology since in all things it seeks those things that are its own and receives rather than bestows something good.[56] The first part is clear because the love of God, which dwells in human beings, loves sinners, evil persons, fools, and weaklings in order to make them righteous, good, wise, and strong. Rather than seeking its own good, the love of God flows out and bestows good.[57] For this reason, sinners are attractive because they are loved; they are not loved because they are attractive. And for this reason human love avoids sinners and evil persons. Thus Christ says [Matt. 9:13]: "For I came to call not the righteous, but sinners." This is the love of the cross, born of the cross, which turns in the direction

---

k This common medieval theological axiom, found in Thomas Aquinas, Bonaventure, and Peter Lombard, has been attributed, alternatively, to Pope Gregory I (c. 540-604), Augustine, or Cassiodorus (485-585). See Cassiodorus, *Expositio psalmorum 85* (MPL 70:611).

l For example, Thomas Aquinas follows Aristotle in his discussion of love in *Summa Theologica* I-I1, Q27, A1: "Love belongs to the appetitive power, which is a passive faculty (*vis passive*). Wherefore, its object stands to it as the cause of its movement (*motus*) or act (*actus*). It is necessary, therefore, that the cause of love be, properly speaking, the object of love." Thomas points out that the proper object of love is the good because love implies a certain connaturality or pleasingness between the lover and the thing loved. Aristotle's distinction between the active and passive intellect became a full-blown metaphysics of knowledge in Aquinas.

where it does not find good, which it may enjoy, but where it may confer good upon the evil and needy person.[58] "It is more blessed to give than to receive" [Acts 20:35], says the Apostle. Hence Ps. 41[:1] states, "Happy are those who consider[m] the poor," for the object of the intellect[n] cannot by nature be that which is nothing (that is, the poor and needy person) but only that of a true and good being.[59] Therefore it judges according to appearances, is a respecter of persons, and judges according to that which can be seen, etc.

THE END

[Explanation to the sixth conclusion][60]

[Whether the human will outside the state of grace is free or rather in bondage and captive?][o]

Conclusion

Outside of grace, the human will [*voluntas*], even when free of all compulsion, is not free from contrary or contradictory actions but is necessarily in bondage and captive.

As proof of this thesis, it must be noted in the first place that contrary actions of the will are willing [*velle*] and willing not [*nolle*], either of which is positive, whereas contradictory actions are willing to [*velle*] and not willing to [*non velle*], also willing not to [*nolle*] and not willing not to [*non nolle*]; that is, at times it wills [to do a thing], but at other times neither wills to nor wills not to [do a thing], but remains neutral and inactive.[61,p] It must be noted, in the second place,

---

m   Latin (reading with the Vulgate): *intelligit*.

n   Latin: *intellectus*.

o   This heading was first added to the Weimar edition of 1883 (WA 1:365).

p   Throughout this discussion *velle* is translated as "willing to," *nolle* as "willing not to," *non velle* as "not willing to," and *non nolle* as "not willing not to."

---

58. Luther speaks here of a love of the cross born from the cross (*natus cruce*), which turns itself around such that it does not discover love where it might be enjoyed but where it might confer good upon the evil and the needy.

59. This passage assumes that the loftier a thing is the more being it has. Lowly things, like the poor and needy, have very little being. Luther argues that the intellect cannot naturally grasp the object of such consideration because the object is nothing, that is, it is not good and true. The Scholastic tradition assumed a proportionality between the lover and the thing loved, and since this proportionality is good, the good is the proper cause of love.

60. The material through p. 112 was first published in 1720. The first section may relate better to theses 13–15 above but also reflects thesis 6 of the *Disputation against Scholastic Theology* (1517), LW 31:9, "It is a falsehood that the will can conform itself to a right precept naturally. Against Biel and [Duns] Scotus [c. 1266-1308]." This reflects the title of the shorter version published in 1545 (*Against the Opinion of Scholastic Theology*). First the Corollary (below, p. 107) begins by quoting the argument of thesis 6 of the *Heidelberg Disputation* directly, while referring back to the distinctions made here.

61. Luther distinguishes between contrary and contradictory propositions. Two propositions are contrary if they cannot be true at the same time, even though they might be false at the same time. Contradictory propositions cannot both be true at the same time nor both be false at the same time. Luther argues that willing a particular thing (*velle*) and willing the negation of that thing (*nolle*) are contraries, but that willing a thing (*velle*) and not willing it (*non velle*) are contradictories.

62. Augustine also ties the freedom of the will (*liberas voluntatis*) to merit and demerit. A free will, however, is not possible for human beings outside of grace because one must will not one's own desires but what God wills.

63. Luther believes his claim is consistent with the will willing apparently contrary or contradictory things.

that we are only speaking of the freedom of the will with respect to merit and lack of merit.[62] With respect to other things inferior to these, I do not deny that the will is free, or indeed considers itself free, with respect to contrary as well as contradictory actions.[63]

With these presuppositions as a basis, I shall now prove the first part of the thesis that the will is without a doubt not free in contradictory actions. Because if it is free not to choose what it wills, it follows that it would also be free to avoid every future sin. But that is false, indeed heretical, and contrary to the statement of St. Gregory: "Sin which is not washed away by penance soon leads to another by its own weight."[q] But if the will is free, it cannot be led into another sin, that is, if the will cannot avoid being led, it is not free. I can also prove this by using the common saying that "the will outside grace cannot long endure without [committing] mortal sin," and hence it is not without the captivity of its freedom. Finally, I can prove this through the statement of the Apostle in 2 Tim. 2[:25, 26]: "[God may perhaps grant . . .] that they escape from the snare of the devil, by whom they are held captive to his will."[r] But it is the will of the devil that they will and do evil.

Second Part of the Conclusion

That the will is not free in contrary actions I will prove by the word of the Lord in Gen. 8[:21]: "For the inclination of the human heart is evil from youth." But if it is at all times inclined to evil, then it is never inclined to good, the contrary of evil. That this, however, takes place freely and at the same time necessarily, I shall prove in this way. Its willing to [do a thing] or willing not to [do a thing] is no less an operation of the natural will than for every natural thing, and it is no more deprived of this function than is any other

---

q   Gregory I, *Moralia in Job*, bk. 25, ch. 9.22.

r   Following the Vulgate.

thing. But it is impossible that willing is constrained and not free. Consequently it is of necessity free and of necessity wills freely. Therefore either of the following is true:

The one falling is unable not to fall except by means of one's own powers.

The one falling is able not to fall except by means of another's powers.[64]

Thus the will outside grace, or constituted by its falling, is unable not to fall and not to will evil by its own powers. It is able, however, by the grace of God not to fall or to stop falling. Thus, I pass over the conclusion as having been briefly proven.

I deduce the following corollary:

Because there is no righteous person on earth who does not sin in doing good, much more does the unrighteous person sin while doing good.[65]

This is proven by the following authorities:

First through the verse in Isa. 64[:6]: "We have all become like one who is unclean, and all our righteous deeds are like a filthy cloth." If righteous deeds are unclean, what will the unrighteous deeds be? And Eccles. 7[:20]: "Surely there is no one on earth so righteous as to do good without ever sinning"; and James 3[:2]: "For all of us make many mistakes"; and Rom. 7[:22-23]: "For I delight in the law of God in my inmost self, but I see in my members another law at war with the law of my mind, making me captive to the law of sin that dwells in my members"; and Psa. 32[:2]: "Happy are those to whom the Lord imputes no iniquity."

Corollary[66]

That the righteous person also sins while doing good is clear from the following:

First, from the verse Eccles. 7[:20]: "Surely there is no one on earth so righteous as to do good without ever sinning." In this connection, however, others say, "Indeed every

64. The statements are modal: the first claims, using one's own powers, it is not possible for a fallen human being not to fall; the second that the only way for a fallen human being not to fall is through another's power (namely, God).

65. Luther claims that every just person who does good sins, while every unjust person sins even more when doing the good. Neither the just nor unjust can avoid sin while engaged in doing the good.

66. The text from the first volume of Luther's Latin works, published in Wittenberg in 1545 begins here. It is titled: *Against the Opinion of the Scholastics.* The first point is word for word from the explanation to thesis 6 above, p. 91f.

righteous person sins, but not when doing good." One may respond to them, "If that is what this verse wishes to say, why waste so many words? Or does the Holy Spirit like to indulge in loquacious and foolish babble? For this meaning would then be adequately expressed by the following: "There is not a righteous person on earth who does not sin." Why does he add "who does good," as if another person were righteous who did evil? For no one except a righteous person does good. Where, however, he speaks of sins outside of good works, he speaks thus [Prov. 24:16], "For though the righteous person falls seven times a day." He does not say, "The righteous person falls seven times a day when doing good."ˢ [This is the comparison: Just as if someone cuts with a rusty and rough hatchet, although the worker is a good craftsman, and nevertheless the hatchet leaves bad, jagged, and ugly gashes, so it is when God works through us, etc.]ᵗ

Second,⁶⁷ from the verse of the Apostle in Rom. 7[:19]: "For I do not do the good I want, but the evil I do not want is what I do," and below: "I delight in the law of God in my inmost self; but I see in my members another law at war with the law of my mind" [Rom. 7:22-23]. See how he delights in and at the same time is displeased with the law of God; at one and the same time he wills good according to the spirit and yet does not do it, but does the contrary. Consequently, this contrary is a certain "willing-not-to" [do a thing], which is always present when the will is present.ᵘ Through this he does good and through that evil. Willing-not-to [do a thing] is from the flesh and willing-to [do a thing] from the spirit. Therefore there is as much sin present as there is "willing-not-to," difficulty, constraint, resistance; and there is as much merit present as there is "willing-to," inclination, freedom, cheerfulness; for these two are mixed together in our entire life and work. But if there is a total "willing-not-to,"

67. What follows in Luther's second and third points is a lengthy exposition of what Luther elsewhere calls *simul iustus et peccator*, that the Christian believer is at the same time righteous and sinner.

---

s   Translated in accordance with the Vulgate.

t   The text in brackets, although in the explanation to thesis 6 above, was added by the editors of the WA to the text here. It is not present in the original version.

u   Latin: *noluntas*, which is derived from *nolle* and must therefore be translated not "unwilling" but "willing not to."

there is already mortal sin and aversion. There is no such thing as a total "willing-to" in this life. Therefore we constantly sin while doing good, sometimes less and sometimes more. That is the reason why there is no righteous person on earth who does good and does not sin. Such a righteous person exists only in heaven. Therefore, just as one is not without this "willing-not-to," so one does not act without it, and for this reason is not without sin. For how can one act without it since one cannot live without it? Scripture also says, "Who can say, 'I have made my heart clean'?" [Cf. Prov. 20:9]. Likewise Gal. 5[:17] states, "For what the flesh desires is opposed to the Spirit, and what the Spirit desires is opposed to the flesh; for these are opposed to each other, to prevent you from doing what you want, etc."

Third, through Ps. 143[:2]: "Enter not into judgment with your servant: for no one living is righteous before you." Here I ask whether that righteous person, who is conceived to be righteous since already actually in [a state of] glorious merit, should also be counted among the living. If a person is among the living, then that person is not righteous. How would this be possible if that person does not sin in his or her own merit?

This I prove by reason:
Anyone who does less than one ought, sins. But every righteous person in doing good does less than such a one ought.[v] I prove the minor premise in the following way: Whoever does not do good out of complete and perfect love of God does less than such a person ought. But every righteous person is of this kind. I prove the major premise through the commandment [Deut. 6:5]: "You shall love the Lord your God with all your soul, and with all your might, etc.," of which the Lord says in Matt. 5[:18], "Not one letter, not one stroke of a letter, will pass from the law until all is accomplished." Therefore we must love God with all our might, or we sin. But the minor premise, that we do not love him with all our

---

v   The implied conclusion: "Therefore the righteous person sins."

might, has been proven above, for the "willing-not-to" in the flesh and in the members hinders this perfection so that not all members or powers love God, but the "willing-not-to" resists the inner will which loves God.

But those persons say: "God does not demand of us this perfect law." I ask: Of whom does God then demand it? Of stone and wood? Or of cattle? This is an error, for it is stated in Rom. 3[:19], "Now we know that whatever the law says it speaks to those who are under the law." Therefore it is a command for us and is demanded of us. Through that entirely false interpretation of the proposition, "God does not demand perfection," the opinion was spread that no sin is involved if a person does something with less than perfect love, since God does not demand it because God pardons it, not because God permits it and it is not sin. If this had been the case, he could have altered his commandment, which is contrary to his own statement [Matt. 5:18], that "Not one letter, not one stroke of a letter will pass from the law until all is accomplished."

I argue now against this:

In the first place, John states in his canonical epistle [1 John 3:9] that "those who are born of God do not sin." Similarly, God gave Abimelech evidence in Gen. 20[:6] that he acted in the simplicity of his heart and consequently did not sin.[68] In Ps. 86[:2] it is written, "Preserve my life, for I am devoted to you." There are other passages that can be applied here.

I answer: Each is true, because one born of God does not sin and yet sins. Unless by chance Paul was not born of God (Rom. 7). Or did indeed John contradict himself when he said [1 John 1:8]: "If we say we have no sin . . . the truth is not in us"? Actually, he sins in the same act because of the will of the flesh; he does not sin because of the contrary will of the spirit.

Thus you say, "How then do we fulfill the law of God?" I answer: because we do not fulfill it, we are therefore sinners and disobedient to God. Nor is this a venial sin in essence or nature, for nothing impure will enter the kingdom of heaven [Rev. 21:27]. For this reason, damnation is demanded for

68. King Abimelech found Abraham's wife Sarah beautiful so the couple told him that they were siblings. Before the king had sexual relations with Sarah, however, he was warned by God that she was married. In Genesis 20:5, the king reports that his intent was formed in the "simplicity of my heart and the innocence of my hands." In the next verse, God replies, "I know that you did this in the simplicity of your heart, and furthermore I protected you from sinning against me."

every sin, for Christ says [Matt. 5:18] that not one letter, not one stroke of a letter, will pass from the law until all is accomplished. Therefore St. Augustine quite correctly states in chapter 19 of the first book of his *Retractions*: "All divine commands are fulfilled when whatever is not done is pardoned."[w] Therefore the commands of God are fulfilled when God pardons for his mercy's sake rather than when a person acts through righteousness, for the mercy of God is greater than the righteousness of human beings. Thus it is that those people say, "God does not demand perfection," whereas they should say, "God pardons." But whom? Those who feel secure and do not believe they sin? Not at all! Rather God pardons those who say [Matt. 6:12], "Forgive us our trespasses," those who recognize and hate their wickedness with a true heart, as in Ezek. 20[:43], "And you shall loathe yourselves for all the evils that you have committed, etc."

That is also what Ps. 32[:6] says, "For this [forgiveness] every saint will pray to you."[x] If one is a "saint" that one has no impiety only through the forgiveness of sin. For what then does one pray? Certainly the saint prays for what must [still] be forgiven, for otherwise the saint gives thanks for the sin that has been forgiven. Then, if [the psalmist] wanted to speak of past sins, he should not have said "every saint," but rather, "every sinner will pray for these things." For a "saint" is the one whose sins have been forgiven, *and* a "saint" prays for the forgiveness of iniquity. This remarkable sentence cannot be resolved by means of their foolish and carnal interpretation: A saint prays for past sins. The prophet is not speaking of himself but of those whom he saw made holy and made saints by virtue of the forgiveness of sins. And nevertheless he says that they pray for forgiveness, unless perhaps the prophet either lies or is flattering them when calling those people holy whose sins were not forgiven.

---

w See Augustine, *Retractions* bk. I, ch. 19.3 (MPL 32:615), where Luther reads "fulfilled" (*implentur*) for "imputed" (*deputantur*).

x Following the Vulgate. Forgiveness is the subject of Ps. 32:5.

But then he should say that they pray "that they might be forgiven" or "in anticipation of the forgiveness of sins."

Therefore:

It is the sweetest mercy of God the Father that God does not save imaginary sinners, but rather real ones, sustaining us in our sins and accepting our works and lives, which are deserving of total rejection, until God perfects and brings us to completion. Meanwhile, we live under the protection and the shadow of his wings [Ps. 17:8] and escape God's judgment through divine mercy, not through our righteousness.

Hence, away with arguments that are like so much human smoke: "One and the same act cannot be accepted and rejected by God. For it follows that it would be both good and not good."[69] I answer: Cannot a person at the same time both fear justice and hope for mercy? I therefore say that every good deed is both accepted and not rejected, and, on the contrary, it is not accepted but rejected. It is accepted through pardon and thus not rejected, for he forgives through mercy that which is less worthy of being accepted: This, however, is rejected, namely, sin, insofar as it is an act from the malice of the flesh.

God nevertheless pardons this sin in his time and demands as much now as in the future. For there is no act which God accepts simply (such are the fictions of the human heart), but God pardons and deals sparingly with all our actions. People presume, however, that there might be someone whom God would accept without pardon, which is false. When therefore God pardons, God neither accepts nor rejects, but pardons. And thus God accepts God's own mercy in our works, that is, the countenance of Job [Job 42:8], namely the righteousness of Christ for us.*y* This is the propitiation of God, who excuses and makes pardonable our works, so that we may substitute God's fullness for that which is deficient in us. For God alone is our righteousness until we are made to conform to the divine image.

---

69. This seems to be a common saying of William of Occam and Duns Scotus. See Luther's 1519 arguments against Johann Eck (1486–1543) in Leipzig (WA 2:420, 12), where the same passage is attributed to Scotus.

y   For a christological interpretation of this text, see Gregory I, *Moralia in Job*, XXXV.8 (13) in MPL 76:757.

I prove this a second time:[70]

1. "Nothing good dwells in me, that is, in my flesh" [Rom. 7:18]. Much less will there be any good in those who are entirely flesh and blood. The Apostle [Paul] speaks of himself and of all righteous people. If therefore these, while doing what is beyond them and according to grace, do not yet do what they should no matter how much they exert themselves, how much more will those, who act without grace according to their ability and do not exert themselves, do the opposite of that which they should! But then they say, "It is true, they do it imperfectly, but this imperfection is not sin." I answer: According to its nature it is sin, but God does not impute it to those lamenting it.

2. Through Gen. 6[:5]: "Every thought of a human heart is inclined to evil from its youth."[z] Here the text does not say "thought," but "every thought," and whatever a person thinks, is evil, because one seeks those things that are to one's advantage and cannot do otherwise without the grace of God.

3. 1 Cor. 13[:5]: Here it is attributed to love alone that it does not insist on its own way. Without it, as the Apostle shows in Phil. 2[:21], all persons "look after their own interests," not those of Christ. But seeking one's own interests is mortal sin.

4. Hos. 13[:9]: "[It is] your destruction," that is, destruction is from you, "O Israel. Your help is from me alone."[a] He does not say, "righteousness," but "destruction," is yours. By yourself you accomplish nothing but destruction.

5. "Nor can a bad tree bear good fruit" [Matt. 7:18].

6. "Whoever is not with me is against me" [Luke 11:23]. But to be against Christ is a mortal sin. And not to be with him is to be outside grace.[b]

---

70. At this point, the 1720 version breaks off. The only source for what follows comes from the first volume of Luther's Latin works of 1545. Luther refers to thesis 13, but see also theses 12 and 16. The following theses state the major premise in a syllogism taken from Scripture (and thus not needing proof), followed occasionally by the minor premise but without drawing what, for Luther, was the obvious conclusion: that human works outside grace and Christ are mortal sins.

---

z   More accurately, a citation of Gen. 8:21 according to the Vulgate, where *cogitatio* is more accurately translated "thought."

a   Citing the Vulgate.

b   See Luther's use of the phrase *extra gratiam* in thesis 63 of the *Disputation against Scholastic Theology* (1517) in LW 31:13.

7. "Whoever does not abide in me is thrown away like a branch and withers; such branches are gathered, thrown into the fire, and burned" [John 15:6]. See, to be outside Christ means to deserve fire and thoroughly wither.[c] In any case, doing whatever is done surely cannot be understood as venial sins.[71]

8. Were not the foolish virgins rejected [Matt. 25:1ff.], not because they had not worked, but because they had worked without oil?[72] They did good things from themselves, but not from grace, for they sought their own glory. A person cannot possibly be free from this vice without grace.

9. "God sends rain on the good and on the ungrateful" [cf. Matt. 5:45]. But that person is ungrateful who does not care about the good things of God received from God, which is a mortal sin. Thus works are of necessity outside grace.

10. "Everyone who commits sin is a slave of sin" [John 8:34]. How is it possible that a slave of the devil and a captive of the sin he serves, can do anything else but sin? How can one who is in darkness do a work of light? How can one who is a fool do the work of a wise man? How can one who is ill do the work of a healthy person? And more examples could be given. Therefore all things that one does are works of the devil, works of sin, works of darkness, works of folly.

11. If a person's being is under the power of darkness, why not also the person's actions?[d] The tree is under the tyranny of the devil, and one cannot deny that its fruits are under the same tyranny![e]

12. That verse in Ps. 94[:11] which the Apostle adduces [1 Cor. 3:20]: "The Lord knows our thoughts, that they are but an empty breath"; and Ps. 33[:10]: "The Lord brings the counsel of the nations to nothing; he rejects the thoughts of the peoples."[f] Here I ask: Do you understand the "thoughts

71. Those things that are actually done outside Christ cannot be understood as venial sins.

72. Here Luther employs a standard allegory that the "oil" is God's grace.

c   Luther uses *extra Christum* here in apposition with his use of *extra gratiam* above.

d   Cf. Augustine, *De nuptiis et concupiscentia*, I.20 (22); *Epistola* 217, 3 (8-11).

e   Cf. Matt. 7:16-20. See point 5 above.

f   Cited according to the Vulgate.

of human beings" to be those which they think up out of themselves? If so, you hear that they are rejected and are not just dead but displeasing before God's judgment. If they are thoughts, however, which human beings do not produce from themselves but from an evil inclination, they ought not to be called "thoughts of human beings." It is certain that God knows those "counsels" that human beings utter by drawing upon natural reason, otherwise God would rather have called them follies. Now God rejects that which is human wisdom; how much more does God reject folly!

13. Prov. 3[:5]: "Do not rely on your own prudence." This must be understood either in general or in particular. If in general, every dictate of reason is rejected and condemned. If in particular, as many think,*g* then it is occasionally permitted to rely upon oneself and one's prudence contrary to this clear text.

14. If people*h* can do something good from themselves without sin, then they can also rightly give themselves glory according to the measure of the good they do. Then they may say that they are good, wise, strong, and the flesh may boast in the sight of God against the Apostle, who specifically says: "Let the person who boasts, boast in the Lord" [1 Cor. 1:31].

15. Psalm 81[:12]: "I gave them over to the desires of their hearts."*i* See, this is the penalty of sin, that one is left at the mercy of one's heart; therefore it is a mortal sin. But "one's heart" is also every human will outside grace whatsoever. Otherwise God would have said, "I gave them over to the desires of an enemy, and they shall go about according to devices of their enemies, but not according to their own."[73]

16. Romans 14[:23]: "For whatever does not proceed from faith is sin." St. Augustine understands this as referring to faith in Christ, although others interpret it as referring to

73. Building on Ps. 80:13, Luther claims that it is the desires of their very own hearts and not some evil force outside human beings.

---

g It has not been possible to track down to whom Luther is referring.
h Singular in the original.
i Cited according to the Vulgate.

the conscience.*j* Nevertheless, faith in Christ is a good conscience, as Peter says [1 Pet. 3:21]: "As an appeal to God for a good conscience." That means that it thoroughly trusts in God. If therefore a work outside faith were not a mortal sin, it would follow that in that text Paul was really troubled about a venial sin, which is false, since no one can live without venial sin. Therefore, everything that does not proceed from faith is a mortal and damnable sin, because it is also contrary to the conscience—the conscience, I say, of faith in Christ—because one is not acting from trust in Christ. For one does not believe one pleases God to merit something and nevertheless acts in such lack of faith and according to his conscience.

17. [Otherwise] the condition of the sinner would be better than that of the righteous person, for righteous persons sin venially in their work and the ungodly do not sin. Therefore it is necessary that one concede that one sins more than venially. Likewise: The righteous are anxious about their works [cf. Job 9:28]. How much more must the works of the godless be feared! Or, again, the condition of the godless is better than that of the righteous, since the latter fears, while the former feels secure.

18. If grace is given to people*k* who "do what is within them," then they can know that they are in grace.[74] This is proven in the following way: People either know that they do what is in them, or do not know it. If they know it, then they know that they have grace, since [the scholastics] say that grace is certainly given to one who does what is in him. If they do not know it, this doctrine is in vain and their consolation ceases. For whatever work they have done, they do not know whether they have done what is in them. Consequently they always remain in doubt.

19. The question is raised: What kind of work is it that people do when they "do what is in them"? If none can be pointed out, why are they so taught to do what they do not

74. Here Luther points out the contradiction in the late medieval theology of persons such as Gabriel Biel. Those who argued that one could be certain that "doing what is in you" attains grace also insisted that one is to remain uncertain about whether one has attained grace to avoid pride.

---

j   Especially Nicholas of Lyra (c. 1270–1349), *Postilla totam Bibliam,* ad loc.

k   Singular in the original.

know what it is? But if there is such a work, let it be pointed out. Some specify the act of loving God above all else as such a work.[75]

Here (if I may digress a little) I say, in the first place: Such teachers attribute nothing to the grace of God except a certain ornamentation of our works, not that it may heal the sick but adorn the strong. We can do works, [they say,] even without [this added] embellishment.[l] Thus, grace is a completely despised thing and a gift that is not necessary because of us, but, as they say, on account of the will and the intention of the one who demands it.[76] What Christian will stand for this outrage? Christ therefore died for us for nothing, for he suffered because of the intention of God. We did not need this, but the intention of the Lawgiver demanded it. If indeed we could have fulfilled the law, God was still not satisfied, for in addition to the law, he wanted to exact his own grace. And thus it is not Pelagius who reappears, but a blasphemer worse than Pelagius.[77] Thus, we discover that God is loved above all things from human nature, and [the scholastic theologian] is not ashamed to say "above all things."

But nevertheless I answer: If the act of loving God is "to do that which is in oneself," it still remains true that one does not know when one loves, and therefore does not know when one "does what is within one," or how and what one must do in order "to do what is within one," or that the person be certain of grace, something which all deny.[m]

If you said: One should try "to do that which is in oneself," I would counter and ask whether one knows that one is trying, and in what way one tries, and what one would do were one to try? If one knows it, one is indeed certain. If one does not know it, the doctrine is entirely worthless. Indeed, this trying is either the same as "doing what is in oneself,"

75. The work (*opus*) in question is the act of loving God above all else (14–15). As in the following paragraph, Luther harshly and consistently attacks William Occam and Gabriel Biel for suggesting that loving God above all things is possible.

76. Biel argued that in a state of sin a person could, using natural powers alone (*ex puris naturalibus*), love God above all else and the neighbor as one's self, but only "according to the substance of the act" but not the "intention of the Lawgiver" (God), who insists that the act must be accompanied by the infused grace that makes acceptable.

77. Pelagius, the opponent of Augustine who insisted that the ability to follow God's commands was the heart of the Christian life.

---

l   Luther's language implies that he is trying to echo Gabriel Biel's position on grace.

m   The technical term, *facere quod in se est*, beloved by Nominalist theologians like Gabriel Biel, is used throughout this paragraph. See n. 74 above on the necessity of doubting whether one is in a state of grace.

78. Luther is continuing his attack on what had started as Gabriel Biel's pastoral solution to the problem of works and grace. By encouraging those wracked with doubt "to do what is in them," so that God would not deny grace, uncertainty regarding God's grace, upon which all medieval systems of justification insisted, remained. Here he uses the same logic to undermine the notion that it was enough if people "try" to do what is in them. This paradoxical paragraph attempts a *reductio ad absurdum*, a form of argument assuming the denial of what is to be demonstrated and deriving a contradiction. But Luther points out that to know that one is trying to do what is within oneself is actually to do that which is within oneself. (How could one know one really tried if one did not actually do it?) But the problem is sin. Clearly, our wills are weak and thus to try to do things does not accomplish what we try.

79. Luther continues this argument from experience through the end of the document.

and the same question recurs, or it is otherwise. Therefore, by not doing what is in oneself, but by striving to do as much as is in oneself, a person does what is in oneself. Therefore, by doing what is within oneself, one does not yet do what is within oneself.[78]

20. Let us stop this senseless talk and consult experience.[79] Let each person do what is within while angry, irritated, and tempted; indeed, let a person prepare for illumination concerning what that one does not know, and let us see whether one accomplishes it. Let a person act (I ask you) and begin, and let us see what such a one does and accomplishes.

21. If one receives grace "by doing what is in oneself," it seems impossible that everyone or at least the majority of people would not be saved. I ask: When one is proud or sins, etc., does one do such a work by that person, or is it done by another? Of course, one does it oneself. Or does one do it by oneself and by one's own strength? Or does another do it using strength other than one's own? One does it by oneself by one's own strength. Therefore, if one sins, one does what is in oneself. Therefore, on the contrary, if one does what is in oneself, that one sins.

But here it is said: I am speaking of a person and of powers that are by nature good, not of powers that are abused. I reply: But the natural powers are always in a state of abuse, because they are diseased. Created man and woman are indeed good, but they are feeble. A person does not act apart from his or her diseases, but acts as one who has become infected with a disease. Therefore a person can only do feeble things, even if that one were good. A person is like a rusty ax made of iron, but, even though it is made of iron, works only like a rusty ax.

22. Why therefore do we concede that concupiscence is invincible?[n] Do what is in you and do not be concupiscent. But you cannot do that. Therefore you do not by nature ful-

---

n   See theses 64–67 of the *Disputation against Scholastic Theology* (1517), LW 31:13–14.

fill the law. But if you do not fulfill it, much less will you fulfill the law of love. Likewise, do what is in you and do not become angry at the one offending you. Do what is in you and do not fear danger.

23. "Do what is in you" and do not fear death. I ask, what person does not shudder, does not despair, in the face of death? Who does not flee it? And yet because God wills that we endure it, it is apparent that we by nature love our will more than the will of God. For if we loved the will of God more, we would accept death with joy, indeed, we would consider it a gain,[o] so that we would consider it to be our will. Therefore we are discussing figments. The person who hates or does not love death (that is, the will of God), loves God far less than himself—even hates God. But we are all such. Where now is the "love of God above all things"? See, we do not love God more than our life and our will. What shall I then say about hell? Who does not hate it?

24. The Lord's Prayer itself is alone sufficient proof that we are poor laborers throughout our lives. For imagine someone, "who does what is in him [or her]," deciding whether to pray: "hallowed be your name, your will be done"; or rather to pray: "it has been hallowed; it has been done." By saying "may it be hallowed," a person thereby confesses that it is defiled. By saying "may it be done," that one thereby confesses disobedience. But if this takes place among sons [and daughters] of God and saints, how much more so among the godless!

In the year 1518

---

o Cf. Phil. 1:21.

A Statement Concerning the Heidelberg Disputation, Made by Luther Apparently Soon after Its Conclusion[p]

These theses were discussed and debated by me to show, first, that everywhere the Sophists of all the schools have deviated from Aristotle's opinion and have clearly introduced their dreams into the works of Aristotle whom they do not understand. Next, if we should hold to his meaning as strongly as possible (as I proposed here), nevertheless one gains no aid whatsoever from it, either for theology and sacred letters or even for natural philosophy. For what could be gained with respect to the understanding of material things if you could quibble and trifle with matter, form, motion, measure, and time—words taken over and copied from Aristotle?

p   In 1528, Michael Stiefel (c. 1487–1567) copied Luther's handwritten note into a copy of the disputation theses pasted into Johannes Bugenhagen's (1485–1558) *Psalmarum interpretatio* of 1526. See WA 9:170, and MLStA 1:187, 218.

The Proceedings at Augsburg

1518

SUZANNE HEQUET

INTRODUCTION

Martin Luther's academic dispute over indulgences, which began with the distribution of the *95 Theses* on 31 October 1517, was followed by two kinds of attacks. To begin with, theologians north of the Alps, such as Johann Tetzel (1465–1519) and Konrad Wimpina (1465–1531), issued counter-theses and counterarguments. When Archbishop Albrecht of Mainz (1490–1545) sent the *Theses* to Rome, however, the academic dispute automatically became an ecclesiastical case, perhaps expanded by a separate brief by Dominicans like Tetzel. First to answer Luther's *Theses* in Rome was the papal court theologian, Silvester Prierias (c. 1456–1523), who in July 1518 published the *Dialogus*, in which he argued that Luther misunderstood his own presuppositions and needed especially to understand papal authority. This publication was an important first step in the papal decision to initiate formal proceedings against Luther.[1]

Meanwhile, by May 1518 Luther had written a defense of the *95 Theses*, the *Explanations of the Ninety-Five Theses*, dedicated to Pope Leo X (1475–1521) and authorized for publication by Luther's ordinary, the bishop of Brandenburg, but not published until August.[2] Also in early 1518, Luther

1. Perhaps as early as June 1518, a summons had been prepared for Luther to appear in Rome within sixty days. For the historical reconstruction here, see Brecht 1:239–65.

2. LW 31:77–252. It also contained a prefatory letter to Johann von Staupitz, the head of the Augustinian Order in Germany, printed in LW 48:64–70. For the letter to Leo X, see WA 1:527–29.

Title page of *Proceedings at Augsburg*,
reprinted in 1518 by Valentin Schumann in Leipzig.

published the *Sermon on Indulgences and Grace*, and in April he was sent to Heidelberg for a meeting of the German chapter of the Augustinian Order. There he defended theses not on indulgences (which were now part of a legal case) but, rather, on questions of justification by faith, law, and gospel, and the "theology of the cross."[a] By the end of August, Luther published his response to Prierias, insisting on a coalition of authorities that he would later use in his encounter with Cardinal Cajetan (also known as Tommaso de Vio [1469–1534]): reason, the fathers of the church, the official church decrees (canon law), and, above all, the Bible.

In the summer of 1518, an imperial diet (parliament) convened in Augsburg, to which the pope sent his legate Cardinal Cajetan. Already on 7 August, Luther had received a summons to face trial in Rome, based upon charges in the *Dialogus*. Matters had moved beyond learned debate to something far more serious, and Luther did not hide his alarm. To complicate matters, during Lent 1518 Luther had delivered a sermon on excommunication and its abuse by church authorities. Opponents had composed a distorted set of theses on the subject under Luther's name and circulated them

---

a For the *Sermon on Indulgences and Grace* and the *Heidelberg Disputation*, see pp. 60–65 and 80–120, respectively.

at the diet.[3] The emperor, Maximilian I (1459–1519), was outraged and called for action. On 23 August the pope delivered to Cajetan a summons for Luther to appear in Rome to answer charges of heresy.[4] On 11 September Cajetan received permission to interrogate Luther in Augsburg and either receive his recantation or condemn him. The pope also sent word to Luther's prince, Elector Frederick (1463–1525), to assist in such an arrest, if such action was necessary.[b] Frederick delayed a few weeks, but then, in a shrewd political move, requested that Luther appear in Augsburg in late September under a letter of safe conduct. Thus, in early October, Luther set out for Augsburg. En route, he was joined in Nuremberg by Wenceslaus Linck (1483–1547), a fellow Augustinian.

At Augsburg, the proceedings between Luther and Cajetan consisted of three meetings from 12 to 14 October. Having received his letter of safe conduct, Luther met with the cardinal for the first time on 12 October. Cajetan had been ordered via a papal communiqué to avoid debate with

3. Luther responded by publishing his own Latin version of the *Sermon on the Ban* (August 1518) in LW 39:3–22.

4. Luther published a copy of this papal summons as part of the *Proceedings*. See below, p. 158–62.

Luther and Catejan at Augsburg.

b For this letter, see Preserved Smith, ed., *Luther's Correspondence and Other Contemporary Letters*, vol. 1 (Philadelphia: Lutheran Publication Society, 1913), 105–6.

5. Because the papal bull *Unigenitus* (1343) was not recorded in all editions of canon law, Luther and others called it *Extravagante* (literally, a [decree] "wandering outside"). Because of the importance of this document, it is translated below, p. 127f.

6. Nominalism, a philosophical and theological "way" of thinking first developed by William of Occam (c. 1287-1347). Sometimes called the *via moderna* (modern way), it contrasted to the philosophy and theology of the *via antiqua* (old way), championed by Thomas Aquinas and his followers, called Thomists.

Luther and simply to demand his recantation.[c] Both Luther's legal representative and Johann von Staupitz (c. 1460-1524), the head of the Augustinian order in Germany, accompanied him to the first meeting, where Cajetan, contrary to the papal instructions, entered into discussion with Luther. That first interview was the longest of the three. Cajetan raised questions on two fronts: challenging thesis 58 of the *95 Theses* and the arguments in the *Explanations* on thesis 7. He defended papal authority to sell indulgences as based on John 20:23 and a papal decree of Clement VI (1291-1352) not found in all collections of canon law, with which he thus assumed Luther was not familiar.[5] Luther was indeed aware of this decree but argued that on the higher authority of Scripture it should be rescinded. The objections raised to Luther's arguments defending thesis 7 touched upon the heart of justification by faith: whether in private confession a person could completely trust the priest's absolution (i.e., God's promise of forgiveness). Cajetan argued, based upon his Augustinian understanding of true humility, that a person should never be certain of his or her standing before God. For Luther, the certainty of God's promise outweighed any doubts, which in any case could not be made the basis of one's relation to God.

In these early discussions, most of Luther's opponents were firm supporters of papal authority. While Luther was an Augustinian friar trained in Nominalism,[6] several of his opponents were Thomists, embracing an Augustinian theology seen through the lens of the Dominican Thomas Aquinas's (1225-1274) theology, which in the sixteenth century routinely defended papal authority in matters of doctrine and practice.[d] Cajetan's line of questioning (which the Italian Thomist had prepared from a careful reading of Luther's work) was designed to convince Luther of the error of his position on indulgences and church authority.

c   Brecht 1:250.

d   For these early opponents, see David V. N. Bagchi, *Luther's Earliest Opponents: Catholic Controversialists, 1518–1525* (Minneapolis: Fortress Press, 1991), 23; and Scott H. Hendrix, *Luther and the Papacy: Stages in a Reformation Conflict* (Philadelphia: Fortress Press, 1981), 46–52.

On the second day, Luther was accompanied again by Staupitz, together with four imperial counselors. Luther requested a public hearing, a request Cajetan denied. Luther then insisted on reading a written statement in response to Cajetan's points raised at their first meeting and asked permission to defend himself and be judged by theologians at one of the universities in Louvain, Basel, Freiburg, or Paris. This request was also denied.

At the third and final meeting, two lawyers from Frederick's court accompanied Luther. He presented a written statement and made three key points. First, a general church council held authority over the pope. Second, a sacrament given to an unbeliever imparted no grace. Third, the doctrine of justification by faith, supported throughout Scripture, was key to understanding the proper meaning of penance and indulgences. After some hesitation, Cajetan accepted the statement and agreed to send it to the pope along with his refutation. But by now, Cajetan was clearly angered. He asked Luther to recant or leave his presence immediately and not return. Luther simply left without recanting.

Luther wrote a letter of apology, again asking for specifics on where he erred, but he received no reply.[e] Hearing that Luther would be arrested, Staupitz released Luther from his monastic vows of obedience and advised him to return to Wittenberg.[7] Before leaving Augsburg, Luther officially appealed Cajetan's decision to Pope Leo X by having his appeal posted on the cathedral door in Augsburg.[f] A month later, when the pope reiterated his support for indulgences, Luther appealed for the first time to a general council. For those who defended the primacy of papal authority over the councils of the church, this was simply a further indication of his heresy. Once back in Wittenberg, Luther wrote his account of these events in his *Proceedings at Augsburg, 1518*, which was published in early December 1518. To it he added

7. This release allowed Luther to return to Wittenberg without fear of having violated his vow of obedience to his superior, in this case, Johann von Staupitz.

e   See LW 48:87–89.

f   See Christopher Spehr, *Luther und das Konzil: Zur Entwicklung eines zentralen Themas in der Reformationszeit* (Tübingen: Mohr Siebeck, 2010), 91.

8. Throughout his lifetime, Luther held that there were multiple layers of authority in the church. Scripture was the first and true authority, with all other authorities (ancient church fathers, decisions of church councils, and even popes) witnessing to the Scripture's message and, hence, falling under its higher authority. Luther held that Clement VI had erred. When Leo X reaffirmed Clement's position, he had to admit that a living pope had erred. At Leipzig, he also admitted that councils could err as well.

a copy of the 23 August papal instructions to Cajetan, which he had somehow obtained.

These proceedings marked a watershed in the Reformation. The very methods of argumentation employed by Cajetan and later at the 1519 Leipzig Debates by Johann Eck (1486–1543) pushed matters beyond simple academic debate and toward a full-blown break in the church over questions of authority.[8,g] Perhaps even more importantly, the arguments over the nature of faith and certainty indicated a shift in thinking that went far beyond the medieval theology of humility and centered instead in the sure and certain word of Christ and faith in that word. Whether this also implied a new human self-understanding in Western thought is still a matter of debate.[h]

g   See Brecht 1:264–65, 317–22.

h   Otto H. Pesch, "'Das heisst eine neue Kirche bauen': Luther und Cajetan in Augsburg," in *Begegnung: Beiträge zu einer Hermeneutik des theologischen Gesprächs*, ed. Otto Pesch et al. (Graz, Vienna, and Cologne: Styria, 1972), 660.

APPENDIX:
THE "*EXTRAVAGANTE*"
OF CLEMENT VI
(*UNIGENITUS DEI FILIUS*)[9, i]

CLEMENT VI to the Archbishop of Tarroco[10] and his suffragens.

The only begotten Son of God . . . "whom God made our wisdom, our righteousness and sanctification and redemption" [1 Cor. 1:30], "entered once for all in the Holy Place taking not the blood of goats and calves but his own blood, thus securing an eternal redemption" [Heb. 9:12]. For "you were ransomed . . . not with perishable things such as silver or gold but with the precious blood of Christ, like that of a lamb without blemish or spot" [1 Pet. 1:18f.]. Immolated on the altar of the Cross though he was innocent, he shed not merely a single drop of blood—although this would have sufficed for the redemption of the whole human race because of the union with the Logos—but a copious flood, like a stream, so that "from the sole of the foot even to the head there was no soundness in him" [Isa. 1:6].

What a great treasure, then, has the good Father acquired for the church militant, if the merciful shedding of blood is not to be empty, meaningless, and superfluous. He wanted to lay it up for his children, so that there might be "an unfailing treasure for mortals; those who get it obtain friendship with God" [Wis. 7:14].

Indeed [God] committed this treasure, not deposited in a handkerchief [cf. Matt. 20:1-16] or buried in a field [cf. Matt. 13:44] but to the care of St. Peter, bearer of the keys of heaven, and to his successors, his own vicars on earth, who

9. *Extravagante*: The designation of a papal or conciliar decree that was not found in earlier editions of canon law and hence was wandering outside (Latin: *extra-vagans*) it. As with all papal bulls, its title, *Unigenitus Dei filius* [the only begotten Son of God] comes from the first words of the Latin.

10. The Latin name for present-day Tarragona, Spain.

---

i From Heinrich Denzinger et al., *Compendium of Creeds, Definitions, and Declarations on Matters of Faith and Morals*, 43rd ed. (San Francisco: Ignatius, 2012), 306–7, par. 1025–27, with some minor additions from WA 2:5.

11. Through the sacrament of penance, eternal punishment for mortal sins was immediately reduced to temporal penalty, which the plenary indulgence decreed here eliminated.

12. Mary.

13. The following translation of the *Acta Augustana 1518* is a revision of that by Harold J. Grimm in LW 31:253–92 based upon WA 2:1–26. The tract was titled *Acta F. Martini Luther Augustiniani apud D. Legatum Apostolicum Augustae* (Wittenberg: J. Grünenberg, 1518). Five reprints are known to exist along with two printings in collections of Luther's early works from 1520.

are to distribute it to the faithful for their salvation. And they are to apply it with compassion, for pious and good reasons, in order that it may benefit those who are truly contrite and who have confessed, at times for the complete remission of the temporal penalty[11] due to sin, at times for the partial remission, either by a general or particular disposition, as before God they judge more expedient.

To the abundance of this treasury, the merits of the blessed Bearer of God[12] and of all the elect from the first just person to the last, also contribute, as we know; nor is at all to be feared that it could be exhausted or diminished, first on account of the infinite merits of Christ, as already mentioned, and further because the more men are drawn to righteousness by having this treasury applied to them, so much more does the store of those merits increase.

Dated Avignon, 27 January [1343], the first year of our pontificate.

THE PROCEEDINGS AT AUGSBURG,[13] 1518

The Proceedings[j] of Friar Martin Luther, Augustinian, with the Lord Apostolic Legate at Augsburg

To the Godly Reader, Friar Martin Luther Extends Greetings

Forgive me, dear reader, for so often wearying you with my trifles. I do this very reluctantly, and again I beg you to realize my critical situation. It has pleased heaven that I

j   Latin: *acta*, a technical term for an official public report of meetings or events.

should become the talk of the people. Nevertheless, I confess that without a doubt I should attribute this not only to the Lord but also to those people whose ears are so pious that they are offended by the most precious and pious truth, even to the extent that they give expression to a godless impiety of heart, mouth, and deed. They have already plagued Johannes Reuchlin, for a long time a privy councilor.[14] Now they plague me, an inquiring disputant (as I might call myself), and they tolerate neither advice nor debates.[15] Therefore we expect that eventually they will plague the dreams and thoughts of all humankind because of their wicked idleness. For who is safe from the jaws of these beasts that devour even those who desire private advice or public instruction? Good God! The desire for instruction and the search for truth is now a new and noteworthy crime. And this occurs in the church, the kingdom of truth, in which it is necessary to give an account to all who demand it. But more on this at another time.[16]

Now, dear reader, what I am doing is this: I see that pamphlets are being published and various rumors are being spread concerning my activities at Augsburg, although I really accomplished nothing more there than the loss of time and money.[17] Probably, however, it was enough of an accomplishment to have heard a new Latin language, namely, that teaching the truth is the same as confusing the church—indeed, that flattering and also denying Christ would be equivalent to pacifying and exalting the church of Christ. For I do not see how you could but appear to be a barbarian to the Romans and the Romans barbarians to you if you did not master this kind of eloquence, even if you were to surpass the eloquence of Cicero.[18] Therefore, to avoid extremes, so that friends of my cause do not excessively elevate it or enemies excessively lower it, I wish to make public the charges against me and my answers to them.

By this testimony I wish to make it known that I excelled in giving the Roman pontiff exceptional and faithful obedience. In the first place, I, poor and weak though I am, set out on foot on a long journey,[19] thus exposing myself to dangers, and I did not take advantage of just and honorable excuses

14. From 1509 to 1516 Johannes Reuchlin (1455–1522), a famous humanist and one of the first northern Europeans to master the three sacred languages (Latin, Greek, and Hebrew), supported the publication of nonbiblical Hebrew texts, especially the mystical *Kabala*. He was opposed especially by theologians at Cologne, a stronghold of Dominican (Thomistic) Scholastic theology, in a case that finally ended in Rome. Many of Luther's early opponents were also Thomists, including Tetzel and Prierias.

15. The recently published *Explanations of the 95 Theses* (LW 31:77–252) still indicated Luther's willingness to debate these issues.

16. It is not clear whether Luther actually returned to this issue. At the very least, it became a main topic in the Leipzig debates with Johann Eck in the summer of 1519. See LW 31:307–25.

17. Luther is thinking of the various writings of Johann Tetzel, Sylvester Prierias, and the unpublished work of Johann Eck. For the falsified theses on the ban that circulated in Augsburg, see the introduction, p. 122f.

18. Cicero (106–43 BCE) was considered the greatest Latin orator of the ancient world.

19. The trip from Wittenberg to Augsburg was about 300 miles

(500 km). Luther set out on 26 September 1518 and arrived on 7 October. See Hendrix, *Luther and the Papacy*, 45.

20. At this juncture, Luther associated his enemies with Scholastic Thomists, among whom Cajetan was one of the most important.

21. The Curia was the papal court and its legion of functionaries, which saw to the disposition of the church's legal cases.

22. 1343 *Unigenitus*, papal bull of Clement VI, called *Extravagante*. For the text of this bull, see the appendix above, p. 127f.

23. DISCUSSIONS ON 12 OCTOBER

24. Because of Elector Frederick's intervention, Luther did not travel to Rome for questioning. Instead, Luther had only to travel to Augsburg to appear before Cardinal Cajetan, the papal legate to the diet that had recently ended there. The concern was for Luther's safety.

for staying away, which all would have judged acceptable. In the second place, I appeared before those whom I could have refused to see, because they belonged on the side of my enemies.[20] However, it seems to me (were I to follow my nose) that these so-called friends have contrived these evil and troublesome conditions and have arranged all matters so that they would more readily contribute to my destruction and not to the search for truth. Nor does it seem as though they expected me to come but hoped that I would obstinately refuse to come so that they could inflict the punishment without a hearing and secretly triumph over me. The not insignificant proof of this I gathered from the fact that the question of the accusation against me was not raised until after my arrival. And up to the present day my writings are in the house of Caiaphas, where they seek false testimony against me and have not yet found it.[k] So this new custom (as I see it) or new law of the Roman Curia[21] has been initiated to first seize Christ and then to look for a charge against him. Nevertheless, I have been accused of two things—really only one—which has the appearance of an accusation, that is, my statement concerning the *Extravagante*,[22] as you will presently learn.

[23] Therefore, because I did not want to permit the illustrious prince, Elector Frederick, duke of Saxony, etc., to labor in vain on my behalf (for he had kindly provided me with both expense money and letters of introduction and had previously graciously seen to it that my cause would be considered outside the city of Rome), I came to Augsburg.[24] Here I was received by the most reverend lord cardinal legate both graciously and with almost too much respect,[25] for he is a man who is in all respects different from those extremely harsh bloodhounds who track down monks among us.[26] After he had stated that he did not wish to argue with me, but to settle the matter peacefully and in a fatherly fash-

k   See the account of Jesus' trial in Matthew 26:57-68 and his appearance before the high priest Caiaphas.

ion,[27] he proposed that I do three things which, he said, had been demanded by the pope: first, that I come to my senses and recant my errors; second, that I promise to abstain from them in the future; and third, that I abstain from doing anything that might disturb the church. Realizing that I could just as well have done these things at Wittenberg without exposing myself to danger and going to so much trouble and that I did not need to seek this papal admonition in Augsburg, I immediately asked to be instructed in what matters I had erred, since I was not conscious of any errors. Then he referred to the *Extravagante* of Clement VI, which begins with the word *Unigenitus*, because in Thesis 58 I had asserted contrary to it that the merits of Christ did not constitute the treasury of merits of indulgences.[l] Then he demanded that I recant, and he confidently pursued the matter, sure of victory, for he was certain and secure in assuming that I had not seen the *Extravagante*, probably relying upon the fact that not all editions of the canon law contain it.[m]

In the second place, he reproached me for having taught in the explanation of Thesis 7 that a person taking the sacrament had to have faith or he would take it to his own damnation,[n] for he wished to have this judged a new and erroneous doctrine. According to him, every person going to the sacrament was uncertain whether or not he would receive grace. By his boldness he made it appear as though I had been defeated, especially since the Italians and others of his companions smiled about this and, according to their custom, even giggled aloud.[28] **I then answered**[29] that I had carefully examined not only this *Extravagante* of Clement, but also the other one of Sixtus IV, which emulated and was similar to it (for I had actually read both and had found them characterized by the same verbosity, which destroys one's faith in their trustworthiness, stuffed as they are with

25. Between 25 September and 29 October, Cajetan composed fifteen tracts in the form of scholastic *Quaestiones*, where Luther's positions were questioned (although Luther was not named). See Brecht 1:250.

26. The first meeting occurred on 12 October 1518. For a reconstruction of these events, see Spehr, *Luther und das Konzil*, 74–75.

27. It appears that Cajetan wanted to allow Luther the opportunity to avoid excommunication by asking for a traditional revocation. See Spehr, *Luther und das Konzil*, 71. This description may also be understood as irony.

28. Luther does not hesitate to play on German suspicions about Italian papal courtiers, also a topic at the recently concluded diet.

29. This phrase was a heading in the original printing.

---

l   See the *95 Theses* above, p. 41f. For the text of *Unigenitus*, also known as the *Extravagante*, see pp. 127–28.

m   See above, n. 22.

n   See the *Explanations of the Ninety-Five Theses* (1518), in LW 31:98.

30. The Bull of Sixtus IV (1414–1484), *Salvator noster* (1476), officially authorized indulgences for the dead. For Cajetan's position on this bull, see Bagchi, *Luther's Earliest Opponents*, 18. For the text of the bull, see Denzinger, *Compendium*, 353–54 (par. 1398).

31. Cajetan had obtained copies of both Luther's *Explanations of the Ninety-Five Theses* and the *Sermo de poenitentia*, and he questioned Luther initially regarding Luther's treatment and use of Scripture in the explanation to thesis 7 and the *Sermo de poenitentia*. See Jared Wicks, *Cajetan Responds: A Reader in Reformation Controversy* (Washington, DC: Catholic University of America Press, 1978), 21–23.

32. In the bull *Pastor aeternus* (14 January 1516), Leo X asserted that the pope had authority over all councils "so that he has the complete right and power to call, transfer, and dissolve them." See Denzinger, *Compendium*, 362 (no. 1445). The Council of Basel was convoked by Pope Martin V (1369–1431) in 1431 and closed in 1449. It worked to assert the authority of church councils over the pope and was dissolved by the pope. After the Reformation, some Roman Catholic scholars refused to view it (in whole or in part) as a general council of the church.

33. At the University of Paris, Jean Gerson (1363–1429) and his followers, termed Gersonists by Luther, called for church reform via a church council, which would be superior to the pope.

ignorance).[30] For many reasons, the *Extravagante* did not impress me as being truthful or authoritative, especially because it distorts the Holy Scriptures and audaciously twists the words (if indeed their customary meaning still should be accepted) into a meaning which they do not have in their context; in fact, they have a contrary meaning. The Scriptures, which I follow in my Thesis 7, are to be preferred to the bull in every case. Nothing is proven in the bull. Only the teaching of St. Thomas is trotted out and reiterated.[31]

Then, in contradiction to what I had said, he began to extol the authority of the pope, stating that it is above church councils, Scripture, and the entire church.[o] With the purpose of persuading me to accept this point of view, he called attention to the rejection and dissolution of the Council of Basel[32] and was of the opinion that the Gersonists as well as Gerson should be condemned.[33] Since this was something new to me, I denied that the pope was superior to the council and Scripture, and I praised the appeal made by the University of Paris.[34] Then in no prearranged order we exchanged words concerning penance and grace.

The second objection caused me much grief, for I scarcely should have feared anything less than that this doctrine would ever be called into question. Thus, in no one point did we even remotely come to any agreement. But as one thing led to another, as is usually the case, a new counter-argument arose. When, however, I saw that nothing was accomplished by such a dispute, except that many points

o   See Cajetan's second article in his *Augsburg Treatises*, 1518, in Wicks' *Cajetan Responds*, 49–55. For more on Cajetan's role at the Fifth Lateran Council in Rome (1512), see Hendrix, *Luther and the Papacy*, 57.

were raised and none solved—indeed we already had battled with nothing but many *"Extravagantes"*[p]—and especially since he was representing the pope and did not wish to appear to yield, I asked that I be given time for deliberation.

[35] On the next day, when four counselors of his majesty the emperor were present, I, with a notary and witnesses who had been brought to the meeting, testified formally and personally by reading in the presence of the most reverend legate the following:

Principally, I, Brother Martin Luther, Augustinian, declare publicly that I cherish and follow the holy Roman Church in all my words and actions—present, past, and future. If I have said or shall say anything contrary to this, I wish it to be considered as not having been said. The most reverend cardinal Cajetan by command of the pope has asserted, proposed, and urged that with respect to the earlier disputation which I held on indulgences, I do these three things: first, to come to my senses and recant my error; second, to pledge not to repeat it in the future; and third, to promise to abstain from all things which might disturb the church.

I, who debated and sought the truth could not have done wrong by such inquiry, much less be compelled to recant, without having been heard or convicted. Today I declare publicly that I am not conscious of having said anything contrary to Holy Scripture, the church fathers, the papal decretals, or right reason.[36] All that I have said today seems to me to have been sensible, true, and catholic.

Nevertheless, since I am a man who can err, I have submitted and now again submit to the judgment and the lawful decision of the holy church and of all who are better informed than I. In addition to this, however, I offer myself personally here or elsewhere to give an account

34. The University of Paris in 1518 had objected to the Concordat of Bologna between Leo X and King Francis I (1494–1547) of France, appealing to a church council.

35. DISCUSSIONS ON 13 OCTOBER

36. "Right reason" refers to using accepted rules for logic. By "papal decretals," Luther means the collections of papal and conciliar decrees that made up most of church law. In the broadest sense, the decretals include all official letters of the pope in which a specific decision or decree is contained. More specifically, the term refers to various collections of such decrees. The *Decretum* [decrees] of Gratian (mid-twelfth century) constituted the first major collection and formed the basis for a code of ecclesiastical laws (*Corpus iuris canonici*). Pope Gregory IX (c. 1145–1241) authorized a collection of the decrees that had appeared after Gratian's collection, which was called the *Decretals of Pope Gregory IX* (1234). Later decrees, nicknamed *Extravagantes* because they "wandered outside" the regular collections, were then included in later editions of this material.

---

[p]   That is, papal bulls.

also in public of all that I have said. But if this does not please the most reverend lord legate, I am even prepared to answer in writing the objections which he intends to raise against me, and to hear the judgment and opinion concerning these points of the doctors of the famed imperial universities of Basel, Freiburg, and Louvain, or, if this is not satisfactory, also of Paris, the parent of learning and from the beginning the university which was most Christian and most renowned in theology.[37]

37. The appeal to the theological faculties of the medieval universities to settle disputes was typical. Luther may have included Paris not only because it was the oldest but also because it was favorable toward conciliarism.

After I had said this, he again referred to yesterday's discussion concerning the first objection, for this one seemed to be very important from his point of view. When I was silent and then, in harmony with my protest, promised to answer in writing, he again became self-confident. Still, when he had agreed to the written response, we parted. The tenor and text of my response is the following.

38. LUTHER'S WRITTEN RESPONSE TO CAJETAN, PRESENTED ON 14 OCTOBER 1518

[38] Greetings to the most reverend father in Christ, Lord Thomas, cardinal of the titular church of St. Sixtus, legate of the apostolic chair, from Friar Martin Luther, Augustinian.

I wish to prove humbly in this letter that I do not refuse to answer and that I freely desire to give account for each individual statement of mine, Most Reverend Father in Christ, in order to meet the objections that you raised yesterday and the day before yesterday. There are two things to which Your Reverend Father objected.

First, I seem to deny in my theses[q] that *Extravagante* of Clement VI beginning with the word *Unigenitus*, in which the treasury of indulgences appears to be identified with the merits of Christ and the saints.

I answer this objection in the following way: That *Extravagante* was not unknown to me when I was engaged in the preparation of my theses. Since I knew for certain, however, that it was the consensus of the entire church that the merits of Christ could not in spirit be entrusted to human beings

q   Theses 58 and 60.

or dispensed through them or by them, as the *Unigenitus* nevertheless seemed to imply, I preferred not to mention the bull and to leave it to better qualified persons to judge what great vexations and anguish I endured to save the honor of the pope.

First of all, it occurred to me and disturbed me that the words of the pope alone would be an ineffective defense against a contentious or heretical person. If one may say that it is scandalous if a secular prince speaks without support of

Portrait of Martin Luther (1483–1546)
from the German translation of
The Babylonian Captivity of the Church
by the artist Hans Baldung Grien
(d. 1545) depicting the reformer
as an Augustinian monk
expounding on the Bible.

CLEMENTE VI. PONT. CC.
Creato del 1342. a' 17. di Maggio.

LEMENTE Sesto di patria Lemonicense, e chiamato prima Pietro, fù prima Monaco, poi Arciuescouo di Roano, e finalmente in Auignone creato Pontefice. Fù di molta dottrina, eloquente, humano assai, e cortese con tutti. Fù eletto a' 7. di Maggio del MCCCXLII. e fù incoronato a' 19. del medesimo mese. Nelle prime quattro tempora del medesimo anno creò dieci Cardinali, de' quali fù vno Guglielmo, figliuolo di sua sorella, & vn suo proprio fratello, ch'era già monaco, & vn'altro certo suo parente. L'anno seguente ne creò due altri, de' quali n'era vno suo nipote, figliuolo d'un'altra sua sorella. E essendo richiesto da Romani, che come hauea Bonifacio ottauo ordinato, che ogni cent'anni, (il qual spatio di tempo era da gli antichi chiamato secolo) fosse il Giubileo, e la remission di tutti i peccati a quelli, che visitauano le Chiese de gli Apostoli, così volesse ridurre a cinquant'anni il Giubileo volentieri si contentò, parendo che l'età dell'huomo a cent'anni non arriuasse, perche hauesse goder potuto questo santo Giubileo. Intendendo, che tutt'Italia fosse in tumulto, e sottosopra, confermò solamente Lucino, e Giouanni Visconti, Vicarij dello

Giubileo a' 50. anni.

B b

An image of Pope Clement VI (r. 1342–1352).
He wears a pallium while to the right is Clement's
coat of arms with the papal triple tiara above.

39. Gratian, *Decretum,* pt. 1, dist. XIX, c. 2 (MPL 187:106), a decree of Pope Agatho (d. 681) in 680. Luther is turning the decree on its head by arguing that papal decrees must be judged by Peter and, hence, by Scripture.

40. Niccolò de' Tudeschi (1386-1445), archbishop of Palermo [Latin: *Panormitanus*], whose annotations on canon law Luther prized highly.

the law, so, likewise, according to Zechariah [Mal. 2:7], not the words of humans but the law of God is demanded from the mouth of a priest. Furthermore, it occurred to me that the *Unigenitus* twists the words of Scripture and abuses them by giving them another meaning, for what was said [in Scripture] concerning justifying grace it applies to indulgences.*r* For this reason, it seemed merely to report and by its pious impression to exhort people, rather than to prove something by a convincing demonstration.

Furthermore, it also disquieted me that it could quite possibly happen that papal decretals occasionally are erroneous and militate against Holy Scriptures and charity. For if one ought to obey the papal decretals as though they were the voice of St. Peter, as it is stated in *distinctio* XIX,[39] still this is to be understood only of those decretals that are in agreement with Holy Scripture and the decretals of previous popes, as stated in the same authority.

Add to this the fact that Peter, when not walking in the truth of the gospel, is actually reprimanded by Paul in Gal. 2[:14]. Therefore it does not appear strange if his successor has erred in some point or other, since indeed it is stated in Acts 15[:1-19] that the teaching of Peter was not accepted until it had been accepted and approved by James the Younger, the bishop of Jerusalem, and agreed to by the entire church. From this seems to have arisen the legal principle that a law becomes established only when it is approved by those living according to its regulations.

Furthermore, how many early decretals are corrected by later ones! Therefore, in time this decretal can also be corrected. Panormitanus, too, in his edition of the *Decretals,*[40] shows that in matters of faith not only is a general council above the pope, but also any believer is, provided such a one uses better authority or reason than the pope, just as Paul does with Peter in Gal. 2[:14]. This is confirmed also in the following statement in 1 Cor. 14[:30]: "If a revelation comes to someone who is sitting down, let the first one be silent." Therefore the voice of Peter must be heard in such a way that

r   See the introduction, p. 127f.

the voice of Paul may more freely be heard when he reprimands Peter. But the voice of Christ must be heard above all others.

I was most troubled, however, by the fact that *Extravagante* appeared to me to contain certain obviously false statements. First of all, it maintains that the merits of the saints constitute a treasure, despite the fact that the entire Scripture states that God rewards far beyond all our worth, as in Rom. 8[:18]: "The sufferings of this present time are not worth comparing with the glory that is to be revealed to us." And St. Augustine[41] says in chapter 19 of the first book of his *Retractions*, "The entire church prays, even to the end of the world, 'Forgive us our debts' [Matt. 6:12]. Therefore it cannot give others that which it itself lacks."[s] Even the wise virgins did not wish to share their oil with the foolish virgins.[t] And St. Augustine says in the ninth book of his *Confessions*, "Woe unto the life of a person, however laudable, if it is judged without mercy."[u] And the prophet said [Ps. 143:2], "Do not enter into judgment with your servant, for no living person is righteous in your sight." Likewise, the saints are saved, not by their merits, but alone by the mercy of God, as I have stated more fully in my *Explanations*.[v]

Indeed, I did not possess the extraordinary audacity to discard so many important clear proofs of Scripture on account of a single ambiguous and obscure decretal of a pope who is a mere human being. Much rather I considered it proper that the words of Scripture, in which the saints are described as being deficient in merits, are to be preferred to human words, in which the saints are said to have more merits than they need. For the pope is not above but under the word of God, according to Gal. 1[:8]: "Even if we, or an angel from heaven, should preach to you a gospel contrary to that

41. Augustine (354–430) was bishop of Hippo in North Africa and the most influential theologian in the Western church during the Middle Ages and beyond. His *Confessions* detailed his life before and slightly after being baptized at the Easter Vigil in 387 by Ambrose (c. 340–397), bishop of Milan.

---

s   Augustine, *Retractiones* I.xix.3 in MPL 32:615.

t   Cf. Matt. 25:9.

u   Augustine, *Confessions*, IX.xiii.34 in NPNF, ser. 1, 1:130 (MPL 32:778).

v   *Explanations of the Ninety-Five Theses* (1518), LW 31:212.

42. This text will continue to play an important role in Luther's understanding of authority. For example, he quotes it in his letter to Charles V (1500–1558), written on 28 April 1521 after Luther had left the Diet of Worms. See LW 48:206.

43. In medieval metaphysics, the taking away of something was not strictly speaking an "entity," although it could be considered a "negative good."

44. By "negative good," Luther means a good that merely removes something but does not confer any new substantial thing to the purchaser. This corresponds to one of Luther's chief arguments in the *95 Theses*. See above, pp. 34–36.

45. That is, the authority of priests and bishops to forgive or retain sins, called "the keys" because of Jesus' words to Peter in Matt. 16:19: "I will give you the keys of the kingdom of heaven, and whatever you bind on earth will be bound in heaven, and whatever you loose on earth will be loosed in heaven."

46. See above, *95 Theses*, p. 42. Luther is arguing against the mercantile

which you received, let him be accursed."[42] Furthermore, it was important to me that the bull stated that this treasure was committed to Peter, about which there is nothing either in the gospel or any part of the Bible.

Perturbed by these annoyances, I decided, as I have said, to remain silent and listen to others, for I believed that my theses were correctly stated, as I still believe today. Now since I am urged to attempt that which I have a right to expect from others, especially from the pope, who alone can explain his own decretals, nevertheless, I will with all my ability and the grace of God and for the sake of the most holy truth, try to bring my theses into agreement with the *Extravagante* and to preserve both in truth.

1. It must be assumed that indulgences are absolutely nothing (metaphysically speaking), for it is certain that they are merely remissions of satisfaction, that is, of good works, such as giving alms, fasting, praying, and the like.[43] Therefore it is also certain that indulgences constitute a negative good, since they only permit the remission of deserved punishments or the performing of burdensome works. From this it necessarily follows that no treasure is received in the proper sense of the term, for nothing positive is conferred. On the contrary, a person is merely permitted to do nothing.[44]

2. It is certain that the pope does not have this treasure, as it were, in a purse or a money chest, but that it consists of a statement connected with the office of the keys.[45] In dispensing the treasure, he does not open a chest but makes known his will and thus grants the indulgence.

3. It therefore follows that the treasure of indulgences is the merits of Christ, not formally or properly but only in effect and nonliterally. The pope does not actually dispense the merits of Christ, but he grants indulgence through the merit of Christ, that is, through the office of the keys, which was given to the church by Christ's merit, for it is by virtue of the office of the keys that satisfaction is remitted. Furthermore, it is clear that I correctly stated in thesis 60 that the office of the keys of the church, given by the merits of Christ, constitutes the treasure. And in this sense, it is true that the merits of Christ are the treasure of indulgences.[46] To be sure,

the treasure and the merits of Christ are to be understood nonliterally. In this sense, it is apparent that the *Extravagante* and my thesis are in agreement.

4. That this is the meaning of the pope in this *Extravagante* is proven by the pope's own words when he says that the treasure was committed to Peter and his successors by Christ. It is firmly established, however, that nothing was committed to Peter except the keys of the kingdom of heaven,[w] which are the merits of Christ (that is, the keys were given by the merits of Christ). But they were given only figuratively and in effect, as I have stated. The other treasure which Christ gave Peter is the treasure of the Word, of which he said, "Feed, nourish, tend my sheep."[x]

5. Still, it is certain that this understanding of the treasure of indulgences is unknown and unrecognized among Christians, as my thesis 56 states.[y] For these words, "treasure," "merit of Christ," and so on, are seldom used except nonliterally and obscurely.[47] Therefore, Christians essentially believe that they themselves obtain an actual and positive good as if it were a gift or grace, when in fact they acquire nothing but the office of the keys, by means of which the satisfaction for their sins is remitted. Thus, they receive a negative good and a treasure that is not a treasure in the usual sense. That treasure is, to be sure, inexhaustible and infinite, because the office of the keys is inexhaustible. The office of the keys rests directly upon the merits of Christ, but indulgences only indirectly. Therefore it can also be said that the merits of Christ are indirectly the treasure of indulgences.

6. Similarly, I might also admit that the merits of the saints constitute this treasure, but only in a nonliteral sense, since the merits of the saints are included through their faith in Christ and are made one with his merits. Thereby their merits are now the same and accomplish the same as the merits of Christ, because the life of the righteous is not

metaphor that underlay not only indulgences but also the notion that any forgiveness of sin demanded payment of punishment.

47. Luther examines the question of what comprises the treasure of the church in theses 56–68, disputing the claim that the treasury could literally, be the merits of Christ and the saints. The "merits of the saints" were those good works done by the saints in heaven while on earth, which accumulated merit for them above any that they needed to satisfy any temporal punishment for sin they may have accrued in life.

---

w   Cf. Matt. 16:19.

x   Cf. John 21:15-17.

y   See above, *95 Theses*, p. 41.

their own but that of Christ living in them. According to Gal. 2[:20], "It is no longer I who live, but Christ who lives in me," for the merits of the saints as saints would be of no value and damnable, as I said above and as St. Augustine said: "Where I am not, there I am the most blessed," because Christ and the church are two in one flesh.[z]

7. Nevertheless, it is most certainly true that the merits of Christ are not synonymous with the treasure of indulgences, in a positive, actual, or direct sense, as though they would confer something, as uneducated people might understand it. If these merits convey an actual gift, they do so not as a treasure of indulgences but as a treasure of life-giving grace. Then they are given formally, actually, directly, without the office of the keys, without indulgences, alone by the Holy Spirit, but never by the pope. Because a person is made one spirit with Christ through love, that one shares in all his benefits. And this is what my thesis 58 stated: "Nor are they the merits of Christ and the saints, because, even without the pope, these merits always work grace for the inner person and cross, death and hell for the outer person."[a]

Briefly, if the *Extravagante* is to be retained as authoritative, it is thus clear that the merits of Christ must of necessity be understood in a twofold sense.[48] On the one hand, according to the literal and formal sense, the merits of Christ are a treasure of the life-giving Spirit. Since they are his very own, the Holy Spirit apportions them to whomever he wills. On the other hand, according to the nonliteral, effective sense, they only signify, according to the letter and the incidental consequences, a treasure created by the merits of Christ. And as the *Extravagante* quotes the Scriptures in a nonliteral sense, so also it understands the treasure, the merits of Christ, and all other concepts in a nonliteral sense.

48. Luther realized that the papal decree had indeed associated Christ's merit with the treasure needed for indulgences. By arguing that this was only true in a nonliteral sense, he hoped to avoid contradicting the decree outright.

---

z   Augustine, *On Continence* c. 13 (29) in MPL 40:309. Andreas Bodenstein from Karlstadt (1486–1541) had first cited this text in his defense of Luther, dated 7 July 1518. See his *Contra D. Joannem Eckium . . . Apologeticae propositiones pro . . . Martino Luther* (Wittenberg, 1518).

a   See above, *95 Theses*, p. 41.

For this reason, it is ambiguous and obscure, and affords a most proper occasion for debate. In my theses, on the other hand, I spoke in terms of the proper sense [of treasure].

Whoever has a better understanding of this, let him give it to me, and I will recant [my understanding], for it is not my duty to interpret the canons of the popes but to defend my theses, lest they may seem to be in opposition to the canons. In humility I expect that if the pope is of a different mind, he will let it be known, and I am willing to comply.[49]

Nevertheless, I intended all these statements out of the reverence for the Apostolic See and the most reverend cardinal. If I am permitted to state my opinion publicly and freely, I contend and can prove that this *Extravagante* is actually, directly, and obviously in opposition to the most reverend cardinal, for the wording of it expressly states that Christ acquired this treasure for the church.[50] This word "acquired" clearly convinces one and conclusively proves that the merits of Christ, by which he acquired a treasure, are something other than the treasure which he acquired, for the cause is one thing and the effect another, as the philosophers also teach. Therefore my thesis remains irrefutable, namely, that the merits of Christ are not the treasure of indulgences, but rather that [the merits] have acquired it. Nevertheless, I submit this opinion to the judgment of the church, as I have stated above.

The other objection is that in thesis 7[51] I stated that no one can be justified except by faith. Thus, it is clearly necessary that individuals[b] must believe with firm faith that they are justified, and in no way doubt that they will obtain grace. For if they doubt and are uncertain, they are not justified but reject grace. My opponents wish to consider this theology new and erroneous.[52]

This I answer by saying:

1. It is an infallible truth that no person is righteous unless such a person believes in God, as stated in Rom. 1[:17]: "The one who through faith is righteous shall live."

49. For this reason, Cajetan immediately had Pope Leo X approve *Extravagante*, leading to Luther's official appeal to a general council, made on 10 December 1518. See WA 2:34–40.

50. For the complete text, see the introduction above, p. 127–28. Luther's pointing out that the papal bull did not make the direct connection to indulgences apparently surprised Cajetan. See Brecht 1:256–57.

51. Luther, *Explanations*, LW 31:98. The following explanation of this thesis presents one of the earliest clear statements of Luther's understanding of justification by faith alone.

52. For Luther and his opponents, novelty in theology was a sure sign of heresy.

b   Luther uses the singular throughout this paragraph.

Likewise [John 3:18], "The one who does not believe is condemned already" and dead. Therefore the justification and life of the righteous person are dependent upon his or her faith. For this reason, all the works of the believer are alive and all the works of the unbeliever are dead, evil, and damnable, as in this passage [Matt. 7:18–19]: "A bad tree cannot bear good fruit. Every tree that does not bear good fruit is cut down and thrown into the fire."

2. Faith, however, is nothing more than believing what God promises and reveals, as in Rom. 4[:3], "Abraham believed God, and he reckoned it to him as righteousness."[c] Therefore the Word and faith are both necessary, and without the Word there can be no faith, as in Isa. 55[:11]: "So shall my word be that goes forth from my mouth; it shall not return to me empty."

3. I must now prove that those[d] going to the sacrament must believe that they will receive grace, and not doubt it, but rather have absolute confidence. Otherwise they will receive the sacrament to their condemnation.

First, I prove this through the word of the Apostle in Heb. 11[:6]: "For whoever would draw near to God must believe that he exists and rewards those who seek him." According to this it is clear that we dare not doubt but must firmly believe that God rewards those who seek him. If we must believe that God is the one who rewards, then we must, above all, believe that he justifies human beings and gives his grace to those living now. Without grace he gives no reward.

Second, in the face of the peril of eternal damnation and the sin of unbelief, we must believe these words of Christ [Matt. 16:19]: "Whatever you loose on earth shall be loosed in heaven." Therefore, if you come to the sacrament of penance and do not firmly believe that you will be absolved in heaven, you come to your judgment and damnation, because you do not believe that Christ speaks the truth when he says [Matt. 16:19], "Whatever you loose . . ."[53] And with your doubt you make a liar of Christ, which is a horrible sin. If, however, you

53. The entire verse from Matt. 16:19 reads: "I will give you the keys of the kingdom of heaven, and whatever; you bind on earth will be bound in heaven, and whatever you loose on earth will be loosed in heaven."

c   See Gen. 15:6.

d   Singular in the original.

say, "What if I am unworthy and unfit for the sacrament?" I answer as I did above. Through no attitude on your part will you become worthy. Through no works will you be prepared for the sacrament, but through faith alone, for only faith in the word of Christ justifies, makes a person alive, worthy, and well prepared. Without faith all other things are acts of presumption and desperation. The just live not by their disposition[54] but by faith. For this reason, you should not harbor any doubt on account of your unworthiness. You go to the sacrament because you are unworthy, so that you may be made worthy and be justified by him who seeks to save sinners and not the righteous.[e] When, however, you believe Christ's word, you honor it and thereby are righteous.

Third, he has commended this faith to us in many ways in the gospel.[55]

First, when he said to the woman of Canaan [Matt. 15:28]: "O woman, great is your faith! Be it done for you as you have believed."[f] This shows that faith in general is not meant here, but the special faith[56] which was concerned with the daughter who was to be healed in answer to her mother's prayer, for she boldly believed that this would be done, that Christ could and would do it, and so her prayer was fulfilled. She never would have obtained this, however, if she had not believed. Therefore she was made worthy of this answer to her prayer, not by her disposition but by faith alone.

Second, when Christ asked those blind men [Matt. 9:28-30], "Do you believe that I am able to do this?" and they answered, "Yes, Lord," he said, "According to your faith let it be done to you." You see, they were certain that it would come to pass as they petitioned. Therefore it came to pass without any preparation on their part. If, however, they had doubted the outcome, they would not have prayed well or received what they had prayed for.

54. Latin: *dispositio*, a technical term for any behavior that a person performs to prepare for God's grace.

55. To prove that his teaching is not new, Luther cites both Scripture and interpretations by later theologians.

56. Luther distinguishes here a "general faith," by which he was reflecting the standard definition of faith as a virtue that accepted as true the teachings of the church, from a "special faith," trusting specific promises of God.

e   Cf. Luke 5:32. Luther would continue to reflect on the believer's unworthiness to receive the sacrament in the LC, "Lord's Supper," par. 55–74 (1529), in BC, 472–74.

f   Both the Greek and Latin texts read: "as you desire." Luther may have conflated this with Matt. 8:13.

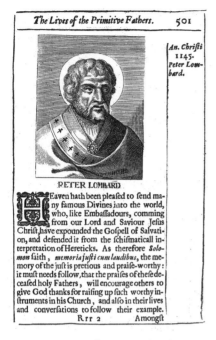

Portrait of Peter Lombard
(c. 1096–1164), bishop of Paris
and author of the standard
medieval textbook for theology,
The Four Books of Sentences.

57. That is, Peter Lombard
(c. 1096–1164), *Sentences* IV.i.3 in
MPL 192:839–40. The *Sentences* quickly
became the basic theological textbook
for medieval theology and earned
for Lombard the title "Master of the
Sentences."

Third, the centurion said [Matt. 8:8], "Only say the word, and my servant will be healed." Certainly he believed in and obtained what was done for him in a specific, immediate way, not according to a general faith.

Fourth, according to John 4[:50]: The official "believed the word that Jesus spoke to him," that is, "Go; your son will live." By means of this faith he saved his son's life. So indeed all persons[g] approaching God should believe that they will receive what they request, or they will not receive it.

Fifth, Christ says in Mark [11:24], "Truly I tell you, whatever you ask in prayer, believe that you receive it, and you will." Notice that he says "whatever," allowing for no exception. It is clear, however, that we ask for something in the sacrament, for no one goes to the sacrament unless it is for grace. Therefore we must listen to Christ when he says, "Believe that you receive it, and you will."[h] Otherwise all things in the church would waver and nothing would stand for certain, which is absurd.

Sixth, this passage [Matt. 17:20]: "If you have faith as a grain of mustard seed, you will say to this mountain, 'Move hence to yonder place,' and it will move; and nothing will be impossible to you." And if you look through the entire gospel you will find many other examples, all of which refer not to a general but to a particular faith and which pertain to achieving some immediate result. For this reason, a firm faith is necessary if a person wishes to receive pardon, since the sacraments of the New Testament, according to the Master [of the *Sentences*], were instituted for motivating and activating our faith.[57]

Seventh, for this reason the Lord often rebuked the disciples, especially Peter, for lack of faith—not lack of general faith, but of special faith concerning a specific, immediate need.[i]

Eighth, James 1[:5-8] says: "If any of you is lacking in wisdom, ask God . . . in faith, never doubting, for the one

g　Singular in the original text.
h　Mark 11:24b.
i　Cf. Matt. 8:26.

who doubts is like the wave of the sea that is driven and tossed by the wind ... who ... must not expect to receive anything from the Lord." That is certainly a most unequivocal statement, which also leads me to the conclusion that no one who doubts about receiving grace or wisdom can receive it. Nor do I see what one can say against this conclusion.

Ninth, the holy Virgin would never have conceived the Son of God if she had not believed the annunciation of the angel. Thus she said, "Let it be to me according to your word" [Luke 1:38], just as Elizabeth proclaimed, "Blessed is she who believed that there would be a fulfillment of what was spoken to her from the Lord" [Luke 1:45]. Hence St. Bernard and the universal church marveled at her faith.[58] Likewise Hannah, the mother of Samuel, after she believed the word of Eli, went her way, "and her countenance was no longer sad."[j] On the other hand, the children of Israel, because they did not believe the word of promise concerning the land of Canaan, perished in the wilderness.

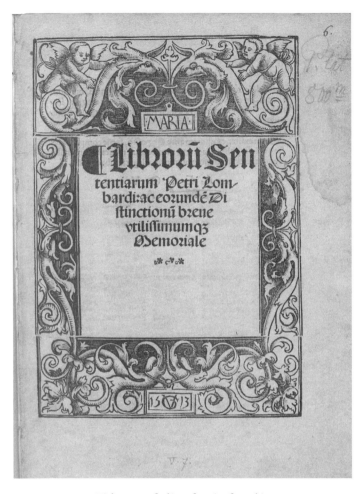

Title page of a list of topics found in Peter Lombard's *The Four Books of Sentences.*

Briefly, whatever remarkable things we read about in the Old and New Testaments, we read that they were accomplished by faith, not by works or general faith, but by faith directed to the accomplishment of an immediate end. Hence

58. Luther is referring to Bernard of Clairvaux's (1090–1153) *Sermon on the Annunciation,* which he cites in his eleventh point below.

j 1 Sam. 1:18

nothing else is so highly praised in Scripture as faith, especially that of Abraham, as in Rom. 4[:1-5], which was a faith in the fact that a son Isaac was to be born to him. Nevertheless, "it was reckoned to him as righteousness."[k] Thus, it is also with us in the sacrament: If we believe, we shall receive grace; if we do not believe, we shall go to our judgment.

Tenth, St. Augustine says in his treatment of the Gospel of St. John, "When the Word is coupled with the element, it becomes a sacrament . . . not because it takes place, but because it is believed."[l] One can see that baptism cleanses a person, not because it takes place, but because that one believes that it cleanses. For this reason, the Lord said in absolving Mary, "Your faith has saved you; go in peace" [Luke 7:50].[59] Hence this common saying: "Not faith's sacrament but the sacrament's faith justifies."[m] Without this faith it is impossible to have peace of conscience, as it is written in Rom. 5[:1], "Therefore, since we are justified by faith, we have peace with God."

Eleventh, St. Bernard says in his first sermon on the annunciation, "You must above all believe that you cannot have forgiveness of sins except through the mercy of God. . . . But add to this that you believe this, too: that your sins are forgiven by God. This is the testimony that the Holy Spirit brings forth in your heart, saying, 'Your sins are forgiven.' Thus the Apostle concludes 'that a person is justified by faith' [Rom. 3:28] out of grace."[60,n]

These and many other explicit passages lead me inexorably to the position stated above. For this reason, Most Reverend Father in Christ, since you are blessed by divine favor with unusual gifts, especially with keen judgment, I humbly

59. Here Luther follows the medieval tradition of associating the unnamed woman in Luke 7 with Mary Magdalene.

60. Bernard of Clairvaux, whom Luther sometimes called the last father of the church, provided important insights for Luther's understanding of justification and faith. Especially his sermons on the Annunciation spurred Luther's theological development. See Franz Posset, *The Real Luther: A Friar at Erfurt and Wittenberg* (St. Louis: Concordia, 2011), 86–128.

---

k   See Gen. 15:6.

l   Augustine, *Tractates in John*, 80.3 in NPNF, ser. 1, 7:344 (MPL 35:1840). The sentence that follows is a paraphrase from the same section of Augustine's sermon on John 15.

m   This saying is also found in Luther's *Conclusions for Investigating the Truth and Consoling Fearful Consciences* (1518) in WA 1:629–33.

n   Bernard of Clairvaux, *Sermon on the Annunciation*, 1.1, 3 (MPL 183:383–84).

beg Your Most Reverend highness to deal leniently with me, to have compassion with my conscience, to show me how I may understand this doctrine differently, and not to compel me to revoke those things which I must believe according to the testimony of my conscience. As long as these Scripture passages stand, I cannot do otherwise, for I know that one must obey God rather than mortals [Acts 5:29].

May it please your highness to intercede with our most holy lord, Leo X,[61] on my behalf, so that he will not proceed against me with such stern rigor that he cast my soul into darkness. I seek nothing but the light of truth, and I am prepared to give up, change, or revoke everything if I am informed that these passages are to be understood in another sense, for I am neither arrogant nor so eager for vainglory that I would be ashamed to revoke ill-founded doctrines. Indeed, it will please me most of all if the truth is victorious. However, I do not want to be compelled to affirm something contrary to my conscience, for I believe without the slightest doubt that this is the meaning of Scripture. May the Lord Jesus direct and preserve you in eternity, Most Reverend Father. Amen.[62]

[63]When I presented Cajetan with the above statement the next day, he at first considered it worthless and said that it consisted of mere words. But then he said that he would send it to Rome. Meanwhile he insisted that I recant, threatening me with the punishments that had been recommended to him, and he said that if I did not recant, I should leave him and stay out of his sight. When I heard this and realized that he was firm in his position and would not consider the Scripture passages, and since I had also determined I would not recant, I left, with no hope of returning. Even though he said and now still boasts that he would have acted toward me as a father and not as a judge, I could not detect any such paternal attitude, except one that was sterner than any court of justice. All he did was demand that I recant against my conscience. At least he did not show a desire or the ability to demonstrate to me where I was wrong or to convince me of my error, for when he saw that I rejected the comments

61. Leo X was pope from 1513 until his death in 1521. He presided over Luther's case and in 1520 promulgated the bull, *Exsurge Domini*, which threatened Luther with excommunication.

62. Luther's written response to Cajetan ends here. This appeal to a conscience bound by Scripture, not unknown in the church's tradition, will recur in Luther's statement at the Diet of Worms. See LW 32:112.

63. THE THIRD MEETING: 14 OCTOBER 1518

64. That is, Cajetan's objections to thesis 58 and the explanation to thesis 7.

65. This canon could not be identified. Here Luther uses irony to contrast his use of Scripture, which included reference to the interpretations of Augustine and Bernard, to what he perceived was Cajetan's spontaneous, personal reinterpretations of the texts from the Bible that Luther had proposed.

66. Cajetan's diffident response brought Luther to state more clearly his objection to papal supremacy in biblical interpretation. See below, *Address to the Christian Nobility*, p. 380f.

of the opinionated scholastics, he promised to take action against me on the basis of Holy Scripture and canon law. What he meant by this, I do not know, for he never produced a syllable from the Holy Scriptures against me, and to the present day he could not do so, even if he were to put forth a special effort, since there is universal agreement that nothing in the Holy Scriptures mentions indulgences. On the contrary, the Scriptures commend faith and are as devoid of references to indulgences as they are full of teaching concerning faith, so that it is impossible for the legate thereby to demolish either one of these two articles.[64]

As a matter of fact, when I quoted the Scriptures to prove my points, that man [Cajetan] began in a paternal way to conjure up glosses out of his own imagination. And while he so readily used the *Extravagante* against me, he cleverly pretended not to know that canon, on the basis of which the church prohibits anyone from interpreting the Scriptures solely on one's own authority.[65] According to Hilary, one should not read meaning into the Holy Scriptures, but extract it from them.[o] Nevertheless, I was not overly annoyed with his distortion of the Bible, knowing that he had become accustomed to that kind of interpretation through his contacts with the long-established practice of the Roman Curia and the work of scholastic quibblers. It has long been believed that whatever the Roman Church says, damns, or wants, all people must eventually say, damn, or want, and that no other reason need be given than that the Apostolic See and the Roman Church hold that opinion.[66] Therefore, since the sacred Scriptures are abandoned and human traditions and words are accepted, it happens that the church of Christ is not nourished "by its own measure of wheat"[p] nor

o Hilary of Poitiers (c. 300–c. 368), *On the Trinity* I.18, in MPL 10:38, a text Luther already quotes in his first lectures on the Psalms (1513, on Psalm 1) in LW 10:13.

p Cf. Luke 12:42.

by the word of Christ, but is usually misled by the indiscretion and rash will of an unlearned flatterer. We have come to this in our great misfortune that these people begin to force us to renounce the Christian faith and deny Holy Scripture.

Furthermore, if that is what is involved in the revocation demanded of me, I foresee only that one revocation will be followed by another and so on *ad infinitum*. For if I should answer one of his statements with a skill equal to his, he would quickly conjure up against me another idol out of his imagination (for Thomistic theology is remarkably fertile in producing subtle distinctions, a veritable Proteus),[67] which I should be compelled to submit to with another revocation. For since he wanders about, not on solid rock, but on the sand of his own ideas,[q] I should be burdened with perpetual revocation.

Therefore, having received the command not to return, I nevertheless remained there that day. Then Cajetan summoned my reverend and most excellent father, Vicar Johann von Staupitz, and, it is said, he urged him to induce me to make a free revocation. I remained another day and received no orders.[68] I remained a third day, that is, Sunday, and sent a letter but received no answer.[69] I remained a fourth day, and nothing happened.[70] There was the same silence on the fifth day. Finally, on the advice of my friends and especially in view of the fact that Cajetan had previously announced that he had an order to throw me and the vicar into jail, and since I had prepared my appeal for public posting,[71] I left, feeling that I had shown sufficient obedience despite my dangerous position.[72]

---

q   Cf. Matt. 7:24-27.

---

67. Proteus was a character from Greek mythology, whose prophetic gifts could be accessed only when bound. To escape capture he would assume various shapes. Luther compares him to the shifty Scholastic debaters among his opponents who, in his view, failed to debate in a straightforward manner. Cf. Homer, *Odyssey* iv.351 and Virgil, *Georgics* iv.386.

68. On 16 October 1518, Luther gave his appeal to a notary. See Spehr, *Luther und das Konzil*, 90, referring to WA 2:27–33.

69. That is, October 17. See WA Br 1:220–21 (trans. in Preserved Smith, *The Life and Letters of Martin Luther* [New York: Barnes & Noble, 1911], 52–53). In this letter Luther expresses regret for having spoken harshly about papal use of Scripture and promises a moratorium of discussion on indulgences, if his opponents agreed. Cajetan did not respond. See also Brecht 1:258–59.

70. On 18 October 1518, Luther wrote a final letter to Cajetan (see LW 48:87–89).

71. This appeal to Pope Leo X over Cajetan's decision was officially posted at the Augsburg Cathedral on 22 October 1518. See Spehr, *Luther und das Konzil*, 91.

72. Luther left Augsburg on 20 October 1518.

73. LUTHER'S REFLECTIONS ON THE
PROCEEDINGS ESPECIALLY IN LIGHT
OF CAJETAN'S LETTER
TO FREDERICK THE WISE

Martin Luther (1483–1546) and Frederick III,
the Elector of Saxony (r. 1483–1525), also known as
Frederick the Wise, kneel before the crucified Jesus.

74. Here Luther answers the charge
of behaving with pride, a mark of
heretics, vis-à-vis his refusal to recant.

[73] Now, my reader, you must listen to me again. I presented my last response with great reverence and at the same time submitted it to the judgment of the pope. You must not, however, believe that I did this because I entertained any doubt concerning the cause itself, or that I should ever change my mind, for divine truth is master over even the pope, and I do not await the judgment of a man when I have learned the judgment of God. But I waited only because I needed to give reverence to him who acted as the pope's representative, and because one should assert and defend that which is undoubtedly true with humility and fear.[74]

It makes no difference what you think of my first explanation,[r] for there is no danger involved, whether it stands or falls. Indulgences gain nothing in importance if that explanation is refuted and proven false, and they lose nothing if it is victorious and proven true, for it has little to do with the main issue at stake, unless by craftily bringing it up an attempt is made to throw doubt upon my *95 Theses* as a whole. If I had wished to act more haughtily in the presence of the legate, I could have refused to utter a single word, for I had already presented and explained the whole matter to the pope so that there was nothing more for me to do but to await his verdict.[s]

---

r   Regarding the *Extravagante*.

s   That is, the *Explanations of the Ninety-Five Theses*, which was dedicated to Pope Leo X. See LW 31:80 and, for a translation of excerpts of the dedication, Smith, *The Life and Letters of Martin Luther*, 44–46.

In the latter answer, however, lies the whole summary of salvation. You are not a bad Christian because you do or do not know about the *Extravagante*. You are a heretic, however, if you deny faith in Christ's word. How much I repress and do not mention here, you will surely notice, good reader, but not without groaning.

One thing, however, I do not wish to conceal from you, namely, that I sought nothing in this hearing except the true meaning of Scripture, which those so-called holy decretals,[t] if they do not actually corrupt, certainly obscure for us in many places with their distorted and malevolent words and hide, as it were, the brightest sun with a cloud. This I will someday treat in greater detail, especially if some Roman flatterer should oppose me.[75] God willing, I will then distinguish myself as a jurist and theologian, even though I shall hardly please anyone, especially not the flatterers of the Roman Curia, for I have recently longed to play war with them, as Joshua waged war against the people of Ai.[u] Meanwhile I am giving you a foretaste of what is to come, namely, that my conclusion is really in opposition to the *Extravagante*, which is in fact false and erroneous and should be revoked. For this reason, I solemnly revoke it in this writing and pronounce it damned.[76]

I also publicly declare that this writing was composed by me and now pleases me so much that I would compose it now if I had not already done so. In the second place, I reject, damn, and detest that *Extravagante* as false and erroneous, deserving of rejection. And I state that it would have been better if it had been put into other words, not because it misrepresents the meaning of its authors, but because it presents an erroneous theological meaning, for its words are used contrary to the most obvious meaning of Scripture.

This is my revocation. I hope that I have satisfied even my enemies. Do you, my reader, think that I am insane or drunk? I am not insane and speak with words of sobriety.

75. Instead, in response to the threat of his excommunication in 1520, Luther consigned a copy of canon law to the flames along with the bull of excommunication, *Exsurge Domini*.

76. Luther uses the traditional language of recantation to "revoke" the authority of *Extravagante* itself.

---

t   See p. 133, n. 36.

u   Cf. Josh. 8:3-29.

77. Refers to Cajetan's letter to Frederick, dated 25 October 1518 (see WA Br 1:233).

78. These examples from canon law distort what for Luther is the obvious meaning of the biblical text.

79. The text is contained in the *Decretals of Pope Gregory IX*, bk. 1, title II ("De constitutionibus"), ch. 3 (beginning with the words "Translato sacerdotio").

To prove this, I will make clear even to the most unlearned that the popes are accustomed to doing violence to the Holy Scriptures in their decretals. The most reverend legate was most displeased with the fact that, as he wrote to the most illustrious Elector Frederick, I had not even spared the holiness of the pope.[77] And he added that I had said "things not deserving of repetition," because I accused the pope of twisting and abusing the Scriptures. Therefore I must make it clear that he cannot deny that the pope forced the meaning of Scripture.[78]

In the first place, the decretal *De Constitutionibus*, beginning with the words *Translato sacerdotio*, states that if the priesthood were changed, the law must also be changed.[79] These are words of the Apostle to the Hebrews [7:12] that the temporal priesthood had ended and the law of Moses had been abrogated by the eternal priesthood of Christ, which succeeded it. This is the true and genuine meaning of these words. But the meaning of this decretal is this: "The priesthood of Christ is transferred from Moses to Christ and from Christ to Peter."ᵛ The jurists interpreted these words in this manner, and the pope either permitted or approved it. Who, however, does not see that this is a distortion and abuse of the meaning of the words? It is indeed such a distortion that, if it is not modified with the greatest industry, it will be both unorthodox and impious. For it is most impious to say that the priesthood of Christ is abrogated and finished, so that Peter may be the priest and lawgiver while Christ is deposed. For this is what the word *translatio*, used by the Apostle, really means. I do not want Peter or Paul to be the priest, since each one is a sinner who has no sacrifice to offer for me or even for himself. I shall say nothing about the most abominable arrogance of which such an interpretation reeks, by maintaining that the priesthood of Christ without a doubt had been conferred upon Peter alone by

---

ᵛ   Luther is quoting the so-called ordinary gloss on the text, comments by Bernard of Parma [Bernard of Botone, d. c. 1266], composed around 1263 and included in all printed versions of Gregory IX's *Decretals*.

Christ, as though the other apostles remained laymen, or were ordained priests and apostles by Peter. Therefore, if I should now state my thesis as follows: "The priesthood of Christ was conferred neither upon Peter nor the pope," and the most reverend legate would then confront me with this decretal, and, with his majestic bearing and thunderous eloquence, he would demand that I recant. And if I should answer that the pope twisted the Scriptures and abused its words—while my thesis was true in a theological sense and the decretal was perchance true in some other, distorted sense—do you think that I should be terrified by the threats of human words used to frighten me, as though I had said something which did not "deserve repetition" and had not spared the holiness of the pope? I will honor the holiness of the pope, but I will worship the holiness of Christ and of truth.

Likewise, if I should treat the passage in Matt. 16[:18-19], "You are Peter, and I will give you the keys to the kingdom of heaven," and "Whatever you loose," either in the classroom or in the pulpit, and should propound this thesis, "By these words one cannot prove that the Roman Church has a higher rank than other churches in the entire world." And the most reverend legate would confront me, no doubt with commotion and indignation over what I had said, with *distinctio* XXI of Gratian's *Decretum*.[w] There Pope Pelagius[80] emphatically states that "not by synodical decrees but by the word of the gospel"—to be sure "by the word," but not the sense—"was the Roman Church given pre-eminence above all other churches." And if he would add this passage of the Apostle Matthew, do you believe that I should abandon the sense of the gospel and embrace the interpretation of [Pope] Pelagius, who boasts that he follows "the word" but not the sense of the gospel? Not that I condemn or deny the new rule of the Romans of our day, but I do not wish the power of Scripture to be reduced to mere words, and I reject the folly of certain very simple-minded men, who would fix the church of

80. Pelagius II (520–590), not to be confused with Pelagius (c. 354–c. 420), the British monk and opponent of Augustine in the fifth century. Later editions of Gratian correct this to read Pope Gelasius (d. 496), in a letter from 494 or 496.

w   Gratian, *Decretum*, dist. xxi, c. 3 (MPL 187:119).

81. Luther refers to the Orthodox churches of eastern Europe, Asia Minor, and North Africa.

82. Pope Gregory I (c. 540–604), one of four patristic teachers [doctores] of the Western church along with Ambrose of Milan, Augustine, and Jerome (c. 347–420). Already Leo I (d. 461) used the term "universal [ecumenical] bishop," an honorific bestowed on the four patriarchs (bishops of Jerusalem, Antioch, Constantinople, and Rome) by the Roman emperor.

83. In his correspondence, beginning with letters to the patriarch of Constantinople, John the Faster (d. 595), Pope Gregory rebukes his Eastern counterpart for using the term "universal bishop" and refuses to accept it for himself. See Gregory's letters, V.18-21, 43; VI.60; VII.13, 34, 40; VIII.30 (MPL 77:738-51, 770-74, 813-14, 867-69, 892-95, 898-900, 931-34); and W. H. C. Frend, *The Rise of Christianity* (Philadelphia: Fortress Press, 1984), 890-92.

84. Cyprian of Carthage (d. 258) corresponded with Cornelius, bishop of Rome (d. 253), during the Decian persecution in 251 to 252. See, e.g., his letter, no. 41 (MPL 3:700). Augustine corresponded with Pope Boniface I (d. 422), among others bishops of Rome. See his letter, no. 98 (MPL 33:359), where he calls Boniface a "co-bishop."

Christ in time and place. As Christ said [Luke 17:20], "The kingdom of God is not coming with signs to be observed." And who dare deny that one can be a Christian who does not submit to the pope and his decretals? Thus, for more than eight hundred years they have thrown out of the church of Christ Christians in all the East and Africa, who never were under the pope or even understood the gospel in that sense.[81] For until the time of St. Gregory, the Roman pope was not addressed as the universal bishop.[82] Even Gregory himself, although he is bishop of Rome, attacks most vehemently the name of the universal bishop and pope of the entire church in more than six letters.[83] Therefore he does not hesitate to call this designation profane, he who alone in our time is called most holy. Just as Peter did not create the other apostles, for this is what ordination of bishops is called today, so the successor of Peter created no successor to the other apostles. Finally, other bishops did not call the Roman pope anything but brother and fellow bishop and colleague, as Cyprian addressed Cornelius and Augustine addressed Boniface and others.[84]

Because of this, the church fathers[85] did not understand Matthew's statement, "I give you . . ." [Matt. 16:19] in the sense of the above holy canon, as though Christ addressed Peter in preference to the others. But they say that "one" stands for "all" in order to express the equality of all, because that which Peter answers, one and all answer. Therefore Matthew also expresses the same meaning in the plural in another place: "Whatever you bind . . ." [Matt. 18:18],[x] so what is said to one is said to all. Finally, the Holy Spirit did not descend upon Peter first on Pentecost [Acts 2], and we do not read that he breathed upon Peter first [John 20:22-23]. Even if the Holy Spirit had actually done so, Peter still would not have become a ruler in preference to the other apostles.

Therefore I admit that canon may be true, but it is true in an improper sense. My thesis on the other hand is true in

---

x   See Matt. 18:18: "Truly I tell you, whatever you bind on earth will be bound in heaven, and whatever you loose on earth will be loosed in heaven."

an evangelical and proper sense. If papal rule can be proven, it should be proven by that passage of the Apostle in Rom. 13[:1]: "For there is no authority except from God, and those that exist have been instituted by God." By virtue of this, strictly speaking, I say that we are subjected to the Roman See as long as it pleases God, who alone, and not the Roman pontiff, changes and establishes authority.[86]

Many such things and others as well, my dear reader, you will find in the sacred decretals, which, if you use "the nose of the bride overlooking Damascus,"[y] that is, a nose of flesh and blood, you often will be offended by the smell.

I now say the following about the *Extravagante*: The merits of Christ are not a treasure of indulgences, for they work grace without the pope.[z] This statement is evangelical, for it is written in many places in the Bible that we are justified by the blood and obedience of Christ. Paul, for example, says in Rom. 5[:19], "By one man's obedience"—I believe this obedience to be the merits of Christ—"many will be made righteous." No one is saved by indulgences, however. To maintain this concerning the merits of Christ is contrary to the clear meaning of the Scriptures. Therefore I do not care whether this statement is contrary to an *Extravagante* or an *Intravagante*.[87] The truth of Scripture comes first. After that is accepted, one may determine whether human words can be accepted as true. I certainly would never dare to assert that people "become friends of God" through indulgences, as the *Extravagante* expressly states when, in reference to a passage in Proverbs concerning participation in eternal wisdom, it applies this to participation in indulgences.[88]

Those Scripture passages were authoritative long before the time of that *Extravagante*, from which they certainly did not obtain their authority. Moreover, one cannot say that they refer to indulgences, since everyone in the church knows that there is nothing in Scripture concerning indulgences. It necessarily follows that if certain passages are interpreted

85. John Chrysostom (c. 347–407), *Homilies on Matthew*, LIV.3 (NPNF, ser. 2, 10:319), refers the "rock" to Peter's faith, as does Erasmus in his *Annotationes* of 1516, where he specifically rejects the application of this text to the Roman popes. Luther is referring to an interpretive tool called synecdoche (where the part signifies the whole), which was used commonly in medieval exegesis, including on this text by Nicholas of Lyra (c. 1270–1349), *Postilla super totam Bibliam*, ad loc.

86. This reduction of papal authority to that of all rulers, inside and outside the church, via Romans 13 will continue to be debated in the ensuing decades. See Hendrix, *Luther and the Papacy*, 67–70.

87. Here Luther makes a play on words. That is, either a canon wandering around outside the earlier editions of canon law, or one wandering around within canon law.

88. See the translation of *Extravagante* above in the introduction, pp. 127–28, and Wisdom of Sol. 7:14, which reads in the Latin: "For [wisdom] is an infinite treasure to human beings, which they that use become the friends of God."

---

y   Cf. Song of Sol. 7:4. Luther, like his contemporaries, understands this text allegorically, as related to the church and Christ.

z   A paraphrase of thesis 58 of the *95 Theses*. See above, p. 42.

as referring to them, as is the case here, violence is done to them, and they are quoted nonliterally and improperly. Nevertheless, I shall out of reverence admit that the *Extravagante* is true, and I attempt to maintain both meanings.[a] Then I am told: "You must follow that meaning (the inferior one) and deny the other (the true one)." Therefore, if I am compelled to call my statement false, I shall do so, but at the same time I shall declare the *Extravagante* doubly false.

For if they accuse me of maintaining an opinion concerning indulgences that is contrary to common belief, I clearly acknowledge this to be the case. Furthermore, I admit that I have done this intentionally for the purpose of bringing up for discussion this common belief that the merits of Christ are called the treasury of indulgences. I knew that this was the common belief, but to me it seemed to ring false. For this reason, I formulated the thesis that the keys,[b] given the church by virtue of the merits of Christ, constituted this treasure.[c] Thus I did not entirely separate the merits of Christ from indulgences, but I interpreted the merits according to a sense other than that held by common opinion. If I had not wished to contradict this common opinion in humility and reverence, I would have refrained from saying that the keys were given by virtue of the merit of Christ, thereby completely excluding the merits of Christ from my discussion. In fact, however, I employed them for the purpose of toning down my contradiction. I should not, however, have committed a mortal sin if I had boldly opposed the *Extravagante* and had quoted St. Jerome.[89] Speaking of those who consider whatever they say to be the law of God, Jerome said, "They disdain to know what the prophets and the apostles thought"—note the word *thought*—"but they accommodate unsuitable testimony to their own interpretation, as though it were a grand and not most vicious kind of teaching to distort passages and to bend the Scripture

89. Jerome was especially known for his biblical interpretation and his translation of the Bible into Latin (the Vulgate).

---

a   That is, both interpretations of the biblical text, Luther's and that of *Extravagante*.

b   See p. 138, n. 45.

c   Thesis 60.

passage which opposes them to suit their wishes."*d* This is certainly what the *Extravagante* does, for it applies words concerning the merits of Christ, by which sins are forgiven, to indulgences. I ask you to note the adaptation whereby this is achieved.

The merits of Christ take away sins and increase the merits of the believer. Indulgences take away the merits and leave the sins.[90] Can the same Scripture text be properly understood to apply to both? I believe that even Orestes would deny this.[91] Nevertheless, out of reverence, I have intentionally admitted it and, although I went too far, affirmed it. Finally, since the *Extravagante* is obscure and indeed wanders about in its words, now saying that the merits of Christ are the treasure of indulgences, and then that they have acquired them, I made a statement which can at once constitute my opinion as opposed to the common one. And now in the face of such dubious twisting of God's words and "falsifying of meaning" (as Jerome calls it), should I make a definite revocation when not convicted of my error? I will not do that. On the contrary, I consistently and confidently deny that the merits of Christ are in any way in the hands of the pope as the words [of *Unigenitus*] state. Let the pope himself see how he understands his *Extravagante*.

May it suffice for the time being that I have shown that the true and proper meaning of Scripture is not found in all the papal decretals. Therefore, one cannot say, maintain, or think otherwise than they prescribe without doing injustice to them, since they themselves assign to the teachers of the church the function of interpreting Scripture and keep to themselves the right of judging between conflicting matters. Accordingly, the juridical competence differs from the theological.[92] Many things are permitted in the former that are prohibited in the latter. Jurists may emphasize their traditions, whereas we theologians preserve the purity of Scripture. We do this particularly because in our time we see evil

90. For a similar argument, see *The Sermon on Indulgences and Grace* above, pp. 62–64. Luther is assuming here a traditional understanding of forgiveness (spoken in the confessional) that led to a person doing (meritorious) good works to lessen the remaining temporal punishment for sin.

91. Orestes, son of Agamemnon and Clytemnestra in Greek mythology, killed his mother to avenge her killing his father. In some versions of the story (notably Aeschylus's *Eumenides*), Orestes goes mad as a result. Luther is saying even a madman would recognize the contradiction.

92. Here Luther is contrasting the judicial use of canon law, which he still views as legitimate, from the work of theology to explicate Scripture.

d Jerome, *Epist.* LIII.7 (MPL 22:544), his letter to Paulinus on the study of the Scriptures.

93. At the request of Emperor Maximillian I and King Louis XII (1462–1515) of France, a council was held in Pisa and Milan in 1511 and 1512 with the aim of "reforming the church in head and members," in this case Pope Julius II (1443–1513). Julius in response called his own council, Lateran V, which met in Rome intermittently from 1512 to 1517. His successor affirmed the Lateran Council and rejected the other, strengthening papal prestige and authority, especially through the papal bull *Pastor aeternus* (above, n. 32).

94. LEGAL BRIEF FROM POPE LEO X TO CARDINAL CAJETAN

95. Technical term for a legal brief used in ecclesiastical cases.

96. Luther is suggesting that someone wrote this letter in Germany and then sent it to the pope to be returned to Cajetan as a special legal brief.

flatterers appear, who elevate the pope over the councils. The consequence is that one council is condemned by another until nothing certain remains for us. And finally, one man, the pope, can crush all things underfoot, since he is at the same time both above the council and within it. He is above it since he can condemn it, within it since he accepts authority from the council as from a higher power, by means of which he becomes higher than the council.[93] There are also those who brazenly state in public that the pope cannot err and is above Scripture. If these monstrous claims were admitted, Scripture would perish and consequently the church also, and nothing would remain in the church but the word of humans. These flatterers actually seek to arouse hatred for the church, and then its ruin and destruction. For this reason, dear reader, I declare before you that I cherish and follow the church in all things. I resist only those who in the name of the Roman Church strive to erect a Babylon for us.[e] And they wish that whatever occurs to them—if only they could move the tongue enough to mention the Roman Church—be accepted as the interpretation of the Roman Church, as if Holy Scripture no longer existed (according to which [as Augustine says][f] we must judge all things), but against which the Roman Church certainly never teaches or acts.

[94] Numbered among those people, I believe, are those suave sycophants who dictated a certain apostolic breve[95] against me, the contents of which I wish to publish so that you may see what clever tricks they used. For I wish to prove, or at least to arouse a suspicion by means of the attached letter, that this breve was composed in Germany and then, with special assiduity, was sent to Rome, and finally, perhaps at the suggestion of some important person of Rome, returned to Germany.[96] This pertains to the account of my hearing.

---

e   See *The Babylonian Captivity of the Church* (1520), in LW 36:3–126.

f   Augustine, *City of God*, XI.3, in NPNF, ser. 1, 2:206.

To our beloved Son Thomas, our cardinal priest of the titular church of St. Sixtus and our legate of the apostolic chair, from Pope Leo X.[g]

Our dear son: greeting and apostolic blessing. After we had learned that one Martin Luther, professor of the Order of Augustinian Hermits, harboring an evil doctrine, had asserted several ideas which are heretical and deviate from the doctrines of the Holy Roman Church, and in addition to this had dared to publish in several parts of Germany his theses and even scandalous pamphlets with extraordinary rashness and obstinacy, indifferent toward obedience and without consulting the Roman Church, the mistress of faith; we, wishing to correct his rashness in a paternal manner, commissioned our Brother Jerome,[97] bishop of Ascoli, general auditor of the Apostolic Chamber of the Curia, to cite this Martin to appear personally before him and to be examined with respect to the above-mentioned accusations and to answer for his faith under threat of certain specified punishments. The said auditor, Jerome, has issued such a citation to the above-mentioned Martin, as we learned later.[98]

Now, however, it has come to our attention that this Martin has abused our kindness and has become more insolent than ever, adding evil to evil and stubbornly persisting in his heresy. He has even gone so far as to publish certain other theses and slanderous pamphlets, in which there are additional heretical and erroneous doctrines. This, indeed, has perturbed us no little.

As it is incumbent upon us, according to our pastoral office, to counteract such actions, and since we wish to prevent a plague of this kind from spreading until it infects the souls of simple people, we command

97. Girolamo Ghinucci of Siena (1480–1541), secretary to Julius II, who named him bishop of Ascoli. Leo X appointed him "auditor," that is, Supreme Justice of the Papal Curia. He became a cardinal in 1538.

98. Luther received this notice on 7 August 1518, as he himself recounts below, p. 163.

g   This title was part of the original. The translation in LW 31:286–89 is based upon Preserved Smith, *Luther's Correspondence and other Contemporary Letters* (1913), 101–4, and retains the officious tone of the Latin original.

99. Maximilian I, Austrian (Habsburg) archduke and Holy Roman Emperor. The references to princes and other authorities is an attempt to list the legal entities that had standing in the empire and were thus represented at the imperial diet. They could thus claim a certain sovereignty and had to be included in any attempt to extirpate Luther's teachings from the Holy Roman Empire.

100. Latin: "*in Albo praetorio.*" This refers to the ancient Roman custom of writing official notices on a white tablet. In this case, the "tablets of the praetor" were the inscribed edicts of the praetor (the Roman magistrate charged with administration of justice). Lewis and Short, *A Latin Dictionary*, q.v. "Albus" and "Praetor." (Published by HarperBrothers, New York, 1879. Now in several electronic search engines.)

through this letter your circumspection—in which we place the greatest confidence in the Lord, on the one hand because of your exceptional learning and experience and on the other because of your sincere devotion toward us and this holy chair, of which you are an honorable member. Thus, as soon as you have received this letter and without any delay, since this matter is by report and also by established fact notorious and inexcusable among us, you drive and compel the said Martin, declared a heretic by the said auditor, to appear personally before you. To accomplish this, secure the support of our most beloved sons in Christ, Maximilian, elected emperor of the Romans, as well as of the remaining German princes, cities, corporations, and other powers, ecclesiastical as well as secular.[99] After he has been handed over to you, hold him in faithful custody until you have a further order from us that he be brought before us and the apostolic chair.

If he should come before you of his own free will, seeking forgiveness for this rashness, and if, after a change of heart, he should show signs of repentance, we give you the authority to receive him into the unity of the holy mother church, which never closes its bosom to one who returns to her. If, however, he perseveres in his stubbornness and defies secular authority, we give you the authority to have him and all his adherents and followers branded in all parts of Germany through public edicts—like those which once upon a time were written on the praetor's tablets[100]—as heretics, excommunicates, anathematized, and damned, and to be shunned as such by all faithful Christians. And that this disease be exterminated more quickly and easily, we give you authority to admonish and require of all prelates, collectively and individually, and other ecclesiastics, both secular and regular of any order, including the mendicant orders, and also dukes, margraves, counts, barons, cities, corporations, and magistrates (with the exception of the said Maximilian, the elected emperor) by our authority, and also under the threat of the sentence of excommunication and other punishments to be enumerated below, that they seize the said Martin and his adherents and followers and hand them over to you, if they desire to be considered believers.

If, however, which God forbid and which we cannot believe will happen, the said princes, cities, corporations, and magistrates, collectively or individually, should in any way receive the said Martin or his adherents and followers or give the same Martin aid, counsel, or public or secret favor, directly or indirectly, for any reason or in any manner whatsoever, we will place under the interdict of the church[101] all the cities, towns, lands, and other places of those princes, cities, corporations, and magistrates, and also the cities, towns, lands, and other places to which the said Martin should go, as long as said Martin should remain there more than three days. Moreover, we also warn collectively and individually the said princes, cities, corporations, and magistrates that, in addition to the said punishment, as far as the ecclesiastics and the said regular clergy are concerned, they will be deprived of their churches, monasteries, and all ecclesiastical benefices. They will also be rendered incapable of holding these in the future. And, as far as the laity is concerned (the emperor excepted) they will also be deprived of their feudal holdings.[102] They will be considered dishonorable and incapable of conducting legal business and will be deprived of Christian burial and of the feudal holdings obtained from us and the Apostolic See or from any secular lords, incurring these punishments, if they do not instantly follow your commands and exhortations without any reservation, contradiction, and opposition, and they do not abstain from giving any counsel, aid, favor, and asylum to those mentioned above.

On the other hand, we grant you by means of this letter the authority to give a plenary indulgence or any compensation or grace to those who are obedient according to your judgment. But you must take into

101. This kind of blanket excommunication of an entire jurisdiction, which differed from individual excommunication for especially heinous sins, had been used most effectively by Gregory VII (c. 1015–1085) against Emperor Henry IV (1050–1106), but its overuse and abuse by later popes made it nearly ineffective as a political or ecclesiastical tool for discipline.

102. This was a typical threatened punishment for those who protected heretics. Excepting the emperor reflects the delicate balance between pope and imperial power and may also have indicated the secular authority that would have done the actual removing from office. By including this letter, Luther was clearly playing upon contemporary suspicions about papal interference in imperial affairs.

103. Priests could obtain (even with the Peter's Indulgence, the target of the *95 Theses*) exemptions from such interdicts, which this breve expressly annuls. Such language was often placed in the proclamation of later plenary indulgences, making previous indulgences invalid at least for a specific time.

104. Breves were always signed by the secretary and sealed in red wax with the official seal of the pope, the fish ring, and they included reference to an important church in Rome, usually, as here, St. Peter's.

105. Jacopo Sadoleto (1477–1547), secretary to Leo X.

106. Sadoleto, a correspondent with Erasmus and later opponent of John Calvin, was known for his elegant Latin.

account no obstructing exemptions, privileges, and favors, whether confirmed by oath, apostolic confirmation, or any other authority, or granted in any way to ecclesiastics and regulars of any order, that is, of mendicant orders, churches, monasteries, or communities, or to secular persons, even though it is expressly stipulated in these exemptions that the persons cannot in any way be excommunicated, suspended, or placed under interdict.[103] The contents of these exemptions we expressly repeal and wish to have considered repealed by virtue of this present decree, despite all things to the contrary, just as though they were inserted word for word in the present decree which invalidates them. Given in Rome at St. Peter's under the ring of the fisherman[104] on the 23rd day of August, 1518, the sixth year of our pontificate.

    Jacopo Sadoleto[105]

The Reflections of Friar Martin Luther upon the Preceding Breve[h]

[i] First, the supreme pontiff addresses all cardinals and bishops as his "venerable brethren." This cardinal priest of the titular church of St. Sixtus, however, he addresses as his "beloved son." This was observed so little that in this breve the remarkable author, forgetting his usual literary skill,[106] writes that Bishop Jerome of Ascoli is called "venerable brother" by the pope. This talebearer should have taken to heart the proverb that states, "A liar must have a good memory."[j]

---

h   This subtitle was part of the original text.

i   The first paragraph of these "Reflections" consisted of eight lines blacked out in the first printing of the *Proceedings*, perhaps because it was seen as too much of an affront to the person of the pope. Inserted here is a translation of a copy that escaped censorship. It was discovered in 1888 and published in WA 9:205.

j   See Quintilian, *De institutione oratoria* IV.2.91.

Furthermore, who told the pontiff that I had abused his kindness, for which reason he had me cited to appear before Cajetan through Jerome? Since at the time this breve was issued, or at least when I was supposed to have abused his goodwill, I had not yet heard anything about the citation, as you will see below. But a certain bungling magpie[107] in Germany, seeing my fidelity, croaked loudly.

Then, that I stubbornly persisted in heresy after the citation and admonition of Jerome and published other pamphlets is an outright lie, for I had stopped publishing books, not only before the date of this breve, but also before the date of the admonition, with the exception of the *Explanations*,[k] which I had completed before being cited. But one can readily see that my popular defense[108] had displeased certain hooded fellows.[109] When I made no concession to them, they conjured up for me a certain pope who prophesies concerning the sequence of events and concerning notoriety and inexcusability. That same Leo X whom they conjure up is perhaps born where there is talk about "the reason of the calculated thing and the reason of the calculating thing."[110]

Finally, and most delightful of all, this breve was issued August 23, but I was cited and admonished August 7. Therefore only sixteen days lapsed between the date of the breve and my receipt of the citation. Figure this out, my reader, and you will find that Jerome, bishop of Ascoli, had begun his process against me, had judged, condemned, and declared me a heretic either before the citation had been handed me or on the sixteenth day after that. So now I ask, where then are the sixty days allowed me in my citation, which began on August 7 and ended about October 7? Is that the custom and procedure of the Roman Curia that on the same day it cites, admonishes, accuses, judges, condemns, and declares one guilty, even one who is far from Rome and knows nothing at all of this? What will they answer, unless that they had forgotten to purge themselves with hellebore[111] while they were preparing to fabricate this lie.

107. An allusion to the black-and-white garb of the Dominican Order, perhaps Johann Tetzel.

108. Luther is referring to his German works, especially to his *Sermon on Indulgences and Grace* (above, pp. 56–65) and to his defense of that sermon against Tetzel's attacks, the *Eine Freiheit des Sermons päpstlichen Ablass und Gnade belangend*, of June 1518 (WA 1:380–93).

109. A clear reference to friars such as Tetzel.

110. Luther is making fun of the hairsplitting logic and terminology of the Scholastics.

111. The dried roots of a plant of that name, used already in classical times as a strong purgative to cure insanity.

k   Luther, *Explanations*, LW 31:77–252.

In conclusion, dear reader, accept my admonition in faith: Whatever may happen to my theses and however much they may have emphasized indulgences, I advise you not to fall into my foolish error. For I once believed that the merits of Christ were actually given me through indulgences, and, proceeding in this foolish notion, I taught and preached to the people that, since indulgences were such valuable things, they should not fail to treasure them, and should not consider them cheap or contemptible. I, most stupid of all stupid people, did not notice that by such talk I virtually established a precept touching salvation, or in any case an indispensable counsel, out of mere permissions, liberties, and relaxations.[112] It was my reason that led me to this, since I was deceived by the obscure words of scholastic opinions and *Extravagantes*. I erred. Bear witness to this, dear reader. I recant. Bear witness to this, dear reader.

However, when I saw with open eyes that all the teachers of the church agreed that it was better to dispense with indulgences than to obtain them, and that those were more blessed who themselves rendered satisfaction than those who purchased indulgences, and that indulgences were nothing but the remission of good works by means of which the satisfaction was fulfilled, I soon saw from what followed that they could be despised, indeed, that it was the most salutary advice to abandon and consider them worthless. But to despise, ignore, and consider worthless the holy, precious, and inestimable merits of Christ (that is, indulgences) sounded horrible. Therefore I judged these words not so much as words of counsel but of mad irreverence.

This brought me to the conclusion that indulgences without reference to the merits of Christ were worthless, that only if they were equated with the merits of Christ were they made the most precious of all treasures, and that thus (alas!) the holy, incomparable merits of Christ might be used as a pretext for the filthiest and ugliest servitude to profit.[113]

What Christian would not gladly give his life, not to mention his money, when the wounds, the blood, the sufferings of our sweetest Savior are described, to say nothing of when they are offered to him? On the other hand, what

112. Luther is referring to the traditional division of commands, required by all, and counsels, followed especially by those under a vow, and he contrasts them to indulgences that he now viewed as undermining the true Christian life of repentance and faith.

113. Luther realizes that without tying indulgences to Christ's merits, no one would buy them, but tying them to such merits, as his opponents were wont to do, meant that the "free" grace of God was for sale.

anguish would be yours if you should see that all this would only serve foul profit and that Christ would be sold not only once by one Judas,[114] but repeatedly by innumerable Judases? Therefore may the name of Christ not deceive you! Remember the prophecy that many false christs will come, who in the name of Christ will do such wonders and signs that they will lead—if it is possible—even the elect into error.[l]

Let us assume that my thesis [58] is wrong and that the merits of Christ *are* the treasure of indulgences; but then think what necessarily follows from this assumption and what you must then say, namely, that the merits of Christ are to be ignored and considered worthless and that those people who do not buy the merits of Christ are more blessed than those who most devoutly seek to obtain them. And although the merits of Christ according to their very nature impel a person to do good works, nevertheless, in indulgences they would exempt a person from good works, which is self-contradictory. What by their nature and by the will of God they should accomplish, they would undo by the will of the pope.

I have done my duty, my reader. If you now err, you err without my being to blame.

Farewell.

114. A reference to Judas betraying Jesus for thirty pieces of silver. See Matt. 26:14-16.

[l] Matt. 24:24.

A Sermon on the Meditation of Christ's Holy Passion

1519

DIRK G. LANGE

INTRODUCTION

Luther wrote his meditation on Christ's passion during Lent 1519 in the hopes of counteracting certain devotional practices of his day, where meditation on Christ's passion and the adoration of the cross were understood as meritorious works designed to stimulate hatred against the Jews and sorrow for sin. On the first Sunday in Lent, 13 March 1519, Luther wrote his friend Georg Spalatin (1484–1545), "I am planning a treatise dealing with the meditation on Christ's passion. I do not know, however, whether I shall have enough leisure to write it out. Yet I will try hard."[a] He completed the meditation by 5 April 1519 and sent it to Spalatin.[b]

This text addresses a central issue of medieval piety, especially during Holy Week: the meditation on the suffering and death of Jesus Christ. The passion story, however, had been supplemented and expanded by popular piety with stories focusing first of all on the various tortures that Christ endured and, second, on various participants in the passion,

Theologian and humanist Georg Burckhardt, also called Georg Spalatin (1486–1563), from Spalt near Nuremberg. This painting by Lucas Cranach the Elder is dated 1509.

a   LW 48:114.

b   See WA Br 1:367.

1. The popular legend recounts how Veronica encountered Jesus on his way to the cross and wiped the sweat and blood off his face. As she did so, an image of Jesus' face was imprinted on the cloth or veil.

2. See the significant contribution that Birgit Stolt has made to an appreciation of the emotions in Luther. Birgit Stolt, *"Laßt uns fröhlich springen!" Gefühlswelt und Gefühlsnavigierung in Luthers Reformationsarbeit* (Berlin: Weidler Buchverlag, 2012), 33f. A chapter of her book appears in English as "'. . . And Feel It in the Heart . . .': Luther's Translation of the Bible from the Perspective of the Modern Science of Linguistics and Translating," *Lutheran Quarterly* 28 (2014): 373–400. She argues that the emotive side of Luther's theology was part and parcel of his intellective side. The gospel message affected those who heard it and allowed them to "jump for joy" (LW 53:219).

from the meal at Bethany (John 12) to Judas's betrayal, as well as on the actions of certain disciples. Emotions, reactions, motives were often invented (as were characters and stories such as Veronica[1]) to encourage a sense of participation in the passion and lead to true contrition, a prerequisite for the sacrament of penance. These stories and artifacts, however, fostered an emotional connection to Christ's suffering, which could lead either to contrition or anger at the Jews, who were widely considered chiefly responsible for Christ's death. Luther observes how people use Christ's suffering to keep from suffering (see below, p. 170). For Luther, this prevents an engagement in Christ's suffering for one's own life.

Luther's "meditation" pushes the believer deeper into a personal engagement with the passion. Luther first criticizes pious practices of his contemporaries. He then introduces his central concern: the meditation on Christ's passion should evoke within a person a deep sense of terror. For Luther, the human being is a psychosomatic unity, in which mind, affects (emotions), and body cannot be divided.[2] The experience of faith and such fruits as prayer and meditation have an impact upon all levels of human existence. Already in his lectures on the Bible, Luther distinguishes between God's alien and proper work. "Terror" or "fright" (*erschrecken*) work first to destroy a person's self-centered claims before God, characterized by boasting in works and merits. As in the *Treatise on Baptism* (below, p. 208f), where Luther argues that the identity human beings claim for themselves is drowned and a new life (new creation) is given by God in baptism, so in the *Meditation on Christ's Passion* Luther describes it "almost like baptism" (below, p. 175).

But, for Luther, with that alien work God also performs a proper work and reveals an immeasurable love for us. One sees Christ's heart with its deep compassion for humanity. With this comes an understanding of how "sweet" this compassion is, and this sweetness strengthens faith (page 177). Luther's use of "sweet," which he shares with various so-called mystical writers, underlines the fact that faith draws one's whole being into relationship with God.

The love of Christ experienced in the meditation on his passion renders the believers firm in Christ (p. 177) so that the Holy Spirit patterns their lives according to the life of Christ. Thus, at the end of the text, Luther lists many ways in which this meditation becomes "active": transforming emotions (whether pride, anger, hatred, etc.), minds (our will to action), and bodies (whether sickness, pain, or the body's many desires, etc.).

A Sermon on the Meditation of Christ's Holy Passion became popular very quickly. In the space of five years, it experienced a total of twenty-four printings, along with a Latin translation. In 1525, it was included by Stephan Roth (1492–1546) in Luther's *Lenten Postil*, where it underwent numerous printings down through the centuries.[3] Its popularity is understandable. Luther explains in simple terms Christ's passage from suffering and death to life, from Good Friday to Easter Sunday. Even more than simply offering an explanation, Luther offers a new approach to this spiritual practice, one that engages believers on all levels of their existence and focuses on what God has done for them.

A MEDITATION ON CHRIST'S PASSION (1519)[4]

1. SOME PEOPLE meditate on Christ's passion by venting their anger on the Jews, singing and ranting about wretched Judas,[6] which satisfies them, just as they are in the habit of complaining about other people, of condemning and reproaching their adversaries. That might well be a meditation on the wickedness of Judas and the Jews, but not on the sufferings of Christ.

2. Some point to the manifold benefits and fruits that grow from contemplating Christ's passion. There is a saying

3. A "postil" in the sixteenth century designated sermons or commentary on the common one-year lectionary. Luther wrote his Christmas postil, or commentary, while at the Wartburg (published in 1522). Stephan Roth in the 1520s and Caspar Cruciger Sr. (1504–1548) in the 1540s published Luther's complete postil on the Sunday and festival Gospel and Epistle lessons, based upon Luther's preaching.

4. The text is based on the original translation by Martin H. Bertram (LW 42:3–15). The original German text, *Ein Sermon von der Betrachtung des heiligen Leidens Christi*, is found in WA 2:136–42.

5. CRITICISMS OF CURRENT PRACTICES

6. Luther alludes to a medieval German hymn, "*O du armer Judas, was hast du getan*" ("Ah, Thou Wretched Judas, What Is It You Have Done?").

This depiction of Jesus as the "man of sorrows" (cf. Isaiah 53:3) was used as a title page illustration for Luther's sermon on the suffering of Christ.

ascribed to St. Albert[7] about this, that it is more beneficial to ponder Christ's passion just once than to fast a whole year or to pray a psalm daily, etc. These people follow this saying blindly[8] and therefore do not reap the fruit of Christ's passion, for in so doing they are seeking their own advantage. They carry pictures and booklets, letters and crosses on their person. Some go so far afield as to imagine that they thus protect themselves against water and sword, fire, and all sorts of perils.[9] Christ's suffering is used to work in them a lack of suffering, contrary to Christ's being and nature.

3. Some feel pity for Christ, lamenting and bewailing his innocence. They are like the women who followed Christ from Jerusalem and were upbraided by Christ that it would be better to weep for themselves and their children [Luke 23:27-28]. They are the kind of people who go far afield in their meditation on the passion, making much of Christ's farewell from Bethany [John 12:1-18][10] and of the Virgin Mary's anguish [John 19:25-27] but never progressing beyond that, which is why so many hours are devoted to the contemplation of Christ's passion.[11] Only God knows whether the purpose is for sleeping or for staying awake.

This group also includes those who have learned what rich fruits the Holy Mass offers. In their simplemindedness they think it enough just to hear Mass. In support of this, several teachers are cited for us who hold that the Mass is *opere operati, non opere operantis*,[12] that it is effective in itself without our merit and worthiness, as if this were all that is needed. Yet the Mass was not instituted for its own worthiness but to make us worthy and to bring us to meditate on Christ's passion. Where that is not done, we turn the Mass into a physical and unfruitful act, even though the Mass is

7. Albert the Great or Albert Magnus (1193-1280) was a Dominican friar and a major Scholastic theologian, often called "*Doctor universalis.*" He was a teacher of Thomas Aquinas (1225-1274).

Jesus is anointed by a woman in the house of Simon
the Pharisee, from Luther's *House Postils* of 1544.

8. Luther argues here that some people have used Albert's words to ignore fasting and praying the psalms and instead to invent new ways of thinking about the passion (such as wearing crosses, etc.). They derive personal satisfaction out of this more than truly meditating.

9. Luther here directs his criticism at those who carry holy pictures, prayer books depicting Christ's suffering (cf. LW 43:5–7), rosaries, etc., as amulets to ward off harm and danger.

10. The veneration of Mary and Martha was widespread in medieval Europe and particularly in Germany. See Giles Constable, "The Interpretation of Mary and Martha," in *Three Studies in Medieval Religious and Social Thought* (Cambridge: Cambridge University Press, 1995), 1–93.

11. It was not unusual for such contemplations to last four or five hours. Often they were much longer.

12. The mere performance of the Mass makes it valid and effective, not the inward intent or disposition of the one who celebrates the Mass. See below, *The Blessed Sacrament of the Holy and True Body of Christ and the Brotherhoods*, p. 245, n. 37.

good in and of itself. But of what help is it to you that God is God if God is not God for you?[c] Of what benefit is it that eating and drinking are good and healthy if they are not healthy for you? And it is to be feared that many Masses will not improve matters as long as we do not seek the right fruit in it.[d]

c   For a more thorough exposition of this aspect of Christian preaching and life, see *The Freedom of a Christian*, below, p. 508.

d   See below, *Treatise on Good Works*, p. 304f.

13. GOOD PRACTICES

[13] 4. They contemplate Christ's passion properly who look at it with a terrified heart and a despairing conscience. This terror must be felt as you witness the stern wrath and the unchanging seriousness with which God looks upon sin and sinners, so much so that God did not want to release sinners to his only beloved Son unless he did such heavy penance for them. As God says in Isaiah 53[:8], "For the sins of my people I have struck him."[e] If the dearest child is punished in this way, what will sinners encounter? An inexpressible and unbearable matter of deadly seriousness must be present for such a great and infinite person to defy it and to suffer and die for it. And if you seriously consider that it is God's very own Son, the eternal wisdom of the Father, who suffers, you will truly be terrified, and the more you consider this the deeper the terror.

5. You must impress this deeply in your mind and not doubt that you are the one who makes Christ suffer in this way, for your sins have certainly caused this. In Acts 2 [:36-37] St. Peter frightened the Jews like a peal of thunder when he said to all of them, "You crucified him." Consequently, on that same day three thousand came to the apostles, terrified and shaking, and asked, "O dear brothers, what should we do now?" Therefore, when you see the nails piercing Christ's hands, you can be certain that it is your work. When you behold his crown of thorns, you may rest assured that these are your evil thoughts, and so on.[14]

14. Concentrating on the suffering of various parts of Christ's body was a time-honored medieval tradition. Luther allegorizes the hands for human action, the head for human thoughts. In the seventeenth century, Paul Gerhardt (1607–1676) translated the Latin hymn by Arnulf of Louvain (c. 1200–1250), from which the well-known hymn "O Sacred Head, Now Wounded" is a part.

6. For every nail that pierces Christ, more than one hundred thousand should in justice pierce you; yes, they should pierce you forever and more painfully! When Christ is tortured by nails penetrating his hands and feet, you should eternally suffer the pain they inflict and the pain of even crueler nails, which will in truth happen to those who allow Christ's passion to be lost on them, because this stern mirror, Christ, will not lie or be trifled with, and whatever it points out must be completely overwhelming.

---

e   Both the Latin Vulgate and the Hebrew read, "he was stricken."

7. St. Bernard[15] drew out from this such terror that he said, "I thought I was secure; I was not aware of the eternal sentence that had been passed on me in heaven until I saw that God's only Son had compassion upon me and offered to bear this judgment for me. Alas, if the situation is that serious, I should not make light of it or feel secure." We read that Christ commanded the women not to weep for him but for themselves and their children [Luke 23:28]. And he adds the reason for this, saying [Luke 23:31], "For if they do this to the green wood, what will happen when it is dry?" It is as if he had said: "From my torture learn what you deserve and what should happen to you." Here the saying applies that the small dog is whipped to frighten the big dog.[f] Thus the prophet said that "on his account all the tribes of the earth will wail for themselves"; the prophet does not say that they will wail for him, but that they will wail for themselves because of him.[g] In like manner the people of whom we heard in Acts 2 [:36-37] were so terrified that they said to the apostles, "O brothers, what should we do?" This is also the song of the church: "I will ponder this diligently and, as a result, my soul will languish within me."[16]

8. On this point, we should truly exercise ourselves, for the main benefit of Christ's passion is that individuals[h] recognize their own true selves and be terrified and crushed by what they see. And when they do not come to this point, they do not yet derive any benefit from Christ's passion. The real and true work of Christ's passion is to conform individuals to Christ, so that as Christ was miserably tormented in body and soul by our sins, we, following him, may be tormented by our sins in our conscience. This does not call for many words but for profound reflection and a great attention to sins. Consider this illustration: a criminal is sentenced to death for the murder of the child of a prince or a king. In

15. Bernard of Clairvaux (1090–1153) was a Cistercian monk and abbot of Clairvaux. Luther held him in high esteem and often quoted him. This particular citation has not yet been identified but may have come from Bernard's own sermon on Christ's passion, *In Feria IV Hebdomadae Sanctae Sermo* (MPL 183:263–70).

16. Most likely a paraphrase of Arnulf of Louvain's hymn, especially the section referring to Christ's heart (MPL 184:1322). See above, n. 14.

---

f   See Wander, 5:1041.

g   Luther is referring to the prophecy in Rev. 1:7 in the Latin, where the verb is reflexive (*plangent se*). Thus, the sorrow of "those who pierced him" is for themselves and what they did.

h   Singular in the original.

17. Like most late medieval thinkers, Luther viewed the destruction of Jerusalem and the Jewish homeland as punishment for Christ's crucifixion. But here, unlike in later writings, he does not limit the guilt to them. See Kirsi Stjerna and Brooks Schramm, eds., *Martin Luther, the Bible, and the Jewish People: A Reader* (Minneapolis: Fortress Press, 2012).

18. At this point in time, Luther did not question the existence of purgatory.

19. FRUITS OF THIS MEDITATION

the meantime you go your carefree way, singing and playing, until you are cruelly arrested and convicted of having incited the murderer. Now the whole world closes in upon you, especially since your conscience also deserts you. You should be terrified even more when you meditate on Christ's passion. For the evildoers, the Jews, whom God has judged and driven out,[17] were only the servants of your sin; you are actually the one who, as we said, by your sin executed[i] and crucified God's Son.

9. The one who is so hardhearted and callous as to be neither frightened by Christ's passion nor led to a knowledge of self, has reason to fear. There is no avoiding being conformed to Christ's image[j] and suffering, whether in this life or in hell. At the very least, you will sink into this terror at the hour of death and in purgatory[18] and will tremble and quake and feel all that Christ suffered on the cross. Since it is horrible to lie waiting on your deathbed, you should pray God to soften your heart and let you ponder Christ's passion in fruitful ways. For unless God buries it in our hearts, it is impossible for us, on our own, to meditate thoroughly on Christ's passion. Neither this meditation nor any other teaching is given to you so that you might jump on it completely on your own in order to master it. Rather, first you should seek and desire God's grace so that you master it not by your own power but by God's grace. That is why the people we referred to above[k] fail to deal correctly with Christ's passion. They do not call upon God's help but look to their own ability to invent their own means of accomplishing this [meditation]. They deal with the matter in a completely human and unfruitful way.

[19] 10. We say without hesitation that those who contemplate God's sufferings for a day, an hour, yes, only a quarter of an hour, do better than to fast a whole year, pray a psalm daily,

---

i   German: *erwürgen*, literally, "strangling," as in an execution by hanging.

j   See 1 Cor. 15:48-49.

k   See above, paragraph nos. 1–3.

yes, better than to hear a hundred Masses.[l] This meditation transforms a person's being and, almost like baptism, gives a new birth. Here the passion of Christ performs its natural and noble work, executing the old Adam and expelling all joy, delight, and confidence that a person could find in other creatures, even as Christ was forsaken by all, even by God.

11. Since this work[20] does not rest with us, it happens that we will sometimes pray for it, and yet not attain it at once. Nevertheless, we should neither despair nor desist. At times this happens because we do not pray for it as God indicates and wishes it, for it must be left free and unfettered. Then a person becomes sad in conscience and grumbles inwardly about the evil in life. It may well be that, even when such a one does not think about Christ's passion, it is working this [death] within, just as these others, who do think of Christ's passion all the time, do not attain self-knowledge through it. For the former the passion of Christ is hidden and genuine, while for the latter it is only an outer shell and misleading. In this way God often reverses matters, so that those who do not meditate on Christ's passion do meditate on it, and those who do not hear Mass do hear it, and those who hear it do not hear it.[21]

12. Until now we have sojourned in Holy Week and rightly celebrated Good Friday. Now we come to the resurrection of Christ, to the day of Easter. After a person becomes aware of sin and terrified at heart, that one must watch that sin does not remain in the conscience, for this would certainly lead to nothing but doubt. Instead, as soon as sins have flowed out from Christ and are recognized, so they must be shaken back on him and the conscience emptied of them.[22] Therefore, watch out that you do not do as those perverse people who gnaw at and devour their hearts with their sins and, running to and fro, strive to get rid of their sins through good works or [penitential acts of] satisfaction, or to work their way out of this by means of indulgences.[m]

20. God's work of killing the old creature and giving life to the new.

21. This way of speaking is related to Luther's theology of the cross. See the *Heidelberg Disputation*, pp. 99–101.

22. In this passage, there are traces of the "Joyous Exchange" (*der fröhliche Wechsel*) that Luther would develop later in his sermon *The Blessed Sacrament of the Holy and True Body of Christ and the Brotherhoods* (see below, p. 240) and in *The Freedom of a Christian* (see below, pp. 499–502).

---

l   Here Luther returns to the comment of Albert the Great. See above, p. 170.

m   See above, *A Sermon on Indulgences and Grace*, p. 62f.

23. Luther continually criticizes pilgrimages as a self-centered work. Pilgrimages were very popular in late medieval Europe (notably the major ones to Rome or to St. James of Compostela, Spain). However, Luther saw such pilgrimages as simply providing an illusion of doing "good work," thereby actually escaping the demands of living faith in daily life.

24. Luther is thinking here of two of the parts of penance, which were customarily appealed to in such sermons. See *Sermon on Penance*, p. 198.

Unfortunately such false confidence in penance and pilgrimages is widespread.[23]

13. You throw your sins off of yourself and onto Christ when you firmly believe that his wounds and sufferings are your sins, that he carries and pays for them, as we read in Isa. 53 [:6], "The Lord has laid on him the iniquity of us all." And St. Peter says [1 Pet. 2:24], "He himself bore our sins in his body on the cross." St. Paul says [2 Cor. 5:21], "For our sake God made him to be sin who knew no sin, so that in him we might become the righteousness of God." You must completely[n] rely on these and similar verses—the more your conscience tortures you, the more you must rely on them. If you do not do that, but presume to still your conscience with your contrition and satisfaction,[24] you will never come to peace and in the end will only doubt. For if we allow sin to remain in our conscience and try to deal with it there, or if we look at sin in our heart, it will be much too strong for us and will live on forever. But if we see that it rests on Christ and is overcome by his resurrection, and then boldly believe this, then sin is dead and nullified. For sin cannot remain on Christ, since it is swallowed up by his resurrection, and so now you see no wounds or no pain in him, that is, no sign of sin. As St. Paul declares [Rom. 4:25], "Christ was handed over to death for our trespasses and was raised for our justification," that is, in his suffering Christ reveals our sin and thereby executes it, but through his resurrection Christ makes us righteous and free of all sin, when we believe this.

14. If, as was said before, you cannot believe, you should ask God for faith. But this too rests entirely in the hands of God who gives faith sometimes openly, sometimes in secret, as was said earlier about suffering. If you wish to rouse yourself to faith, first of all, you should no longer contemplate the suffering of Christ (for this has already done its work and terrified you). Instead, pass through that and see Christ's friendly heart and how full of love it is toward you

---

n   German: *mit ganntzem wag*, literally, "by wagering everything."

that it impels him to carry with heaviness your conscience and your sin. Then your heart will be sweet[25] toward him, and the confidence of faith will be strengthened. Now go further and rise through Christ's heart to God's heart, and you will see that Christ would not have shown this love for you if God, to whom Christ with his love for you is obedient, did not want to hold [you] in eternal love. There you will find the divine, good, fatherly heart, and, as Christ says [cf. John 6:44], you will be drawn to the Father through him. Then you will understand the words of Christ [John 3:16], "For God so loved the world that he gave his only Son...." That is, we know God properly when we grasp God not in God's power or wisdom (which is terrifying), but in God's kindness and love. Then faith and confidence are able to exist, and then a person is truly born anew in God.

15. When your heart has thus become firm in Christ, and you have become an enemy of sin from love and not the fear of suffering, then from that day on Christ's passion should become an example for your entire life, and you will now see his passion differently. Until now we regarded it as a sacrament[26] that is active in us while we are passive, but now we find that we too must be active, namely, in the following ways:

If pain or sickness afflicts you, consider how paltry this is in comparison to the thorny crown and the nails of Christ.

If you are obliged to do or to refrain from doing things against your will, ponder how Christ was captured and bound and led here and there.

If you are assailed by pride, see how your Lord was mocked and ridiculed along with criminals.

If unchastity and lust assail you, remember how bitterly Christ's tender flesh was scourged, pierced, and beaten.

If hatred, envy, and vindictiveness trouble you, recall how Christ, who indeed had more reason to avenge himself, interceded with tears and cries for you and for all his enemies.

If sadness or any adversity, physical or spiritual, distresses you, strengthen your heart and say, "Well, why should I not be willing to bear a little distress, when agonies and fears caused my Lord to sweat blood in the Garden of Gethsem-

25. Here, by borrowing the emotive language of so-called mystics, Luther reflects how faith affects both the mind and the emotions.

26. The notion of Christ's death as saving action (*sacramentum*) and example (*exemplum*) goes back to Augustine (354–430) and comes to the fore again in Luther's *The Freedom of a Christian*, below, pp. 487–531. In the list that follows, Luther borrows frequently from standard meditations on Christ's passion but now seen as the result of God's grace, not its cause.

ane?*° Those who lay in bed while their Lord struggles in the throes of death are indeed lazy and disgraceful servants."

So then, this is how we find strength and encouragement from Christ against every vice and failing. This is the proper contemplation of Christ's passion, and such are its fruits. And those who exercise themselves in this way do better than listening to all the stories of Christ's passion or reading all the Masses. This is not to say that Masses are of no value, but they do not help us in this meditation and exercise.

Those who thus make Christ's life and name a part of their own lives are true Christians as St. Paul says [Gal. 5:24]: "Those who belong to Christ Jesus have crucified the flesh with its passions and desires." Christ's passion must be handled not with words or appearance but with life and truth. Thus St. Paul[27] exhorts us [Heb. 12:3], "Consider him who endured such hostility against himself from sinners, so that you may not grow weary or lose heart." And St. Peter writes [1 Pet. 4:1], "Since therefore Christ suffered in the flesh, strengthen and arm yourselves by meditating on this."*° However, such meditation has gone out of fashion and become rare, even though the letters of St. Paul and St. Peter abound with it. We have transformed the essence into an appearance and have only painted our meditations on Christ's passion on walls and in pamphlets.

27. Luther both held to the Pauline authorship of Hebrews and questioned it.

---

o   Luke 22:39-46.

p   Luther is giving a close paraphrase of the Vulgate.

This engraving of the crucifixion is by the artist
Hans Schäufelein (c. 1480–1539), as found
in Martin Luther's *Operationes in Psalmos* of 1519.

Sermon on the Sacrament of Penance

1519

DIRK G. LANGE

INTRODUCTION

The year 1519 brought with it many tensions in Luther's work and life. More than half the year was overshadowed by the preparations for the debate with Johann Eck (1486–1543), which finally took place in Leipzig in the summer of 1519. Since the beginning of the year, Luther lived in the uncertainty of whether the debate would happen or not. Luther had received mixed signals from various church and political authorities.[a] In addition, leading up to the debate, Luther addressed the issue of papal authority, already implied in the *95 Theses*.[b] Luther's friends tried to dissuade him from entering into a debate over this question, but during the dispute Eck forced Luther into defining his position vis-à-vis papal authority in light of his understanding of righteousness. Luther's understanding of the "keys" is further developed in this sermon.[1]

In the midst of dealing with the ecclesial and political implications of his case with Rome, sparked by the spread of the *95 Theses*, Luther continued to concern himself with

1. The "power of the keys" refers to Matt. 16:19, where Jesus gives the keys of the kingdom of heaven, that is, the power to forgive sin, to Peter. In medieval Western theology, this was interpreted to lodge final authority in the church in the "see of Peter," the bishop of Rome or pope. For a broader discussion, see Ronald Rittgers, *The Reformation of the Keys: Confession, Conscience, and Authority in Sixteenth-Century Germany* (Cambridge: Harvard University Press, 2004).

a   Brecht 1:299–322.
b   See above, *95 Theses*, introduction, p. 28.

2. See LW 14:279–349 and
LW 27:151–410.

3. See LW 44:3–20 (marriage), LW
42:95–116 (preparing to die), LW
42:83–93 (procession), LW 42:15–81
(Lord's Prayer) and, in this volume,
pp. 169–79 (Christ's suffering). For
the instruction on confession, see WA
2:57–65.

4. The Duchess Margaretha von
Braunschweig-Lüneburg (b. before
1472, d. in the 1530s) was the
daughter of Count Konrad V
von Rietberg (d. 1472).

Duchess Margaretha
von Braunschweig-Lüneburg
(1469–1528).

questions of spiritual care. In the same year as the debate
with Eck, Luther began his second round of lectures on the
Psalms (published by 1521) and prepared his lectures on
Galatians for publication in 1519.[2] His concern for spiritual
and pastoral care are evidenced in the subjects of a series
of German sermons and writings from this year on how to
make confession, on marriage, on preparing to die, on contemplating the suffering of Christ, on prayer and procession
of the cross, and on the Lord's Prayer for laypersons.[3] Finally,
toward the end of the year and at the prompting of friends,
Luther wrote three important sermons on the sacraments:
penance, baptism, and the Lord's Supper.

The *Sermon on the Sacrament of Penance* was composed
in October 1519. This sermon, as well as the two that followed on baptism and the holy and true body of Christ,
were dedicated to the Margaretha von Rietberg, duchess
of Braunschweig-Lüneberg,[4] to whom Luther wrote a brief
introductory paragraph. It is unclear whether Luther knew
the duchess. He had been encouraged to dedicate the sermons to her because of her piety.

For Luther, theology and practice were intimately linked
in all of these writings. The *95 Theses* themselves primarily
criticized the practice of indulgences and their relation to
contrition and confession in the sacrament of penance.[c] In
the *Sermon on the Sacrament of Penance*, Luther continues to
develop and deepen this critique, already popularized in the
Sermon on Indulgences and Grace (1518)[d] and further explained
in the *Sermon on Preparing to Die*. By the time Luther wrote
the *Sermon on the Sacrament of Penance*, he was fully express-
ing his critical assessment of relying on human works to
make satisfaction (the third part of penance). Here he also
focuses on ministry (authority) and, most significantly, on
a redefinition of the sacraments in light of the role of faith.

Already in the *Sermon on Preparing to Die*, Luther begins
to reorient the sacraments away from human works and

c   See above, *The 95 Theses,* pp. 20–22.

d   See above, pp. 60–65.

toward their source as God's gracious gift to human beings. The sacraments "contain nothing but God's words, promises, and signs,"[e] and faith relies upon and joyfully engages God's signs and promises.[f]

The *Sermon on Preparing to Die* was apparently written in much haste.[g] It had been commissioned by a princely councilor, Markus Schart (d. 1529). Luther probably wrote it just before the *Sermon on the Sacrament of Penance*. In the latter, Luther delineates more clearly the contours of a sacrament, outlining three things that make up a sacrament and, in particular, the sacrament of penance (first, the word of absolution spoken by a priest—an audible, tangible word; second, God's grace, the forgiveness of sins and peace; and third, faith that receives—literally, "makes"—the sacrament). In this delineation, we see Luther already foreshadowing his major work *The Babylonian Captivity of the Church* (1520).[h]

In late medieval piety, preparation for dying (including the sacrament of extreme unction)[5] and the sacrament of penance were closely linked, given that both placed a person into a state of grace and, thus, on the way to heaven. Additionally, in Luther's mind this association is witnessed not only by the proximity of composition but also by the fact that in one printed edition of the sermon from 1520, Luther wrote the name of Markus Schart on the title page. As Luther writes the *Sermon on the Sacrament of Penance*, he is thinking about what it means to prepare for death. Confessing and absolution as dying, as a continual dying and rising again, preparing the believer for bodily death, weaves its way into his understanding of the work of the sacraments and makes the link between penance and baptism particularly strong. Penance is one way in which baptismal dying and rising are practiced.

5. One of the seven sacraments of the medieval Western church, extreme unction (now called anointing of the sick) consisted of anointing a dying person with consecrated oil (based upon James 5:14). Through the infusion of grace associated with the sacrament, a person moved from a state of sin into a state of grace, preparing the believer for a blessed death.

e   LW 42:109.
f   LW 42:110: "Faith must be present for a firm reliance and cheerful venturing on such signs and promises of God."
g   Brecht 1:354–55.
h   LW 36:3–126.

At this point in his theological development, Luther brings into focus his tripartite definition of the sacraments: a sacrament has a tangible element, with a command and promise of Jesus attached to it. He has also reduced the number of sacraments from seven to three (baptism, Lord's Supper, penance), an opinion that he refines in *The Babylonian Captivity of the Church*. Depending upon the definition of sacraments used, later Lutherans continue to debate the sacramental nature of penance.[i]

Most significant in these "sacramental" sermons is the central role accorded to faith. In the sacrament of penance, faith is to be the "chief thing, the inheritance through which one attains the grace of God." Good works always follow such faith, and, in fact, it is impossible that they would not. "Works of Satisfaction" (the traditional third part of the sacrament) do not complete or fulfill absolution but, rather, become for Luther a joyful response.

Faith itself, however, is also not a human work but the work of the Holy Spirit in the believer. Faith is a particular form of life or relation to God that renders the human being totally receptive to God. Faith is the way of pure and simple welcome.[j] Through faith, the Holy Spirit establishes the gracious relationship with God that constitutes life. Believing is not a cognitive act of accepting but of being enveloped and losing oneself in that movement.[6] Throughout the sermon, Luther employs words that attempt to describe this dependence on God's word, especially *aufnehmen* (receiving) and *empfangen* (welcome). Belief in the word of absolution is itself given by the Holy Spirit.

This faith, this simple trust in the word of absolution, is then also a radical critique of authority. The word itself is that which gives authority (not ecclesial positions giving authority to the word). This theme continually surfaces in this sermon, particularly in Luther's comments throughout

6. See, from the same time, Luther's first *Commentary on Galatians* (1519), in LW 27:172: "Therefore if you take notice, you will easily realize that this feeling is not in you because of your own strength."

i   For a later discussion, see Philip Melanchthon, *Apology of the Augsburg Confession*, XIII.3–17, in BC, 219–21.

j   Berndt Hamm, *The Early Luther: Stages in a Reformation Reorientation*, trans. Martin J. Lohrmann (Grand Rapids: Eerdmans, 2014), 22–24.

the tract on Matthew 16:19, "Whatever you bind on earth will be bound in heaven, and whatever you loose on earth will be loosed in heaven." At the heart of the sacrament is the word of absolution. It is the priest's responsibility to deliver this word. Through the reorientation of the function of ministry, Luther redefines authority as it was held in the church of his day. The only authority a pope, bishop, or priest has is that of service. The keys were not given to one person, Peter (and his successors), but to the whole people.

Eyn Sermon von dem Sacrament der pusz, D. M. L. was originally written in German and first published by Johann Grünenberg in Wittenberg. It appeared about mid-October 1519 and not, as some had supposed, during the same year as Luther's *Sermo de poenitentia.*[k] Before the end of 1519 there were four printings, one of them appearing in Leipzig. Within two years ten more editions were out, coming from printers in Nuremberg, Augsburg, Erfurt, and Strasbourg.

DEDICATORY LETTER[l]

TO THE ILLUSTRIOUS and highborn princess and lady, Lady Margarethe, née von Rechberg, duchess of Braunschweig-Lüneberg,[7] my gracious Lady, I, Martin Luther, Augustinian in Wittenberg, offer all my good riches in God: God's grace and peace in Christ our Lord.

Highborn Princess, gracious Lady! Some of my good friends, cousins, and lords[8] have requested me to write something spiritual and Christian for Your Noble Grace, in order to express my gratitude and show my obedient service

7. Margaretha was the daughter of Count Konrad V von Rietberg and Countess Jacobe von Neuenahr (c. 1430–1492). On 10 March 1483, Margaretha married Duke Friedrich von Braunschweig-Lüneberg, who was deposed in 1484 and died childless on 5 March 1495. She died in the early 1530s. See MLStA 1:245, n. 2.

8. Chiefly, Georg Spalatin (1484–1545). See MLStA 1:245, n. 5.

k WA 1:317–24; 9:779, published in 1518.

l Written somewhere around 15 October 1519. See WA Br 1:537. This translation is based on WA 2:713.

to Your Noble Grace's gracious will and pleasure which she bears toward me, an unworthy man. To this goal, my own duty had certainly also driven me many times. Still, this has been difficult, since I have not found so many [of my writings], with which I might satisfy this desire and duty, especially since I certainly consider that long ago our only master, Christ, has come to Your Noble Grace long, long before me. Finally, I have let myself be moved to publish in Your Noble Grace's name meditations on Holy Scripture (which is highly valued by me), namely, several sermons: on the holy, reverend, and comforting sacraments of Penance, Baptism, and the Lord's Supper. [I have done this] in light of the fact—as I myself have also experienced—that so many sad and anxious consciences are found who neither recognize these holy and grace-filled sacraments nor are able to use them. Instead, they sadly take upon themselves to still [their consciences] with their works rather than to seek peace in God's grace through the holy sacraments—given the extent to which the holy sacraments have been covered over and taken from us through human teachings. I beseech Your Noble Grace that you will accept this my lowly service in grace and not be angered with me for my brazenness [at addressing you]. For I am obediently prepared to serve Your Noble Grace at all times. May God let her be commended to him far and wide! Amen.

A SERMON
ON THE SACRAMENT
OF PENANCE[9]

9. The text is based on the translation by E. Theodore Bachmann (LW 35:9–23). The original text is that of the Wittenberg printer Grünenberg, a copy of which is in the Duke August Library in Wolfenbüttel (WA 2:714–23).

The first page of *Sermon on the Sacrament of Penance,* printed in 1519.

10. L.A.W. = Luther Augustiner [Augustinian] Wittenberg. Luther signed his works with his monastic nomenclature "Augustiner" well into the 1520s. In other words, Luther is still writing and preaching as a friar.

11. For this basic Scholastic distinction between guilt (*culpa*) and punishment (*poena*) in the effect of sin, see above, *95 Theses*, p. 35.

12. See Luther's explanation in the *Sermon on Indulgences and Grace*, p. 60f. Already in the *95 Theses* (above, p. 35), Luther distinguished between the satisfaction of punishment imposed by church regulations and punishment of sin imposed by God. In late medieval theology, fasting, almsgiving, and prayer were considered works of satisfaction that reduced or satisfied both kinds of punishment. The attaining of indulgences eliminated the need for such works.

13. This description of the conscience remains a significant theme for Luther. See below, *The Freedom of a Christian*, p. 532. Later Lutherans preserved this in the *Formula of Concord* (Solid Declaration, VI.17), in BC, 590.

By Doctor Martin L.A.W.[10]

1. FORGIVENESS is of two kinds in the sacrament of penance: forgiveness of punishment and forgiveness of guilt.[11] Concerning the first, the forgiveness of punishment, or satisfaction, enough has been said in the treatise on indulgences that appeared some time ago.*m* It is not very significant and is an immeasurably lesser thing than the forgiveness of guilt, which one might call a divine or heavenly indulgence, one that only God can grant from heaven.

2. Here is the difference between these two types of forgiveness: indulgence or forgiveness of punishment does away with works and efforts of an imposed satisfaction and thus reconciles a person outwardly with the Christian church.[12] But the forgiveness of guilt, the heavenly indulgence, does away with the heart's fear and timidity before God; it makes the conscience lighthearted and merry inwardly[13] and reconciles a person with God. And this is what true forgiveness of sins really means, that people's sins no longer bite or make them uneasy, but rather that a joyful confidence, that God has forgiven them their sins forever, overwhelms them.

3. Persons, however, who do not find within themselves nor feel such a conscience and joyful heart regarding God's grace cannot be helped by any indulgence even though they were to buy all the letters of indulgence ever issued. For a person may be saved without any letters of indulgence or making satisfaction or paying for sin by death. No one, however, is saved without a joyful conscience and a light heart toward God (that is, without the forgiveness of guilt). So it would be much better not to buy indulgences at all than to forget this forgiveness of guilt or, even more, to neglect exercising it every day.

4. For [arriving at] such forgiveness of guilt and for calming the heart in the face of its sins, there are various ways

m   See above, *Sermon on Indulgences and Grace*, pp. 60–65.

and methods. Some think they can accomplish this through letters of indulgence. They run to and fro, to Rome or to St. James,[14] buying indulgences here and there. But this is mistaken and all in vain. It makes things even worse, for God alone must forgive sins and grant peace to the heart. Some wear themselves out with many good works, even too much fasting and effort so that some have ruined their bodies and gone out of their minds, thinking that by the power of works [they can] do away with their sins and soothe their heart. Both of these types are defective in that they want to do good works before their sins are forgiven, whereas on the contrary, sins must be forgiven before good works can happen. For works do not drive out sin, but driving out of sin produces good works. For good works must be done with joyful heart and good conscience toward God, that is, out of the forgiveness of guilt.

[15]5. The true way and the right manner, besides which no other can be found, is that most worthy, gracious, and holy sacrament of penance that God gave for the comfort of all sinners when [God] gave the keys to St. Peter on behalf of the whole Christian Church and in Matt. 16[:19], said, "Whatever you bind on earth will be bound in heaven, and whatever you loose on earth will be loosed in heaven." Each Christian must take to heart these holy, comforting, and gracious words of God and memorize them with great thanks. For the sacrament of penance consists of forgiveness of sin, comfort and peace of conscience, every joy and blessedness of the heart over and against all sins and terrors of conscience and against all despair and assaults*n* from the gates of hell.*o*

6. Now there are three things in the holy sacrament of penance.[16] The first is absolution. These are the words of the priest that show, tell, and proclaim*p* to you that you are free

n German: *Anfechtung.*

o See Matt. 16:18.

p The use of the word *show* recalls Augustine's definition of a sacrament as a "visible word." See below, n. 17.

14. St. James the Apostle was said to have been buried at St. James of Compostela (Santiago de Compostela), a city in northwestern Spain. Next to Jerusalem and Rome, this was the most famous place of pilgrimage in the Middle Ages.

15. THE SACRAMENT FOR THE COMFORTING OF SINNERS

16. Luther expands the classic bipartite medieval definition of a sacrament (dating back to St. Augustine) to three parts. To "sign" and "signification" Luther adds "faith." The sign is the material element and action. The signification is the meaning of the sacrament (what the sign indicates). By adding "faith" as the third component, Luther includes the individual within the action of the sacrament. For Luther, the significance of the sacrament shapes the life of the participant through faith.

and that your sins are forgiven by God according to and by virtue of the above-quoted words of Christ to St. Peter. The second is grace, the forgiveness of sins, the peace and comfort of the conscience, as the words declare. This is why it is called a sacrament, a holy sign; in it one hears the words externally that signify spiritual gifts within, gifts by which the heart is comforted and set at peace. The third is faith, which firmly believes that the absolution and words of the priest are true, by the power of Christ's words, "Whatever you loose . . . shall be loosed," etc.

Everything, then, depends on this faith, which alone makes the sacraments accomplish what they signify, and everything becomes true that the priest says. For as you believe, so it happens to you.[q] Without this faith all absolution and all sacraments are in vain and indeed do more harm than good. There is a common saying among the teachers that goes like this: Not the sacrament, but the faith that believes the sacrament is what removes sin. St. Augustine says this: The sacrament removes sin, "not because it takes place, but because it is believed."[17] For this reason, in the sacrament one must studiously discern faith; and this we wish now to sketch out further.

7. It follows, then, in the first place, that the forgiveness of guilt, the heavenly indulgence, is granted to no one on account of the worthiness of their contrition over their sins, nor on account of any works of satisfaction, but only on account of faith in the promise of God [Matt. 16:19], "Whatever you loose . . . shall be loosed." Although contrition and good works are not to be neglected, one is nevertheless not to build upon them, but only upon the sure words of Christ, who pledges to you that when the priest frees you, you shall be free. Your contrition and works may deceive you, and the devil will quickly annihilate them in death and assaults,[18] but Christ your God will not lie to you, nor will he waver; neither will the devil turn Christ's word against him. And if you build upon them with a firm faith, you will be standing

17. See Augustine, *Tractates on John,* 80.3 (NPNF, ser. 1, 7:344), on John 15:3: "The word is added to the element, and there results the Sacrament, as if itself also a kind of visible word. . . . And whence has water [in Baptism] so great efficacy, as in touching the body to cleanse the soul, save by the operation of the word; and that not because it is uttered, but because it is believed?"

18. German: *Anfechtung.* Luther is referring both to fears in the face of death and attacks throughout life.

q   See Matt. 8:13; 9:29.

on the rock against which the gates and all the powers of hell cannot prevail.*

8. It follows further that the forgiveness of guilt is not within the province of any human office or authority, be it pope, bishop, priest, or any other. Rather, it depends exclusively upon the word of Christ and your own faith. For Christ did not intend to base our comfort, our salvation, our confidence on human words or deeds but only upon himself, upon his words and deeds. Priests, bishops, and popes are only servants who hold before you the word of Christ, upon which you should rely and sit upon[19] with a firm faith as upon a solid rock. Then the word will keep you, and your sins will have to be forgiven. Therefore, the word is not honored because of the priests, bishops, or pope; but priests, bishops, and pope are to be honored because of the word, as those who bring to you the word and message of your God that you are freed from sins.

9. In addition, it follows that in the sacrament of penance and forgiveness of guilt a pope or bishop does nothing more than the lowliest priest.* Indeed, where there is no priest, each individual Christian—even a woman or child—does as much.[20] For any Christian can say to you, "God forgives you your sins in the name [of the Father, Son, and Holy Spirit]," and if you can grasp that word with a confident faith, as if God were saying it to you, then in that same faith you are surely absolved. So completely does everything depend on faith in God's word. No pope, bishop, or priest can do anything to your faith; neither can anyone give someone else a better word of God than that common word Christ spoke to St. Peter [Matt. 16:19], "Whatever you loose . . . shall be loosed." This word must be in every absolution; indeed every absolution depends upon it.

Even so one should observe, and not despise, the established orders of authority. Only, make no mistake about the sacrament and its effect, as if it counted for more when given

19. Luther employs the image of a large rock upon which one can sit.

20. Here Luther begins to develop an aspect of the common priesthood of all Christians where, in the absence of a priest or pastor or in an emergency, any baptized Christian can fulfill the public office. See below, *Address to the Christian Nobility*, p. 382, and *The Freedom of a Christian*, p. 506.

---

r   See Matt. 16:18 and, perhaps, 1 John 5:4.

s   See above, the *95 Theses*, p. 37.

by a bishop or a pope than when given by a priest or a layperson. As the priest's Mass and baptism and distribution of the holy body of Christ are just as valid as if the pope or bishop were doing them, so it is with absolution, that is, the sacrament of penance. The fact that they reserve certain cases for absolution does not make their sacrament any greater or better.[t] It is the same as if for some reason they withheld from anybody the Mass, baptism, or the like. Nothing would thereby be either added to or taken away from baptism and the Mass.

10. Therefore if you believe the word of the priest when the priest absolves you (that is, when the priest absolves you in the name of Christ and in the power of the words, saying, "I absolve[21] you from your sins"), then your sins are assuredly absolved also before God, before all angels and all creatures—not for your sake or for the priest's sake but for the sake of the very Word of Christ, who cannot be lying to you when he says [Matt. 16:19], "Whatever you loose . . . shall be loosed." Should you, however, not believe that your sins are truly forgiven and removed, then you are a heathen, not a Christian, and an unbeliever toward your Lord Christ. And this is the most serious sin against God of all. By no means should you go to the priest if you do not want to believe the absolution; you are doing yourself great harm by your disbelief. By such disbelief you make your God to be a liar when, through the priest, God says to you, "You are absolved from your sins," and you retort, "I don't believe it" or "I doubt it," as if you were more certain in your opinion than God is in God's words. Whereas you should let all [your] opinions go, and with unshakeable faith accede to the word of God spoken through the priest. For if you doubt whether your absolution is approved of God and whether you are rid of your sins, that is the same as saying, "Christ has not spoken the truth, and I do not know whether he

---

21. In German, *lossen* means both "loosen" and "absolve," thus echoing Matt. 16:19 throughout this paragraph. Luther is referring to the words said by the priest in private confession: "I absolve you."

---

t   See above, *95 Theses*, p. 35, and also Luther's criticism in *The Babylonian Captivity of the Church* (1520), LW 36:86–88. In "reserved cases" only the bishop, pope, or one appointed by them could absolve.

approves his own words, when he says to Peter, 'Whatever you loose . . . shall be loosed.'" O God, spare everybody from such diabolical disbelief.

11. When you are absolved from your sins, indeed when amid your awareness of sin some devout Christian—man or woman, young or old—comforts you, then receive this absolution in such faith that you would readily let yourself be torn apart or killed over and over again, or readily renounce everything else, rather than doubt that you have been truly absolved before God. Since by God's grace it is commanded of us to believe and to hope that our sins are forgiven, how much more then ought you to believe it when God gives you a sign of it through another person! There is no greater sin than not to believe this article of "the forgiveness of sins" which we pray daily in the [Apostles'] Creed. And this sin is called the sin against the Holy Spirit.[22] It strengthens all other sins and makes them forever unforgivable. So look what a gracious God and Father we have who not only promises us forgiveness of sins but also commands using the most grievous sin that we should believe that they are forgiven. With this very command God presses us toward a joyful conscience, and with this grievous sin he drives us away from sins and from a bad conscience.[23]

12. A number of people have been teaching us that one should and must be uncertain about absolution and doubt whether we have been restored to [the state of] grace and had our sins forgiven—on the grounds that we do not know whether our contrition has been adequate or whether sufficient satisfaction has been made for our sins.[24] And because this is not known, the priest may not assign a completely appropriate penance.*u* Be on guard against these misleading and un-Christian prattlers. The priest is necessarily uncertain as to your contrition and faith, but this is not what matters. It is enough that you make confession and seek an

22. For Luther, such unbelief defines the sin against the Holy Spirit. In his commentary on Psalm 1 in *Operationes in Psalmos* (LW 14:289), based upon lectures begun half a year before this sermon, Luther notes that unbelief is godlessness. In his commentary on Galatians published in 1519 (LW 27:154), Luther contrasts this definition of sin with his opponents' insistence that sins against the papacy are the worst.

23. For Luther, God's command to believe prevents the penitent from falling into the unforgivable sin of disbelief and thus becomes a gracious warning from God.

24. This uncertainty was thought of as a form of humility to keep a person from becoming secure and failing to do good works. Luther's defense in the *Explanations of the 95 Theses* of thesis 7 (LW 31:100), which insists that Christians believe with certainty in the absolution, would become a major point of disagreement with Cardinal Cajetan (1469–1534) in Augsburg (see above, p. 131). The sacrament of penance moved a person from a state of sin into a state of grace.

---

u   German: *Buße*. For the three meanings of this term and its Latin equivalent, *poenitentia*, see above, p. 27, n. 12. Here Luther is using the term to designate works of satisfaction that a penitent must do upon receiving absolution.

absolution; the priest should give you the absolution and is in fact obliged to do so. The priest should leave to God and to your faith whatever will come of the confession and absolution. You should not first be discussing whether or not your contrition is sufficient. Rather you should be assured of this: that after all your efforts your contrition is not sufficient and that this is why you flee to the grace of God, hear God's completely certain word in the sacrament, receive[v] it in free and joyful faith, and never doubt that you have come to grace—not by your own merits or contrition but by God's gracious and divine mercy, which promises, offers, and fulfills for you complete and free forgiveness of sins. Then, in the face of all the assaults[w] of sin, conscience, and the devil, you learn to boast and glory not in yourself or your own actions but in the grace and mercy of your dear Father in heaven. As a result of this, be all the more contrite and render satisfaction as you are able, but let only this simple faith in the unmerited forgiveness promised in the words of Christ go on before and remain the captain on the field [of battle].

13. Those, however, who do not desire peace think then that they have produced adequate contrition and works—besides which, they make Christ a liar, flirt with the sin against the Holy Spirit, and on top of it all, treat the most worthy sacrament of penance unworthily. So they receive their deserved reward: they build on sand,[x] trusting themselves more than God. The result must necessarily be an ever-greater unease of conscience, a vain striving after impossible things, seeking assurance and comfort but never finding it, until the end-products of such reversals follow: despair and eternal damnation. For what else are they seeking but to achieve certainty by their efforts? It is as if they wanted by their own works to strengthen God's word, through which

v   German: *aufnehmen*. In Luther's day, the word meant "to understand" or "to adopt" and was construed for the most part passively.
w   German: *Anfechtung*.
x   See Matt. 7:26.

they are supposed to be strengthened in faith. They begin to shore up heaven, to which rather they should be clinging. That is, they will not let God be merciful. They want God only as judge, as if God ought not forgive anything freely unless something were first paid out. Yet in the entire gospel we read of no one of whom God required anything but faith; out of grace and free of charge God showered all of his benefits upon the unworthy, bidding them afterward to live well and to go in peace, and the like.[y]

14. It is all the same whether a priest errs, is bound,[25] or absolves carelessly. As you just receive the words sincerely and believe them, even if you either do not know or care about the priest being in error or bound, you are nevertheless absolved and have the full sacrament. For, as already indicated, this sacrament does not depend on the priest, nor on your own actions, but entirely on your faith. You have as much as you believe. Without this faith, you could have all the contrition in the world, but it would still be only the remorse of Judas that angers rather than reconciles God. For nothing reconciles God better than when one honors God as truthful and gracious; and no one does this except the one who believes God's words.[z] Thus David praises God [Ps. 86:15, Vulgate]: "Lord, you are slow to anger, merciful, and truthful." And this same truth saves us from all sins, if we cling to it by faith.

[26]15. It follows that the "keys" or the authority of St. Peter is not an authority at all but a service; and the keys have not been given to St. Peter but to you and me.[a] The keys are yours and mine. For St. Peter, insofar as he is a pope or a bishop, does not need them; to him they are neither necessary nor helpful. Their entire virtue lies rather in this, that they help sinners by comforting and strengthening their conscience. So Christ established that authority in the church should

25. Even if a priest's own sins were "bound" (Matt. 16:19), that is, not forgiven, one can still trust the word of absolution.

26. THE AUTHORITY OF THE "KEYS" IS SERVICE

---

y   Luther is thinking here of Jesus' statements in Mark 5:34; Luke 7:50; 8:48.

z   See below, *The Freedom of a Christian*, p. 497.

a   See above, p. 191, n. 20.

be service, and that by means of the keys the clergy should not be serving themselves but only us. For this reason, as one sees, the priest does no more than to speak a word, and the sacrament is already there. And, as God has promised, this word is God's word. The priest, moreover, has sufficient evidence and reason to grant absolution when he sees that one desires it from him.[b] Beyond that, he is not obligated to know anything. I say this in order that the most gracious virtue of the keys should be cherished and honored, and not despised because of abuses by some who do little more than threaten, annoy, and pronounce the ban,[27] creating nothing but tyranny out of this lovely and comforting authority (as if Christ only instituted the will and dominion of the priests with the keys), not knowing to what purpose the keys should be used.

16. Just so no one accuses me again of forbidding good works,[c] let me say that one should with all seriousness be contrite and remorseful, confess, and do good works.[28] But, I maintain as best I can that in the sacrament we let faith be the chief thing, the inheritance through which one attains the grace of God. Then we can do a lot of good—glorifying God alone and being useful to our neighbor—but not depending upon these as sufficient payment for our sin. For God gives us grace freely and without cost; so we should also serve God freely and without cost.

Besides, everything that I have said about this sacrament is said to them whose conscience is troubled, uneasy, erring, and terrified, who would gladly be freed from their sin and be righteous but do not know where to begin. For these are the very ones who also have true contrition—indeed too much contrition—and are fainthearted. God comforts people like these through the prophet Isaiah, chapter 40, "Cry to the fainthearted and say to them, *consolamini*, be comforted,

27. The "ban" refers to the practice of excommunication, often used to political ends in medieval Christianity by excommunicating entire countries. Pope Leo X had already threatened this in Luther's case.

28. An echo of the three traditional parts of penance (contrition, confession, and satisfaction).

The coat of arms of Leo X (r. 1513–1521), the first of the Medici popes, displaying the papal tiara and keys of Peter.

b   See the third section of *The Blessed Sacrament of the Holy and True Body of Christ and the Brotherhoods*, below, p. 242f., note c.

c   For this charge against Luther, see below, *Treatise on Good Works*, p. 268.

you faint of heart; behold your God.'"[d] And in Matt. 11[:28], Christ says, "Come to me, all you that are weary and are carrying heavy burdens, and I will give you rest." The hard-hearted, however, who do not yet desire comfort for their conscience, have likewise not yet experienced this same suffering. To them this sacrament is of no use. One must first make them weak and fearful with the terrible judgment of God, so that they too learn to seek and sigh for the comfort of the sacrament.

17. In confession, if a priest wishes to ask or if you want to examine yourself, as to whether or not you are truly contrite, I have no objections.[29] Just so no one becomes so bold in the sight of God and claims to have sufficient contrition, for such an attitude is presumptuous and fabricated; no one has sufficient contrition for sin. The inquiry could even be much broader as to whether a person firmly believes the sacrament, that sins are forgiven as Christ said to the paralytic [Matt. 9:2], "My son, have faith and your sins are forgiven you"; and to the woman [Matt. 9:22], "Have faith, my daughter, your faith has made you well."[e] Such inquiry has become quite rare in this sacrament; we are only concerned with contrition, sin, satisfaction, and indulgence. And so one blind person is always leading another [Matt. 15:14]. Actually in this sacrament the priest through a word brings God's message about sin and the forgiveness of guilt. Therefore the priest should indeed be the one who inquires and discerns most of all whether a person is receptive to the message. Such receptivity can never consist in anything other than faith and the desire to embrace this message. Sin, contrition, and good works should be treated in sermons separate from the sacrament and confession.

18. It may happen that God does not let a person sense[f] the forgiveness of guilt so that the turbulence and uneasiness

29. Among others, the late medieval theologian Gabriel Biel had argued that one entered a state of grace at the moment of true contrition (not at the moment of absolution) and thus went to the priest to determine whether the contrition was real, just as people went to the Levitical priests to determine if leprosy was gone. In 1522, Luther published an exposition of Luke 17:11-19 (healing of the ten lepers; WA 8:336–97) to refute this notion.

---

d   Luther combines Isa. 40:1, 9. As was typical among late medieval preachers, he cites the Latin text in the midst of his paraphrase.

e   Translating from the Vulgate.

f   German: *befinden*, which in Luther's German could also mean "experience" or "feel."

of conscience persist after the sacrament as before. Here one must deal wisely, for the deficiency is in faith. It is impossible that the heart would not be joyful when it believes its sins are forgiven, just as it is impossible that it not be troubled and uneasy when it does not believe its sins are forgiven. Now if God allows faith to remain weak, one should not despair on that account, but rather recognize it as a temptation and affliction[g] by means of which God tests, provokes, and drives a person to cry out all the more and plead for such faith, saying with the father of the possessed boy in the gospel, "I believe, help my unbelief!" [Mark 9:24], and with the apostles, "[Lord], increase our faith" [Luke 17:5]. In this way a person learns that everything is God's grace: the sacrament, forgiveness, and faith, until completely letting go, despairing of self, a person comes to hope exclusively and holds on unceasingly to God's sheer grace.

19. Now penitence and the sacrament of penance are two different matters.[h] As said above[i] the sacrament consists in three things: in the word of God, that is, the absolution; in faith in this absolution; and in peace, that is, the forgiveness of sins that surely follows faith. But penance has also been divided into three parts: contrition, confession, and satisfaction.[30]

Now just as in contrition there is many an abuse, as has already been noted, so it is also in the case of confession and satisfaction. There are a host of books on these subjects[31] but unfortunately very few on the sacrament of penance. Where, however, the sacrament proceeds well in faith, there penance (confession, contrition, and satisfaction) is easy and never in danger of being too little or too much. For the faith of the sacrament makes all the crooked straight and levels all the uneven ground.[j] So no one who has the faith of the sacrament can err, whether in contrition, confession, or satisfaction; and even if someone should err, it would not harm him

---

30. The *Summa Theologica* III, q. 90, compiled by a student of Thomas Aquinas (1225–1274), holds that while satisfaction is a "fruit" of penance-as-a-virtue, it is nonetheless a "part" of penance-as-a-sacrament.

31. The sacrament of penance with its private confession gave rise to a legal casuistry contained in penitential manuals (*canones* or *libri poenitentiales*), written to guide confessors and spurred on by the Fourth Lateran Council (1215), which made auricular confession obligatory. They assigned certain "penance" for each sin.

---

g   German: *Anfechtung.*
h   German: *Buß*, see above, p. 27, n.12.
i   See above, p. 189f.
j   Cf. Isa. 40:3-4.

or her. Where there is no faith, however, neither contrition, nor confession, nor satisfaction is adequate, which is why so many books and teachings stream forth on contrition, confession, and satisfaction through which many hearts become very frightened and confess so often that they do not know whether the sins they confess are venial or mortal.[32] Yet on this subject, we desire to say a little more:

20. One need not confess venial sins to the priest, but only to God. Now, however, another question arises: What are mortal and venial sins? There has never yet been a teacher, nor will there ever be one, learned enough to give us a dependable rule for distinguishing venial from mortal sins, except in such obvious offenses against God's commandments as adultery, murder, theft, falsehood, slander, betrayal, hatred, and the like. It is, moreover, entirely up to God to judge what other sins are to be regarded as mortal. It is impossible for human beings to recognize this, as Ps. 19[:12] says, "But who can detect their errors? Clear me from hidden faults." Therefore private confession is no place for [reciting] sins other than those which one openly recognizes as deadly, those which at the time are oppressing and frightening the conscience. For if one were to confess all one's sins, a person would have to be confessing every moment, since in this life we are never without sin.[33] Even our good works are not pure and without sin. Yet it is not without benefit to confess the slighter sins, particularly if one is not aware of any mortal sins. For as has been said, in this sacrament God's word is heard, and faith is strengthened more and more. And even if one should have nothing to confess, it would still be profitable often to hear the absolution and God's word for the sake of faith so that one would grow accustomed to believing in the forgiveness of sins.[k] This is why I said that the faith of the sacrament does everything, even though the confession might be too much or too little. Everything benefits the one who believes God's sacrament and word.

32. German: *täglich* and *tödlich*, the customary translations of the time for venial and mortal sin. In medieval theology, a mortal sin, which put a person in a state of sin and thus liable to eternal damnation, had three components: gravity of the sin and the full knowledge and deliberate consent of the sinner. A venial sin, by contrast, lacked one or more of these characteristics and was a minor infraction, done in ignorance or without the consent of the will.

33. Here Luther is attacking the medieval requirement to confess all known mortal sins. Luther's own earlier anxieties about the confessional may be reflected here.

---

k   Luther continues to see private confession in this light. See the *Small Catechism*, "Baptism," 18 and 24, in BC, 360–61; and the LC, "Confession," 13 and 21, in BC, 477-78.

34. Luther is referring to the practice of confessors assigning certain prayers to satisfying the temporal punishment remaining for their sins. This often involved praying the rosary (reciting the Lord's Prayer and Ave Maria a required number of times).

Concerning satisfaction let this now suffice: the best kind of satisfaction is to sin no more[l] and to do all possible good toward your neighbor, whether enemy or friend. This kind of satisfaction is rarely mentioned. We think to pay for everything simply through assigned prayers.[34]

21. This is the authority of which Christ speaks, in Matt. 9[:6-8], to the unbelieving scribes, "'But so that you may know that the Son of Man has authority on earth to forgive sins'—he then said to the paralytic—'stand up, take your bed and go to your home.' And he stood up and went to his home. When the crowds saw it, they were filled with awe, and they glorified God, who had given such authority to human beings."[m] Now this authority to forgive sins is nothing other than what a priest—indeed, when there is necessity, any Christian—may say to another when one sees another afflicted or anxious in their sins. They can joyously speak this verdict, "Take heart, your sins are forgiven" [Matt. 9:2]. And whoever receives[n] this and believes it as a word of God, their sins are surely forgiven.

Where, however, there is no such faith, it would do no good even if Christ or God himself spoke the verdict. For God cannot give a person something that that person does not want to have. Whoever does not want to have it does not believe that it is being given; such a person does the word of God a great dishonor, as was said above. You see, then, that the whole church is filled with the forgiveness of sins. But there are few who really receive and welcome it.[o] For they do not believe it and would rather rely upon their own works.

l For this German adage (*Nimmer tun ist höchster Buß*), see Wander, 1:520 (no. 2). Luther's comment caused the pope to condemn Luther (see *Defense and Explanation of All the Articles* [1521] in LW 32:38–42), and it became a point of debate between Philip Melanchthon (1497-1560) and Johann Agricola (1494–1566) in 1527 over the cause of repentance (see *Instruction by the Visitors for the Parish Pastors of Saxony* [1528], in LW 40:293–96).

m The appointed gospel for the nineteenth Sunday after Trinity, which fell on 30 October in 1519.

n German: *aufnehmen*. See above, p. 191, note v.

o German: *aufnehmen und empfahen*. Luther understands this reception of faith not as a work but as an experience wrought by God and God's promise.

So it is true that a priest genuinely forgives sin and guilt, although he is in no position to give to the sinner that faith which receives and welcomes the forgiveness. For this faith God must give. Nevertheless, the forgiveness is genuine, as true as if God had spoken it, whether it is grasped by faith or not. No one in the Old Testament, neither high priest nor ordinary priests, neither kings nor prophets, nor anyone else among the people possessed such authority to forgive sins, and thus to render a verdict in God's place. The only exceptions occurred at God's express order, as when Nathan confronted King David (2 Sam. 12:1-15). But in the New Testament every Christian has this authority to forgive sins when a priest is not at hand. A Christian has it through the promise of Christ, when he said to Peter [Matt. 16:19], "Whatever you loose on earth shall be loosed in heaven." Had this been said to Peter alone, then in Matt. 18[:18] Christ would not have said to all in general, "Whatever you loose on earth shall be loosed in heaven." There he is speaking to all Christendom and to each [Christian] in particular. This is the great thing then about a Christian: Were nothing more given to us than to hear someone speak such a word to us, God could not be fully loved and praised. Now the world is full of Christians, yet no one pays any attention to this or gives God thanks.

The last page of the *Sermon on the Sacrament of Penance.*

Summa Summarum[p]

For the one who believes:
{ everything is helpful
nothing is harmful. }

For the one who does not believe:
{ everything is harmful
nothing is helpful. }

---

p Latin for "To sum it all up."

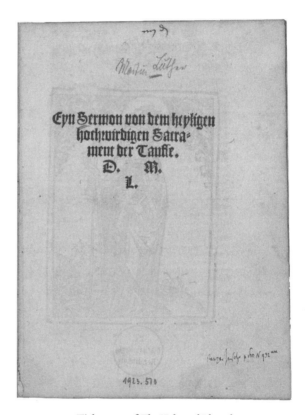

Title page of *The Holy and Blessed
Sacrament of Baptism*
with signature of Martin Luther.

The Holy and Blessed Sacrament of Baptism

1519

DIRK G. LANGE

INTRODUCTION

The sermon or treatise on baptism is part of the trilogy dedicated to the Duchess Margaretha of Braunschweig-Lüneburg (c. 1472–c. 1535).[a] It was first printed on "the Wednesday before [St.] Martin's [Day]" (9 November 1519), two days before the anniversary of Martin Luther's own baptism.[b] Luther develops here his baptismal theology that undergirds his understanding of the forgiveness of sins and the implications, throughout the life of a Christian, of practicing penitence. Luther notes that the sacrament of penance—confession and absolution—is a remembrance of baptism, for in baptism "we are forgiven."[c] Throughout this sermon, Luther expands upon this remembering.

In medieval Christianity, baptism, though continually present as a practice, was not central to the life of a Christian. Penance, in fact, had become the central practice[d] and also the one most abused (e.g., through the sale of indulgences).

---

a   See above, p. 185f.
b   WA 2:724.
c   See below, p. 217.
d   Brecht 1:360–61.

No wonder that in 1517 Luther began by dealing with the issue of indulgences (and the sacrament of penance), not the sacrament of baptism. Having developed significantly his thinking on penance, Luther now turns to the other sacraments and continues to explore the meaning and role of the sacraments. Not only does he highlight the close connection between baptism and penance, but also, by including the sacrament of the altar, Luther defines the fundamental characteristics of Christian life through these sacraments.

Luther's work on the sacraments is more fully developed in *The Babylonian Captivity of the Church*.[e] The three sermons in this volume depict important steps toward the changes that Luther proposes in *The Babylonian Captivity*. For the medieval church, the sacraments had a double function. They were seen as tools for increasing grace. If properly performed, they channeled grace into the souls of individuals. At the same time, they were stepping-stones to an ever-fuller participation in God's glory, again brought about through a proper "performance" of the rite. Luther challenges this time-honored tradition. The sacrament of penance is the word of absolution spoken here and now, not a means of channeling grace (understood as a substance) into the soul, creating a new "disposition" (*habitus*) there or preparing the recipient for greater graces through works of satisfaction. While Luther by no means abandons the language of "means of grace" or instrumentality, he shifts its meaning from the ontological and moral to places of lasting encounter with God.[f]

These three sermons do more than simply apply Luther's understanding justification by faith alone to the sacraments. The sacraments and their ritual and material embodiment provide Luther with an even fuller understanding of what

---

e   LW 36:3–126.

f   See, e.g., the *Schwabach Articles*, art. 8, in *Sources and Contexts of The Book of Concord*, ed. Robert Kolb and James A. Nestingen (Minneapolis: Fortress Press, 2001), 90, which became the basis of art. 5 of *The Augsburg Confession*, in BC, 40.

is implied by faith "alone." For him, baptism lies at the beginning of the Christian life, of a life of faith. Everything else refers back to it or is grounded in this action that God accomplishes. A sacrament does not divide the world into sacred and secular; it is not a secret access into God's heavenly reality. Instead, God encounters needy persons in the world. In that encounter with death and life in Christ, faith is created and life is reoriented.

In the sacraments, the recipient encounters Jesus Christ. Jesus Christ promises that he is "in baptism, the Supper, and preaching until the end of the age, until he comes."[g] This encounter reveals humanity's greatest need so that the sacraments speak to human vulnerability and incapacity to become holy. At the same time, one cannot understand or rationalize the sacraments: they are intended to oppose human reason and drive to faith.

In order to reach this major shift in sacramental theology, Luther introduces faith as a primary element of the sacrament. The sacraments, since Augustine (354–430), were defined as having two parts: sign (the material or physical component or action) and signification (their meaning). Luther expands this to three elements, adding faith as that which human beings experience in the very action of the sacrament. Already in the *Sermon on Penance*, he added the third element, "faith."[h] Now, in the sermon on baptism, Luther underscores faith's centrality even further. Faith is received and welcomed. Luther is still struggling to find an appropriate language for this radical passivity or dependence on the part of human beings. As Berndt Hamm describes the early Luther, "For Luther, faith is the path of pure reception, of being gifted with the righteousness of Jesus Christ."[i]

Though this treatise is not "polemical," in that Luther is not rejecting the baptismal practice of his day as he had

---

g   Martin Luther, *The Marburg Colloquy* (1529), LW 38:29.

h   See above, p. 190.

i   Berndt Hamm, *The Early Luther: Stages in a Reformation Reorientation*, trans. Martin J. Lohrmann (Grand Rapids: Eerdmans, 2014), 24.

1. This is related to Luther's
understanding of the justified person
as *simul iustus et peccator* (at the same
time righteous and sinner). See also
Leif Grane, *The Augsburg Confession:
A Commentary* (Minneapolis: Augsburg,
1987), 40–49.

rejected the practice of indulgence and the system of satisfaction in the medieval sacrament of penance, it nonetheless makes some important claims that are then later developed in both the *Small Catechism* and *Large Catechism* (1529).
Most notably, Luther retrieves Augustine's understanding
that baptism does not remove sin but forgives it. In this
retrieval, the framework in which the medieval church had
placed baptism and penance is broken apart. Baptism is not
limited to the washing away of original sin and restoring
the sinner to a state of grace. For Luther, baptism's work
of forgiveness and new life remains forever. Baptism establishes a new relationship with God (not a new "character"
in the person baptized).[1] This forgiveness (absolution) is
renewed daily through penance. Penance itself is not a work
that must be added to the believer after the grace of baptism
has been sinned away but, instead, it is a way to practice
baptism.

Second, we find throughout the sermon an insistence on
the sign, that is, on the body of the sacrament and in the
sacrament. In the first paragraph, Luther already states that
full immersion is preferable (even if other methods such as
sprinkling are acceptable) because full immersion also helps
the body understand what the sacrament is all about. A person's entry into the sacrament of baptism and the practice
of baptism is not through cognitive assent but through a
drowning and rising, that is, a participation in Christ's
death and resurrection that continues throughout life. A
Christian life is about this continual return to baptism.

Third, Luther develops what could be called a baptismal
spirituality. "Therefore this whole life is nothing else than a
spiritual baptism."[j] All of life is a continual dying to sin and
a daily rising up again to live from God. The journey metaphor, which entered Western Christian thought with Augustine, is not foreign to Luther, who used it quite frequently.
For him, however, the journey is not a "work" of improve-

j   See below, p. 218.

ment but an action by the Holy Spirit, who throughout life exercises the faith of the baptized. This work of the Spirit begins in baptism, is sustained through penance, and nurtured at the table.

✳

THE HOLY AND BLESSED SACRAMENT OF BAPTISM[2]

D.M.A.[3]

1. BAPTISM[k] MEANS *baptismos* in Greek, and *mersio* in Latin, that is, to plunge something completely into the water so that the water covers it. Although in many places it is no longer customary to thrust and submerge infants into the font, instead pouring baptismal water over them with the hand, nevertheless, the former is what should be done.[4] It would be proper, according to the meaning of the word *Taufe*, that the infant, or whoever is to be baptized, should be put in and sunk completely into the water and then drawn out again. For even in the German language the word *Taufe* comes undoubtedly from the word *tieffe* [deep] and means that which is baptized is sunk deeply into the water.[5] This usage is also demanded by the significance of baptism itself. For baptism, as we shall hear, signifies that the old creature and the sinful birth of flesh and blood are to be wholly drowned by the grace of God. We should therefore do justice to its meaning and make baptism a true and complete sign of the thing it signifies.

2. Johann Grünenberg published the first edition in Wittenberg in 1519. Between 1519 and 1523, fifteen separate printings appeared. The present translation is based upon WA 2:(724) 727–37, as well as on the text translated by Charles M. Jacobs and revised by E. Theodore Bachmann (LW 35:29–45).

3. D.M.A. for Doctor Martinus Augustiner [Augustinian].

4. While various forms of baptizing have apparently been practiced in all periods of the church, immersion may have been one of the most ancient. All forms of baptism with water were considered equally valid. The oldest baptismal order of the diocese of Münster (ca. 1400–1414) prescribed triple immersion, while the 1521 order of the Schwerin diocese allowed a choice between immersion and washing [*abwaschen*]. While Luther prefers immersion, he, too, is open to other practices. See the LC, "Baptism," par. 65, in BC, 465: "This act or ceremony consists of being dipped into the water, which covers us completely, and being drawn out again."

5. Later German linguists have substantiated Luther's etymology. See DWB 21:187. It is thus related to the English words *dip* and *deep*.

---

k   German: *die Taufe*.

2. Baptism is an external sign or token. It separates us from all those not baptized so that we are known as a people of Christ, our commander,[l] under whose banner (which is the holy cross) we continually fight against sin. In this holy sacrament we must therefore pay attention to three things: the sign, the significance, and faith.

6. THE SIGN OF BAPTISM

[6] The sign consists in this, that we are thrust into the water in the name of the Father and of the Son and of the Holy Spirit; however, we are not left there but are drawn out again. This accounts for the expression: *aus der Taufe gehoben.*[m] The sign must thus consist of both parts, the putting in and the drawing out.

7. THE SIGNIFICANCE OF BAPTISM

[7] 3. The significance of baptism is a blessed dying to sin and a resurrection in the grace of God, so that the old creature, conceived and born in sin, is drowned, and a new creature, born in grace, comes forth and rises. Thus, in Titus 3[:5] St. Paul calls baptism a "washing of new birth," since in this washing a person is born again and made new. As Christ also says, in John 3[:5], "Unless you are born a second time of water and the Spirit (of grace) you may not enter the kingdom of heaven." For just as a child is drawn out of his mother's womb and is born and through this fleshly birth is a sinful person and a child of wrath [Eph. 2:3], so one is drawn out of baptism and is born spiritually. Through this spiritual birth a person is a child of grace and a justified person. Therefore sins are drowned in baptism, and in place of sin, righteousness arises.

4. The significance of baptism—the dying or drowning of sin—is not fulfilled completely in this life. Indeed this does not happen until a person passes through bodily death and completely decays to dust. As we can plainly see, the sacrament or sign of baptism is quickly over. But the spiritual

---

l   German: *Hertzogen* ("duke," originally and literally, "leader of an army").

m   Literally, "lifted up out of the baptismal water," a common expression in the passive voice for the one baptized and in the active voice for "stand as sponsor."

baptism, the drowning of sin, which it signifies, lasts as long as we live and is completed only in death. Then it is that a person is completely sunk in baptism, and that which baptism signifies comes to pass.

Therefore this whole life is nothing else than a spiritual baptism that does not cease until death. The one who is baptized is condemned to death as if the priest, when he baptizes, were to say, "See, you are sinful flesh. Therefore I drown you in God's name and in God's name condemn you to death, so that all your sins along with you die and perish." Wherefore St. Paul, in Rom. 6[:4], says, "we have been buried with Christ by baptism into death." The sooner a person dies after baptism, the sooner baptism is completed. For sin never ceases entirely while the body lives, which is so completely conceived in sin that sin is its very nature, as the prophet says, "Indeed, I was born guilty, a sinner when my mother conceived me" [Ps. 51]. There is no help for the sinful nature unless it dies and is destroyed with all its sin. Therefore the life of a Christian, from baptism to the grave, is nothing else than the beginning of a holy death. For at the Last Day, God will make that person altogether new.

5. Similarly, the lifting up out of the baptismal water is quickly done, but the thing it signifies—spiritual birth, the increase of grace and righteousness—certainly begins[n] in baptism but continues until death, indeed, until the Last Day. Only then will everything that baptism signifies be complete. Then will we arise from death, from sins, and from all evil, pure in body and soul, and then we will live eternally. Then will we be truly lifted up out of baptism and be completely born and we will put

Image of infant baptism from a 1545 Leipzig printing of Luther's *Small Catechism*.

---

n   German: *hebt woll an*. This phrase also has the sense of being lifted up or out. The beginnings of a life of faith are in this lifting up out of death.

8. This paraphrases the words spoken (by the priest) while the sponsors dress the child in a baptismal gown in the medieval rite with which Luther was familiar. See LW 53:101 for Luther's 1523 translation of it.

on the true baptismal robe of immortal life in heaven. As the sponsors say, when they raise the child up out of baptism, "See, your sins are now drowned, and we receive you in God's name into an eternal life of innocence,"[8] so the angels will also raise up all baptized, upright Christians at the Last Day and fulfill what baptism and the sponsors signify, as Christ declares in Matt. 24[:31], "And he will send out his angels . . . and they will gather his elect from the four winds, from one end of heaven to the other."

6. Baptism was foreshadowed in Noah's flood, when the whole world was drowned, except for Noah with his three sons and their wives, eight souls, who were saved in the ark. That the people of the world were drowned signifies that in baptism sins are drowned. But that the eight in the ark, with animals of every sort, were preserved, signifies—as St. Peter explains in his second epistle [2 Pet. 2:5]—that through baptism a person becomes holy. Now baptism is by far a greater flood than was that of Noah. For that flood drowned people for no more than one year, but baptism drowns all sorts of people throughout the world from the birth of Christ even to the Day of Judgment. Moreover, while that was a flood of wrath, this is a flood of grace, as is declared in Ps. 29[:10, paraphrase], "God will make a continual new flood."[9] For without doubt many more people have been baptized than were drowned in the flood.

7. From this it follows, to be sure, that when someone comes forth out of baptism, that person is truly pure and completely innocent from sin.[o] Still, there are many who do not properly understand this. They think that sin is no longer present, and so they become lazy and negligent in the killing of their sinful

Noah's ark shaped like a rectangular box (as was the tradition), with graphic images of the corpses of people and animals, as well as the dove with an olive branch, from a 1527 publication.

o   German: *Unschuldig*, which means "guiltless" (the meaning of the Latin word *innocens*) or "owing nothing."

nature, just as some do after they have gone to confession. For this reason, as I said above, it should be properly understood and known that our flesh, so long as it lives here, is by nature evil and sinful. *p*

In order to help them, God has devised the plan of making our flesh altogether new, even as Jer. 18[:4-6] shows. For the potter, when the vessel "was spoiled in the potter's hand," thrust it again into the lump of clay and kneaded it, and afterward made another vessel, as seemed good to the potter. "So," says God, "are you in my hands." In the first birth it did not turn out well for us; therefore God thrusts us into the earth again by death, and makes us over at the Last Day, that we may turn out well and without sin.

This well-being, as has been said, begins*q* in baptism, which signifies death and the resurrection at the Last Day. Therefore, so far as the sign of the sacrament and its significance are concerned, sins along with the person are already dead and the person has risen again; so the sacrament has taken place. But the work of the sacrament has not yet fully happened, that is, death and the resurrection at the Last Day are still before us.

8. Each is therefore sacramentally altogether pure and innocent. This is to say nothing other than that such individuals*r* have the sign of God, namely, baptism, by which is signified that all their sins shall be dead and that they, too, shall die in grace and at the Last Day rise again to everlasting life, pure, sinless, and innocent. With respect to the sacrament, then, it is true that they are without sin and guilt. Yet because all has not yet been completed and they still live in the sinful flesh, they are neither without sin nor pure in all things, but instead they have started to become pure and innocent.

Therefore, when a person comes of age, the natural and sinful appetites—wrath, impurity, lust, greed, pride, and the

9. Luther bases his paraphrase on the Vulgate Latin translation, which reads: *"Dominus diluvium inhabitare facit"* (literally, "The Lord makes the flood to dwell"). Nicholas of Lyra (1270–1349), the premier medieval interpreter of the Bible, also suggests the connection to baptism in comments on this text in his *Postilla moralis.*

---

p   For the importance of this argument in Luther's theology, see the introduction above, p. 206, n. 1

q   German: *hebt er an*; see above, p. 209, note *n.*

r   Singular in the original.

10. While medieval theologians argued that the remnants of sin, concupiscence, remained after baptism, Luther insists that the person justified in baptism remains at the same time a sinner. By arguing that sin itself remains in the person until the last day, Luther views baptism as an eschatological promise. Already in his lectures on Romans 7 (1515–1516), he made the same point. See LW 25:322–43.

like—begin to stir; none of these would appear if all sins were drowned and dead in the sacrament. Now it only signifies that they will be drowned through death and the resurrection at the Last Day. So St. Paul, in Rom. 7[:17-20], and the saints with him, though they were baptized and were holy, lament that they are sinners and have sin in their nature because the natural and sinful appetites are always active so long as we live.[10]

9. You ask, "How does baptism help me, if it does not altogether blot out and remove sin?" This is the place for a right understanding of the sacrament of baptism. This blessed sacrament of baptism helps you because in it God allies himself with you and becomes one with you in a grace-filled, comforting covenant[s] [in the following ways].

In the first place, you give yourself up to the sacrament of baptism and its significance. That is, you desire to die, together with your sins, and to be made new at the Last Day according to the signification of the sacrament, as has been said. God receives this from you and grants you baptism. From that hour God begins[t] to make you a new person. God pours into you grace and the Holy Spirit, who begins to kill nature and sin and to prepare you for death and the resurrection at the Last Day.

In the second place, you bind yourself to remain [in Baptism] and to kill your sin more and more as long as you live, up to your dying day. This, too, God receives and trains and tests you all your life long with many good works and with all kinds of suffering. Thereby God accomplishes what you have desired in baptism, namely, that you want to become free from sin, die, and rise again at the Last Day, and so fulfill your baptism. Therefore, we read and see how bitterly God let the saints be tortured and suffer so much, in order that, at the point of being slain, they fulfilled the sacrament of baptism, died, and were made new. For when this does not

---

s   German: *Bund*, literally, "a binding," to which Luther then refers in the following paragraphs.

t   German: *anheben*. See above, p. 209, note n.

happen and we do not suffer or are exercised, then one's evil nature overwhelms a person, makes baptism useless, falls into sin, and remains the same old creature as before.

10. As long as your binding to God stands, God in turn is gracious and binds himself to you, not imputing to you the sins that remain in your nature after baptism: neither taking them into account nor condemning you because of them. God is satisfied and well pleased if you are constantly striving and desiring to put these sins to death and at your death to be rid of them. For this reason, although evil thoughts and appetites stir, indeed even though at times you may sin and fall, as you rise up again and enter again into this covenant, they are done away with through the power of the sacrament and binding, as St. Paul says in Rom. 8[:1].[11] No one who believes in Christ is condemned by the evil, sinful inclination of nature, as long as that person does not follow it and give in to it. St. John the Evangelist writes in his epistle [1 John 2:1-2], "But if anyone does sin, we have an advocate with God, Jesus Christ, who has become a forgiveness of our sins."[u] All this takes place in baptism, where Christ is given us, as we shall hear in the sermon that follows.[12]

11. Now if this covenant did not exist and God were not so merciful as to wink at our sins,[v] then, no matter how small the sin, it would condemn us. For God's judgment can endure no sin. Therefore there is no greater comfort on earth than baptism, for through baptism we come under the sentence of grace and mercy, which does not condemn our sins but with many exercises[w] drives them out. There is a fine statement of St. Augustine that says, "Sin is altogether forgiven in baptism; not in such a manner that it is no longer present, but in such a manner that it is not imputed."[13] It is as if he were to say, "Sin remains in our flesh even until death

11. "There is therefore now no condemnation for those who are in Christ Jesus."

12. See below, *The Blessed Sacrament of The Holy and True Body of Christ and the Brotherhoods*, p. 230. This indicates how closely connected these three tracts were in Luther's mind.

13. Augustine wrote in *On Marriage and Concupiscence*, bk. I, ch. 28 (25) (in NPNF, ser. 1, 5:275): "If the question arises, how this concupiscence of the flesh remains in the regenerate . . . the answer to be given is this: Carnal concupiscence is remitted, indeed, in baptism; not so that it is put out of existence, but so that it is not to be imputed for sin." Here Luther understands by concupiscence not, as had the Scholastic theologians, simply the "matter" of sin but not "formed" into true sin by the will, but as sin itself.

---

u A close paraphrase of the Vulgate, rendering "propitiator" with "forgiveness."

v Literally: if God did not mercifully peek through his fingers. See below, *Treatise on Good Works*, p. 283, note s.

w German: *ubungen*: For Luther this includes the trials and discipline described above.

and works without ceasing, but as long as we do not desire it or remain in it, sin is so overruled by our baptism that it does not condemn us and is not harmful to us. Rather, in us it is daily being destroyed, ever more and more until our death."

For this reason, no one should be terrified if they feel evil lust or love, nor should they despair even if they fall. Rather, they should remember their baptism and comfort themselves joyfully in it, knowing that there God has covenanted to destroy sin for them and not count it towards damnation, so that they do not desire or remain in sin. Moreover, these wild thoughts and appetites, and even a fall into sin, should not be regarded as an occasion for despair. Regard them rather as an admonition from God that we should remember our baptism and what was spoken there, that we should call upon God's mercy and exercise ourselves in striving against sin, that we should even desire death that we may be rid of sin.

14. THE THIRD THING: FAITH

[14] 12. Here, then, is the place to discuss the third thing in the sacrament: faith. Faith means that one firmly believes all this: that this sacrament not only signifies death and the resurrection at the Last Day, by which a person is made new to live without sin eternally, but also that the sacrament assuredly begins and achieves it, binding us to God so that we want to fight against sin and kill it till we die. On the other hand, God will be merciful to us and deal graciously with us, not judging us with severity because, in this life, we are not without sin until purified by death.

So you understand how in baptism a person becomes innocent, pure, and sinless, and yet remains full of evil inclinations. Human beings[x] can be called pure in the sense that they have started to become pure and have a sign and covenant of this purity. They are to become ever purer, which is why God will not count against them their former impurity, and thus they are pure through God's gracious reckoning, not on account of their own nature. As the prophet says in

---

x   Singular in the original.

Ps. 32[:1-2], "Happy are those whose transgression is forgiven, whose sin is covered. Happy are those to whom the Lord imputes no iniquity."

This faith is the most necessary of all things, for it is the ground of all comfort. Those[y] who do not possess such faith must despair of their sins, for the sin that remains after baptism makes it impossible for any good work to be pure before God. For this reason, one must boldly and without fear cling to baptism and hold it up[z] against all sins and terrors of conscience, humbly saying, "I know full well that I cannot do any work that is pure, but I am baptized, and through my baptism God, who cannot lie, has bound himself to me. God will not count my sin against me, but will kill it and blot it out."

13. So, then, we understand that the innocence that is ours by baptism is so called simply and solely because of God's mercy, through which God has begun this work in us and bears patiently with our sin and regards us as if we were sinless. This also explains why Christians are called in the Scriptures the children of mercy, a people of grace and of God's good will.[a] It is because through baptism they have started to become pure. Through God's mercy, they are not condemned for the sin that remains; until, finally, through death and at the Last Day, they become totally pure just as baptism and its sign attest.

Therefore those who think that through baptism they have become totally pure are greatly mistaken. They go about in their ignorance and do not kill their sin. They do not want to let go of their sin and simply persist in it, thereby making nothing of their baptism. They continue to depend only on a few external works. Meanwhile pride, hatred, and other evils in their nature, which they disregard, grow worse and worse.

y Singular in the original.
z See above, p. 209, note n.
a See, perhaps, Eph. 5:1, 9; 1 Pet. 2:9-10; and Luke 2:14, respectively.

15. Luther is combating the view that the innate concupiscence of human beings is not really sin but only an inclination toward sin, the "tinder of sin," a teaching finally promulgated as dogma in a decree of the Council of Trent (1546). For arguments defending Luther's view (as expressed in CA II), see Philip Melanchthon (1497–1560), Ap II.4-14 (1531), in BC, 112–14.

16. On "satisfaction," see above, *Sermon on Indulgences and Grace*, p. 160, n. 10.

No! It is not so! Sin, evil inclination, must be recognized as real sin.[15] That it does not harm us, however, is to be ascribed to the grace of God. God will not count sin against us as long as we struggle against it through many exercises, works, and sufferings, and, in the end, through death, kill it. To those who do not do this, God will not pardon their sins. For they do not follow in their baptism and its covenant, and they hinder the work of God and baptism that has commenced.

14. Those who presume to blot out and set aside their sin through "satisfaction"[16] are the same sort of people. They go so far as to disregard their baptism, as if they had no more need of it beyond the fact of having been once baptized. They do not know that baptism is in force all through life, even until death, yes even to the Last Day, as was said above. And so they presume to find another way of blotting out sin, namely, by works. They fashion for themselves and for all others, evil, terrified, and uncertain consciences; they despair at the hour of death; and they do not know how they stand with God, thinking that by sin they have now lost their baptism and that it profits them no more.

Guard yourself against this error with your life. For as has been said, if individuals[b] have fallen into sin, they should all the more remember their baptism, how God has bound himself to them to forgive all their sins, so that they may fight against them even until death. Upon this truth and covenant with God, a person must joyfully dare to rely. Then baptism again goes into force and to its work. Then the heart again becomes peaceful and glad, not in one's own works or "satisfaction," but in the mercy of God promised to each one in baptism, a mercy that God will keep forever. One must hold this faith firmly and cling to it even though attacked by everything and all sins, given that all[c] who let themselves be forced away from this faith make God a liar for binding himself to the sacrament of baptism.

b   Singular in the original.
c   Singular in the original.

15. The devil attacks this faith most of all. If he can over-throw it, he has won. For the sacrament of penance (of which we have already spoken)[17] also has its foundation in this sac-rament, inasmuch as sins are forgiven only to those who are baptized, that is, to those whom God has promised to for-give sin. The sacrament of penance thus renews and points again to the sacrament of baptism. It is as if in the absolu-tion the priest were saying, "See, God has now forgiven you your sin, as God long since promised you in baptism, and has commanded me, by the power of the keys, to assure you of this forgiveness. So now you come again into the work and power of baptism." Believe, and you have it. Doubt, and you are lost. So we find that because of sin baptism may well be hindered in its work of forgiving and slaying sin, yet only by not believing baptism's work is it canceled out. Faith, in turn, removes the hindrance to baptism's work. Thus every-thing depends on faith.

To speak quite plainly, it is one thing to forgive sins and quite another thing to put them aside or drive them out. Faith attains the forgiveness of sins, although they are not entirely driven out. But to drive sins out is to struggle[d] against them, and, in the end, to die, for in death sin per-ishes completely.[e] Both the forgiveness and the driving out of sins are the work of baptism as the Apostle writes to the Hebrews [Heb. 12:1], those who are baptized and whose sins were forgiven, that they "should lay aside the sin which clings to them."[f] For so long as I believe that God will not count my sins against me, my baptism is in force and my sins are forgiven, even though they may still be present in great measure. It follows then that sins are driven out through sufferings, death, and the like. This is what we confess in the article [of the Apostles' Creed], "I believe in the Holy Spirit . . . the forgiveness of sins," and so forth. Here there is special reference to baptism, in which the forgiveness takes

17. See above, pp. 187–201. Deriving the sacrament of penance (confession and absolution) from baptism was a unique contribution of Martin Luther.

---

d   German: *ubung*, that is, "exercise against sin."

e   Literally, "goes completely under" (as in drowned).

f   Hebrews 12:1: "Therefore . . . let us also lay aside every weight and the sin that clings so closely."

18. FAITH: A BAPTISMAL LIFE

19. See examples below.

20. Luther uses the traditional teaching that divided society into three arenas: the married, the clerics, and the rulers. For him, all of life is a continual practice of dying and thus part of baptism, forcing people to look beyond themselves to help others.

place through God's covenant with us; therefore we must not doubt this forgiveness.

[18] 16. It follows, then, that baptism makes all sufferings, and especially death, profitable and helpful, as they must simply serve baptism in the doing of its work, that is, in the slaying of sin. It cannot be otherwise. For the one who would complete[g] the work and purpose of baptism and be rid of sin must die. Sin, however, does not like to die, and for this reason it makes death so bitter and so horrible. God is gracious and powerful so that sin, which brought death, is driven out again by its own work, by death itself.

You find many people who want to live in order to become righteous and who say that they would like to be righteous. Now there is no shorter way or manner than through baptism and the work of baptism, which is suffering and death. Yet as long as they do not want to go this way, it is a sign that they do not properly intend or know how to become righteous. Therefore God instituted many walks of life in which all[h] shall learn to exercise themselves[19] and to suffer. To some God has commanded marriage, to others clerical orders, to others temporal rule, and to all God has commanded that they shall toil and labor to kill the flesh and accustom it to death.[20] Because for all who are baptized, their baptism has made the repose, ease, and prosperity of this life a pure poison, a hindrance to its work. For in such a life no one learns to suffer, to die with gladness, to get rid of sin, or to live in harmony with baptism. Instead, there grows only love of this life and horror of eternal life, fear of death, and unwillingness to blot out sin.

17. Consider now the lives of human beings, many of whom fast, pray, go on pilgrimage, and perform similar exercises, thinking only to heap up merit and sit down in the high places of heaven, but who no longer learn to kill their

g   "*Genug thun,*" the German equivalent of the Latin *satisfactio*. Luther suggests that satisfaction is only accomplished through continually dying. See above, *95 Theses*, theses 1–4, p. 34f.

h   Singular in the original.

evil vices. Fasting and all such exercises should be aimed at holding down and overcoming the sinful nature, the old Adam,[i] and accustoming it to do without all that is pleasing for this life, thus preparing it more and more each day for death so that the work and purpose of baptism may be fulfilled. And all of these exercises and toils are to be measured not by their number or their greatness but by the demands of baptism. That is, individuals[j] are to take upon themselves those works that are good and necessary for the suppressing of their sinful nature, sending it to death, and they are to increase or diminish these works as they find sin increasing or diminishing.[k] As it is, people go their way and take upon themselves this, that, and the other task, doing now this, now that, according to the appearance or reputation of the work. Afterward they let it drop just as quickly and thus become altogether inconstant, till in the end they amount to nothing. Indeed some of them so rack their brains over the whole business, and so abuse nature, that they are useless both to themselves and to others.

All this is the fruit of that doctrine with which we have been so infatuated as to think that after repentance or baptism we are without sin and that our good works are to be heaped up for their own sake or as a "satisfaction" for sins already committed but not for the blotting out of sin as such. This is encouraged by those preachers who unwisely preach the legends and works of the blessed saints and hold them up as examples for all. The ignorant easily fall for these things and bring about their own destruction from the examples of the saints. God has given every saint a special way and a special grace to follow in their baptism.[21] But baptism and its significance set a common standard for everyone, according to which all individuals[l] may examine themselves according to their station in life and find what is the best way to fulfill the work and purpose of their baptism: namely, to kill sin

21. Following one's baptism is to practice one's baptism.

---

i   Cf. 1 Cor. 15:21-22, 45-49; Rom. 5:12-21.

j   Singular in the original.

k   See below, *Treatise on Good Works*, p. 324.

l   Singular in the original.

22. Luther followed the traditional view that King Solomon authored Ecclesiastes.

23. Here Luther is attacking the widely held view that especially monastic vows were equivalent to a second baptism. See, e.g., Thomas Aquinas (1225-1274), *Summa Theologica* II/II, q. 88, 186–89.

24. Luther here is comparing the ordained priest or monk and a layman.

and to die in order that Christ's burden may grow light and easy [Matt. 11:30] and not be carried with worry and care. This is what Solomon[22] says about it [Eccles. 10:15], "The toil of fools only wears them out, because they do not know the way to town." For just as those who wish to go to the city and cannot find their way become fearful, so it is also with these [ignorant of baptism] whose life and work become bitter to them and yet accomplish nothing.

18. Here belongs the more general question whether baptism, and the vow which we make to God in baptism, is something more or greater than the vows of chastity, of the priesthood, or of the clergy.[23] Since baptism is common to all Christians, it is supposed that the clergy have taken a special and higher vow.

I answer: From what has been said, this is an easy question to answer. For in baptism we all make one and the same vow: to kill sin and to become holy through the work and grace of God, to whom we submit and offer ourselves, as clay to the potter [Jer. 18:4-6]. In this no one is any better than another. However, for a life that practices baptism for the purpose of killing sin, there is not one method or special station in life. This is why I said that all[m] must examine themselves so that they may determine in which station they may best kill sin and subdue their nature. It is true, then, that there is no vow higher, better, or greater than the baptismal vow. What more can we promise than to drive out sin, to die, to hate this life, and to become holy?[n]

Over and above this vow, we may indeed bind ourselves to a walk of life that will be suitable and helpful for the completion of baptism. It is just as though two people went to the same city, and the one went by the walking path, the other by the highway, just as each thought best. So the one who binds himself[24] to marriage walks in the toils and sufferings that belong to that station and lays upon himself its burdens, in order that he may grow used to pleasure and sorrow, avoid sin, and prepare himself for death better than he

m   Singular in the original.
n   Cf. Matt. 16:24-26 and John 12:25.

could do outside of that station. But the one who seeks more suffering and by much exercise would speedily prepare himself for death and soon attain the work of their baptism, let them bind themselves to chastity or to a clerical order.[o] For this clerical walk of life—if it is as it ought to be—should be full of suffering and trials, which exercise him more in the work of his baptism than the married life. Through such trials he quickly grows used to welcoming death with joy and so reaches the goal of their baptism.

Now above this station there is yet a higher one that rules in the spiritual order: the station of bishop, pastor, and so forth.[25] Those persons should be well practiced in sufferings and works, and at every hour be ready for death—to die not only for their own sake, but also for the sake of those who are their subjects.

Yet in all these walks of life the measure mentioned above should never be forgotten, namely, that all[p] should so exercise themselves only to the end that sin may be driven out and should not be guided by the number or the greatness of the works. But—alas!—just as we have forgotten our baptism and what it means, what vows we made there and how we are supposed to walk in its works and reach its goal, so, too, we have forgotten about the ways and walks of life to reach that goal. We hardly know to what end these stations in life were instituted, or how we are to live in them in order to fulfill our baptism. They have been made into a glittering show,[q] and little more remains of them than a worldly display. As Isaiah [1:22] states, "Your silver has become dross, your wine is mixed with water." On this, God have mercy! Amen.

19. If, then, the holy sacrament of baptism is a matter so great, gracious, and full of comfort, each should diligently see to praising, thanking, and honoring God for it ceaselessly, joyfully, and heartily. For I fear that our thanklessness has caused us to become blind and unworthy of recognizing such grace. The whole world has been and still is full of

25. Luther still maintains a particular hierarchy in this passage of the married man, the monk or cleric, and the bishop and pastor (German: *pfarrherr*; the chief minister of a parish). This distinction will begin to fade already in *The Freedom of a Christian*. He will insist throughout his life on a hierarchy of office in the household, government, and church but will emphasize even more that before God (that is, in the spiritual realm) all are equal in their baptism before God. Even in this passage, what sets the bishops and others apart is the cross and suffering.

---

o   German: *geystlichen orden*, literally, "spiritual order."
p   Singular in the original.
q   Literally, "pomp."

26. Luther explores this idea more fully in *The Babylonian Captivity of the Church* (1520), in LW 36:57–58.

baptism and the grace of God,[26] but we have been led astray into our own anxious works, into indulgences and other similar false comforts. We have thought that we are not to trust God until we are righteous and have made satisfaction for our sin, as though we would buy God's grace or pay God for it.

In truth, the one who is not mindful of God's grace—how it puts up with a person as a sinner and will make a person holy—and who looks only to God's judgment will never be joyful in God and neither love nor praise God. But when we hear and firmly believe that in the covenant of baptism God receives us sinners, spares us, and makes us pure each day, then our heart has to become joyful, and love and praise God. Thus God says through the prophet [Mal. 3:17], "I will spare them as a father spares his child." It is therefore necessary that we give thanks to the most-praised Majesty, who is so gracious and merciful toward us poor condemned little worms. And the work, as it truly is, we must magnify and recognize.

20. At the same time, however, we must also beware that a false sense of security does not creep in and say, "If baptism is so gracious and great a thing that God will not count our sins against us, and as soon as we turn again from sin everything is right by virtue of baptism, then for the present I will live and act according to my own will. Afterward, or when I am close to death, I will remember my baptism, remind God of his covenant, and thus fulfill my baptism."

To be sure, there is something so great about baptism that if you turn again from sins and appeal to the covenant of baptism, your sins are forgiven. But watch out, when you sacrilegiously and wantonly sin against grace, that the judgment does not lay hold of you and anticipate your turning back. Even if you then desired to believe or trust in your baptism, your assault,[r] by God's decree, might be so great that your faith will not able to stand. If those who do not sin or

---

r   German: *Anfechtung*, see above, *Sermon on the Sacrament of Penance*, p. 190, n. 18.

only fall because of sheer weakness scarcely remain, then what will become of your ungodliness, which has tempted and mocked God's grace?[27]

Let us then walk in fear,[s] so that we may hold fast to the riches of God's grace with a firm faith and joyfully give thanks to God's mercy forever and ever. AMEN.

[27] Luther may be thinking of 1 Pet. 4:18, "If it is hard for the righteous to be saved, what will become of the ungodly and the sinners?"

[s] German: *furchten*. See, e.g., Neh. 5:9.

The Blessed Sacrament of the Holy and True

Body of Christ, and the Brotherhoods

1519

DIRK G. LANGE

INTRODUCTION

On 29 November 1519 Martin Luther wrote to Georg Spalatin (1484–1545), "Of its kind, the sermon on the Eucharist is the wordiest!"[a] This sermon is Luther's first writing specifically on the Lord's Supper. It is the third sermon in the trilogy[b] dedicated to Duchess Margaretha von Braunschweig-Lüneburg (c. 1472–c. 1535) and composed in October–November 1519.

Like the sacrament of penance, the sacrament of the altar or Mass was subject to numerous abuses in Luther's time. It eventually became a theme on which Luther wrote profusely, not only in opposition to the Roman Church but also later in opposition to other reformers, especially Andreas Bodenstein from Karlstadt (1486–1541) and Ulrich Zwingli (1484–1531), and their understanding of the sacrament, either of whom could have appealed to some comments in this tract to defend portions of their position.[1]

1. See Martin Luther, *The Sacrament of the Body and Blood of Christ—Against the Fanatics* (1526), LW 36:329–61; *That These Words of Christ, 'This Is My Body,' etc., Still Stand Firm against the Fanatics* (1527), LW 37:99–150; *Confession Concerning Christ's Supper* (1528), LW 37:151–372. The debate came to a head at the Marburg Colloquy, 1–4 October 1529 (cf. LW 38:3–89). Luther and Zwingli disagreed on the principle matter: the real presence of Christ's body and blood in the bread and wine and whether the sacraments were only signs of human community (Zwingli) or also means of grace (Luther).

---

a   LW 48:134. "A most verbose treatise on the Eucharist is in the press."

b   See *The Sermon on the Sacrament of Penance* and *The Holy and Blessed Sacrament of Baptism* in this volume.

For Luther, it was essential that there was clarity about the sacrament itself and its movement. This sacrament, more than the other two, stood at the junction of the religious and superstitious (or magical). Unfortunately, what Luther and the people experienced in the sacrament was something that resembled magic (by the mere performance of the rite [*ex opere operato*] something happened) and superstition (the consecrated elements were to be adored in and for themselves). The sacrament had been turned into a sacrifice to God that the priest performed, a work done for himself and the people. It was yet another form of interposing human works into one's relation to God, similar to an indulgence. The more "Masses" someone could afford to buy, the less time they would have to spend in purgatory. The people could also buy Masses for their dead relatives to relieve their time of suffering in purgatory. In this sermon, Luther rejects this whole notion of works and sacrifice.

Luther begins the sermon by noting the need for both bread and wine. Again we see his concern for the material elements of the sacrament. Ideally, both kinds (bread and wine) are to be used, that is, they are to be eaten and drunk (and not just adored or worshiped in a tabernacle or monstrance). Of course, his suggestion that both kinds be distributed (no matter how diplomatically and conciliatory he makes the proposal in this sermon) caused quite a stir. In fact, it created considerable backlash, necessitating Luther to write a postscript to the third printing of the sermon. The uproar was aggravated by the fact that the printer, without consulting Luther, had added two woodcuts to the title page—one of a monstrance and another a monstrance and chalice.

In the first paragraph, Luther reiterates and develops his three-part definition of a sacrament—as sign, significance, and faith. Faith is now more than just connecting the sign

Roman Catholic observance of the Mass as depicted in Luther's *Sermon on the New Testament*, published 1520.

to its significance[c] but translates the sacrament into daily life. That is, the sacrament becomes the way one exercises and lives faith. The whole embodiment of the Christian life and the foundation for good works is to be found in this sacrament.

And this life is the fellowship (or communion) of the saints. The fellowship is unique in that not only does Christ bear all that burdens recipients and in exchange gives them all his benefits, but also they are called to bear the sufferings and sins of the neighbor. Participants share all things, spiritual and material, with all those who gather at the table, with the faith community.[d] This allows Luther to begin to break down the late medieval anxiety that accompanied receiving the Supper impurely or unworthily and replace it with an emphasis on the benefits and blessing received.

In this tract, there is an early reference to what was to become a major theme in later works as well—namely, the "joyous exchange" (*das fröhliche Wechsel*) of Christ's righteousness for the believer's sin. This exchange is further explained in Luther's treatise *The Freedom of a Christian*. In his German version, he calls it the joyous exchange for the first time.[e] Throughout his life, he continues to refer to this exchange (especially in the Galatians commentary from 1535).[f] It is widely acknowledged that Luther derived the idea of exchange, among other places, from medieval mysticism.[g]

A monstrance (or ostensorium) was the vessel in which the eucharistic host was displayed. From Luther's *The Blessed and True Sacrament of the Holy Body of Christ*, published in 1520.

c   Brecht 1:362.

d   See above, p. 207.

e   For a translation of the Latin text, see below, p. 499f. For the German translation, see Philip and Peter Krey, eds., *Luther's Spirituality* (Mahwah, NJ: Paulist, 2007), 76. In his 1519 Palm Sunday sermon on Phil. 2:5-11, which became *Two Kinds of Righteousness* (printed the same year; see LW 31:295–306, esp. 297-99), one finds the same concepts.

f   See LW 26:284.

g   Oswald Bayer, *Martin Luther's Theology: A Contemporary Interpretation*, trans. Thomas H. Trapp (Grand Rapids: Eerdmans, 2008), 225–30. See also Heiko A. Oberman, *Luther: Man between God and Devil*, trans. Eileen Walliser-Schwarzbart (New Haven: Yale University Press, 1989), 184–85; Berndt Hamm, *The Early Luther: Stages in a Reformation*

2. For Luther's use of the word *sacramentum* in relation to the "mystery" of the joyous exchange, see *The Freedom of a Christian*, below, p. 500, n. 78.

Here, however, he employed it for describing the sacrament of the altar. Again, Luther links this sacrament with significant insights into his ever-growing understanding of justification through faith alone.[2] In this sermon, Luther names the mystery a "gracious exchange."[h]

In the second half of the sermon, Luther offers a sustained critique of the sacrificial interpretation of the sacrament as he attacks the term medieval theologians consistently used to describe the grace in the New Testament sacraments as effective *ex opere operato* (by the mere performance of the rite). Here Luther demands that, in order to be effective, the sacrament does not simply need to be properly performed but that it must engage the participant, that is, be used in faith, and that the fellowship (communion) is not esoteric but a real fellowship in which the burdens of all are carried by the community.[i] A sacrament is not a sacrifice (a work on the participant's part, something to be performed) but a benefit that God gives and that redefines life.

The sermon concludes with a critique of the brotherhoods. These were fraternities mostly for devotional purposes but often organized according to the varying guilds.[j] They originated in the monasteries, though they quickly developed from the thirteenth century onward as also vocationally based brotherhoods linked closely to the various guilds. Members were obligated to the recitation of certain prayers and the attendance upon certain Masses at stipu-

---

Reorientation (Grand Rapids: Eerdmans, 2014), 200–203. The original source for describing the relation of the believer to Christ as one of marriage is Augustine of Hippo (354–430).

h   See below, p. 242 [sec. 17].

i   For this same connection to prayer, see *Treatise on Good Works* (1520), below, p. 314f.

j   For Luther's criticism of brotherhoods, see *Address to the Christian Nobility* (1520), below, p. 440f.

lated times. Each member was believed to participate—and, most important of all, even after death—in the benefits accruing from these "good works" of all the other members. In the case of most of the sodalities,[3] membership (for which the fees, generally steep, varied) entitled the member to the enjoyment of certain indulgences. In the late Middle Ages, Cologne had approximately 120 such brotherhoods. In 1520 Wittenberg boasted of twenty such fraternities, and Hamburg had more than one hundred. In 1519 Degenhard Pfeffinger (1471–1519), of Wittenberg, was a member of eight such fraternities in his home city and, through their cartel relationships, derived benefits from twenty-seven more in other places. (The brotherhood of St. Peter in Salzburg, for example, was united in fellowship with eighty other fraternities.) They chose the names of powerful or well-beloved saints, such as Mary, Mother of God, St. Anne (according to legend the mother of the Virgin Mary), St. Sebastian (martyr in Rome under Diocletian, who was emperor in 284–305), St. James, St. Francis, and more. They could also be Third Orders[4] attached to different monasteries and convents.

For Luther, these so-called brotherhoods or communities were a disgrace. They modeled the exact opposite of that fellowship nurtured at the Lord's Table. They were self-serving, offering Masses only for themselves, rather than going out to help their neighbor. His criticism here reveals the reason for his stress on fellowship, love, and unity in the first half of the tract. The "brotherhoods" undermined the true unity of brothers and sisters at the Lord's Supper.

In discussions of Luther's understanding of the Lord's Supper, this sermon is sometimes sidelined as a radical, early work, one that he apparently tempered in later debates with the Swiss reformers in particular. It, however, cannot be so easily dismissed. The reader finds here the main themes of Luther's understanding of the sacraments relating to justification (especially the "joyous exchange"), to the importance of the physical elements and their action (eating and drinking), and to the benefits derived from the sacrament (the immeasurable grace and mercy of God, along with fellowship and love). These themes are always in the background

3. A sodality was a kind of fraternity that flourished in the sixteenth century. The members were connected through devotional practices, such as reciting certain prayers and attending stipulated Masses. By participating in such a fraternity, each member was believed to benefit from the good works of all the members. Membership in most sodalite fraternities entitled members to benefit from certain types of indulgences.

4. Members of a Third Order were laymen or women (or ordained men or women) who did not take traditional religious vows, such as those connected to a "first order" (Dominicans, Franciscans, Augustinians, etc.) or "second order" (nuns associated with the "first order").

of many of Luther's subsequent writing, most importantly *The Babylonian Captivity of the Church.*[k]

The first edition of this text appeared in Wittenberg some time before 24 December 1519. The postscript (p. 254f) is from Edition C.[l] By 1525, a total of fourteen printings had appeared in German, along with a translation in Latin. As with other early sermons of Luther, we find here numbered paragraphs, a common technique in late medieval sermons.[m]

✳

THE BLESSED SACRAMENT OF THE HOLY AND TRUE BODY OF CHRIST, AND THE BROTHERHOODS[5]

5. This translation is based on the first edition that appeared in Wittenberg some time before 24 December 1519 and can be found in WA 2:(738) 742–58, as well as on the translation by Jeremiah J. Schindel and updated by E. Theodore Bachmann (LW 35: 49–73).

6. INTRODUCTION: SIGN AND SIGNIFICANCE

[6] FIRST OF ALL, the holy sacrament of the altar, or of the holy and true body[n] of Christ, also has three parts that we must know. The first is the sacrament or sign. The second is the significance of this sacrament. The third is the faith required with each of the first two. These three parts must be found in every sacrament. The sacrament must be external and visible, having some physical form[o] or appearance. The significance must be

---

k   LW 36:3–126.

l   WA 2:739, a 1520 reprint by the Wittenberg printer, Johannes Grünenberg.

m   See above, *Sermon on Indulgences and Grace*, pp. 60–65.

n   German: *Leichnam*. Although the word now means "body given to death" or "corpse" in today's German, in the sixteenth century it was a synonym for body.

o   Throughout the sermon, Luther used the words *leiblich* or *eyngeleybt*, which have usually been translated as "physical" and/or

The first page of the first printing of *The Blessed Sacrament
of the Holy and True Body of Christ and the Brotherhoods.*

internal and spiritual, within the spirit of the person. Faith
must make both of them useful and effective.

2. The sacrament, or external *sign*, consists in the form and
appearance of bread and wine, just as baptism has water as
its sign; only the bread and wine must be used in eating and
drinking, just as the water of baptism is used by immersion
or pouring. For the sacrament, or sign, must be received or
at least desired, if it is to be beneficial.[7] Of course, at present

7. See section 8 of this sermon for the
work or benefits of the sacrament.
These comments already mark a shift
from watching the priest celebrate the
meal to the actual reception of the
sacrament.

"incorporated," respectively. However, the two German words carry
a far deeper resonance with the body (as in the English "bodily" or
"embodied"). Each time any form of these words appears in Luther's
text, it will be indicated in the footnotes.

8. Meaning both bread and wine.

9. The custom of giving only the bread but not the wine to the laity, while stretching back centuries in the medieval church, became required church practice after the decree of the Council of Constance (1414–1418), which reacted against the criticisms of the practice by John Wycliffe (c. 1320–1384) and John Hus (c. 1369–1415). See Heinrich Denzinger, *Compendium of Creeds, Definitions, and Declarations on Matters of Faith and Morals*, 43rd ed. (San Francisco: Ignatius Press, 2012), 325 (par. 1198).

10. Luther was cautious in his proposal at this point in time, upholding the current practice but suggesting a fuller practice in section 3. In 1520, in *The Babylonian Captivity of the Church* (LW 36:19–28), Luther would name the withholding of the cup the first captivity of the sacrament. He would also express himself more forthrightly on the advisability of both kinds and the wickedness of forbidding both kinds in *A Treatise on the New Testament, That Is, the Holy Mass* (also 1520), LW 35:106–7.

11. The Council of Basel (1431–1449) had concluded the *Compactata* of Prague (30 November 1433), which reversed the decision of Constance to the extent of allowing the followers of Hus to administer the sacrament in both kinds, a decree never approved by the pope.

12. Luther insists on the fullness of the physical sign as a way of understanding the sacrament, thus linking sign and signification.

both kinds[8] are not given to the people daily, as in former times.[9] But this is not necessary since the priesthood partakes of it daily in sight of the people. It is enough that the people desire it daily and at present receive one kind, as the Christian Church ordains and provides.[10]

3. For my part, however, I would consider it a good thing if the church should again decree in a general council[11] that all persons be given both kinds, like the priests. Not because one kind is insufficient, since indeed the desire of faith is alone sufficient, as St. Augustine says: "Why do you prepare stomach and teeth? Only believe, and you have already partaken of the sacrament."[p] But it would be fitting and fine that the form, or sign, of the sacrament be given not in part only, but in its entirety, just as I said of baptism: it would be more fitting to immerse in the water than to pour it for the sake of the completeness and perfection of the sign.[12] For

An illustration for a 1519 Basel reprint of Luther's *Sermon on the Blessed Sacrament*, showing the host being offered to a layman.

---

p   Augustine, *Tractates on John*, XXV.12. For an English translation see NPNF, ser. 1, 7:164."

this sacrament [of the Body of Christ], as we shall see, signifies the complete union and the undivided fellowship of the saints;[13] and this is poorly and unfittingly indicated by [distributing] only one part of the sacrament. Nor is there as great a danger in the use of the cup as is supposed,[14] since the people seldom go to this sacrament.[15] Besides, Christ was well aware of all future dangers, and yet he saw fit to institute both kinds for the use of all his Christians.

4. The *significance* or effect of this sacrament is the fellowship of all the saints. From this it derives its common name *synaxis*[q] or *communio*,[r] that is, fellowship. The Latin *communicare* means to participate in this fellowship, or as we say in German, *zum sacrament gehen*.[s] So it is that Christ and all saints are one spiritual body [Rom. 12:5; 1 Cor. 12:5], just as the inhabitants of a city are one community and body, each citizen being a member of the other and of the entire city. All the saints, therefore, are members of Christ and of the church, which is a spiritual and eternal city of God (Isa. 60:14; Heb. 12:22; Rev. 3:12). And whoever is taken into this city is said to be received into the community of saints and to be incorporated into Christ's spiritual body and made a member of him. On the other hand, *excommunicare* [excommunicate] means to put out of the community and to sever a member from this body; and that is called in German "putting one under the ban"—though there are degrees here, as I shall show in the following treatise, concerning the ban.[16]

To receive this sacrament in bread and wine, then, is nothing else than to receive a sure sign of this fellowship and incorporation[t] with Christ and all saints. It is as if citizens were given a sign, a document, or some other pledge to assure them that they are citizens of the city, members of that particular community. St. Paul says this very thing in 1 Cor. 10[:17, paraphrase], "we who are many are one body, for we all partake of the one bread and of one cup."

13. As early as 1515–1516, in his lectures on Romans [12:13], in LW 25:461–62, Luther distinguished between the contemporary understanding of "saints" as those who "are blessed and participating in glory" and the biblical understanding of "saints" as "all those who believe in Christ." This second sense, including both clergy and laity, is implicit in Luther's use of the term here and throughout the treatise.

14. Especially the fear of wine spilling on the floor.

15. In 1215 the Fourth Lateran Council stipulated that every Christian had to receive the Lord's Supper once a year between Easter and Corpus Christi day. See *Receiving Both Kinds in the Sacrament* (1522) in LW 36:249. Luther sought, throughout his life as a reformer, to increase participation. See his comments in the *Small Catechism* and *Large Catechism* (BC, 360, 471).

16. See *Sermon on the Ban* (1520) in LW 39:7ff., where Luther distinguishes between the external ban (excommunication) that excludes from the church's sacramental fellowship and the internal ban (sin and unbelief) that excludes from fellowship with Christ.

q   A Greek term.
r   The Latin equivalent.
s   Literally, "go to sacrament," that is, taking part in the sacrament's fellowship.
t   German: *ein leybung*, literally, "embodiment." See above, p. 230, note o.

[17] 5. This fellowship consists in this, that all the spiritual possessions of Christ and his saints are shared with and become the common property of the one who receives this sacrament. Again all sufferings and sins also become common property; and thus love is ignited through love and unites. To stay with our simple comparison, it is like a city where every citizen shares with all the others the city's name, honor, freedom, trade, customs, usages, help, support, protection, and the like, while at the same time sharing all the dangers of fire and flood, enemies and death, losses, taxes, and the like. For the one who would share in the profits must also share in the costs, and always recompense love with love. Here we see that whoever injures one citizen injures an entire city and all its citizens; whoever benefits one [citizen] deserves favor and thanks from all the others. So also in our natural body, as St. Paul says in 1 Cor. 12[:25-26], where he gives this sacrament a spiritual explanation: "the members may have the same care for one another. If one member suffers, all suffer together with it; if one member is honored, all rejoice together with it." This is obvious: if anyone's foot hurts, yes, even the little toe, the eye at once looks at it, the fingers grasp it, the face puckers, the whole body bends over to it, and all are concerned with this small member; again, once it is cared for, all the other members are benefited. This comparison must be noted well if one wishes to understand this sacrament, for Scripture uses it for the sake of the simple.

6. In this sacrament, therefore, individuals*u* are given through the priest a sure sign from God that they are thus united with Christ and his saints and hold all things in common, that Christ's sufferings and life are God's own, together with the lives and sufferings of all the saints. Therefore whoever does injury to such people, does injury to Christ and all the saints, as God says through the prophet [Zech. 2:8], "Truly, one who touches you touches the apple of my eye." On the other hand, whoever does a kindness to

---

u   Singular in the original throughout.

one does it to Christ and all his saints; as he says in Matthew 25[:40], "Truly I tell you, just as you did it to one of the least of these . . . you did it to me." Again, they must be willing to share all the burdens and misfortunes of Christ and his saints, the cost as well as the profit. Let us consider more closely both of these aspects.

7. Now suffering assails us in more than one form. There is, in the first place, the sin that remains in our flesh after baptism: the inclination to anger, hatred, pride, unchastity, and so forth.[18] This sin assails us as long as we live. Here we not only need the help of the community and of Christ in order that they might struggle with us against this sin, but it is also necessary that Christ and his saints intercede for us before God, so that we are not held accountable for this sin by God's strict judgment. Therefore, in order to strengthen and encourage us against this sin, God gives us this sacrament, as much as to say, "Look, many kinds of sin are assailing you; take this sign by which I give you my pledge that this sin is assailing not only you but also my Son, Christ, and all his saints in heaven and on earth. Therefore take heart and be bold. You are not fighting alone. Great help and support are all around you." King David speaks of this bread [Ps. 104:15, paraphrase], "The bread strengthens a person's heart." And the Scriptures in numerous places ascribe to this sacrament the property of strengthening, as in Acts 9[:18-19] [where it is written] of St. Paul, "Then he got up and was baptized, and after taking some food, he regained his strength."[19]

In the second place, the evil spirit assails us unceasingly with many sins and afflictions. In the third place, the world, full of wickedness, entices and persecutes us and is altogether bad. Finally, our own guilty conscience assails us with our past sins; and there is the fear of death and the pains of hell. All of these make us weary and weak, unless we seek strength in this fellowship, where strength is to be found.

8. Those who are in despair, distressed by a sin-stricken conscience or terrified by death or carrying some other burden upon their heart, if they wish to be rid of it all, let them go joyfully to the sacrament of the altar and lay down their

18. Here Luther breaks with medieval tradition that argued only the "material aspect" of sin, namely concupiscence, remained after baptism, but not sin itself. Instead, Luther argued that a believer is, at the same time, righteous and sinner.

19. Here Luther uses a form of allegory, common in the Middle Ages, by associating all mention of bread in the Bible with the bread of the Lord's Supper. Like most Christians of that day, Luther assumed that many, if not all, of the psalms were written by King David.

20. German: *Anfechtung.* This important word for Luther's theology means such things as tribulation, anguish, or struggle.

21. Luther turns love from being a goal that believers strive for (to always love more and more and be better and better, etc.) to a gift that God gives and that sends recipients into the world to serve the neighbor.

sorrow in the midst of the community and seek help from the entire company of the spiritual body. Just as a citizen whose property has suffered damage or misfortune at the hands of enemies will lodge a complaint with the town council and fellow citizens and ask them for help. The immeasurable grace and mercy of God are given us in this sacrament to the end that we might put from us all misery and tribulation[20] and lay it upon the community [of saints], and especially on Christ. Then we may with joy find strength and comfort, and say, "Though I am a sinner and have fallen, though this or that misfortune has befallen me, nevertheless I will go to the sacrament to receive a sign from God that I have on my side Christ's righteousness, life, and sufferings, with all holy angels and the blessed in heaven and all righteous people on earth. If I die, I am not alone in death; if I suffer, they suffer with me. [I know that] all my misfortune is shared with Christ and the saints, because I have a sure sign of their love toward me." See, this is the fruit and [proper] use of this sacrament by which the heart cannot but rejoice and be strengthened.

9. When you have partaken of this sacrament, therefore, or desire to partake of it, you must in turn share the misfortunes of the fellowship, as has been said. But what are these? Christ in heaven and the angels, together with the saints, have no misfortunes, except when injury is done to the truth and to the Word of God. Indeed, as we have said, every bane and blessing of all the saints on earth affects them. Here your heart must go out in love and learn that this is a sacrament of love.[21] As you experience love and support, so in turn you give it to Christ in his needy ones. You must feel the pain of all dishonor done to Christ in his Holy Word, all the misery of Christendom, all the unjust suffering of the innocent, with which the world is everywhere filled to overflowing. You must fight, work, pray, and—if you cannot do more—have heartfelt sympathy.[v] See, this is what it means to bear in your turn the misfortune and adversity of Christ and

---

v   German: *hertzlich mit leyden haben.* This expression is more intense than "sympathy," implying suffering deep within the heart.

The Blessed Sacrament of the Holy and True
Body of Christ, and the Brotherhoods
237

his saints. As the saying of Paul puts it [Gal. 6:2], "Bear one another's burdens, and in this way you will fulfill the law of Christ." See, as you carry all of them, so they all in turn carry you; and all things are in common, both good and evil. Then all things become easy, and the evil spirit cannot stand up against this fellowship.

When Christ instituted the sacrament, he said [Luke 22:19, paraphrase], "This is my body which is given for you, this is my blood which is poured out for you. As often as you do this, remember me." It is as if he were saying, "I am the Head, I will be the first to give myself for you. I will make your suffering and misfortune my own and will bear them for you, so that you in your turn may do the same for me and for one another, allowing all things to be common property, in me, and with me. And I leave you this sacrament as a sure sign of all this, in order that you may not forget me, but daily exercise and admonish one another with what I did and am still doing for you, in order that you may be strengthened, and also bear one another in the same way."

10. This is also a reason, indeed the chief reason, why this sacrament is received many times, while baptism is received but once. Baptism is the taking up or entering upon a new life, in the course of which countless adversities assail us, with sins and sufferings, both our own and those of others. There is the devil, the world, and our own flesh and conscience, as I have said, that never cease to chase and hunt us down. Therefore we need the strength, support, and help of Christ and of his saints that are promised to us here, as in a sure sign, by which we are united with them, made into one body,[w] and all our sorrow is laid down in the midst of the community.

For this reason, it even happens that this holy sacrament is of little or no benefit to those who have no misfortune or anxiety, or who do not feel their misfortune. For it is given only to those who need strength and comfort, who have timid hearts and terrified consciences, and who are assailed by sin, or have even fallen into sin. How could it do anything

---

w   German: *eyngeleybt*, see above, p. 230, note o.

22. The appellation for the Virgin Mary already in the ancient church and part of the christological controversies, when Nestorius (c. 386–450), patriarch of Constantinople, called Mary instead only the "Christ bearer." See Luther's discussion of the name in *The Magnificat* (1521), LW 21:326–27.

23. Following Matt. 26:20-25 and Mark 14:17-21, Luther places the announcement of the betrayal prior to the institution of the Lord's Supper.

24. Luther moves worthiness from a moral category to a deeper level of human existence where faith and unbelief stand as opposites. Worthiness is no longer equated with moral uprightness but with longing for the sacrament out of weakness. Concerning this distinction, see Luther's commentary on Psalm 1 in *Works on the First Twenty-Two Psalms* (1519–1521), LW 14:289.

for untroubled and secure spirits, who neither need nor desire it? For the Mother of God[22] says [Luke 1:53, paraphrase], "God fills only the hungry, and comforts them that are distressed."[x]

11. In order that the disciples, therefore, might by all means be worthy and well prepared for this sacrament, Christ first made them sorrowful, held before them his departure and death, by which they became exceedingly troubled. And then he greatly terrified them when he said that one of them would betray him. When they were thus full of sorrow and anxiety, disturbed by sorrow and the sin of betrayal, then they were worthy, and he gave them his holy body to strengthen them.[23] By this he teaches us that this sacrament is strength and comfort for those who are troubled and distressed by sin and evil. St. Augustine says the same thing, "This food demands only hungry souls, and is shunned by none so greatly as by a sated soul which does not need it."[y] Thus the Jews were required to eat the Paschal lamb with bitter herbs, standing and in haste [Exod. 12:8, 11]; this too signifies that this sacrament demands souls that are desirous, needy, and sorrowful.

Now the ones[z] who make the afflictions of Christ and of all Christians their own, defend the truth, oppose unrighteousness, and help bear the needs of the innocent and the sufferings of all Christians, will find affliction and adversity enough to say nothing of what the evil human nature, the world, the devil, and sin daily inflict on them daily. And it is God's will and purpose to set so many dogs upon us, chasing us, and everywhere to "prepare bitter herbs for us," so that we may long for this strength and take delight in the holy sacrament, and thus be worthy (that is, desirous) of it.[24]

---

x　Like others from this period, Luther often cites Scripture paraphrastically to interpret it.

y　A paraphrase of Augustine's commentary on Ps. 22:26 in his *Expositions on the Book of Psalms*, XXI.27. For an English translation see NPNF, ser. 1, 8:60.

z　Singular in the original.

12. It is Christ's will then that we partake of it frequently, in order that we may remember him and exercise ourselves in this fellowship according to his example. For if his example were no longer kept before us, the fellowship also would soon be forgotten. At present, we see with sorrow that many Masses are held and yet the Christian fellowship that should be preached, practiced, and kept before us by Christ's example has virtually perished.[a] So much so that we hardly know any more what purpose this sacrament serves or how it should be used. Indeed with our Masses we frequently destroy this fellowship and pervert everything. This is the fault of the preachers who do not preach the gospel or the sacraments, but rather their humanly devised fables about the many works to be done and the ways to live well.[25]

But in times past this sacrament was so properly used and the people were taught to understand this fellowship so well, that they even gathered food and material goods in the church, and there—as St. Paul writes in 1 Cor. 11[:12]—distributed among those who were in need.[26] We have a vestige of this [practice] in the little word "collect" in the Mass, which means a general collection, just as a common fund is gathered to be given to the poor.[27] Those were the days, too, when so many became martyrs and saints. There were fewer Masses, but much strength and blessing resulted from them; Christians cared for one another, supported one another, sympathized with one another, bore one another's burdens and affliction. This has all disappeared. What remain now are only numerous Masses and many people receiving this sacrament without in the least understanding or practicing what it signifies.

13. There are those, indeed, who would gladly share in the benefits but not in the costs. That is, they like to hear that in this sacrament the help, fellowship, and support of all the saints are promised and given to them. But they are unwilling in their turn to belong to this fellowship. They do not want to help the poor, to put up with sinners, to care

25. Here again Luther criticizes the medieval understanding of satisfaction as works that must be done in order to be right with God.

26. Given that Justin Martyr's (c. 100–165) *Apology* was first translated into Latin in 1565, it is doubtful that Luther knew of it. It contained a description of the practice Luther refers to here. See Justin Martyr, *Apologia* I, 67, 7.

27. Luther's perception reflects a common understanding about the "Collect," which was actually the prayer collecting the main thoughts of the appointed readings in the Mass that day. Collections for the poor in the "community chest" (*Gemeinde Kasten*), which predated the Reformation, would become an important component of the worship life of Reformation parishes. See Luther's later comments in the preface to *Ordinance of a Common Chest* (1523) and *Concerning the Order of Public Worship* (1523), in LW 45:159–94 and 53:7–14.

---

a   For Luther's attack on private Masses, hinted at here, see below, *Treatise on Good Works*, p. 305.

for the sorrowing, to suffer with the suffering, to intercede for others, to defend the truth or, risking life, property, and honor, to seek the betterment of the church and of all Christians. They are unwilling because they fear the world. They do not want to have to suffer disfavor, harm, shame, or death, although it is God's will that they be thus driven—for the sake of the truth and of their neighbors—to desire the great grace and strength of this sacrament. They are self-seeking persons, whom this sacrament does not benefit. Just as we could not put up with a citizen who wanted to be helped, protected, and made free by the community, and yet in turn would do nothing for it nor serve it. No, we must make the evil of others our own, if we wish Christ and his saints to make our evil their own. Then will the fellowship be complete and justice be done to the sacrament. The sacrament has no blessing and significance unless love grows daily and so transforms persons that they are made one with all others.

14. To signify this fellowship, God has established signs of this sacrament that completely serve this purpose and by their form attract and motivate us to this fellowship. For just as the bread is made out of many grains ground and mixed together, and out of the bodies of many grains there comes the body of one bread,[28] in which each grain loses its form and body and takes upon itself the common body of the bread; and just as the grapes for wine, in losing their own form, become the body of one common wine and drink, so it is and should be with us, if we use this sacrament properly. Christ with all saints, by his love, takes upon himself our form [Phil. 2:7], fights with us against sin, death, and all evil. This enkindles in us such love that we take on his form, rely upon his righteousness, life, and blessedness. And through the interchange of his blessings and our misfortunes, we become one loaf, one bread, one body, one drink, and have all things in common.[29] O this is a great sacrament,[b] says

28. This ancient figure goes back at least into the second century, as attested by a document unknown to Luther, *The Didache* 9:4, "As this [bread] lay scattered upon the mountains and became one when it had been gathered, so may your church be gathered into your kingdom from the ends of earth." Kurt Niederwimmer, *The Didache: A Commentary*, Hermeneia, trans. Linda M. Maloney (Minneapolis: Fortress Press, 1998), 144.

29. Luther would work out this notion of exchange more fully in *The Freedom of a Christian* (1520). See below, p. 500.

b　In the Vulgate of St. Jerome (c. 347–420), the Greek word *mysterion* ("mystery") in Eph. 5:32 is translated *sacramentum*. Compare Luther's later discussion of the term in LW 36:93–95.

St. Paul, that Christ and the church are one flesh and bone [Eph. 5:32]. Again through this same love, we are to be transformed and to allow the infirmities of all other Christians to be our own; we are to take upon ourselves their form and their necessity, and let them have all the good that we are capable of so that they may benefit from it. That is the real fellowship and the true significance of this sacrament. In this way we are changed into one another and are made into a community by love. Without love there can be no such change.

15. Christ appointed these two forms of bread and wine, rather than any other, as a further indication of the very union and fellowship that is in this sacrament. For there is no more intimate, deep, and indivisible union than the union of food with the one who is fed. For the food enters and is assimilated by a person's nature, and becomes one being with the one eating. Other unions, achieved by such things as nails, glue, rope, and the like, do not make one indivisible being out of the objects joined together. Thus in the sacrament we too become united with Christ, and are made one body[c] with all the saints, so that Christ takes us upon himself and acts in our behalf as if he were what we are, taking up what concerns us as if it were his concern, taking it up even more than we do. In turn, we also wish to take Christ upon ourselves, as if we were what he is, which indeed will finally happen—we shall be conformed to his likeness. As St. John says [1 John 3:2], "when he is revealed, we will be like him": so deep and complete is the fellowship of Christ and all the saints with us. Thus our sins assail him, while his righteousness protects us. For the union makes all things common until at last Christ completely destroys sin in us and makes us like himself, at the Last Day. Likewise by the same love we are to be united with our neighbors, we in them and they in us.

16. Besides all this, Christ did not institute these two forms only and alone, but gave his true natural flesh in the

---

c   German: *eyngeleybet*. See above, p. 230, note o.

30. German: *Vorwandelt*, the German equivalent of the Latin word *transubstantiation*. Luther uses the term while rejecting all Scholastic speculation concerning substance (see below, p. 243) and explicitly calls into question that doctrine as "the second captivity of the sacrament" in *The Babylonian Captivity of the Church* (LW 36:28–35).

bread and his natural true blood in the wine that he might give a really perfect sacrament or sign. For just as the bread is changed into his true natural body[30] and the wine into his natural true blood, so truly are we also drawn and changed into the spiritual body, that is, into the fellowship of Christ and all saints and by this sacrament put into possession of all the virtues and mercies of Christ and his saints, as was said above of a citizen who is taken and incorporated into the protection and freedom of the city and the entire community. For this reason, Christ instituted not simply the one form, but two separate forms—his flesh under the bread, his blood under the wine —to indicate that not only his life and good works, shown by his flesh and accomplished in his flesh, but also his passion and martyrdom, shown by his blood and in which he poured out his blood, are all our own. And we, being drawn into them, may use and enjoy them.

17. So it is clear from all this that this holy sacrament is nothing else than a divine sign, in which Christ and all saints together with all their works, sufferings, merits, mercies, and possessions, are pledged, granted, and imparted for the comfort and strengthening of all who are in anxiety and sorrow, persecuted by the devil, sins, the world, the flesh, and every evil. And to receive the sacrament is nothing else than to desire all this and firmly to believe that it happens this way.

31. FAITH

32. Luther now summarizes his previous discussion using the phrase "gracious exchange" (*gnediger wechsell*). See the introduction, p. 227.

[31] Here, now, follows the third part of the sacrament, that is, the *faith*[d] on which everything depends. For it is not enough to know what the sacrament is and signifies. It is not enough that you know it is a fellowship and a gracious exchange[32] or blending of our sin and suffering with the righteousness of Christ and his saints. You must also desire it and firmly believe that you have received it. Here the devil and human nature wage their fiercest fight, so that faith cannot stand. There are those who practice their arts and subtleties by try-

d   The word "faith" (*Glaube*) is capitalized in the original.

ing [to fathom] what becomes of the bread when it is changed into Christ's flesh and of the wine when it is changed into his blood and how the whole Christ, his flesh and blood, can be encompassed in so small a portion of bread and wine. It does not matter if you do not search for it.[e] It is enough to know that it is a divine sign in which Christ's flesh and blood are truly present. The how and the where, we leave to him.[33]

18. See to it here that you exercise and strengthen your faith, so that when you are sorrowful or when your sins press you and you go to the sacrament or hear Mass, you do so with a hearty desire for this sacrament and for what it signifies. Then do not doubt that you have what the sacrament signifies; that is, be certain that Christ and all his saints are coming to you with all their virtues, sufferings, and mercies, to live, work, suffer, and die with you, and that they desire to be completely yours, having all things in common with you. If you will exercise and strengthen this faith, then you will experience what a rich, joyous, and bountiful wedding feast your God has prepared for you upon the altar. Then you will understand what the great feast of King Ahasuerus signifies [Esther 1:5]; and you will see what that wedding feast is for which God slew his oxen and fat calves, as it is written in the gospel [Matt. 22:2ff.]. Then your heart will become truly free and confident, strong and courageous against all enemies [Ps. 23:5]. For who will fear any misfortune if they are sure that Christ and all his saints are with them and have all things, evil or good, in common with them? So we read in Acts 2[:46] that the disciples of Christ broke this bread and ate with great

33. This begins Luther's critique of transubstantiation. See *The Babylonian Captivity of the Church* (LW 36:34). In a later treatise written against Ulrich Zwingli, Luther is even more explicit about human reason's inability to know. See *That These Words of Christ, 'This Is My Body,' Etc., Still Stand Firm against the Fanatics* (1527), LW 37:28–29.

The great feast of King Ahasuerus (Xerxes), shown here with his retinue, in the book of Esther, chapter 1.

e   Although WA 2:750, n. 1 suggests a typographical error and reads *siehist* ("see") rather than *suchist* ("search"), we follow MLStA 1:280, n. 60.

gladness of heart. Since this work is so great that the smallness of our souls would not dare to desire it, to say nothing of hoping for or expecting it, it is good and necessary to go often to the sacrament, or at least in the daily Mass to exercise and strengthen this faith on which the whole thing depends and for the sake of which it was instituted.[34] For if you doubt, you do God the greatest dishonor and make him out to be a faithless liar; if you cannot believe, then pray for faith, as was said earlier in the other treatise.[f]

19. See to it also that you give yourself to everyone in fellowship and by no means exclude anyone in hatred or anger; for this sacrament of fellowship, love, and unity cannot tolerate discord and disunity. You must take to heart the infirmities and needs of others, as if they were your own. Then offer to others your strength, as if it were their own, just as Christ does for you in the sacrament. This is what it means to be transformed into one another through love, out of many particles to become one bread and drink, to lose one's own form and take on that which is common to all.

For this reason, slanderers and those who wickedly judge and despise others cannot but receive death in the sacrament, as St. Paul writes in 1 Cor. 11[:29]. For they do not do to their neighbor what they seek from Christ or what the sacrament indicates. They begrudge others anything good; they have no sympathy for them; they do not care for others as they themselves desire to be cared for by Christ. And then they fall into such blindness that they do not know what else to do in this sacrament except how, with their own prayers and devotion, they may fear and honor Christ as present.[35] When they have done this, they think they have done their whole duty. But Christ has given his holy body for this purpose that the thing signified by the sacrament—the fellowship, the transformation wrought by love—may be put into practice. And Christ values his spiritual body, which is the fellowship of his saints, more than his own natural body. To

f   For Luther's discussion of unbelief, see above, *The Sacrament of Penance*, p. 198.

The Blessed Sacrament of the Holy and True
Body of Christ, and the Brotherhoods
245

him it is more important, especially in this sacrament, that faith in the fellowship with him and with his saints may be properly exercised and become strong in us; and that we, in keeping with it, may properly exercise our fellowship with one another. Blind worshipers do not perceive Christ's purpose. In their devoutness they go on daily reciting and hearing Mass, but they remain every day the same; indeed every day they become worse but do not perceive it.

Therefore take heed. It is more needful that you discern the spiritual than the natural body of Christ; and faith in the spiritual body is more necessary than faith in the natural body. For the natural without the spiritual benefits us nothing in this sacrament; a transformation must occur and be exercised through love.

20. There are many who, regardless of this exchange[g] of love and faith, rely upon the fact that the Mass or the sacrament is, as they say, *opus gratum opere operato*,[36] that is, a work which of itself pleases God, even though they who perform it are not pleasing. From this they conclude that it is a good thing to have many Masses no matter how unworthily they are said, since harm comes [only] to those who say or use them unworthily. I will leave everyone to their own opinion, but such fables do not please me. For, [if you desire] to speak in such terms, there is no creature or work that does not of itself please God, as is written in Genesis 1[:31, paraphrase], "God saw all God's works and they pleased God." What is the result if bread, wine, gold, and all good things are misused, even though of themselves they are pleasing to God? Why, the consequence of that is condemnation. So also here: the more precious the sacrament, the greater the harm which comes upon the whole community from its misuse. For it was not instituted for its own sake, that it might please God, but for our sake, that we might use it right, exercise our faith by it, and through it become pleasing to God. If it is merely an *opus operatum*,[37] it works only harm everywhere; it must become an *opus operantis*.[38] Just as bread and wine, no

36. That is, a work (that is) acceptable by virtue of the work having been performed. Here begins Luther's critique of the medieval sacramental system and particularly its sacrificial character. The sacrament is not complete simply by virtue of being properly performed. The ritual is not a work by which we are saved.

37. *Opus operatum*, an action that is done without reference to the status of the doer, a shortened form of the phrase cited above.

38. *Opus operantis*, the action of the one acting, is an action considered with reference to the doer of it. These technical terms were first coined by Augustine in his struggle against the Donatists over the worthiness of some clerics, supposedly tainted by persecution, to baptize, celebrate the Lord's Supper, or ordain. Augustine argued that God's grace in the New Testament sacraments was powerful enough to be effective *ex opere operato*, by the mere performance of the work. By contrast, the Old Testament sacrifices and circumcision were effective *ex opere operantis* (by the work or contribution of the one participating in the action). Peter Lombard (c. 1096–1164) then included this distinction in his basic theological textbook, used throughout the Middle Ages. In its later usage, an *opus operatum* was effective whatever the state of the participants, so that Masses could even be said for the dead. See below, n. 40.

g   German: *wechsels*, see above, p. 242, n. 32.

39. Here Luther argues that the action itself (the *opus operatum*), whether the celebration of the Mass or Christ's death on the cross, does not in itself do good but requires faith.

40. According to Alexander of Hales (d. 1245), in agreement with Thomas Aquinas (1225–1274), sacraments of the New Testament are in their own right signs *and causes* of invisible grace, and hence superior to the Old Testament rites that were merely signs but *not causes*. Thus the sacraments of the Old Testament *signified* the passion of Christ and its effects, but they had no *power* to justify; their effect depended rather on the faith that they were able to stimulate in the believer. The sacraments of the New Testament, on the other hand, in and of themselves effectively impart grace *ex opere operato*, i.e., by the

matter how much they may please God in and of themselves, work only harm if they are not used, so it is not enough that the sacrament be merely performed (that is, *opus operatum*); it must also be used in faith (that is, *opus operantis*). We must take care that such dangerous interpretations do not make us lose the sacrament's power, and faith completely perish through the false security of the "enacted" sacrament.[h]

All this comes from the fact that they pay more attention in this sacrament to Christ's natural body than to the fellowship, the spiritual body. Christ on the cross was also an "enacted work"[39] that was well pleasing to God. But to this day the Jews have found it a stumbling block because they did not construe it through faith as a useful work. See to it then that the sacrament is for you an *opus operantis*, that is, a work that is made use of, that is well pleasing to God not because of what it is in itself but because of your faith and your good use of it. The Word of God, too, is in itself pleasing to God, but it is harmful to me unless it also pleases God in me. In short, such expressions as *opus operatum* and *opus operantis* are vain words of human beings, more of a hindrance than a help.[40] And who could tell of all the abominable abuses and misbeliefs which daily multiply about this blessed sacrament, some of which are so spiritual and holy that they might almost lead an angel astray?

Briefly, those[i] would understand the abuses need only keep before them the above-mentioned use and faith of this sacrament. Namely, that there should be a troubled, hungry soul, who desires heartily the love, help, and support of the entire community, of Christ and of all Christendom, who does not doubt that in faith these are obtained and who then becomes one with everyone: whoever does not take this as the point of departure for arranging and ordering their hearing or reading of Masses and receiving of the sacrament is in error and does not use the sacrament in a holy manner. It is for this reason also that the world is overrun with pes-

---

h German: *gemachte sacramentis.* Luther's translation of the Latin *operatum.*

i Singular in the original.

tilences, wars, and other horrible plagues, because with our many Masses we only bring down upon us greater disfavor.*j*

21. We see now how necessary this sacrament is for those who must face death, or other dangers of body and soul, so that they are not left alone in them but are strengthened in the fellowship of Christ and all saints. This is why Christ instituted it and gave it to his disciples in the hour of their extreme need and peril. Since we are all daily surrounded by all kinds of danger, and must in the end die, we should humbly and heartily give thanks with all our powers to the God of all mercy for giving us such a gracious sign, by which (as we hold fast to it in faith) God leads and draws us through death and every danger to God's self, to Christ and all saints.

Therefore it is also useful and necessary that the love and fellowship of Christ and all saints be hidden, invisible, and spiritual, and that only a bodily, visible, and outward sign of it be given to us. For if this love, fellowship, and support were apparent to all, as is temporal, human fellowship, we would not be strengthened or trained by it to desire or put our trust in the things that are unseen and eternal [2 Cor. 4:18]. Instead, we would be trained to put our trust only in things that are temporary and visible, and would become so accustomed to them as to be unwilling to let them go; we would not follow God, except so far as visible and tangible things led us. We would be prevented from ever coming to God. For everything that is bound to time and sense must fall away, and we must learn to do without them if we are to come to God.[41]

For this reason, the Mass and this sacrament are a sign by which we train and accustom ourselves to let go of all visible love, help, and comfort, and to trust in the invisible love, help, and support of Christ and his saints. For death takes away all the things that are seen and separates us from human beings and transient things. To face death, we must have the help of the invisible and eternal, and these are indicated to us in the sacrament and sign, to which we cling

mere performance of the rite, apart from any act of the soul. For Thomas, faith was a prerequisite for receiving the sacrament's effect. Bonaventure (1221–1274) regarded faith as something supplementary to the *opus operatum*. Gabriel Biel (c. 1420–1495), with whose works Luther was intimately familiar, defined the subjective condition not so much in terms of a positive disposition as of the absence of any impediment, such as mortal sin. Thus the Scholastics differed as to the extent to which faith was necessary for the *reception* of that grace. By arguing that the effect of the sacrament did not depend on any disposition on a person's part but solely on God and the sufferings of Christ, Biel reduced any disposition on the part of the recipient to negative passivity. See Heiko Oberman, *Harvest of Medieval Theology* (Cambridge: Harvard University Press, 1963), 467. Ultimately, Luther's proposal lay not in the preference for *operantis* over *operatum* but in the rejection of the *opus* altogether. The sacrament is not a good work or sacrifice on our part but a testament or promise on the part of God, to be received by us in faith— not an *officium* (duty) but a *beneficium* (benefit). See *Treatise on the New Testament* (1520), LW 35:93, and *The Babylonian Captivity of the Church* (1520), LW 36:35–57.

41. This suspicion of temporal and material things shows the influence of certain forms of medieval theology especially influenced by Platonism.

---

j For Luther's equating such misuse of the Mass with God's disfavor, see 1 Cor. 11:29-30.

by faith until we finally also attain them openly with the senses.

Thus the sacrament is for us a ford, a bridge, a door, a ship, and personal transport,[k] by which and in which we pass from this world into eternal life. Therefore everything depends on faith, because the one who does not believe is like the person who is supposed to cross the sea, but who is so timid as not to trust the ship; and so such a one must remain and never become holy out of unwillingness to embark and cross over. This is caused by sensuality and unexercised faith that shrinks from the passage across the Jordan of death—and the devil too has a gruesome hand in it.

22. This was signified long ago in Josh. 3[:14-17]. After the children of Israel had gone dry-shod through the Red Sea [Exod. 14:21ff.], which points to baptism, they also went through the Jordan in the same way.[42] But the priests stood with the ark in the Jordan, and the water below them was cut off, while the water above them rose up like a mountain, which points to this sacrament. The priests hold and carry the ark in the Jordan when, in the hour of our death or danger, they preach and administer to us this sacrament, the fellowship of Christ and all saints. As we then believe, the waters below us depart; that is, the things that are seen and temporary do nothing but flee from us. The waters above us, however, well up high; that is, the horrible torments and images of death from another world terrify us as if they would overwhelm us. If, however, we pay no attention to them and walk over with a firm faith, then we shall enter with dry feet, unharmed into eternal life.

We have, therefore, two principal sacraments in the church, baptism and the bread. Baptism leads us into a new life on earth; the bread guides us through death into eternal life.[43] And the two are signified by the Red Sea and the Jordan, and by the two lands, one beyond and one on this side of the Jordan. This is why our Lord said at the Last Supper [Matt. 26:29], "I tell you, I will never again drink of this fruit of the vine until that day when I drink it new with you in my

42. Nicholas of Lyra (1270–1349), in his *Postilla Moralis super totam Bibliam*, by contrast, connects both crossings to baptism, but he, too, emphasizes the office of ordained priests.

43. Luther defines with great simplicity the difference between the two sacraments. With one (baptism) we begin a new life here, on earth, and to reach our goal, God feeds us along the way (sacrament of the altar).

---

k   German: *Tragba(h)r*, a sedan chair or litter.

The Blessed Sacrament of the Holy and True
Body of Christ, and the Brotherhoods
249

Father's kingdom"—so entirely is this sacrament intended and instituted for a strengthening against death and an entrance into eternal life.

In conclusion, the blessing of this sacrament is fellowship and love, by which we are strengthened against death and all evil. This fellowship is twofold: on the one hand we partake[l] of Christ and all saints; on the other hand we permit all Christians to be partakers of us, in whatever way they and we are able. By means of this sacrament, then, all self-seeking love is rooted out and gives way to love that seeks the common good of all. Through the change wrought by love there is one bread, one drink, one body, one community. This is a true unity of Christian kinship.[m] Let us see, therefore, how the neat-looking brotherhoods, of which there are now so many, compare and square with this.

Concerning the Brotherhoods[44]

1. Let us consider the evil practices of the brotherhoods. Gluttony and drunkenness is one of these. After one or more Masses are held, the rest of the day and night, and other days besides, are given over to the devil; they do only what displeases God. Such mad reveling has been introduced by the evil spirit, and he calls it a brotherhood, whereas, it is more a debauch and an altogether pagan, yes, a swinish way of life. It would be far better to have no brotherhoods in the world at all than to sanction such misconduct. Temporal lords and cities should unite with the clergy in abolishing it. For by it God, the saints, and all Christians are greatly dishonored; and the divine services and feast days are made into a laughingstock for the devil. Saints' days are supposed to be kept and hallowed by good works. And the brotherhood is also

44. For these brotherhoods ("fraternities," "confraternities") or associations, designed to foster meritorious works and Masses, see the introduction, p. 229f., esp. n. 3 (on solidalities).

---

l   German: *geniessen*. In Early New High German, the word suggests intense participation with one another, a community. See Jacob Grimm and Wilhelm Grimm, eds., *Deutsches Wörterbuch*, 33 vols., (Leipzig: Hirzel, 1854–1954), 5:3451ff.

m   Literally, "true Christian brotherly unity." See Psalm 133. Luther uses this term to foreshadow his criticism of brotherhoods.

supposed to be a special convocation of good works; instead it has become a collecting of money for beer. What have the names of Our Lady, St. Anne, St. Sebastian,[n] or other saints to do with your brotherhoods, in which you have nothing but gluttony, drunkenness, useless squandering of money, howling, yelling, chattering, dancing, and wasting of time? If a sow were made the patron saint of such a brotherhood, she would not consent. Why then do they afflict the dear saints so miserably by taking their names in vain in such shameful practices and sins, and by dishonoring and blaspheming with such evil practices the brotherhoods named after these saints? Woe to those who do this and those who permit it!

2. If individuals[o] desire to maintain a brotherhood,[45] they should gather provisions and feed and serve a tableful or two of poor people, for the sake of God. The day before they should fast, and on the feast day remain sober, passing the time in prayer and other good works. Then God and his saints would be truly honored; there would be improvement too, and a good example would be given to others. Or they should gather the money that they intend to squander for drink, and collect it into a common treasury, each guild for itself. Then in cases of hardship, needy fellow workers might be helped to get started and be lent money, or a couple of young people in the same craft might be fitted out respectably from this common treasury. These would be works of true brotherhood; they would make God and God's saints look with favor upon the brotherhoods, of which they would then gladly be the patrons. But where people are unwilling to do this, where they insist on following the old ways of simulated brotherhood, I admonish them not to do it on the saints' days, nor in the name of the saints or of the brotherhood. Let them take some other weekday and leave the names of the saints and of their brotherhoods alone, in case the saints one day punish it. Although there is no day that is not dishonored by doing such things, at least the fes-

45. Though there were third orders attached to the monasteries (especially noteworthy is the Third Order of Saint Francis) to which women, men, and couples belonged, the brotherhoods seem to have consisted primarily of men.

---

n   See the introduction, p. 229.

o   Singular in the original.

tivals and the names of the saints should be spared. For such brotherhoods call themselves brotherhoods of the saints while they do the work of the devil.

3. There is another evil feature of the brotherhoods, and it is a spiritual evil, a false opinion that their brotherhood is to be a benefit to no one but themselves, those who are members on the roll or who contribute. This damnably wicked opinion is an even worse evil than the first, and it is one of the reasons why God has brought it about that with their gluttony, drunkenness, and the like, the brotherhoods are becoming such a mockery and blasphemy of God. For in them they learn to seek their own good, to love themselves, to be faithful only to one another, to despise others, to think themselves better than others, and to presume to stand higher before God than others. And so the communion of saints, Christian love, and true kinship,[p] which are established in the holy sacrament, go under while selfish love flourishes in them. By means of these many external brotherhoods devoted to works, they oppose and destroy the one, inner, spiritual, essential kinship common to all saints.

When God sees this perverted state of affairs, God perverts it still more, as is written in Ps. 18[:26, following the Vulgate], "With the perverse you will be perverted." So God brings it to pass that they make themselves and their brotherhoods a mockery and a disgrace. And God casts them out of the common fellowship[q] of saints, which they have opposed and with which they do not make common cause, and into their own brotherhood of gluttony, drunkenness, and unchastity; so that they, who have neither sought nor thought of anything more than their own, may find their own. Then, too, God blinds them so that they do not recognize it as an abomination and disgrace but adorn their misconduct with the names of saints, as though they were doing the right thing. Beyond this, God lets some fall into so deep

p   German: *Bruderschaften*, literally, "brotherhood." The term is
    translated more inclusively when Luther uses it more broadly.
    All changes will be footnoted.

q   In the original: "brotherhood."

an abyss that they boast publicly and say that whoever is in their brotherhood cannot be condemned; just as if baptism and the sacrament, instituted by God himself, were of less value and more uncertain than that which they have concocted out of their mindless heads. Thus will God dishonor and blind those who, with their crazed conduct and swinish practices of their brotherhoods, mock and blaspheme the feasts, name, and saints of God, to the detriment of that common Christian fellowship*r* that flowed from the wounds of Christ.

4. For a correct understanding and use of the brotherhoods, therefore, one must learn to distinguish correctly between them. The first is the divine, the heavenly, the noblest, which surpasses all others as gold surpasses copper or lead—the communion of saints—of which we spoke above. In this we are all brothers and sisters, so closely united that a closer relationship cannot be conceived. For here we have one baptism, one Christ, one sacrament, one food, one gospel, one faith, one Spirit, one spiritual body [Eph. 4:4-5], and each person is a member of the other [Rom. 12:5]. No other fellowship*s* is so close and strong. For, to be sure, natural kinship*t* consists of one flesh and blood, one heritage and home; yet they must separate and join themselves to the blood and heritage of others [in marriage]. The organized brotherhoods have one membership roll, one Mass, one kind of good works, one festival day, one fee; and, as things are now, their common beer, common gluttony, and common drunkenness. But none of these penetrates so deeply as to produce one spirit, for that is done by Christ's fellowship*u* alone. For this reason, too, the greater, broader, and more comprehensive it is, the better it is.

Now all other brotherhoods should be so conducted as to keep this first and noblest kind constantly before their eyes and regard it alone as great. With all their works they

r In the original: "brotherhood"
s In the original: "brotherhood."
t In the original: "brotherhood."
u In the original: "brotherhood."

should be seeking nothing for themselves; they should rather do them for God's sake, entreating God to keep and prosper this Christian community and fellowship[v] from day to day. When a brotherhood is formed, they should let it be seen that the members step in[w] for others and do something special for Christendom with their prayers, fasting, alms, and good works, not in order to seek selfish profit or reward, or to exclude others, but to serve as the free servants of the whole community of Christians.

If there were such a correct conception, God would also in return restore good order, so that the brotherhoods might not be brought to shame by debauchery. Then blessing would follow: a general fund could be gathered, whereby material aid too could be given to other persons. Then the spiritual and material works of the brotherhoods would be done in their proper order. And whoever does not want to follow this order in his brotherhood, I advise him to let the brotherhood go, and get out of it; it will [only] do him harm in body and soul.

But suppose you say, "If I do not get something special out of the brotherhood, of what use is it to me?" I answer: True, if you are seeking something special, of what use indeed is the brotherhood or sisterhood? But if by it you serve the community and other people, as the way of love does, you will have your reward for this love, without seeking it or desiring it on your part. If, however, you consider the service and reward of love too small, this is evidence that yours is a perverted brotherhood. Love serves freely and without charge, which is why God in return gives to it every blessing, freely and without charge. Since, then, everything must be done in love, if it is to please God at all, the brotherhood too must be one of love. It is the nature of that which is done in love, however, not to be self-seeking [1 Cor. 13:5], or to seek its own profit, but to seek that of others, and above all that of the community.

---

v   In the original: "brotherhood."

w   German: *herausspringen*, literally, "jump out in front of."

5. To return once more to the sacrament, since Christian fellowship is at present in a bad way, such as it has never been before, and is daily growing worse, especially among those in high places, and since all places are full of sin and shame, you should be concerned not about how many Masses are said, or how often the sacrament is celebrated—for this will make things worse rather than better—but about how much you and others grow in the meaning and faith of this sacrament; for in that alone lies improvement. And the more you find yourself being incorporated[x] into the fellowship of Christ and his saints, the better you stand. That is, as you find that you are becoming strong in the confidence of Christ and his beloved saints, that you become certain that they love you and stand by you in all the trials of life and of death; and more, that you, in turn, take to heart the shortcomings of all Christians and of the entire community and the lapses of any individual Christian, and your love goes out to each one and you desire to help everyone, hate no one, suffer with all, and pray for all—see, then is the sacrament's work right! And you will come many times to weep, lament, and mourn over the wretched condition of Christendom today. If, however, you find no such confidence in Christ and his saints and if the needs of Christendom and of every single neighbor do not trouble or move you, then beware of all other good works, by which you think you are righteous and will be made holy. They are surely nothing but hypocrisy, sham, and deceit, for they are without love and fellowship; and without these nothing is good.

To sum it all up: *Plenitudo legis est dilectio* [Rom. 10:13], "Love is the fulfilling of the law." AMEN.

[Postscript][46]

There are some who have unnecessarily rejected this treatise because I said in the third paragraph: I should consider it a good thing if a Christian council were to decree that

46. This paragraph is found only in two of the Wittenberg printings, Editions C (WA 2:739) and N (WA 9:791), apparently the only two corrected by Luther himself.

x   German: *eyngeleybet*. See above, p. 230, note o.

both kinds be given to everyone. They have opened their mouth so wide that they are saying, "This is an error and it is offensive." God in heaven have mercy! That we should live to see the day when Christ, noble Lord and God, is publicly insulted and blasphemed by his own people, who rebuke his ordinance as an error! It would have been enough had they allowed it to remain a permissible order and not turned it into a command. Then, at least, it would not be forbidden or regarded as an error.[47] Yet I beg them to look carefully at the second and third paragraphs,[y] in which I have stated clearly that one kind is sufficient. I have also experienced that my writings are being rejected only by those who have not read them and who do not intend to do so. To such persons I send my greetings and inform them that I am paying no attention to their blind and frivolous criticism. As long as God grants me life, I do not intend to tolerate that they so brazenly condemn and blaspheme my Lord Christ as an erring, offensive, and revolutionary teacher—they can act accordingly.

47. Luther expresses his wish that the Council had not made a strict law out of communion in only one kind but had left it open.

y   See above, pp. 231–33.

Treatise on Good Works

1520

TIMOTHY J. WENGERT

INTRODUCTION[1]

In late March of 1520, one month after he started to prepare for publication a "sermon" on good works, Martin Luther wrote to his contact at the Saxon court, Georg Spalatin (1484–1545): "It will not be a sermon but rather a small book, and if my writing progresses as well as it has, this book will be the best work I have published so far."[a] Although the better-known pamphlets of 1520 were still to appear—*Address to the Christian Nobility*, *The Babylonian Captivity of the Church*, and *The Freedom of a Christian*[b]—the finished *Treatise on Good Works* fulfilled Luther's prediction as one of the clearest and most accessible introductions to Luther's reforming work and theology. Luther's main goal was to commend a new, down-to-earth piety to all Christians. This piety was new, because at its center was a radically different meaning of good works that would transform the way believers practiced their faith. That different meaning, it turned out, was

1. This introduction is a revision of the "Translator's Introduction" by Scott Hendrix, in Martin Luther, *Treatise on Good Works*, trans. Scott Hendrix (Minneapolis: Fortress Press, 2012), 2–11. The translation that follows is also a revision of the work by Hendrix.

---

a WA Br 2:75 (March 25, 1520).

b For the *Address* and *Freedom of a Christian*, see below, p. 369 and 467. For the *Babylonian Captivity*, see LW 36:3–126.

easy to misunderstand and required a detailed explanation that Luther offered in this "small book."

Today the term "good works" is often associated with acts of charity in general, but in late medieval theology it designated acts of religious devotion and charity that made up for sins committed by believers and thus were considered meritorious for salvation. Already in the Sermon on the Mount, Jesus said, "Let your light shine before others, so that they may see your good works and give glory to your Father in heaven."[2] Augustine of Hippo (354–430), the bishop and theologian whom Martin Luther cited more than any other, debated with his Pelagian opponents the place of good works in the Christian life.[3] Augustine was the source of Luther's claim that actions that appear to be good works are in fact sinful unless done in faith.[c]

In the *Rule of St. Benedict* (c. 480–542), "good works" are given a primary role in monastic life. Chapter 4, titled "The Instruments of Good Works," concludes with the following admonition: "Behold, these are instruments of the spiritual art, which, if they have been applied without ceasing day and night and approved on judgment day, will merit for us from the Lord that reward which he has promised." These "instruments" of merit are also evident in a definition from a popular medieval dictionary of theology printed in 1517: "Certain works are directed toward our neighbor and pertain to love of neighbor, while others are directed toward God alone and pertain to divine worship and adoration."[d] By the sixteenth century, such good works were a required part of the Christian life that applied to every believer who desired eternal life. Often, these basic religious works were outlined by another part of the Sermon on the Mount, where Jesus talked about prayer, almsgiving, and fasting.

When confronted with Martin Luther's basic message, readers and listeners were sometimes confused or angered

---

2. Matt. 5:16. The term "good works" also appears in the Vulgate text of 2 Pet. 1:10 and was therefore present in the Latin Bible of the Middle Ages; but the phrase, for which there is only moderate textual evidence, is absent from most English translations of 2 Pet. 1:10.

3. In his later career, Augustine's opponents included the British monk, Pelagius (354–420) and his adherents, who insisted that human beings were born with the ability to resist sin and could thus fulfill God's gracious commandments. These "Pelagians" were condemned in various councils of the ancient church.

---

c   Hans-Ulrich Delius, *Augustin als Quelle Luthers,* 3d ed. (Berlin, 1984), 66.

d   Johannes Altenstaig (d. c. 1525), *Vocabularius theologiae* (Hagenau, 1517), fol. 169b.

by what they read and heard about good works. In sermons and pamphlets, Luther and his colleagues claimed that salvation came by faith alone and not by works. Their assertion was based on their reading of biblical verses like Rom. 3:28, "For we hold that a person is justified by faith apart from works prescribed by the law"; or Eph. 2:8-9, "For by grace you have been saved through faith, and this is not your own doing; it is the gift of God—not the result of works, so that no one may boast." Even though, they argued, Paul's message did not overthrow the law, understood especially as the Ten Commandments, still the origin of Christian good works came from faith.[4]

Some of Luther's readers and listeners charged that his position implied that believers were free from the obligation to perform any good works at all—a complaint to which not only Luther but also other early preachers who defended Luther's views had to respond. One preacher described the opposing attitude this way: "If it is true, all the better, we need to perform no good works; we will gladly take faith alone. And if praying, fasting, holy days, and almsgiving are not required, then we will lie near the stove, warm our feet on its tiles, turn the roasting apples, open our mouths, and wait until grilled doves fly into them."[5]

The late medieval believers who heard that good works would not save them associated those good works with religious activities that were no longer necessary for salvation. The quotation above mentions praying, fasting, worship, and almsgiving, which Luther and his supporters viewed as appropriate works for believers. But the list of unnecessary works included acquiring indulgences, venerating and praying to saints, making pilgrimages to their shrines, holding private Masses (said by a priest without communicants), requiring clerical celibacy, making binding monastic vows, venerating relics, and so on.[6] In the *Treatise on Good Works*, Luther takes pains to distinguish these activities, which he calls the "wrong kind of good works," from the "right kind of good works," namely, those nurturing faith and obeying the Ten Commandments out of faith. For that reason, the treatise shows how faith, by which one is saved, leads

4. See, e.g., Rom. 3:31; 10:4; and Gal. 2:15-21.

5. Urbanus Rhegius (1489–1541), a preacher at Augsburg, *Anzeigung, daß die römische Bulle merklichen Schaden in Gewissen mancher Menschen gebracht und nicht Doctor Luthers Lehre* (Augsburg, 1521), C4r–v. These examples of leisure relate to *Schlaraffenland*, an imaginary place mentioned in European fairy tales that was alleged to contain a surplus of everything. Luther also alludes to it in this *Treatise*, p. 359, n. 126.

6. For an exhaustive list of religious practices Luther regarded as for the most part unnecessary in the "true Christian church," see his *Exhortation to All the Clergy* (1530), written during the Diet of Augsburg (LW 34:54–59).

inevitably to obedience, that is, how properly fulfilling the first commandment ("You shall have no other gods") leads to obedience of the remaining commandments—and all of this not as a human work at all but as a gift and work of the Holy Spirit. This theme appears repeatedly throughout the composition, as if to say: the right kind of good works follow from faith, just as the last nine commandments follow the first. Another significant theme attacks the late medieval distinction between commands and counsels, where lay believers in a state of grace had to fulfill the Ten Commandments but those under a vow and hence in a state of perfection also could also fulfill Jesus' "counsels" of poverty, chastity, and obedience as a higher level of Christian obedience. For Luther, there is enough simply in the Ten Commandments to keep every Christian busy.

Luther preached on the Ten Commandments throughout his career. His *Small Cathechism* and *Large Catechism* (1529) remain the best-known expositions of the commandments, but prior to 1529 Luther had preached and written on them six times: 1516–1517, 1518, 1520, 1522, 1525, and 1528. A sermon from 1528 reveals why Luther deemed the Ten Commandments so important—namely, to foster a proper understanding of Christian freedom: "It used to be that the Sabbath was 'made holy' in that after hearing a Mass we spent the day getting drunk. Now, too, we abuse the Sabbath, going in and out of the church by habit to hear a sermon but not observing the word. You go in [to church] and come out no wiser than before, snoring and sleeping in church. But that does not sanctify the Sabbath."[7] In other words, Christian freedom from the law and works does not imply license to abuse that freedom by spurning the fruits of faith.

The *Treatise on Good Works* was written with strong encouragement from Georg Spalatin, secretary and court chaplain to Elector Frederick III of Saxony (1463–1525), to whom, as noted above, Luther enthusiastically reported on his progress. One month before that letter, however, Spalatin had reminded him of a promise to compose a sermon on good works. Luther replied that he did not remember the

[7]. WA 31/1:66, 29–32. See also LC, "Ten Commandments," par. 96–97, in BC, 399.

promise and, besides, had already published so much that nobody would buy it. Two days later, however, he wrote to Spalatin that he did remember and would get down to work.

It was the beginning of a very busy twelve months. On 9 January 1520, the legal proceedings against Luther were reopened in Rome, and Pope Leo X (1475–1521) had appointed three commissions to prepare a denunciation of the German professor. In June, the denunciation was issued in the form of a papal edict, *Exsurge Domine*, which threatened Luther with excommunication if he did not recant. The papal ban of excommunication itself took effect in January of 1521. Meanwhile, Luther was lecturing on the Psalms and composing one important work after another. His rejection of the pope's claim to be the vicar of Christ and to rule over the entire church appeared in May of 1520 under the title *The Papacy at Rome*.[8]

8. LW 39:49–104.

In the midst of the confrontation between Luther and the papal Curia, this tract on good works appeared. Judging by the number of reprints and editions, it was popular and sold well. The first edition was printed by Melchior Lotter Jr. (c. 1490–1542) in Wittenberg and appeared in late May or early June of 1520. Before the end of the year, the treatise had been reprinted eight times, with another six reprints appearing in 1521. That same year, a Latin translation was published in Leipzig and then reprinted in Wittenberg. It was followed by translations into other languages: English, French, Dutch, and Low German, a dialect spoken in the lowlands of northern Germany.

Some refer to the treatise as the *Sermon on Good Works*, presumably because it started as a sermon and because the title of at least one edition claimed that it had been preached. The title of the first edition, however, is simply *Von den guten Werken*, best rendered in English as *Good Works* or literally as *Concerning Good Works*. As Luther said, however, it turned out to be a small book, and therefore this edition uses the title *Treatise*, as did the American edition of Luther's works.

Luther argues that the Ten Commandments define all the good works for the Christian life. The first commandment is fulfilled through faith, which is the first and chief

Von den guten
Wercken:
D.M.
L

Wittenberg.

This historiated title page border of Luther's *Treatise on Good Works* features the crest of the printer, Melchior Lotter the Younger, at the foot. It has been attributed to Lucas Cranach the Elder or to his workshop.

good work that leads to and undergirds all the others. Reflecting a late medieval approach to good works that emphasized Christian virtues, Luther defines the kind of good work proceeding from that faith for each commandment. Thus, the second commandment is fulfilled by praise (of God and thus not of the self), the third by worship (understood as attending Mass, hearing preaching, and prayer [especially corporate prayer]), the fourth by obedience to superiors and solicitude to underlings, the fifth by gentleness, the sixth by purity and chastity, the seventh by generosity, and the eighth by truth telling.[9] Additionally, when Luther is ready to explain the second commandment against taking God's name in vain, he does it under the heading of "the second good work." He then discusses the ways through which the second commandment is obeyed, and he identifies four of those ways, each of which he calls a work of the second commandment. In this case, the term "good work" refers both collectively to obeying the second commandment and specifically to the ways in which that obedience can take place. His explanations of the third and fourth commandments are also extensive, but after that Luther, perhaps realizing that his sermon had indeed become a book, devotes less space to the last six commandments. His commentary on the last two commandments is compressed into one paragraph.

The headings under which the work or works of each commandment are explained are not uniform. At the fourth commandment, the traditional division of the commandments into two tables leads Luther to call the fourth commandment "the first commandment of the second table

9. Unlike the later Reformed penchant for numbering the commandments according to the Hebrew text (and thus adding a second commandment against images), Luther follows the tradition of the Greek and Latin texts by dividing the commandments of Moses." As in many of Luther's early writings, the paragraphs are numbered consecutively throughout the entire treatise, a customary way of dividing late medieval tracts and sermons. Here Luther numbers the paragraphs consecutively through the first two commandments, but after that the numbering of paragraphs starts over within each commandment. His explanations of the first four commandments are much longer than those of the last six, and his treatment of prayer, which is the third work of the third commandment, is a little treatise in itself.

Biblical passages are translated as Luther cited or phrased them rather than according to modern translations. At this point in Luther's career, there was no standard German translation of the Bible (Luther's German New Testament appeared first in 1522). As was common among late medieval preachers, Luther had in mind or sometimes even cited a text in Latin and rendered it into German as a paraphrased translation. Thus, although his citations may not appear to today's readers as accurate, they are in fact a blend of citation and explanation not at all unusual for his day. Luther's biblical citations arise from the Vulgate, or Latin version of the Bible, much of which he knew by heart.

On the advice of Spalatin, Luther dedicated the treatise to Duke John (1486–1532), the brother of Luther's first prince, Elector Frederick III of Saxony. In 1525, Elector Frederick died, and Duke John became the new elector. John was firmly committed to Luther and his colleagues and did all he could to ensure the survival of Wittenberg theology and practice in Saxony and beyond. Besides leading the Saxon delegation at the Diet of Augsburg and signing the *Augsburg Confession* (1530), Elector John led the reform of the University of Wittenberg and endorsed the inspection and reorganization of parishes (starting in 1527), in which the evangelical forms of worship and piety recommended by Luther were often utilized. Although Luther could not have foreseen it in 1520, he could not have dedicated a more fitting piece to Duke John than the *Treatise on Good Works*.

The translation of the treatise is based primarily on the text in Luther's German edited by Hans-Ulrich Delius and

to covet into two, and he views the prohibition of images as a special expansion of the first commandment for the Israelites.

Duke John of Saxony.
Portrait by Lucas Cranach
the Elder, 1534.

Rudolf Mau in *Martin Luther Studienausgabe*, with constant reference to the critical "Weimar" edition of Luther's works.*ᵉ* That text is taken from the first printed edition that came from the press of Melchior Lotter Jr. in Wittenberg around the end of May 1520. The editors also took into consideration the text of Luther's manuscript that was discovered in 1892. A comparison of the printed edition with the manuscript reveals a number of variations and alterations, some of which come from the printer. In addition, other modern versions have been consulted.*ᶠ*

TREATISE ON GOOD WORKS[10]

JESUS.[11]

TO THE ILLUSTRIOUS AND NOBLE prince and lord, John, Duke of Saxony, Landgrave of Thuringia, Margrave of Meissen, my gracious lord and patron.

Illustrious and noble prince, gracious lord, with my humble prayer I am always at the service of your princely majesty.

---

10. See the final paragraph of the introduction.

11. Following a monastic tradition, Luther began many of his early writings and letters with this word.

---

e　*Martin Luther Studienausgabe*, vol. 2, ed. Hans-Ulrich Delius (Berlin: Evangelische Verlagsanstalt, 1982), 12–88; and WA 6:196–276. The manuscript in Luther's hand is found in WA 9:226–301.

f　*Die guten Werke*, in *Martin Luther Taschenausgabe*, vol. 4, *Evangelium und Leben*, ed. Horst Beintker (Berlin: Evangelische Verlagsanstalt, 1983), 36–131; *Von den guten Werken*, ed. Werner Jetter, in *Martin Luther Ausgewählte Schriften*, vol. 1: *Aufbruch zur Reformation*, ed. Karin Bornkamm and Gerhard Ebeling, 2d ed. (Frankfurt am Main: Insel, 1983), 38–149.

Gracious prince and lord. For some time I have wanted to acknowledge my humble devotion and duty to your grace with one of the spiritual wares that suit my position, but I found myself unfit for the task of creating a gift that would be worthy of you. Now, however, my most gracious Lord Frederick, Duke of Saxony, Elector of the Holy Roman Empire, Vicar, etc.,[12] and brother of your princely grace, has not disdained to receive my amateurish little book, which was dedicated to him and now much to my surprise has been published.[13] I am encouraged by his gracious example and make bold to presume that, just as both of you have the same noble blood, you also have the same noble spirit evident in a mild and beneficent disposition. I hope, therefore, that your princely grace will not scorn my poor, humble offering, which I have found more necessary to publish than any of my other sermons or pamphlets, because good works, which involve much greater deception and cunning than anything else, have provoked the most controversy. In this matter, it is easy to take advantage of ordinary people, and for that reason our Lord Christ commanded us to beware of sheep's clothing that hides the wolf underneath.[g] Good works have more things added to and subtracted from them than any gold, silver, precious stones, or other expensive things, even though such works must have the same, simple goodness; otherwise, they are mere fakes that sparkle with pretty colors.

I know full well and hear daily that many people belittle my poverty and say I produce only little pamphlets and sermons in German for the uneducated laity. That does not bother me, however. Would God that I had worked my whole life and devoted all my ability to the improvement of one layperson! I would be satisfied with this, give thanks to God, and willingly let all my little books turn to dust. I will let others judge whether or not writing many thick books is a scholarly method that serves Christendom well; but if I wanted to write big books in their way, I think I could produce them faster than they could prepare a small sermon in

12. Following courtly protocol, Luther lists Elector Frederick's chief offices. "Vicar," a position in the political hierarchy of the Holy Roman Empire (the official surrogate for the emperor when he was absent, was held by Duke John's brother, Elector Frederick, who was Luther's overlord. After Frederick's death in 1525, his brother, John, to whom Luther is dedicating this writing, succeeded him as elector.

13. *Fourteen Consolations for Those Who Labor and Are Heavy-Laden*, written for and dedicated to the ailing Elector Frederick in August 1519 (LW 42:117–66; WA 6:99–134). Georg Spalatin produced a German translation that was made from Luther's Latin manuscript, and both versions were published at Wittenberg in February of 1520, the same month that Spalatin reminded Luther of a promise to write a treatise on good works.

g   An allusion to Matt. 7:15.

my way. If reaching a goal were as easy as pursuing it, then Christ would long since have been thrown out of heaven and the throne of God overturned. "Even though we cannot all be authors, we want to be critics all the same."[h] I will happily let others have the honor of great accomplishments and will not be ashamed to preach and write in German for the uneducated laity. Although I can only do a little, I am of the mind that Christendom would have benefited much more from such activities (had we occupied ourselves with it sooner and tried to keep it up) than from the learned tomes and disputations conducted only by scholars at the universities. Moreover, I have never forced or invited anyone to listen to me or read my sermons. I have openly and dutifully served the community[i] with what God has given me, and whoever is not pleased can read and listen to someone else. Nor does it bother me if my contribution is not needed. For me it is more than enough that a few of the laity, especially the most eminent of them, deign to read my sermons.

Even if other incentives were lacking, I have plenty now that I have learned how much your princely grace has been pleased by these German pamphlets and desires to know more about good works and faith. It has pleased me to provide this service as diligently as I can, and as your humble subject I request your princely grace kindly to accept this opus of mine until God grants me time to offer a full explanation of faith. For now I wanted to indicate how we should practice and use faith in every good work and allow it to be the noblest work of all. If God permits, at another time I will treat the [Apostles'] Creed and how we should daily pray and recite it.[j] Herewith I commend myself humbly to your princely grace.

---

h A rhymed German adage also found in the Latin. See Wander, 1:582.

i *Gemeinde*: his Wittenberg congregation and community.

j German: *den Glauben* (the faith). Luther published an explanation of the Apostles' Creed in 1520 along with explanations of the Ten Commandments and the Lord's Prayer that had been printed in 1518 and 1519 (WA 7:194–229).

Wittenberg, the twenty-ninth day of March, one thousand five hundred and twenty years after the birth of Christ.

Your princely grace's obedient chaplain, Doctor Martin Luther, Augustinian at Wittenberg.

[Introduction]

1. It should be known, first of all, that no good works exist other than those that God has commanded, just as there is no sin other than what God has forbidden. Whoever wishes to recognize and perform good works need only learn God's commandments.[14] Accordingly, Christ says in Matt. 19[:17]: "If you wish to enter life, keep the commandments." And when the young man asks in Matt. 19[:16-19] what he has to do to be saved, Christ holds up to him the Ten Commandments and nothing else. Therefore we must learn to distinguish among good works from God's commandments and not from the appearance, magnitude, or quantity of the deeds themselves or from human opinion, laws, or approaches. We have seen how this happened in the past and still happens owing to our blindness and complete disdain for God's commandments.

14. Luther is setting up a contrast between the God-given Ten Commandments, on the one hand, and human regulations and Christ's so-called counsels, on the other.

[The First Good Work]*k*

2. The foremost and noblest good work is faith in Christ, just as he himself said in John 6[:28-29] when the Jews asked him what they should do in order to perform good works of God. He answered: "This is the (good) work of God, that you believe in him whom he has sent." Now when we hear this or preach it, we pass right over it, thinking it is a small thing that is easy to do. We should instead pause here a long time and ponder it in depth. For all good works have to be

---

k   Luther relates this first good work, faith, to the first commandment, beginning below in par. 9 (p. 274).

15. A reference to the medieval practice of a lesser noble receiving a grant of land from his lord, so that the former must live totally from the benevolence of the latter. So all good works arise out of faith.

16. Luther investigates a first aspect of faith: its relation to works.

17. Luther refers here to medieval Scholastic theologians who insisted believers could not be certain whether they were in a state of grace, where they would receive due reward for their good works. See Luther's encounter with Cardinal Cajetan (1469–1534) in 1518, above, pp. 141–47.

18. See Matt. 6:1-18, used in the Middle Ages to define three categories of good works. This begins Luther's discussion of the first level of faith.

included in this one and receive their goodness from it, as if receiving a fief.[15] We have to make it simple and clear so that it can be understood.[16] We find that many people pray, fast, create pious endowments, do this and that, and lead respectable lives in the opinion of others; but if you ask them whether or not they are certain that God is pleased with what they do, they do not know or at least have their doubts. Moreover, they cite learned scholars who do nothing but teach good works and claim it is unnecessary to have such certainty.[17] See here! All these good works are performed apart from faith; they amount to nothing and are completely dead, because the attitude of your conscience before God determines the goodness of the works that proceed from it. If there is no faith or good conscience toward God, your works are decapitated, and your life and goodness amount to nothing at all. Now you see why, whenever I exalt faith and reject as false those works done without it, they accuse me of forbidding good works, although my real desire is to teach the genuine good works that belong to faith.[*]

3. If you then ask these people the following: when they are on the job, walking or standing still, eating, drinking, sleeping, or engaging in any activity that sustains the body or promotes the common good, do they consider their actions to be good works pleasing to God? You will find they say no. They define good works very narrowly and confine them to church-related activities like praying, fasting, and giving alms.[18] The rest are done in vain, people think, and lack significance in the eyes of God. Thus, their contemptible unbelief causes them to minimize and trivialize the service of God, who on the contrary is served by everything, whatever it may be, that is done, spoken, or conceived in faith. Eccl. 9[:7-9] teaches the same: "Go forth with joy, eat and drink, knowing that your work pleases God. Always clothe yourself in white and keep your head anointed with oil. Spend your

l   See charges 31 and 32 in the papal bull, *Exsurge Domini*, published in October 1520. For a later example of this same charge, see the *Augsburg Confession* XX.1–2 in BC, 52–53.

life with the wife you love all the days of these uncertain times that are granted to you."[19] For our clothing *always* to be white means that without distinction all our works are good, no matter what we call them. They are white when I am certain and believe that they please God; then the head of my soul will never lack the oil of a good conscience. Therefore Christ says in John 8[:29], "I always do what is pleasing to him." How could it have been "always" unless it included those times when he was eating, drinking, and sleeping? And St. John says in 1 John 3[:19-22]: "By this we know that we stand in the truth, when we can comfort our hearts and have confidence in his presence. Even if our heart afflicts us with remorse, God is greater than our heart . . . and we have assurance . . . that we will receive that which we have sought because we keep his commandments and do what pleases him."[m] Again [1 John 3:9]: "Those who have been born of God" (that is, believe and trust God) "do not sin . . . (and) cannot sin." And Ps. 34[:22]: "None of those who trust in him shall sin." And Ps. 2[:11]: "Blessed are those who trust in him."[n] If this is true, then everything they do must be good, or the evil they do must be quickly forgiven. Now do you see why I exalt faith so highly and gather all works within it and reject all works that do not flow from faith?

4. All individuals[o] are able to tell and feel whether or not what they do is good. If their hearts are confident that their work is pleasing to God, then it is good even if it were something as trivial as picking up a straw. If the heart is unsure instead of confident, then the work is not good even if it raised all the dead and the doers gave their bodies to be burned.[p] Paul teaches that very thing in Rom. 14[:23]: "For whatever does not proceed from faith is sin." We are called believers in Christ only on the basis of faith as the chief work and not on the basis of other works, which can also be done

19. Luther's rendering of Eccl. 9:7-9. In his commentary on the Bible, Nicholas of Lyra (c. 1270–1349) associated white clothing with a holy life but the oil with divine grace. Following the general pattern of biblical translation before his own translation of 1522, Luther renders texts freely according to the Latin Vulgate. See the editor's introduction above, p. 263.

---

m   Luther's rendering of the text.

n   In both psalms, Luther renders the Vulgate's "hope" (NRSV: "take refuge") with "trust."

o   Singular in the original.

p   See 1 Cor. 13:3.

20. Luther's term for adherents of Islam, who were familiar to sixteenth-century Europeans primarily as Muslims from the Ottoman Turkish Empire.

21. Luther attacks the cornerstone of late medieval, Aristotelian ethics, that a person becomes good by doing good and that faith, hope, and love are simply (theological) virtues. See *The Freedom of a Christian* below, p. 487.

22. For medieval theologians, the term *habitus* referred to a disposition infused in the soul, created by grace, and containing the virtues faith, hope, and love. Luther objected to this concept because *habitus* was not a biblical term and because it emphasized faith as a static quality of the soul instead of trust in God.

by pagans, Jews, Turks,[20] and sinners. Firm trust, however, that God is pleased with them is possible only for Christians enlightened and fortified by grace.

The reason that speaking this way seems strange and I have been called a heretic comes about because these people adhere to blind reason and pagan ways of thinking and have not set faith above other virtues but on the same level with them and assigned to faith its own work, which is then isolated from the works of other virtues.[21] Faith alone, however, validates all other works and makes them acceptable and worthy, as long as the doers trust God and do not doubt that God approves everything they do. Those who criticize me, however, have not allowed faith to remain a work but have made of it a *habitus*,[22] although nowhere does Scripture call anything a divine good work except faith alone.[q] No wonder, then, that they are blind and have become leaders of the blind.[r] This faith [of which I speak] is soon joined by love, peace, joy,[s] and hope. To those who trust God, God immediately gives the Holy Spirit, as St. Paul tells the Galatians [Gal. 3:2]: "You have received the Spirit not because of your good works but because you have believed God's word."[t]

5. In this faith all works become equal. One is like the other, and all distinctions among them disappear whether they are large or small, short or long [in duration], many or few. Works are pleasing not for their own sake but because of faith, which is present in one and the same way in every work. That faith is alive and efficacious no matter how different the works are from one another, just as our bodily members derive their life, functions, and names from the head and without the head would have none of those. Moreover, it follows that a Christian who lives in this faith does

q   John 6:29. For Luther, faith is a work that God effects in human beings.

r   A reference by Jesus to the Pharisees in Matt. 15:14.

s   Love, peace, and joy are named fruits of the Spirit in Gal. 5:22.

t   Citing the text as a statement, not a question.

not need to be taught good works and instead does whatever is there to be done. And it is well done, as St. Samuel[u] said to Saul [1 Sam. 10:6-7]: "[When] the Spirit . . . will possess you, you will . . . be turned into a different person, and . . . do whatever you see fit to do, for God is with you." Thus, we also read about St. Hannah, Samuel's mother, that when she believed the priest Eli, who assured her of God's grace, she went home happy and content, and from that time on she no longer wandered around from place to place. That is, whatever happened was all the same to her.[v] St. Paul Paul also says [2 Cor. 3:17]: "Where the Spirit of Christ is, everything is free."[w] Faith does not allow itself to be bound to any work nor to be deprived of any work. Instead, as Ps. 1[:3] says: They "yield their fruit in its time," that is, as the time comes and goes.

6. We may illustrate this with a common, down-to-earth example. When a husband or wife cherishes and pleases the other spouse and truly believes it, who needs to teach them how to act or what to do, when to speak or not, or what to think about the other? Their own confidence alone teaches all that and more. There is no difference in the works they do, be they great or small, extended or brief, many or few. They do them all with joyful, serene, and confident hearts and are completely free.[x] But if uncertainty is present, they look for the best thing to do and thus begin imagining there to be differences among the works by which they may gain the other's affection. Then they must walk around with heavy hearts and with no enthusiasm, completely trapped, half despairing, and as often as not they end up acting the fool.

---

u Luther, like most in his day, regarded the patriarchs, prophets, and other faithful women and men of Hebrew Scripture as saints.

v 1 Sam. 1:6-28, esp. vv. 18-19.

w The NRSV, following the Greek and Latin, has "Spirit of the Lord."

x Literally: "a completely free journeyman," a saying derived from the guilds and the "graduation" from apprentice to journeyman. An English equivalent might be "As free as the wind."

23. Here and elsewhere, Luther attacks a cornerstone of late medieval piety and theology, that a person must always doubt his or her standing before God, not knowing for certain whether one's sorrow for sin or subsequent good works truly please God. This humility of uncertainty was seen as an especially important good, meritorious work over against the sin of pride.

24. The burial shrine of St. James at Santiago de Compostela in northwestern Spain was a favorite destination for pilgrims.

25. Luther later recalled that he visited some of the holy places in Rome during his sojourn in late 1511 and early 1512.

26. The trip to Rome has been convincingly redated (from 1510 to 1511) by Hans Schneider, "Martin Luthers Reise nach Rom neu datiert und neu gedeutet," in *Studien zur Wissenschafts- und Religionsgeschichte*, ed. Akademie der Wissenschaften zu Göttingen (Berlin: De Gruyter, 2011), 1–157.

27. Special prayers ascribed to Bridget (Birgitta), a Swedish saint who died in Rome in 1373, were popular among late medieval Christians.

28. Luther introduces a second aspect of faith.

Individual Christians,[y] therefore, who live with this confidence in God, know all things,[z] are able to do all things, take responsibility for all that needs to be done, and do it all joyfully and freely, not in order to accumulate merits and works but in order to fulfill their desire to please God in this way, to serve God simply without return, being satisfied that God is pleased. On the other hand, those who are not one with God or uncertain about it begin to look anxiously for ways to make satisfaction and sway God with many works.[23] They run to St. James,[24] Rome,[25, 26] Jerusalem, here or there, pray to St. Bridget (d. 1373) to grant this or that,[27] fast on this or that day, make confession here, make confession there, beseech this or that person, and yet they find no rest. And they do all this with such great heaviness, doubts, and lack of enthusiasm in their hearts that Hebrew Scripture calls such good works *aven amal*, in German "toil and trouble."[a] They are not good works at all but a complete waste. This matter has driven many people mad and made them miserable with anxiety. The Wisd. of Sol. 5[:6-7] states about them: "We have worn ourselves out on unrighteous paths and we have taken ways that are arduous and bitter; we have not known the way of God and the sun of righteousness has not risen over us."[b]

7. Given that in such works, faith is still paltry and weak, let us inquire further about cases when people suffer with respect to their body, property, reputation, friends, or anything else.[28] Do they then believe they are still pleasing to God and—be their suffering and adversity great or small—that God is still mercifully disposed toward them? In this situation, when all our senses and understanding tell us that God is angry, it is an art to trust in God and to regard oneself as better cared for than it appears. In this situation,

y   Singular in the original.

z   Cf. 1 Cor. 2:15-16.

a   Ps. 90:10. But see also Job 4:8; 5:6; Pss. 10:7; 55:11; Isa. 10:1.

b   A close paraphrase of Wisd. of Sol. 5:6-7. Throughout his career, Luther cited passages from the Apocrypha, to which he later accorded a secondary authority but also included in his translation of the complete Bible in 1534.

God is hidden,[c] just as the bride says in the Song of Sol. [2:9]: "Look, there he stands behind our wall gazing in at the windows."[29] That is: during our sufferings, which try to separate us from God like a wall or even a barrier, he stands there hidden and yet sees me and does not leave me. He is standing ready to help with grace and allows himself to be seen through the window of a dim faith. In Lam. [3:31-33, paraphrased], Jeremiah says: "God rejects mortals but never with callous disregard." They have no experience with this kind of faith but instead give up, thinking that God has abandoned them and become their enemy. They attribute their affliction to other people and the devil, and there is no trust in God whatsoever. For this reason, they forever view their suffering as offensive and harmful, and then they go out and do what they think are good works without recognizing any lack of faith on their part. But those who in the midst of such suffering trust in God and are completely confident that God is pleased with them consider their suffering and adversity to be nothing but costly merits and precious assets, the value of which no one can appreciate. For faith and confidence render precious before God everything that to others is the worst that can happen. That applies even to dying, according to Ps. 116[:15]: "The death of the saints is considered precious in the eyes of God." As much as confidence and faith are greater and stronger at this level than they are when there is no suffering, so also the afflictions that are endured in faith are likewise superior to any and all works done in faith. In this way, suffering produces immeasurably greater advantages than such works can ever provide.

8. Above these is the highest level of faith of all,[30] which is required when God torments the conscience not with earthly afflictions but with death, hell, and sin and withholds divine grace and mercy, as if God wanted to condemn and stay angry forever, something that only a few people experience, as David laments in Ps. 6[:1]: "Do not . . . discipline me in your wrath."[31] To trust that God is gracious

29. Luther, like many other interpreters before him, applied the Song of Solomon to the relation of the believer and Christ.

30. Luther's third aspect of faith.

31. This idea is similar to the medieval *resignatio ad infernum*. For an earlier example, see Luther's *Lectures on Romans* (1515–1516), in LW 25:379–84.

---

c   This argument is closely related to Luther's theology of the cross. See the *Heidelberg Disputation*, above, pp. 98–101.

in this situation is the finest work that can occur in and through any creature. The "work saints" and "doers of good deeds" know nothing about this; for how could they be certain of God's goodness and grace, since they are not certain regarding their own works and have doubts about even the lowest level of faith?

Now you can see why I have insisted that faith should always be praised and that every work done without faith should be rejected: to lead the people away from the false, hypocritical, pharisaical, faithless good works that now fill to overflowing the cloisters, churches, houses, and all levels of society, and to direct them toward the true, genuinely good and faithful works. No one contradicts me except the unclean animals with uncloven hooves, as Moses says in the law,[d] who cannot stand to make any distinction among good works. Instead, they fall into the trap of thinking that when they have prayed, fasted, endowed Masses, and made confession and satisfaction,[e] everything will be well with them, even though they are not confident of receiving divine grace and blessing. For the most part, they consider it good when they have performed many great things over a long period without such confidence and only then expect good things for themselves after the works are done. Thus, they count on them instead of on God's goodwill; that is, they build on sand and water and must suffer a horrible collapse, as Christ says in Matt. 7[:26-27]. On Christmas night, the angels proclaimed this kindness and goodwill from heaven when they sang: "*Gloria in excelsis Deo*. Glory to God in the highest, peace on earth and goodwill to all people."[f]

9. Do you see? This is the work of the first commandment: "You shall not have other gods."[32] That is to say: Since I alone am God, all your confidence, trust, and faith should be placed only in me and no one else. You do not "have a

32. Following these introductory paragraphs about faith and its three aspects (fruits, suffering, and resignation), Luther now turns to an exposition of the first commandment (Exod. 20:3; Deut. 5:7). Luther associates this commandment with faith throughout his career. See, e.g., LC, "Ten Commandments," par. 1–4 (BC, 386).

d Cf. Lev. 11:1-8. An indirect, sarcastic use of allegory to refer to those who in fact disagreed with his view of good works.

e Two parts of the sacrament of penance.

f Luke 2:14. Luther is citing a translation of the Greek reflected in the Vulgate and the Latin Mass and used in sixteenth-century German and English translations.

god" when all you do is mouth the word or worship by bowing the knee or making external gestures instead of trusting God from the heart and counting on God's goodness, grace, and favor in all that you do or suffer, in living and dying, in weal and in woe, just as Christ said to the Samaritan woman in John 4[:24]: "I say to you, whoever worships God must worship in spirit and truth." And this faith, trust, and confidence, which come from the bottom of the heart, are the true fulfillment of the first commandment. Without them no work of any kind can satisfy its demand. Just as this commandment is the first, highest, and best, from which and to which all the others flow and by which they are evaluated and judged, so also the work that fulfills it (trust and confidence in God's favor at all times) is the first, noblest, and best work from which and to which all the others flow, in which they abide and by which they must be judged and evaluated. To do other works against this one is to act as if neither the first commandment nor God existed. Hence St. Augustine rightly calls the work that fulfills the first commandment faith, hope, and love.[g] It was said above that such confidence and faith bring with them love and hope. In fact, rightly considered, love should be first or at least on the same level with faith. For I cannot trust God without believing that he is favorably inclined toward me. As a consequence, I am favorably inclined toward God and moved to trust him from the heart and rely on him for everything good.

10. Now consider all those who do not trust God all the time nor expect divine favor and benevolence in all their working or suffering, living or dying, but instead look for those things elsewhere or from themselves. They do not keep this commandment and are in fact practicing idolatry even though they were to perform the works of all the other commandments and, in addition, pile up prayer to all the saints along with fasting, obedience, patience, chastity, and innocence. The chief work is not there, without which all the

---

g "God is to be worshiped with faith, hope, and love." Augustine, *Enchiridion* 1, 3 in *Basic Writings of Saint Augustine*, ed. Whitney J. Oates (New York: Random House, 1948), 1:658 [= MPL 40:232].

others are nothing but pure glitter, show, and makeup with nothing underneath. Christ warns us against this in Matt. 7[:15]: "Beware of false prophets who come to you in sheep's clothing." That means all those who try to make themselves pleasing to God through many good works (as they call them) and buy God's favor as if God were a peddler or a day laborer, who did not want to give away his grace and favor for nothing. Such characters are the most perverse people on earth; they can never or only with great difficulty be turned in the right direction. Others act like them when in adversity they run to and fro seeking counsel, help, and consolation from everyone and everything except God, from whom they are strictly commanded to request it. The prophet Isaiah in chapter 9[:13] chastises these people in this way: "The unwise folk do not turn to him who strikes them." God struck them by sending them suffering and adversity so that they would seek and trust God, but they ran away instead to other people, sometimes in Egypt, sometimes in Assyria, and even to the devil. That idolatry is recorded by the same prophet and in the books of Kings.[h] All holy hypocrites act the same way: when something bad happens, instead of running to God they flee away in fear, wondering how they can get rid of their troubles either by themselves or with others' help and yet be regarded by themselves and others as godly.

11. In many places, St. Paul holds this opinion and attributes so much to faith that he writes [Rom. 1:17], *"Justus ex fide sua vivit,"* that is (in German), that "righteous persons have life from their faith" and that "on account of faith they are accounted righteous before God."[33] If righteousness consists in faith, it is clear that faith alone fulfills all the commandments and makes all their works righteous, especially since nobody is just unless all the commandments are kept and, contrariwise, that no works are able to justify in God's sight apart from faith. Moreover, the holy apostle rejects works and praises faith so completely that some people have taken umbrage at his words and said: "Then we will do no

33. Rom. 1:17; 3:28. Following the typical pattern of late medieval preachers, Luther first cites the Latin of Rom. 1:17 and provides a translation, but then adds Rom. 3:28. Singular in the original.

---

h   See, e.g., 1 Kgs. 36:1-30 or Isaiah 36.

more good works." He condemns such people as mistaken and simpleminded.[i]

Nevertheless, the same thing is still going on now. Whenever we reject impressive, showy works done without faith today, people say that they should only believe and do nothing good at all—as if the first commandment were to be obeyed now by singing, reading, playing the organ, saying Mass, and praying at Matins, Vespers and other appointed times, by endowing churches, altars and cloisters and adorning them with bells, expensive ornaments, vestments, and altar ware, and even by collecting treasures[34] or running to Rome or to the shrines of the saints. If that were true, then, whenever we don our vestments and bow, genuflect, pray the rosary and the Psalms, and do all that not before an idol but before the holy cross of God or a picture of his saints, that is what we would call honoring and worshiping God and, according to the first commandment, having no other gods. Any usurer, adulterer, or sinner of any kind could do that every day. So it is, but if we do these things with the kind of faith that we hold pleases God, then they are praiseworthy not for the sake of their virtuous quality but because of this very faith that makes all works equal, as has been said. If we doubt this, however, or do not believe that God is gracious to us and takes pleasure in us, or measure ourselves to be God pleasing only according to our works, then it is pure deception to honor God externally but internally to elevate ourselves as an idol. That is why I so often have spoken out against and

34. Treasures: perhaps a reference to collections of relics.

Page from the *Heiligthumsbuch*, illustrated by Lucas Cranach and published in 1518, describing the relics from the Castle Church, Wittenberg. The caption reads: "[This reliquary contains] 4 pieces of the mount from which sermon on the mount was delivered; 3 from where Jesus prayed; 2 from where he taught the Lord's Prayer; a stone Jesus stood on in Jerusalem; a piece of the middle of the world; a stone where he wept over Jerusalem; a stone from where Jesus got on the donkey; 2 pieces of the earth where Jesus was arrested. In total: 14 [15] particles."

---

i   See Rom. 6:1-19. Luther picks up this theme in *The Freedom of a Christian* (below, p. 518).

denounced such works, pomp, and lavishness: so that it is clear as day how they not only take place in doubt or without such faith but also that there is scarcely one person in a thousand who does not set faith in such things, presuming that works make them acceptable to God and eligible for grace. They even make a business of it. God, who has freely promised favor, cannot abide this and instead wants people to begin to rely on his favor and through it accomplish all works whatever their names.

12. From this, note the gap between fulfilling the first commandment only with external works and fulfilling it with innermost trust. The latter makes genuine and living children of God, while the former produces a ruinous idolatry and the most harmful hypocrites on earth. With their pretentious displays, they lead countless people astray, keep them from faith, and leave them woefully seduced, in external mirages and specters. Christ warns us in Matt. 24[:23] about these hypocrites: "Beware of those who say to you, 'Here is the Christ or there he is.'" And in John 4:[21, 23]: "I tell you the time will come that you will worship God neither on this mountain nor in Jerusalem . . ., for the Father seeks those who worship spiritually."

These verses and others like them have caused me and should cause everyone to reject that pompous display of bulls, seals, and banners surrounding indulgences,[35] with which the poor folk are enticed to build churches, make contributions, set up endowments, and offer prayers, even as faith is passed over in silence or, better said, completely suppressed. Since faith makes no distinction among works, it cannot tolerate that some are grossly exaggerated and touted over others but desires only genuine worship and refuses to place that honor or name on any other works unless faith itself imparts it to them. Faith does this so that each work arises in and from faith. This type of mischief is foreshadowed in the Old Testament where the Jews abandon the temple and offer sacrifices in other places, like pleasure gardens and on the mountaintops.*j* Our hypocrites act the same way: eager to perform every work while ignoring the chief work of faith completely.

35. For a description of the ceremonies surrounding indulgences and Luther's criticism in the *95 Theses*, see above, p. 18f.

A typical papal bull, this one by Pope Gregory XIII, who concedes
to the Compagnia di San Paolo the authority to operate a "Monte di Pietà,"
a pawnshop giving charitable loans to the poor, March 1, 1579.

13. Where now are those who ask which works are good,
or what they should do, or how they can become righteous?[k]
Moreover, where are those who, when we preach about faith,
accuse us of denying that any good work should be taught
or done?[l] Is it not true that the first commandment by itself

j   See, e.g., 1 Kgs. 13:33 and Isa. 65:3-7. Luther interprets these events
    typologically.
k   In Luther's German the word *fromm*, which now means "godly" or
    "pious," meant "upright" and was a synonym for *gerecht* (righteous).
l   In the manuscript version of this tract's introduction, Luther points
    to this charge as the basis for writing. See WA 9:229, n. 1.

demands more than anybody can do? Even if a single person became a thousand people or all people or every living creature, there would be enough demanded and more than enough, since it commands each person at every moment to conduct one's life with faith and confidence in God at all times, putting such trust in nothing else, and hence to have no other god than the one true God.

Since, therefore, human nature requires us at every moment to be active or passive, suffering something or fleeing from it (for life never rests, as we see), so then begin here. Let those*m* who desire to be upright and to abound in good works practice faith always, in every situation of life and in all works; let them learn constantly to do or avoid everything in that trust. Then they will discover how much there is to accomplish, how everything is comprehended in faith, and how you can never be idle, because even idleness occurs within the practice and work of faith. In short, when we believe, as we should, that everything that is or happens in us or to us pleases God, then it has to be good and meritorious. Therefore St. Paul says: "So, brothers [and sisters], whether you eat or drink or whatever you do, do everything" "in the name of Jesus Christ our Lord."*n* Now it cannot happen in his name if it does not happen in faith. Rom. 8[:28]: "We know, however, that all things work together for the best for God's holy ones."

When some people say that good works are forbidden when we preach faith alone, it is similar to this. Supposed I advised a sick person: "If you were healthy, your body could perform all its functions, but without your health everything you do is nothing," and someone upon hearing this concluded that I had forbidden the sick man's body to perform any of its functions, even though what I meant was that health had to be there first, which could then stimulate the actions of all the bodily members. Likewise, in all works, faith must be the master artisan*o* and the captain, or they amount to nothing at all.

---

m   Singular in the original.

n   1 Cor. 10:31 with Col. 3:17.

14. Now you might respond: If, through the first commandment, faith does everything, why are there so many ecclesiastical and secular laws, along with rituals in the churches, cloisters, and shrines, which urge and encourage people to do good works?[36] The answer: Precisely because not all of us have faith or pay attention to it. If everyone had it, we would need no law at all, for everyone would perform good works spontaneously all the time, just as such trust would certainly teach them.[37]

Now there are four kinds of people. The first sort (just mentioned) need no law. Paul refers to them in 1 Tim. 1[:9] when he says "the law is not laid down for the righteous person (that is, to the one who has faith), for they do voluntarily what they know and what pleases them, as long as they do it alone with firm trust that in all they do God's good pleasure and favor hover over them. The second kind intends to abuse this freedom by relying on it improperly and becoming lazy. Saint Peter says about them in 1 Pet. 2[:16]: "You should live as those who are free, but do not use this freedom to cloak your sin," as if he were saying: "The freedom of faith does not give free rein to sin and will not cover it up, but it does allow you to do all kinds of works and to suffer whatever comes your way,[p] so that no one is restricted only to this or that specific work." Thus, Paul also says in Gal. 5[:13]: "Take care that this freedom not become a pretext for you to live according to the flesh." Such people have to be prodded with laws and kept in line by teaching and warnings. The third kind consists of malicious persons who are always thinking of ways to sin. Like wild horses and dogs, they must be restrained by the force of ecclesiastical and civil laws and, if that fails, removed from society by the civil sword, as Paul says in Rom. 13[:3-4]: "Civil authority bears the sword and with it serves God . . . not for the godly but to instill fear in the ungodly." The fourth sort of people, who understand this faith and spiritual life in immature

36. Luther is most likely thinking especially of the commands for fasting, praying, confessing one's sins, and receiving the Supper as well as the encouragements to go on pilgrimages, support the poor and the mendicant friars, pray the rosary, and the like.

37. See Luther's exposition of this theme in *The Freedom of a Christian*, below, p. 512.

o   German: *Werkmeister*, that is, the guild master who oversees the work of apprentices.

p   Literally: "as they come before your hands." See Eccl. 9:10a.

and childlike ways, have to be enticed and lured like young children with rituals, rules, and external things—readings, praying, fasting, singing, going to church and adorning them, playing organ music, and whatever else is observed in cloisters and churches—until they, too, learn to acknowledge faith. To be sure, a great danger lurks here when—as is happening now—the leaders so emphasize and hammer away at these very rituals and external matters as if they were the true works while ignoring faith. For they should be teaching both things just as a mother gives her children other food along with milk until finally the children can eat solid food by themselves.

15. Because we are not all the same, we must have patience with those people and take upon ourselves and observe what they take upon themselves and observe.[38] We should not despise them but direct them in the proper path of faith. Saint Paul teaches as much in Rom. 14[:1]: "Receive the weak in faith and instruct them." And he did that himself in 1 Cor. 9[:20]: "To those who are under the law I became as one under the law, although I was not under it." Moreover, Christ in Matt. 17[:24-27], as he was about to pay the temple tax even though he was not obligated to do so, discussed with Peter whether taxes were paid by the children of kings or only by others. Peter answered, "Only by the others." Then Jesus said: "Thus, the children of kings are exempt from taxation. However, so that we give them no offense, go to the sea and cast out a line. Take the first fish you catch, and in his mouth you will find a penny. Give it for you and me."[39]

Here we see that works and other matters are free for a Christian through faith. And yet, because others still do not believe, individual Christians[q] take upon themselves and observe what they are not obligated to. Christians do it freely because they are certain that it surely pleases God. Moreover, they do it gladly, take it on themselves like any other free work that presents itself without their having chosen it. For they seek and desire nothing more than simply to act in faith in a way that pleases God.

38. For a similar argument, see *The Freedom of a Christian* below, p. 532.

39. Luther calls the coin a *pfennig*, a coin originally made of 1/240th of a pound of silver but often much less. In the sixteenth century, the coin could still be worth a substantial amount, depending on where it had been minted.

---

q   Singular in the original.

In this essay,[r] we have undertaken to teach which works are truly good and, in this section, which work is supreme. It is obvious that we are not talking about the second, third, or fourth kind of people, but about the first group, to which the others should aspire. The first group should, however, bear patiently with the others and instruct them. For this reason, one should not despise those still weak in faith, who would like to do good and learn better and still do not understand, on account of their ceremonies to which they cling so tightly. It is not as if they are completely lost. Instead, blame their ignorant and blind instructors, who never taught them faith and led them so deeply into works. Carefully and gradually, as if handling a sick person, they must once again be led out into faith but still be allowed for a while to cling to some works for the sake of their conscience and practice them as if necessary for salvation until they understand faith correctly. In this way, they will not be torn from these things so quickly lest their weak conscience be so completely destroyed or confused that they retain neither faith nor works. We should not, however, even bother with obstinate folk who are stuck in works and ignore what is said about faith and even fight against it. This Christ did and taught when he said [Matt. 15:14]: "Let them alone; they are blind guides of the blind."

16. You may ask, however: "How can I be sure that all my works are pleasing to God, since from time to time I fall short, for example, by talking, eating, drinking, or sleeping too much or by crossing the line in some other way, none of which I seem able to avoid?" The answer is: "Your question demonstrates that you consider faith to be like any work and fail to set it over all works. Faith is the highest and best work precisely because it persists and it erases everyday sins by not doubting that God is so well disposed toward you that such pitfalls and mistakes are, as it were, invisible,[s] even if a

---

r   In German, *sermo* was a loan word from Latin and could mean
      "sermon" or, as in this case, "essay."

s   Literally, "looks through his fingers," a favorite expression of Luther
      for God's toleration of human sin.

40. In the early church, murder, adultery, and apostasy were considered mortal sins, capable of killing the soul by making it liable to eternal damnation. By the Middle Ages, not only the so-called seven deadly sins (wrath, greed, sloth, pride, lust, envy, and gluttony) but any sin that a person deliberately committed was consider mortal sin.

mortal sin[40] were committed (although that should never, or at most seldom, happen to those whose lives are filled with faith and trust in God). Despite this, faith stands up again and does not doubt that its sin has already been removed, as it is written in 1 John 2[:1-2]: "I am writing this to you, my children, so that you may not sin. But if anyone does sin, then we have an advocate with God, Jesus Christ. He is the atonement for our sins." Moreover, Wisd. of Sol. 15[:2] states: "Even if we sin, we are still yours and acknowledge that you are great." And Prov. 24[:16]: "The righteous may fall seven times, but every time they rise again." For this reason, this trust and faith have to be so strong and exalted so that a person may know that before God's judgment seat all their works and their entire life are purely damnable sins, as it is written in Ps. 143[:2]: "No one living is righteous before you."[t] Moreover, such a person must be so uncertain about their works that they can only be good when they are done in this very faith, which does not expect judgment but only divine grace, favor, and mercy, as David says in Ps. 26[:3]: "For your mercy is forever before my eyes, and I walk cheerfully in your truth."[u] Again in Ps. 4[:6-7]: "The light of your countenance hovers over us," that is, the awareness of your grace through faith, and "with it you have made my heart glad," for we receive what we expect.

Now you see that works are blameless, forgiven, and good not by their own nature but by the mercy and grace of God for the sake of the faith that relies on this mercy. Because of works we can only be frightened, but because of God's grace we can comfort ourselves, as Ps. 147[:11] says: "The Lord takes pleasure in those who fear him and yet still trust in his mercy."[v] For this reason, we pray with complete trust, "our Father," and still ask "forgive us our debts"—his children and yet still sinners; we are precious to him and yet fail to

---

t   See thesis 3 of the *Heidelberg Disputation*, above, p. 89.

u   Luther and his contemporaries assumed that most if not all of the psalms were written by David.

v   In Luther's unique rendering of the psalm.

satisfy him.[41] Faith, fortified in the goodness and favor of God, does all of this.

17. You may ask, however, where faith and confidence come from or where they may be found. To know this is more necessary than anything else. First, without a doubt, it does not come from your works or merits but alone from Jesus Christ, who has freely promised it and bestows it, as St. Paul says in Rom. 5[:8]: "God makes his love so sweet and agreeable in that Christ died for us while we were still sinners." It is as if Paul wanted to say: "Does this not make for a strong and invincible confidence that Christ died for our sins even before we asked for it or were concerned about it, indeed, while we were still wandering further and further into sin?" Paul continues [5:9-10]: "If Christ died for us a long time ago, while we were still sinners, much more surely then will we be saved through him now that we have been justified by his blood. For if while we were still enemies we were reconciled with God through the death of his Son, we will certainly be saved by his life now that we are reconciled."

Look here! You must imprint Christ in yourself and see how God holds up his mercy before you, offering it without any prior merit on your part. From this picture of his grace you must derive faith and confidence that all your sins are forgiven. Thus, faith does not originate with works, nor do works manufacture faith. Instead, faith must spring and flow from the blood, wounds, and death of Christ.[42] When in this death you see that God is so loving to you that he even gave his Son for you,[w] then your heart simply melts[x] and in turn becomes pleasing to God. In this way confidence grows out of pure favor and love, that is, out of God's love for you and your love for God. We thus have never read that the Holy Spirit was given to anyone when he or she performed works but always when people heard the mercy of God and the gospel of Christ. Today and in every age, faith comes only from that same word and from nowhere else. For Christ

41. An expression of Luther's assertion that the believer is "simultaneously saint and sinner" (*simul iustus et peccator*).

This woodcut by Lucas Cranach the Elder is taken from the last printed leaf of the third Wittenberg printing of *Sermon on Good Works*. It shows the Apostle John, Mary the mother of Jesus, Mary Magdalene, and three soldiers gathered before the cross.

42. For this description of faith's origin, Luther borrows from the language of the so-called Christ-mysticism of the Middle Ages, found already in Bernard of Clairvaux (1090–1153) down to Johann von Staupitz (c. 1460–1524).

---

w   Cf. John 3:16.

x   Literally: becomes sweet.

is the rock from which a person sucks butter and honey, as Moses says in Deut. 32[:13].[43]

The Second Good Work [44]

18. Up to this point, we have treated the first work and the first commandment, but very briefly and in broad strokes since much more could be said. Now we move on to works related to the other commandments.

The second work, following immediately after faith, is prescribed by the second commandment that we should honor God's name and not use it in vain.[y] Like all other works, this one cannot be accomplished without faith, and if attempted without it, the result is pure hypocrisy and pretense. Next to faith, we can do nothing greater than to extol, preach, and sing God's praises, honor, and name, lifting them up and magnifying them in every way we can.

Although I said above (and it is true) that no differences exist among works in which faith is present and active, nevertheless this may be understood only when those works are measured against faith and its work. If, however, works are compared with one another, then differences do exist and one is greater than another. Just as in the body, when its members are considered together and measured against the health of the entire body, there is no difference among them and all are equally healthy; but still there is a difference among the works of individual members, and one work is greater, nobler, and more useful than another. In this case as well, to praise God's honor and name is a greater work than those that fulfill the commandments that follow. Nonetheless, both this work and those that follow must proceed from the very same faith.

I know full well that this work has been so devalued as to have become almost unknown. We will therefore examine it further. Moreover, it cannot be stressed enough that this work must be done in the faith and confidence that it pleases

43. Luther, like others, including the medieval commentator Paul of Burgos (c. 1351–1435), understood this passage as a prophecy of Christ. Later, following Nicholas of Lyra, Luther interpreted it as Moses' admonition to the Israelites (see LW 9:290–99).

44. This heading ("second good work") appears in the printed editions and encompasses four "good works" that fulfill the second commandment and are discussed in sections 21–31. Luther and later Lutherans numbered the Decalogue (Ten Commandments) according to the Greek Septuagint and Latin Vulgate, interpreting the command about graven images, which the Hebrew Bible and Reformed Christians count as the second commandment, as an expansion of the first commandment applicable only to the Israelites. See, e.g., *Against the Heavenly Prophets*, 1525 (LW 40:86).

y Exod. 20:7; Deut. 5:11.

God very much. In fact, there is no other work in which trust and faith are experienced and felt so noticeably as in giving honor to God's name. It also helps strengthen and increase faith, although all the other works help as well, as St. Peter says in 2 Pet. 1[:10]: "Dear brothers [and sisters], be diligent to confirm your call and election through good works."[z]

19. The first commandment forbids us to have other gods. As a consequence, it commands us to have the one true God by means of firm faith, trust, confidence, hope, and love.[45] With these works alone can we possess, honor, and hold fast to the one God. No other work enables us to draw close to God or depart from God. This only happens through faith or unbelief, through trust or doubt. No other work ever reaches up to God. In the same way, the second commandment prohibits us from taking God's name in vain. But that is not all. It also commands us to honor, invoke, praise, proclaim, and exalt his name. That is to say, it is not possible to avoid dishonoring God's name when it is not properly honored. For although it may be honored with the mouth, genuflections, kisses,[a] or other actions, when they do not proceed from the heart through faith, trusting God's favor, the result is nothing but pretense and a hypocritical appearance.

See how many good works a person can do all day long in this commandment and never be without the good works of this commandment, even if undertaking no more pilgrimages or visits to shrines.[46] So tell me, does a moment ever pass in which we do not continuously receive God's blessings or suffer evil misfortune? What are these things but constant admonitions and encouragements to praise, honor, and bless God and to call upon him and his name? Even if you did nothing in other matters, would you not have enough to do with this commandment alone by blessing, singing to, praising, and honoring God's name unceasingly?

45. Here, as elsewhere, Luther insists that a negative (or, elsewhere, positive) command always implies the opposite. See his explanations of the Decalogue in the *Large Catechism* and *Small Catechism*.

46. A person could visit countless local shrines, many of which honored the Virgin Mary or a local saint. There were also more famous pilgrimage sites, such as St. James in Santiago de Compostela and the tombs of the apostles in Rome.

z   The phrase "through good works" is from the Latin Vulgate. It did not appear in Erasmus's version of the Greek text (an absence mentioned in Erasmus's annotations) and, thus, not in Luther's 1522 German translation of the New Testament.

a   By kissing crosses, relics, or images.

Why else were tongue, voice, language, and mouth created? As Ps. 51[:14-15] says: "Lord, open my lips and my mouth will declare your praise," and "My tongue shall lift up your mercy." Is there any work done in heaven besides the second commandment, as we read in Ps. 84[:4]: "Happy are those who live in your house and forever sing your praise."[b] David indicates the same in Ps. 34[:1]: "God's praise shall continually be in my mouth." And St. Paul says in 1 Cor. 10[:31]: "Whether you eat or drink or whatever you do, do it all to the honor of God." Likewise Col. 3[:17]: "Whatever you do, in word or deed, do it in the name of the Lord Jesus Christ, giving thanks and praise to God the Father." If we took the work of this commandment to heart, we would have heaven on earth and enough to do forever, just like the blessed in heaven.

20. From this arises the astonishing but just judgment of God, that sometimes a poor person, whom no one can imagine doing many and great works, when at home alone praises God joyfully when things are going well or calls upon God with complete confidence when something bad happens. In so doing that individual performs a greater, more God-pleasing work than another person who frequently fasts, prays, endows churches, makes pilgrimages, and is busy doing great deeds everywhere. Such a fool gawks and looks for even greater works to the point of being so completely blinded as to miss the greatest work of all. In the eyes of such fools,[c] praising God is a very small thing in contrast to the fabulous image of these self-invented works, in which such individuals presumably praise themselves more than God or which please them more than God does. With their good works they rage against the second commandment and its works. The Pharisees and the public sinner in the Gospel [Luke 18:9-14] offer examples of both. In his transgressions, the sinner invokes and praises God, thus fulfilling the two greatest commandments, to believe in and honor God. The hypocrite fails to do either and parades

---

b   Luther interprets this psalm anagogically as a description of heaven.

c   Singular in the original.

around with other works through which he extols himself more than God and puts more trust in himself than in God. Rightly, therefore, the hypocrite is deservedly rejected while the sinner is chosen.

This happens all the time, that the greater and better the works, the less pretentious they are, so that everyone thinks they are easy to do because it appears that almost no one gives more of an impression of extolling God's name and honor like those who in reality are not doing it. With such hypocrisy—since their hearts lack faith—they make the most precious work despicable. In Rom. 2[:23-24] the Apostle Paul dares to say openly that those who blaspheme God's name the most [are] those who boast of the law of God. It is easy to speak God's name and to record his glory on paper and walls; but to praise God completely, to bless him for his benevolence, to call upon him for consolation in every distress— these are, next to faith, truly the greatest and rarest of works. When we realize how seldom they are encountered in Christendom, our sadness might make us despair. Despite this, the grand, beautiful, and glorious works devised by human imagination keep multiplying; superficially they appear identical to genuine works, but below the surface they lack faith and trust and, in short, have nothing good about them. For this reason, Isa. 48[:1] also admonishes the people: "Listen up, you who bear the name as if you truly were Israel, you who swear by the name of God but do not pay homage to him with truth and righteousness." That is, they did not do it with genuine faith and trust (which are the real "truth and righteousness") but were trusting in themselves, their works, and their own abilities, all the while invoking and praising the name of God. These two things,[47] however, cannot be reconciled with each other.

21. The first work of this commandment is thus to praise God for all his benefits, which are so numerous that such praise and thanksgiving would have neither interruptions nor an end. For who could praise God adequately for our physical existence, to say nothing of all the temporal and eternal blessings? As a result, through one part of this commandment, everybody is inundated with good and precious

47. Trusting oneself and yet invoking God's name.

works. If they[d] do them with genuine faith, they have in no way existed [on earth] in vain. By contrast, no one sins more gravely than the worst hypocritical holy folk, who please themselves and who like to boast and to hear the world praise, honor, and extol them.

It follows, then, that the second work of this commandment is to guard yourself against all worldly honor and praise, avoiding and fleeing from them, seeking nothing for your own name, reputation, and acclaim so that everyone would talk about you and sing your praises. This is a dangerous sin but still one of the most common despite its being regarded as a minor offense. Everyone, no matter how insignificant, wants to count for something and not be the least of all, so deep is the corruption of human nature in its conceit and false trust in itself, contrary to the first and the second commandments.

Because in this world people consider this horrible offense to be the noblest virtue, it is perilous for them to read pagan books or listen to pagan stories if they are not already well acquainted with God's commandments and stories from Holy Scripture. All pagan books are suffused with this poison of seeking praise and honor. A person learns from them in accord with blind reason: people cannot be or become capable and reputable unless motivated by praise and honor. Nor can they be ranked among the best if they do not chase after glory and honor above everything else: body, life, friends, and possessions. All the holy fathers[48] have denounced this vice and unanimously decided that it is the most difficult of all to overcome. According to St. Augustine, all other vices are expressed in evil deeds, but pride and vanity express themselves in good works.[e]

If therefore people[f] had nothing else to do except this second work of this commandment, they would have more than enough to do for a lifetime, in battling this vice that is

48. Early church theologians, including the four doctors of the Western church: Ambrose (c. 340–397), St. Augustine, St. Jerome (c. 347–420), and Pope Gregory I (c. 540–604).

---

d　Singular in the original.

e　A paraphrase of a statement attributed to Augustine by Prosper of Aquitaine (c. 390–c. 455), *Sententiae ex operibus S. Augustini* (MPL 45, col. 1863).

f　Singular in the original.

so widespread, sneaky, and slippery, and so hard to uproot. We, however, turn our backs on this good work and practice other lesser good works and by so doing even toss this one aside and forget it completely. In this way, the holy name of God, which alone ought to be honored, is dishonored and taken in vain by our own accursed name, self-satisfaction, and desire for fame. In God's eyes, this sin is graver than murder and adultery, but the evil it harbors is harder to discern than murder because of its subtlety since this happens in the spirit, not in the crude flesh.

22. According to some people, it is well for young people to do good deeds when they are motivated by fame and honor or, on the contrary, by shame and disgrace. For there are many who do good and avoid evil out of love of honor and fear of shame and in no way would have behaved otherwise. I will let them think what they want. Now, however, we are looking for how a person ought to do truly good works. Thus, those who are so disposed need not be motivated by fear of shame or by love of honor. Instead, they have and should have a better and much nobler impetus, namely, the commandment of God, the fear of God, the favor of God, along with their faith in and love of God. Those who lack this impetus or despise it and let themselves be driven by shame or honor receive their reward, as the Lord says in Matt. 6[:2, 5]. In their case, the deed and the reward correspond to the motivation, and there is nothing good about it except in the eyes of the world.

In my opinion, however, one can habituate and drive a young person [to good behavior] more easily with the fear of God and the divine commandments than anything else. When that does not work, we have to put up with other motivations like shame and honor to get a young person to do good and avoid evil. In the same way, we must tolerate the sinful or imperfect people described above.[g] We can do no more than to tell them: "What you are doing is neither right nor sufficient in the eyes of God" and let them go until they also learn to do good for the sake of God's commandment.

g   See above, p. 281f.

This is just how small children, by means of rewards and promises from their parents, are encouraged to pray, fast, learn, and so on. It would not be desirable, however, for children to be impelled like that all their lives and never to learn to do good in the fear of God or, worse yet, to become so accustomed to doing it only for the sake of praise and honor.

23. It is true, however, that we must still have a good name and reputation, and everyone should behave so that no one speaks ill of them or is offended by them, as St. Paul says in Rom. 12[:17]: "We should be diligent to do good not only before God but in the sight of all."[h] And in 2 Cor. 4[:2]: "We have such integrity that no one can find anything wrong with us." Great diligence and caution must prevail here, however, so that honor and a good name do not lead to a swollen head that is overly pleased with itself.[49] The saying of Solomon [Prov. 27:21] applies here: "As the fire in the furnace tests gold, so a person is tested by being praised." There are only a few, highly spiritual people who, in the presence of honor and praise, remain free and serene and unaffected. They are not bothered by it and develop no conceit; instead, they remain unencumbered, attributing all of their honor and good name to God alone, letting God be responsible for them and using them only to honor God and to improve the lives of others instead of using them for their own advantage. As a result, they do not measure themselves against or place themselves above the least capable and most despised people on earth, but they regard themselves as God's servants to whom God has granted the honor of serving both God and their neighbors. This is no different than if God had commanded them, for God's sake, to distribute a few precious coins among the poor. Jesus says therefore in Matt. 5[:16]: "Let your light shine before others so that they may see your good works and give glory to your Father in heaven." He does not say "they should give glory and praise to you" but rather, "your work should only serve to improve their lives so that they will praise God both in themselves and in you." This is the proper use of a good name and respect: when God

49. Luther reflects here many aspects of Augustinian and monastic humility.

h Luther conflates 2 Cor. 8:20-21 with Rom. 12:17.

is praised through the betterment of others. If people want to praise us, however, instead of God in us, we should not tolerate it and with all our might guard ourselves against this sin, fleeing from it at all costs as from the severest sin and thievery of divine honor.

24. This is why God many times allows individuals[i] to fall into grave sin, and even to remain there, so that they may become dishonored in their own eyes and others'. Otherwise, had they survived with their great gifts and virtues intact, they might not have avoided the formidable vice of [trusting] their pure honor and reputation. God, so to speak, protects us from this sin using other serious sins, so that his holy name alone remains honored. Thus, because of our twisted depravity, which not only does what is evil but also misuses all that is good, one sin becomes the medicine to heal another.[50]

See how much individuals[j] have to do if they want to perform good works, for countless opportunities surround them all the time! And see how they squander [these opportunities] everywhere and blindly ignore them, and seek and pursue other works according to their own thoughts and pleasure, so that no one can speak against this enough nor find enough protection against it. All the prophets had to deal with this, and some were even killed simply because they condemned these very self-made works[51] and only proclaimed God's command. One of them, Jeremiah, says in chapter 7[:21-23]: "Take your burnt offerings and add them to your sacrifices and eat their flesh. I have not commanded anything like that, but I have commanded you to listen to my voice"—that is, do not listen to what you imagine is correct and good but to what I command you—"and walk only in the way that I have commanded you." And in Deut. 12[:8, 32]: "You shall not do what appears right and good to you, but that which your God has commanded."

These verses and countless others are intended to tear people away not only from their sins but also from the works

50. Because Luther is arguing that, next to faith, honoring God's reputation is the highest Christian work, he can say that other sins that cause shame cure the (worse) sin of conceit.

51. Cf. Col. 2:23 ("self-chosen spirituality"), which Luther contrasts to works commanded by God.

---

i   Singular in the original.
j   Singular in the original.

that they imagine are good and to direct them instead to the simple meaning of God's commandments, so that at all times they diligently heed them alone. As it is written in Exod. 13[:9]: "You shall let these commandments be a sign on your hand and a constant image before your eyes." And, Ps. 1[:2]: "Upright persons speak to themselves, day and night about God's commandment."[k] We have more than enough to do, indeed too much, if we are simply to satisfy the divine commandments. God has given them to us, so that when we comprehend them we will not be idle for a second and can rightly forget all other works. But the evil spirit, who never rests, when unable to lead us into committing evil works on the left side, attacks us on the right with our own self-fabricated works that appear good. Against both, God has commanded in Deut. 28[:14] and Josh. 23[:6], "You shall not depart from my commandments either to the right or to the left."

25. The third work of this commandment is to call on God's name in all distress. For this greatly reveres God's name and keeps it holy: that we invoke it and call upon it when under affliction or in distress.[l] This, finally, is the reason God inflicts us with suffering, affliction, distress, and even death and lets us live with many sinful urges so that through them he may impel us and cause us to run to him, cry out, and call upon his holy name. By so doing, we perform this work of the second commandment, as God says in Ps. 50[:14, 15]: "Call upon me in your distress and I will help you," and "You shall venerate me for I desire a sacrifice of praise."[m] For this reason, this is the way through which we may come to salvation, for through this work a person discovers and experiences what God's name is and how power-

---

k In the singular in the original. Luther paraphrases the word *meditate* according to the Hebrew "speak to oneself."

l German: *anfechtung und nodt*, two crucial terms for Luther's lifelong view of the Christian life as under assault and beset by direst needs, and thus obliged to pray. He often links the second commandment, prayer, and especially the first petition of the Lord's Prayer.

m Luther also cites this in the LC, "Lord's Prayer," par. 19 (BC, 434).

ful it is in helping everyone who calls upon it. Through this, our trust and faith will grow very strong and thereby will also fulfill the first and greatest commandment. David experienced this, in Ps. 54[:6-7]: "You have delivered me from all distress; therefore I will make known your name and declare that it is lovely and sweet." And in Ps. 91[:14-15] God says: "I will deliver them because they hope in me; I will aid them because they have acknowledged my name."

Look here! Is there a person on earth who would not have enough to do regarding this work to last a lifetime? Who is not under attack every hour? I will skip over those countless attacks caused by adversities. The most pernicious kind comes when there is no attack at all and everything is running smoothly, lest in such a situation the person forgets God and through lack of restraint misuses the good times. Here it is ten times more necessary to call upon God's name than in the midst of adversity. As it is written in Ps. 91[:7]: "A thousand may fall at your left hand, ten thousand at your right hand." Everyday human experience shows us as plain as day that horrible sins and vices flourish more during good times when there is peace and things are cheap than when we are afflicted by war, pestilence, sickness, and other misfortune. For example, Moses feared for his people, that there would be no greater cause for them to forsake God's commandments than that they became too stuffed and had too much leisure, as he says in Deut. 32[:15]: "My dear people have become rich, sated, and fat; therefore they have turned against their God." Consequently, God also allowed many of their enemies to survive and refused to drive them away, so that the people could not relax but had to keep practicing the commandments, as is described in Judg. 3[:1-5]. God is dealing with us in the same manner when he allows us to suffer all kinds of misfortune. He is so concerned about us that he teaches us, indeed drives us, to honor and call upon his name, to gain faith and trust in him and thereby to fulfill the first two commandments.

26. Here foolish people behave dangerously, especially self-righteous, holier-than-thou folk and all those who desire to be something special. They promote the use of

52. Pious phrases, alleged to have come from heaven and sometimes worn as amulets for protection against personal harm, illness, or death.

53. Practices quite common in Luther's day and universally condemned by Christian teachers.

incantations; some people shield themselves with [heavenly] letters,[52] others seek out fortune-tellers, some search for one thing, others for another, all in order to be safe and avoid misfortune. Words alone cannot describe the devilish specter that reigns in this game, through magic, conjuring, and superstition,[53] all of which occurs because people simply have no need of God's name and trust God in nothing. Here God's name and the first two commandments are greatly dishonored, because they seek from the devil, other people, and creatures what they ought to seek and find in God alone through a pure, simple faith, trust, joyous hope, and invocation of God's holy name.

Now judge for yourself whether or not it is a fatuous perversion that some people have to believe in the devil, other people, or some creature and trust them for good fortune and have nothing to fall back on for help except this kind of faith and trust. What remuneration should God, who is true and just, offer people so that they trust God as much as or more than other people and the devil? He not only promises help and solid support but also commands us to count on it, and he gives us all kinds of reasons and prods us to put our faith and trust in him. Is this not a terrible pity both that either the devil or human beings, who command and force nothing but only make promises and give assurances, are set over God, who actually promises, urges, and commands, and that they are held in greater esteem than God? We should rightly be ashamed and learn a lesson from those who have faith in the devil or human beings. For if the devil, who is an evil, deceitful spirit, keeps faith with those who ally themselves with him, how much more, incomparably more, will the most benevolent and faithful God stay true to anyone who trusts him? A rich man trusts and relies upon his money and property, and are we unwilling to trust and rely on the living God and believe that he can and will help us? As they say, "Gold makes bold,"[n] as Bar. 3[:17] states: "Gold is something in which people put their trust." Much

n   A German proverb: "*Gut macht Mut!*" literally, "Possessions make [a person have] courage."

greater, however, is the boldness created by the eternal and highest Good, on which none but the children of God rely.

27. Even if none of these adversities[o] compelled us to trust and call upon God, sin alone would be more than sufficient to make us practice this work. Sin besieges us with three mighty armies—our own flesh, the world, and the evil spirit—which harry and attack us without respite. God uses them to cause us constantly to do good works, that is, to do battle against sin and these enemies. The flesh seeks titillation and leisure; the world seeks wealth, favor, power, and acclaim; the evil spirit looks for arrogance, fame, conceit, and disdain of others.

Together they are so potent that even one of them is enough to overpower a person. And yet we can without a doubt overcome them but only by calling upon the holy name of God with a firm faith, as Solomon says in Prov. 18[:10]: "The name of God is a strong tower; the faithful flee to it and are lifted up." Thus, David says in Ps. 116[:13]: "I will drink the cup of salvation and call upon God's name." Again in Ps. 18[:3]: "I will call upon God with praise, so shall I be saved from all my enemies." We have become ignorant of these works and the strength of the divine name, because we are unaccustomed ever to struggle earnestly with sin and therefore to have need of God's name. This causes us to practice only our self-contrived works, which we are able to perform through our own powers.

28. Also included among the works of this commandment are the following: that we should not swear, curse, lie, deceive, or practice magic using God's holy name, or misuse it in any other way. These are crude examples with which everyone is familiar, but until now these sins were for the most part the only ones named in preaching and proclamation. Included here is also preventing others from lying, swearing, deceiving, cursing, practicing magic, or committing other sins using God's name. These are all good reasons to do good and to guard against evil.

---

o See par. 25 above.

54. Here Luther reflects his own behavior toward his opponents. In the *Large Catechism* Luther ties this criticism to both the second and eighth commandments. See LC, "Ten Commandments," pars. 54, 284 (BC, 393, 424).

55. The *summum bonum*, the most desirable purpose and goal of human existence, a concept derived from Greek philosophy that Christian theologians applied in various ways to life in God or eternal blessedness.

The most important and difficult work of this commandment[54] is to protect God's holy name against all those who misuse it spiritually and spread such misuse everywhere. It is not enough for me to praise the divine name for myself alone or to call upon it in good and bad times just for me. I must step forward and for the sake of God's name and honor take upon myself the hostility of everyone else, as Christ said to his disciples [Matt. 10:22]: "You will be hated by all because of my name." We cannot help but bring upon ourselves the anger of father, mother, and our best friends. In this matter, we must confront the authorities, both spiritual and temporal, and be rebuked as disobedient. Indeed, everyone the world admires—the rich, the learned, the holy—will turn against us. And although particularly those who are charged with preaching God's word are under this obligation, it is also expected of every Christian when circumstances demand it. In fact, we should invest all that we have on behalf of God's holy name and prove with our actions both that we love God and his name, his honor and his glory, above anything else and that we trust God above all things and expect all our blessings from him. In this way, we confess publicly that we consider God as the highest good[55] and for his sake forsake and leave behind all other goods.

29. First of all, we must strive against all injustice when the truth or righteousness is impugned by force and adversity. We must not make any distinction here among persons, as some do who fight with great diligence and persistence against injustice that has been done to the rich and powerful or to their friends but remain silent and passive when it happens to the poor and despised or to their enemies. They do not see the name and honor of God as they really are but look through rose-colored glasses[p] and measure truth and justice according to the people affected. They will never be aware of their distorted vision because they privilege the person over the matter itself. They are arch-hypocrites and only appear to defend the truth. They realize they run no risk when they support the rich, the powerful, the learned,

---

p   Literally, painted glass.

or their friends, who in turn will protect, respect, and otherwise be useful to them. It is very easy, therefore, to protest injustices done to popes, kings, princes, bishops, and other bigwigs. In these situations that are not so dire, everyone wants to show how righteous they are. Alas, how insidious is the false Adam with his petitions![56] How finely he dresses up his desire for self-advancement in the garb of truth, justice, and divine honor! When, however, something bad happens to a poor and insignificant person, this false pair of eyes sees no advantage to be gained but only a threat of losing favor with the powerful. Thus, such a one prudently leaves the poor person without aid. Who can describe how much this depravity has corrupted Christendom? God declares in Ps. 82[:2-4]: "How long will you judge unjustly and show partiality to the wicked? Give justice to the poor and the orphan; give the afflicted and the destitute their due. Rescue the needy and forsaken; deliver them from the hand of the wicked." But no one does this, and thus the psalm continues [v. 5]: "They have neither knowledge nor understanding and walk around in darkness." That is, they do not see the truth but cling only to the reputation with the bigwigs regardless of how unjust they are and ignore the poor even if justice is all on their side.

30. See how many good works are close at hand here! The vast majority of the rich, the powerful and "friends," act unjustly and oppress the poor, the forgotten, and their opponents. The more powerful they are, the more despicable their actions. If they cannot be resisted with force in order to assist the truth, then we should at least speak the truth publicly and bolster it with words, not giving our consent to what they do or implying that it is just but instead stating the truth openly.

What benefit would individuals[q] gain from doing all kinds of good things, like visiting Rome and other holy places, acquiring every indulgence, or endowing all church buildings and other religious foundations,[57][r] if they were

56. That is, the old creature: Human nature in bondage to sin.

57. Luther's own prince, Elector Frederick, had seen to extensive renovations of the All Saints' Foundation and Church in Wittenberg. Money or income from land holdings were to fund such foundations, the members of which might be responsible to recite private Masses for the dead, teach at universities, or the like.

---

q   Singular in the original.

r   German: *alle kirchenn unnd stiffte.*

found guilty, in the name and honor of God, of silencing and forsaking that very name and instead considering their possessions, reputation, connections, and friends more important than the truth, which is God's very name and honor? To whom does this good work not come knocking at the door daily, with the result that it is unnecessary to roam far from home or inquire where good works can be found? When we consider how people everywhere live so rashly and frivolously in regard to this matter, then with the prophet we have to exclaim: *Omnis homo mendax!* "Every human being is false, lies, and deceives."[s] For they set aside the true, central good works and adorn and paint themselves with the least important, using them to look righteous and quietly to pave their way into heaven.

You may ask: why does God not do this himself since God obviously knows how to and can help every person? God certainly can do this but prefers not to do it alone. God wants us to work together with him and does us the honor of desiring to accomplish his work with and through us. If we decline to accept this honor, then God will do it alone and help the poor. Those people, however, who did not wish to help God and scorned that great honor God will condemn along with all the unrighteous and consider as supporters of the unrighteous. Although God alone is blessed, he still wants to give us the honor and not be blessed by himself but share that blessedness with him. Were God to act alone, then the commandments would be given to us in vain, because no one would have cause to exercise themselves in the great works of these very commandments. Nor would anyone make an effort to view God and his name as the greatest good or to stake everything on him.

31. It also belongs to this work to oppose all false, seductive, errant, and heretical teachings and any abuse of the clerical authority. This is extremely serious because these teachings use God's holy name to fight against God's name. Thus, to oppose these people looks daunting and

---

s   "Every person is a liar." From the Vulgate reading of Ps. 116:11, which Luther renders freely in German. See also Rom. 3:4.

risky, because they claim that whoever opposes them also opposes God and all the saints, in whose seat these people claim to sit[58] and wield authority. They allege that the words of Christ were spoken to them: "Whoever hears you hears me; whoever rejects you rejects me."[59]t They rely strictly on these words and have no compunction about saying, doing, or not doing whatever they want. They ban, curse, rob, kill, and perpetrate all the evildoings as they please without any restraint.[60] In no way did Christ mean that we should obey them in everything they say and do but only when they speak his word, the gospel, and not their own words and do his work and not their own. Otherwise how could we know whether or not to avoid their lies and sins? There must certainly be a rule that tells us to what extent we should obey and follow them—a rule that cannot be set by them but must be set over them by God according to which we can judge, as we shall hear in the fourth commandment.u

Thus, at present, it must needs be the case that most of the clergyv preach false doctrine and abuse their spiritual authority, so that we have reason to do the work of this commandment. And we are being put to the test concerning what we will do or leave undone against such blasphemers for the sake of God's honor.

If only we were conscientious [about doing this], how often the official buffoons would impose their papal and episcopal excommunications in vain and how those Roman thunderbolts would be reduced to a whisper![61] How often would some people, to whom the world now has to listen, be forced to shut their mouths. How few preachers would be found in Christendom! But things have gotten to the point that whatever they claim must all be right. Now no one fights for God's name and honor, and I hold that there is no graver or more widespread sin in the public matters than this one.[62] For it is so difficult that, given the risk,

58. This paragraph reflects Luther's case with Rome. The papacy laid claim to be the successor to Peter and his see in Rome. See also 2 Thess. 2:4, which Luther took as a reference to anti-Christ.

59. This text played an important role in discussions of clerical authority throughout the Reformation. See, e.g., the *Augsburg Confession* XXVIII.21-28 (BC, 94-95).

60. Luther here is reflecting both common complaints about abuse of clerical power and his own particular struggle with the Roman hierarchy.

61. That is, papal decrees would have little effect. In October 1520, Luther would receive the official papal bull threatening excommunication, *Exsurge Domini*.

62. Namely, the sin of not opposing such misuse of God's name. Luther here is setting up a defense of his own outspoken criticisms of the papacy and its defenders.

t   Luke 10:16.

u   See below, pp. 337–41.

v   Here and elsewhere, literally, "the spiritual estate," the common designation of the entire clergy.

few understand how to attack when armed only with God's name and power. But the prophets in ages past and the apostles (St. Paul especially) were masters at it. It did not bother them whether the most or least important priest said or did something in God's name or his own. They focused on the words and actions and held them up against God's commandment regardless of who spoke or acted—a big fish or a small fry[w]—in the name of God or some human being. For that reason, the apostles and prophets had to die, and in our day there would be much more to say [against such people] because it is much worse now. But Christ and Saints Peter and Paul are forced to adorn all of this [teaching] with their holy names, with the result that no more ignominious name exists on earth than the holiest and exalted name of Jesus Christ.[63]

By itself, this abuse and blasphemy against God's holy name ought to scare people to death, and I fear that if it keeps up, we will start openly worshiping the devil as a god, given that the clerical authorities and scholars continue to handle these matters with such indescribable coarseness. It is high time that we earnestly ask God to make his name holy. But blood will be the price, and those who now sit among the holy martyrs' possessions, having gained it through the martyrs' blood, must themselves now make martyrs. More about that at another time.[64]

On the Third Commandment[65]

1. We have just seen how many good works are contained in the second commandment, but they are not good in and of themselves but only when they are done in faith and with confidence in divine benevolence.[x] And we see now how much we have to do when we observe only this commandment and how many others, who do not understand this

63. Luther is arguing that present false teaching uses Christ's and the apostles' names for legitimacy. The popes claimed to be successors to Peter and Paul, whose basilica in Rome was the object of the money raised by the Peter Indulgence.

64. Luther is intimating that the papacy has become demonic to the point of making new martyrs while living off the reputation of the church's early martyrs. See his *Address to the Christian Nobility* (p. 435f) and *The Babylonian Captivity of the Church* (LW 36:11–18), both written later in 1520.

65. The heading for this section specifies the commandment instead of the work or works of the commandment as in previous headings. The numbering of the subsections starts over as Luther moves through the commandments in order. See Exod. 20:8 and Deut. 5:12: "Remember the sabbath day and keep it holy."

---

w   Literally, "a big Hans or a small Nick."

x   A reference back to the first commandment.

commandment, unfortunately busy themselves with other works. Now comes the third commandment: "You shall keep the Sabbath holy." How our hearts should behave toward God in thoughts is commanded in the first commandment, and how the mouth should behave in words is commanded in the second. In the third commandment is commanded how we should behave toward God in our deeds. These commandments are written on the first tablet of the law of Moses that he held in his right hand and that govern human beings on the right side, that is, in those matters relating to God which concern God's dealings with humans and humans' with God apart from the mediation of any creature.[66]

The first work of this commandment, which we commonly called worship,[y] is unsophisticated and easily grasped: attending Mass, praying, and listening to the sermon on Sundays and holy days.[67] According to this definition, this commandment entails only a few works. If, however, they are not done with faith and trust in God's goodwill, they are nothing, as we said earlier. Consequently, it would really be good if there were fewer holy days, especially since in our day those activities—killing time, eating and drinking too much, playing games, and doing other evil deeds—are for the most part worse than what we do on workdays.[68] In addition, attending Mass and hearing a sermon have no positive effect on people, and the prayers are said without faith. It has almost come to the point where people think it is enough that we watch the Mass with our eyes, hear the sermon with our ears, and say the prayers with our lips. It is all external, so that we do not consider that we receive something from the Mass into our hearts; learn and retain something from the sermon; and seek, desire, and expect something from prayer. True, the bishops, priests, and those responsible for preaching[69] are even more at fault because they fail to preach the gospel or teach people how they ought to view the Mass, listen to the sermon, and say their prayers. For that reason, we will treat each of these works in more detail.

66. The Bible mentions two tablets but not a division into three and seven commandments that were inscribed on the tablets. The division apparently originated in rabbinic Judaism.

67. In later expositions of the Ten Commandments, Luther associates prayer exclusively with the second commandment. Here he highlights corporate prayer. Throughout this tract, Luther uses the word *Mass* to denote the regular Sunday worship with preaching, readings, prayers, and the Lord's Supper.

68. Before the Reformation, the major and minor festivals of the church year had become so numerous that attempts were made in certain regions to prune the calendar. See LW 53:14 (WA 12:37).

69. In Luther's day, bishop, priest, and preacher were three chief clerical offices in the church.

---

y The German word is *Gottesdienst*, literally, "the service of God." The second "work" of this commandment begins below, p. 321.

70. Luther will take up some of these themes later in the year in the *Babylonian Captivity of the Church* (LW 36:3–126, esp. 37–44).

71. Luther uses the term for an endowed Mass that was said yearly on the date of someone's death but to refer to Christ's institution at the last supper and therefore all celebrations of the Lord's Supper.

72. "Under" means "under the forms of bread and wine," based upon a Latin formulation used by the Fourth Lateran Council (1215) to denote that the body and blood of Christ were contained under the forms (*species*) of bread and wine. For Luther's explanation of the Supper as a testament and for his rejection of this philosophical explanation for Christ's presence in the Supper, called transubstantiation, see *The Babylonian Captivity* (LW 36:28–35).

2. At Mass, it is necessary that we be present with our heart as well; this happens when we practice faith in our hearts. We have to repeat the words that Christ spoke when he instituted the Mass: "'Take and eat; this is my body given for you.' In the same manner, he took the cup and said: 'Take and drink from it, all of you; that is a new, eternal covenant in my blood, which is poured out for you and for many for the forgiveness of sins. As often as you drink it, do it in remembrance of me.'"[70, z] With these words, Christ established for himself a memorial or anniversary Mass[71] to be celebrated for him daily throughout Christendom. And he attached to it a glorious, rich, and generous will and testament, which grants and establishes for us not annuities, money, or worldly possessions but the forgiveness of all our sins, grace, and mercy unto eternal life, so that everyone who comes to this memorial shall possess this testament. Christ has died so that the testament became durable and irrevocable. Instead of leaving us a sealed document, he has left us as a proper sign and "legal instrument" his own body and blood under the bread and wine.[72]

It is necessary for individuals[a] to practice the first work of this commandment properly in that they not doubt that it is a testament and a trustworthy one at that, so that they do not make Christ into a liar. If you do nothing at Mass but stand there without realizing or believing that through this testament Christ has promised and bestowed the forgiveness of all your sins, how is that different from saying: "I do not know or I do not believe that forgiveness of my sins is promised and bestowed here"? Countless Masses are now said throughout the world, but very few hear them with this kind of faith and practice! It provokes God's anger, and as a result, none can participate in the Mass fruitfully except for those[b] who are disconsolate, yearn for divine grace, and desire to be rid of their sins or even for those with an evil

z   A conflation of Matt. 26:26-28 and 1 Cor. 11:23-25, reflecting the text of the Latin Mass in Luther's day.

a   Singular in the original.

b   Singular in the original.

intention [to sin],[73] as long as they are transformed during the Mass and desire the benefits of this testament. For that reason, in former times [only] notorious, public sinners were not admitted to the Mass.[74]

When, however, this faith is in order, the heart draws joy from the testament, warms itself in God's love to the point of melting. Then, praise and thanksgiving follow with a sweetened heart.[75] For this reason, the Greek word for "mass" is *Eucharist*, or "thanksgiving." We should praise and thank God for such a consoling, rich, and sublime testament, just as a person would exult, be thankful, and rejoice for inheriting a thousand gulden or more from a friend.[c] All too often, however, Christ receives the same response as those who have made people rich through their wills. The heirs quickly forget them, and they never receive praise or thanks for what they did. The same happens now with our Masses: they are merely celebrated, but we do not know why or what purpose they serve. We do not thank, love, or praise but remain barren and hardened, and just continue saying our little prayers.[76] More about this at another time.[d]

3. The sermon should be nothing other than the proclamation of this testament. But who will hear it if no one proclaims it, and those who should be preaching it scarcely comprehend it themselves! The sermons wander around in completely useless fables with the result that Christ is forgotten. Our situation is similar to that of the man in 2 Kgs. 7[:19]: "We see our goods, but we cannot enjoy them." Eccles. [6:1-2] also refers to it: "It is a great misfortune when God gives people riches but does not allow them to be enjoyed." We see innumerable Masses but do not know whether they are testaments or something else entirely, as if they were run-of-the-mill good works in and of themselves. O God, how totally blinded we are! Wherever this testament is rightly preached, however, it is necessary that we listen attentively, comprehend and retain it, continually meditate on it, and

73. As in the *Explanations of the Ninety-Five Theses* (LW 31:106–7), Luther insists that the sacraments are precisely intended for true sinners. For this he was condemned in the papal bull of excommunication. See Luther's response in LW 32:12–19.

74. They were not allowed to receive Communion, and in early Christianity they were not permitted to attend Mass or were restricted to an area away from the assembly of worshipers.

75. Here and elsewhere Luther uses highly emotive language, often found in late medieval German mystical writings as well as in later Lutheran hymnody.

76. Luther is referring to the common late medieval practice of practicing private devotions during the Mass. The Mass bells would then ring to get people to focus on the Mass at the crucial moments of transubstantiation and elevation (when the unbloodied sacrifice of Christ was offered to the Father).

c   That is, millions of dollars.

d   Namely, in *The Babylonian Captivity of the Church* (LW 36:3–126), which was published later in 1520.

thereby strengthen faith against all attacks of sin—past, present, or future.

This is the only ceremony or practice that Christ instituted in which Christians are to assemble, practice, and hold in harmony. Unlike other ceremonies, Christ has not permitted this one to be a mere work but instead placed in it an abundant and overflowing treasure, which is offered to and possessed by all who believe in it.

The sermon should entice sinners to feel remorse for their sin and inflame the desire for this treasure. It follows that it must be a grave sin for those who do not listen to the gospel and spurn this treasure and the rich meal to which they are invited. A much graver sin, however, is committed by those who do not preach the gospel and thereby allow those who would gladly have heard it go to ruin, although Christ has steadfastly commanded them to preach the gospel and this testament. In fact, he did not want the Mass to be celebrated unless the gospel was also preached. Thus he says: "As often as you do it, do it in remembrance of me." That is, as St. Paul said [1 Cor. 11:24-26]: "You are to proclaim his death." For this reason, it is a frightening and horrifying task to be a bishop, pastor, or preacher today, for no one knows about this testament anymore, let alone that they are to preach it as their single highest duty and obligation. It will be difficult for them to account for so many souls who go to ruin because such preaching was lacking.

4. People should pray, but not in the customary way by turning pages in a prayer book or counting beads on the rosary.[77] Instead, we should bring particularly pressing needs [before God], earnestly seek aid, and place our faith and trust in God so intently that we have no doubt we will be heard. Saint Bernard told his [monastic] brothers this very thing: "Dear brethren, do not belittle your prayers as if they were said in vain; for in truth I tell you that before you utter the words they are already written down in heaven. And you should be quite certain that your prayer will be answered or, if not, that it was not in your best interest for it to be answered."[e]

77. Luther here calls into question traditional modes of praying. The rosary was a form of medieval devotion popularized by the Dominican Order. The "Hail Mary," the Lord's Prayer, the Gloria Patri, and other prayers were repeated in groups of ten that were tracked by fingering beads on a string or cord.

e   From a Lenten sermon, which Luther often cited, by Bernard of

Prayer is therefore a special exercise of faith, which consequently makes it so absolutely acceptable [to God], for either the prayer is answered directly or something better than what was requested is granted. As St. James says [1:6-8]: "Let whoever prays ask in faith, never doubting . . . for whoever doubts . . . does not expect to receive anything from God." That is a straightforward declaration that simultaneously promises and denies. All who do not believe receive nothing—neither what they asked for nor anything better.

In order to awaken such faith, Christ himself also said (in Mark 11[:24]): "I tell you, whatever you ask for, believe that you will receive it and it will certainly happen."[f] And in Luke 11[:9-13]: "Ask and it will be given you, search and you will find, knock and it will be opened for you. For whoever asks receives, whoever searches finds, and whoever knocks, for them it is opened. What father among you gives his son a stone when he asks for bread, or a snake when he asks for fish, or a scorpion when he asks for an egg? If you, then, who by nature are not good, know how to give good gifts to your children, how much more will your heavenly Father give a good spirit to all who ask."[g]

5. Who is so callous and hardhearted that such powerful words do not move such a person to pray joyously, gladly, and with complete trust? But think how many prayers would have to be rewritten if someone wanted to pray rightly according to these words! Every church and cloister is without question full of praying and singing. How, then, can it happen that they bring so little improvement or benefit and things keep getting worse? The reason can only be what St. James indicates [4:3]: "You pray much, but you receive nothing because you pray in the wrong way." For where this faith and trust are lacking in prayer, then it is dead and nothing

Clairvaux, a prominent Cistercian abbot, theologian, and churchman. See MPL 183:180. For the list of citations by Luther, see MLStA 2:45, n. 335.

f Following the Latin Vulgate.

g Luther follows the Vulgate, which read "good spirit." His translation of the New Testament from 1522 reads (with the Greek): "Holy Spirit."

but toil and effort; even if something is received, it is only useful in a temporal way, offering no benefits or help for souls but instead blinding them and causing them great harm. They go rattling on, without noticing whether or not they receive what they request or even desire or expect [an answer]; they remain obdurate in this unbelief, which is a deplorable habit that contradicts both the exercise of faith and the essence of prayer.

From this it follows that the individuals[h] who pray properly never doubt that their prayer is pleasing to God and heard, even if they do not receive exactly what they asked for. For in prayer one should lay all one's needs before God but never limit God to a certain amount, ways and means, place or purpose. Instead, if God wants to give something better or different from what we imagine, we should leave it to God's discretion, "for often we do not know what we ask," as St. Paul says in Rom. 8[:26], and, as he says in Eph. 3[:20], "God can do and give far more than we can grasp." Hence, as far as prayer goes, let there be no doubt that it is pleasing to God and is heard. But, still, let God choose the time and place, the amount and the purpose, let God make things turn out as they should. The ones who pray rightly "pray to God in spirit and truth."[i] For those who do not believe they will be heard sin against this commandment on the right side through their unbelief, wandering far from it. Those who place a limit on the answer to their prayer sin on the left side by wandering too close in testing God. Hence God has forbidden both things so that no one deviates from the commandment in either direction—either with unbelief or with testing God—but with pure faith stays on the right road, trusting God without any restrictions.

6. Thus, we see that this commandment, like the second, is nothing other than a matter of practicing and reflecting on the first commandment, which consists of faith, trust,

---

h   Singular in the original.
i   John 4:24. Luther here uses the terms *Anbeter* and *anbeten*, derived from the word "to pray" (*beten*), which could also be translated "adorer" and "adore."

confidence, hope, and love of God. And we see that the first commandment is the captain and that faith is the chief work and life of all other works, which cannot be good without it, as I said.

Now you may ask, "What if I cannot believe that my prayer will be heard and is pleasing to God?" Answer: this is why faith, prayer, and other good works are commanded, so that you might see what you can and cannot do. Then, when you find that you are unable to believe and act in this manner, you may humbly lament this before God and with a small spark of faith you may begin to strengthen it more and more each day by applying it through all of life in every action. For there is no one on earth who has not been afflicted with a weakness of faith (itself the first and highest commandment). In the gospels even the holy apostles—Peter most of all—were weak in faith so that they even begged Christ [Luke 17:5], "Lord, increase our faith!" And he frequently scolded them for having such little faith.

Do not, therefore, despair and throw up your hands if you discover that in prayer or other works you do not believe as strongly as you should and would like to believe. Instead, you should give thanks to God from the bottom of your heart that he has revealed your weakness to you and thereby teaches and admonishes you how necessary it is for you to practice your faith and strengthen it daily. Look at how many people go on praying, singing, reading [Masses], working, and appearing to be great saints, without ever coming to the realization about how it is going for them with faith, the chief work. In this way they blind themselves and lead others astray, imagining that everything is as it should be. Thus, they calmly build upon the sand of their own works[j] without any faith and not upon God's grace and promise with a sound and pure faith.

For this reason, as long as we live, however long that might be, we have our hands full with remaining pupils of the first commandment and of faith with all its works and troubles, never ceasing to learn. No one knows what it

---

j   See Matt. 7:26.

78. The "spiritual walks of life" included all clergy, monks, and nuns. The term *Fathers* was used for prominent Christians in the early church, especially some so-called Desert Fathers, that is, monks in Egypt, some of whom practiced continuous prayer.

means to trust God alone except the person who makes a beginning and tries to put it into practice.

7. Consider this. If no other good work were provided, would not prayer alone be enough to exercise faith for the entire span of human life? For this very reason, those in spiritual walks of life were pledged to this work. For example, in former times some Fathers prayed day and night.[78] Of course, no Christian has time to "pray without ceasing,"[k] but I am talking about spiritual prayer. That is, no one is so occupied by work that they cannot, if they wish, talk with God while working and place before him their own needs and the needs of others, beg and plead for help, and in so doing exercise and fortify their faith.

The Lord meant just that in Luke 18[:1], when he said to pray continuously without letting up, but at the same time in Matt. 6[:5-7] he forbade using many words and long prayers. In so doing he was chastising the hypocrites, not that he says that praying aloud for a long time is evil but that it is not the kind of true prayer that can happen at all times and that it is nothing without the inner prayer of faith. For we also have to practice outward prayer when appropriate, especially at Mass (as is also required by this commandment) and wherever it promotes inward prayer and faith—whether at home, in the fields, or during any kind of labor whatsoever. There is no time to say more about this here. It belongs to the exposition of the Lord's Prayer, in which all petitions and oral prayers are succinctly summarized.[l]

8. Where are the people who want to learn about and perform good works? Let them take up praying alone and practice it properly; then they will find that what the holy Fathers said is true: nothing is quite the work that prayer is.[m]

k   See 1 Thess. 5:17.

l   Luther is probably thinking of his 1519 *An Exposition of the Lord's Prayer for Simple Laypeople* (LW 42:15–81; WA 2:74–130). For another interpretation from 1519 (but also published in 1522), see his *Personal Prayer Book* (LW 43:3–35; WA 10/2:339–406). Later expositions include the LC, "The Lord's Prayer" (BC, 440–56; from 1529), and *A Simple Way to Pray* (LW 43:189–211; from 1535).

m   Luther is citing the *Vitae Patrum* (*Lives of the [Desert] Fathers*) V.12.1, a saying of Agathon (MPL 73:941).

Murmuring orally is easy or thought to be easy, but to accompany the words with authentic devotion and heartfelt earnestness, that is, with yearning and faith so that the heart truly desires what the words say and does not doubt they will be heard—that is a remarkable deed in God's eyes.

The evil spirit, however, opposes prayer with all its might. O how often it takes away the desire to pray by allowing no time and place for it or awakens so much doubt about whether a person is worthy to ask something of a majestic figure like God. It sows confusion until people themselves do not know whether it is important to pray or not, whether or not their prayers are pleasing to God, and many other fanciful thoughts. For the evil spirit fully appreciates how mighty each person's faith-filled prayers are, how much damage they inflict on that very spirit, and how useful they are for everyone. Consequently, it tries at all costs to stifle such prayer. Thus, people[n] must be truly wise and firmly hold that they and their prayers are not worthy before such an immense Majesty, in no way relying on their own worthiness nor letting their unworthiness prevent them from praying. But instead, they must look to God's commandment, hold it up to the devil, and declare: "Nothing is instigated because of my worthiness and nothing is prevented because of my unworthiness. I pray and act only because God, solely out of divine goodness, has promised to grant a hearing and grace to every unworthy person—and not only promised but also strictly, at the risk of earning his eternal anger and wrath, commanded me to pray, to trust, and to receive. Since it was not too much for the high Majesty to obligate in such a invaluable way his small unworthy worms to pray, to believe and to receive from him, would it be too much for me to accept this commandment joyfully, no matter how worthy or unworthy I might be?" This is how one must cast out the devil's insinuations—with God's command. Only then will he cease—otherwise never.

9. What hardships and other matters must a person present and lament before the almighty God in prayer in order

---

n   Singular in the original.

to exercise faith? Answer: first, one's own pressing hardships and afflictions. David says in Ps. 32[:7]: "You are my refuge amid the anguish that surrounds me and my assurance that I will be saved from all the evil round about." And in Ps. 142[:1-2]: "With my voice I appeal to God and with my mouth I implore the Lord. I will spread out my prayer before his countenance and pour out before him everything that oppresses me." Therefore, in the Mass a Christian should take up what seems lacking or is too much to bear and pour it out openly before God with tears and groans, as pitiably as possible, just as to a faithful father who is ready to help. If you are not aware of what you need or experience no attacks, then you should realize you could not be worse off. For the greatest attack occurs when you are so obdurate, hard-hearted, and insensitive as to be oblivious to any attacks.[o]

There is no better mirror for seeing what you need than the Decalogue, in which you discover what you lack and what you should seek. If, then, you find yourself with a weak faith, little hope, and scant love of God, or, alternatively if you find that you do not honor and praise God but, desiring your own honor and reputation instead, you prefer above everything else the approval of others, or, again, if you would rather not attend Mass or listen to the sermon or are too lazy to pray—in these matters no one is without failings—you should take these shortcomings more seriously than damage to your property, your body, or your honor. They are worse than any fatal disease, worse even than death itself. Next, you should earnestly lay these things before God, cry out to him, ask for help, and with complete confidence expect that you have been heard and that you will receive both help and mercy. Then go on to the second table of the commandments and discover how disobedient you have been, and still are, toward parents and others in authority; with how much anger and hatred you have verbally abused your neighbors;

o   See sec. 25 above, under "The Second Good Work": "The most pernicious kind comes when there is no attack at all and everything is running smoothly." See also WA 50:272, where Luther refers to a sermon on the Song of Songs by Bernard of Clairvaux, XXXIII.16 (MPL 183:959).

and how you have attacked your neighbor with unchastity, avarice, and injustice in word and deed. Then you will see without a doubt that you are full of needs and misery and have reason enough to cry tears of blood, if you could.

10. I know full well that many people are so foolish that they will not ask for such things unless they see themselves as pure beforehand, thinking that God hears no one who remains in sin. All false preachers do this by not being devoted to faith and trust in God but emphasizing instead teachings about one's own works.

Consider this, you poor soul: if you have broken a leg or fallen into mortal danger, then you call on God, invoke this or that saint, and keep at it until your leg is healed and the danger is past. Now, you are not so foolish as to think that God listens to no one who has broken a leg or is in mortal danger. Indeed, you assume that God must listen to you even more if you are in severe distress and anguish. So, why, then, are you so foolish in the face of incomparably greater need and eternal harm? And so do you refuse to ask all the more for faith, hope, love, humility, obedience, chastity, gentleness, peace, and righteousness, as if you had no unbelief, doubt, arrogance, disobedience, anger, avarice, or unrighteousness whatsoever? Instead, the more you find yourselves lacking in all these things the more fervently and diligently you should pray and cry out for them.

We are so blind that we run to God with physical ailments and needs, but for illnesses of the soul we run away from God and are determined not to return until we are cured—as if there were two gods, one to help the body and one to aid the soul, or as if we ourselves could take care of spiritual needs, although they are greater than the physical. This is really a devilish bit of advice and counsel.

No, my dear! If you want to be cured of your sin, you must not pull back from God but run to him with more confidence than ever, entreating him as if you had suddenly been struck with some physical malady. God is not the enemy of sinners except for unbelievers, that is, for those who do not acknowledge and rue their sins or ask God for help. Instead, they want to cleanse themselves in advance by their presumption, to admit no need of divine grace, and do not allow God to be God, who gives to everyone and takes nothing in return.

11. The preceding pertains to prayer for personal needs in general.*p* The kind of prayer, however, that actually belongs to this commandment and is designated a work of the Sabbath is much better and more significant and should be offered for the assembly of all Christians, for the needs of all people, enemies and friends, and especially for those who reside in one's own parish or diocese. Saint Paul wrote to his disciple Timothy [1 Tim. 2:1-3]: "I charge you to make sure that prayer and supplication is made for everyone, for kings and all rulers, so that we can lead a quiet and peaceable life in the service of God and with integrity. For that is good and pleasing to God our Savior." Likewise, Jeremiah (in chapter 29[:7]) ordered the people of Israel to pray for the city and the land of Babylon, because "the peace of the city is your peace." Bar. 1[:11-12] states: "Pray for the life of the king of Babylon and for the life of his son, so that we may live in peace under their rule."*q*

This common prayer is precious and most powerful. It is the reason we gather. On this basis, moreover, the church is called a house of prayer,*r* so that we likewise, as one, should gather up our needs and the needs of all people and bring them before God, appealing for grace. It must be done, however, with deep feeling and earnestness, so that the needs of all penetrate our hearts and, while actually suffering with them, we pray for them in faith and trust. If that kind of prayer is not offered during the Mass, it is better to have no Mass at all. For how does this square with coming together bodily in a house of prayer—given that the act of gathering itself shows we ought to pray in common for the whole community—if we scatter the prayers and divide them up so that each person prays only for personal needs and no one bothers with or cares for the needs of anybody else? How

---

p   Sections 9-10.

q   The book of Baruch in the Apocrypha is written as a letter from Baruch, Jeremiah's secretary, to the people and priests of Jerusalem.

r   See Luke 19:46.

then is it possible for prayer to be beneficial, good, pleasing, and "in common," or a work of "the Sabbath" or "of the assembly,"[79] if people say only their private little prayers—one for this, another for that—and have nothing but self-serving and self-seeking prayers to which God is averse?

12. An expression of common prayer has remained in use for a long time—when, after the sermon, one recites the confession of sin and prays for all of Christendom from the pulpit. But that should not suffice as is now the custom and practice. Instead, it should become an admonition to offer prayer throughout the Mass for these needs, to which the preacher urges us and, so that we may pray in a worthy manner, reminds us of our sin and humbles us. But this should be done as briefly as possible so that the people together as one community may lament their sin before God and pray for everyone with sincerity and faith.

Would God that every group would attend Mass and pray in this way so that together the earnest, heartfelt cry of all the people would ascend to God. Think what immeasurable value and support would result from such prayer! What could confront all evil spirits more menacingly? How could there be here on earth any greater work that would sustain so many upright people and convert so many sinners?

In truth, the Christian church on earth possesses no greater force or work than such common prayer to counter everything that harasses it. The evil spirit knows this quite well and does everything it can to hinder this prayer. It lets us build pretty churches, create numerous endowments, play instruments, read and sing, celebrate many Masses, and promote unlimited pomp. It has no regrets about this but even encourages us to imagine such things are the finest and to think that with them we have done everything just right. When prayer that is communal, strong, and effective dies out, such hypocrisy smothers it. Where prayer is covered over, no one can diminish that spirit or defeat it. But when it sees that we do want to engage in this prayer, whether it happens in a thatched cottage or a pigsty, the evil spirit cannot ignore it but has more fear of that sty than of any tall, beautiful churches whatsoever, with their steeples and bells,

79. The "common prayers" labeled the general prayers of the assembled congregation. Luther is asking how they can be called common, shared prayers when no one shares them.

in which such prayer is not present. The places and buildings in which we assemble do not matter, but rather only this invincible prayer that we truly offer in common and lift up to God.

13. We observe the effectiveness of this prayer in Abraham, when he prayed long ago for the five cities, Sodom, Gomorrah, and so on, and eventually convinced God not to destroy them if ten godly persons—two in each city—could be found.[s] Think what could happen if many people in a congregation appealed to God with sincere and heartfelt trust! James writes: "Beloved, pray for one another that you may be saved. For the prayer of godly persons can do very much if it is constant and does not let up"[t] (that is, does not cease asking God—as many irresolute people do—even if they do not immediately receive that for which they are praying). James uses Elijah as an example [James 5:17-18]: "He was a human being like us and prayed that it might not rain, and for three years and six months it did not rain. Then he prayed again and it rained, and everything bore fruit." Many utterances and examples in Scripture encourage us to pray, but always in earnest and with faith, as David says: "God's eyes look upon the devout, and his ears listen to their prayers."[u] Likewise [Ps. 145:18]: "God is near to all those who call upon him, to all who call upon him in truth." Why does the psalmist add "in truth"? Because it is not praying or calling upon God when only the mouth mumbles.

What is God supposed to do when you come to church with your mouth, a prayer book, and a rosary and set your mind on nothing other than getting through the words the prescribed number of times?[80] If someone asks you, however, what the point was or what you intended to pray for, you will have no idea because it has not occurred to you to place this or that concern before God or to ask for anything. Your only reason for praying is because so many prayers have been prescribed for you, which you now want to perform and get

A man with a sword holds a rosary.
Published in Luther's
Sermon on Saint Michael, 1522.

80. At private confession, the priest would often assign the penitent a certain number of prayers like the Our Father and the Ave Maria to be said as penance. The rosary helped a person keep track of the number of times these prayers were recited.

---

s Gen. 18:22-33.

t James 5:16 from the Latin Vulgate.

u Combining Ps. 33:18 with 39:12 in the Vulgate.

through. Is it any wonder, then, that thunder and lightning so often set church buildings on fire, since we turn houses of prayer into houses of ridicule by calling this prayer, when we ask for nothing and bring no concerns to God? When we pray, we should behave like those who bring petitions to powerful princes. Such petitioners do not intend to run on at the mouth; otherwise, the prince would think they were crazy or making fun of him. On the contrary, they plan out precisely what they are going to say and present their request with great care while at the same time committing it to his gracious favor, confident that the petition will be heard. Likewise, we must talk with God about specific matters, identify some pressing needs by name, entrust it to his grace and goodwill and not doubt that it will be heard. God has promised to hear such prayers, and that is more than any earthly lord has promised.

14. We are masters of this way of praying: when we suffer from illness or other bodily afflictions, then we invoke St. Christopher[81] and St. Barbara,[82] or we vow to make a pilgrimage to St. James or to go here and there.[v] In such cases, we discover earnest imploring and absolute confidence, that is, everything that belongs to proper prayer. But when we attend Mass in church, we stand there like statues[w] and can think of nothing to ask or nothing to lament. The rosary beads clack, the prayer book rustles, and the mouth babbles, but nothing more than that.

81. A completely legendary figure who was included among the fourteen auxiliary saints, or "holy helpers," Christopher first became popular when the bubonic plague swept Germany in the fourteenth century. He was allegedly a martyr during the third century. As "Christ-bearer" (the meaning of his Greek name), legend had it that this giant could not carry the Christ child across a stream he controlled. Still known today as the patron of travelers, in the Middle Ages he was also invoked against epilepsy and plague.

82. Also one of the "holy helpers," Barbara, whose name first appeared in the seventh century, supposedly

The martyrdom
of St. Barbara.

v See p. 272 above.

w German: *Ölgötzen* (oil gods), people who stand there rigid without saying anything; derived from oil paintings of saints and perhaps connected to Peter sleeping on the Mount of Olives (Matt. 26:30, 40-46).

suffered martyrdom in the third or fourth century after being handed over to Roman authorities by her pagan father; her aid was sought against perils of storms and fire. Legend had it that people who prayed at her grave were healed of their diseases.

St. Christopher carrying Christ across a stream.

If you ask what you should request and lament in prayer, the Ten Commandments and the Lord's Prayer will easily teach you. Open your eyes wide and look hard at your life and all the lives in the whole Christian church,[x] especially those in the spiritual walk of life,[y] and you will find that faith, hope, love, obedience, chastity, and other virtues are trampled underfoot and that all kinds of horrible vices prevail. You will also see that good preachers and religious leaders are scarce and that knaves, children, fools, and women are in control so that, given this terrible anger of God, it is imperative all over the world to pray nonstop with nothing but tears of blood. It is all too true that never before has it been so necessary to pray as from now until the world ends. If these awful afflictions do not move you to wailing and lamenting, do not let your spiritual walk of life, your [monastic] orders, your good works, or your prayers deceive you. There is not a Christian muscle or quality in you, however pious you may be. This was all prophesied: that at the very time God's anger is hottest and the distress of Christendom at its worst, no one can be found who will cry out to God and make intercession. Thus Isaiah laments in chapter 64[:5, 7]: "You are angry with us, but there is no one to stand up and hold you back." Likewise, Ezek. 22[:30-31] states: "And I sought for anyone among them who would repair the wall and stand in the breach before me; but I found no one. Therefore I have poured out my anger upon them and devoured them in the blaze of my wrath." With these words, God shows how he wants us to stand before him and protect one another from his wrath, just as is often written about the prophet Moses that he restrained God from pouring out his anger upon the people of Israel.[z]

15. What will become of those who not only ignore the harm done to the whole Christian church and say no prayers

---

x   Here and in pars. 15–16, the German is *Christenheit*, literally, "Christianity" or "Christendom." It is Luther's term for the entirety of the Christian church.

y   See p. 310, n. 78.

z   Exod. 32:11-14; Num. 14:13-19; 21:7-9; Ps. 106:23.

for it but instead even laugh and take delight in passing judgment on their neighbors' sins and gossiping about them in the worst way? And yet, without fear or shame, they attend church, hear the Mass, say prayers, and see themselves and want to be seen as godly Christians. They need to be prayed for twice over, while we need pray only once for those whom they judge, slander, and ridicule. That such people would exist was presaged by the crucified thief on Christ's left hand, who blasphemed Christ in his suffering, pain, and misery, and by all those who likewise reviled Christ on the cross when they should have been helping him.*

My God, how blind, how mad we Christians have become! When, heavenly Father, will this anger cease? That we make fun of, curse, and judge the sorry state of Christendom, which we gather in the church and at Mass to pray for, comes from our stupid minds. When the Turks devastate towns and the countryside with their inhabitants and destroy churches,[83] we think immediately that huge damage has been done to Christendom. We complain and force kings and the princes into battle. When, however, faith disappears, love becomes cold, God's word is neglected, and all kinds of sins gain the upper hand, no one steps forth to fight them. Even though pope, bishops, and priests ought to join the spiritual battle as generals,*b* captains, and commanders against this far worse spiritual "Turk." They are themselves this "Turk" and the princes and leaders of the devil's army, just as Judas was for the Jews when they arrested Christ.*c* To initiate the process of putting Jesus to death, it took one of the best: an apostle, bishop, and priest. In the same manner, Christendom must be brought to ruin by those who should be guarding it. They remain so deluded, however, that they want to devour the Turk while they set their own houses and sheepfolds on fire and let them burn along with the sheep and everything in them. Nonetheless, they are still worried

83. The Muslim Ottoman Empire and its troops, called by Luther the "Turks," threatened central Europe in the 1520s and 1540s. Belgrade and much of Hungary fell to the invading armies in 1521.

---

a Luke 23:35-39.

b German: *Herzogen*, usually translated "dukes," but here taken literally, "those who lead an army."

c Matt. 26:47-50.

about the wolf in the bush. This is our sentence; this is our reward for the ingratitude we have shown for the endless grace that Christ has freely acquired for us with his precious blood, his arduous labor, and his bitter death.

16. Now where are the idlers who do not know how to do good works? Where are those who run to Rome and St. James [of Compostela], to this place or another? Take only the work connected with the Mass as your own. Look at the sins and failures of your neighbors, have pity on them, let yourself be moved to cry out to God and pray for them. Do the same for all the hardships we suffer throughout Christendom, particularly for its rulers whom God allows to be seduced and fall so woefully—to the unbearable punishment and plague of us all. If you do that consistently, be assured that you are one of the best soldiers and commanders not only against the Turks but also against the devil and the powers of hell. And if you do not do this, how would it help you even if you performed every miracle of all the saints, or strangled all the Turks and yet were found guilty of not having heeded the needs of your neighbor and therefore having sinned against love? On the last day, Christ will not ask how often you prayed for yourself, fasted, made a pilgrimage, and did this or that, but how often you did something good for others, especially for the least of all.[d] Among the least are also those who live in sins, spiritual poverty, captivity, and need who are far more numerous than those who suffer from physical maladies. Watch out, therefore, because our self-chosen good works lead us back into ourselves, so that we seek only our own benefit and blessedness. But God's commandments force us to our neighbors, so that we only benefit them and their blessedness. Just as Christ on the cross prayed not for himself alone but rather for us when he said [Luke 23:34]: "Father, forgive them, for they know not what they are doing," so we must also pray for one another. Everyone is able to see from this how perverted and reprehensible people are who slander, despise, and brazenly judge others; they do nothing but revile those for whom they should be

d Matt. 25:31-46.

praying. No one is more deeply immersed in these vices than those who for the sake of their beautiful, sparkling selves do many and various good works of their own merely in order to outshine others and gain their approval.

17. The spiritual meaning of this commandment[84] contains an even greater work that encompasses human nature in its entirety. Here one has to realize that in Hebrew *sabbath* means "cease working"[e] or "rest," because (Gen. 2[:2]) "on the seventh day God rested from all the works that he had done." For this reason, God also commanded us to rest on the seventh day and refrain from the works that we have been doing the other six days. For us, this very Sabbath has been transformed into Sunday, and the other days are called workdays, but Sunday is called a day of rest or a feast day or a holy day. Would God that there were in Christendom no feast days except Sunday and that the feast days of Our Lady[85] and of the saints were all moved to Sundays. As a consequence, by laboring on workdays, many more vices would be avoided, and the land would not be so poor and devastated.

This rest or cessation of works is twofold: bodily and spiritual; hence, the commandment must be understood in two ways. Physical refraining from work and resting were addressed earlier: we stop the work of our hands and our labor in order to assemble in church, be present at Mass, listen to God's word, and pray communally and with one accord. To be sure, this rest is physical and not commanded by God for the Christian church, as the apostle says in Col. 2[:16-17]: "Let no one obligate you . . . to observe any feast day . . . for these were only prefiguring of what is to come." Now, however, truth has been fulfilled so that every day is a feast day of rest, as Isa. 66[:23] says: "One feast day will follow the next," and every day will be free from work.[f] Nonetheless, such a rest day is necessary and has been set up by the whole Christian church for the sake of those not under a

84. Luther uses spiritual or "allegorical" interpretations of Scripture throughout his career, borrowing insights from the ancient and medieval traditions and using them to emphasize faith's dependence on God's word. This is his second main point regarding this commandment. See above, p. 303.

85. Mary, the mother of Jesus. When feasts of Mary and the saints fell on weekdays, work was stopped in favor of special Masses and processions.

---

e German: *feyr.* This word means both rest and, in a transferred meaning, "festival" or "feast."

f German: *werckel tag,* a day of little or no work or chores.

86. Literally, "the imperfect ones." Medieval theologians distinguished between believers in a state of grace and those under a vow who were said to be in a state of perfection, not that they were themselves perfect but rather that they were in a place where their good works were more valuable for reaching the goal of perfection before God.

87. The so-called Divine Office, or times of prayer at intervals throughout the day, was observed in cloisters and chapters of clergy as Matins, Lauds, Terce, Sext, None, Vespers, and Compline. The Divine Office provided for the entire Psalter to be recited each week.

vow[86] and working folk so that they have time to come and hear the word of God. For, as we see, priests and monks say the Mass every day, pray the hours,[87] and exercise themselves in the word of God by studying, reading, and hearing it read. For that reason, they are, over and above others, exempted from work, supported by regular incomes, have a day of rest every day and perform the works of Sabbath every day. They have no days for small chores, and one day is like another. If all of us were perfect and well versed in the gospel, then we could work every day if we wished or have a day of rest whenever we could. For now such rest is not necessary or commanded except to learn God's word and to pray.

Spiritual rest, for which above all else God intended this commandment, entails not only laying down our work and labor but—much more—letting God alone work in us without applying any power of our own at all. How does that take place? As follows: Humankind, damaged by sin, has an inordinate love and predilection for all things sinful. As Scripture says in Gen. 8[:21], "The human heart and mind always aspire to evil," that is, to arrogance, disobedience, anger, hate, avarice, unchastity, and so on. To sum it up: in all that individuals do or leave undone they seek their own will, advantage, and honor more than that of God or the neighbor. All their works, words, and thoughts, even their entire lives, are evil and not godly.

If God is to work and live in them, all these vices and corruption must be strangled and stamped out so that a rest and ceasing of all our works, words, thoughts, and lives may take place—so that from now on, as Paul says in Gal. 2[:20], "not we, but Christ lives in us," acts and speaks. This does not happen in the midst of sweet and pleasant days; instead, here one must inflict pain on human nature and suffer such pain. Now comes the conflict between spirit and flesh,[g] with the spirit resisting anger, lust, and pride while the flesh prefers lasciviousness, honor, and security. Thus, Paul says in Gal. 5[:24]: "Those who belong to our Lord Christ have crucified their flesh with its vices and desires." Here is the source

g　See Gal. 5:16-17.

of good works like fasting, keeping vigils, and performing strenuous labors,[88] about which some people talk and write a great deal, although they are unaware of their origin and purpose. Hence we will say a few things about them.

18. This kind of rest, in which our working ceases and God alone works in us, happens in two ways: first, through our own practice and, second, through the external practice and pressure from others.[h] Our own practice should be done and ordered as follows. First, we observe where our flesh, senses, will, and thoughts are inciting us and then resist them and not follow them, as the wise man says in Sir. [18:30]: "Do not follow your base desires." Likewise, Deut. 12[:8]: "Do not do . . . what appears right to you."[i]

Every day a person must use the prayers said by David [Ps. 119:35, 37]: "Lord, guide me onto your path . . . and prevent me from going my own way," and many similar utterances, all of which can be summarized in one petition: "Your kingdom come to us."[j] So many base desires exist in such great variety and the leading of the evil one is so clever, polished, and appealing that individuals[k] are unable to control themselves and stay on the straight and narrow. They must let go and entrust themselves to God's rule, relying in no way on their reason. As Jeremiah says [10:23]: "I know, O LORD, that the way of human beings is not in their control." This was manifested when the children of Israel departed from Egypt through a wilderness where there was no road, no food, no drink, and no aid. Therefore, "God went ahead of them by day in a pillar of cloud and by night in a pillar of fire," fed them from heaven with heavenly bread, and prevented their clothes and their shoes from wearing out, as we read in the books of Moses.[l] Thus we pray, "'Your kingdom come,' so that you, God, rule over us and not we ourselves." Nothing is more dangerous than our own reason and will. This is the

88. "Vigils" involved staying awake in prayer and meditation, especially on the eve of a festival. "Labors" were associated with monastic practice of "prayer and labor" (*ora et labora*) and were also understood as penitential.

h   For this second kind of rest, see below, par. 22.
i   Rendered in line with the Vulgate.
j   From the Lord's Prayer (Matt. 6:10; Luke 11:2).
k   Singular in the original.
l   See Exod. 13:21; 16:4; and Deut. 29:5.

first and best work of God in us and the best practice for letting go of our works: to shut down our reason and will, to rest and entrust oneself to God in all things, especially when these works appear to be spiritual and good.

19. Discipline of the flesh follows from this: practices for slaying its coarse, evil desires and creating rest and repose. We must put the flesh to death and quiet it with fasting, vigils, or labors; and for that reason, we are teaching why and to what extent we should fast, perform vigils, or labor.

Unfortunately, there are many blind people who practice chastising themselves, whether through fasting, vigils, or labor, only because they imagine that these things are good works through which they may merit a great deal. They dive in and at times so overtax themselves that they wreck their bodies and drive themselves mad. Those people are even blinder who rate their fasting not according to how little they eat or how long they refrain from eating but by the kind of food from which they abstain. Fasting is worth more, they believe, if they eat no meat, butter, or eggs. Above these are those who try to fast like the saints and choose certain days like Wednesday, or Saturday, or the feast days of St. Barbara and St. Sebastian, and the like.[89] In such fasting, all of these folk seek only the work itself and, when they have accomplished this, assume they have done well. I will not mention those who fast and yet get completely drunk or those who "fast" by eating so much fish and other foods that they approximate genuine fasting and preserve its benefits as much as if consuming meat, butter, and eggs instead. That kind of "fasting" is not fasting at all but rather a mockery of fasting and of God.

Therefore, I would permit individuals to select for themselves certain days, specific foods, or the extent of their fasts as they wish, as long as they do not restrict it to the activity but take into consideration their own "flesh." They should correlate the extent of their fasting, vigils, and other labors with the degree to which their flesh is lustful and arrogant and no more, in spite of what the pope, the church, a bishop, a father confessor, or whoever may have commanded. For the extent of fasting, vigils or labors should not be measured

89. The Feast of St. Barbara (December 4) was often designated as a special fast day during Advent, and the Feast of St. Sebastian (January 20), who according to legend was martyred by being tied to a tree and shot with arrows, was celebrated as the day when the sap returned to the trees and, hence, a day for eating fruit.

by the specific foods, days, or amount but by the increase or decrease of carnal lust and arrogance. Damping down and slaying those vices is the only reason that fasting, vigils, and labors were instituted. If those vices did not exist, then eating would be as good as fasting, sleeping as good as vigils, and leisure as good as labors. One would be as good as another—without distinction.

20. Suppose someone discovers that fish causes more arrogance in the flesh than eggs or meat, then that person should eat meat instead of fish. Or again, if fasting drives someone mad or ruins the stomach or body, or is unnecessary for slaying the flesh's arrogance, then that person should omit it entirely and eat, sleep, and relax as much as it takes to stay healthy, even if it contradicts the precepts of the church and the rules of religious orders and societies.[90] For no precept of the church and no rule of a religious order can set a higher standard for fasting, vigils, or labor or demand more observance than it takes to tame or slay the flesh and its desires. Where this goal is exceeded and fasting, eating, sleeping, and keeping vigils either demand more than the flesh can bear or than is necessary to slay lust or ruin the body and crush the mind, no one would think that a person has done a good work or can appeal to the church's precepts or other regulations as an excuse.[91] People will think such persons[m] are guilty of self-neglect or have as much as become their own murderers. The human body was not created for killing its life and natural functions but only for slaying its arrogance. Even were that arrogance so strong and mighty that it could not be adequately resisted without ruining and damaging bodily life, still, as I said, in fasting, keeping vigils, and laboring, attention should not be fixed on the activities themselves—neither the days, nor the amount, nor the kind of food—but on the arrogant and lustful Adam[92] in order to ward off its cravings.

21. On this basis we can evaluate how wisely or foolishly some women act when they are pregnant and how a person should behave toward sick people. Women who foolishly

90. In addition to orders of monks and friars, in the late Middle Ages guilds and other groups of laypeople formed themselves into religious confraternities with a variety of religious duties.

91. Limiting fasting for health reasons was a standard part of medieval pastoral advice.

92. That is, the Old Creature, mired in sin and self-worship.

m   Singular in the original.

insist on fasting would rather risk great danger to themselves and their fetuses than to forgo fasting with other people. They make something a matter of conscience where there is none, and where they should follow their conscience they do not.[n] It is all the fault of the preachers who carry on about fasting without clarifying its correct use, extent, fruits, cause, or goal. For the same reason, people who are sick should be allowed to eat and drink every day as much as they wish. In short: once the arrogance of the flesh has come to an end, every reason for fasting vigils, labor, eating only this or that has already ended, too, and no binding commandment exists any longer.

At the same time, a person should not let a careless laziness about slaying the flesh's arrogance emerge from this freedom. The wily [old] Adam has many tricks by which to find a way to pretend that the head or body is being ruined. So some people seize on this and say that it is neither necessary nor obligatory to fast or chastise themselves and that they can eat any food they want—as if they had been diligently practiced fasting for a long time when in fact they have never tried it.

We should be no less cautious, however, about giving offense to those who are inadequately informed and consider it a grave sin if someone else does not fast or eat the same way they do. In this case, one should patiently instruct them and not simply despise them openly or spite them by consuming this or that food, but instead show them the cause for doing this and lead them with forbearance to the same insight. If, however, they are too stubborn and refuse to listen, let them go their own way while we do what we know is right.[o]

22. The second practice[p] arises when others attack us, namely, when we are harmed by other people or by devils that take our property and our honor, make our bodies ill, and in every possible way drive us to anger, impatience, and

---

n   That is, they strictly kept fasting, instead of caring for the safety of themselves or their child.

o   Luther will express this same concern for the weak in his so-called Invocavit Sermons of March 1522 (LW 51:71-73).

p   For the first practice, see par. 18 above.

unrest. For God's work reigns in us according to God's wisdom, not our reason, and according to God's purity and virtue, not the arrogance of our flesh. For God's work is wisdom and purity; our work is foolishness and impurity—and they should cease. Thus, God's work should reign in us according to God's peace and not our anger, impatience, and turmoil. Peace is also God's work; impatience is the work of our flesh that should cease and die, so that we may keep in every respect a spiritual Sabbath, stopping our own activity and letting God work in us.

In order to put to death our works and the [old] Adam, God hangs around our necks many unpleasant burdens that make us angry, much suffering that tries our patience, and finally death and the world's contempt. By doing these things, God is simply trying to expunge our anger, impatience, and turmoil and replace them with his work, that is, with his peace. As Isaiah says in chapter 28: "God undertakes a strange work" in order to arrive at his proper work.[93]q What does this mean? He means that God sends us suffering and turmoil in order to teach us patience and peace. God permits us to die in order to make us alive until each person is so peaceful and quiet that it does not matter whether things go well or poorly, whether one lives or dies, is honored or dishonored. At that point, God alone dwells there and human works are no more. This is what it means to keep the Sabbath rest and make it holy in the right way. Here there is no human control, delight, or sorrow at all. Instead, God alone leads each human being, and nothing is present but divine delight, joy, and peace along with all the other works and virtues.

23. God esteems these works so highly that he commands us not only to observe the Sabbath but also to make or "keep it holy."[94] In this way, God indicates that nothing is more precious than suffering, dying, and misfortune; for they are sacred and make individuals holy by leading them away from

93. This notion of God's alien and proper work, related to the distinction between law and gospel, is also tied to Isaiah 28 by Philip Melanchthon (1497–1560) in the *Apology of the Augsburg Confession*, XII.51–54 (BC, 195). See also the *Heidelberg Disputation*, above, p. 90.

94. Luther now turns to explaining the second half of the commandment, "and keep it holy." See Exod. 20:8 and Deut. 5:12.

q   Isa. 28:21: "For the Lord will rise up as on Mount Perazim, he will rage as in the valley of Gibeon to do his deed—strange is his deed!—and to work his work—alien is his work!"

their works to God's work in the same way that dedicating a church turns a regular building into a house of worship. Likewise, people should regard suffering and misfortune as holy things, and be glad and thank God when they strike. For when they come, they make people holy so that they may fulfill this commandment, be saved and redeemed from their sinful works. Thus David says [Ps. 116:15]: "The death of his holy ones is precious in his sight."

To strengthen us, God not only commanded us to rest—for nature does not like to suffer and die so that it is a bitter day of rest when its works become useless and dead—but God also comforted us with many words from Scripture, as it says in Ps. 91[:15]: "I am with them in all their suffering and will rescue them," and Ps. 34[:18]: "The Lord is near to all who suffer and will help them."

Since not even that was enough, God provided a convincing example, his dearest and only Son, Jesus Christ, our Lord. On that Sabbath, an entire day of rest,[95] he lay in the grave divested of all his works and became the first to fulfill this commandment, although he did not need it for himself. He did it to comfort us, so that in suffering and dying we could be still and at peace. Given that Christ was raised after his Sabbath rest and from that point on lived only in God and God in him, so also, through slaying our [old] Adam (which is completed only after the death and burial of the body), we are raised into God, so that God lives and works in us eternally. Look! There are three sides of human nature—reason, desire, and aversion—into which all human works may be classified. They must be choked out by these three practices: God's rule, self-discipline, and suffering inflicted by others. Then we can take our rest spiritually in God and leave God room to do his work.

24.[96] These actions and suffering should take place in faith and in confident expectation of divine succor so that all works stay rooted in the first commandment and in faith, as we said above, and faith is exercised and strengthened in those actions. All the other commandments and works are set up for the sake of faith. Notice how a beautiful golden ring is made from the first three commandments and how

95. Holy Saturday between Good Friday and the first Easter.

96. The following summarizes Luther's interpretation of the first three commandments and their relation to faith.

the second commandment flows into the third from the first commandment and faith, and likewise the third commandment runs through the second and into the first. For the first work is faith: having a good heart and trusting in God, from which flows the second good work: praising God's name, acknowledging God's grace, and giving honor to God alone. After that comes the third work: worshiping God by praying, attending to the sermon, and contemplating and meditating on God's blessings, then by chastising and subjugating the flesh.

When the evil spirit notices such faith, honor, and worship of God, it goes on a rampage and starts persecution. It attacks our body, property, reputation, and life, and brings down upon us illness, poverty, shame, and death—all of which God has preordained and imposed on us for our own good.[97] Note that with this begins the other work or rest of the third commandment, in which faith "is severely tested like gold in the fire."[r] It is a remarkable thing to keep on trusting in God, although God brings death, disgrace, sickness, and poverty, and to maintain that God is still the kindest Father of all when faced with such a cruel example of wrath. But that must happen regarding this work of the third commandment. Suffering forces faith to call upon and praise God's name during the suffering. In this way, the third commandment again returns to the second commandment, and through the invocation and praise of God's name faith grows and comes into its own, and it becomes stronger through these two works of the second and the third commandments. So faith goes forth into those works and through those works returns to itself, just as "the sun rises until its setting and then returns to the place of its rising."[s] In Scripture, the daytime is dedicated to the peaceful life with works and the night to the suffering life with adversity. Faith, however, lives and is active in both, "goes in and out," as Christ says in John [10:9].[t]

97. Here Luther reframes the evil intent of bodily injury caused by persecution into a tool of God for discipline. Luther may even have his own attacks in mind.

r   Sir. 2:5.

s   Ps. 19:6, reading with the Vulgate.

t   Both the German and Latin texts have John 6. But see John 10:9: "[they] will come in and go out and find pasture."

25. In the Lord's Prayer, we offer petitions according to this order of good works in the commandments. First we say, "Our Father in heaven," words of the first work, faith, which, according to the first commandment, does not doubt that it has a merciful God and Father in heaven. Second, "Hallowed be your name," through which faith desires God's name, honor, and glory to be praised and calls upon God's name in all times of need, as the second commandment says. Third, "Your kingdom come," in which we ask for the true Sabbath and day of rest, for our works to cease and for God's work alone to be in us and for God to reign in us as in his own kingdom, as he himself says [Luke 17:21]: "See, the kingdom of God is nowhere but in you yourselves." In the fourth part, "Your will be done," we ask that we may obey the seven commandments of the second table and hold fast to them. Faith is also exercised in their works, which are directed toward the neighbor, just as it is exercised in the works of the first three commandments, which are directed toward God. The first three petitions of the Lord's Prayer contain the words "you" and "your" so that these petitions seek only what belongs to God. The other petitions all say "us" and "our," because in them we are asking for things that are good for us and for our salvation. All we have recounted up to now pertains to the first table of Moses and has painted the noblest good works in broad strokes for the simple folk. Now comes the second table.

The First Commandment
of the Second Table of Moses[98]

"Honor your father and mother."[u]

From this commandment we learn that after the noble works required by the first three commandments there is no greater work than to obey and serve those whom God has appointed as authorities over us. For this reason, dis-

98. Commandments 4–10. See also above, p. 303, n. 66.

u Exod. 20:12; Deut. 5:16.

obedience is even worse than murder, unchastity, theft, dishonesty, and anything else covered by the last six commandments. For making distinctions among sins—which ones are more serious than others—can be difficult for us to recognize except by observing the order of God's commandments, even though there is also a distinction among the works within each commandment. For who does not know that cursing is worse than being angry, killing worse than cursing, killing father and mother worse than killing just anyone? These seven commandments teach us how we ought to practice good works toward others and, first of all, toward those placed over us.

1. **The first work** of this commandment is to honor our biological fathers and mothers. This honor does not only consist in outward gestures but also in obedience to them, keeping their words and deeds in mind, showing them respect and treating them as important, agreeing with what they say, remaining quiet, and putting up with how they treat us unless it violates the first three commandments, and providing them as needed with food, clothing, and shelter. God said on purpose that we should *honor* them, not that we should *love* them, although we should do that as well. Honor is superior to simple love and includes a certain fear that is joined with love and makes people more afraid to insult their parents than punishment would do—just as we honor a holy place with a certain fear but do not flee from it as we would from punishment but flock to it. That kind of fear mixed with love is true honor. Fear without love, however, opposes the things that we despise or flee, as a person fears punishment or the executioner. No honor is present there, only fear without love; indeed, it is fear with hatred and hostility. There is an adage in St. Jerome: "What we fear we also hate."[v] God will not be feared or honored with such fear, nor

---

v   Jerome, Letter 82 to Theophilus (d. 412), bishop of Alexandria, par. 3: "There is an old saying: whomever one fears, one hates; whomever one hates, one wishes to see dead" (MPL 22, col. 737). The saying, which Luther cites elsewhere (WA 13:435), is attributed to the Roman poet Quintus Ennius (239–169 BCE).

does he want parents to be honored that way but honored instead with fear that is combined with love and trust.[w]

2. This work may seem easy, but few people take it seriously enough. If the parents are upright and do not love their children according to the flesh[x] but, as they should, direct them and point them toward serving God in word and deed according to the first three commandments, then the selfish will of their children is broken continuously so that they must constantly do, avoid, or suffer exactly what their own nature would rather not do. As a result, the children have reason to despise their parents, murmur against them, or do worse things. Love and fear cannot survive in a child as long as God's grace is not present. Similarly, when parents exercise discipline and punishment as they should—even unjustly at times, although it does no harm to the soul's salvation—one's corrupt nature receives it grudgingly. Above all this, some children are so wicked that they are ashamed of their parents if they are poor, lowborn, unsightly, or dishonorable. Such things matter more to those children than the exalted commandment of God, who is over everything else and gives them such parents out of thoughtful care in order to exercise and train them in his command. It becomes worse when the children have their own children, for whom their love grows, while the love and respect toward their own parents decreases greatly.

What is commanded and said in respect to parents also applies to those who stand in their stead when the parents are not present or have died: friends, stepparents, godparents, civil lords, and spiritual fathers. Everyone must be ruled and be subject to others.[99] Hence we see how many good works are taught in this commandment, since it subjects our entire lives to other people. And from this arises this high praise of obedience and the fact that it comprises all kinds of virtue and good works.

99. In Luther's political and religious world, this was the case. Only close friends were considered equals.

---

w   Luther would continue to make this connection throughout his career. See the *Small Catechism*, "Ten Commandments," 1–2 (BC, 351), and the LC, "Ten Commandments," 322–25 (BC, 429–30).

x   That is, "do not spoil them."

3. There is a second way of dishonoring parents that is more subtle and dangerous than the first and yet is dressed up and made presentable as genuine honor. It happens whenever natural love causes parents to let children have their own way. Honor and love are present, to be sure, and everyone is delighted; father and mother are pleased, and so are the children.

The plague is so common that examples of the first kind of dishonor (that is, disobedience) are scarcely ever seen. It all happens because parents are so blind that they neither acknowledge nor honor God in the first three commandments and therefore cannot see what their children lack and how they as parents should teach and rear them. As a result, children are taught to value worldly honor, desires, and material goods in order to please other people and go far in life. The children, of course, are quite content and happy to be obedient without any disagreement whatsoever.

Under this seemingly good appearance, however, God's commandment crashes to earth, and what is written in Isaiah and Jeremiah about children being devoured by their own parents is being fulfilled.*y* The parents are acting just like King Manasseh, who let his own child be sacrificed to the idol Moloch and immolated.*z* How is offering one's own child to an idol and immolating it different from parents rearing their children to care for the world more than for God? Such parents simply let their children wander off and be burned up by worldly lust and affections, earthly pleasures, goods, and honor, while love for God, divine honor, and the desire for eternal goods are extinguished.

O how dangerous it is to be a father or mother when only flesh and blood rule! For truly this commandment determines whether or not the first three and the last six are accepted and obeyed, because parents are commanded to teach their children such things, as in Ps. 78[:5-6]. It states: "He commanded our parents to teach . . . their children that the next generation might know them and the child of their

---

y Isa. 57:5; Jer. 7:31; 32:35.

z 2 Kgs. 21:6; 23:10.

child might proclaim them to their children."[a] This is the reason that God commands that parents be honored, that is, be loved with fear; for the love just described lacks fear and is consequently more like disrespect than honor.

Now see if it is not true that everyone has enough good works to do, whether a parent or a child! But we who are blind overlook these things and search elsewhere for all kinds of works that are not commanded.

4. When parents are so foolish as to rear their children in a worldly manner, their children should not obey them at all, for according to the first three commandments, God should be more highly esteemed than parents.[100] By the term "rearing in a worldly manner," I mean that children are taught to seek only the pleasure, honor, property, or power of this world.

Of course, it is a necessity and no sin at all to dress appropriately and to earn one's bread honestly. Nevertheless, in their hearts children must be or learn to be reconciled to the fact that it is a pity that this bleak earthly life may hardly begin or be lived without more fancy clothing and possessions than needed for covering the body, warding off the cold, and obtaining enough to eat. Thus, children, while preferring not to do what the world wants and for the sake of something better, must put up with such foolishness and profligacy in order to avoid something even worse. For this reason Queen Esther wore her royal crown and nevertheless said to God: "You know that the symbol of royalty on my head has never pleased me; I consider it no better than filthy rags and never wear it when I am alone but only in public when I must."[b] Whoever thinks like this in their heart wears finery without danger, for they wear it as if not wearing it, dance as if not dancing, live well as if not living well. These

a   A close paraphrase of the Vulgate.
b   These words occur in the prayer of Esther that appears only in an expanded Greek version of the book as part of the Apocrypha. These Greek additions were translated into Latin and placed at the end of Esther in the Vulgate and in the 1530s translated into German and for the Wittenberg Bible. In the NRSV, the words quoted by Luther appear in the English translation of the Greek version of Esther and contained in addition C of "Esther with Additions," 14:16.

are secret souls, the hidden brides of Christ, but they are rare because it is hard not to desire fine clothes and jewels. At the command of her parents, St. Cecilia wore robes embroidered with gold, but underneath against her body she wore a hair shirt.[101]

Some parents ask: "How am I supposed to introduce my child to society and ensure for them an honorable marriage? I have to display some finery." Tell me, are these not the words of a heart that doubts God and trusts its own caring about such things more than God's, even though St. Peter teaches [1 Pet. 5:7]: "Cast all your care upon him and be certain that he cares for you"? It is a sign that these parents have never thanked God for their children, never prayed for them in the right way, and never commended them to God. Otherwise they would have learned and experienced how they should expectantly pray to God regarding their children's marriage. Therefore, God lets them follow their own course filled with cares and worries and yet without any chance of success.

5. Thus, it is true, as they say, that parents, if they had done nothing else, can gain salvation by means of their children. And if parents raise them for serving God, then they really have both hands full of good works for themselves. For who are the hungry, thirsty, naked, imprisoned, sick, and strangers[c] save the souls of your own children? With them God makes your house into a hospice with you as the administrator. You are to watch over them, by giving them "food and drink" with good words and works so that they learn to trust, believe, fear, and put their hope in God; honor God's name; refrain from swearing and cursing; and discipline themselves with prayer, fasting, keeping vigils, working, worshiping, hearing God's word, and observing the Sabbath.[102] In this way they will learn to disdain temporal things, endure misfortune with equanimity, face death without fear, not holding this life too dear.

Do you see what an important lesson it is and how many good works are right there for you in your own house with your child, who needs all kinds of things as a hungry, thirsty,

101. According to tradition, Cecilia was an early Christian martyr who was made a saint in the Roman Church. The detail mentioned by Luther appears in the account of her life in the *Golden Legend*, a popular collection of saints' lives compiled in the thirteenth century by Jacobus de Voragine (c. 1230-1298). Strictures against such finery were a standard part of late medieval preaching, on which Luther based his comments here. See his work from 1516 on the Ten Commandments, WA 1:452, 15-453, 10.

102. Here Luther summarizes his comments about the works of the first three commandments.

c Matt. 25:31-46.

naked, poor, imprisoned, and sick soul? Oh what a blessed marriage and household that would be where such parents resided; yes, it would be a true church, an elect cloister, even a paradise. About this Ps. 128[:1-4] states: "Blessed are those who fear God and walk in his commandments. You will be nourished with the labor of your hands; therefore, you will be blessed and it will go well with you. Your wife will be like a fruitful vine in your house, and your children will be like young shoots of the olive tree around your table. Behold, therefore, how blessed are those who fear the Lord!" Where are such parents? Where are those who ask about good works? No one wants to come forward. Why? The devil, flesh, and blood draw away from what God has commanded. It does not glitter and therefore counts for nothing. One person runs off to St. James;[d] another makes vows to Our Lady. No one vows to honor God by governing and teaching themselves and their children well. Those whom God has commanded to guard their children in body and soul abandon them and instead want to serve God somewhere else that has not been commanded. There is no bishop who forbids such perverse behavior or preacher who condemns it. In fact, for the sake of avarice these leaders approve such behavior and daily invent more pilgrimages, canonize more saints, and sell more indulgences![103] May God have pity on such blindness!

6. At the same time, there is no easier way for parents to earn hell than with their own children in their own house when they neglect their children and fail to teach them the things listed above. What good would it do parents if they fasted themselves to death, prayed, made pilgrimages, and did all kinds of good works? Neither at their death nor at the last day will God ask about these things but rather demand that they account for their children whom God entrusted to them—as demonstrated by the words of Christ in Luke 23[:28-29]: "You daughters of Jerusalem, do not cry over me but over yourselves and your children. The days will come when you will say: 'Blessed be the wombs that have never

103. Pilgrim sites were always associated with particular saints and had specific amounts of indulgence connected to them.

---

d   See p. 272, n. 24.

given birth and the breasts that have never suckled.'" Why will they lament in this way if not because their damnation stems from their own children; if the parents had not had them, they might have been saved! To be sure, these words should really open the eyes of parents so they can look spiritually at the souls of their children, lest these poor children be deceived by their parents' false, fleshly love into thinking they had properly honored their parents by not being cross with them or by obeying them in worldly ostentation. Then the children's self-will becomes stronger, although this commandment would have parents be honored when the self-will of their children is broken and they become humble and gentle.

What was said about the other commandments—that they should arise out of the most important work of all[e]—applies here also. No parents should imagine that their discipline or teaching by itself suffices for their children, unless it be done in reliance on God's favor, without any doubt that God is pleased with such works. And let such works be nothing other than for encouraging and practicing one's faith: to trust God and to expect from his merciful will all that is good. Without such faith, no work is efficacious, good, or pleasing; for many unbelievers have reared their children beautifully, but all to no avail because of unbelief.

7. **The second work** of this commandment is to honor and obey our spiritual mother, the holy Christian church, and its spiritual authorities. We should follow whatever they command, forbid, set down, order, ban, or allow. Just as we honor, fear, and love our natural parents, so also we should let the spiritual authorities be right in all matters that do not contradict the first three commandments.[104]

This second work is almost more difficult than the first. The spiritual authorities are supposed to punish sin with the ban and other legal measures and to urge their spiritual children to be upright, so they might have cause to perform these works and exercise themselves by obeying and honoring the authorities. One sees no such diligence now, however,

104. Luther would continue throughout his life to urge obedience to pastors and other spiritual authorities, but always with this caveat, which was where he thought the papacy fell short.

_e_   That is, from faith.

and they set themselves against their subjects like the mothers who run away from their children to their lovers, as Hos. 2[:7] states.[f] They do not preach, teach, guard against anything, or punish anybody. There is no longer any spiritual authority in Christendom.

What then can I say about this second work? There still remain some fast days and festivals that ought to be abolished. But no one pays any attention to this. Excommunication is customarily used only against people in debt, but it should not be that way. The job of the spiritual authorities is to punish severely public sins and scandalous behavior such as adultery, unchastity, usury, gluttony, worldly ostentation, fancy dress, and the like and to see to it that behavior improves. Moreover, they should provide due oversight of clerical chapters, cloisters, parishes, and schools and to ascertain that worship services are properly held. In the schools and cloisters, they should provide learned, upright men[g] for the youth, boys and girls, so that all of them are properly educated, their elders provide good examples, and Christendom is filled and adorned with fine young folk. St. Paul writes to his disciple Titus [2:1-10] that he should instruct and be guide to every station in life—young and old, men and women. Now, however, all[h] who want to may apply, and those who have only themselves for supervisors and teachers get the job. Alas, it has come to the point that the places in which one should learn the right things have become nothing but schools for rogues and no one cares about the wild young people at all.

8. If this order were followed, then one could say how honor and obedience should take place. But now what is happening is the same as with natural parents who let children have their own way. The spiritual authorities impose a penalty, but then they offer a dispensation, take money for

---

f   By using the German word *Bullen* for "lovers," Luther may be alluding to papal bulls.

g   *Männer* (*Menner* in Luther's text), that is, male teachers. Later, Luther would encourage hiring female teachers for the girls. See *To the Councilmen of Germany* (1524), LW 45:368-71.

h   Singular in the original.

it, and let people get by with more than they should.[105] I will say nothing further. We see that there is more of this than there should be. Greed sits on the throne, and the authorities actually teach what they should prevent. Anyone can see that the spiritual estate[i] is worldlier in all matters than the worldly estate itself. Because of this, Christendom will perish and this commandment will cease to exist.

If there existed a bishop who would diligently provide care and oversight for all such walks of life,[j] make official visits to all the parishes, and stay on top of things, as he ought, then one city alone would truly be too much for him. At the time of the apostles, when Christendom was at its best, every city had its own bishop, even though Christians were a minority in those cities. How could that possibly work today when one bishop has so much to care for, another perhaps more, yet another who claims the whole world, and another half the world?[106] Now is the time to ask God for mercy. We have too many "spiritual authorities" but little or no spiritual governance. Meanwhile, let those who can see to it that clerical chapters, cloisters, parishes, and schools are properly organized and supervised. It would also be the job of spiritual authorities to reduce the number of cloisters and schools if they cannot be provided for. It is much better to have no cloister or clerical chapter than one with bad governance, which would make God angrier.

9. Because these authorities have totally neglected and twisted their proper duties, it must surely follow that they will abuse their power and undertake improper and corrupt works, like parents who command something that is against God. Hence we must be wise, for the Apostle [Paul] has said it will be a dangerous time when such authorities govern,[k] because it will look as if one is challenging their authority if one fails to carry out or defend every order issued by them. We must take the first three commandments and the right

105. A reference to the widespread practice of allowing dispensations from canon law. For example, illegitimate sons could purchase legitimacy so that they could become priests; Archbishop Albrecht von Brandenburg of Mainz (1490–1545) purchased a dispensation to hold more than one episcopal see; in the form of indulgences, priests could purchase the right to celebrate Mass in a territory under the ban.

106. That is, not only are the dioceses too large to provide the pastoral care and supervision they should, but also papal claims to rule the entire church (and world) are also at fault.

---

i   See p. 301, note v.

j   Here and throughout these paragraphs the German is *Stand* or (plural) *Stände*, see above, p. 310, n. 78.

k   See 1 Tim. 4:1-3 and 2 Tim. 3:1-5.

107. Especially notorious was the awarding of bishoprics to members of prominent families on the basis of the candidate's ability and willingness to pay in return. The buying and selling of church offices, known as simony (after Simon Magus in Acts 8:18-24), was strongly condemned in the Middle Ages. Foundations established benefices, that is, guaranteed income attached to clerical duties at a particular place. Holders of such benefices sometimes never even visited them but simply paid an underling (curate) to do the pastoral work involved. Luther also makes similar complaints in the *Address to the Christian Nobility*. See below, p. 405f.

tablet[*l*] in our hands and be certain of this: that no person—neither bishop, pope, nor angel—has the right to command or dictate anything that contradicts, hinders, or fails to promote those three commandments with their works. If they do try it, it is invalid and will not stand up, and we commit sin if we obey or follow such things or just stand by and allow it.

It is easy to understand why the rules about fasting do not apply to sick people, pregnant women, or to any and all[*m*] who cannot fast without injury to themselves. But let us go further. In our day, nothing comes out of Rome but a yearly fair of spiritual goods that are publicly and shamelessly bought and sold: indulgences, parishes, cloisters, bishoprics, and cathedral chapters—along with all kinds of foundations far and wide set up for the service of God.[107] In this way, not only is all the world's money and property pushed and pulled toward Rome—something that does only minor damage—but parishes, bishoprics, and other prelatures are disrupted, abandoned, and desolate. As a result, the people are completely neglected, God's word, name, and honor are vanishing, and faith is obliterated. In the end, those clerical offices and institutions will belong not only to unlearned and unskilled clerics but also to the biggest Roman buffoons in the world. Thus, everything instituted for God's service—preaching to, guiding, and improving the people—must now be done by stable boys and mule drivers or, lest I put it even more crudely, by Roman whores and buffoons. But still, the only thanks we receive is that they ridicule our people as fools.

10. Seeing that such unbearable shenanigans take place in the name of God and St. Peter, as if God's name and spiritual authority were instituted in order to blaspheme God's honor and to destroy the whole Christian church in body and soul, it is our duty to resist it as much as we can, like upright children whose parents have gone mad. We must first examine the origin of the right that whatever has been

l   For the two tablets of the law, see p. 303, n. 66.

m   Singular in the original.

established in our lands for the service of God and the welfare of our children should benefit Rome, while here, where it should be a benefit, it is neglected. How can we be so dumb?

Since our bishops and spiritual prelates stand stock-still and neither defend themselves or are frightened [about the abuses] and cause Christendom to go to ruin, we should first humbly ask God to help us ward off these things and then get to work putting up roadblocks for these papal courtiers and envoys[108] and, in a mild and reasonable manner, solemnly ask them whether or not they intend to care properly for their benefices, live on-site, and improve the people by means of preaching and setting a good example. If not, and they continue to live in Rome or elsewhere and let their churches become weak and desolate, let the pope in Rome, whom they serve, feed them.[109] It is not right for us to support the pope's servants and his people, that is, his buffoons and whores, to the ruin and injury of our souls.

Do you see? They are the real Turks[n] whom the kings, princes, and nobility should attack first, not for themselves but only for the betterment of Christendom and to prevent blasphemy and the shame done to God's name. Thus, princes should treat these spiritual authorities as they would a father who has lost his wits, where, if one failed to take him into custody and restrain him (albeit with deference and respect), he would ruin his children, his legacy, and everyone else. In like manner, we should hold the Roman authorities in honor as our supreme father but, seeing that they have become so mad and foolish, not allow their schemes so that they cannot use them to destroy Christendom.

11. Some people think we should present this issue to a general council, but I say no to this because we have held many councils where this was proposed, namely, at Constance, Basel, and the last at Rome.[110, 111] Nothing was accomplished, and things got even worse. Such councils are useless because the shrewd minds at Rome devised a ploy that the kings and princes must swear to let them remain as they

108. Messengers who delivered indulgence letters and papal edicts from Rome to other places. Luther may be thinking of the likes of the legate Karl von Miltitz (c. 1490–1529), who had most recently been negotiating with the electoral Saxon court about this case.

109. At this time, some of Germany bishops and other church leaders were, in fact, absentee Italians living in Rome. This was a typical complaint raised in *gravamina* brought to the diets of the Holy Roman Empire. See also the *Address to the Christian Nobility*, below, p. 402.

110. Three late medieval councils whose agendas included church reform: Constance (1414–1418), Basel (1431–1439), and the Fifth Lateran, at Rome (1512–1517).

111. In his struggles with Rome, Luther twice appealed to a general council above the papal decisions, and this continued to comprise a part of the Evangelicals' negotiating position at least through 1530 and the Diet of Augsburg.

n   See p. 319 above.

112. As throughout his life and based upon late medieval usage, Luther employs the term *reformacion* to mean not "the Reformation" but substantial or lasting reform of ecclesial institutions.

are with what they possess. Thus, they slammed the door to fend off any kind of reformation[112] and gave free rein and sanction to every kind of villainous behavior, despite the fact that such an oath is required, demanded, and taken against God and the rule of law—and it even excludes the Holy Spirit, who should govern councils. The best and indeed the only remaining remedy would be for kings, princes, the nobility, cities, and communities to take the first step in the matter so that the bishops and clergy, who are now fearful, would have cause to follow. For here one should and must look no further than to God's first three commandments, against which neither Rome, nor heaven, nor earth can command or forbid anything. Imposing the ban and using threats, by which they try to resist such things, makes no difference, just as it makes no difference for a crazed father to threaten a son harshly who resists or challenges him.

12. **The third work** of this commandment is to obey civil authorities, as Paul teaches in Rom. 13[:1-7] and Titus 3[:1] and as St. Peter teaches in 1 Pet. 2[:13-17]. Be subject to the king as the supreme ruler and to the princes as his delegates and to all the ranks of worldly power. Its work is to protect those subject to it and to punish thievery, robbery, and adultery, as St. Paul writes in Rom. 13[:4]: "It does not bear the sword in vain; it serves God by instilling fear in those who are evil [and promoting] the well-being of the godly."

You can sin against civil authorities in two ways. First, when one lies to, deceives, or proves disloyal to them, or fails to carry out with body or property what they have ordered or commanded. Even if the civil authorities commit an injustice, as did the king of Babylon against the people of Israel,[o] God will have them obeyed without any subterfuge or threats. Second, [you sin against civil authorities] when one speaks evil of the authorities, curses them, or, because it is impossible to take revenge, disparages them publicly or in secret with murmuring and destructive criticism.

In all of this, we should bear in mind what St. Peter commanded us to remember: whether the authorities exercise

o Jer. 27:8-15; Bar. 2:19-26.

their power justly or unjustly, it cannot hurt the soul but only the body and what we possess.[p] Even if it happened that they wanted to force us publicly to commit injustice against God or other people, as rulers did in ages past when they were not yet Christian or, as some report, the Turk still does, to suffer injustice destroys no one's souls but instead improves them, even though it may well diminish one's body and property. To commit injustice, however, destroys the soul even if it benefits the entire world.[q]

13. This is why, when injustice is done, civil authorities pose less danger than spiritual ones. Civil authority cannot do harm because it has nothing to do with preaching, faith, and the first three commandments.[113] But spiritual authority does harm not only when it commits injustice but also when it abandons its office and does something different, even if it were better than the best possible action by civil authority. Hence one must resist spiritual authorities when they act unjustly but must not resist civil authorities even though they act equally unjustly. The poor commoners believe and do what they see and hear from the spiritual authorities, and if they do not see and hear it, they will not believe or do anything, because spiritual authority has been established for no reason other than to lead the people in faith to God. All this is not the job of civil authority. For it may do and leave undone whatever it wants, and my faith in God is completely independent and acts on its own, because I do not have to believe whatever civil authority believes. In God's eyes, civil authority is a small matter and is regarded by him as far too insignificant for a person—solely because of it (whether it acts justly or unjustly)—to oppose, disobey, or quarrel with it. On the contrary, spiritual authority is a great, overflowing good and is regarded by God as much too

113. In the 1530s, Luther would modify his opinion and insist that the Christian prince has responsibility to see to it that blasphemy is avoided in his lands.

---

p   Luther appears to conflate Matt. 10:28 and 1 Pet. 2:18-20.

q   Luther has in mind the common Latin proverb cited in the works of Cicero (*Tusculanae disputationes* 5, 19, 56 [106–43 BCE]): "It is better to suffer injustice than to commit it." See MLStA 2:71, n. 614. Luther's *Table Talk* contains the proverb in the following form: "It is better for us to bear than to do injury, for we sin when we do it but not when we bear it" (WA TR 4:308, no. 4427).

precious, for even the humblest Christian to suffer in silence when it deviates from its own office by even a hair's breadth, not to mention when it completely violates its office as we observe every day.

14. There are also various abuses connected to civil authority, first, by succumbing to flatterers, which is a common and particularly damaging scourge to this authority. No one can guard against or watch out for this enough. It is led around by the nose, rides roughshod over the poor commoners, and becomes a government, as the sage said, like a spider's web that catches small flies but lets the millstones pass right through.[114] The laws, orders, and governance of civil authority catch the small fry but let the big fish escape. If the lord is not bright enough to do without his advisers' counsel or is not so well regarded that they fear him, then their authority must needs be childish, unless God somehow performs a miracle.

For this reason, God has deemed evil and incompetent rulers the worst plague of all and added this threat in Isa. 3[:1]: "I will take all brave men from you and give you children and childish rulers." In the Scriptures (Ezek. 14[:12-23]), God has identified four plagues. The first and least of these, which David also chose, is pestilence;[r] the second is uncontrolled inflation; the third is war; the fourth, all kinds of wild beasts—lions, wolves, serpents, and dragons. These beasts stand for evil rulers because, wherever they are, not only does the land suffer ruin in body and possessions, as in the first two plagues, but it also suffers the loss of honor, discipline, virtue, and the salvation of souls. For pestilence and inflation make people upright and rich, but war and wicked rulers destroy everything that makes for earthly and eternal well-being.

15. It takes a really intelligent lord not always to force the issue even though he may have justice and the best possible case on his side. It is a much nobler virtue to put up with injury to one's rights than to property and the body, since

114. A common European proverb, found also in Spanish and Russian, and often used by Luther. See Wander, 4:723.

r   2 Sam. 24:10-17.

the subjects benefit from such restraint, especially given that earthly justice only depends on temporal goods.

Thus, this is a foolish saying: "I have a right to that, and I will take it by force and keep it although it brings nothing but misfortune to another."[115] We read that the emperor Octavian[116] would not go to war no matter how just the cause, unless there was some indication it would do more good than harm or that the harm would not be unbearable. He said: "War is like fishing with a golden net; one never catches enough to make up for the risk of losing much more."[s] Someone leading a wagon must travel quite differently than when he is simply walking alone. The latter can walk, jump, and do as he pleases, but when leading, he must steer and conduct himself in such a way that the horse and wagon can follow, and he must pay more attention to them than to his own wishes. The same is true of a lord, who leads the public with him. He must not travel or act as he pleases but in accord with the public's abilities, and he must consider what is necessary and most useful to them more than his own will and desires. For when a lord rules only according to his crazy ideas and only follows his own discretion, he is like a crazy driver who hurtles their horses and wagons wildly over unfamiliar roads and bridges through thickets, hedges, ditches, rushing streams, hills, and valleys. He won't drive very far before it ends in a complete wreck.

For this reason, it would be best for rulers if, starting in their youth, they would read or have read to them histories from both sacred and pagan books, in which they would discover more examples about the art of ruling than all the law books. One can read in Esther 6[:1-2] that the kings of Persia did this. Examples and histories always offer and teach more than laws and jurisprudence. The former teaches on the basis of sure and certain experience, while the latter teaches using uncertain, untried words.

115. A saying similar to the Latin: *Fiat iustitia et pereat mundus* ("Let justice be done, and let the world perish"), also attributed Pope Adrian VI (1459–1523), who became pope in the 1522. See MLStA 2:73, n. 629.

116. Gaius Octavius (63 BCE–CE 14), that is, Caesar Augustus, the first Roman emperor.

Octavian Augustus.
Bust kept since 1589
in Palace Bevilacqua, Verona.

---

s   For this common proverb, see MLStA 2:73, n. 633. The Roman historian Flavius Eutropius (4th cent.), *Breviarium ab urbe condita* VII.14, used this phrase to describe and criticize Caesar Augustus's successor, Nero (37–68). For Caesar Augustus's reluctance to go to war, see Suetonius (69– d. after 122), *Divus Augustus*, 21, 2.

117. By "this land" Luther is thinking of the German lands of the Holy Roman Empire. For a broader discussion of the topic in sections 16 and 17, see *Address to the Christian Nobility*, pp. 460–64, below.

118. German: *Zinskauf*. It was the practice of paying a sum of money from the buyer to the seller, which then made the seller responsible for paying the buyer a fixed percentage of the purchase price each year in perpetuity. Originally, it involved land and thus was a purchase of the land's income. These contracts were first constructed to circumvent the church's strictures on charging interest. See Luther's extensive criticism in *Trade and Usury* (final version: 1524) in LW 45:295–310, a section first published in a 1520 sermon attacking the practice.

119. Luther refers to a German saying that the "three Jews" (a term of obvious derision) are "shorn Jews" (i.e., priests), "Jews carrying golden rings" (Christian merchants who charge more interest than Jewish bankers), and "circumcised Jews" (the actual Jewish people). Because Christians were not supposed to charge interest to fellow Christians, the task of loaning money often fell to Jewish people, which became yet one more basis for anti-Jewish propaganda. See Wander, 2:1034f.

120. German: *Officiel*. This was the title of a specific episcopal officer, who carried out the bishop's will.

16. In our day, all rulers, especially in this land, have three especially necessary works to perform.[117] First, they should do away with the dreadful habits of gluttony and drunkenness, not only because of the excess but also because of the expense. Owing to the spice trade and the like, without which one could live quite well, there has been no small decline in temporal goods in this land, and it continues each day. The secular government would have enough on its hands to prevent both these rampant vices that have pervaded the land far and wide, and it could perform no better service for God, and it would improve its own land. Second, they should restrict the outlandish cost of clothing, on which so much wealth is wasted and which merely serves the world and the flesh. It is appalling that this abuse is so prevalent among a people that is pledged, baptized, and dedicated to the crucified Christ and should carry the cross with him and should daily prepare themselves for that other life through dying. If this practice were only observed in a few cases due to imprudence, it would be more bearable; but since it is done freely, with impunity, and without hindrance or shame, and since both praise and fame are sought for doing it, such waste is truly an un-Christian enterprise. Third, the rulers should abolish the usurious practice of purchasing income,[118] which ruins, devours, and destroys all kinds of lands, cities, and people all over the world through its devious appearance of not really being usury at all, when in fact it is worse than usury because one does not take precautions as one does when usury is obvious. See, this is the three Jews (as it is said) who suck out the entire world.[119] On this point, the lords should not sleep or be lazy if they want to give God a good account of their office.

17. The chicanery perpetrated by church officials[120] and other episcopal and clerical officers should be pointed out here. For the sake of making a penny, they place tremendous burdens on the poor commoners through excommunications, subpoenas, harassment, and coercion. Such actions should be prohibited by secular authority*t* because no other assistance or means of stopping this are available.

O would God in heaven that once such a government, as the people of Israel had, would also start to abolish houses of prostitution![u] It is an un-Christian image and a public sin for Christians to maintain such houses that in earlier times were completely unheard of. A new law should require that boys and girls be married in a timely fashion in order to avoid this vice. Both spiritual and civil authorities should support such an ordinance and practice. If it was possible for the Jews, why should it not also be possible for Christians? Indeed, if such a law is possible in villages, market towns, and a few cities, as is evident, why is it not possible everywhere?

What prevents this is that there is no government in the world. No one wants to work, and so the artisans have to lay their journeymen off. Then they run wild and no one can tame them. If there were an ordinance that they would have to obey their masters and that no one would hire them elsewhere, this loophole for evil would be closed. God help me, I worry that desiring such a law is only wishful thinking, but we are not thereby excused.

Please notice that I have identified only a few works of those in authority, but nevertheless they are so beneficial and so many that they have a surfeit of good works with which they can serve God every minute. Like all the others, these works should arise from faith and exercise faith, so that no one does them to curry favor with God but rather, certain of his graciousness, does them to the honor and praise of their dear and merciful God and to serve and be useful to one's neighbors.

18. **The fourth work** of this commandment is for household servants to obey the man and woman of the house and for workers to obey their masters and mistresses. On this matter, St. Paul says in Titus 2: "Preach . . . to laborers or servants[v] that they are to hold their masters in honor, obey

---

t Literally, "the worldly sword," the common designation for temporal government.

u See Lev. 19:29; Deut. 23:17-18.

v German: *den knechten odder dienern*: Luther's standard paraphrase for the Latin *servi* ("servants" or "slaves").

them, do what pleases them, and neither deceive nor resist them. By so doing, they also do credit to the teaching of Christ and to our faith, so that nonbelievers will have no reason to complain about or resent us."*w* Saint Peter says [1 Pet. 2:18-19]: "Servants, obey your masters out of fear of God, not only those who are kind and gentle but also those who are capricious and rough, for it is pleasing to God when a person innocently bears injustice."

One of the biggest complaints in the world is about servants and workers, how they are disobedient, disloyal, crude, and greedy, in short, a plague from God.[121] Truth be told, obedience is the only job of servants by which they can be saved; they really do not need to take off on pilgrimages or do anything else of the kind. They have enough to do if their hearts are set in the right direction, gladly doing or avoiding what they know will please their masters and mistresses and doing it all in simple faith, not that they thereby would merit a lot but that they do everything relying on God's grace, where all merit is located,*x* working without reward, purely out of love and goodwill toward God that has grown out of this trust. Moreover, they should allow all such work to be a kind of exercise and admonition that will increase their faith and trust more and more. As we have said now many times, this faith makes all works good. Indeed, faith itself must do them and be the "master artisan."*y*

19. At the same time, masters and mistresses should not rule their servants, maids, and workers with an iron hand or be too exacting. Instead, now and then they should ease up and overlook some things to keep peace.*z* For the same criteria may not fit equally at all times for all situations of life, because here on earth we lead imperfect lives. Saint Paul says in Col. 4[:1]: "Masters, treat your slaves justly and fairly and remember that you also have a master in heaven." Just as

121. In Luther's day, servants (German: *Knechte*) were usually young people indentured for a time to a household to learn agriculture or a trade. They received wages, room and board, and they could become householders or artisans in their own right. Day laborers (German: *Tagelöhner*) were paid daily wages by farmers or other householders. Lifelong slavery and serfdom were unknown in Luther's day in Saxony.

w A conflation of Titus 2:1a, 9-10 with 1 Tim. 6:1-2.

x The word for "merit" in German also means "earn."

y German: *Werkmeister*. See above, p. 281, note o.

z Literally, "look through the fingers," a favorite phrase of Luther also for how God overlooks sin.

masters do not wish to be treated harshly by God but rather want many things to be overlooked through grace, so also they should treat their servants all the more gently and overlook some things, while at the same time making sure that their servants do right and learn to fear God.

Look at the good works a mistress and master can do and look at the fine way in which God constantly makes good works available to us in such variety and so directly that we have no need to inquire about them and can now ignore the other showy and popular works that people have dreamed up, for example, pilgrimages, building churches, acquiring indulgences, and the like. Here I should also mention that a wife should be subject to her husband as her superior, obey and yield to him, be silent, and let him be in the right as long as it is not against God. At the same time, a man should love his wife, let some things go, and not be too strict or exacting in dealing with her. Saints Peter and Paul said a great deal about this matter,[a] but it properly belongs to a longer treatment of the commandments and is easily grasped from these passages.

20. Everything we have said about these works is covered by two words: *obedience* and *solicitude*. Obedience is the duty of subjects, and solicitude is the duty of superiors, who should be diligent in ruling their subjects well, dealing with them kindly, and doing everything in their power to be useful and helpful to them. That is their way to heaven and the best work they can do on earth, more pleasing to God than if they would perform nothing but miracles. Therefore, St. Paul says in Rom. 12[:8], "Let the works of those in authority be solicitude." As if he were saying: "These individuals[b] are not led astray by what people with a different rank or walk of life are doing; they do not try to copy this or that work, whether glittering or drab; rather, they attend to their own walk of life and consider how they can be useful to those under their authority. They persist in that and refuse to be torn away even if heaven stood open before them or to

---

a   Eph. 5:22-25; Col. 3:18-19; 1 Pet. 3:5-7.

b   Singular in the original.

flee even if hell itself were running after them. That is the right road, which will take them to heaven."

Truly, those people, therefore, who attend only to themselves and their own walk of life and stand by them will quickly become people who are rich in good works, but so quietly and secretly that no one will see it but God. Now, however, we let all this go and instead one person runs to the Carthusians,[122] another here, another there, just as if good works and God's commandments were thrown in a corner and covered up. In Prov. 1[:20-21], on the contrary, it is written: "Wisdom cries out openly in the streets, in the midst of the people, and at the gates of the city." This demonstrates that good works are available in abundance everywhere, all the time, in all walks of life. Christ himself proclaimed it in Matt. 24[:23-26]: "When they tell you that Christ is here or he is there, do not believe them; when they say, 'Look, he is in the wilderness,' do not go out, or 'Look, he is hidden inside the house,' do not believe it. They are false prophets and false Christians."[c]

21. At the same time, obedience is the obligation of subjects, who with all diligence and thoroughness are to do or avoid whatever those over them demand, not allowing themselves to be sidetracked from this, regardless of what others are doing. They should never imagine they would be better off doing other good works—be it prayer or fasting or whatever it is called—that would divert them from carrying out their duties with careful and persistent effort.

Should it ever happen, however, as it often does, that temporal power and authority, whatever their titles, force subjects to act against God's commandment or keeps them from obeying it, then obedience ceases and duty is set aside. In that case, one must say what St. Peter said to the leaders of the Jews: "One must obey God more than mortals."[d] He did not say: "mortals should not be obeyed," for that would

122. A monastic order founded in 1084 in France and known for its strict vows of renunciation and silence.

---

c   The term "false Christians" appears in the Latin text.

d   Acts 5:29. The Latin text may be rendered either "rather than" or, as Luther does here, "more than."

be false, but "God . . . more than mortals." If a prince, for example, wanted to start a war but it was known that the cause was unjust, then no one should follow him or help him because God has commanded that we should not kill our neighbors or do them an injustice. Likewise if the prince commanded giving false testimony, robbing, lying, deceiving someone, and the like. One should instead let property, honor, and life go so that God's commandment may abide.

On the Fifth Commandment[e]

The first four commandments do their work on human reason. That is, they take human beings captive, rule them, and make them subjects, so that they do not rule themselves, think for themselves, or think too much of themselves but instead show humility and let themselves be led in order to protect against arrogance. The following commandments take up human desires and lusting in order to slay them.[123]

1. There are the angry and vengeful passions of which the fifth commandment speaks: "You shall not kill." The work of this commandment is very comprehensive, drives out vice, and is called gentleness. This gentleness is of two kinds. The first kind sparkles beautifully, but there is nothing behind it. We direct it to friends and to others who help and support us in matters that concern our property and reputation or who do not injure us in word or in deed. Such gentleness can also be expressed by irrational animals, lions and snakes, pagans, Jews, Turks, fools, murderers, and evil women.[124] All of them can be gentle and serene as long as one does what they want or leaves them in peace. Not a few people, deceived by such apparent gentleness, however, then try to justify and excuse their anger by saying: "I would not be angry if everyone left me in peace." Oh, sure, my dear! Under these circumstances the evil spirit would also be gentle if everything went its way. Sorrow and strife overwhelm you because they are meant to show you to yourself—how stuffed full of anger

123. Luther employs a basic philosophical distinction between intellect (reason) and will (desires).

124. Luther expresses typical disdain for outsiders to his community. The term "evil woman" often specifically referred either to prostitutes or witches.

e   Exod. 20:13; Deut. 5:17.

and malice you are. In this way, you are admonished to strive toward gentleness and to expel your anger.

The other kind of gentleness is good to the core and is revealed toward adversaries and enemies. It does not hurt them, does not take revenge; does not curse, insult, or spread lies about them; does not even wish bad things on them, even though they might have taken away property, reputation, body, friends—everything. Wherever possible, this gentleness returns good for evil, speaks well of them, wishes them the best, and prays for them. For Christ says in Matt. 5[:44]: "Return good for evil; pray for your persecutors and those who revile you." And Paul says in Rom. 12[:14]: "Bless those who curse you; do not curse them but treat them well."

2. Now see just how this precious and exalted work has disappeared among Christians! Nothing reigns more powerfully over all people but quarreling, war, strife, anger, hate, envy, gossip, cursing, blaspheming, doing injury, taking vengeance, and other expressions of anger in word and deed. Yet we go on celebrating feast days, hearing Mass, saying little prayers, endowing churches and [providing them with] ornaments that God has not commanded. We show off these works splendidly and extravagantly, as though we were the holiest Christians the world had ever seen. Meanwhile, using all these mirrors and facades, we allow God's commandment to perish to the point that no one realizes how near or far he [or she] is from gentleness and the fulfillment of this divine commandment, even though God said that those who keep the commandments will enter into eternal life, not those who do these other works.[f]

There is no one alive on earth to whom God does not give an indicator of their[g] own anger and iniquity, that is, by way of their enemies and adversaries, who harm their property, their honor, their bodies, or their friends. In this way, God tests whether or not anger is still present and whether or not they can be gracious to their enemies, speak well of them, treat them kindly, and intend them no harm. Given this,

f   See Matt. 19:16-17; Mark 10:17-19; Luke 18:18-20.

g   Singular in the original throughout this paragraph.

now let those come forth who ask what they should do in order to perform good works, please God, and be saved. Let them visualize their enemies and place them before the eyes of their hearts in order to bend and accustom themselves to thinking well of their enemies, wishing the best for them, caring and praying for them, and when the opportunity presents itself, speaking well of them and doing good to them. Whoever attempts this and does not have enough to do for an entire lifetime may prove me a liar and declare all this talk to be false. Since, however, God will have it this way and not be remunerated in any other way, what does it profit us to go around with great works that are not commanded and to ignore this command? Therefore, God says in Matt. 5[:22]: "If you are angry with a neighbor, you will be liable to judgment; those who say to their neighbors *racha* (that is, a cruel, angry, horrid form of abuse) are liable to the council; those who call their neighbors fools (that is, all kinds of cursing, swearing, insulting, gossiping) are liable to eternal fire." If angry words and thoughts are condemned so severely, how will the actions of the hands—beating, wounding, killing, injuring, wreaking damage, and the like—be judged?

3. Where a profound gentleness is present, the heart bewails every evil that happens to one's enemy. These are the genuine children and heirs of God, the brothers [and sisters] of Christ, who did the same for all of us on the holy cross. Thus we see that an upright judge sorrowfully pronounces a verdict on those who are guilty and is greatly pained by the death sentence required by law for such people. This deed appears as if it arose from anger and cruelty, but the gentleness is so profoundly good that it persists under the angry deeds; indeed, it wells up from the heart most powerfully just when it has to be angry and serious.

We must beware, however, lest we are gentle against God's honor and commandment. For it is written of Moses [Sir. 45:4] that he was the gentlest man on earth, and yet, after the Jews had worshiped the golden calf and angered God, he had many of them killed to placate God once again.[h] It

---

h   Exod. 32:28.

is not fitting, therefore, for the authorities to take it easy and allow sin to rule and for us to remain silent about this. I should not be so concerned about my property, my honor, or injury done to me that I become angry; but we must defend God's honor and commandment and guard against injury and injustice done to our neighbors—those who govern using the sword and others using words and rebukes, yet all filled with sorrow for the one who has earned such punishment.

This precious, fine, and sweet work can be learned easily wherever we do it in faith and exercise our faith in doing it. Just as faith does not doubt God's love in that it has a gracious God, so also it can easily be gracious and kind to our neighbors, no matter how seriously they have transgressed [against us], for we have committed even worse transgressions against God. Yes, it is but a short commandment, but it offers within it a long and great exercise for good works and faith.

The Sixth Commandment

"You shall not commit adultery" [i]

1. A good work is also commanded in this commandment. It includes many things, drives out many vices, and is called purity or chastity. About this much has been written and preached so that almost everyone knows about it, even if they do not take it to heart and practice it as diligently as they do the works that are not commanded. (We are quite ready to do what is not commanded and to leave undone what is commanded!) We observe that the world is full of shameful deeds of unchastity, scandalous sayings, fables, and ditties. Moreover, incentives daily pile up to indulge in gluttony, drunkenness, idleness, and excessive displays of jewelry and finery. Meanwhile, we carry on as if we were Christians when we have attended church, said our little

---

i   Exod. 20:14; Deut. 5:18.

prayers, and observed our fasts and feast days as if that were enough.

If, however, no other work than chastity were commanded, we would have our hands full obeying it alone. Unchastity is a very dangerous and rabid vice that infects all our members: the heart through our thoughts; the eyes in our looking; the ears through what we hear; the mouth in what we say; our hands, feet, and entire body through what we do. To keep it in check requires enormous work and effort. In this way, God's commandment teaches us what a formidable thing is involved in honest good works. Indeed, it is impossible out of our own powers even to conceive a good work, to say nothing about beginning to do it or bringing it to completion. According to St. Augustine, the struggle for chastity is for individual Christians[j] the hardest struggle of all simply because they must daily defend themselves against it without ceasing and seldom defeat it.[k] All the saints have bemoaned it and shed tears over it, as St. Paul says in Rom. 7[:18]: "I find within me, that is, in my flesh, nothing good."[125]

2. The work of chastity, should it endure, results in many other good works: fasting and moderation against gluttony and drunkenness; vigils and early rising against laziness and oversleeping; labor and effort against idleness. Gluttony, drinking to excess, oversleeping, laziness, and idleness are weapons of unchastity that can quickly overcome chastity. Over against these, the holy Apostle Paul [Rom. 13:12-13] lists fasting, vigilance, and labor as godly weapons that keep unchastity in check, although, as mentioned above, these very disciplines should go no further than to curb unchastity, not to damage one's health.

The strongest defense of all consists of prayer and the word of God. When evil lust stirs, a person should flee to prayer, beg God for mercy and aid, read and contemplate the gospel, and gaze on the suffering of Christ depicted there.

125. The comments in this section especially reflect Luther's situation as an Augustinian friar. Later comments in his 1521 tract, *The Judgment of Martin Luther on Monastic Vows* (LW 44:243–400], and elsewhere demonstrate how he reexamined his understanding of chastity in the years to come.

---

j   Singular in the original.

k   The statement is found in a sermon, still attributed to Augustine in Luther's day, but now assigned to pseudo-Augustine, *Sermon* 293 (MPL 39:2302).

Psalm 137[:9] says: "Blessed are those who seize the children of Babylon and smash them against a rock."[l] This means: as long as our evil thoughts are in their infancy and just beginning, run to the Lord Christ, who is a rock that will pulverize and destroy them.

Do you see? Each and every person will be completely swamped, find enough to do for oneself and be overwhelmed in him- or herself with countless good works. At present, however, no one uses praying, fasting, alertness, and labor to ward off vice; they are considered ends in themselves, even though they were instituted to accomplish the work of this commandment and to cleanse us more and more each day.

Others have identified more things to avoid: soft beds and clothing; expensive jewelry; and the company, conversation, and eyeing of women or men (as the case may be) along with similar things that promote chastity. In such matters, no one can prescribe a binding rule or a fixed amount. All individuals[m] must judge for themselves which of these things—in what amount and used for how long—promote chastity. Then they must choose and keep at them. If they cannot, for a while they should be given into the care of another, who will hold them to what they have chosen until they are able to control themselves. Long ago, cloisters were established for this reason, namely, to teach young people discipline and purity.

3. More obviously than for any other commandment, a sound and robust faith helps in doing this work. For that reason, Isa. 11[:5] states: "Faith is the girdle of his loins," that is, a guardian of chastity; for those who live expecting all grace to come from God are well pleased by spiritual purity. For this reason, they are able to resist more easily the unchastity of the flesh, and in this faith the Spirit tells them how to avoid evil thoughts and everything else that stands

---

l Luther uses a not unusual allegorical interpretation of this psalm, one that the authors of the *Confutation of the Augsburg Confession* also used as support for clerical celibacy. See Robert Kolb and James A. Nestingen, eds., *Sources and Contexts of The Book of Concord* (Minneapolis: Fortress Press, 2001), 126.

m Singular in the original.

in the way of chastity. Just as faith in divine love lives continually and effects every good work, so it never omits the Spirit's admonitions about everything that either pleases or displeases God, as St. John says in his letter [1 John 2:27]: "You have no need of anyone to instruct you, for God's anointing," meaning God's Spirit, "teaches you all things."

We should not despair when we cannot rid ourselves quickly of such attacks, and we should not imagine that we will be free of them as long as we live. We should consider them as nothing other than inducements and admonitions to pray, fast, do vigils, labor, and practice other things, in order to suppress the flesh and especially to promote and practice faith in God. The chastity to prize is not the kind that comes easily, but rather the kind that takes to the field to battle unchastity and to drive out all the poison that the flesh and evil spirit have injected. Saint Peter says [1 Pet. 2:11]: "I admonish you to keep away from carnal lust and desire that constantly fight against the soul." And St. Paul in Rom. 6[:12] says: "Do not give in to the passions of the body." These verses and others like them demonstrate that no one lacks sinful lust but should and must resist it every day. Although this brings with it unrest and unpleasantness, to God it is still an acceptable work, and for us that should be our consolation and our sufficiency. Those who think they can control such attacks by giving in to lust only make it burn hotter. Even though it may subside for a while, it returns at another time stronger than before and finds human nature weaker than ever.

The Seventh Commandment

"You shall not steal" [n]

[1.] This commandment, too, includes a work that consists of many good works and opposes many vices. In German, it is called "generosity." This is a work that involves each and

---

[n] Exod. 20:15; Deut. 5:19.

every individual being ready to use whis or her possessions to help and serve. It fights against not only theft and robbery but any damage to worldly possessions that one person can inflict on another, for example, through greed, usury, overcharging, cheating, selling inferior goods, or using false weights and measures. Who can recount all the clever new tricks that increase every day in business? Everyone searches for an advantage to the disadvantage of others; they forget the law that says [Matt. 7:12]: "Whatever you wish others to do to you, do also to them." All who keep this rule in mind in their crafts, business, and trade with the neighbor will soon find how they should buy and sell, take and give, lend and give at no charge, make promises and keep them, and the like. When we observe the nature of the world, to what extent avarice prevails everywhere, we not only should have enough to do nourishing ourselves with God and honorable [living], but also we also should become filled with dread and fright at this perilous and miserable life that is so weighed down by, besmeared with, and captive to anxiety about daily sustenance and dishonest searching after it.

2. Not in vain does the wise man say [Sir. 31:8-9]: "Blessed is the rich person who is found blameless, who does not run after gold or put trust in its treasures. Who is that person that we may offer praise, for a miracle has been accomplished in that life?" It is as if the author wanted to say, such people are very rare or do not exist at all. Indeed, there are very few people who notice or admit to such addiction to gold; for avarice has a very attractive and respectable cover, namely, bodily nourishment and other natural necessities. Under that cover, greed acts without limits or bounds. Thus, as Sirach says, those who try to live without being touched by greed must indeed accomplish miraculous signs and wonders in their lives.

Now consider this. Those individuals*o* who want to perform not only good works but also miracles, which God praises and that please him, what else would they need to

---

o   Singular in the original throughout this paragraph.

investigate? Let them examine themselves and make sure they do not run after gold or set their trust in money, but let the gold run after them and the money wait upon their pleasure. If they avoid setting their heart on it or liking it too much, then they are indeed generous miracle workers and blessed ones, as Job 31[:24] states: "I have never relied on gold nor let money be my comfort and confidence." And Ps. 62[:10]: "If riches increase, do not set your heart on them." Christ teaches the same thing in Matt. 6[:31-32]: "We are not to worry about what we eat or drink or how we will clothe ourselves; for God knows what we need and provides it all."

Some people say: "Okay, rely on God, do not worry, and see whether or not a roast hen flies into your mouth."[126] On the contrary, I am not saying we should not work or look for food, but that we should not worry or be greedy or doubt we will have enough. For in Adam, we have all been sentenced to hard work, as God says [Gen. 3:19]: "In the sweat of your face you shall eat your bread." And Job 5[:7]: "As birds are born to fly, so human beings are born to work."[p] As birds fly around without feeling worried or greedy, so we should work without worry and avarice. If you are anxious and greedy to such an extent that you are waiting for a roast hen to fly into your mouth, then be anxious and greedy to see if you are fulfilling God's commandment and going to be saved.

3. Faith by itself teaches the work of this commandment. For if the heart anticipates God's favor and relies on it, how is it possible for faith to be greedy and full of cares? It must be certain beyond any doubt that God receives us. For this reason faith does not cling to any money at all but instead uses it with joyful generosity for the benefit of others—knowing all along that it will have enough for any needs because the God in whom it trusts will never deceive or forsake it, as Ps. 37[:25] says: "I have been young and now am old, yet I have not seen" a believer who trusts in God, that is, "a righteous person forsaken or such a one's children

126. Luther is referring to what happens in a popular medieval tale about a land where roasted fowl fly directly into one's mouth and fried fish jump from the water to one's feet. See p. 259, n. 5 above.

---

p   Luther cites the Vulgate, which has "birds" in place of "sparks" (NRSV).

begging bread."[q] This is why the only sin that the Apostle [Paul] calls idolatry is greed [Col. 3:5], because it is the crudest example of not trusting God and expecting more benefit from wealth than from God. Through trust God is truly honored or dishonored, as I said earlier.[r]

Indeed, in this commandment one can clearly see how all good works must arise from and be done in faith. For everyone can see without a doubt that the cause of avarice is mistrust, while the cause of generosity is faith because the person who trusts God is generous and does not have doubts about not having enough at any time. And vice versa: a person is greedy and anxious because of not trusting God. Just as faith is the master artisan[s] and driving force behind the good work of generosity in this commandment, so it is with all the other commandments. Without such faith, generosity accomplishes nothing but seems rather like a careless waste of money.

4. Here it is also important to realize that this same generosity must be extended to enemies and opponents. For as Christ himself teaches in Luke 6[:32-34]: "What kind of good deed is it if you are generous only to your friends? For wicked people do the same for their friends." Even irrational animals are kind and generous to their own species. A Christian, however, must go further and show generosity to those who have not earned it, to evildoers, enemies, and ungrateful folk, and like the heavenly Father "let the sun rise on the evil and on the good and send rain on the grateful and the ungrateful."[t]

Here it becomes clear how difficult it is to do good works according to God's commandment and how human nature resists, squirms, and stalls because it much prefers its own easier, self-chosen works. Therefore, try approaching your

---

q   Luther places his interpretive gloss in front of the biblical text ("a righteous person").

r   See Luther's treatment of the second commandment, above, p. 269f.

s   German: *Werkmeister*. See above, p.281, note o.

t   Matt. 5:45.

enemies, who show no gratitude, and do good to them. Then you will see how far you are from obeying this commandment and how you will have to work at practicing this work your whole life long. When your enemies need your aid and you fail to help them even though you could, that is just the same as if you had stolen from them, because you are obligated to help them. Thus St. Ambrose says: "Feed the hungry, for if you do not, then you have slain them insofar as it was in your power."*u* Works of mercy belong to this commandment, and Christ will ask you about them at the Last Day.[127] Nevertheless, princes and cities should see to it that vagrants, pilgrims,*v* and other nonresident beggars are either banned or allowed residency with proper "restrictions and ordinances,"*w* so that troublemakers posing as beggars are not permitted to get away with their drifting and villainy, of which there is plenty. I have said more about the works of this commandment in my sermon on usury.[128]

The Eighth Commandment

*"You shall not bear false witness against your neighbor"*x*

[1.] This commandment appears trivial at first but is in fact so vast that whoever would keep it correctly must stake everything—body and life, goods and reputation, friends and all possessions—on it. And yet it involves only the work of one small bodily member: the tongue. In German, it is

127. "Works of mercy" is a technical term for the works listed in the parable of the sheep and the goats in Matt. 25:35-36.

128. The "large" tract on usury (1520: WA 6:36-60). In the autumn of 1519 Luther had composed a much shorter essay on usury, which he revised and expanded for publication in early 1520 not long before he began to write the *Treatise on Good Works*. In 1524 the expanded treatise on usury was reissued together with a new essay on business practices and monopolies under the title *Trade and Usury* (LW 45:231-310; WA 15:279-313).

---

u Cited by Luther from medieval canon law, where it is listed with citations from Ambrose of Milan. According to MLStA 2:85. n. 764, it is found in Anselm of Canterbury (c. 1033-1109), citing Polycarp (69-155), and in many other medieval sources, including Bernard of Clairvaux and Gabriel Biel (c. 1420-1495).

v Literally, "*Jakobsbrüder*" (or James's brothers), that is, pilgrims allegedly on their way to or from the shrine of St. James at Compostela in northwestern Spain.

w German: *Masse und Ordnung*, a technical legal phrase of the sixteenth century, often found in city ordinances of the time.

x Exod. 20:16; Deut. 5:20.

called speaking the truth and refuting lies wherever necessary. Thus, many of the tongue's evil works are forbidden here: both those that happen through speaking and those that occur in silence. Through speaking, for example, when someone has a fraudulent case in a court of law and tries to defend it with falsehoods or to trick one's neighbor with deceit—using anything to make one's own case look better and stronger while passing over in silence and downplaying anything that would help the good case of the neighbor. With such behavior, however, these individuals are not treating the neighbor as they would like the neighbor to treat them.[y] Some people act that way out of selfishness, and others do it to avoid damages or disgrace, but either way they are seeking what they want more than God's commandment. As an excuse, they use the saying, "Vigilanti iura subveniunt," (the law helps those who are vigilant),[z] as if they were not obligated to watch out for their neighbor's case as much as for their own. Thus, they intentionally allow their neighbors' case, which they know is just, to be lost. This outrage is so common that I fear no legal judgment or action can take place without one party or the other sinning against this commandment. Even if they cannot succeed in carrying out their intentions, they still had the unjust desire and intention in wanting the just case of their neighbor to lose and their own fraudulent one to be upheld. This sin is especially prevalent in cases where the other party is a big shot[a] or an enemy, because a person wants to take revenge on an enemy and no one wants to antagonize a big shot. Out come the flattery and the smooth talk or even just silence about the truth. No one will risk falling from grace or favor, being injured, or risking any danger for the sake of the truth, and consequently God's commandment must founder. That is

---

y   See Matt. 7:12. Singular in the original.

z   An adage from jurisprudence, often cited by Luther. See MLStA 2:86, n. 776. A longer form (in both Latin and German) reads: "Law is written for the vigilant not for the sleeping." See Wander, 3:1520, n. 46.

a   German: *grosse Hansen* ("big Johns").

pretty much the way the world runs, and those who would resist it have their hands full with good works fulfilled simply by using the tongue. In addition, how many people let themselves be silenced from telling the truth by gifts and bribes, so that in every respect it is truly a noble, great, and rare work for a person not to bear false witness against one's neighbor.

2. Beyond that, however, is a still greater witness of the truth in which we must fight against the evil spirits.[129] And it arises not because of worldly goods but for the sake of the gospel and the truth of the faith, which the evil spirit has never been able to tolerate, and therefore it unceasingly induces the most powerful among the people to oppose the gospel and to persecute it to the point that one can scarcely withstand them. About this Ps. 82[:3-4] states: "Rescue the needy from the power of the unjust and help the forsaken maintain the justice of their cause." The spiritual prelates[130] are at fault for the fact that such persecution has now become rare. They have not emphasized the gospel but have allowed it to be forgotten. In this way, they buried the very thing that caused the persecution and made this witness necessary. In place of the gospel, they teach their own laws and whatever else pleases them. The devil can now remain quiet because, by triumphing over the gospel, he has also crushed faith in Christ so that everything is going according to his plan. If, however, the gospel is emphasized and heard once again, the whole world will assuredly rouse itself and rebel—the majority of the kings, princes, bishops, teachers, clergy, and everything high and mighty will oppose it and become enraged. This has always happened when the word of God comes to light because the world cannot tolerate what comes from God. This is proven in Christ, who was and is the noblest, dearest, and best that God has. Yet the world not only failed to receive him[b] but also persecuted him more hideously than anything else that God ever sent. As in his time and at all times, only a few stand up for divine truth and risk life and limb, reputation and possessions and

129. What follows is a thinly veiled description for Luther's readers of his own experience.

130. Especially bishops and abbots or heads of orders, but Luther could mean all clergy.

---

b See John 1:11.

everything they have, as Christ himself promised [Matt. 24:9-10]: "Everyone will hate you for my name's sake," and "I will be a stumbling block for many." If this truth had been attacked by peasants, shepherds, stable boys, and unimportant people, who would not have been ready to profess and bear witness to it? But when the same truth is attacked by the pope and bishops along with princes and kings, everyone disappears, remains silent, and becomes a hypocrite, in order not to lose their possessions, the approval of others, their reputation, or their lives.

3. Why do people do that? Because they have no faith in God and expect from God nothing good for themselves. Where this confidence and faith are present, there is also a courageous, valiant, and dauntless heart that risks everything and stands by the truth though risking one's neck or station in life,[131] even against pope and kings, as we see that those precious martyrs once did. For such a heart remains content and gentle because it has a God that shows grace and favor, and thus it disdains the favor, graciousness, kindness, and honor coming from others, letting go of or taking in stride all transient things, as Ps. 15[:4] says: "This one despises those who despise God and honors those who fear God," that is, such a heart does not fear tyrants or the mighty who persecute the truth and despise God but disregards and despises them. At the same time, this same heart supports, stands by, watches over, and honors those who are persecuted for the truth and fear God more than human powers. It does not care who might disapprove, as Heb. 11[:27] says of Moses: "He stood by his brothers despite the mighty king of Egypt."

Look here! In this commandment, you will once again see that faith must be the master artisan[c] of this work, because without faith no one is bold enough to do it. Hence all works rest in faith, as has been said often enough. For apart from this faith all works are dead, no matter how much they gleam and call themselves good. Just as no one

---

131. German: *es gelt hals odder mantel,* literally, "it is worth neck or cloak." This unique saying in Luther is translated in the 1521 Latin version as *"sive capitis, sive pallii sit periculum"* (literally, "let there be danger to the head or cape"). The pallium often referred to a sign of episcopal office, although it could even refer to a monk's or friar's habit.

---

c German: *Werkmeister.* See above, p. 281, note *o.*

This engraving is the last in a series of twelve illustrating
the consecration of a bishop. The pallium is a long
woolen cloth embroidered with six small black crosses
sent to the bishop by the pope. The ceremony of bestowal
of the pallium must take place in the new bishop's own diocese.
Here the new bishop kneels before the presiding bishop,
who places the pallium over his chasuble.

does the work of this commandment without a firm and fearless reliance on God's favor, so no one does any work of all the other commandments without this same faith. Using this commandment, individuals[d] can easily test and determine whether or not they are Christians and believe in Christ the right way and whether they do good works or not. Now we realize how the all-powerful God has placed before us our Lord Jesus Christ not only as the one in whom we should confidently believe but also as an example of this very confidence and of such good works, so that we might trust him, follow him, and abide forever in him, as he says in John 14[:6]: "I am the way, the truth, and the life," the way on which we follow him, the truth that we believe in him, and the life that we live eternally in him.

From all of this, it is now obvious that all those works that have not been commanded are perilous and easy to identify: building and decorating churches, going on pilgrimages, and all the many others that are described in detail in canon law.[132] They lead astray, burden, and corrupt the world, create anxious consciences, and they have silenced and enfeebled faith. Since people[e] have their hands full with obeying the commandments God has given, even if they used all their strength and neglected everything else, and still cannot do all these good works, why should people look for other works that are neither necessary nor commanded and ignore the ones that are?

The last two commandments,[f] which forbid the evil bodily appetites, lust, and envy of worldly goods are clear in themselves and remain in place without harming the neighbor. Even so these things remain right up to the grave, and the internal struggle against them remains until death. For that reason, in Rom. 7[:7] St. Paul merged these two com-

132. Canon law, a collection of papal and conciliar decrees, included rules for penitential acts of satisfaction.

d   Singular in the original.
e   Singular in the original.
f   "You shall not covet your neighbor's house; you shall not covet your
     neighbor's wife, or male or female slave, or ox, or donkey, or anything
     that belongs to your neighbor" (Exod. 20:17; Deut. 5:21).

mandments into one and set one goal for them that we do not reach but can only envision until death. No one has ever been so holy that no evil inclination was felt when the cause and the stimulus were right there. For original sin is by nature innate in us. It can be dampened but never rooted out except by bodily death, which for that reason is both useful and desirable. May God help us. Amen.

Printed at Wittenberg in the press of Melchior Lotter the Younger in the year 1520.

An den Christlichenn
Adel teutscher Nation:
von des Christlichen
stantes besserung:
D. Martinus
Luther.

Durch yhn selbs ge-
mehret vnd corrigirt.

Buittemberg.

Title page of *Address to the Christian Nobility*. This historiated title page
border features the arms of the city of Wittenberg at the head and
the crest of the printer, Melchior Lotter the Younger, at the foot.
The woodcut has been attributed to Lucas Cranach the Elder.

To the Christian Nobility
of the German Nation Concerning the

Improvement of the
Christian Estate

1520

JAMES M. ESTES

INTRODUCTION

This treatise is Luther's first appeal to secular authorities for help with the reform of the church. For more than two years, starting with the *95 Theses* in 1517, Luther's appeals for reform had been addressed to the ecclesiastical hierarchy, whose divinely imposed responsibility for such things he took for granted. By the early months of 1520, however, Luther had come to the conclusion that nothing could be expected from Rome but intransigent opposition to reform of any sort.[a] It was only at this point that he began to write of the need for secular rulers to intervene with measures that would clear the way for ecclesiastical reform. In the *Treatise on Good Works* (in print by 8 June 1520), Luther argued that the abuses of "the spiritual authorities" were causing "Christendom to go to ruin," and that, in this emergency, anyone who was able to do so should help in whatever way possible. Specifically, "The best and indeed the only remaining remedy would be for kings, princes, the nobility, cities, and communities

---

a   See James M. Estes, *Peace, Order, and the Glory of God: Secular Authority and the Church in the Thought of Luther and Melanchthon, 1518–1559* (Leiden: Brill, 2005), 7–17. See also Brecht 1:369–79.

1. The Dominican, Silvestro Mazzolini, known as Sylvester Prierias (after his birthplace Priero in Piedmont), was "master of the sacred palace" at the Roman Curia, which meant that he was the pope's theological adviser and censor of books. Given charge of the Luther case in 1518, he became Luther's first Italian literary opponent, publishing four polemical treatises against him in the years 1518–1520. The third of these, the *Epitome*, was published at Perugia in 1519.

2. See below, p. 376. Offers of support, including armed protection, received in the early months of 1520 from the imperial knights Ulrich von Hutten (1488–1523), Franz von Sickingen (1481–1523), and Silvester von Schaumberg (c. 1466–1534) appear to have given Luther a sense of political support outside Saxony that encouraged him to hope that an appeal to the nobility might well produce a positive response; see Brecht 1:369–70.

to take the first step in the matter so that the bishops and clergy, who are now fearful, would have cause to follow."[b] He made the same point in the treatise *On the Papacy in Rome* (in print by 26 June 1520), asserting that "the horrible disgrace of Christendom" has gone so far "that there is no more hope on earth except with secular authority."[c]

Meanwhile, just as the *Treatise on Good Works* was coming off the presses, Luther received a copy of the *Epitome of a Response to Martin Luther* (*Epitoma responsionis ad Martinum Lutherum*) by the papal theologian Silvester Prierias (c. 1426–1523).[1] The *Epitome* was a bold assertion of papal absolutism, insisting that papal authority was superior to that of a council and even to Scripture itself. To Luther, this "hellish book" was conclusive evidence that the Antichrist was reigning in Rome and that there was no possibility of a reform initiated or approved by it. It was therefore necessary to abandon "unhappy, hopeless, blasphemous Rome" and seek reform elsewhere.[d]

It was in this frame of mind that on 7 June 1520 Luther announced to Georg Spalatin (1484–1545) his intention "to issue a broadside to [Emperor] Charles and the nobility of Germany against the tyranny and baseness of the Roman Curia."[e] By 23 June, the "broadside" had grown into a major treatise, the manuscript of which Luther sent to his friend Nicholas von Amsdorf (1483–1565), together with the letter that became the preface to the treatise when it was published in mid-August.[f] In the letter, Luther describes the treatise as "a few points on the matter of the improvement of the state of Christendom, to be laid before the Christian nobility of the German nation, in the hope that God may help his church through the laity, since the clergy, to whom this task more properly belongs, have grown quite irresponsible."[2] What could the laity do to remedy the failure of the clergy?

b   See above, p. 342.

c   LW 39:102–3.

d   WA 6:328–29 (Luther's preface to the annotated edition of the *Epitome* that he published in mid-June 1520).

e   WA Br 2:120.

f   See below, pp. 376–78.

Luther's answer was that the leaders of the lay community could summon a church council.[g] But how could that be done against the will of the pope? Luther's answer to that question was a fundamental contribution to the thought of the Reformation.

The treatise itself is divided into three sections. In the first, Luther attacks the "three walls" behind which the "Romanists" have shielded themselves from reform: (1) the claim that spiritual authority is higher than secular authority and therefore not subject to secular jurisdiction; (2) the claim that the pope alone has the authority to interpret the Scriptures; and (3) the claim that only the pope can summon a council. The second section is a brief discussion of measures to be discussed at councils to curb the "thievery, trickery, and tyranny" of Rome. The third and by far the longest of the three sections, which appears to have been tacked on at the last moment, is a set of twenty-seven proposals for action by either secular authority or a council (as appropriate) for improving "the dreadful state of affairs" in Christendom. In these last two sections, Luther denounces a long list of ecclesiastical abuses, particularly those of the Roman Curia, which would have been familiar to his readers. Many of them are taken directly from the lists of "*Gravamina* [grievances] of the German Nation Against Rome" that had been brought forward at virtually every meeting of the imperial diet since the middle of the fifteenth century, most recently at the Diet of Augsburg in 1518.[h] In so doing, Luther identified himself with the conciliarist, patriotically German, anti-Roman sentiment that pervaded German ecclesiastical and political life at the time. This was well calculated to secure widespread popular approval for the treatise, but

---

g   For Luther's suspicions about church councils, see p. 341 above.

h   See Martin Luther, *Sämmtliche Werke*, ed. Johann Georg Walch et al., 2d ed., vol. 15: *Reformations-Schriften, erste Abtheilung, zur Reformationshistorie gehörige Documente: A. Wider die Papisten aus den Jahren 1517 bis 1524.* (St. Louis: Concordia, 1899), 453–71. For the more extensive list presented at the Diet of Worms in 1521, see RTA 2:661–718.

it is Luther's attack on the three walls that accounts for the enduring importance of the treatise. In that attack he redefines the relationship between clergy and laity and elaborates the view of the role of secular government in church reform to which he would adhere virtually without change for the remainder of the 1520s, before adapting it to new circumstances in the 1530s.

To the Christian Nobility has often been described as the work in which Luther called upon the German princes to assume responsibility for the reform of the church.[i] In fact, however, the most striking feature of the treatise is Luther's refusal to attribute to secular rulers any authority at all in matters of faith or church governance. Although the classical formulation of what is sometimes labeled the "Doctrine of the Two Kingdoms" was still three years in the future,[j] Luther was already clearly committed to the view that secular authority extends only to the secular realm of human affairs and that it has no jurisdiction in the spiritual realm. As he put it in the *Treatise on Good Works*, secular jurisdiction is limited to matters covered by the Second Table of the Decalogue (the commandments regulating the conduct of human beings toward one another), and that it has nothing to do with the First Table (the commandments regulating the duties of human beings toward God).[k] How, then, could Luther justify any role at all for secular government in the reform of the church? The answer, already prefigured in the *Treatise on Good Works* and *The Papacy at Rome* and now fully elaborated in *To the Christian Nobility*, was necessarily somewhat complicated.

---

i   See, e.g., John Dillenberger's introduction to the treatise in *Martin Luther: Selections from His Writings* (New York: Random House, 1961), 403: "In this work of 1520 . . . Luther calls upon the ruling class to reform the Church, since the Church will not reform itself." See also Roland Bainton, *Here I Stand: A Life of Martin Luther* (New York/ Nashville: Abingdon, 1950), 152: "[B]y what right, the modern reader might well inquire, might Luther call upon [the German nobility] to reform the Church?"

j   In the treatise *On Secular Authority, To What Extent It Should Be Obeyed* (LW 45:75–129).

k   See above, pp. 342–44.

First of all, many of the most glaring ecclesiastical abuses in need of correction fell into the category of secular crimes (robbery and theft) committed by "spiritual" persons (the clergy and monks). Thus defined, such abuses (e.g., raising money by peddling indulgences) could be viewed as the direct responsibility of secular rulers, to whom God had assigned the duty of protecting the goods and property of their subjects. One had only to dispose of the claimed exemption of "spiritual" persons from secular jurisdiction. "Spiritual" crimes, on the other hand, were a more difficult matter. Given his definition of the limits of secular authority, Luther could not appeal to secular rulers *as such* to deal with such matters. He could, however, argue that, *as baptized Christians*, secular rulers shared in the right and duty of all Christians to interpret Scripture and to adhere to the correct interpretation if the pope errs. This meant that in an emergency with which the pope could not or would not deal, they shared in the right and duty of all baptized Christians to do what they could to restore ecclesiastical authority to its proper function. It meant further that, *because of their commanding position in society*, they had a special obligation to do so. On this basis, Luther could appeal to the emperor and the German princes to serve their fellow Christians in an emergency by summoning a church council, in which "bishops and clergy," hitherto intimidated and frustrated by papal opposition to reform, would be free to do their duty to provide reform. The aim, in other words, was to restore the proper functioning of established ecclesiastical authority, not to transfer it to secular rulers.[1]

The response to Luther's appeal to "the Christian nobility of the German nation" came at the Diet of Worms in 1521. Instead of summoning a reform council, the assembled princes outlawed Luther and his followers. But the reform movement continued to spread rapidly, particularly in cities and towns, and Luther defended the right of such communities to reform themselves despite the objections of

---

1   See Estes, *Peace, Order, and the Glory of God*, 17–30.

Luther is shown as an Augustinian monk debating the pope,
a cardinal, a bishop, and another monk.

ecclesiastical authority.[m] When, moreover, hostile Catholic governments tried to suppress these reform efforts, Luther angrily denounced them for arrogating to themselves a power in spiritual matters that was not theirs by right.[n] By the late 1520s, however, the spontaneous spread of the Reformation in Saxony had reached the point at which church life urgently needed to be regulated in the interest of unity and good order. But Saxony had no bishop to provide the

m See LW 39:305–14 (*That a Christian Assembly or Congregation Has the Right and Power to Judge All Teaching and to Call, Appoint, and Dismiss Teachers, Established and Proven by Scripture*, 1523).

n *On Secular Authority* (1523).

necessary leadership. In this emergency, Luther once again appealed to secular authority for help with ecclesiastical reform, using essentially the same arguments that he had advanced in 1520. He called on the elector, in his capacity as Christian brother, to serve his fellow Christians by appointing an ecclesiastical visitation commission that would establish uniformity of doctrine and practice on the churches in his domains.[o] Since, however, Luther expected the elector *as prince* to enforce the established uniformity, it was clear that his distinction between the prince *as prince* (secular authority *as such*), without authority in spiritual matters, and the prince as Christian brother, entitled to intervene only in emergencies, no longer fit the situation as well as it had at the beginning of the decade. Luther himself was aware of this and, starting in 1530, he rethought his position in conversation with Philipp Melanchthon (1497–1560). By 1534 he and Melanchthon were in agreement that, the necessary distinction between secular and spiritual authority notwithstanding, it was the duty of a Christian prince to establish and maintain true religion among his subjects.[p]

---

o   LW 40:263–320.

p   See Estes, *Peace, Order, and the Glory of God*, ch. 5. In Luther's case, the key texts are his commentaries on Psalms 82 (1530) and 101 (1534–35), particularly the latter; see LW 13:51–60, 166–201.

Portrait of Nicholaus von Amsdorf, whom Luther consecrated as bishop of Naumburg in the 1540s, by the German painter and printmaker Peter Gottlandt.

3. The present translation is a twice-revised version of that by Charles M. Jacobs in *Works of Martin Luther with Introductions and Notes*, ed. Luther Reed et al., 6 vols. (Philadelphia: Holman, 1915), 2:61–164. The first revision was by James Atkinson for LW 44:123–217. The German text used is that of MLStA 2:96–167, edited by Karlheinz Blaschke. Much information from Blaschke's notes has found its way into this translation. See also WA 6:381–469, and Karl Benrath, ed., *An den christlichen Adel deutscher Nation von des christlichen Standes Besserung* (Halle: Verein für Reformationsgeschichte, 1884), referred to below as Benrath.

TO THE CHRISTIAN NOBILITY OF THE GERMAN NATION CONCERNING THE IMPROVEMENT OF THE CHRISTIAN ESTATE, 1520[3,4]

JESUS.[q]

TO THE ESTEEMED and Reverend Master, Nicholas von Amsdorf, Licentiate of Holy Scripture, and Canon of Wittenberg, my special and kind friend, from Doctor Martin Luther.

The grace and peace of God be with you, esteemed, reverend, and dear sir and friend.[r]

The time for silence is past, and the time to speak has come, as Eccles. [3:7] says. I am carrying out our intention to put together a few points on the matter of the improvement of the state of Christendom, to be laid before the Christian nobility of the German nation, in the hope that God may help his church through the laity, since the clergy, to whom this task more properly belongs, have grown quite irresponsible. I am sending the whole thing to you, reverend sir, [that you may give] an opinion on it and, where necessary, improve it.

I know full well that I shall not escape the charge of presumption, because I, a despised, cloistered person, venture to address such high and great estates on such weighty mat-

q See above, p. 264, n. 11.

r An early example of Luther's use of a "Pauline greeting" (cf. 1 Cor. 1:3) here combined with an older form where he simply employed the word "Jesus." By 1522 this new form, an indication of identification of his office with that of the Apostle Paul, would completely replace the other.

ters, as if there were nobody else in the world except Doctor Luther to take up the cause of Christendom and give advice to such highly competent people. I make no apologies no matter who demands them. Perhaps I owe my God and the world another work of folly. I intend to pay my debt honestly. And if I succeed, I shall for the time being become a

A fool is pictured with a feather hat,
about to trip himself with a cane; one shoe on
and one off; and three children running about him.

court jester. And if I fail, I still have the one advantage that no one need buy me a cowl or provide me with a cockscomb.[5] It is a question of who will put the bells on whom.[s] I must fulfill the proverb, "Whatever the world does, a monk must be in the picture, even if he has to be painted in."[t] More than once a fool has spoken wisely, and wise men have often been arrant fools. Paul says, "He who wishes to be wise must

4. In the German phrase *der christliche Stand* ("the Christian Estate"), the word *stand* can mean "estate" as used in such phrases as "estates of the realm" or "imperial estates," but it can also mean "status" in the sense of standing or rank, as well as "state" in the sense of condition or walk of life. Nowhere in the treatise does Luther address himself to a Christian or "spiritual" estate that stands apart from another, presumably secular or worldly estate in society. Indeed, one of his principal arguments is that all baptized Christians are of the same "spiritual status" and that there is no distinction in this regard between clergy and laity (see below, pp. 381–83). Moreover, the list of reforms that he proposes requires action by both spiritual authority and secular authority, which he views as Christian. "The Christian estate," in other words, is the entire body of Christians viewed as one entity, often referred to as Christendom, in which all are of the same spiritual rank or standing. Luther finds that entity to be in terrible condition and thus sorely in need of reform. Bertram Lee Woolf captured this meaning when he took the liberty of turning *von des christlichen Standes Besserung* into "as to the Amelioration of the State of Christendom"; see Woolf, *Reformation Writings of Martin Luther* (New York: Philosophical Library, 1953), 101.

5. A cowl and a red rooster's comb were traditional signs of a clown or jester. Luther did not need them because he was already equipped with a monk's cowl and tonsure.

s   I.e., who will declare whom to be a clown.
t   The proverb *monachus semper praesens* is attested in Wander, 3:703, n. 130.

6. Luther's authority to speak on controversial matters of doctrine and practice derived from his status as a doctor of theology. In the process of being awarded his doctorate (19 October 1512), he took a solemn oath to teach the Holy Scriptures faithfully and to combat heresy and error. With the doctorate, moreover, he acquired full academic freedom to discuss without hindrance all questions of scriptural interpretation. See Brecht 1:126–27.

7. During the Great Schism in the Western church (1378–1417), when there were two (and, for a time, three) rival popes, and ecclesiastical abuses (most of them rooted in the ruthless exploitation of papal authority to raise money) got worse, a sustained attempt was made to deal with the situation by means of a general council. Canonists argued that supreme authority in the church rested not with the pope, but with the universal community of believers, and that in an emergency that authority could be exercised by a council, which could be convoked by some authority (e.g., the emperor) other than the pope. The resulting "conciliar movement" assigned to a general council the task of restoring the unity of Christendom under one pope and of reforming the church, beginning with a thorough reform of the papacy itself. The Council of Constance (1414–1417) managed to restore unity under one undisputed pope, but it did not successfully address the problem of church reform. There followed a struggle

become a fool" [1 Cor. 3:18]. Moreover, since I am not only a fool, but also a sworn doctor of Holy Scripture, I am glad for the opportunity to fulfill my doctor's oath,[6] even in the guise of a fool.

I beg you, give my apologies to those who are moderately intelligent, for I do not know how to earn the grace and favor of the super-intelligent. I have often sought to do so with the greatest pains, but from now on I neither desire nor value their favor. God help us to seek not our own glory but his alone. Amen.

At Wittenberg, in the monastery of the Augustinians, on the eve of St. John Baptist [June 23] in the year fifteen hundred and twenty.

To His Most Illustrious, Most Mighty, and Imperial Majesty, and to the Christian Nobility of the German Nation, from Doctor Martin Luther.

Grace and power from God, Most Illustrious Majesty, and most gracious and dear lords.

It is not from sheer impertinence or rashness that I, one poor man, have taken it upon myself to address your worships. All the estates of Christendom, particularly in Germany, are now oppressed by distress and affliction, and this has stirred not only me but everybody else to cry out time and time again and to pray for help. It has even compelled me now at this time to cry aloud that God may inspire someone with his Spirit to lend a helping hand to this distressed and wretched nation. Often the councils have made some pretense at reformation, but their attempts have been cleverly frustrated by the guile of certain men, and things have gone from bad to worse.[7] With God's help I intend to expose the wiles and wickedness of these men, so that they are shown up for what they are and may never again be so obstructive and destructive. God has given us a young man of noble birth as our ruler,[8] thus awakening great hope of good in many hearts. Presented with such an opportunity we ought to apply ourselves and use this time of grace profitably.

The first and most important thing to do in this matter is to prepare ourselves in all seriousness. We must not start something by trusting in great power or human reason, even if all the power in the world were ours. For God cannot and will not suffer that a good work begin by relying upon one's own power and reason. He dashes such works to the ground; they do no good at all. As it says in Ps. 33[:16], "No king is saved by his great might and no lord is saved by the greatness of his strength." I fear that this is why the good emperors Frederick (I) Barbarossa and Frederick II and many other German emperors, even though all the world feared them, were in former times shamefully oppressed and trodden underfoot by the popes.[9] It may be that they relied on their own might more than on God, and therefore had to fall.

Frederick I Barbarossa.

between the restored papacy, which rejected the very idea of conciliar supremacy and feared reforms that would reduce papal income, and the conciliarists, who were numerous among theologians, bishops, and secular rulers, and who continued to call for limitations on papal authority and a thorough reform of the church "in head and members." With the help of Europe's secular rulers, to whom they made far-reaching concessions of authority to appoint bishops and other clergymen as well as of a share of ecclesiastical revenues, the popes defeated the conciliar movement, which had its last stand at the Council of Basel (1431–1449). But because of abuse and lack of reform in the "Renaissance papacy," conciliarism retained widespread appeal, particularly north of the Alps.

8. Charles V (1500–1558) was now twenty years old.

9. The Hohenstaufen emperors Frederick (I) Barbarossa (1152–1190) and his grandson, Frederick II (1212–1250), the last of the Hohenstaufens, both pursued dynastic and imperial interests in Italy that brought them into conflict with the cities of Lombardy and the popes (in their capacity as Italian territorial rulers). Both were excommunicated, and Frederick II was even deposed; both experienced catastrophic losses on the battlefield at the hands of their Italian enemies. Meanwhile, particularly in the reign of Frederick II, the German princes secured concessions that put an end to all hope of the establishment of a powerful national monarchy hereditary in the Hohenstaufen family.

Imperial authority survived in northern Italy and Germany but real power was in the hands of the great commercial cities of Italy and the German territorial princes.

10. Known as "the warrior pope," Julius II (1443–1513) spent much of his reign (1503–13) personally leading military campaigns aimed at recovering papal territory that had been alienated by his predecessors or annexed by Venice. In these struggles, France and Venice numbered among his enemies, but the German emperor Maximilian I (1459–1519) was his occasional ally.

11. I.e., the advocates of papal supremacy in the church.

What was it in our own time that raised the bloodthirsty Julius II to such heights? Nothing else, I fear, except that France, the Germans, and Venice relied upon themselves.[10] The children of Benjamin slew forty-two thousand Israelites because the latter relied on their own strength, Judg. 20[:21].[*u*]

That it may not so fare with us and our noble Charles, we must realize that in this matter we are not dealing with human beings, but with the princes of hell. These princes might well fill the world with war and bloodshed, but war and bloodshed do not overcome them. We must tackle this job by renouncing trust in physical force and trusting humbly in God. We must seek God's help through earnest prayer and fix our minds on nothing else than the misery and distress of suffering Christendom without regard to what evil men deserve. Otherwise, we may start the game with great prospects of success, but when we get into it the evil spirits will stir up such confusion that the whole world will swim in blood, and then nothing will come of it all. Let us act wisely, therefore, and in the fear of God. The more force we use, the greater our disaster if we do not act humbly and in the fear of God. If the popes and Romanists[11] have hitherto been able to set kings against each other by the devil's help, they might well be able to do it again if we were to go ahead without the help of God on our own strength and by our own cunning.

The Romanists have very cleverly built three walls around themselves. Hitherto they have protected themselves by these walls in such a way that no one has been able to reform them. As a result, the whole of Christendom has fallen horribly.

In the first place, when secular authority has been used against them, they have made decrees and declared that secular authority has no jurisdiction over them, but that, on the contrary, spiritual authority is above secular authority.[*v*] In the second place, when the attempt is made to reprove

u　The biblical text mentions only twenty-two thousand slain.

v　See p. 384, n. 18.

them with the Scriptures, they raise the objection that only the pope may interpret the Scriptures.ʷ In the third place, if threatened with a council, their story is that no one may summon a council but the pope.ˣ

In this way they have cunningly stolen our three rods from us, so that they may go unpunished. They have ensconced themselves within the safe stronghold of these three walls so that they can practice all the knavery and wickedness that we see today. Even when they have been compelled to hold a council,[12] they have weakened its power in advance by putting the princes under oath to let them remain as they were.ʸ In addition, they have given the pope full authority over all decisions of a council, so that it is all the same whether there are many councils or no councils. They only deceive us with puppet shows and sham fights. They fear terribly for their skin in a really free council! They have so intimidated kings and princes with this technique that they believe it would be an offense against God not to be obedient to the Romanists in all their knavish and ghoulish deceits.

May God help us and give us just one of those trumpets with which the walls of Jericho were knocked down [Josh. 6:20] to blow down these walls of straw and paper as well and set free the Christian rods for the punishment of sin,[13] [as well as] bring to light the craft and deceit of the devil, to the end that through punishment we may reform ourselves and once more attain God's favor.

Let us begin by attacking the first wall. It is pure invention that pope, bishop, priests, and monks are called the spiritual estate while princes, lords, artisans, and farmers are called the secular estate. This is indeed a piece of deceit and hypocrisy. Yet no one need be intimidated by it, and for this reason: all Christians are truly of spiritual status, and there is no difference among them except that of office. Paul says in 1 Cor. 12[:12-13] that we are all one body, yet every

12. The most recent was the Fifth Lateran Council, 1512–1517. See n. 40, p. 398.

13. "Rod" is used in the Bible to mean an instrument of God's wrath; see, e.g., Ps. 2:9 and Rev. 2:27.

---

w   For the claim of sole authority to interpret Scripture, see Friedberg 1:58–60 (*Decret. prima pars*, dist. 19, can. 1f).

x   See n. 37.

y   See above, *Treatise on Good Works*, p. 341f.

member has its own work by which it serves the others. This is because we all have one baptism, one gospel, one faith, and are all Christians alike; for baptism, gospel, and faith alone make us spiritual and a Christian people.

But if a pope or bishop anoints, tonsures, ordains, consecrates, and prescribes garb different from that of the laity, he can perhaps thereby create a hypocrite or an anointed priestling, but he can never make anyone into a Christian or into a spiritual person by so doing. Accordingly, we are all consecrated priests through baptism, as St. Peter says in 1 Pet. 2[:9], "You are a royal priesthood and a priestly realm." And the Apocalypse says, "Thou hast made us to be priests and kings by thy blood" [Rev. 5:9-10]. For if we had no higher consecration than that which pope or bishop gives, such consecration by pope or bishop would never make a priest, and no one could say Mass or preach a sermon or give absolution.

Therefore, when a bishop consecrates it is nothing else than that in the place and in the name of the whole community, all members of which have the same power, he selects one person and charges him with exercising this power on behalf of the others. It is just as if ten brothers, all the sons and equal heirs of a king, were to choose one of their number to rule the inheritance for them: even though they are all kings and of equal power, one of them is charged with the responsibility of ruling. To put it still more clearly: suppose a group of earnest Christian laypeople were taken prisoner and set down in a desert without an episcopally ordained priest among them. And suppose they were to come to a common mind there and then in the desert and elect one of their number, whether he were married or not,[z] and charge him to baptize, say Mass, pronounce absolution, and preach the gospel. Such a man would be as truly a priest as if he had been ordained by all the bishops and popes in the world. This is why in cases of necessity anyone can baptize and give absolution.[14] This would be impossible if we were not all

14. On emergency baptism see, e.g., the bull *Exultate Deo* (1439), which decreed that in case of necessity anyone, "not only a priest or deacon but also a woman or, indeed, even a pagan or a heretic, has the power to baptize" (Carl Mirbt and Kurt Aland, eds. *Quellen zur Geschichte des Papsttums und des römischen Katholozismus*, 6th ed. (Tübingen: Mohr Siebeck, 1967), 485, no. 774, §10). The idea that in an emergency when no priest is available an ordinary layperson can hear confession and pronounce absolution can be traced to a statement of St. Augustine (354–430) that was incorporated into the *Decretum Gratiani* (cf. following note); Friedberg 1:1374.

z   The word here translated as "married," *ehelich*, can also mean "of legitimate birth." Canon law made both marriage and illegitimate birth a disqualification for ordination.

priests. Through canon law[15] the Romanists have almost destroyed and made unknown the wondrous grace and authority of baptism and Christian status. In times gone by, Christians used to choose their bishops and priests in this way from among their own number, and they were confirmed in their office by the other bishops without all the fuss that goes on nowadays. St. Augustine, Ambrose, and Cyprian each became [a bishop in this way].[16]

Since those who exercise secular authority have been baptized with the same baptism, and have the same faith and the same gospel as the rest of us, we must admit that they are priests and bishops, and we must regard their office as one that has a proper place in the Christian community and is useful to it. For whoever has crawled out of the water of baptism can boast that he is already a consecrated priest, bishop, and pope, even though it is not seemly that just anybody should exercise such an office. Because we are all priests of equal standing, no one must push himself forward and take it upon himself, without our consent and election, to do that for which we all have equal authority. For no one dare take upon himself what is common to all without the authority and consent of the community. And should it happen that someone chosen for such office were deposed for abuse of it, he would then be exactly what he was before. Therefore, a priest in Christendom is nothing else but an officeholder. As long as he holds office, he takes precedence; where he is deposed, he is a peasant or a townsman like anybody else. Indeed, a priest is never a priest when he is deposed. But now the Romanists have invented *characteres indelebiles* and blather that a deposed priest is nevertheless something different from a mere layman. They fancy that a priest can never be anything other than a priest, or ever become a layman.[17] All this is just contrived talk and human law.

It follows from this that there is no true, basic difference between laymen and priests, princes and bishops, or (as they say) between spiritual and secular, except that of office and work, and not that of status. For they are all of spiritual status, all are truly priests, bishops, and popes. But they do not

15. The term Luther uses here (and elsewhere) is *das geystlich recht* ("spiritual law"), a term that refers to church law as codified in the later medieval period into what is now known as the *Corpus Iuris Canonici*. Of the five collections that make up the *Corpus*, Luther referred most often to the two oldest: the *Decretum Gratiani* (c. 1140), and the *Decretals*, i.e., the *Liber Decretalium Gregorii IX* (1234). His attitude toward canon law was ambiguous. On the one hand, he hated it as the embodiment in law of papal tyranny. On the other hand, he found in it much useful evidence about the wholesome practices and teachings of the ancient church, and he became adroit at citing it to prove his contention that the "Romanists" ignored their own law when it suited their interests to do so. (On 10 December 1520 Luther burned a copy of canon law along with the papal bull of excommunication.)

16. St. Augustine, bishop of Hippo (354–430); St. Ambrose, bishop of Milan (c. 340–397); St. Cyprian, bishop of Carthage (d. 258).

17. The doctrine that ordination impresses on the soul an indelible mark that distinguishes the recipient from all those who have not received it was given authoritative formulation in the 1439 bull *Exultate Deo* of Pope Eugene IV (1383–1447); see Mirbt-Aland 484–85, no. 774, §9. Thus, a man in orders could cease functioning as a priest, but he could never again be a mere layman.

all have the same work to do, just as priests and monks do not all have exactly the same work. This is the teaching of St. Paul in Rom. 12[:4-5] and 1 Cor. 12[:12] and in 1 Pet. 2[:9], as I have said above, namely, that we are all one body of Christ the Head, and all members one of another. Christ has neither two bodies nor two kinds of body, one secular and the other spiritual. There is but one head and one body.

Therefore, just as those who are now called "spiritual," that is, priests, bishops, or popes, are neither different from other Christians nor superior to them, except that they are charged with the administration of the word of God and the sacraments, which is their work and office, so it is with secular government, which has the sword and rod in hand to punish the wicked and protect the good. A cobbler, a blacksmith, a peasant—each has the work and office of his trade, and yet they are all alike consecrated priests and bishops, and everyone should benefit and serve everyone else by means of their own work or office, so that in this way many kinds of work may be done for the bodily and spiritual welfare of the community, just as all the members of the body serve one another [1 Cor. 12:14-26].

Now consider how Christian the decree is which says that the secular power is not above the "spiritual estate" and has no right to punish it.[18] That is as much as to say that the hand should not help the eye when it suffers pain. Is it not unnatural, not to mention un-Christian, that one member should not help another and prevent its destruction? In fact, the more honorable the member, the more the others ought to help. I say therefore that since secular authority is ordained of God to punish the wicked and protect the good, it should be left free to perform its office in the whole body of Christendom without restriction and without respect to persons, whether it affects pope, bishops, priests, monks, nuns, or anyone else. If it were sufficient for the purpose of preventing secular authority from doing its work to say that among Christian offices it is inferior to that of preacher, confessor, or anyone of spiritual status, one would also have to prevent tailors, cobblers, stonemasons, carpenters, cooks, innkeepers, farmers, and the practitioners of all other secu-

18. The claim that spiritual authority was superior to all secular authority and not subject to correction by it was classically formulated in the 1302 bull *Unam sanctam* of Boniface VIII (c. 1235–1303). An important corollary of this view was the claim that clergymen had the *privilegium fori*, i.e., that they were exempt from the jurisdiction of the secular courts, even when charged with secular crimes. See nn. 21, 22 below.

lar trades from providing pope, bishops, priests, and monks with shoes, clothes, house, meat, and drink, as well as from paying them any tribute. But if these laypeople are allowed to do their proper work without restriction, what then are the Romanist scribes[19] doing with their own laws, which exempt them from the jurisdiction of secular Christian authority? It is just so that they can be free to do evil and fulfill what St. Peter said: "False teachers will rise up among you who will deceive you, and with their false and fanciful talk, they will take advantage of you" [2 Pet. 2:1-3].

For these reasons, Christian secular authority ought to exercise its office without hindrance, regardless of whether it is pope, bishop, or priest whom it affects. Whoever is guilty, let him suffer [punishment]. All that canon law has said to the contrary is the invention of Romanist presumption. For thus St. Paul says to all Christians, "Let every soul (I take that to mean the pope's soul also) be subject to governing authority, for it does not bear the sword in vain, but serves God by punishing the wicked and benefiting the good" [Rom. 13:1, 4]. St. Peter, too, says, "Be subject to all human ordinances for the sake of the Lord, who so wills it" [1 Pet. 2:13, 15]. He has also prophesied in 2 Pet. 2[:1] that such men would arise and despise secular government. This is exactly what has happened through canon law.

So I think this first paper wall is overthrown. Inasmuch as secular rule has become a part of the Christian body, it is part of the spiritual estate, even though its work is physical. Therefore, its work should extend without hindrance to all the members of the whole body, to punish and use force whenever guilt deserves or necessity demands, without regard to whether the culprit is pope, bishop, or priest. Let the Romanists hurl threats and bans as they like. That is why guilty priests, when they are handed over to secular law, are first deprived of their priestly dignities.[20] This would not be right unless the secular sword previously had had authority over these priests by divine right. Moreover, it is intolerable that in canon law so much importance is attached to the freedom, life, and property of the clergy,[21] as though the laity were not also as spiritual and as good Christians

19. An allusion to references in the Gospels to "scribes and Pharisees."

20. A clergyman found guilty of a secular crime by an ecclesiastical court was first deprived of his priestly office and then surrendered to the secular authorities for punishment.

21. In addition to the *privilegium fori* (see previous note), members of the clergy and religious orders enjoyed the *privilegium canonis*, according to which anyone who laid a hand on a clergyman or monk automatically incurred excommunication, the lifting of which was reserved to the pope. Canon law also declared that ecclesiastical persons and property were exempt from most of the general obligations (e.g., military service) and taxes required of laypeople (*privilegium immunitatis*).

22. An interdict banned the administration of the sacraments and other ecclesiastical rites (e.g., Christian burial) in a given jurisdiction, even an entire kingdom (as in the case of England, placed under interdict by Pope Innocent III [c. 1160–1216] in 1208). The use of interdict was not uncommon in the Middle Ages, but by 1500 its frequent use for trifling infractions of church law or clerical privilege was a common grievance of the laity against the clergy.

23. In his *Epitome* (see p. 370, n. 1), Sylvester Prierias had quoted this provision of canon law against Luther: "An undoubtedly legitimate pope cannot be lawfully deposed or judged by either a council or the entire world, even if he be so scandalous as to lead people with him *en masse* into the possession of the devil in hell." See WA 6:336.

as they, or did not also belong to the church. Why are your life and limb, your property and honor, so cheap and mine not, inasmuch as we are all Christians and have the same baptism, the same faith, the same Spirit, and all the rest? If a priest is murdered, the whole country is placed under interdict.[22] Why not when a peasant is murdered? How does this great difference come about between two men who are both Christians? It comes from the laws and fabrications of men.

It can, moreover, be no good spirit that has invented such exceptions and granted such license and impunity to sin. For if it is our duty to strive against the words and works of the devil and to drive him out in whatever way we can, as both Christ and his apostles command us, how have we come to the point that we have to do nothing and say nothing when the pope or his cohorts undertake devilish words and works? Ought we merely out of regard for these people allow the suppression of divine commandments and truth, which we have sworn in baptism to support with life and limb? Then we should have to answer for all the souls that would thereby be abandoned and led astray!

It must, therefore, have been the chief devil himself who said what is written in the canon law, that if the pope were so scandalously bad as to lead crowds of souls to the devil, still he could not be deposed.[23] At Rome they build on this accursed and devilish foundation, and think that we should let all the world go to the devil rather than resist their knavery. If the fact that one man is set over others were sufficient reason why he should not be punished, then no Christian could punish another, since Christ commanded that all people should esteem themselves as the lowliest and the least [Matt. 18:4].

Where sin is, there is no longer any shielding from punishment. St. Gregory writes that we are indeed all equal, but guilt makes a person inferior to others.[a] Now we see how the Romanists treat Christendom. They take away its freedom without any proof from Scripture, at their own whim. But God, as well as the apostles, made them subject to the

---

a   Pope Gregory the Great (c. 540–604), *Regula pastoralis* 2.6.

secular sword. It is to be feared that this is a game of the Antichrist,[24] or at any rate that his forerunner has appeared.

The second wall is still more loosely built and less substantial. [The Romanists] want to be the only masters of Holy Scripture, although they never learn a thing from the Bible all their life long. They assume the sole authority for themselves, and, quite unashamed, they play about with words before our very eyes, trying to persuade us that the pope cannot err in matters of faith, regardless of whether he is righteous or wicked.[25] Yet they cannot point to a single letter.[b] This is why so many heretical and unchristian, even unnatural, ordinances stand in the canon law. But there is no need to talk about these ordinances at present. Since these Romanists think the Holy Spirit never leaves them, no matter how ignorant and wicked they are, they become bold and decree only what they want. And if what they claim were true, why have Holy Scripture at all? Of what use is Scripture? Let us burn the Scripture and be satisfied with the unlearned gentlemen at Rome who possess the Holy Spirit! And yet the Holy Spirit can be possessed only by upright hearts. If I had not read the words with my own eyes,[c] I would not have believed it possible for the devil to have made such stupid claims at Rome, and to have won supporters for them.

But so as not to fight them with mere words, we will quote the Scriptures. St. Paul says in 1 Cor. 14[:30], "If something better is revealed to anyone, though he is already sitting and listening to another in God's word, then the one who is speaking shall hold his peace and give place." What would be the point of this commandment if we were compelled to believe only the man who does the talking, or the man who is at the top? Even Christ said in John 6[:45] that all Christians shall be taught by God. If it were to happen that the pope and his cohorts were wicked and not true Christians, were not taught by God and were without understanding, and at the same time some obscure person had a right

24. Luther and his contemporaries believed the appearance of the Antichrist was prophesied in 2 Thess. 2:3-10; 1 John 2:18, 22; 4:3; and Revelation 13. It was precisely at this time that Luther's suspicion that the papacy was the Antichrist turned to conviction and was expressed publicly in his response to the *Epitome* of Prierias; see the introduction, p. 370, n. 1 and note d.

25. Papal infallibility did not finally become official doctrine of the Catholic Church until 1870. In Luther's day, it was an opinion that had long been vigorously asserted by champions of papal authority, particularly at the Curia in Rome, but was not universally accepted. In his attack on the *95 Theses*, for example, Sylvester Prierias had argued, without citing Scripture, that "whoever does not rely on the teaching of the Roman church and the supreme pontiff as an infallible rule of faith, from which even Holy Scripture draws its vigor and authority, is a heretic" (*D. Martini Lutheri Opera Latina varii argumenti*, vol. 1: *Scripta 1515–1518* [Frankfurt/Main: Heyder & Zimmer, 1865], 347). But in the wake of Luther's excommunication in 1521, there were many in Germany and elsewhere who did not believe that he was a heretic just because the pope said so.

---

b   I.e., to a single letter of Scripture to support their claim.

c   Luther is referring to the passage quoted in n. 25.

understanding, why should the people not follow that one? Has the pope not erred many times? Who would help Christendom when the pope erred if we did not have others[d] who had the Scriptures on their side and whom we could trust more than him?

Therefore, their claim that only the pope may interpret Scripture is an outrageous fancied fable. They cannot produce a single letter [of Scripture] to maintain that the interpretation of Scripture or the confirmation of its interpretation belongs to the pope alone. They themselves have usurped this power. And although they allege that this power was given to St. Peter when the keys were given him, it is clear enough that the keys were not given to Peter alone but to the whole community.[e] Further, the keys were not ordained for doctrine or government, but only for the binding or loosing of sin. Whatever else or whatever more they arrogate to themselves on the basis of the keys is a mere fabrication. But Christ's words to Peter, "I have prayed for you that your faith fail not" [Luke 22:32], cannot be applied to the pope, since the majority of the popes have been without faith, as they must themselves confess. Besides, it is not only for Peter that Christ prayed, but also for all apostles and Christians, as he says in John 17[:9, 20], "Father, I pray for those whom thou hast given me, and not for these only, but for all who believe on me through their word." Is that not clear enough?

Just think of it! The Romanists must admit that there are among us good Christians who have the true faith, spirit, understanding, word, and mind of Christ. Why, then, should we reject the word and understanding of good Christians and follow the pope, who has neither faith nor intelligence? To follow the pope would be to deny the whole faith as well as the Christian church. Again, if the article, "I believe in one holy Christian church," is correct, then the pope cannot be the only one who is right.[f] Otherwise, we would have

d   Singular in the original.
e   Matt. 16:19; 18:18; and John 20:23. See above, pp. 195–96 (*The Sacrament of Penance*, 1519). For the "Keys," see above, p. 37, n. 36.
f   Citing the Nicene Creed, according to the standard German translation.

to pray, "I believe in the pope at Rome." This would reduce the Christian church to one man, and be nothing else than a devilish and hellish error.

Besides, if we are all priests, as was said above,[g] and all have one faith, one gospel, one sacrament, why should we not also have the power to test and judge what is right or wrong in matters of faith? What becomes of Paul's words in 1 Cor. 2[:15], "A spiritual person judges all things and yet is judged by no one"? And 2 Cor. 4[:13], "We all have one spirit of faith"? Why, then, should not we perceive what is consistent with faith and what is not, just as well as an unbelieving pope does?

We ought to become bold and free on the authority of all these texts, and many others. We ought not to allow the Spirit of freedom (Paul's appellation [2 Cor. 3:17]) to be frightened off by the fabrications of the popes but ought rather to march boldly forward and test all that they do or leave undone by our faithful understanding of the Scriptures. We must compel the Romanists to follow not their own interpretation but the better one. Long ago Abraham had to listen to Sarah, although she was in more complete subjection to him than we are to anyone on earth [Gen. 21:12]. And Balaam's donkey was wiser than the prophet himself [Num. 22:21-35]. If God spoke then through a donkey against a prophet, why should he not be able even now to speak through a righteous person against the pope? Similarly, St. Paul rebukes St. Peter as someone in error in Gal. 2[:11-12]. Therefore, it is the duty of every Christian to espouse the cause of the faith, to understand and defend it, and to denounce every error.

The third wall[26] falls of itself once the first two are down. For when the pope acts contrary to the Scriptures, it is our duty to stand by the Scriptures, to reprove him, and to constrain him, according to the word of Christ, Matthew 18[:15-17], "If your brother sins against you, go and tell it to him, between you and him alone; if he does not listen to you, then take one or two others with you; if he does not

26. See p. 381 (first wall) and p. 387 (second wall).

g   See p. 383f.

listen to them, tell it to the church; if he does not listen to the church, consider him a heathen." Here every member is commanded to care for every other. How much more should we do this when the member that does evil is responsible for the government of the church, and by that one's evildoing is the cause of much harm and offense to the rest. But if I am to accuse such a person before the church, I must naturally call the church together.

[The Romanists] have no basis in Scripture for their claim that the pope alone has the right to call or confirm a council.[27] It is just their own law, and it is only valid as long as it is not harmful to Christendom or contrary to the laws of God. But if the pope deserves punishment, this law ceases to be valid, for it is harmful to Christendom not to punish him by authority of a council.

Thus we read in Acts 15 that it was not St. Peter who called the Apostolic Council but the apostles and elders. If then that right had belonged to St. Peter alone, the council would not have been a Christian council, but a heretical *conciliabulum*.[h] Even the Council of Nicaea, the most famous of all councils, was neither called nor confirmed by the bishop of Rome, but by the emperor Constantine.[28] Many other emperors after him have done the same, and yet these councils were the most Christian of all.[29] But if the pope alone has the right to convene councils, then these councils would all have been heretical. Further, when I examine the councils the pope did summon, I find that they did nothing of special importance.

Therefore, when necessity demands it, and the pope is an offense to Christendom, the first one who is able should, as true members of the whole body, do what can be done to bring about a truly free council. No one can do this so well as the secular authorities, especially since they are also fellow-Christians, fellow-priests, fellow-participants in spiritual authority, sharing power over all things. Whenever it is necessary or profitable, they ought to exercise the office and work that they have received from God over everyone.

27. The claim, asserted in several decrees of canon law, had been advanced against Luther by Prierias in his *Epitome*: "[W]hen there is one undisputed pontiff, it belongs to him alone to call a council." Moreover, "the decrees of councils neither bind nor constrain unless they are confirmed by the authority of the Roman pontiff" (WA 6:335).

28. The Council of Nicaea (325), the first general council, was called by Emperor Constantine (c. 272–337) to deal with the Arian Controversy.

29. Besides Nicaea, there were the councils of Constantinople (381), Ephesus (431), and Chalcedon (451). More recently, Emperor Maximilian I and King Louis XII (1462–1515) of France had convoked the Second Council of Pisa (1511), but Pope Julius II countered by summoning the Fifth Lateran Council to Rome (1512).

---

h   I.e., a miserable little invalid gathering rather than a true council.

Would it not be unnatural if a fire broke out in a city and everybody were to stand by and let it burn on and on and consume everything that could burn because nobody had the authority of the mayor, or because, perhaps, the fire broke out in the mayor's house? In such a situation is it not the duty of every citizen to rouse and summon the rest? How much more should this be done in the spiritual city of Christ if a fire of offense breaks out, whether in the pope's government or anywhere else! The same argument holds if an enemy were to attack a city. The person who first rouses the others deserves honor and gratitude. Why, then, should that person not deserve honor who makes known the presence of the enemy from hell and rouses Christian people and calls them together?

All their boasting about an authority that dare not be opposed amounts to nothing at all. Nobody in Christendom has authority to do injury or to forbid the resisting of injury. There is no authority in the church except to foster improvement. Therefore, if the pope were to use his authority to prevent the calling of a free council, thereby preventing the improvement of the church, we should have regard neither for him nor for his authority. And if he were to hurl his bans and thunderbolts, we should despise his conduct as that of a madman, and we should instead ban him and drive him out as best we can, relying completely upon God. For his presumptuous authority is nothing, nor does he possess it. He is quickly defeated by a single text of Scripture, where Paul says to the Corinthians, "God has given us authority not to ruin Christendom, but to build it up" [2 Cor. 10:8]. Who will leap over the hurdle of this text? It is the power of the devil and of Antichrist, which resists the things that serve to build up Christendom. Such power is not to be obeyed, but rather resisted with life, property, and with all our might and main.

Even though a miracle were to be performed against secular authority on the pope's behalf, or if somebody were struck down by the plague—which they boast has sometimes happened—it should be considered as nothing but the work of the devil designed to destroy our faith in God.

Statue of Emperor Constantine.

Christ foretold this in Matt. 24[:24], "False Christs and false prophets shall come in my name, who shall perform signs and miracles in order to deceive even the elect." And Paul says in 2 Thess. 2[:9] that Antichrist shall, through the power of Satan, be mighty in false miracles.

Let us, therefore, hold fast to this: Christian authority can do nothing against Christ. As St. Paul says, "We can do nothing against Christ, only for Christ" [2 Cor. 13:8]. But if an authority does anything against Christ, then it is that of the Antichrist and the devil, even if it were to rain and hail miracles and plagues. Miracles and plagues prove nothing, especially in these evil latter days. The whole of Scripture foretells such false miracles. This is why we must cling to the word of God with firm faith, and then the devil will soon drop his miracles!

With this I hope that all these wicked and lying terrors, with which the Romanists have long intimidated and dulled our consciences, have been overcome and that they, just like all of us, shall be made subject to the sword. For they have no right to interpret Scripture merely on their own authority and without learning. They have no authority to prevent a council, much less at their mere whim to put it under obligation, impose conditions on it, or deprive it of its freedom. When they do such things, they are truly in the fellowship of Antichrist and the devil. They have nothing at all of Christ except the name.

Let us now look at the matters that ought to be properly dealt with in councils, matters with which popes, cardinals, bishops, and all scholars ought properly to be occupied day and night if they loved Christ and his church. But if this is not the case, let ordinary people[i] and the secular authorities take action,[j] without regard to papal bans and fulminations, for [suffering under] an unjust ban is better than ten just and proper absolutions, and [trusting] one unjust,

Papal coat of arms showing
a triple-crowned tiara.

---

i   Luther's word is *der hauff* (literally, "the crowd," i.e., ordinary people without ecclesiastical office).

j   I.e., convoke a council and do whatever else they can to restore health to the church.

improper absolution is worse than ten just bans. Therefore, let us awake, dear Germans, and fear God more than mortals [Acts 5:29], lest we suffer the same fate of all the poor souls who are so lamentably lost through the shameless, devilish rule of the Romanists, and the devil grow stronger every day—as if it were possible that such a hellish regime could grow any worse, something that I can neither conceive nor believe.

First. It is horrible and shocking to see the head of Christendom, who boasts that he is the vicar of Christ and successor of St. Peter, going about in such a worldly and ostentatious style that neither king nor emperor can equal or approach him. He claims the title of "most holy" and "most spiritual," and yet he is worldlier than the world itself. He wears a triple crown, whereas the highest monarchs wear but one.[30] If that is like the poverty of Christ and of St. Peter, then it is a new and strange kind of likeness! When anybody says anything against it, [the Romanists] bleat, "Heresy!" They refuse to hear how un-Christian and ungodly all this is. In my opinion, if the pope were to pray to God with tears, he would have to lay aside his triple crown, for the God we worship cannot put up with pride. In fact, the pope's office should be nothing else but to weep and pray for Christendom and to set an example of utter humility.

Be that as it may, this kind of splendor is offensive, and the pope is bound for the sake of his own salvation to set it aside. It was for this reason that St. Paul said, "Abstain from all practices which give offense" [1 Thess. 5:22], and in Rom. 12[:17], "We should do good, not only in the sight of God, but also in the sight of all people." An ordinary bishop's mitre ought to be good enough for the pope. It is in wisdom and holiness that he should be above his fellows. He ought to leave the crown of pride to Antichrist, as his predecessors did centuries ago. The Romanists say he is a lord of the earth. That is a lie! For Christ, whose vicar and vicegerent he claims to be, said to Pilate, "My kingdom is not of this world" [John 18:36]. No vicar's rule can go beyond that of his lord. Moreover, he is not the vicar of Christ glorified but of Christ crucified. As Paul says, "I was determined

30. The tiara or triple crown, the papal headdress on nonliturgical occasions, was first used in the fourteenth century. The symbolism of the three layers of the crown was variously interpreted, but it undoubtedly included the assertion of the pope's elevation above all secular authority as well as his headship of the church.

to know nothing among you save Christ, and him only as the crucified" [1 Cor. 2:2], and in Phil. 2[:5-7], "This is how you should regard yourselves, as you see in Christ, who emptied himself and took upon himself the form of a servant." Or again in 1 Cor. 1[:23], "We preach Christ, the crucified." Now the Romanists make the pope a vicar of the glorified Christ in heaven, and some of them have allowed the devil to rule them so completely that they have maintained that the pope is above the angels in heaven and has them at his command.[31] These are certainly the proper works of the real Antichrist.

Second. Of what use to Christendom are those people called cardinals? I shall tell you. Italy and Germany have many rich monasteries, foundations,[k] benefices, and livings. No better way has been discovered of bringing all these to Rome than by creating cardinals and giving them bishoprics, monasteries, and prelacies for their own use and so overthrowing the worship of God. You can see that Italy is now almost a wilderness: monasteries in ruins, bishoprics despoiled, the prelacies and the revenues of all the churches drawn to Rome, cities decayed, land and people ruined because services are no longer held and the word of God is not preached. And why? Because the cardinals must have the income! No Turk[32] could have devastated Italy and suppressed the worship of God so effectively!

Now that Italy is sucked dry, the Romanists are coming into Germany.[l] They have made a gentle beginning. But let us keep our eyes open! Germany shall soon be like Italy. We have some cardinals already. The "drunken Germans" are not supposed to understand what the Romanists are up to until there is not a bishopric, a monastery, a parish, a benefice, not a single penny left. Antichrist must seize the treasures of the earth, as it is prophesied [Dan. 11:39, 43]. It works like this: they skim the cream off the bishoprics, monasteries, and benefices, and because they do not yet ven-

31. Cf. LW 32:74-75. This claim was advanced by Augustinus de Ancona (known as Augustinus Triumphans [1243-1328]) in Quaestio 18 of his *Summa de potestate ecclesiastica*, 1326 (first printed at Augsburg in 1473). See Blasius Ministeri, "De vita et operibus Augustine de Ancona, O.E.S.A. (d. 1328)," *Analecta Augustiniana* 22 (1953): 115, 156.

32. Luther's term for adherents of Islam, who were familiar to sixteenth-century Europeans primarily as Muslims from the Ottoman Turkish Empire. Besides being his word for subjects of the Ottoman Turkish Empire, "Turk" was Luther's word for "Muslim." Islam was familiar to sixteenth-century Europeans primarily via their confrontation with the Ottoman Turks, who were long a military threat on the eastern borders of the Holy Roman Empire as well as in the Mediterranean.

k German: *Stift*. This refers to university foundations and the collegiate foundations of cathedrals.

l Cf. *Treatise on Good Works*, above, p. 340f.

ture to put them all to shameful use, as they have done in Italy, they in the meantime practice their holy cunning and couple together ten or twenty prelacies. They then tear off a little piece each year so as to make quite a tidy sum after all. The provostship of Würzburg yields a thousand gulden; that of Bamberg also yields a sum, [as do] Mainz, Trier, and others. In this way, one thousand or ten thousand gulden may be collected, so that a cardinal could live like a wealthy monarch at Rome.

When we have gotten used to that, we shall appoint thirty or forty cardinals in one day.[33] We shall give to one of them the Münchenberg at Bamberg,*[m]* along with the bishopric of Würzburg, with a few rich benefices attached to them, until churches and cities are destitute, and then we shall say, "We are Christ's vicars, and shepherds of Christ's sheep. The foolish, drunken Germans will just have to put up with it."

My advice, however, is to make fewer cardinals, or to let the pope support them at his own expense. Twelve of them would be enough, and each of them might have an income of a thousand gulden.[34] How is it that we Germans must put up with such robbery and extortion of our goods at the hands of the pope? If the kingdom of France has prevented it, why do we Germans let them make such fools and apes of us?[35] We could put up with all this if they stole only our property, but they lay waste to the churches in so doing, rob Christ's sheep of their true shepherds, and debase the worship and word of God. If there were not a single cardinal, the church would not perish. The cardinals do nothing to serve Christendom. They are only interested in the money side of bishoprics and prelacies, and they wrangle about them just as any thief might do.

Third. If ninety-nine percent of the papal court were abolished and only one percent kept, it would still be large enough to give answers in matters of faith. Today, however, there is such a swarm of parasites in that place called Rome, all of them boasting that they belong to the pope, that not even Babylon saw the likes of it. There are more than three

m   I.e., the Michaelsberg Abbey in Bamberg.

33. On 1 July 1517, Pope Leo X (1475–1521) named thirty-one cardinals, the largest number ever created in a single consistory until 1946. At the end of Leo's reign, the total number of cardinals was forty-eight, seventeen more than it had been at the time of his election in 1513, but only three more than it had been at the time of the election of Julius II in 1503.

34. It was a common complaint that the College of Cardinals was too large, its size fed more by the income derived from the fees charged for an appointment to it than by the needs of the church. The fifteenth-century reform councils of Constance and Basel had wanted the total number fixed at twenty-four. The actual number at this time tended to hover at around twice that (see n. 33). The idea that the cardinals should be assigned a fixed income rather than endowed with benefices was also a common suggestion in the literature for church reform. The Council of Constance recommended an income of three to four thousand gulden.

35. In 1438 King Charles VIII (1470–1498) of France presided over a synod of French clergy and nobility at Bourges that adopted the so-called

Pragmatic Sanction, which applied to France some of the reform decrees of the Council of Basel. In effect, the Pragmatic Sanction took control over the election of bishops, abbots, and other benefice holders in France away from the pope and bestowed it on the crown, thus severely reducing the income derived from such appointments by the pope or his nonresident appointees. The payment of annates (see n. 37) to the pope was forbidden. In 1516 Pope Leo X and King Francis I (1494–1547) concluded the Concordat of Bologna, which replaced the Pragmatic Sanction but kept many of its provisions. The right of nomination to bishoprics and other high offices was expressly reserved to the crown, the pope retaining the right to withhold confirmation from appointments that violated canonical requirements. The matter of annates, however, was passed over in complete silence, which meant that the pope was tacitly given permission to collect them again. In Germany, relations between the pope and the German church were regulated by the Concordat of Vienna, concluded by Pope Nicholas V (1397–1455) and Emperor Frederick III (1415–1493) in 1448. By its terms, the pope had much greater freedom in appointments to ecclesiastical office and in collection revenues.

36. The papal court, or Curia, consisted of all the officials engaged in conduct of papal business as well as the pope's personal "household." According to a list published at Rome in 1545, there were in that year 949 curial positions that were available for the one-time payment of a fee. This

thousand papal secretaries alone. Who could count the other officials? There are so many offices that one could scarcely count them.[36] These are all the people lying in wait for the endowments and benefices of Germany as wolves lie in wait for sheep. I believe that Germany now gives much more to the pope at Rome than it used to give to the emperors in ancient times. In fact, some have estimated that more than three hundred thousand gulden a year find their way from Germany to Rome."[n] This money serves no use or purpose. We get nothing for it except scorn and contempt. And we still go on wondering why princes and nobles, cities and endowments, land and people, grow poor. We ought to marvel that we have anything left to eat!

Since we have now come to the heart of the matter, we will pause a little and let it be seen that the Germans are not quite such crass fools that they know nothing about or do not understand the sharp practices of the Romanists. I do not here complain that God's command and Christian law are despised at Rome, for things are not going so well throughout Christendom, especially in Rome, that we may complain of such exalted matters. Nor do I complain that natural law, or secular law, or even reason count for nothing. My complaint goes deeper than that. I complain that the Romanists do not keep their own fabricated canon law, even though it is in fact plain tyranny, avarice, and temporal splendor rather than genuine law. This we shall see.

In former times, German emperors and princes permitted the pope to receive annates from all the benefices of the German nation. This sum amounts to one-half of the revenue of the first year from every single benefice.[37] This permission was given, however, so that by means of these large sums of money the pope might raise funds to fight against the Turks and infidels in defense of Christendom, and, so that the burden of war might not rest too heavily upon the nobility, the clergy too should contribute something toward it. The popes have so far used the splendid and simple devotion of the German people—they have received this money for more

n   See RTA 2:675, par. 11.

than a hundred years and have now made it an obligatory tax and tribute, but they have not only amassed no money [for this defense], they have used it to endow many posts and positions at Rome and to provide salaries for these posts, as though annates were a fixed rent.

When they pretend that they are about to fight the Turks, they send out emissaries to raise money. They often issue an indulgence on the same pretext of fighting the Turks. They think that those half-witted Germans will always be gullible, stupid fools, and will just keep handing over money to them to satisfy their unspeakable greed. And they think this even though it is public knowledge that not a cent of the annates, or of the indulgence money, or of all the rest, is spent to fight the Turks. It all goes into their bottomless moneybag. They lie and deceive. They make laws and they make agreements with us, but they do not intend to keep a single letter of them. Yet all this is done in the holy names of Christ and St. Peter.

In this matter, the German nation, bishops and princes, should now consider that they, too, are Christians. They should govern and protect the physical and spiritual goods of the people entrusted to them and defend them against these rapacious wolves who, dressed in sheep's clothing, pretend to be shepherds and rulers.º And since annates have been so shockingly abused, and not even kept for their original agreed purpose, [the bishops and princes] should not allow their land and people to be so pitilessly robbed and ruined contrary to all law. By decree either of the emperor or of the whole nationᵖ the annates should either be kept here at home or else abolished. Since the Romanists do not abide by their agreement, they have no right to the annates. Therefore, the bishops and princes are responsible for punishing such thievery and robbery, or even preventing it, as the law requires.

In such a matter, they ought to help the pope and strengthen his hand. Perhaps he is too weak to prevent such

number did not include the members of the papal household or the officials responsible for the government of the city of Rome and the papal states. See Benrath, 88, n. 18; 95–96, n. 36.

37. *Annates* consisted of the first year's revenue of an ecclesiastical benefice (or a specified portion of that revenue) paid to the papal treasury in return for appointment to that benefice. The rate of half the annual revenue was set by Pope John XXII (1244–1334) in 1317. It was an onerous tribute and much resented. The Council of Constance (1415) limited the payment of annates to bishoprics, abbacies, and other benefices with an income of more than twenty-four gulden, a rule that was applied to Germany in the Concordat of Vienna (1448).

---

o   Cf. Matt. 7:15.

p   That is, by decree of the imperial diet.

38. Ever since the early fourteenth century, popes had claimed the authority to reserve to themselves the right of appointment to all ecclesiastical benefices, a right that might in specific cases be graciously conceded to others (Friedberg 2:1259–61). Abolished in France, "reservations" were still valid in Germany. The Concordat of Vienna (1448) provided for the free election of bishops and abbots, subject to confirmation by the pope, who could object to persons deemed unsuitable. If the election were found to violate canon law, the pope was to provide a candidate. In the case of canonries and other benefices below those of highest rank, those that fell vacant in the even-numbered months of the year were reserved for appointment by the pope. In the odd-numbered months, local authorities exercised their right of election.

39. Charles V (1500–1558) was Holy Roman Emperor from 1519 to 1556. His empire included Spain and the Habsburg Empire that extended across Europe from Spain and the Netherlands to Austria and the Kingdom of Naples.

40. The ecclesiastical jurisdiction of the Holy Catholic Church in Rome.

abuse single-handedly. Or, in those cases where he wants to defend and maintain this state of affairs, they ought to resist him and protect themselves from him as they would from a wolf or a tyrant, for he has no authority to do evil or defend it. Even if it were ever desirable to raise such funds to fight the Turks, we ought to have at least enough sense to see that the German nation could better manage these funds than the pope. The German nation itself has enough people to wage war if the money is available. It is the same with annates as it has been with many other Romanist schemes.

Then, too, the year has been so divided between the pope and the ruling bishops and chapters that the pope has six months in the year (every other month) in which to bestow the benefices that become vacant in his months. In this way, almost all the best benefices have fallen into the hands of Rome, especially the very best prebends and dignities.[38] And when they once fall into the hands of Rome, they never come out of them again, though a vacancy may never occur again in the pope's month. In this way the chapters are short-changed. This is plain robbery, and the intention is to let nothing escape. Therefore, it is high time to abolish the "papal months" altogether. Everything that has been taken to Rome in this way must be restored. The princes and nobles ought to take steps for the restitution of the stolen property, punish the thieves, and strip the privilege of those who have abused that privilege. If it is binding and valid for the pope on the day after his election to make regulations and laws in his chancellery by which our endowed chapters and livings are stolen from us—a thing he has absolutely no right to do—then it should be still more valid for Emperor Charles,[39] on the day after his coronation, to make rules and laws that not another benefice or living in all Germany should be allowed to pass into the hands of Rome by means of the "papal months." The livings that have already fallen into the hands of Rome should be restored and redeemed from these Romanist robbers. Charles V has the right to do this by virtue of his authority as ruler.

But now this Romanist See[40] of avarice and robbery has not had the patience to wait for the time when all the benefices would fall to it one by one through this device of the "papal months." Rather, urged on by its insatiable appetite to get them all in its hands as speedily as possible, the Romanist See has devised a scheme whereby, in addition to the "annates" and "papal months," the benefices and livings should fall to Rome in three ways.[q]

First, if anyone who holds a "free" living[r] should die in Rome or on a journey to Rome, his living becomes the property in perpetuity of the Romanist—I ought to say roguish—See. But the Romanists do not want to be called robbers on this account, though they are guilty of robbery of a kind never heard of or read about before.

Second, if anyone belonging to the household of the pope or cardinals holds or takes over a benefice, or if anyone who had previously held a benefice subsequently enters the household of the pope or cardinals, [his living becomes the property in perpetuity of the Romanist See]. But who can count the household of the pope and cardinals? If he only goes on a pleasure ride, the pope takes with him three or four thousand on mules, in disdain of all emperors and kings! Christ and St. Peter went on foot so that their successors might have all the more pomp and splendor. Now Avarice has cleverly thought out another scheme, and arranges it so that many even outside Rome have the name "member of the papal household" just as if they were in Rome. This is done for the sole purpose that, by the simple use of that pernicious phrase "member of the pope's household," all benefices may be brought to Rome and bound there for all time. Are not these vexatious and devilish little inventions? Let us beware! Soon Mainz, Magdeburg, and Halberstadt will quietly slip into the hands of Rome, and then the cardinalate will cost a pretty penny![41] After that they will make all the German bishops cardinals, and then there will be nothing left.

Portrait of Holy Roman
Emperor, Charles V.

41. The reference is to the accumulation of bishoprics in the hands of Albrecht von Brandenburg (1490–1545), who in 1513 became archbishop of Magdeburg and administrator of the bishopric of Halberstadt, and in the following year archbishop-elector of Mainz. In 1518 he was made cardinal. The need to raise money to pay the enormous fees for the dispensations from the canonical ban on such accumulation of benefices was in part behind the sale of indulgences by Johann Tetzel (c. 1460–1519). Luther objected to this indulgence in the *95 Theses* but was unaware of Albrecht's financial dealings. See above, p. 17f.

q   Here Luther summarizes provisions of the Concordat of Vienna.

r   I.e., one not previously subject to appointment by the pope.

Third, when a dispute has started at Rome over a benefice, [it reverts to Roman control]. In my opinion this is the commonest and widest road for bringing livings into the hands of Rome. Even when there is no real dispute, countless knaves will be found at Rome who will unearth one and snatch the benefices at will. Thus many a good priest must lose his living or pay a sum of money to avoid having his benefice disputed. Such a living, rightly or wrongly contested, becomes the property of the Roman See forever. It would be no wonder if God were to rain fire and brimstone from heaven and sink Rome into the abyss, as he did Sodom and Gomorrah of old [Gen. 19:24]. Why should there be a pope in Christendom if his power is used for nothing else than for such gross wickedness and to protect and practice it? O noble princes and lords, how long will you leave your lands and your people naked and exposed to such ravenous wolves?

Since even these practices were not enough, and Avarice grew impatient at the long time it took to seize all the bishoprics, my Lord Avarice devised the fiction that the bishoprics should be nominally abroad but that their origin and foundation is at Rome. Furthermore, no bishop can be confirmed unless he pays a huge sum for his pallium and binds himself with solemn oaths to the personal service of the pope.[42] That explains why no bishop dares to act against the pope. That is what the Romanists were seeking when they imposed the oath [of allegiance]. It also explains why all the richest bishoprics have fallen into debt and ruin. I am told that Mainz pays twenty thousand gulden.[s] That is the Romanists all over! To be sure, they decreed a long time ago in canon law that the pallium should be given without cost, that the number in the pope's household be reduced, disputes lessened, and the chapters and bishops allowed their liberty. But this did not bring in money. So they turned over a new leaf and have taken all authority away from the bishops and chapters. These sit there like ciphers and have neither office nor authority nor work. Everything is con-

42. The pallium, a woolen shoulder cape that had to be secured from Rome, was the emblem of the office of archbishop as well as a symbol of his close ties to the papacy. A newly elected archbishop was required to acquire the pallium within three months of his election. In the early history of the church, it had been granted free of charge, but by Luther's day it had long since become an extremely expensive acquisition.

---

s Elsewhere Luther put the price at thirty thousand; see LW 39:60 (*On the Papacy in Rome*).

trolled by those arch-villains at Rome, almost right down to the office of sexton and bell ringer. Every dispute is called to Rome, and everyone does just as he pleases, under cover of the pope's authority.

What has happened in this very year? The bishop of Strasbourg wanted to govern his chapter properly and reform it in matters of worship. With this end in view, he established certain godly and Christian regulations. But our dear friend the pope and the Holy Roman See wrecked and damned this holy and spiritual ordinance, all at the instigation of the priests.[43] This is called feeding the sheep of Christ! That is how priests are strengthened against their own bishop, and how their disobedience to divine law is protected! Antichrist himself, I hope, will not dare to shame God so openly. There is your pope for you! Just as you have always wanted! Why did the pope do this? Ah! If one church were reformed, that would be a dangerous breakthrough. Rome might have to follow suit. Therefore, it is better that no priest be allowed to get along with another and, as we have grown accustomed to seeing right up to the present day, that kings and princes should be set at odds. It is better to flood the world with Christian blood, lest the unity of Christians compel the Holy Roman See to reform itself!

So far we have been considering how they deal with benefices that become vacant and are unoccupied. But for tender-hearted Avarice the vacancies are too few. Therefore, he has kept a very close watch even on those benefices still occupied by their incumbents, so that these too can be made vacant, even though they are not now vacant. He does this in several ways.

First, Avarice lies in wait where fat prebends or bishoprics are held by an old or sick man, or even by one with an alleged disability. The Holy See then provides a coadjutor, that is, an assistant, to an incumbent of this kind. This is done without the holder's consent or permission, and for the benefit of the coadjutor, because he is a member of the pope's "household," or because he has paid for it, or has otherwise earned it by some sort of service to Rome. In this case, the free rights of the chapter or the rights of the incumbent

43. Although he became a determined opponent of the Reformation, Wilhelm III, Count of Honstein (c. 1470–1541), bishop of Strasbourg from 1506 to 1541, had a long history of failed attempts to reform the clergy of his diocese. It is not clear what particular event Luther is referring to here, but he appears to have learned of it from Georg Spalatin; see WA Br 2:130, 20.

44. To be awarded a benefice *in commendam* was to be assigned the income from it without being obligated to perform the spiritual office that went with it (which would usually be assigned to a paid deputy or curate). *Commenda* had long been used to supplement the income of students, professors, ecclesiastical diplomats, cardinals, and others. The appointment of cardinals or even laymen as abbots *in commendam* was a longstanding abuse that was not effectively dealt with until the Council of Trent.

45. A monk who had abandoned his monastery without permission was deemed "apostate." In Luther's day, such renegade monks, wandering about in their garb and exercising the rights and privileges of their order, were a common sight. They were a nuisance to the resident parish clergy and often disrupted parish life.

46. Offices that cannot be combined in the hands of one officeholder.

47. In this context, "gloss" means a specious, self-serving interpretation and application of a word or expression. Luther is not referring to the "ordinary glosses" (*glossa ordinaria*), which were the authoritative commentaries on canon law by medieval jurists (glossators).

48. The *datarius* was the head of the *Dataria apostolica*, the bureau of the

are disregarded, and the whole thing falls into the hands of Rome.

Second, there is the little word *commenda*.[44] This means the pope puts a cardinal, or another of his underlings, in charge of a rich, prosperous monastery, just as if I were to give you a hundred gulden to keep. This does not mean to give the monastery or bestow it. Nor does it mean abolishing it or the divine service. It means quite simply to give it into his keeping. Not that he to whom it is entrusted is to care for it or build it up, but he is to drive out the incumbent, receive the goods and revenues, and install some apostate, renegade monk or another,[45] who accepts five or six gulden a year and sits all day long in the church selling pictures and images to the pilgrims, so that neither prayers nor Masses are said in that place anymore. If this were to be called destroying monasteries and abolishing the worship of God, then the pope would have to be called a destroyer of Christendom and an abolisher of divine worship. He certainly does well at it! But this would be harsh language for Rome, so they have to call it a "*commenda*," or an entrusting for taking over the charge of the monastery. The pope can make "*commenda*" of four or more of these monasteries in one year, any single one of which may have an income of more than six thousand gulden. This is how the Romanists increase the worship of God and maintain the monasteries! Even the Germans are beginning to find that out!

Third, there are some benefices they call *incompatabilia*,[46] which, according to the ordinances of canon law, cannot be held at the same time, such as two parishes, two bishoprics, and the like. In these cases, the Holy Roman See of Avarice evades canon law by making glosses to its own advantage,[47] called *unio* and *incorporatio*. This means that the pope incorporates many *incompatabilia* into one single unit, so that each is a part of every other, and all of them together are looked upon as one benefice. They are then no longer *incompatabilia*, and the holy canon law is satisfied because it is no longer binding, except upon those who do not buy these glosses from the pope or his *datarius*.[48] The *unio*, that is, the uniting, is very similar. The pope combines many such benefices like a bundle of sticks, and they are all regarded as one benefice. There is at present a certain papal courtier[t] in Rome who alone holds twenty-two parishes, seven priories, as well as forty-four benefices.[49] All these are held by the help of that masterly gloss, which declares that this is not against canon law. What the cardinals and other prelates get out of it is anybody's guess. And this is the way the Germans are to have their purses emptied and their insolence deflated.

Another of these glosses is the *administratio*. This means that a man may hold, in addition to his bishopric, some abbacy or dignity and all its emoluments, without having the title attached to it. He is simply called the "administrator."[50] At Rome it is sufficient to change a word or two but leave the actuality what it was before. It is as if I were to teach that we were now to call the brothel-keeper the mayor's wife. She still remains what she was before. This kind of Romish regime Peter foretold in 2 Pet. 2[:1, 3], "False teachers will come who will deal with you in greed and lying words for their gain."

Our worthy Roman Avarice has devised another technique. He sells and bestows benefices on the condition that the vendor or bestower retains reversionary rights to them. In that event, when the incumbent dies the benefices automatically revert to him who had sold, bestowed, or surrendered them in the first instance. In this way, they have made hereditary property out of the benefices. Nobody else can come into possession of them except the man to whom the seller is willing to dispose of them, or to whom he bequeaths his rights at death. Besides, there are many who transfer to another the mere title to a benefice, but from which the titleholder does not draw a cent. Today, too, it has become an established custom to confer a benefice on a man while reserving a portion of the annual income for oneself. This used to be called simony.[51] There are many more things of this sort than can be counted. They treat benefices more shamefully than the heathen soldiers treated Christ's clothes at the foot of the cross.

papal Curia responsible for drafting, registering, and dating (hence the name) such written decisions of the pope as dispensations, appointments to benefices, and so forth. Fees were charged for its services.

49. The papal courtier referred to by Luther has not been identified. But there is documentation for two Germans, Johannes Zink (d. c. 1527) and Johannes Ingenwinkel (1469–1535), who accumulated papal appointments in Rome. In the period 1513 to 1521, Zink received fifty-six appointments; in the years 1496 to 1521 Ingenwinkel received 106. See Aloys Schulte, *Die Fugger in Rom 1495–1523*, vol. 1 (Leipzig: Verlag von Duncker, 1904), 282–306.

50. As, for example, in the case of Albrecht von Brandenburg, who was the administrator of Halberstadt; see above, n. 41.

51. Simony (named for Simon Magus; cf. Acts 8:18-20) was the buying or selling of an ecclesiastical office for money, favors, or any kind of material reward. It was strictly against canon law but widely practiced nonetheless.

t   Luther's word is *kurtisan* (from the Latin *curtisanus*), the common (pejorative) term for a member of the papal Curia, or for a clergyman who secured his appointment from the Roman Curia.

52. From 1484 popes claimed and occasionally exercised the right to issue decrees, the content of which had been determined by the pope *motu proprio* ("of his own accord"), without consulting the cardinals or any other authorities, for reasons that he himself found sufficient.

But all that has been said up till now has been going on for so long that it has become established custom at Rome. Yet Avarice has come up with something else, which I hope may be his last and choke him. The pope has a noble little device called *pectoralis reservatio*, meaning mental reservation,[u] and *proprius motus*, meaning the arbitrary exercise of his authority.[52] It goes like this. A certain man goes to Rome and succeeds in procuring a benefice. It is duly signed and sealed in the customary manner. Then another candidate comes along, who brings money or else has rendered services to the pope, which bears no mention here, and desires the same benefice of the pope. The pope then gives it to him and takes it away from the other. If anybody complains that this is not right, then the Most Holy Father has to find some excuse lest he be accused of a flagrant violation of [canon] law. He then says that he had mentally reserved that particular benefice to himself and had retained full rights of disposal over it, although he had neither given it a thought in his whole life nor even heard of it. In this way, he has now found his usual little gloss. As pope he can tell lies, deceive, and make everybody look like a fool. And all this he does openly and unashamedly. And yet he still wants to be the head of Christendom, but lets himself be ruled by the evil spirit in obvious lies.

The pope's arbitrary and deceptive reservation now creates such a state of affairs in Rome that it defies description. There is buying, selling, bartering, exchanging, trading, pretense, deceit, robbery, theft, luxury, whoring, knavery, and every sort of contempt of God. Even the rule of the Antichrist could not be more scandalous. Venice, Antwerp, and Cairo[53] have nothing on this fair at Rome and all that goes on there. In these places there is still some regard for right and reason, but in Rome the devil himself is in charge. And out of this sea the same kind of morality flows into the whole world. Is it any wonder that people like this are terrified of reformation and of a free council, and prefer rather to set all the kings and princes at enmity lest in their unity they

53. Three major ports in the commerce of the day, famed as centers of vice.

---

u   Literally, "reservation in the breast or heart."

should call a council? Who could bear to have such villainy brought to light?

Finally, the pope has built his own emporium for all this noble commerce, that is, the house of the *datarius* in Rome.[v] All who deal in benefices and livings must go there. Here they have to buy their glosses, transact their business, and get authority to practice such arch-knavery. There was a time when Rome was still lenient. In those days, people just had to buy justice or suppress it with money. But Rome has become so expensive today that it allows no one to practice such knavery unless he has first bought the right to do so. If that is not a brothel above all imaginable brothels, then I do not know what brothels are.

If you have money in such an emporium, you can obtain all the things we have just discussed. Indeed, not just these! Here usury[54] becomes honest money; the possession of property acquired by theft or robbery is legalized. Here vows are dissolved; monks are granted freedom to leave their orders. Here marriage is on sale to the clergy. Here the children of whores can be legitimized. Here all dishonor and shame can be made to look like honor and glory. Here every kind of fault and blemish is knighted and ennobled. Here marriage within the forbidden degrees or otherwise forbidden is rendered acceptable. O what assessing and fleecing take place there! It seems as though canon law were instituted solely for the purpose of setting a great many money traps from which anyone who wants to be a Christian must purchase his freedom. In fact, here the devil becomes a saint, and a god as well. What cannot be done anywhere else in heaven or on earth, can be done in this emporium. They call these things *compositiones*! Compositions indeed! Better named confusions.[55] Compared with the exactions of this holy house the Rhine toll is a poor sum indeed.[56]

Let no one accuse me of exaggeration. It is all so open that even in Rome they have to admit that the state of affairs there is more atrocious than anyone can say. I have not yet stirred the real hellish dregs of their personal vices—nor do

54. Canon law still condemned as usury the charging by Christians of interest on loans to other Christians.

55. *Compositiones* were the fees paid for dispensations from the provisions of canon law. Luther makes a pun on *compositiones* (literally, "things in good order") and *confusiones* ("things in disorder").

56. Princes and nobles who had fortresses along the Rhine commonly exacted tolls from passing merchant ships.

v   See n. 48 above.

57. The Fugger firm of Augsburg was the greatest international banking house of the sixteenth century. It numbered popes, bishops, emperors, kings, and princes among its clients and benefactors. The Fuggers advanced to Charles V the funds needed to secure his election as emperor. Similarly, they advanced to Albrecht von Brandenburg the monies required for the purchase from Rome of the dispensations he needed to become archbishop of Mainz (see p. 399, n. 41).

58. A bull is a solemn mandate of the pope on any subject under his authority (the definition of doctrine, the granting of privileges, etc.). The name "bull" derives from the Latin *bulla*, a term for the seal attached to an official document.

59. Certificates that entitled the bearer to choose his or her own confessor and authorized the confessor to confer absolution for offenses normally reserved to the jurisdiction of bishops or the pope.

60. *Butterbriefe* was the popular term for written dispensations to consume butter, cheese, and milk during Lent.

61. The Campo de' Fiore was a Roman marketplace that Pope Eugene IV and his successors restored and developed at great expense. The Belvedere, originally a garden house in the Vatican, was turned into an elegant banquet hall and then used by Pope Julius II to store his collection of ancient art (e.g., the Apollo Belvedere). Luther hints that indulgence money was lavished on such projects rather than used for constructing St. Peter's in Rome as advertised.

I want to. I speak only of ordinary, well-known matters, and still cannot find adequate words for them. Bishops, priests, and above all the theologians in the universities ought to have done their duty and with common accord written against such goings-on and cried out against them. This is what they are paid to do! But the truth is found on the other side of the page.[w]

I must take leave of this subject with one final word. Since this Boundless Avarice is not satisfied with all this wealth, wealth with which three great kings would be content, he now begins to transfer this trade and sell it to the Fuggers of Augsburg.[57] The lending, trading, and buying of bishoprics and benefices, and the commerce in ecclesiastical holdings, have now come to the right place. Now spiritual and secular goods have become one. I would now like to hear of somebody clever enough to imagine what Roman Avarice could do more than what it has already done, unless perhaps Fugger were to transfer or sell this present combination of two lines of business to somebody else. I really think it has just reached the limit.

As for what they have stolen in all lands, and still steal and extort, through indulgences, bulls,[58] confessional letters,[59] butter letters,[60] and other *confessionalia*—all this is just patchwork. It is just as if one were rolled dice with a devil right into hell. Not that these things bring in little money—for a powerful king could well support himself on such proceeds—but it is not to be compared with the streams of treasure referred to above. I shall say nothing at present about where this indulgence money has gone. I shall have more to say about that later. The Campo de' Fiore and the Belvedere and certain other places probably know something about that.[61]

Since, then, such devilish rule is not only barefaced robbery, deceit, and the tyranny of the gates of hell but also ruinous to the body and soul of Christendom, it is our duty to exercise all diligence to protect Christendom from

---

w I.e., the opposite is the case.

such misery and destruction. If we want to fight against the Turks, let us begin here where they are worst of all. If we are right in hanging thieves and beheading robbers, why should we let Roman Avarice go free? He is the worst thief and robber that has ever been or could ever come into the world, and all in the holy name of Christ and St. Peter! Who can put up with it a moment longer and say nothing? Almost everything Avarice possesses has been procured by theft and robbery. It has never been otherwise, as all the history books prove. The pope never purchased such extensive holdings that the income from his *officia*ˣ should amount to one million ducats, over and above the gold mines we have just been discussing and the income from his lands. Nor did Christ and St. Peter bequeath it to him. Neither has anyone given or lent it to him. Neither is it his by virtue of ancient rights or usage. Tell me, then, from what source could he have obtained it? Learn a lesson from this, and watch carefully what they are after and what they say when they send out their legates to collect money to fight the Turks.

Now, although I am too insignificant a man to make concrete proposals for the improvement of this dreadful state of affairs, nevertheless I shall sing my fool's song through to the end and say, so far as I am able, what could and should be done, either by secular authority or by a general council.

1. Every prince, every noble, every city should henceforth forbid their subjects to pay annates to Rome and should abolish them entirely. The pope has broken the agreement and made the annates a robbery to the injury and shame of the whole German nation. He gives them to his friends, sells them for huge sums of money, and uses them to endow offices. In so doing he has lost his right to them and deserves punishment. Consequently, secular authority is under obligation to protect the innocent and prevent injustice, as Paul teaches in Romans 13, and St. Peter in 1 Pet. 2[:14], and even the canon law in Case 16, Question 7, [canon 31], *de filiis*.[62] From this came the basis for saying to the pope and his own

62. The correct name of the canon is *Filiis vel nepotibus*; Friedberg 1:809. It provides that when the endowment provided for a church is misused, and appeals to the bishop and archbishop fail to correct the abuse, the heirs of the person who established the endowment may appeal to the secular courts. Luther wants this principle applied to annates as well.

ˣ   The curial offices that could be purchased; see p. 396, n. 36.

63. Although Luther here adheres to the traditional threefold division of society into priests, rulers, and workers (or farmers), he does so in accordance with the position taken in his assault on the first wall (pp. 381–85), namely that secular rulers have the obligation to protect their subjects against secular crimes committed by the clergy.

[the clergy], "*Tu ora*, thou shalt pray"; to the emperor and his servants, "*Tu protege*, thou shalt protect"; to the common man, "*Tu labora*, thou shalt labor," not, however, as though each person were not to pray, protect, and labor. (For the one who performs any task diligently does nothing but pray, protect, and labor.) But to each a special work is assigned.[63]

2. Since the pope with his Romish tricks—his *commenda*, coadjutors, reservations, *gratiae expectativae*, papal months, incorporations, unions, pensions, *pallia*, chancery rules, and such knavery[y]—usurps for himself all the German foundations without authority and right and gives and sells them to foreigners at Rome who do nothing for Germany in return, and since he robs the local bishops of their rights and makes mere ciphers and dummies of them, and thereby acts contrary to his own canon law, common sense, and reason, it has finally reached the point where the livings and benefices are, out of sheer greed, sold to coarse, unlettered donkeys and ignorant knaves at Rome. Pious and learned people do not benefit from their service or skill. Consequently the poor German people must go without competent and learned prelates and be destroyed.

For this reason, the Christian nobility should set itself against the pope as against a common enemy and destroyer of Christendom for the salvation of the poor souls who perish because of this tyranny. The Christian nobility should ordain, order, and decree that henceforth no further benefice shall be drawn into the hands of Rome, and that hereafter no appointment shall be obtained there in any manner whatsoever, but that the benefices should be dragged from this tyrannical authority and kept out of his reach. The nobility should restore to the local bishops their right and responsibility to administer the benefices in the German nation to the best of their ability. And when a papal courtier comes along,[z] he should be given a strict order to keep out, to jump into the Rhine or the nearest river, and give the

---

y   With the exception of *gratiae expectivae* (promises to bestow a benefice not yet vacant), these "tricks" were explained earlier; see above, pp. 401–5, with the explanatory notes.

z   Cf. p. 403, n. 49 and note *t*.

Romish ban with all its seals and letters a nice, cold bath. If this happened, they would sit up and take notice in Rome. They would not think that the Germans are always dull and drunk but have really become Christian again. They would realize that the Germans do not intend to permit the holy name of Christ, in whose name all this knavery and destruction of souls goes on, to be scoffed at and scorned any longer, and that they have more regard for God's honor than for the authority of mortals.

3. An imperial law should be issued that no bishop's cloak [*pallium*] and no confirmation of any dignity whatsoever shall henceforth be secured from Rome, but that the ordinance of the most holy and famous Council of Nicaea be restored. This ordinance decreed that a bishop shall be confirmed by the two nearest bishops or by the archbishop.[64] If the pope breaks the statutes of this and of all other councils, what is the use of holding councils? Who has given him the authority to despise the decisions of councils and tear them to shreds like this? Perhaps we should depose all bishops, archbishops, and primates[65] and make ordinary pastors of them, with only the pope as their superior, as he now is. The pope allows no proper authority or responsibility to the bishops, archbishops, and primates. He usurps everything for himself and lets them keep only the name and the empty title. It has even gone so far that by papal exemption the monasteries, abbots, and prelates as well are removed from the regular authority of the bishops.[66] Consequently there is no longer any order in Christendom. The inevitable result of all this is what has happened already: relaxation of punishment and the license to do evil all over the world. I certainly fear that the pope may properly be called "the man of sin" [2 Thess. 2:3]. Who but the pope can be blamed for there being no discipline, no punishment, no government, no order in Christendom? By his usurpation of power he ties the prelates' hands and takes away their rod of discipline. He opens his hands to all those set under him, and gives away or sells them freedom.[a]

64. Canon 4 of the Council of Nicaea (325). Here Luther still assumes that the existing ecclesiastical hierarchy would be preserved and reformed.

65. A primate was the highest-ranking archbishop of a country; in the Empire it was the archbishop of Mainz.

66. It was common practice for monastic houses to be removed from the jurisdiction of the local bishop and placed directly under that of the pope. Indeed, it was all but universal in the case of the houses of the mendicant orders.

_____

a I.e., freedom from the jurisdiction of the local prelate.

67. This was actually a decree of the Council of Sardica (343), but it was incorporated into canon law with inaccurate attribution to the Council of Nicaea; see Friedberg 1:520.

68. The councils of Constance and Basel had both tried to put an end to the evocation of secular cases to the Roman Curia, but it remained one of the most often-repeated of the grievances of the Holy Roman Empire against Rome. See Benrath, 97–98, n. 43; RTA 2:672, par. 1.

Lest the pope complain that he is being robbed of his authority, it should be decreed that in those cases where the primates or the archbishops are unable to settle a case, or when a dispute arises between them, then the matter should be laid before the pope, but not every little thing. It was done this way in former times, and this was the way the famous Council of Nicaea decreed.[67] Whatever can be settled without the pope, then, should be settled in such a way that his holiness is not burdened with such minor matters, but gives himself to prayer, study and the care of all Christendom. This is what he claims to do. This is what the apostles did. They said in Acts 6[:2-4], "It is not right that we should leave the Word of God and serve tables, but we will hold to preaching and prayer, and set others over that work." But now Rome stands for nothing else than the despising of the gospel and prayer, and for the serving of tables, that is, temporal things. The government of the apostles and of the pope have as much in common as Christ has with Lucifer, heaven with hell, night with day. Yet the pope is called "Vicar of Christ" and "Successor to the Apostles."

4. It should be decreed that no secular matter is to be referred to Rome, but that all such cases shall be left to secular authority, as the Romanists themselves prescribe in that canon law of theirs, which they do not observe.[68] It should be the pope's duty to be the most learned in the Scriptures and the holiest (not in name only but in fact) and to regulate matters that concern the faith and holy life of Christians. He should hold the primates and archbishops to this task, and help them in dealing with these matters and taking care of these responsibilities. This is what St. Paul teaches in 1 Cor. 6[:7], and he takes the Corinthians severely to task for their concern with worldly things. That such matters are dealt with in Rome causes unbearable grief in every land. It increases the costs, and, moreover, these judges do not know the usage, laws, and customs of these lands, so that they often do violence to the facts and base their decisions on their own laws and precedents. As a result, the contesting parties often suffer injustice.

Moreover, the horrible fleecing practiced by the officials[69] must be forbidden in every diocese, so that they no longer assume jurisdiction over anything except matters of faith and morals and leave matters of money and property, life and honor, to the secular judges. Secular judges, therefore, should not allow sentences of excommunication and banishment in cases where faith and morals are not involved. Spiritual authority should rule over matters that are spiritual, as reason teaches. Spiritual goods, however, do not consist of money or material things but rather of faith and good works.

One might, nonetheless, grant that cases concerning benefices or livings be tried before bishops, archbishops and primates. Accordingly, whenever disputes or conflicts needed to be resolved, the primate of Germany could hold a general consistory with its jurists and judges, which would have the same authority as that of the *signatura gratiae* and *signatura justitiae* in Rome.[70] Cases in Germany would, by means of appeal, be brought before it and transacted in good order. One could not be required to pay for this by occasional presents and gifts, as is the case at Rome, as a result of which they have grown accustomed to the selling of justice and injustice. This is because the pope does not pay them a salary, but lets them grow fat from gifts. For no one at Rome cares anything about what is right or wrong, only about what is money and what is not. One might, rather, pay for this [court] from the annates, or in some other way devised by those who are better informed and more experienced in these things than I am. All I seek to do is to arouse and set to thinking those who have the ability and inclination to help the German nation be free and Christian again after the wretched, heathenish, and un-Christian reign of the pope.

5. Reservations should no longer be valid,[b] and no more benefices should be seized by Rome, even if the incumbent dies or there is a dispute, or even if the incumbent is a member of the pope's household or on the staff of a cardinal. And it must be strictly forbidden and prevented for any

69. The *officialis* was the presiding judge of a bishop's court.

70. The supreme tribunal of the church was the *Signatura*, which was divided into the *Signatura gratiae*, presided over by the pope himself, and the *Signatura justitiae*, headed by a cardinal. The latter resolved conflicts of jurisdiction among various legal entities in the Curia. The former handled the pope's responses to requests for privileges or favors and in so doing could grant exemptions from church law. The proposal to turn the honorary primacy of the archbishop of Mainz into the effective headship of a German church with extensive administrative independence of Rome was first advanced by the Alsatian humanist Jakob Wimpfeling (1450–1528) in a memorandum submitted to Emperor Maximilian I in 1510. A shortened version of the memorandum had been published in May 1520, but Luther appears to have had access to the full manuscript. See Benrath, 98, n. 45.

b   See p. 398, n. 38.

papal courtier[c] to contest any benefice whatsoever, to summon pious priests to court, harass them, or force them into lawsuits. If, in consequence of this prohibition, any ban or ecclesiastical pressure should come from Rome, it should be disregarded, just as though a thief were to put a man under the ban because he would not let him steal. Indeed, they should be severely punished for blasphemous misuse of the ban and the divine name to strengthen their hand at robbery, and for desiring, by means of lies and fabrications, to compel us to endure and praise such blasphemy of God's name and such abuse of Christian authority, and to be participants in their rascality in the sight of God. We are responsible before God to oppose them, as St. Paul in Rom. 1[:32] reproves as worthy of death not only those who do such things, but also those who approve and permit them to be done. Most unbearable of all is the lying *reservatio pectoralis,*[d] whereby Christendom is so scandalously and openly put to shame and scorn because its head deals with open lies and for filthy lucre unashamedly deceives and fools everybody.

6. The *casus reservati*, reserved cases,[71] should also be abolished. They are not only the means of extorting much money from the people, but by means of them the ruthless tyrants ensnare and confuse many tender consciences, intolerably injuring their faith in God. This is especially true of the ridiculous, childish cases they make such a fuss about in the bull *Coena Domini,*[72] sins which should not even be called everyday sins, much less so great that the pope cannot remit them by indulgence. Examples of these sins are hindering a pilgrim on his way to Rome, supplying weapons to the Turk, or counterfeiting papal briefs.[73] They make fools of us with such crude, silly, clumsy goings-on! Sodom and Gomorrah, and all the sins that are or may be committed against the commandments of God, are not reserved cases. But what God has never commanded and they themselves have imagined—these must be reserved cases, in order that no one be prevented from bringing money to Rome, so that

71. Those cases in which the granting of absolution was reserved to the pope.

72. Since the fourteenth century it had been the custom to publish at Rome on Maundy Thursday an updated version of the bull *In coena Domini*, a catalog of heresies and offenses punishable by excommunication, absolution for which was reserved to the pope. After his excommunication in 1521, Luther's name was added to the list of heretics.

73. A decree in the form of a letter emanating from the pope, simpler in form than a bull but of comparable authority.

c   See p. 403, n. 49.

d   I.e., mental reservation; see above, p. 404.

they may live in the lap of luxury, safe from the Turks and by their wanton, worthless bulls and briefs keep the world subjected to their tyranny.

Such knowledge should properly be available from all priests or be a public ordinance, namely, that no secret, undenounced sin constitutes a reserved case; and that every priest has the power to remit every sin no matter what it is.[e] Where sins are secret, neither abbot, bishop, nor pope has the power to reserve one of them to himself. If they did that, their action would be null and void. They ought even to be punished as people who without any right at all presume to make judgments in God's stead, and thereby ensnare and burden poor and ignorant consciences. In those cases, however, where open and notorious sins are committed, especially sins against God's commandments, then there are indeed grounds for reserved cases. But even then there should not be too many of them, and they should not be reserved arbitrarily and without cause. For Christ did not set tyrants in his church, but shepherds, as Peter said in the last chapter of his first epistle [1 Pet. 5:2-3].

7. The Roman See should do away with the *officia*[f] and cut down the creeping, crawling swarm of vermin at Rome, so that the pope's household can be supported out of the pope's own pocket. The pope should not allow his court to surpass the courts of all kings in pomp and extravagance, because this kind of thing not only has never been of any use to the cause of the Christian faith but also has kept the courtiers from study and prayer until they are hardly able to speak about the faith at all. This they proved quite flagrantly at this last Roman council,[74] in which, among many other childish and frivolous things, they decreed that the human soul is immortal and that every priest must say his

74. The Fifth Lateran Council (1412–1417), convened by Julius II.

---

e   Thesis 6 (*95 Theses*, above, p. 35) stated, "The pope cannot remit any guilt except by declaring and confirming its remission by God or, of course, by remitting guilt in [legal] cases reserved to himself." In terms of divine grace and the removal of guilt, priests simply announced God's forgiveness. Regarding especially heinous sins, ecclesiastical absolution was restricted to the papal see.

f   See p. 396, n. 36.

prayers once a month unless he wants to lose his benefice. How can the affairs of Christendom and matters of faith be settled by people who are hardened and blinded by gross avarice, wealth, and worldly splendor, and who now for the first time decree that the soul is immortal? It is no small shame to the whole of Christendom that they deal so disgracefully with the faith at Rome. If they had less wealth and pomp, they could pray better and study to be worthy and diligent in dealing with matters of faith, as was the case in former times, when bishops did not presume to be the kings of all kings.

8. The harsh and terrible oaths that the bishops are wrongfully compelled to swear to the pope should be abolished. These oaths bind the bishops like servants and are decreed in that arbitrary, stupid, worthless, and unlearned chapter, *Significasti*.[75] Is it not enough that they burden us in body, soul, and property with their countless foolish laws by which they weaken faith and waste Christendom, without also making a prisoner of the bishop both as a person as well as in his office and function? In addition, they have also assumed the investiture,[76] which in ancient times was the right of the German emperor, and in France and other countries investiture still belongs to the king. They had great wars and disputes with the emperors about this matter until finally they had the brazen effrontery to take it over, and have held it until now; just as though the Germans more than all other Christians on earth had to be the silly fools of the pope and the Romanist See and do and put up with what no one else will either put up with or do. Since this is sheer robbery and violence, hinders the regular authority of the bishop, and injures poor souls, the emperor and his nobles are duty-bound to prevent and punish such tyranny.

9. The pope should have no authority over the emperor, except the right to anoint and crown him at the altar, just as a bishop crowns a king. We should never again yield to that devilish pride which requires the emperor to kiss the pope's feet, or sit at his feet, or, as they say, hold his stirrup or the bridle of his mule when he mounts to go riding. Still less should he do homage and swear faithful allegiance to

75. It provided that no pallium (above, p. 400, n. 42) was to be bestowed on an archbishop until he had sworn an oath of allegiance to the Holy See; Friedberg 2:49–50.

76. Investiture was the ceremony of installing a bishop in office by bestowing on him the staff and ring that were the symbols of his authority. In Germany this was a matter complicated by the fact that most bishops were the secular rulers of an imperial territory (e.g., the electorate of Mainz) as well as the overseers of an ecclesiastical benefice (e.g., the archbishopric of Mainz). In the eleventh and twelfth centuries, this situation had produced a bitter struggle between pope and emperor over who controlled the investiture of bishops. The Concordat of Worms (1122) took away from the emperor the right to invest bishops with ring and staff and left him with only the right to invest them with authority as secular rulers.

the pope, as the popes brazenly demand as though they had a right to it. The chapter *Solite*,[g] which sets papal authority above imperial authority, is not worth a cent, and the same goes for all those who base their authority on it or pay any deference to it. For it does nothing else than force the holy words of God, and wrest them out of their true meaning to conform to their own fond imaginations, as I have shown in a Latin treatise.[h]

This most extreme, arrogant, and wanton presumption of the pope has been devised by the devil, who under cover of this intends to usher in the Antichrist and raise the pope above God, as many are now doing and even have already done. It is not proper for the pope to exalt himself above the secular authorities, except in spiritual offices such as preaching and giving absolution. In other matters, the pope is subject to the crown, as Paul and Peter teach in Rom. 13[:1-7] and 1 Pet. 2[:13], and as I have explained above.[i]

The pope is not a vicar of Christ in heaven but only of Christ as he walked the earth. Christ in heaven, in the form of a ruler, needs no vicar, but sits on his throne and sees everything, does everything, knows everything, and has all power. But Christ needs a vicar in the form of a servant, the form in which he went about on earth, working, preaching, suffering, and dying. Now the Romanists turn all that upside down. They take the heavenly and kingly form from Christ and give it to the pope, and leave the form of a servant to perish completely. He might almost be the Counter-Christ, whom the Scriptures call Antichrist,[j] for all his nature, work, and pretensions run counter to Christ and only blot out Christ's nature and destroy his work.

It is also ridiculous and childish for the pope, on the basis of such perverted and deluded reasoning, to claim in his decretal *Pastoralis* that he is rightful heir to the emperorship

---

g   Friedberg 2:196.

h   *Resolutio Lutheriana super propositione XIII de potestate papae* (1519) in WA 2:217-21, 8, part of the Leipzig Debate with Johann Eck in 1519.

i   See pp. 364-85.

j   See p. 387, n. 24.

77. This document, the *Donation of Constantine* (Mirbt-Aland, no. 504), purported to be the testament of Emperor Constantine. It conferred on the pope temporal sovereignty in Rome, Italy, and "all the western regions" and was used to bolster not only papal claims to secular rule in Italy but also the claim that the secular authority of kings and emperors was a gracious concession from the pope, in whom supreme secular and ecclesiastical authority were united. In 1440 the Italian humanist Lorenzo Valla (c. 1407–1457) demonstrated that the *Donation* was a forgery. Shortly before writing this treatise, Luther had read the edition of Valla's treatise published by Ulrich von Hutten in 1517. For an abbreviated English version, see Henry Bettenson and Chris Maunder, eds., *Documents of the Christian Church*, 4th ed. (New York: Oxford University Press, 2011), 102–6.

78. Since 1060, popes had claimed feudal sovereignty over the kingdom of Naples and Sicily, where much land had been given to the church since late antiquity. These claims, justified on the basis of the *Donation of Constantine* (see preceding note), were hotly contested.

79. At this time the kingdom was contested between the royal houses of France and Spain. Emperor Charles V was also King Charles I of Spain.

in the event of a vacancy.[k] Who has given him this right? Was it Christ when he said, "The princes of the Gentiles are lords, but it shall not be so among you" [Luke 22:25-26]? Or did Peter bequeath it to him? It makes me angry that we have to read and learn such shameless, gross, and idiotic lies in canon law and must even hold them as Christian doctrine when they are devilish lies.

That impossible lie, the *Donation of Constantine*,[77] is the same sort of thing. It must have been some special plague from God that so many intelligent people have let themselves be talked into accepting such lies. They are so crude and clumsy that I should imagine any drunken peasant could lie more adroitly and skillfully. How can a person rule and at the same time preach, pray, study, and care for the poor? Yet these are the duties which most properly and peculiarly belong to the pope, and they were so earnestly imposed by Christ that he even forbade his disciples to take cloak or money with them [Matt. 10:9-10]. Christ commanded this because it is almost impossible for anybody to fulfill these duties if they have to look after one single household. Yet the pope would rule an empire and still remain pope. This is what those rogues have thought up, who under the cover of the pope's name would like to be lords of the world and would gladly restore the Roman Empire to its former state through the pope and in the name of Christ.

10. The pope should restrain himself, take his fingers out of the pie, and claim no title to the kingdom of Naples and Sicily.[78] He has exactly as much right to that kingdom as I have, and yet he wants to be its overlord. It is property gotten by robbery and violence, like almost all his other possessions. The emperor, therefore, should not grant him this realm, and where it has been granted, he should no longer give his consent.[79] Instead, he should draw the pope's attention to the Bible and the prayer book, that he preach and pray and leave the government of lands and people—especially those that no one has given to him—to the lords.

---

k   *Clem.* lib 2, tit. 11. cap. 2 (Friedberg 2:1151–53).

The same goes for Bologna, Imola, Vicenza, Ravenna, and all the territories in the March of Ancona, Romagna, and other lands that the pope has seized by force and possesses without right.[80] Moreover, the pope has meddled in these things against every express command of Christ and St. Paul. For as St. Paul says, "No one should be entangled in worldly affairs who should tend to being a soldier of God."[l] Now the pope should be the head and chief of these soldiers, and yet he meddles in worldly affairs more than any emperor or king. We have to pull him out of these affairs and let him tend to being a soldier. Even Christ, whose vicar the pope boasts he is, was never willing to have anything to do with secular rule. In fact, when somebody sought a judgment from him in the matter of a brother's action, he said to that man, "Who made me a judge over you?" [Luke 12:14]. But the pope rushes in without invitation and boldly takes hold of everything as if he were a god, until he no longer knows who Christ is, whose vicar he pretends to be.

11. Further, the kissing of the pope's feet should cease.[m] It is an un-Christian, indeed, an anti-Christian thing for a poor sinful man to let his feet be kissed by one who is a hundred times better than himself. If it is done in honor of his authority, why does the pope not do the same to others in honor of their holiness? Compare them with each other— Christ and the pope. Christ washed his disciples' feet and dried them, but the disciples never washed his feet [John 13:4-16]. The pope, as though he were higher than Christ, turns that about and allows his feet to be kissed as a great favor. Though properly, if anyone wanted to do so, the pope ought to use all his power to prevent it, as did St. Paul and Barnabas, who would not let the people of Lystra pay them divine honor, but said, "We are mortals like you" [Acts 14:15]. But our flatterers have gone so far as to make an idol [of the pope] for us, so that no one fears or honors God as

80. All these were components of the states of the church, the conglomeration of territories in central Italy over which the pope exercised direct secular rule. It was in large measure the result of claims to secular authority in Italy that the papacy was inextricably involved in the political and military struggles of Italy and western Europe.

l This is a free rendering of the Vulgate text of 2 Tim. 2:4.

m See above, p. 414 and below, n. 81., p. 418.

81. Both kissing the pope's feet and his being carried were depicted in *Passional Christi und Antichristi* (1521; WA 9:677–715 with the appendix), with woodcuts by Lukas Cranach Sr. (1472–1553) and comments by Philip Melanchthon and Martin Luther contrasting papal practices with Christ's passion. For depiction of this, see below, p. 523.

The pope being carried in a procession.

much as he fears and honors the pope. They will stand for that, but not for diminishing the pope's majesty by so much as a hairsbreadth. If they were only Christian and esteemed God's honor more than their own, the pope would never be happy to see God's honor despised and his own exalted. Nor would he let anyone honor him until he saw that God's honor was once more exalted and raised higher than his own.[81, n]

Another example of the same scandalous pride is that the pope is not satisfied to ride or be driven, but, although strong and in good health, has himself borne by men like an idol and with unheard-of splendor. Dear readers, how does such satanic pride compare with Christ, who went on foot, as did all his disciples? Where has there ever been a worldly monarch who went about in such worldly pomp and glory as he who wants to be the head of all those who ought to despise and flee from the pomp and vanity of this world, that is, the Christians? Not that we should bother ourselves very much about him as a person, but we certainly ought to fear the wrath of God if we flatter this sort of pride and do not show our indignation. It is enough that the pope rants and plays the fool in this way. But it is too much if we approve of it and grant it to him.

What Christian heart can or should take pleasure in seeing that when the pope wishes to receive communion, he sits quietly like a gracious lord and has the sacrament brought to him on a golden rod by a bowing cardinal on bended knee? As though the holy sacrament were not worthy that the pope, a poor, stinking sinner, should rise and show respect to his God, when all other Christians, who are much holier than the Most Holy Father the pope, receive it with all due reverence! Would it be a wonder if God sent down a plague upon us all

---

n   The remainder of this section was not included in the first printing of the treatise. Along with two other passages indicated in the

because we tolerate and praise such dishonor of God by our prelates, and make ourselves participants in this damnable pride by our silence or flattery?

It is the same when the pope carries the sacrament in procession. He must be carried, but the sacrament is set before him like a jug of wine on a table. At Rome Christ counts for nothing, but the pope counts for everything. And yet the Romanists want to compel us—and even use threats—to approve, praise, and honor these sins of the Antichrist, even though they are against God and all Christian doctrine. Help us, O God, to get a free, general council, which will teach the pope that he, too, is a mortal and not more than God, as he presumes himself to be!

12. Pilgrimages to Rome should either be abolished or else no one should be allowed to make such a pilgrimage simply out of curiosity or pious devotion, unless his parish priest, his town authorities, or his overlord confirm that he has a good and sufficient reason for doing so.[82] I say this not because pilgrimages are bad, but because they are ill advised at this time. For at Rome they do not see a good example, but rather pure scandal. The Romanists themselves devised the saying, "The nearer Rome, the worse the Christians."[o] They bring back [from Rome] contempt for God and his commandments. They say the first time a man goes to Rome he seeks a rascal; the second time he finds one; the third time he brings him back home with him.[p] Now, however, they have become so accomplished that they can make three pilgrimages in one and have truly brought back to us from Rome such things that it would be better never to have seen Rome or known anything about it.

Even if this were not the case, there is still another and a better reason: simple people are led into a false estimation

82. Although there were many other popular destinations for pilgrims, like Jerusalem or Santiago de Compostela, Rome with its holy places was by far the favorite.

notes below, it was inserted into the second printing, published at Wittenberg in November 1520.

o   A common proverb in German and Latin; see Wander, 3:1714, no. 21f.

p   Wander, 3:1717–18, no. 72. See the remark of Ulrich von Hutten in his *Vadiscus*: "Three things there are which those who go to Rome usually bring back with them: a bad conscience, a ruined stomach, and an empty purse." See *Ulrich von Hutten Schriften*, ed. Eduard Böcking, vol. 4: *Gespräche* (Leipzig, 1860), 169.

and misconception about the divine commandments. For they think that going on a pilgrimage is a precious good work, which is not true. It is scarcely a good work—frequently a wickedly deceptive work, for God has not commanded it. But God has commanded that a man should care for his wife and children, perform the duties of a husband, and serve and help his neighbor. Today it happens that a man makes a pilgrimage to Rome, spends fifty, maybe a hundred, gulden, something that nobody commanded him to do, and leaves his wife and child, or his neighbor at any rate, to suffer want back home. And yet the silly fool thinks he can gloss over such disobedience and contempt of the divine commandment with his self-assigned pilgrimage, which is really nothing but impertinence or a delusion of the devil. By encouraging this with their false, feigned, foolish "golden years,"[83] by which the people are excited, torn away from God's commandments and drawn to the seductive papal enterprise, the popes have done the very thing they ought to have prevented. But it has brought in money and fortified their counterfeit authority. That is why it had to go on, even though it is contrary to God or the salvation of souls.

To eradicate such false, seductive faith from the minds of simple Christian people, and to restore a right understanding of good works, all pilgrimages should be abolished. For there is no good in them, no commandment and no duty, but only countless occasions for sin and disdain of God's commandments. This is why there are so many beggars who commit all kinds of mischief by going on these pilgrimages, and who learn to beg when there is no need and become accustomed to it. This accounts for vagabondage and many ills about which I shall not speak here.

Whoever wants to go on a pilgrimage today or vow to make a pilgrimage should first explain the reasons for doing so to his priest or his lord. If it turns out that he wants to do it for the sake of a good work, then let the priest or lord put his foot down firmly and put an end to the vow and the good work as a devilish delusion. Let priest and lord show him how to use the money and effort [to be expended] on the pilgrimage for God's commandments and for works a

83. "Golden" or "jubilee" years were established by Pope Boniface VIII (c. 1235–1303) in 1300. Initially, every hundredth year was to be a jubilee, but by mid-fourteenth century it had become every fifty years, and by Luther's time it was every twenty-five years. During jubilee years, plenary indulgences were offered to pilgrims to Rome who visited the churches of the apostles a specified number of times. The pope received a handsome share of the pilgrims' free offerings, and the local economy benefited from their presence. Luther was doubtless aware that a large number of Germans went on pilgrimage to Rome in 1500.

thousand times better by spending it on his own family or on his poor neighbors. If, however, he wishes to make the pilgrimage out of curiosity, to see other lands and cities, he may be allowed to do so. But if he made the vow during an illness, then that vow must be annulled and canceled. God's commandment should be emphasized, so that henceforth he will be content to keep the vow made in baptism as well as the commandments of God.[q] Nevertheless, he may be allowed to perform his foolish vow just once to quiet his conscience. Nobody wants to walk in the straight path of God's commandments common to all of us. Everybody invents new ways and vows for himself as if he had already fulfilled all of God's commandments.

[13.] Next we come to the great crowd of those who make many vows but keep few. Do not be angry, my noble lords! I really mean it for the best. It is the bittersweet truth that the further building of mendicant cloisters[84] should not be permitted. God help us, there are already too many of them. Would God they were all dissolved, or at least combined into two or three orders! Their wandering around the countryside [begging] has never done any good and never will do any good. My advice is to join together ten of these houses or as many as need be, and make them a single institution for which adequate provision is made so that begging will not be necessary. It is far more important to consider what the common people need for their salvation than what St. Francis, St. Dominic, and St. Augustine,[85] or anyone else has established as a rule, especially because things have not turned out as they planned.

The mendicants should also be relieved of preaching and hearing confession, unless they are called to do this by the bishops, parishes, congregations, or the civil authorities. Nothing but hatred and envy between priests and monks has come out of this kind of preaching and confessing, and this has become a source of great offense and hindrance to the common people. It ought to stop because it can well

84. In contrast to monks, who lived by the Benedictine rule (cf. n. 94), mendicant friars (see the following note) sustained themselves in part by begging. Many cities had designated areas where this begging was permitted.

85. Luther is referring to the three principal mendicant orders, the Franciscans (founded by Francis of Assisi [c. 1181–1226]), the Dominicans (founded by Dominic [1170–1221]), and the Augustinian Hermits (his own order, which supposedly used a rule written by Augustine, bishop of Hippo).

---

q   In *The Babylonian Captivity* of 1520 and in Martin Luther's *Judgment against Monastic Vows* of 1521, Luther will again emphasize baptismal vows. See above, p. 220.

St AVGVSTINE *the Learned and painfull Bishop of Hippo, in Africa, for the space of 40 yeares where he dyed, in the 70th yeare of His Age, about ÿ yeare of or Lord 430.*
W. Marshall sculp.

Engraving of St. Augustine, bishop of Hippo,
by William Marshall (d. 1649).

86. This applies particularly to the Franciscans and Augustinians. By the fifteenth century, both orders were divided between the Observants, who favored strict adherence to their order's rule, and the Conventuals, who took a more flexible view. Johann von Staupitz (c. 1460-1524), the head of the Augustinian order in Germany and Luther's own confessor, tried to unite the two groups. Luther's journey to Rome in 1511 was part of the legal conflict that this attempt produced.

be dispensed with. It looks suspiciously as though the Holy Roman See has purposely increased this army lest the priests and bishops, unable to stand the pope's tyranny any longer, some day become too powerful for him and start a reformation. That would be unbearable to his holiness.

At the same time, the manifold divisions and differences within one and the same order should be abolished. These divisions have arisen from time to time for very trivial reasons; they have been maintained for even more trivial reasons, and they quarrel with each other with unspeakable hatred and envy.[86] Nevertheless, the Christian faith, which can well exist without any of these distinctions, comes to grief because of both parties, and a good Christian life is valued and sought after only according to the standards of outward laws, works, and methods. Nothing comes of this but hypocrisy and the ruination of souls, as all can plainly see.

The pope must also be forbidden to found or approve any more of these orders; in fact, he must be ordered to abolish some and reduce the numbers of others. Inasmuch as faith in Christ, which alone is our chief possession and exists without any kind of orders, suffers no little danger in that people, confronted with so many and varied works and ways, will be easily led astray to live according to such works and ways rather than to pay heed to faith. And unless there are wise prelates in the monasteries who preach and stress faith more than the rule of the order, it is impossible for that order not to harm and mislead the simple souls who have regard only for works.

But in our day the prelates who did have faith and who founded the orders have passed away almost everywhere. It is just as it was centuries ago among the children of Israel. When the fathers who had known the wonders and the works of God had passed on, their children, ignorant of

God's works and of faith, immediately elevated idolatry and their own human works.[r] In our day, unfortunately, these orders have no understanding of God's works or of faith, but make wretched martyrs of themselves by striving and working to keep their own rules, laws, and ways of life. Yet they never come to a right understanding of a spiritually good life. It is just as 2 Tim. 3[:5, 7] declares, "They have the appearance of a spiritual life, but there is nothing behind it: they are constantly learning, but they never come to a knowledge of what true spiritual life is." If the ruling prelate has no understanding of Christian faith, it would be better to have no monastery at all; for such a superior cannot govern an order without causing damage and destruction, and the holier and better the prelate appears to be in his external works, the more this is the case.

To my way of thinking, it would be a necessary measure, especially in our perilous times, to regulate convents and monasteries in the same way that they were regulated in the beginning, in the days of the apostles and for a long time afterward. In those days, convents and monasteries were all open for everyone to stay in them as long as they pleased. What else were the convents and monasteries but Christian schools where Scripture and the Christian life were taught, and where people were trained to rule and to preach?[87] Thus we read that St. Agnes went to school,[88] and we still see the same practice in some of the convents, like that at Quedlinburg and elsewhere. And in truth all monasteries and convents ought to be so free that God is served freely and not under compulsion. Later on, however, they became obsessed with vows and made of them an eternal prison. Consequently, these monastic vows are more highly regarded than the vows of baptism.[89] We see, hear, read, and learn more and more about the fruit of all this every day.

I can well suppose that this advice of mine will be regarded as the height of foolishness, but I am not concerned about that at the moment. I advise what seems good to me; let those who will reject it. I see for myself how the vows are

87. This is a prominent theme in Luther's views on monasticism; see his treatise *The Judgment of Martin Luther on Monastic Vows* (1521), in LW 44:312–13, 355, 367.

88. St. Agnes of Rome, fourth-century virgin and martyr (cf. LW 45:312). According to legend, the thirteen-year-old Agnes was on her way home from school when she encountered the young man who, incensed by her rejection of his passionate advances, made the false accusations that led to her martyrdom.

89. Most medieval theologians maintained that monastic vows conveyed the same grace as baptism; see, e.g., Thomas Aquinas (1225–1274), *Summa Theologica* II.2, q. 189, a. 3 ad 3. The same theologians drew a distinction between "precepts of the gospel" (the observance of which was necessary to salvation) and "counsels of perfection" (the observance of which, especially in monastic life, enabled one to achieve salvation "better and more quickly"). See Bonaventure (1221–1274), *Breviloquium* V.9, and Aquinas, *Summa Theologica* II.2, q. 108, a. 4. Luther attacks this notion in *The Treatise on Good Works* (see above, p. 267).

r   Cf. Judg. 2:6-23.

kept, especially the vow of chastity. This vow has become universal in these monasteries, and yet it was never commanded by Christ. On the contrary, chastity is given to very few, as he himself says [Matt. 19:11-12], as well as St. Paul [1 Cor. 7:7]. It is my heartfelt wish that everybody be helped and that Christian souls not become entangled in self-contrived human traditions and laws.

14. We also see how the priesthood has fallen, and how many a poor priest is overburdened with wife and child, his conscience troubled. Yet no one does anything to help him, though he could easily be helped. Though pope and bishops may let things go on as they are and allow what is heading for ruin to go to ruin, yet I will redeem my conscience and open my mouth freely, whether it vexes pope, bishop, or anybody else. And this is what I say: according to the institution of Christ and the apostles, every city should have a priest or bishop, as St. Paul clearly says in Titus 1[:5]. And this priest should not be compelled to live without a wedded wife but should be permitted to have one, as St. Paul writes in 1 Tim. 3[:2, 4] and Titus 1[:6-7], saying, "A bishop shall be a man who is blameless, and the husband of but one wife, whose children are obedient and well behaved," etc. According to St. Paul, and also St. Jerome, a bishop and a priest are one and the same thing.[s] But of bishops as they now are the Scriptures know nothing. They have, rather, been established by an ordinance of the Christian community, so that one priest will have authority over many others.

So then, we clearly learn from the Apostle that it should be the practice in Christendom for every town to choose from among the community a learned and pious citizen,

The martyrdom of St. Agnes.

---

s   For St. Paul, cf. Luther's interpretation of 1 Cor. 4:1 in *Concerning the Ministry* (1523), LW 40:35. For St. Jerome (c. 347–420), see his *Commentary on Titus* (PL 26:52) and *Epistulae* 146 (PL 22:1192–95).

entrust to him the office of the ministry, and support him at the expense of the community. He should be free to marry or not. He should have several priests or deacons, also free to marry or not as they choose, to help him minister to the masses and the community with word and sacrament, as is still the practice in the Greek church. Because there was afterwards so much persecution and controversy with heretics, there were many holy fathers who voluntarily abstained from matrimony so that they might better devote themselves to study and be prepared at any moment for death and conflict.

But the Roman See has interfered and out of its own wanton wickedness turned this into a universal commandment that forbade priests to marry.[90] This was done at the bidding of the devil, as St. Paul declares in 1 Tim. 4[:1, 3], "There shall come teachers who bring the devil's teaching and forbid marriage." Unfortunately so much misery has arisen from this that tongue could never tell it. Moreover, this gave the Greek church cause to separate,[91] and discord, sin, shame, and scandal were increased to no end. But this always happens when the devil starts and carries on. What, then, shall we do about it?

My advice is to restore freedom to everybody and leave every man the free choice to marry or not to marry. But then there would have to be a very different kind of government and regulation of church property; the whole canon law would have to be demolished; and few benefices could be allowed to get into Roman hands. I fear that greed is a cause of this wretched, unchaste celibacy. As a result, everyone has wanted to become a priest and everyone wants his son to study for the priesthood, not with the idea of living in chastity, for that could be done outside the priesthood, but rather to provide themselves with temporal livelihood without work or worry, contrary to God's command in Gen. 3[:19] that "in the sweat of your face you shall eat your bread." The Romanists have artfully decorated this text to mean that their labor is to pray and say Mass.

I here take no account of popes, bishops, cathedral canons, and monks, whose offices were not instituted by God.

90. The earliest papal proscription of clerical marriage dates back to the fourth century, but a serious effort at enforcing clerical celibacy in the Western church began only in the eleventh century. It reached its apex in the twelfth century, when the first and second Lateran councils (1123 and 1139) made clerical marriage not only unlawful but invalid, which meant that all sexual relations between a priest and a woman, whether they were married or not, was classed as fornication, and their children were illegitimate. The decrees of the Lateran council were incorporated into canon law, despite which clerical concubinage remained common. See James A. Brundage, *Law, Sex, and Christian Society in Medieval Europe* (Chicago: University of Chicago Press, 1987), 214–23, 251–53, 401–5, 474–77, 536–39.

91. In the Eastern church, priests and deacons can marry before ordination (though not afterward), but bishops must remain celibate. This was a point of contention between the Eastern and Western churches, but not one of the major issues in the Great Schism (1054) between them.

They have taken these burdens upon themselves, so they themselves will have to bear them. I want to speak only of the ministry that God has instituted, which consists of presiding over a community with word and sacrament, living among them, and maintaining a household. The same should be given liberty by a Christian council to marry to avoid temptation and sin. For since God has not bound them, no one else may or should bind them, even if he were an angel from heaven,[t] let alone a pope. Everything that canon law decrees to the contrary is mere fable and blather.

Furthermore, my advice to anyone henceforth being ordained a priest or anything else is that he in no wise vow to the bishop that he will remain celibate. On the contrary, he should tell the bishop that he has no right whatsoever to require such a vow, and that it is a devilish tyranny to require it. But if anyone is compelled to say, or even wants to say, "*so far as human frailty permits*," as indeed many do, let him frankly interpret these same words in a negative manner to mean "*I do not promise chastity.*" For *not human frailty* but only *the strength of angels and the power of heaven permit chaste living.*[u] In this way, a person should keep the conscience free of all vows.

I will advise neither for nor against marrying or remaining single. I leave that to a common Christian ordinance and to everyone's better judgment. I will not conceal my real opinion or withhold comfort from that pitiful band who with wives and children have fallen into disgrace and whose consciences are burdened because people call their wives priests' whores and their children priests' bastards. I say this freely by virtue of my right as court jester.[92]

You will find many a pious priest against whom nobody has anything to say except that he is weak and has come to shame with a woman, even though from the bottom of their hearts both are of a mind to live together in lawful wedded

92. The role in which Luther had cast himself in the introductory letter to Amsdorf; see above, pp. 377–78.

---

t   Cf. Gal. 1:8.

u   The italicized words are in Latin in the original and reflect Luther's ironic reference to monastic and ordination vows, always recited in Latin.

love, if they could do it with a clear conscience. But even though they both have to bear public shame, the two are certainly married in the sight of God. And I say that where they are so minded and live together, they should unburden their consciences. Let the priest take and keep her as his lawful wedded wife and live honestly with her as her husband, whether the pope likes it or not, whether it be against canon or human law. The salvation of your soul is more important than the observance of tyrannical, arbitrary, and wanton laws, which are neither necessary to salvation nor commanded by God. You should do as the children of Israel did who stole from the Egyptians the wages they had earned[v] or as a servant who steals from his wicked master the wages he has earned: steal from the pope your wedded wife and child! Let the man who has faith enough to venture this boldly follow my advice. I shall not lead him astray. Though I do not have the authority of a pope, I do have the authority of a Christian to advise and help my neighbor against sins and temptations—and that not without [good] cause or reason!

First, not every priest can do without a woman, not only because of human frailty, but much more because of keeping house. If he may have a woman [for keeping house], which the pope allows, and yet may not have her in marriage, what is that but leaving a man and a woman alone together and yet forbidding them to fall? It is just like putting straw and fire together and forbidding them to smoke or burn.

Second, the pope has as little power to command celibacy as he has to forbid eating, drinking, the natural movement of the bowels, or growing fat. Therefore, no one is bound to obey such a command, and the pope is responsible for all the sins that are committed against it, for all the souls that are lost, and for all the consciences that are confused and tortured because of it. He has strangled so many wretched souls with this devilish rope that he has long deserved to be driven out of this world. Yet it is my firm belief that God has been more gracious to many souls at their last hour than the

v   Cf. Exod. 12:35-36.

pope was to them in their whole lifetime. No good has ever come nor will come out of the papacy and its laws.

Third, even though the law of the pope is against it, it is nonetheless the case that when a marriage is entered into against the pope's law, then his law is already at an end and is no longer valid. For God's commandment, which enjoins that no man shall put husband and wife asunder [Matt. 19:6], is above the pope's law. And the commandments of God must not be broken or neglected because of the pope's commandment. Nevertheless, many foolish jurists, along with the pope, have devised impediments and thereby prevented, broken, and brought confusion to the estate of matrimony, so that God's commandment concerning it has altogether disappeared.[93] Need I say more? In the entire canon law of the pope there are not even two lines that could instruct a devout Christian, and, unfortunately, there are so many mistaken and dangerous laws that nothing would be better than to make a bonfire of it.[w]

But if you say that [clerical marriage] is scandalous, and that the pope must first grant dispensation, I reply that whatever scandal there is in it is the fault of the Roman See, which has established such laws with no right and against God. In the sight of God and the Holy Scriptures marriage of the clergy is no offense. Moreover, if the pope can grant dispensations from his greedy and tyrannical laws for money, then every Christian can grant dispensations from these very same laws for God's sake and for the salvation of souls. For Christ has set us free from all humanly devised laws, especially when they are opposed to God and the salvation of souls, as St. Paul teaches in Gal. 5[:1] and 1 Cor. 10[:23].

15. Nor must I forget the poor monasteries.[94] The evil spirit, who has now confused all the estates of life and made them unbearable through human laws, has taken possession of some abbots, abbesses, and prelates. As a result, they govern their brothers and sisters in such a way that they quickly go to hell and lead a wretched existence here and now, as do all the devil's martyrs. That is to say, these supe-

93. Because it was a sacrament, marriage was entirely a matter of church law that had to be adjudicated in ecclesiastical courts. The most common impediment to marriage was too close a degree of consanguinity (within the first four degrees), which meant, for example, that second cousins could not legally marry. Even the relationship between godparents and godchildren was defined as a forbidden degree of "spiritual consanguinity." Dispensations from these impediments were readily available to those who could pay for them.

94. Having dealt with the mendicant friars above (pp. 421–22), Luther now turns to monks and nuns, such as Benedictines and Cistercians, who lived by the Rule of St. Benedict.

w   This is exactly what Luther did; see p. 383, n. 15.

riors have reserved to themselves in confession all, or at least some, of the mortal sins that are secret, so that no brother can absolve another, on pain of excommunication. Now then, we do not find angels at all times and in all places, but also flesh and blood, which would rather undergo all excommunications and threats rather than confess secret sins to prelates and appointed confessors. Thus these people go to the sacrament with such consciences that they become irregulars and even worse.[95] O blind shepherds! O mad prelates! O ravenous wolves!

To this I say: if a sin is public or notorious, then it is proper for the prelate alone to punish it, and it is only these sins and no others that he may reserve and select for himself. He has no authority over secret sins, even if they were the worst sins that ever are or can be found. If the prelate reserves them, then he is a tyrant. He has no such right and is trespassing upon the prerogative of God's judgment.

And so I advise these children, brothers and sisters: if your superiors are unwilling to permit you to confess your secret sins to whomever you choose, then take them to your brother or sister, whomever you like, and be absolved and comforted. Then go and do what you want and ought to do. Only believe firmly that you are absolved, and nothing more is needed. And do not be distressed or driven mad by threats of excommunication, being made irregular, or whatever else they threaten. These [penalties] are valid only in the case of public or notorious sins that no one will confess. They do not apply to you. What are you trying to do, you blind prelates, prevent secret sins by threats? Relinquish what you obviously cannot hold on to so that God's judgment and grace may work in the people under your care! He has not given them so entirely into your hands as to let them go entirely out of his own! In fact, you have the smaller part under you. Let your statutes be merely statutes. Do not exalt them to heaven or give them the weight of divine judgments!

16. It is also necessary to abolish completely the celebration of anniversary Masses for the dead,[96] or at least to reduce their number, since we plainly see that they have become

95. Irregulars were monks who had violated the *regula* (rule) of their order and were no longer members in good standing.

96. I.e., Masses said for the repose of the souls of one or more persons on the anniversary (or appointed day of remembrance) of their deaths. Endowments were commonly provided for this purpose.

97. Endowed Masses for departed members were particularly popular with religious fraternities, and Luther had already voiced criticism of the immoderate eating and drinking that accompanied their celebration; see *Sermon on the Blessed Sacrament*, pp. 249–53.

98. Vigils were preparatory observances (prayers, Scripture readings, etc.) on the eve (or the entire day) before a major church festival, or they were prayers or observances said throughout the night as a special religious discipline, which is the sense in which Luther is using the word.

nothing but a mockery. God is deeply angered by these, and their only purpose is money-grubbing, gluttony, and drunkenness.[97] What pleasure can God take in wretched vigils and Masses that are so miserably rattled off and neither read nor prayed.[98] And if they were prayed, it would not be for God's sake and out of love, but for the sake of money and of getting the job done. But it is impossible for a work that is not done out of unconstrained love to please God or secure anything from him. So it is altogether Christian to abolish, or at least to diminish, everything we see that is becoming an abuse and that angers God rather than appeases him. I would rather—in fact, it would be more pleasing to God and much better—that a chapter, church, or monastery combine all its anniversary Masses and vigils and on one day, with sincerity of heart, reverence, and faith, hold one true vigil and Mass on behalf of all its benefactors, than hold thousands every year for each individual benefactor without reverence and faith. O dear Christians, God does not care for much praying but for true praying. In fact, he condemns long and repetitive prayers, and says in Matt. 6[:7; 23:14], "They will only earn the more punishment thereby." But Avarice, which cannot put its trust in God, brings such things to pass, for it fears that it will die of hunger.

17. Certain penalties or punishments of canon law should be abolished, too, especially the interdict,[x] which without any doubt was invented by the evil spirit. Is it not a devilish work to correct one sin through many and great sins? It is actually a greater sin to silence or suppress the word and worship of God than if one had strangled twenty popes at one time, to say nothing of a priest, or had appropriated church property. This is another of the tender virtues taught in canon law. One of the reasons this law is called "spiritual" is that it comes from "the spirit": not from the Holy Spirit but from the evil spirit.

Excommunication must never be used except where the Scriptures prescribe its use, that is, against those who do not

---

x   See above, p. 386, n. 22.

hold the true faith or who live in open sin, but not for material advantage. But today it is the other way around. Everybody believes and lives as he pleases, especially those who use excommunication to fleece and defame other people. All the excommunications are for material advantage, for which we have nobody to thank but the holy canon law of unrighteousness. I have said more about this in an earlier discourse.[y]

The other punishments and penalties—suspension, irregularity, aggravation, reaggravation, deposition,[99] lightning, thundering, cursings, damnings, and the rest of these devices—should be buried ten fathoms deep in the earth so that their name and memory not be left on earth. The evil spirit unleashed by canon law has brought such a terrible plague and misery into the heavenly kingdom of holy Christendom, having done nothing but destroy and hinder souls by canon law, that the words of Christ in Matt. 23[:13] may well be understood as applying to them, "Woe to you scribes! You have taken upon yourselves the authority to teach and have closed the kingdom of heaven to the people, for you do not enter and you stand in the way of those who go in."

18. All festivals should be abolished, and Sunday alone retained. If it were desired, however, to retain the festivals of Our Lady and of the major saints, they should be transferred to [the nearest] Sunday, or observed only by a morning Mass, after which all the rest of the day should be a working day. Here is the reason: since the feast days are abused by drinking, gambling, loafing, and all manner of sin, we anger God more on holy days than we do on other days.[z] Things are so topsy-turvy that holy days are not holy, but working days are. Nor is any service rendered God and his saints by so many saints' days. On the contrary, they are dishonored;

99. For "irregularity," see above, n. 95. "Aggravation" was the threat of excommunication; "reaggravation" was the excommunication itself. "Deposition" was permanent dismissal from clerical office, as opposed to temporary "suspension."

---

y   In the *Sermon on the Power of Excommunication*, published in Latin in 1518 (WA 1:638–43), and in the *Sermon on the Ban*, preached in German in December 1519 and published early in 1520 (LW 39:5–22).

z   Cf. Luther's similar observations concerning the excessive number and riotous celebration of saints' days in the *Treatise on Good Works*, p. 321.

100. Otilie (Odilia), feast day 13 December (c. 662–c. 720), was the patron saint of Alsace, and her shrine at Odilienberg was a well-known place of pilgrimage. The much more widely known and venerated St. Barbara (feast day 4 December) was the patron saint of gunners, miners, and others who work with explosives. See the *Treatise on Good Works* (p. 317, n. 82).

although some foolish prelates think that they have done a good work if each, following the promptings of his own blind devotion, celebrates a festival in honor of St. Otilie or St. Barbara.[100] But they would be doing something far better if they honored the saint by turning the saint's day into a working day.

Over and above the spiritual injury, the average man incurs two material disadvantages from this practice. First, he neglects his work and spends more money that he would otherwise spend. Second, he weakens his body and makes it less fit. We see this every day, yet nobody thinks of correcting the situation. In such cases, we ought not to consider whether or not the pope has instituted the feasts, or whether we must have a dispensation or permission [to omit them]. Every community, town council, or government not only has the right, without the knowledge and consent of the pope or bishop, to abolish what is opposed to God and injurious to men's bodies and souls, but indeed is bound, at the risk of the salvation of its souls to abolish it, even though popes and bishops, who ought to be the first to do so, do not consent.

Above all, we ought to abolish completely all church anniversary celebrations, since they have become nothing but taverns, fairs, and gambling places, and only increase the dishonoring of God and foster the damnation of souls.[101] It does not help matters to boast that these festivals had a good beginning and are a good work. Did not God set aside his own law, which he had given from heaven, when it was perverted and abused? And does he not daily overturn what he has set up and destroy what he has made because of the same perversion and abuse? As it is written of him in Ps. 18[:26], "You show yourself perverse with the perverted."

19. The grades or degrees within which marriage is forbidden, such as those affecting godparents or the third and fourth degree of kinship,[a] should be changed. If the pope in Rome can grant dispensations and scandalously sell them for money, then every priest may give the same dispensations

101. The anniversary of the consecration of a church, to which often a special indulgence was attached, was a feast day in that parish. The frequently raucous and disorderly celebration of these local feast days was a common topic of complaint from clerical reformers and public officials. See the *Explanations of the 95 Theses* (1518), LW 31:198.

---

a   See above, n. 93.

without charge and for the salvation of souls. Would God that every priest were able to do and remit without payment all those things we have to pay for at Rome, such as indulgences, letters of indulgence, butter letters, Mass letters, and all the rest of the *confessionalia* and skullduggery at Rome[102] and free us from that golden noose, canon law, by which the poor people are deceived and cheated of their money! If the pope has the right to sell his noose of gold and his spiritual snares (I ought to say "law")[b] for money, then a priest certainly has more right to tear these nooses and snares apart, and for God's sake tread them underfoot. But if the priest does not have this right, neither does the pope have the right to sell them at his disgraceful fair.

Furthermore, fasts should be left to individual choice and every kind of food made optional, as the gospel makes them.[c] Even those gentlemen at Rome scoff at the fasts and leave us commoners to eat the fat they would not deign to use to grease their shoes, and then afterward they sell us the liberty to eat butter and all sorts of other things. The holy Apostle says that we already have freedom in all these things through the gospel.[d] But they have bound us with their canon law and robbed us of our rights so that we have to buy them back again with money. In so doing they have made our consciences so timid and fearful that it is no longer easy to preach about liberty of this kind because the common people take offense at it and think that eating butter is a greater sin than lying, swearing, or even living unchastely. Do with it what you will, it is still a human work decreed by human beings, and nothing good will ever come of it.

20. The chapels in forests and the churches in fields,[103] such as Wilsnack,[104] Sternberg,[105] Trier,[106] the Grimmenthal,[107] and now Regensburg[108] and a goodly number of others that recently have become the goal of pilgrimages, must be leveled. Oh, what a terrible and heavy reckoning

102. For indulgences and butter letters, see above, p. 406, n. 60 [*Butterbriefe*]. Mass letters (*messbriefe*) were certificates entitling the bearer to the benefits of Masses celebrated by confraternities. See above, p. 229, n. 3.

103. Chapels built in the countryside as goals of pilgrimage, not as parish churches.

104. Bad Wilsnack in Brandenburg became a pilgrimage site after 1384, when three consecrated hosts (communion wafers) reportedly survived a fire undamaged and with a drop of Christ's blood in each.

105. From 1491 the Augustinian monastery at Sternberg in Mecklenberg was a popular goal of pilgrims because of a "bleeding host" (consecrated bread) displayed there.

106. The cathedral at Trier possessed one of the many cloaks claiming to be the seamless robe of Christ for which his executioners had cast lots (John 19:23-24).

107. Grimmenthal (near Meiningen) had a pilgrimage church (rebuilt and expanded 1499–1507) with a statue of the Virgin Mary that was said to effect miraculous cures.

108. In 1519, when the Jews were expelled from Regensburg, the synagogue was torn down and replaced with a chapel dedicated to the Virgin Mary. "The Fair Virgin of Regensburg," a painting in the chapel, quickly became an object of veneration and pilgrimage.

b Luther makes an untranslatable pun on *geistliche netz* ("spiritual snares") and *geistlich recht* ("spiritual law" = canon law).

c Cf. Matt. 15:11.

d 1 Cor. 10:23; Col. 2:16.

The pilgrimage shrine of St. Mary's in Regensburg, built on the site of a recently destroyed synagogue. Woodcut by Michael Ostendorfer (c. 1490–1559).

those bishops will have to give who permit this devilish deceit and profit by it. They should be the first to prevent it, and yet they regard it all as a godly and holy thing. They do not see that the devil is behind it all, to strengthen greed, to create a false and fictitious faith, to weaken the parish churches, to multiply taverns and whoring, to lose money and working time to no purpose, and to lead ordinary people by the nose. If they had read Scripture as well as the damnable canon law, they would know how to deal with this matter!

The miracles that happen in these places prove nothing, for the evil spirit can also work miracles, as Christ has told us in Matt. 24[:24]. If they took the matter seriously and forbade this sort of thing, the miracles would quickly come to an end. But if the thing were of God, their prohibition would not hinder it.[e] And if there were no other evidence that it is not of God, the fact that people come running to them like herds of cattle, as if they had lost all reason, would be proof enough. This could not be possible if it were of God. Further, since God never gave any command about all this, there is neither obedience nor merit in doing it. Therefore one should step in boldly and protect the people. For whatever has not been commanded and is done beyond what God commands is certainly the devil's doing. It also works to the disadvantage of parish churches, because they are held in less respect. In short, these things are signs of great unbelief among the people, for if they really had faith they would find all they need in their own parish churches, to which they are commanded to go.

e Acts 5:39.

But what shall I say now? Every bishop thinks only of how he can set up and maintain such a place of pilgrimage in his diocese. He is not at all concerned that the people believe and live aright. The rulers are just like the people. The blind lead the blind [Luke 6:39]. In fact, where pilgrimages do not catch on, they set to work to canonize saints, not to honor the saints, who would be honored enough without being canonized, but to draw the crowds and bring in the money. At this point, pope and bishops lend their aid. There is a deluge of indulgences. There is always money enough for these. But nobody worries about what God has commanded. Nobody runs after these things; nobody has money for them. How blind we are! We not only give the devil free rein for his mischief, but we even strengthen and multiply his mischief. I would rather the dear saints were left in peace and the simple people not led astray! What spirit gave the pope authority to canonize saints? Who tells him whether they are saints or not? Are there not enough sins on earth already without tempting God, without interfering in his judgment and setting up the dear saints as decoys to get money?

My advice is to let the saints canonize themselves. Indeed, it is God alone who should canonize them. And let all stay in their own parishes, where they will find more than in all the shrines even if they were all rolled into one. In one's own parish one finds baptism, the sacrament, preaching, and one's neighbor, and these things are greater than all the saints in heaven, for all of them were made "saints" by God's word and sacrament. As long as we esteem such wonderful things so little, God is just in his wrathful condemnation in allowing the devil to lead us where he likes, to conduct pilgrimages, found churches and chapels, canonize saints, and do other such fool's works, so that we depart from true faith into a novel and wrong kind of belief. This is what the devil did in ancient times to the people of Israel, when he led them away from the temple at Jerusalem to countless other places. Yet he did it all in the name of God and under the pretense of holiness. All the prophets preached against it, and they were martyred for doing so. But today nobody preaches against it. If somebody were to preach against it all, perhaps bishop,

109. Antoninus (1389–1459), archbishop of Florence, achieved renown as reformer of the Dominican order. When Luther wrote this treatise, the procedure of canonizing Antoninus (completed in 1523) was already under way.

pope, priest, and monk would possibly martyr him, too. St. Antoninus of Florence[109] and certain others must now be made saints and canonized in this way, so that their holiness, which would otherwise have served only for the glory of God and set a good example, may be used to bring fame and money.

Although the canonization of saints may have been a good thing in former days, it is certainly never good practice now, just as many other things that were good in former times—feast days, church treasures and ornaments—are now scandalous and offensive. For it is evident that through the canonization of saints neither God's glory nor the improvement of Christians is sought, but only money and reputation. One church wants to have the advantage over the other and would not like to see another church enjoy that advantage in common. In these last evil days spiritual treasures have even been misused to gain temporal goods, so that everything, even God himself, has been forced into the service of Avarice. This only promotes schisms, sects, and pride. A church that has advantages over others looks down on them and exalts itself. Yet all divine treasures are common to all and serve all and ought to further the cause of unity. But the pope likes things as they are. He would not like it if all Christians were equal and one with each other.

It is fitting to say here that all church privileges, bulls, and whatever else the pope sells in that skinning house of his in Rome should be abolished, disregarded, or extended to all. But if he sells or gives indults,[110] privileges, indulgences, graces, advantages, and faculties[111] to Wittenberg, Halle, Venice, and above all to his own city of Rome, why does he not give these things to all churches in general? Is it not his duty to do everything in his power for all Christians, freely and for God's sake, even to shed his blood for them? Tell me, then, why does he give or sell to one church and not to another? Or must the accursed money make so great a difference in the eyes of His Holiness among Christians, who all have the same baptism, word, faith, Christ, God, and all else?[f] Do the Romanists want us to be so blind to all these things, though we have eyes to see, and be such fools, though

110. An indult is a permission or a privilege, awarded to an individual or group by competent ecclesiastical authority (the pope or a bishop), granting exemption from a particular norm of canon law.

111. "Faculties" were extraordinary powers to grant indulgences and absolution in reserved cases. They were usually bestowed on papal legates or commissioners but could be bestowed on local church officials.

we have a perfectly good faculty of reason, that we worship such greed, skullduggery, and pretense?[g] The pope is your shepherd, but only so long as you have money and no longer. And still the Romanists are not ashamed of this rascality of leading us hither and thither with their bulls. They are concerned only about the accursed money and nothing else!

My advice is this: If such fool's work is not abolished, then all upright Christians[h] should open their eyes and not permit themselves to be led astray by the Romanist bulls and seals and all their glittering show. Let them stay at home in their own parish church and let their baptism, their gospel, faith, Christ, and God, who is the same God everywhere, be what is best to them. Let the pope remain a blind leader of the blind.[i] Neither an angel nor a pope can give you as much as God gives you in your parish church. Indeed, the pope leads you away from God's gifts, which are yours for free, to his gifts, for which you have to pay. He gives you lead for gold, hide for meat, the string for the purse, wax for honey, words for goods, the letter for the spirit.[112] You see all this before your very eyes, but you refuse to take notice. If you intend to ride to heaven on his wax and parchment, this chariot will soon break down and you will fall into hell, and not in God's name![j]

Let this be your one sure rule. Whatever you have to buy from the pope is neither good nor from God. For what God gives is not only given without charge, but the whole world is punished and damned for not being willing to receive it as a free gift. I am talking about the gospel and God's work. We have deserved God's letting us be so led astray because we have despised his holy word and the grace of baptism. It is as St. Paul says, "God shall send a strong delusion upon all those who have not received the truth to their salvation, so

112. The imagery here is that of a papal bull, which was written on parchment (animal hide) and to which was attached with wax a cord from which the seal hung. For "letter and spirit," see 2 Cor. 3:6.

---

f   Cf. Eph. 4:4-6.

g   German: *Spiegelfechten*, literally, "standing in front of a mirror and pretending to fight"; in other words, being pretentious, hypocritical, or phony.

h   Singular in the original.

i   Cf. Matt. 15:14.

j   Echoing 2 Kgs. 2:1-12.

that they believe and follow lies and knavery" [2 Thess. 2:11], as they deserve.

21. One of the greatest necessities is the abolition of all begging in all of Christendom. Nobody ought to go begging among Christians. It would indeed be a very simple matter to make a law to the effect that every city should look after its own poor, if only we had the courage and the intention to do so.[113] No beggar from outside should be allowed into the city, whether he call himself pilgrim or mendicant monk. Every city should support its own poor, and if it was too small, the people in the surrounding villages should also be urged to contribute, since in any case they have to feed so many vagabonds and evil rogues who call themselves mendicants. In this way, too, it could be known who was really poor and who was not.

There would have to be an overseer or warden who knows all the poor and informs the city council or the clergy what they needed. Or some other better arrangement might be made. As I see it, there is no other business in which so much skullduggery and deceit are practiced as in begging, and yet it could all be easily abolished. Moreover, this unrestricted universal begging is harmful to the common people. I have figured out that each of the five or six mendicant orders[k] visits the same place more than six or seven times every year. In addition to these, there are the common beggars, the ambassador beggars,[114] and the pilgrims. This adds up to sixty times a year that a town is laid under tribute. This is over and above what the secular authorities demand in the way of taxes and assessments. All this the Romanist See steals in return for its wares and consumes for no purpose. To me it is one of God's greatest miracles that we can still go on existing and find the wherewithal to support ourselves.

To be sure, some think that if these proposals were adopted the poor would not be so well provided for, that fewer great stone houses and monasteries would be built, and fewer so well furnished. I can well believe all this. But none of it is necessary. Whoever has chosen poverty ought

113. Luther is breaking with the medieval tradition, in which begging was a respectable activity for those who had fallen into poverty or for those who, like mendicant friars and pilgrims, chose to support themselves in that fashion. By the early sixteenth century, urban populations increasingly viewed the large numbers of beggars as a threat to good order. While Catholic authorities sought to regulate begging, Protestant authorities outlawed it and established laws and institutions for the care of the poor. By 1522, for example, Wittenberg had outlawed begging and established a Poor Chest Ordinance. In the following year, Luther provided a preface for the *Ordinance of a Common Chest* enacted by the Saxon town of Leisnig (LW 45:161–94).

114. Luther's word is *botschafften* ("messengers" or "ambassadors"). The reference is to the so-called *stationarii* (*stationirer* in German), members of religious orders who exploited the gullibility of peasants and villagers by enrolling them, in return for an annual fee, on lists of beneficiaries of the intercession of the saint whose messenger they claimed to be (e.g., St. Valentine). The supposed benefit derived was freedom from certain diseases (epilepsy in the case of Valentine). See Benrath, 105–6, n. 79, and cf. p. 441, note *m*.

---

k   Franciscans, Dominicans, Augustinians, Carmelites, Servites.

not be rich. If he wants to be rich, let him put his hand to the plow and seek his fortune from the land. It is enough if the poor are decently cared for so that they do not die of hunger or cold. It is not fitting that one person should live in idleness on another's labor, or be rich and live comfortably at the cost of another's hardship, as it is according to the present perverted custom. St. Paul says, "Whoever will not work shall not eat" [2 Thess. 3:10]. God has not decreed that anyone shall live off the property of another, save only the clergy who preach and have a parish to care for, and they should, as St. Paul says in 1 Corinthians 9[:14], on account of their spiritual labor. And also as Christ says to the apostles, "Every laborer is worthy of his wage" [Luke 10:7].

22. It is also to be feared that the many Masses that have been endowed in ecclesiastical foundations[115] and monasteries are not only of little use, but arouse the great wrath of God. It would therefore be beneficial to endow no more of such Masses, but rather to abolish the many that are already endowed. It is obvious that these Masses are regarded only as sacrifices and good works, even though they are sacraments just like baptism and penance, which profit only those who receive them and no one else. But now the custom of saying Masses for the living and the dead has crept in, and all things are based on them. This is why so many Masses are endowed, and why the state of affairs that we see has developed out of it.

But this is perhaps a too bold and an unheard-of proposal, especially for those who are concerned that they would lose their job and means of livelihood if such Masses were discontinued. I must refrain from saying more about it until we arrive again at a proper understanding of what the Mass is and what it is for. Unfortunately, for many years now it has been a job, a way to earn a living. Therefore, from now on I will advise a person to become a shepherd or some sort of workman rather than a priest or a monk, unless he knows well in advance what this celebrating of Masses is all about.

I am not speaking, however, of the old collegiate foundations and cathedral chapters, which were doubtless established for the sake of the children of the nobility. According

115. For example, in 1519 the All Saints' Foundation at Wittenberg's Castle Church, consisting of sixteen foundation canons, some of whom were teachers at the University of Wittenberg, recited over six thousand private Masses for the dead (mostly deceased members of the Saxon elector's family).

to German custom, not every one of a nobleman's children can become a landowner or a ruler. It was intended that these children should be looked after in such foundations, and there be free to serve God, to study, to become educated people, and to educate others. I am speaking now of the new foundations that have been established just for the saying of prayers and Masses, and because of their example the older foundations are being burdened with the same sort of praying and Mass celebrating, so that even these old foundations serve little or no purpose. And it is by the grace of God that they finally hit the bottom, as they deserve. That is to say, they have been reduced to choir singing, howling organs, and the reading of cold, indifferent Masses to get and consume the income from the endowments. Pope, bishops, and university scholars ought to be looking into these things and writing about them, and yet they are precisely the ones who do the most to promote them. Whatever brings in money they let go on and on. The blind lead the blind [Luke 6:39]. This is what greed and canon law accomplish.

It should no longer be permissible for one person to hold more than one canonry or benefice. Each must be content with a modest position so that someone else may also have something. This would do away with the excuses of those who say that they must hold more than one such office to maintain their proper station [in life]. A proper station could be interpreted in such broad terms that an entire country would not be enough to maintain it. But greed and a mistrust of God go hand in hand in this matter, so that what is alleged to be the needs of a proper station is nothing but greed and mistrust.

23. Brotherhoods,[116] and for that matter, indulgences, letters of indulgence, butter letters, Mass letters, dispensations, and everything of that kind,[l] should be snuffed out and brought to an end. There is nothing good about them. If the pope has the authority to grant you a dispensation to eat butter, to absent yourself from Mass and the like, then he ought also to be able to delegate this authority to priests,

116. Brotherhoods (*bruderschaften*)—also known as fraternities, sodalities, religious guilds, and (most often in English) confraternities—were associations of laymen created for the purpose of promoting the religious life of their members. Any town of any size had several; in 1520 Wittenberg had twenty. Frequently certain indulgences were attached to membership and attendance at Masses or other rituals at appointed times. Great importance was attached to the endowment of Masses for the souls of departed members. Although brotherhoods could become deeply involved in the charitable and cultural as well as the religious life of their communities, they were often criticized, in Germany at any rate, as drinking clubs whose members missed no opportunity for gluttony and drunkenness. Luther's jaundiced view of them is more fully expressed in his *Sermon on the Blessed Sacrament*, pp. 249–53 above. Cf. Benrath, 105–6, n. 79.

l   See nn. 55, 59, 60, and 102.

from whom he had no right to take it in the first place. I am speaking especially of those brotherhoods in which indulgences, Masses, and good works are apportioned. My dear friend, in your baptism you have entered into a brotherhood with Christ, with all the angels, with the saints, and with all Christians on earth. Hold fast to these and do right by them, and you will have brotherhoods enough. Let the others glitter as they will, compared with the true brotherhood in Christ those brotherhoods are like a penny compared with a gulden. But if there were a brotherhood that raised money to feed the poor or to help the needy, that would be a good idea. It would find its indulgences and its merits in heaven. But today nothing comes of these groups except gluttony and drunkenness.

Above all, we should drive out of German territory the papal legates[m] with their faculties,[n] which they sell to us for large sums of money. This traffic is nothing but skullduggery. For example, for the payment of money they make unrighteousness into righteousness, and they dissolve oaths, vows, and agreements, thereby destroying and teaching us to destroy the faith and fealty that have been pledged. They assert that the pope has authority to do this. It is the devil who tells them to say these things. They sell us doctrine so satanic, and take money for it, that they are teaching us sin and leading us to hell.

If there were no other base trickery to prove that the pope is the true Antichrist, this one would be enough to prove it. Hear this, O pope, not of all men the holiest but of all men the most sinful! O that God from heaven would soon destroy your throne and sink it in the abyss of hell! Who has given you authority to exalt yourself above your God, to violate and "loosen"[117] what he has commanded, and teach Christians, especially the German nation, praised throughout history for its nobility, constancy, and fidelity, to be inconstant, perjurers, traitors, profligates, and faithless?

117. A play on the power to bind and loose sins, first given to Peter (Matt. 16:19) and claimed by later popes as their exclusive right.

---

m   The word again is *botschafften*, but here it appears to mean not the *stationarii* of n. 114 but, rather, actual papal commissioners.

n   See n. 111.

118. In 1443 Vladislaus III, king of Poland (1424–1444) and (as Uladislaus I) king of Hungary, signed at Szeged a ten-year truce with the Turks. In the following year, Vladislaus allowed himself to be persuaded by the papal legate, Cardinal Cesarini (1398–1444), that the truce was invalid because the Turks could not be trusted to keep their word. So he renewed the war, as a result of which both he and the legate were killed at the battle of Varna on 10 November 1444.

119. Like Luther after him, the Bohemian reformer Jan Hus (1372–1415), lecturer at the University of Prague and popular preacher in the Bethlehem Chapel in Prague, rejected papal authority, demanded free preaching of the gospel, insisted on the right of the laity to receive communion in both kinds, and denounced clerical vices such as simony and the sale of indulgences. He was excommunicated in 1410, and when his supporters in Prague took to the streets in his defense, the city was placed under interdict (1412). Summoned to appear at the Council of Constance, Hus did so under a safe-conduct granted by Emperor Sigismund (1368–1437). But the council decreed that, according to divine and human law, no promise made to a heretic was binding. Hus was arrested, imprisoned, put on trial, and on 6 July 1415 burned at the stake. Luther is mistaken in assuming that Hus's colleague Jerome of Prague (1379–1416), who journeyed to Constance to support Hus, was also given a safe-conduct. Like Hus, he was arrested and burned at the stake.

God has commanded us to keep word and faith even with an enemy, but you have taken it upon yourself to loosen his commandment and have ordained in your heretical, anti-Christian decretals that you have his power. Thus through your voice and pen the wicked Satan lies as he has never lied before. You force and twist the Scriptures to suit your fancy. O Christ, my Lord, look down; let the day of your judgment burst forth and destroy this nest of devils at Rome. There sits the man of whom St. Paul said, "He shall exalt himself above you, sit in your church, and set himself up as God, that man of sin, the son of perdition" [2 Thess. 2:3-5]. What else is papal power but simply the teaching and increasing of sin and wickedness? Papal power serves only to lead souls into damnation in your name and, to all outward appearances, with your approval!

In ancient times the children of Israel had to keep the oath that they had unwittingly been deceived into giving to their enemies, the Gibeonites [Josh. 9:3-21]. And King Zedekiah was miserably lost along with all his people because he broke his oath to the king of Babylon [2 Kgs. 24:20—25:7]. In our own history, a hundred years ago, that fine king of Hungary and Poland, Ladislaus, was tragically slain by the Turk along with a great many of his people because he allowed himself to be led astray by the papal legate and cardinal and broke the good and advantageous treaty and solemn agreement he had made with the Turk.[118] The pious Emperor Sigismund had no more success after the Council of Constance when he allowed those scoundrels to break the oath that had been given to John Hus and Jerome.[119] All the trouble between the Bohemians and us stems from this. Even in our own times—God help us!—how much Christian blood has been shed because of the oath and the alliance which Pope Julius made between Emperor Maximilian and King Louis of France, and afterward broke![120] How could I tell all the trouble the popes have stirred up by their devilish presumption with which they annul oaths and vows made between powerful princes, making a mockery of these things, and taking money for it? I hope that the judgment day is at hand. Things could not possibly be worse than the state of

IOANNES HVSSVS BOHEMVS.
Cæsaris huic violata fides, damnatus iniqué es't
Vir pius et vera relligiōis amans.
Nonne (inquit) lapsos post centum iugiter annos
Danda deo ratio est impia turba tibi?
Cum priuill.

Portrait of Jan Hus (c. 1369–1415).
Engraved by Hendrik Hondius (1573–1650),
whose initial is at the upper right.

120. In 1508, Pope Julius II, King Louis XII of France, Emperor Maximilian I, and King Ferdinand of Aragon (1452–1516) formed the League of Cambrai against Venice. After the defeat of Venice at the hands of the French in 1509, Julius abandoned the League and in 1510 concluded with Ferdinand of Aragon, Emperor Maximilian, Henry VIII of England (1491–1547), and the Swiss a new alliance, the Holy League, aimed at expelling the French from Italy. This aim had been largely achieved by the death of Louis XII in 1515, but only temporarily. The Italian wars—essentially a dynastic power-struggle between the Valois of France (Francis I) and the Habsburgs of Spain and Burgundy (Charles V)—would continue, with brief periods of respite, until 1559, with frequently disastrous consequences for the papacy and the Italian states, especially with the sack of Rome in 1527 by the troops of Charles V.

121. Following the burning of Hus at Constance, the Hussite nobles and cities in Bohemia rallied to the defense of their reform movement. This led to a Hussite revolution, which five "crusades" mounted by Sigismund, Holy Roman Emperor and king of Bohemia, could not put down (1419–1431). In 1436, a peace treaty between the Council of Basel, Emperor Sigismund, and the Hussites was concluded, guaranteeing the continued existence of the Hussite communities and the right of Hussites to hold public office. Rome never officially accepted this agreement, but it remained in force in Bohemia nonetheless. This

affairs the Romanist See is promoting. The pope suppresses God's commandment and exalts his own. If he is not the Antichrist, then somebody tell me who is. But more of this another time.[o]

24. It is high time we took up the Bohemian question and dealt seriously and honestly with it.[121] We should come to an understanding with them so that the terrible slander,

---

[o] Luther may have been referring to his recently published tract (26 June 1520), *On the Papacy in Rome, against the Most Celebrated Romanist in Leipzig* (LW 39:49–104).

meant that there were two confessions in one Christian country: Hussites (predominantly Czech speaking) and Catholics (German speaking).

122. Because Luther denied that the pope ruled the church by divine right, his enemies had accused him of teaching "the Bohemian heresy" of Hus, a charge made by Johann Eck (1486–1543) at the Leipzig Debate in 1519. On that occasion, as here, Luther insisted that Hus had been erroneously and unjustly condemned as a heretic. See Brecht 1:319–21 and LW 31:314.

hatred, and envy on both sides comes to an end. As befits my folly, I shall be the first to submit an opinion on this subject, with due deference to everyone who may understand the case better than I.

First, we must honestly confess the truth and stop justifying ourselves. We must admit to the Bohemians that John Hus and Jerome of Prague were burned at Constance against the papal, Christian, imperial oath, and promise of safe-conduct. This happened contrary to God's commandment and gave the Bohemians ample cause for bitterness. And although they should have acted as perfect Christians and suffered this grave injustice and disobedience to God by these people, nevertheless, they were not obliged to condone such conduct and acknowledge it as just. To this day they would rather give up life and limb than admit that it is right to break and deal contrarily with an imperial, papal, and Christian oath. So then, although it is the impatience of the Bohemians that is at fault, yet the pope and his crowd are still more to blame for all the misery, error, and the loss of souls which have followed that council.

I will not pass judgment here on the articles of John Hus, or defend his errors, although I have not yet found any errors in his writings according to my way of thinking.[122] I firmly believe that those who violated a Christian safe-conduct and a commandment of God with their faithless betrayal gave neither a fair judgment nor an honest condemnation. Without doubt they were possessed more by the evil spirit than by the Holy Spirit. Nobody will doubt that the Holy Spirit does not act contrary to the commandment of God, and nobody is so ignorant as not to know that the violation of good faith and of a promise of safe-conduct is contrary to the commandment of God, even though they had been promised to the devil himself, to say nothing of a mere heretic. It is also quite evident that such a promise was made to John Hus and the Bohemians and was not kept, and that he was burnt at the stake as a result. I do not wish, however, to make John Hus a saint or a martyr, as some of the Bohemians do. But at the same time I do acknowledge that an injustice was done to him, and that his books and doctrines were unjustly condemned. For the judgments of God are secret and terrible, and no one save God alone should undertake to reveal or utter them.

I only want to say this. John Hus may have been as bad a heretic as it is possible to be, but he was burned unjustly and in violation of the commandment of God. Further, the Bohemians should not be forced to approve of such conduct, or else we shall never achieve any unity. Not obstinacy, but the open admission of the truth must make us one. It is useless to pretend, as was done at the time, that the oath of safe-conduct given to a heretic need not be kept. That is as much as to say that God's commandments need not be kept so that God's commandments may be kept. The devil made the Romanists insane and foolish so that they did not know what they had said and done. God has commanded that a promise of safe-conduct ought to be kept. We should keep such a commandment though the whole world collapses. How much more, then, when it is only a question of freeing a heretic! We should overcome heretics with books, not with fire, as the ancient fathers did. If it were wisdom to vanquish heretics with fire, then public hangmen would be the most learned scholars on earth. We would no longer need to study books, for he who overcomes another by force would have the right to burn him at the stake.

Second, the emperor and princes should send a few really upright and sensible bishops and scholars [to the Bohemians]. On no account should they send a cardinal or a papal legate or an inquisitor, for such people are most unversed in Christian things. They do not seek the salvation of souls, but, like all the pope's henchmen, only their own power, profit, and prestige. In fact, these very people were the chief actors in this miserable business at Constance. The people sent into Bohemia should find out from the Bohemians how things stand in regard to their faith, and whether it is possible to unite all their sects.[123] In this case, the pope ought, for the sake of saving souls, relinquish his power [of appointment] for a time and, in accordance with the decree of the

123. After the death of Hus, his followers divided into two groups. The more moderate group was known as the Utraquists or the Calixtines because of their demand for communion in both kinds (*sub utraque*), i.e., that the cup (*calix*) be administered to the laity. Otherwise they were essentially Catholic in doctrine. The other group, know as Taborites (after Mount Tabor, their fortified stronghold near Prague) were socially and theologically more radical and sought to extend the kingdom of God by force of arms. In the 1420s they split into two groups, the more moderate joining the Utraquists, the radicals surviving only to be annihilated on the battlefield in 1434. In the 1460s a radical group of Utraquists broke away to form the Bohemian Brethren (also known as the Unity of the Brotherhood), who rejected private property, oaths and all other civic obligations, and sought to live simple Christian lives away from urban centers. In the 1470s the Utraquists again began to splinter in two directions. A conservative faction sought to reestablish their connections with Rome, while the more radical faction, now called the New Utraquists, deliberately distanced themselves from Rome. By 1519 leaders of this group were in communication with Martin Luther. See *Oxford Encyclopedia of the Reformation*, ed. Hans Hillebrandt, 4 vols. (New York & Oxford: Oxford University Press, 1996), 1:185–86 s.v. "Bohemian Brethren"; 2:278–80, s.v. "Hussites"; and 4:206–8, s.v. "Utraquists."

truly Christian Council of Nicaea,[p] allow the Bohemians to choose an archbishop of Prague from among their number and let him be confirmed by the bishop of Olmütz in Moravia, or the bishop of Gran in Hungary, or the bishop of Gnesen in Poland, or the bishop of Magdeburg in Germany. It would be enough if he is confirmed by one or two of these, as was the custom in the time of St. Cyprian.[q] The pope has no right to oppose such an arrangement, and if he does oppose it, he will be acting like a wolf and a tyrant; no one ought to obey him, and his ban should be met with a counterban.

If, however, in deference to the chair of Peter, it were desired to do this with the pope's consent, then let it be done this way—provided that it does not cost the Bohemians a single penny and provided that the pope does not put them under the slightest obligation or bind them with his tyrannical oaths and vows as he does all other bishops, contrary to God and right. If he is not satisfied with the honor of being asked for consent, then let them not bother anymore about the pope or his vows and his rights, his laws and his tyrannies. Let the election suffice, and let the blood of all the souls endangered by this state of affairs cry out against him. No one ought to consent to what is wrong. It is enough to have shown courtesy to tyranny. If it cannot be otherwise, then an election and the approval of the common people can even now be quite as valid as confirmation by a tyrant, though I hope this will not be necessary. Someday some of the Romanists or some of the good bishops and scholars will take notice of the pope's tyranny and repudiate it.

I would also advise against compelling the Bohemians to abolish both kinds in the sacrament, since that practice is neither un-Christian nor heretical. If they want to, I would let them go on in the way they have been doing. Yet the new bishop should be careful that no discord arises because of such a practice. He should kindly instruct them that neither practice is wrong,[124] just as it ought not to cause dissension that the clergy differ from the laity in manner of life and

---

124. Luther defends communion in both bread and wine for the laity in *The Babylonian Captivity of the Church* (1520), LW 36:19–28, but still permitted communion in one kind, a position maintained (for the sake of the weak) in his *Invocavit* sermons, preached upon his return from Wartburg in March 1522 (LW 51:90–91) and in the *Instruction by the Visitors for the Parish Pastors of Saxony* from 1528 (LW 40:288–92).

---

p   See p. 409, n. 64.

q   See p. 383, n. 16.

dress. By the same token, if they were unwilling to receive Roman canon law, they should not be forced to so do, but rather the prime concern should be that they live sincerely in faith and in accordance with Holy Scripture. For Christian faith and life can well exist without the intolerable laws of the pope. In fact, faith cannot properly exist unless there are fewer or none of these Romanist laws. In baptism we have become free and have been made subject only to God's word. Why should we become bound by the word of any man? As St. Paul says, "You have become free; do not become a bond-servant of mortals,"[r] that is, of those who rule by human laws.

If I knew that the Pickards[125] held no other error regarding the sacrament of the altar except believing that the bread and wine are present in their true nature, but that the body and blood of Christ are truly present under them, then I would not condemn them but would let them come under the bishop of Prague. For it is not an article of faith that bread and wine are not present in the sacrament in their own essence and nature, but this is an opinion of St. Thomas and the pope.[126] On the other hand, it is an article of faith that the true natural body and blood of Christ are present in the natural bread and wine. So then, we should tolerate the opinions of both sides until they come to an agreement, because there is no danger in believing that the bread is there or that it is not.[s] We have to endure all sorts of practices and ordinances that are not harmful to faith. On the other hand, if they held heterodox beliefs, I would rather think of them as outside [the church], although I would teach them the truth.

Whatever other errors and schisms are discovered in Bohemia should be tolerated until the archbishop has been restored and has gradually brought all the people together again in one common doctrine. They will certainly never be united by force, defiance, or by haste. Patience and gentleness

125. Strictly speaking, the word *Pickards*, a corruption of *Beghards*, applies to the communities of pious laymen (members of corresponding sisterhoods were known as Beguines) that arose, chiefly in the Low Countries, in the twelfth and thirteenth centuries and were suspected of heresy by the ecclesiastical hierarchy. But, as here, the name was often applied to Hussites in Bohemia.

126. Since the Fourth Lateran Council of 1215, it has been official Catholic doctrine that in the Eucharist the whole substance of the bread and wine are transubstantiated into the whole substance of the body and blood of Christ, only the accidents (i.e., the outward appearances of bread and wine) remaining. The doctrine received its classical formulation from St. Thomas Aquinas, who employed the categories of substance and accidents found in Aristotelian metaphysics.

---

r   Cf. 1 Cor. 7:23; Gal. 5:1.

s   Luther's views were more fully developed in *The Babylonian Capitivity of the Church* (1520) in LW 36:28–35.

are needed here. Did not even Christ have to tarry with his disciples and bear with their unbelief for a long time until they believed his resurrection? If only the Bohemians had a regular bishop and church administration again, without Romanist tyranny, I am sure that things would soon be better.

The restoration of the temporal goods that formerly belonged to the church should not be too strictly demanded, but since we are Christians and each is bound to help the rest, we have full power to give them these things for the sake of unity and allow them to retain them in the sight of God and before the eyes of the world. For Christ says, "Where two are in agreement with one another on earth, there am I in the midst of them" [Matt. 18:19-20]. Would God that on both sides we were working toward this unity, extending to each other the hand of brotherhood and humility. Love is greater and is more needed than the papacy at Rome, which is without love. Love can exist apart from the papacy.

With this counsel I shall have done what I could. If the pope or his supporters hinder it, they shall have to render an account for having sought their own advantage rather than their neighbor's, contrary to the love of God. The pope ought to give up his papacy and all his possessions and honors, if thereby he could save one soul. But today he would rather let the whole world perish than yield one hair's-breadth of his presumptuous authority. And yet he wants to be the holiest of all! Herewith I am excused.

25. The universities, too, need a good, thorough reformation. I must say this, no matter whom it annoys. Everything the papacy has instituted and ordered serves only to increase sin and error. What else are the universities, unless they are utterly changed from what they have been hitherto, than what the book of Maccabees calls *gymnasia epheborum et graecae gloriae*?[127] What are they but places where loose living is practiced, where little is taught of the Holy Scriptures and Christian faith, and where only the blind, heathen teacher Aristotle rules far more than Christ?[128] In this regard my advice would be that Aristotle's *Physics, Metaphysics, Concerning the Soul*, and *Ethics*, which hitherto have been thought to

127. I.e., schools in which young men were taught the Greek way of life, including the worship of other gods, rather than Jewish law. Cf. 2 Macc. 4:7-17.

128. Although Luther greatly appreciated the value of Aristotle's works for the discipline of logical reasoning, he agreed with Erasmus and other humanists (not to mention some medieval scholars) that Aristotle had had a baneful influence on Scholastic theology. He took particular exception to Aristotle's teaching that human beings become good by doing good, which, in his judgment, encouraged the mistaken attribution of efficacy to human effort, apart from grace, in the process of justification.

be his best books, should be completely discarded along with all the rest of his books that boast about nature, although nothing can be learned from them either about nature or the Spirit. Moreover, nobody has yet understood him, and many souls have been burdened with fruitless labor and study, at the cost of much precious time. I dare say that any potter has more knowledge of nature than is written in these books. It grieves me to the quick that this damned, arrogant, villainous heathen has deluded and made fools of so many of the best Christians with his misleading writings. God has sent him as a plague upon us on account of our sins.

This wretched fellow in his best book, *Concerning the Soul*, even teaches that the soul dies with the body, although many have tried without success to save his reputation. As though we did not have the Holy Scriptures, in which we are fully instructed about all things, things about which Aristotle has not the faintest clue! And yet this dead heathen has conquered, obstructed, and almost succeeded in suppressing the books of the living God. When I think of this miserable business, I can only believe that the evil spirit has introduced the study [of Aristotle].

For the same reasons his *Ethics* is the worst of all books. It flatly opposes divine grace and all Christian virtues, and yet it is considered one of his best works. Away with such books! Keep them away from Christians. No one can accuse me of overstating the case, or of condemning what I do not understand. Dear friend, I know what I am talking about. I know my Aristotle as well as you or the likes of you. I have lectured on him and have been lectured at on him,[129] and I understand him better than St. Thomas or Duns Scotus did.[130] I can boast about this without arrogance, and if necessary, I can prove it. It makes no difference to me that so many great minds have devoted their labor to him for so many centuries.

Scottish philosopher and theologian Duns Scotus (c. 1266–1308), also known as Doctor Subtilis (the subtle doctor). Painting by Justus Van Ghent (1410–1480).

129. During his first year in Wittenberg (1508–1509), Luther gave lectures on Aristotle's *Nichomachean Ethics*. He had been required to study Aristotle during his student years. See above, pp. 76–78.

130. Duns Scotus (c. 1266–1308), as thoroughgoing an Aristotelian as Thomas Aquinas, was the latter's chief rival for first place among medieval theologians.

131. I.e., the commentaries by the Scholastics. By this time, the curriculum at Wittenberg had all but discarded medieval commentators in rhetoric and logic in favor of Philipp Melanchthon's humanist work (published in 1519 and 1521 [on rhetoric] and 1520 [on logic]).

132. These subjects, with the exception of history, were part of the curriculum in Wittenberg since 1518.

133. In addition to the basic arts faculty, discussed in the previous paragraph, there were three higher faculties at all medieval universities: medicine, law, and theology.

134. German: *in seynis hertzen kasten*, which is Luther's rendering of the Latin *in scrinio pectoris* (further on in

Such objections do not disturb me as once they did, for it is plain as day that other errors have remained for even more centuries in the world and in the universities.

I would gladly agree to keeping Aristotle's books *Logic*, *Rhetoric*, and *Poetics*, or at least keeping and using them in an abridged form, as useful in training young people to speak and to preach properly. But the commentaries and notes must be abolished,[131] and as Cicero's *Rhetoric* is read without commentaries and notes, so Aristotle's *Logic* should be read as it is without all these commentaries. But today nobody learns how to speak or how to preach from it. The whole thing has become nothing but a matter for wearying disputation.

In addition to all this, there are, of course, the Latin, Greek, and Hebrew languages, as well as the mathematical disciplines and history.[132] But all this I commend to the experts. In fact, reform would come readily if only we devoted ourselves seriously to it. Actually a great deal depends on it, for it is here in the universities that the Christian youth and our nobility, with whom the future of Christendom lies, will be educated and trained. Therefore, I believe that there is no work more worthy of pope or emperor than a thorough reform of the universities. And on the other hand, nothing could be more devilish or disastrous than unreformed universities.

I leave it to the physicians to reform their own faculties; I take the jurists and theologians for myself.[133] I say first that it would be a good thing if canon law were completely blotted out, from the first letter to the last, especially the Decretals.[t] More than enough is written in the Bible about how we should behave in all circumstances. The study of canon law only hinders the study of the Holy Scriptures. Moreover, the greater part smacks of nothing but greed and pride. Even if there were much in it that was good, it should still be destroyed, for the pope has the whole canon law imprisoned in the chamber of his heart,[134] so that hence-

---

t I.e., the *Liber Decretalium Gregorii IX* (1234); see p. 383, n. 15. It was an important subject in the faculty of theology.

forth any study of it is just a waste of time and a farce. These days canon law is not what is written in the books of law, but whatever the pope and his flatterers want. Your cause may be thoroughly established in canon law, but the pope always has his "chamber of the heart" in the matter, and all law, and with it the whole world, has to be guided by that. Now it is often a villain, and even the devil himself who controls the chamber, and they proudly boast that it is the Holy Spirit who controls it! Thus they deal with Christ's poor people. They impose many laws upon them but obey none themselves. They compel others to obey these laws or buy their way out with money.

Since then the pope and his followers have suspended the whole canon law as far as they themselves are concerned, and since they pay it no heed but give thought only to their own wanton will, we should do as they do and discard these volumes. Why should we waste our time studying them? We could never fathom the arbitrary will of the pope, which is all that canon law has become. Let canon law perish in God's name, for it arose in the devil's name. Let there be no more "doctors of the Decretals" in the world, but only "doctors of the papal chamber [of his heart]" that is, the pope's flatterers. It is said that there is no better secular government anywhere than among the Turks,[135] who have neither canon law nor secular law but only their Koran. But we must admit that there is no more shameful rule than ours with its canon and secular law, which has resulted in nobody living according to common sense, much less according to Holy Scripture anymore.

Secular law—God help us—has become a wilderness.[136] Though it is much better, wiser, and more honest than the spiritual law,*u* which has nothing good about it except its name, there is nevertheless far too much of it. Surely, wise rulers, along with Holy Scripture, would be more than enough law. As St. Paul says in 1 Cor. 6[:5-6], "Is there no one among you who can judge his neighbor's cause, that you must go to law before heathen courts?" It seems just

this paragraph and in the one that follows, he uses the Latin phrase), traditionally translated into English as "shrine of the heart." A *scrinium* was a chest or box for the storage of books and papers and, later, relics. According to Pope Boniface VIII, the pope had all laws in his *scrinium pectoris* (literally, "in the storage box of his heart") and was the final judge of its meaning and application. See Friedberg 2:937; LW 31:385 (*Why the Books of the Pope and His Disciples Were Burned*, 1520); and *Smalcald Articles*, III.8.4, in BC, 322.

135. See p. 394, n. 32.

136. By "secular law" Luther means primarily Roman law as codified in the *Corpus Iuris Civilis*, which, together with the *Corpus Iuris Canonici,* constituted the "common law" (*ius commune*) of the Holy Roman Empire (i.e., the law that applied to all cases not governed by a recognized local law, custom, or privilege). In addition, there were various versions of Germanic law that

u I.e., canon law.

were in the process of being replaced by Roman law or integrated into it, to the advantage of centralizing governments and the disadvantage of local customs and privileges. See Gerald Strauss, *Law, Resistance, and the State: The Opposition to Roman Law in Reformation Germany* (Princeton: Princeton University Press, 1986), ch. 3.

137. By 1530 Luther would have arrived at a far more positive attitude toward Roman law, deeming it the epitome of God-given wisdom in the secular realm, and a correspondingly harsher attitude toward Germanic law, which he found barbarous in its severity and frequently unfair in its application. See James Estes, "Luther's Attitude toward the Legal Traditions of His Time," *Luther-Jahrbuch* 76 (2009): 87–88, 96–99.

138. That is, on the *Four Books of Sentences* (*Sententiarum libri quatuor*) in which the twelfth-century theologian Peter Lombard (c. 1096–1164), who was known as "the Master of the *Sentences*," collected and briefly explained the opinions (*sententiae*) of ancient church fathers on a wide range of theological subjects. As part of their progress toward doctorates, theologians (including Luther) had to lecture on the *Sentences*, which in Luther's day was still the basic textbook for theological instruction.

139. The first degree granted to a candidate in theology was that of bachelor of the Bible (*baccalaureus biblicus*), which qualified the recipient to lecture on the Bible. The next

to me that territorial laws and customs should take precedence over general imperial laws, and that the imperial laws be used only in case of necessity. Would God that every land were ruled by its own brief laws suitable to its gifts and peculiar character. This is how these lands were ruled before these imperial laws were designed, and as many lands are still ruled without them! Rambling and farfetched laws are only a burden to the people, and they hinder cases more than they help them. But I hope that others have already given more thought and attention to this matter than I am able to do.[137]

My dear theologians have saved themselves worry and work. They just leave the Bible alone and lecture on the *Sentences*.[138] I should have thought that the *Sentences* ought to be the first study for young students of theology, and the Bible left to the doctors. But today it is the other way round. The Bible comes first and is then put aside when the baccalaureate is received. The *Sentences* come last, and they occupy a doctor as long as he lives.[139] There is such a solemn obligation attached to these *Sentences* that a person who is not a priest may well lecture on the Bible, but the sentences must be lectured on by someone who is a priest. As I see it, a married man may well be a Doctor of the Bible, but under no circumstances could he be a Doctor of the *Sentences*.[140] How can we prosper when we behave so wrongly and give the Bible, the holy word of God, a back seat? To make things worse, the pope commands in the strongest language that his words are to be studied in the schools and used in the courts, but very little is thought of the gospel. Consequently, the gospel lies neglected in the schools and in the courts. It is pushed aside under the bench and gathers dust so that the scandalous laws of the pope alone may have full sway.

If we bear the name and title of teachers of Holy Scripture, then by this criterion we ought to be compelled to teach the Holy Scripture and nothing else, although we all know that this high and mighty title is much too exalted for a person to take pride in it and allow being designated a Doctor of Holy Scripture. Yet that title might be permitted if the work justified the name. But nowadays, the *Sentences* alone dominate in such a way that we find among the theologians more pagan and human darkness than holy and certain doctrine of Scripture. What are we to do about it? I know of nothing else to do than to pray humbly to God to give us such real doctors of theology as we have in mind. Pope, emperor, and universities may make doctors of arts, of medicine, of laws, of the *Sentences*; but be assured that no one can make a doctor of Holy Scripture except the Holy Spirit from heaven. As Christ says in John 6[:45], "They must all be taught by God himself." Now the Holy Spirit does not care about red or brown birettas[141] or other decorations. Nor does he ask whether a person is young or old, lay or cleric, monk or secular, unmarried or married. In fact, in ancient times he actually spoke through a donkey against the prophet who was riding it [Num. 22:28]. Would God that we were worthy to have such doctors given to us, regardless of whether they were lay or cleric, married or single! They now try to force the Holy Spirit into pope, bishops, and doctors, although there is not the slightest sign or indication whatever that he is in them.

The number of books on theology must be reduced and only the best ones published. It is not many books that make people learned or even much reading. It is, rather, a good book frequently read, no matter how small it is, that makes a person learned in the Scriptures and upright. Indeed, the writings of all the holy Fathers should be read only for a time so that through them we may be led into the Scriptures. As it is, however, we only read them these days to avoid going any further and getting into the Bible. We are like people who read the signposts and never travel the road they indicate. Our dear Fathers wanted to lead us to the Scriptures by their writings, but we use their works to get away from the Scriptures. Nevertheless, the Scripture alone is our vineyard in which we must all labor and toil.[142]

Above all, the foremost reading for everybody, both in the universities and in the schools, should be Holy Scripture—and for the younger boys, the Gospels. And would God that every town had a girls' school as well, where the girls would be taught the gospel for an hour every day either in German

degree was that of bachelor of the sentences (*baccalaureus sententiarius*), which obligated the recipient to lecture on Lombard's *Sentences*. After mastering the first two of the four books of the *Sentences*, the candidate became a *baccalaureus sententiarius formatus* or licentiate, which obliged him to participate in disputations and other academic functions. Then came the doctorate. For Luther's (unusually rapid) traversal of these stages of promotion, see Brecht 1:125–27.

140. At Wittenberg, this pattern was reversed in the case of Philip Melanchthon, who received his bachelor of Bible in 1519 under Luther's direction but never lectured on the *Sentences*. Instead, he was married (in 1520) and developed a new kind of lecture on main topics of Christian doctrine, derived especially from Paul's letter to the Romans, which were published in 1521 as the *Loci communes theologici* ("Theological Common Places").

141. A red biretta was the headdress of a doctor of theology; a brown or russett (*braunrot*) one was that of a master in the arts faculty.

142. Cf. the much later painting by Lucas Cranach Jr. (1515–1586), in the Wittenberg City Church, "The Vineyard of the Lord," which depicted the reformers as vinedressers.

or in Latin.[v] But real schools! Monasteries and nunneries began long ago with that end in view,[w] and it was a praiseworthy and Christian purpose, as we learn from the story of St. Agnes and of other saints.[x] Those were the days of holy virgins and martyrs when all was well with Christendom. But today these monasteries and nunneries have come to nothing but praying and singing. Is it not only right that every Christian know the entire holy gospel by the age of nine or ten? Does not each person derive name and life from the gospel? A spinner or a seamstress teaches her daughter her craft in her early years. But today even the great, learned prelates and the very bishops do not know the gospel.

Oh, how irresponsibly we deal with these poor young people who are committed to us for training and instruction. We shall have to render a solemn account of our neglect to set the word of God before them. Their lot is as described by Jeremiah in Lam. 2[:11-12], "My eyes are grown weary with weeping, my bowels are terrified, my heart is poured out upon the ground because of the destruction of the daughter of my people, for the youth and the children perish in all the streets of the entire city. They said to their mothers, 'Where is bread and wine?' as they fainted like wounded men in the streets of the city and gave up the ghost on their mothers' bosom." We do not see this pitiful evil, how today the young people of Christendom languish and perish miserably in our midst for want of the gospel, in which we ought to be giving them constant instruction and training.

Moreover, even if the universities were diligent in [the teaching of] Holy Scripture, we should not send everybody there as we do now, where their only concern is numbers and where everybody wants a doctor's degree. We should send only the most highly qualified students who have been well trained in the lower schools. Every prince or city coun-

---

v   On this, including the need of schools for girls, see Luther's *To the Councilmen of All Cities in Germany, That They Establish and Maintain Christian Schools* (1524), LW 45:339-78.

w   See p. 423, n. 87.

x   See p. 423, n. 88.

cil should see to this, and permit only the well qualified to be sent. I would advise no one to send his child where the Holy Scriptures are not supreme. Everything that does not unceasingly pursue the study of God's word must corrupt, and because of this we can see what kind of people there are and will be in the universities. Nobody is to blame for this except the pope, the bishops, and the prelates, for it is they who are charged with the welfare of young people. The universities only ought to turn out people who are experts in the Holy Scriptures, who can become bishops and priests, and can stand in the front line against heretics, the devil, and the whole world. But where do you find that? I greatly fear that the universities, unless they teach the Holy Scriptures diligently and impress them on the young students, are wide gates of hell.

26.*y* I know full well that the gang in Rome will allege and trumpet mightily that the pope took the Holy Roman Empire from the Greek emperor and bestowed it upon the Germans, for which honor and benevolence he is said to have justly deserved and obtained submission, thanks, and all good things from the Germans.[143] For this reason they will, perhaps, undertake to throw all attempts to reform themselves to the four winds and will not allow us to think about anything but the bestowal of the Roman Empire. For this cause they have persecuted and oppressed many a worthy emperor so willfully and arrogantly that it is a shame even to mention it.*z* And with the same adroitness they have made themselves overlords of every secular power and authority, contrary to the holy gospel. I must therefore speak of this, too.

There is no doubt that the true Roman Empire, which the writings of the prophets foretold in Num. 24[:17-24] and Dan. 2[:36-45], has long since been overthrown and come

143. Through a series of military conquests, Charles the Great (a.k.a. Charlemagne, c. 742–814), king of the Franks, managed to unite most of western Europe under one rule for the first time since the collapse of the western Roman Empire in the fifth century. In the year 800 Charles had himself crowned "Emperor of the Romans" by Pope Leo III (750–816) in St. Peter's Basilica, an act that nullified any claim by the Byzantine emperors in Constantinople to authority in what had been the western Empire. Thereafter Charlemagne and his successors as German kings were known as Roman emperors. In later struggles with the German emperors over who possessed the highest jurisdiction, medieval popes interpreted Charlemagne's coronation by Leo as the act of someone who, by virtue of his supreme jurisdiction in both secular and spiritual matters, had the authority to take imperial power from the Greek emperor and bestow it on the Frankish king. The pope's confirmation was deemed necessary for the election of the German king/ Roman emperor to be deemed valid, and that confirmation could be withheld or withdrawn.

---

y   This entire section is missing from the first printing of the treatise; Luther added it to the second printing; see p. 418, note *n.*

z   See p. 379, n. 9.

144. Luther here dissociates himself in part from the conception of "world history" that had prevailed in western Europe in the Middle Ages. It was based on the prophecy in Daniel 2 (repeated in variant form in Daniel 7) of the rise and fall of the four great empires of "gold," "silver," "bronze," and "iron" (with the latter to be divided into empires of "iron" and "clay") that would precede the apocalypse and the establishment of Christ's kingdom. Medieval exegetes identified the four empires as Babylon, Persia, Greece (Macedonia), and Rome. For as long as the apocalypse had not occurred, it remained necessary to argue that the Roman Empire still existed. Hence, theologians argued that the collapse of the western Roman Empire in 476 left imperial authority intact in the eastern Empire (Byzantium) and that the papal coronation of Charlemagne in 800 effected a transfer of imperial rule from the Greeks to the Germans (*translatio imperii a Graecis ad Germanos*). See above, n. 143.

to an end,[144] as Balaam clearly prophesied in Num. 24[:24] when he said, "The Romans shall come and overthrow the Jews, and afterward they also shall be destroyed."[145] That happened under the Goths,[146] but more particularly when the empire of the Turks began almost a thousand years ago. Then eventually Asia and Africa fell away, and in time France and Spain, and finally Venice broke away, and nothing was left to Rome of its former power.

When, then, the pope could not subdue to his arrogant will the Greeks and the emperor at Constantinople, who was the hereditary Roman emperor, he invented a little device to rob this emperor of his empire and his title and to turn it over to the Germans, who at that time were warlike and of good repute. In so doing, [the Romanists] brought the power of the Roman Empire under their control so that it had to be held as a fief from them. And this is just what happened. [Imperial authority] was taken away from the emperor at Constantinople, and its name and title given to us Germans, and thereby we became servants of the pope. There is now a second Roman Empire, built by the pope upon the Germans, for the former one, as I said earlier, has long since fallen.

So, then, the Roman See now gets its own way. It has taken possession of Rome, driven out the German emperor, and bound him by oaths not to dwell at Rome.[a] He is supposed to be Roman emperor, and yet he is not to have possession of Rome; and besides, he is to be dependent on and move within the limits of the good pleasure of the pope and his supporters. We have the title, but they have the land and the city. They have always abused our simplicity to serve their own arrogant and tyrannical designs. They call us crazy Germans for letting them make fools and monkeys of us as they please.

Now then, it is a small thing for God to toss empires and principalities to and fro. He is so gentle with them that once in a while he gives a kingdom to a scoundrel and takes one from a good man, sometimes by the treachery of wicked,

a According to the *Donation of Constantine* (cf. n. 110); see Mirbt-Aland, 255, no. 504, §§17–19.

faithless men, and sometimes by inheritance. This is what we read about the kingdoms of Persia and Greece, and about almost all kingdoms. It says in Dan. 2[:21] and 4[:34-35], "He who rules over all things dwells in heaven, and it is he alone who overthrows kingdoms, tosses them to and fro, and establishes them." Since no one, particularly a Christian, can think it a very great thing to receive a kingdom, we Germans, too, need not lose our heads because a new Roman Empire is bestowed on us. For in God's eyes it is but a trifling gift, one that he often gives to the most unworthy, as it says in Dan. 4[:35], "All who dwell on earth are as nothing in his eyes, and he has the power in all the kingdoms of men to give them to whom he will."

But although the pope used violence and unjust means to rob the true emperor of his Roman Empire, or of the title of his Roman Empire, and gave it to us Germans, yet it is nevertheless certain that God has used the pope's wickedness to give such an empire to the German nation, and after the fall of the first Roman Empire, to set up another, the one that now exists. And although we had nothing to do with this wickedness of the popes, and although we did not understand their false aims and purposes, we have nevertheless paid tragically and far too dearly for such an empire with incalculable bloodshed, with the suppression of our liberty, the occupation and theft of all our possessions, especially of our churches and benefices, and with the suffering of unspeakable deception and insult. We carry the title of empire, but it is the pope who has our wealth, honor, body, life, soul, and all that we possess. This is how they deceive the Germans and cheat them with tricks.[b] What the popes have sought was to be emperors themselves, and though they could not achieve this, they nonetheless succeeded in setting themselves over the emperors.

Since the Empire has been given us by the providence of God as well as by the plotting of evil men, without any guilt

145. NRSV: "But ships shall come from Kittim and shall afflict Asshur and Eber." Luther follows the Vulgate, which translates "They will come in ships from Italy and be over the Assyrians and destroy the Hebrews," In the 1523 translation into German, Luther leaves the Hebrew Kittim in the text and in a marginal note insists that it applies rather to Macedonia (Greece) and Alexander the Great (356-323 BCE). In his lectures on Genesis from 1537, Luther associates Kittim primarily with Greece but also with the coasts of Italy and France (LW 2:191). In the 1545 edition of the German Bible, he explains that Kittim refers to both Alexander the Great and the Romans, whose kingdoms will collapse, leaving only Israel (WA DB 8:514–15).

146. The Visigoths sacked Rome in the year 410.

---

b   *Szo sol man die Deutschen teuschen und mit teuschen teuschen*, a pun on *Deutchen* ("Germans"), *teuschen* ("deceive," "cheat"), and *teuschen* ("tricks," "deceptions") that cannot be duplicated in English.

on our part, I shall not advise that we give it up, but rather that we rule it wisely and in the fear of God, as long as it pleases him for us to rule it. For, as has been said already, it does not matter to him where an empire comes from; his will is that it be governed regardless. Though the popes were dishonest in taking it from others, we were not dishonest in receiving it. It has been given us through evil people by the will of God, for which we have more regard that for the fraudulent intention to be emperors themselves, and indeed more than emperors, and only to mock and ridicule us with the title. The king of Babylon also seized his kingdom by robbery and violence. Yet it was God's will that that kingdom be ruled by the holy princes Daniel, Hananiah, Azariah, and Mishael.[c] Much more, then, is it God's will that this empire should be ruled by the Christian princes of Germany, no matter whether the pope stole it, got it by force, or established it anew. It is all God's ordering, which came to pass before we knew about it.

Therefore, the pope and his followers have no right to boast that they have done the German nation a great favor by giving us the Roman Empire. In the first place, they did not mean it for our good. Rather, they took advantage of our simplicity when they did it in order to strengthen their proud designs against the real Roman emperor at Constantinople, from whom the pope took his empire against God and right, which he had no authority to do. In the second place, the pope's intention was not to give us the Empire, but to get it for himself, so that he might bring all our power, our freedom, our wealth, our souls, and our bodies into subjection to himself, and through us (had God not prevented it) to subdue all the world. He clearly says so himself in his Decretals,[d] and has attempted to do so by means of many wicked wiles with a number of the German emperors. Thus have we Germans been beautifully neatly taught our

c   Dan. 1:6-7; 2:48; 5:29. The latter three are renamed in Dan. 1:7—
    Shadrach, Meshach, and Abednego.
d   See, e.g., the decretal *Venerabilem fratrem* (1202). See Mirbt-Aland
    307, no. 596; Friedberg 2:80.

German.[e] While we supposed we were going to be lords, we became in fact servants of the most deceitful tyrants of all time. We have the name, the title, and the insignia of empire, but the pope has its treasures, authority, rights, and liberties. The pope gobbles the kernel while we are left playing with the husk.

Now may God, who (as I said) tossed this empire into our lap by the wiles of tyrants and has charged us with its rule, help us to live up to the name, title, and insignia and to retrieve our liberty. Let the Romanists see once and for all what it is that we have received from God through them. If they boast that they have bestowed an empire on us, let them. If that is true, then let the pope give us back Rome and all that he has gotten from the Empire; let him free our land from his intolerable taxing and fleecing; let him give us back our liberty, our rights, our honor, our body and soul; and let the Empire be what an empire should be, so that the pope's words and pretensions might be fulfilled.

If he will not do that, then what is he playing at with his false, fabricated words and his deceptions? Has there not for so many centuries now been enough of his ceaseless and uncouth leading of this noble nation around by the nose? It does not follow that the pope must be above the emperor because he crowns or appoints him. The prophet St. Samuel anointed and crowned the kings Saul and David at God's command, and yet he was their subject.[f] The prophet Nathan anointed King Solomon,[g] but he was not set over the king on that account. Similarly, St. Elisha had one of his servants anoint Jehu king of Israel, but they still remained obedient and subject to the king.[h] It has never happened in all the history of the world that he who consecrated or crowned the king was over the king, except in this single instance of the pope.

---

e   Probably a pun similar to note *b*, p. 457, meaning "We Germans have been tricked [by the popes]."

f   1 Sam. 10:1; 16:13.

g   1 Kgs. 1:39. It was in fact Zadok the priest who anointed Solomon.

h   2 Kgs. 9:6.

The pope permits himself to be crowned by three cardinals who are beneath him, but he is nonetheless their superior. Why should he then go against his own example, against universal practice, and against the teaching of Scripture by exalting himself above secular authority or imperial majesty simply because he crowns or consecrates the emperor? It is quite enough that he is the emperor's superior in the things of God, that is, in preaching, teaching, and the administration of the sacraments. In these respects, any bishop and any priest is over everybody else, just as St. Ambrose in his diocese was over the emperor Theodosius,[147] the prophet Nathan over David, and Samuel over Saul. Therefore, let the German emperor be really and truly emperor. Let neither his authority nor his power be suppressed by such sham pretensions of these papist deceivers as though they were to be excepted from his authority and were themselves to rule in all things.

27.[i] Enough has now been said about the failings of the clergy, though you may and will find more if you look in the right place. Let us now take a look at some of those of the secular realm.

In the first place, there is a great need for a general law and decree in the German nation against boundlessly excessive and costly dress, because of which so many nobles and rich people are impoverished.[j] God has certainly given us, as he has to other countries, enough wool, flax, linen, and everything else necessary for the seemly and honorable dress of every class. We do not need to waste fantastic sums for silk, velvet, golden ornaments, and foreign wares. I believe that even if the pope had not robbed us with his intolerable fleecing, we would still have more than enough of these home-grown robbers, the traders in silk and velvet. We see that now everybody wants to be like everybody else, and pride and envy are thereby aroused and increased among us, as we deserve. All this misery and much more besides would

147. In the year 390, St. Ambrose, bishop of Milan, refused to admit Emperor Theodosius I (347–395) to communion until after he had done public penance for having ordered the indiscriminate slaughter of seven thousand inhabitants of Thessalonica following the murder there of the Roman governor by rioters.

i   In the first printing of the treatise, this section followed immediately after section 25 and was numbered 26.

j   Such a law (part of a larger *Polizeiordunung*) was proposed at the Diet of Worms in 1521; see RTA 2:335–41.

probably be avoided if only our ardor [for such things] would let us be thankfully content with the good things God has already given us.

It is also necessary to restrict the traffic in spices, which is another of the great ships in which money is carried out of the German lands. By the grace of God, more things to eat and drink grow here than in any other country, and they are just as tasty and good. Perhaps my proposals seem foolish, impractical, and give the impression that I want to ruin the greatest of all trades, that of commerce. But I am doing my best, and if there is no general improvement in these matters, then let him who will try his hand at improving them. I do not see that many good morals have ever come to a country through commerce, and in ancient times God made his people Israel dwell away from the sea because of this and did not let them engage in much commerce.[k]

But the greatest misfortune of the German nation is certainly the *zynskauf*.[148] If that did not exist, many people[l] would have to leave unpurchased their silks, velvets, golden ornaments, spices, and display of every kind. This traffic has not existed much longer than a hundred years, and it has already brought almost all princes, endowed institutions, cities, nobles, and their heirs to poverty, misery, and ruin. If it goes on for another hundred years, Germany will not have a penny left, and the chances are we shall have to eat one another. The devil invented the practice, and by confirming it the pope has brought woe upon the whole world.

Therefore, I beg and pray at this point that everyone open their eyes and see the ruin of their children and heirs. Ruin is not just at the door, it is already in the house. I pray and beseech emperor, princes, lords, and city councilors to condemn this trade as speedily as possible and prevent it from now on, regardless of whether the pope with all his unjust justice objects, or whether benefices or monasteries are based upon it. It is better for a city to have one benefice supported by honest legacies or revenue than to have a hundred

148. *Zinskauf* in modern German, a synonym for *Rentenkauf*, i.e., the purchase of an annuity (a yearly rent) in return for the use of a sum of money or a piece of property. Because the buyer was theoretically purchasing something and could not recall the sum paid, the annual payments could not be called interest. In this way the biblical and canon-law prohibitions of lending at interest to other Christians (usury) was circumvented. Luther, who was more conservative on the subject of charging interest than were his Catholic opponents, like Johann Eck, insisted that the *Zinskauf* was indeed usurious unless rigorous standards of fairness (e.g., equal risk on the part of both buyer and seller) were met. See his *Treatise on Good Works* (p. 346, n. 118), and his *Long Sermon on Usury* (early 1520); LW 45:233–43 (helpful introduction), 273–95 (text); and Brecht 1:356–57.

---

k   See Ezek. 27:3, 8; and Isa. 23:1, 8, where Tyre is described, in contrast to Israel, as having merchant ships and being engaged in commerce.

l   Singular in the original.

benefices supported by *zynskauf*. Indeed, a benefice supported by a *zynskauf* is more grievous and oppressive than twenty supported by legacies. In fact, the *zynskauf* must be a sign and proof that the world has been sold to the devil because of its grievous sins and that at the same time we are losing both temporal and spiritual possessions. And yet we do not even notice it.

In this connection, we must put a bit in the mouth of the Fuggers and similar companies.*ᵐ* How is it possible in the lifetime of one person to accumulate such great possessions, worthy of a king, legally and according to God's will? I don't know. But what I really cannot understand is how a person with one hundred gulden can make a profit of twenty in one year. Nor, for that matter, can I understand how a person with one gulden can make another—and make it not from tilling the soil or raising cattle, where the increase of wealth depends not on human wit but on God's blessing. I leave this to people who understand the ways of the world.[149] As a theologian I have no further reproof to make on this subject except that it has an evil and offending appearance, about which St. Paul says, "Avoid every appearance or show of evil" [1 Thess. 5:22]. I know full well that it would be a far godlier thing to increase agriculture and decrease commerce. I also know that those who work on the land and seek their livelihood from it according to the Scriptures do far better. All this was said to us and to everybody else in the story of Adam, "Cursed be the ground when you work it; it shall bear you thistles and thorns, and in the sweat of your face you shall eat your bread" [Gen. 3:17-19]. There is still a lot of land lying fallow and neglected.

Next comes the abuse of eating and drinking, which gives us Germans a bad reputation in foreign lands, as though it were a special vice of ours. Preaching cannot stop it so deeply is it rooted and so firmly has it got the upper hand. The waste of money would be insignificant were it not for all the vices that accompany it—murder, adultery, stealing, blasphemy, and every other form of immorality. Govern-

149. Luther here reflects the Aristotelian economic principle that money is simply an object like a chair or table and thus incapable of making money.

m See p. 406, n. 57.

ment can do something to prevent it; otherwise, what Christ says will come to pass, that the last day shall come like a secret snare, when they shall be eating and drinking, marrying and wooing, building and planting, buying and selling.[n] It is so much like what is now going on that I sincerely hope the Judgment Day is at hand, although very few people give it any thought.

Finally, is it not lamentable that we Christians tolerate open and common brothels in our midst, when all of us are baptized unto chastity?[o] I know perfectly well what some say to this, that is, that it is not a custom peculiar to one nation, that it would be difficult to put a stop to it, and, moreover, that it is better to keep such a house than that married women, or girls, or others of still more honorable estate should be molested. Nevertheless, should not secular and Christian governments consider that one ought not to counteract these things in such a heathen manner? If the children of Israel could exist without such impropriety, why cannot Christians do as much? In fact, how do so many cities, country towns, market towns, and villages do without such houses? Why can't large cities do without them as well?

In this matter and in the other matters previously mentioned, I have tried to point out how many good works secular government could do, and what the duty of every government should be, so that everyone may learn what an awful responsibility it is to rule and sit in high places. What use would it be if a ruler were himself as holy as St. Peter, if he did not diligently try to help his subjects in these matters? His very authority would condemn him. It is the duty of governing authority to seek the best for its subjects. But if the authorities were to give some thought to how young people might be brought together in marriage, the hope of married life would greatly help every one of them to endure and resist temptation.

But today everybody is attracted to the priesthood or the monastic life, and among them, I am sorry to say, there is

n   Cf. Luke 21:34; 12:45, and Matt. 24:36-44.
o   See above, *Treatise on Good Works*, p. 347.

not one in a hundred who has any other reason than that he seeks a living and doubts that he will ever be able to support himself in married life. Therefore, they live wildly enough beforehand, and wish, as they say, to get it out of their system, but experience shows that it is only more deeply embedded in them. I find the proverb true, "Despair makes most monks and priests."[p] That is what happens and that is how it is, as we see.

I will, however, sincerely advise that to avoid the many sins that spread so shamelessly, neither youths nor maidens should bind themselves to chastity or clerical life before the age of thirty. Chastity, as St. Paul says, is a special gift [1 Cor. 7:7]. Therefore, I would advise those upon whom God has not conferred his special gift to abstain from clerical life and making vows. I say further that if you trust God so little that you fear you won't be able to support yourself as a married man, and you wish to become a cleric only because of this distrust, then I beg you for your own soul's sake not to become a cleric at all, but rather a farmer or anything you like. For where a single measure of faith in God is needed to earn your daily bread, there must be ten times that amount of faith to remain a cleric. If you do not trust God to provide for you in temporal things, how will you trust him to support you in spiritual things? Alas, unbelief and distrust spoil everything and lead us into all kinds of misery, as we see in all walks of life.

Much more could be said of this pitiful state of affairs. Young people have nobody to watch over them. They all do as they please, and the government is as much use to them as if it did not exist. And yet the care of young people ought to be the chief concern of the pope, bishops, rulers, and councils. They want to exercise authority far and wide, and yet they help nobody. For just this reason a lord and ruler will be a rare sight in heaven, even though he build a hundred churches for God and raise up all the dead!

Let this suffice for the moment. [I think I have said enough in my little book *Treatise on Good Works*[q] about what

p   Wander, 4:1625.

the secular authorities and the nobility ought to do. There is certainly room for improvement in their lives and in their rule, yet the abuses of the temporal power are not to be compared with those of the spiritual power, as I have shown in that book.][r]

I know full well that I have sung rather grandly. I have made many suggestions that will be considered impractical. I have attacked many things too severely. But how else ought I to do it? I am duty-bound to speak. These are the things I would do if I were able. I would rather have the wrath of the world upon me than the wrath of God. The world can do no more to me than take my life. In the past I have made frequent overtures of peace to my enemies, but as I see, God has compelled me through them to open my mouth ever wider and to give them enough to say, bellow, shout, and write because they have nothing else to do. Well, I know another little song about Rome and the Romanists. If their ears are itching to hear it, I will sing that one to them, too—and pitch it in the highest key! You understand what I mean, dear Rome.[150]

Moreover, I have many times offered my writings for investigation and hearing, but to no avail because, as I too know full well, if my cause is just, it must be condemned on earth and be justified by Christ alone in heaven. For all the Scriptures bear witness that the cause of Christians and of Christendom must be judged by God alone, and no cause has ever yet been justified on earth by human effort because the opposition has always been too great and too strong. It is still my greatest concern and anxiety that my cause may not be condemned, by which I would know for certain that it is not yet pleasing to God. Therefore, just let them go hard at it, pope, bishop, priest, monk, or scholar. They are just the ones to persecute the truth, as they have always done. May God give us all a Christian mind and grant to the Christian nobility of the German nation in particular true spiritual courage to do the best they can for the poor church. Amen.

Wittenberg, in the year 1520.

150. The "little song" is *The Babylonian Captivity of the Church* (LW 36:3–126), which was also written in 1520, shortly after this treatise was published.

q   See above, pp. 342–47.
r   The bracketed passage was inserted into the second edition of the treatise. See above, p. 418f., note *n*.

DE LIBER
TATE CHRISTIANA DIS,
SERTATIO MARTINI
LVTHERI, PER AV
TOREM RECO
GNITA.

EPISTOLA EIVSDEM AD
LEONEM DECIMVM
SVMMVM PON
TIFICEM.

Title page of *The Freedom of a Christian*
from a 1521 printing of the second edition.

The Freedom of a Christian

1520

TIMOTHY J. WENGERT

INTRODUCTION

The movement within Western Christianity that began in 1517 with the posting of Martin Luther's *95 Theses*, now known as the Reformation, was by no means a foregone conclusion in its earliest stages. Starting with the papal legate, Cardinal Cajetan's (1469–1534) interview of Luther in October 1518,[1] various attempts were made first to avoid or mitigate Luther's impending condemnation by the pope and, later, to find ways around the papal condemnation and the impending judgment of the imperial diet (parliament) that finally met in Worms in April 1521. One such embassy fell on the shoulders of Karl von Miltitz (c. 1490–1529), who throughout 1520 tried to find ways around the impasse between Luther and his supporters (along with his protector prince, the Elector Frederick of Saxony [1463–1525]) on the one side and the papal court and its defenders on the other.[2]

Luther left the final meeting with von Miltitz with instructions to write a reconciliation-minded letter to Pope Leo X (1475–1521), which he did in the weeks that followed and to which he appended a nonpolemical tract describing the heart of his beliefs. (Indeed, compared to other major tracts he produced in 1520, *The Freedom of a Christian* has

1. See above, pp. 121–65.

2. For the details of the historical record, see Brecht 1:400–415, and Berndt Hamm, *The Early Luther: Stages in a Reformation Reorientation* (Grand Rapids: Eerdmans, 2014), 172–89.

3. These tracts include two others in this volume, *Sermon on Good Works* and *Address to the Christian Nobility*, and *The Babylonian Captivity of the Church*, in LW 36:3–126.

4. Hamm, *The Early Luther*, 172–89.

5. For a translation of the German preface, see LW 31:333. For a translation of the entire German tract, see Philip Krey and Peter Krey, eds., *Luther's Spirituality* (Mahwah, NJ: Paulist, 2007), 69–90.

a remarkably temperate tone.)[3] The dedicatory letter to Leo X represents what might be called a "case study" in the proposal found in *The Freedom of a Christian*, where Luther shows both his deep respect for the pope and his surprising freedom in proclaiming the gospel. While it is clear that these two documents should, therefore, be read in tandem, several accidents of history allowed for their own separate existence.[4]

In September 1520, probably working from a detailed Latin outline, Luther first completed the German version of *The Freedom of a Christian* and its epistle dedicatory to Leo X. Because the letter to Leo X arrived first at the printer, however, Johann Grünenberg (d. c. 1525)—knowing a bestseller when he saw one—printed it separately, forcing Luther to write a second, perfunctory preface for the German version to Hermann Mühlpfort (c. 1486–1534), mayor of Zwickau. Thus, some copies of the German version of *The Freedom of a Christian* circulated with both prefaces.[5] At nearly the same time and working off the same outline (so that many sections of the German and Latin correspond closely but were never quite word-for-word translations of each other), Luther then completed the Latin version, adding an introduction and a lengthy appendix not found in the German. The differences between the two tracts also arose in part out of the slightly different audiences for them: the one addressed to theologians, clerics, and church leaders (for whom Latin was the common language), and one addressed to the German-speaking public, which included the nobility, townsfolk, many from the lesser clergy, and others who could read (or have Luther's writings read to them).

Printing History

The Freedom of a Christian was a bestseller. Including the original Latin and German versions published in Wittenberg, there were between 1520 and 1526 thirty printings: nineteen in German, one in the dialect of the German lowlands, and eight in Latin, along with translations of the Latin into German (!) and English. It now appears that Luther sent a corrected copy to a cathedral canon in Augsburg, who forwarded it to Beatus Rhenanus, a famous humanist and early supporter in Basel (Switzerland), who added his own marginal headings and sent it on to the printer Adam Petri in Basel. The latter corrected typographical errors and probably in March 1521, published this corrected version in time for the Frankfurt book fair, titling it *A Discourse on Christian Freedom Revised by the Author*.[6] Later in the same year, Melchior Lotter reprinted this version, simply noting that it was "revised in Wittenberg."[a] With the few exceptions mentioned in the footnotes, all of the subheadings used in the following translation have been taken from Petri's edition.

The Letter to Leo X

The letter to Leo has all of the characteristics of polished Renaissance Latin prose expected for a writing that addresses the pope. Not only is the Latin itself among Luther's best writings, but the letter's argument also bears the marks of typical Latin style. Thus, Luther prosecutes two separate arguments, according to the painstaking analysis of the German linguist Birgit Stolt.[b] Her analysis is reflected in the headings of this translation. The Renaissance context of this letter, like that to Archbishop Albrecht von Brandenburg of Mainz (1490–1545), helps explain the tone of the

6. *De liberate Christiana dissertatio per autorem recognita* (Basel: A. Petri, 1521). Rhenanus (1485–1547) was an important humanist who worked from 1511 to 1526 in Basel at the famous Froben press and was favorable toward Luther's work. (In January 1520, Martin Bucer sent him a copy of Luther's commentary on Galatians.) Philipp Melanchthon was also a great supporter of the tract. His letter from April 1521 to an unknown recipient in Schaffhausen reflects many of the themes of *The Freedom of a Christian* and even refers his correspondent to it. See *Melanchthons Briefwechsel*, vol. T1: *Texte 1–254 (1514–1522)*, ed. Richard Wetzel (Stuttgart-Bad Cannstatt: Frommann-Holzboog, 1991), 276–78 (no. 137). Wetzel notes that in 1524 this letter was included with a Nuremberg printing of *The Freedom of a Christian*.

---

a   See WA 7:40, "E": *Epistola Lutheriana ad Leonem Decimum summum pontificem. Liber de Christiana libertate, continens summam Christianae doctrinae, quo ad formandam mentem, & ad intelligendam Euangelii vim, nihil absolutius, nihil conducibilius neque a veteribus neque a recentioribus scriptoribus perditum est. Tu Christianae lector, relege iterum atque iterum, & Christum imbibe. Recognitus Wittembergae* (Wittenberg: Melchior Lotter, 1521). English: *A Lutheran Letter to Pope Leo X. A Book on Christian Freedom, Containing the Sum of Christian Teaching, Concerning Which Nothing More Absolute or More in Line with Either Ancient or More Recent Writers Has Been Produced for Forming the Mind and for Understanding the Power of the Gospel. You, Christian Reader, Reread This Again and Again and Drink in Christ. Reedited in Wittenberg.* For the publication, authorships, and dating of these printings, see James Hirstein's article in *Revue d'histoire et de philosophie religieuses* (forthcoming).

b   Birgit Stolt, *Studien zu Luthers Freiheitstraktat mit besonderer Rücksicht auf das Verhältnis der lateinischen und der deutschen Fassung zu einander und die Stilmittel der Rhetorik* (Stockholm: Almzvist & Wiksell, 1969).

piece—what to modern ears might appear stilted and even obsequious at times. *Not* to have addressed the pontiff with such respect would itself have been considered a shocking breech of etiquette and further proof of Luther's contempt for all authority in the church and government. To read this letter as if Luther were hiding his true feelings or even being deceitful imposes modern sensibilities on a very different age and with its very different expectations.

This letter also gives evidence of Luther's paradoxical view of the Christian's life as both free (in the gospel) and bound to the neighbor. To be sure, Luther was bound and determined to put to rest the (unfounded) rumor that he had attacked the pope's person. While he would insist that the papal court was to blame for the sorry state of the church in his day, he had no particular criticism of Leo X himself. Instead, he took direct aim at his bitterest opponent and one of the instigators of the papal bull of excommunication, Johann Eck (1486–1543). Thus, he expressed himself in the letter with remarkable freedom against his opponents—a freedom that arose for him from Christ himself. Luther could even call to mind the behavior of one of his favorite medieval theologians, Bernard of Clairvaux (1090–1153), who had written sternly to Pope Eugene III (1383–1447). This appeal to Leo, however, went unanswered.

The Freedom of a Christian

As the letter to Leo already indicates, Luther was a child of the Renaissance. This meant that his Latin prose especially was carefully shaped according to the rhetorical rules and conventions of his day. In the case of *The Freedom of a Christian*, this means that the reader today can still detect the basic outline of his argument as it followed these conventions.[c] Even the marginal notes added to the second edition often identify these various parts. Based upon classical writings on rhetoric by Cicero (106–43 BCE) and Quintilian (c. 35–c. 100), late medieval rhetorical handbooks divided a speech

---

c Ibid.

or tract into six parts: exordium, division of the tract, the exposition of the theme, confirmation or proof of the theme, an answer to objections to the theme, and a peroration.

Observing closely how Luther develops the argument in *The Freedom of a Christian* can help the reader in understanding the document. Luther begins by talking about the nature of faith, a key subject of debate in his case with Rome. Thereby, he intends to arouse his readers' interest in the subject and to present himself as a reliable witness or authority concerning faith. This constitutes a proper exordium, which Luther uses to encourage readers to see the importance of understanding faith, now defined not as a virtue but as an experience of struggle and mercy.

As the marginal gloss from the 1521 text notes, Luther then states the "themes" (*themata*) of his writing about Christian freedom and servitude. Yet, according to late medieval rules of rhetoric, these "themes" are not, as modern readers might think, outlining the subject of his essay (which was faith), but instead announce the proper division of the overall argument into two nearly equal sections, the first on the freedom of a Christian and the second on a Christian's servitude. It is first in the brief exposition of the themes, the so-called *narratio* following the themes' statement, that the reader discovers Luther's actual subject: *not* to divide freedom and servitude but to explain how, given their relation to faith and their use by the Apostle Paul, they cohere.

The body of the first part, or "theme," of the work consists in the *confirmatio* where Luther attempts to prove his claim that freedom and servitude cohere in the Christian life. Luther insists that the whole human being may be viewed as both inner and outer and that not works but only God's word received in faith constitutes true Christian freedom. From this premise, Luther then introduces three benefits or fruits of faith, concentrating most of his efforts on the third fruit: the marriage of the soul and Christ by faith alone. With this "joyous exchange" (as he calls it in the German version) between human sin and Christ's righteousness, the believing person receives, in addition, Christ's priesthood and kingship. Yet, by priesthood Luther does not mean having an office in the church but, rather, praying and proclaiming Christ's love; and by kingship Luther is not talking about power but the spiritual kingship of peace. Christian freedom then consists precisely in these gifts, fruits, and benefits of faith, so that Christians are lords over sin, death, the devil, and anything else that threatens them.

When Luther arrives at what he calls the second theme, that Christians are servants of all, he introduces it not as a separate theme at all but, rather, again following the rules of rhetoric, as an answer to the chief objections to the first section and its description of law and gospel, faith and its blessings. This standard component of good rhetoric since the time of Cicero, called the *confutatio*, anticipated opponents' arguments aimed at refuting the main point of a speech or writing. Here, the chief objection takes the form of derision. Opponents who were convinced that Luther's teaching on faith would lead to lawlessness and disorder, giving believers license to sin, had made exaggerated claims to that effect. Luther rebukes them ("Not so, you wicked people") and answers their objections using a series of examples from Scripture and experience that show how faith freely produces good works and, hence, serves the neighbor.[7] Throughout this section of the tract, however, Luther also restates his basic point that Christian faith does not depend upon works but only on God's mercy. Running throughout this section is a criticism of Aristotelian ethics, which dominated late medieval thinking, that a person becomes virtuous (or righteous) by doing virtuous acts. Luther argues the opposite, namely that only the one declared righteous by Christ through faith alone can bear fruit of righteousness.

The close of any proper speech or writing was the peroration, which consisted either of a summary conclusion to the argument or an appeal to the reader or listener. Indeed, Luther even signals this transition with the words, "We conclude."[8] In this case, Luther concludes that Christians live in Christ through faith and their neighbors through love. After his final "Amen," however, Luther adds a lengthy appendix that answers another misunderstanding of his argument by

7. See below, p. 510.

8. See below, p. 530.

ceremonialists, namely, that he really is supporting license and an abandonment of all good order among Christians.

His refusal to equate reform with abandoning past practices while still rebuking ceremonialists, coupled with his concern for the weak in faith, led Luther in 1522, upon returning from protective custody in the Wartburg Castle, to put the brakes on the reform movement that had arisen during his absence from Wittenberg—not on the basis of objections to the practices favored by these reform-minded colleagues (including not only Andreas Bodenstein from Karlstadt [1486–1541] but also Philip Melanchthon and Nicholas von Amsdorf [1483–1565], among others) but because such changes in practice would upset the faith of weak Christians who would not understand why they were taking place.[9] This reticence about changing forms of worship—foreign to his Roman opponents and to other leaders of reform (for example, Ulrich Zwingli [1484–1531] in Zurich and early Anabaptists)—stands as a unique mark of Wittenberg's brand of theology and may be traced to Luther's comments in *The Freedom of a Christian*.

9. See Martin Luther, *Invocavit Sermons* (March 1522), in LW 51:67–100.

10. The present translation is a revision of *Martin Luther, Freedom of a Christian: Luther Study Edition*, trans. Mark Tranvik (Minneapolis: Fortress Press, 2008), itself a revision of the version in LW 31:327–77, first translated by W. A. Lambert and revised by Harold J. Grimm. The present revision is based primarily upon WA 7:39–73, but also using the more recent version with extensive notes, ed. Hans-Ulrich Delius, in MLStA 2:260–309. The headings, except where noted, are translated from the Basel edition of 1521, printed by Adam Petri (1454–1527).

11.   **EXORDIUM**

12. Referring to the pope's ecclesiastical jurisdiction in Rome.

13. Luther addresses here an important part of his case with Rome. In 1518, after Pope Leo X had reaffirmed his predecessors' statements about indulgences, Luther made a formal appeal to a general council. Especially to those theologians who championed papal authority over that of a church council, this was prima facie evidence of Luther's heresy, as decrees of Pius III (1439–1503) and Julius II (1443–1513) stated. By laying the blame on the pope's advisers and Leo's generally despised predecessors, Luther sought to defend his action. (This appeal remained an important part of the Evangelical struggle with Rome throughout Luther's lifetime and is reflected in the prefaces to the *Augsburg Confession* and Luther's own *Smalcald Articles*.)

LUTHER'S EPISTLE TO LEO X, SUPREME PONTIFF [10,d]

JESUS.[e]

MARTIN LUTHER sends greetings to Leo X, Roman Pontiff, in Christ Jesus our Lord. Amen.

[11,f]Surrounded by the monsters of this age, with which I have struggled and battled for three years, I am compelled at times to look to you and to think of you, Leo, most blessed father. Indeed, since you are widely held to be the sole cause of my battles, I cannot but think of you. And although the godless flatterers around you, who rage against me without cause, forced me to appeal from your see[12] to a future Council (given that I have no respect for the completely vain decrees of your predecessors, Pius and Julius, who with foolish tyranny prohibited such appeals),[13] nevertheless, throughout this time I have never turned my soul away from Your Holiness so as neither to desire with all my powers the very best for you and for your see nor, as far as was in me, to

---

d   Using marginal notes found in WA 7:40, "D": *Epistola Lutheriana ad Leonem Decimum summum pontificem. Dissertatio de libertate Christiana per autorem recognita Wittembergae* (Basel: Adam Petri, 1521). See the Introduction above.

e   See above, p. 264, n. 11.

f   Throughout this letter, marginal notes on the letter's structure follow the structural analysis made by Stolt.

seek the same with earnest and heartfelt prayers to God.[14] I nearly started to despise and declare victory over those who up to now have tried to frighten me with the majesty of your authority and name, except I see that there remains one thing which I cannot despise and which has been the reason for my writing to Your Holiness for a second time.[g] That is, I realize that I am accused of impertinence, now twisted into my greatest vice,[15] because I am judged to have attacked your person.[16]

[Part One: Luther's Defense]

[17]However, so that I may confess this matter openly,[18] whenever your person has been mentioned, I am aware of having only said the greatest and best things. But if I had done otherwise, I could under no circumstances condone it; I would vote in favor of their judgment against me every time, and I would recant nothing more freely than this my impertinence and godlessness. I have called you a Daniel in Babylon, and every one of my readers knows fully well how, with extraordinary zeal, I have defended your remarkable innocence against your defiler, Sylvester [Prierias].[19] Your reputation and the fame of your blameless life, chanted in the writings of so many men the world over, are too well known and dignified to be possibly assailed in any way by anyone, no matter how great. Nor am I so foolish to attack someone whom absolutely everyone praises. As a matter of fact, I have even tried and will always try not to attack even those whom public opinion dishonors. For I take pleasure in no one's faults, since I myself am conscious enough of the log in my own eye.[h] Nor do I want to be the first who throws a stone at the adulteress.[i]

14. The heightened rhetoric here and throughout this letter, addressed to a Renaissance pope, indicates the care with which Luther wrote it. None of the headings in this letter come from the original.

15. Luther's opponents often construed his highly charged language as impudence and exaggeration. Erasmus of Rotterdam (1466–1536) nicknamed him *doctor hyperbolicus*, "the exaggerating teacher."

16. Personal attacks of governmental or ecclesiastical rulers were viewed as especially inappropriate.

17. **Answering Three Questions in His Defense**
1. Whether He Committed the Offense

18. Luther answers the charges according to the three questions of the judicial genre of speech: whether he committed the offense; what he actually did; whether he acted rightly.

19. Luther stated this in his 1518 tract, *Response to the Dialogue of Sylvester Prierias concerning the Power of the Pope* (WA 1:679, 5–7). Sylvester (Mazzolini) Prierias (1456–1523) was named after the city of his birth (Prierio). A Dominican (as was Johann Tetzel [1460–1519]), he strongly defended papal authority and infallibility in matters of teaching and practice. Luther viewed this as an insult to the pope because it exalted him over Christ and the Scriptures.

---

g   The first time was the preface to the *Explanations of the Ninety-Five Theses* of 1518. See WA 1:527–29.

h   Matt. 7:3.

i   John 8:1-11.

20.   *2. What Luther Actually Did and*
Whether This Was Proper

20 Now, generally I have sharply attacked ungodly teachings, and I have been quick to snap at my opponents not because of their bad morals but because of their godlessness. I do not repent of this in the least, as I have resolved in my soul, despite the contempt of others, to persist in this fervent zeal, following the example of Christ, who in his zeal called his adversaries "a brood of vipers," "blind," "hypocrites," and "children of the devil."*ʲ* And Paul branded the Magician [Elymas] a "son of the devil . . . full of deceit and villainy."*ᵏ* Others he ridiculed as "dogs," "deceivers," and "adulterators."*ˡ* If you consider any sensitive audience, no one will seem more biting and unrestrained than Paul. What is more biting than the prophets? The mad multitude of flatterers imitates the ever so sensitive ears of our rational age, so that, as soon as we sense disapproval of our ideas, we cry that we are bitten. As long as we can rebuff the truth by labeling it something else, we flee from it under the pretext of its being snappish, impatient, and unrestrained. What good is salt if it has lost its bite?*ᵐ* What use is the edge of a sword if it does not cut? "Accursed is the one who does the Lord's work deceitfully."*ⁿ*

21.   *3. Summary Conclusion*

21 For this reason, most excellent Leo, I beg you to admit that this letter vindicates me. And I beg you to convince yourself that I have never thought ill of your person and, moreover, that I am the kind of person who eternally wishes the very best things happen to you and that for me this strife is not with any person over morals but over the Word of truth alone. In everything else I will yield to anyone. I cannot and

j   See Matt. 23:33, 13, 17; and John 8:44, respectively.

k   Acts 13:10.

l   Phil. 3:2; 2 Cor. 11:13; 2:17 (following the Latin; NRSV: "peddlers").

m   Classical Latin authors often compared salt (especial "black salt") with sharpness (e.g., Pliny [the Elder] (23–79), *Historia naturalis*, 10, 72, 93, par. 198) and sarcasm (e.g., Catullus [c. 84-54 BCE], 13, 5). See also Matt. 5:13.

n   Jer. 48:10 (Vulgate).

will not yield or deny the Word. If a person has thought something else about me or otherwise interpreted my positions, then that one is not thinking straight nor interpreting my true positions.

[22] However, I have rightly cursed your see, called the Roman Curia,[23] which neither you nor any human being can deny is more corrupt than Babylon or Sodom[24] and, as far as I can tell, is composed of depraved, desperate, and notorious godlessness. And I have made known that, under your name and under the cover of the Roman Church, the people of Christ are being undeservedly deceived. Indeed, I have thus resisted and will continue to resist [the Curia], as long as the Spirit of faith lives in me—not that I would strive for the impossible or that I would hope that, given the furious opposition of so many flatterers, my works alone would improve anything in that chaotic Babylon, but I do acknowledge the debt owed to my fellow Christians,° whom I must warn so that fewer may perish or at least have milder symptoms from that Roman plague. Indeed, as you yourself know, for many years nothing else has been flooding the world from Rome than the devastation of possessions, bodies, and souls, and the worst examples of the worst possible things. All this is clearer than day to everyone. Moreover, out of the Roman Church, once the holiest of all, has been fashioned a completely licentious den of thieves, the most shameless of all brothels, the kingdom of sin, death, and hell, so that were the Antichrist to come, he could hardly think of anything that would add to its wickedness.[25]

22.   **Proof That Luther**
            Acted Properly
      1. The Corruption in the Roman Curia

23. The papal court (Latin: *curia*), consisting of cardinals, bishops, and other clerical functionaries.

24. Rev. 18:2-24 and 11:8, respectively names for the powers opposed to Christ and Christians during the end times.

25. Faced with what he perceived as the Roman Curia's intransigence, Luther moved from granting the papacy human authority over the churches to condemning it (but not individual bishops of Rome) as in league with or identified with the Antichrist. By the late Middle Ages, many Christian thinkers assumed that at the world's end an Antichrist would arise to do battle with God's elect.

o   Literally, "brothers."

26. *2. Luther's Compassion for the Pope*

27. An attempt to poison Leo X had indeed been made in 1517.

28. Luther was quoting Baptista Mantuanus (1447–1516), *Varia ad Falconem Sinibaldum epigrammata,* a collection of epigrams against corruption in Rome. Luther also quoted this text in *On the Bondage of the Will* (LW 33:53) and used Mantuanus's work in his 1545 tract *Against the Roman Papacy: An Institution of the Devil* (LW 41:257–376). Gout was considered an incurable disease.

29. *3. What the Pope Should Do*

30. He was a member of the powerful de Medicis. From this point on, Luther uses the word *gloria* (glory or fame or boasting) to describe the situation in Rome and with his enemies.

[26] In the meantime, you, Leo, sit as a lamb in the midst of wolves, as Daniel in the midst of lions, and you dwell with Ezekiel among the scorpions.[p] How can you alone oppose these monsters? Add three or four of your best and most learned cardinals! "What are they among so many?"[q] Before you had even begun setting up the remedy, you would have all been poisoned to death.[27] It is all over for the Roman Curia. The wrath of God has fallen upon it completely. It hates councils; it fears being reformed; it cannot allay its raging godlessness; and it fulfills the eulogy written for its "mother," about whom is said, "We tried to heal Babylon, but she has not been healed. Let us forsake her."[r] To be sure, it was part of your office and that of your cardinals to heal these ills, but "this gout derided the physician's hands,"[28] and neither horse "nor chariot responds to the reins."[s] Touched by deep affection, I have always been grieved, most excellent Leo, that you, who were worthy of far better times, became pope in this day and age. For the Roman Curia is not worthy of you or people like you but only Satan himself, who now actually rules in that Babylon more than you do.

[29] O that, having cast aside the glory that your completely accursed enemies heap upon you, you would instead live on the small income of a parish priest or on your family's inheritance.[30] Only the Iscariots, sons of perdition,[t] are worthy of glorying in this kind of glory. For what are you accomplishing in the Curia, my Leo, except that the more wicked and accursed a person is, the more happily such a one uses your name and authority to destroy the wealth and souls of human beings, to increase wickedness, and to suppress faith and truth throughout the church of God? O truly most unhappy Leo, sitting on that most dangerous throne—I am telling you the truth, because I wish you well! For if Bernard

---

p   Matt. 10:16; Dan. 6:16; and Ezek. 2:6, respectively.

q   See John 6:9.

r   Jer. 51:9 (Vulgate).

s   Virgil (70–19 BCE), *Georgics*, 1, 514.

t   The family of Judas Iscariot, as he was labeled in John 17:12.

had compassion on Pope Eugenius,[31] when the Holy See—although already then very corrupt—still governed with more hope [for improvement], why should we not complain about the three hundred years of corruption and ruin that has been added since then? Is it not true that under the great expanse of heaven nothing is more corrupt, pestilential, and despicable than the Roman Curia? For it even surpasses by any measure the godlessness of the Turks, so that, truth be told, what was once the gate of heaven is now the very gaping mouth of hell—such a mouth that because of the wrath of God cannot be blocked. This leaves only one option in these

31. Bernard of Clairvaux, a Cistercian monk, wrote *On Consideration* (MPL 182:727–808), addressing it to Pope Eugene III (d. 1153) and warning about the dangers connected to the papal office.

A seventeenth-century depiction of Bernard of Clairvaux (1090–1153), Cistercian monk and theologian.

miseries: perhaps we can call back and rescue a few from this Roman abyss (as I said)."

32. *4. Recapitulation of Part One*

[32] Observe, my father Leo, my reason and design for raving against that pestilential see. For I completely avoided raging against your person because I even hoped that I would gain your favor and cause your rescue—if I could have quickly and decisively broken open that prison of yours or, rather, your hell. For it would have been useful for your sake and your rescue, along with that of many others, had an attack by all talented, able people been able to mitigate some of the confusion in that godless Curia. Those who harm the Curia serve your office; those who by any and all means curse it glorify Christ. In short, Christians are those who are not "Romans."

[Part Two: A Narrative of Luther's Case]

33. *1. The Real Cause of the Dispute*

34. Luther considered his unguarded remarks at the Leipzig Debate were the real cause of the problem and demanded explanation for a successful defense of his case before Leo. He returns to the debate in the next section when describing events chronologically.

[33] But, to enlarge upon this, attacking the Roman Curia or raising questions about it had never crossed my mind at all.[34] For seeing that all remedies for saving it had failed, I had only contempt for it, served it divorce papers,[v] and said to it, "Let the evildoer still do evil, and the filthy still be filthy."[w] I devoted my time to the peaceful and quiet studies of Holy Scripture, by which I wanted to assist my brothers around me. When I made some progress in this, Satan opened his

u See above, p. 475.
v See Jer. 3:8.
w Rev. 22:11.

eyes and goaded his servant Johann Eck,[35] a noted enemy of Christ, with an uncontrollable desire for glory. This resulted in Eck dragging me into an unexpected arena for combat and trapping me on one little word that in passing I let slip concerning the primacy of the Roman Church.[36] This glorious "Thraso,"[37] foaming at the mouth and gnashing his teeth, boasted that he would risk everything "for the glory of God" and "for the honor of the Holy Apostolic See." Puffed up with the prospect of abusing your power for himself, he expected nothing but certain victory, seeking not so much the primacy of Peter as his own preeminence among the theologians of this age. To achieve that goal, he imagined no small advantage in triumphing over Luther. When [the debate] ended unhappily for the Sophist,[38] an incredible madness seized the man, for he sensed that whatever of the Roman shame had come to light through me was his fault alone.[39]

35. Johann Eck, professor of theology at the University of Ingolstadt, opposed Luther already in 1518 and challenged Luther's colleague Andreas Bodenstein from Karlstadt to a debate in Leipzig, to which Luther then was added as an opponent. It took place in June 1519. See LW 31:307–25 for some of the 1519 documents from the proceedings.

36. Luther admitted in a publication leading up to the debate that the papacy of the last four hundred years was in error (proposition 13 in LW 31:318). At the debate, he admitted that councils could also err. Luther's intentions seemed more focused than he was admitting to Leo.

37. A vain character in the Roman author Terence's (d. 159 BCE) comedy *The Eunuch*, known for rhetorical bombast.

38. In the Renaissance, the label "sophist" implied someone who could nitpick about logic while missing the point of an argument. The universities established to judge the debate found in Eck's favor, but Luther won in the court of public opinion through the early publication of several accounts favorable to him.

39. After the Leipzig Debates, Eck made several trips to Rome to secure Luther's condemnation as a heretic. He also constantly wrote against Luther and his Wittenberg colleagues throughout his life.

40.   *2. The Progression of the Case*

41. Luther had to prove that he had done everything in his power to avoid this conflict.

42. Cardinal Cajetan (Tommaso de Vio), was also known by the name of St. Sisto's in Rome, where he was cardinal presbyter. As part of the Dominican order, he was a famous Renaissance interpreter of Thomas Aquinas (1225–1274). He was papal legate (ambassador) to the 1518 imperial Diet of Augsburg.

43. See Luther's *Proceedings at Augsburg*, above, pp 121–65. Although Luther describes Cajetan's behavior as overstepping his mandate as legate, Cajetan only may have violated the specific agreement with the Elector of Saxony, Luther's prince.

44. Karl von Miltitz was the papal ambassador north of the Alps in 1518 and 1519 with instructions to resolve the dispute with Luther.

45. Luther's own prince and the patron of the University of Wittenberg.

46. At the 1521 Diet of Worms, in addition to his public appearance before the diet, Luther met at several points with the archbishop of Trier, Richard von Greiffenklau zu Vollrads (1467–1531).

[40] Therefore, most excellent Leo, allow me this once to make my case[41] here and to accuse your true enemies. I believe you are aware what your legate, Cardinal St. Sisto,[42] an unwise and unfortunate—indeed, untrustworthy—person, had wanted [to do] with me. When out of reverence for your name I placed myself and the entire affair into his hands, he did not attempt to establish peace—which he could easily have done with one simple word, since at the time I had promised to be silent and make an end to my case if he commanded my adversaries to do likewise. Instead, as a man seeking glory, he was not content with this agreement and instead began to defend my adversaries, to allow them freedom [of speech] and to command me to recant, even though this was not part of his mandate at all.[43] So, just when the case was in a very favorable place [for resolution], he came with his ill-natured tyranny and made it much worse. Thus, the blame for whatever followed this was not Luther's but totally Cajetan's, who did not permit me to remain silent and quiet as I at the time had requested with all my might. What more could I have possibly done?

Next followed Karl Miltitz, also a nuncio of Your Holiness.[44] He traveled back and forth in various negotiations, omitting nothing in regards to restoring the case's status quo, which Cajetan had rashly and arrogantly upset. Finally, with great difficulty but assisted by the Most Illustrious Prince, Elector Frederick,[45] he managed to speak with me several times privately, where once again I yielded to your authority and was prepared to keep silent, even accepting as a judge [in the case] either the Archbishop of Trier or the Bishop of Naumburg.[46] And thus it was settled and so ordered. While these good things were occurring and held the prospect [for success], behold, your other great enemy Eck[x] madly rushed in with the Leipzig disputation, which he set up with Dr. Karlstadt. And when a new question arose concerning the primacy of the pope, he turned

---

x   Luther is making a play on words: "Ecce . . . Eck" (Behold . . . Eck).

his concealed weapons on me and thoroughly destroyed the plans for peace. In the meantime, Karl Miltitz waited. The disputation was held, judges were chosen, and yet no decision was reached. Small wonder, given Eck's lies, deceptions, and trickery, that everything everywhere was so completely stirred up, aggravated, and confused that, whatever the outcome of the decision, a greater conflagration would have flared up. For he sought glory not truth. Here, too, I left nothing undone that I should have carried out.

I concede that on this occasion much of Roman corruption came to light. But in this matter, whatever wrong was committed was Eck's fault. He took on a task beyond his abilities. While striving furiously for his own glory, he revealed the shame of Rome to the whole world. This one is your enemy, my Leo, or rather, the enemy of your Curia. We can learn from his example that no enemy is more pernicious than a flatterer.[y] For what did his flattery accomplish other than a kind of evil that not a single king would have been able to accomplish? For today the name "Roman Curia" reeks the world over, and papal authority languishes. Its notorious ignorance is now despised.[z] We would have heard nothing of this had Eck not upset the peace agreement between Karl and me. He himself senses this plainly and, too late and to no avail, is offended by the subsequent publication of my books. He should have thought of this earlier, when, just like a bleating goat, he madly raved about his own glory and sought nothing but his own advantage with you—at your great peril. That completely vain man hoped that I would stop and be silent out of fear for your name, since I do not believe that he supposed his own intelligence and learning would be enough. Now, because he realizes that I have confidence and continue to speak out, he understands albeit with overdue sorrow for his rash behavior—if he understands at

The coat of arms of
Thomas Cardinal Cajetan,
also called Tommaso de Vio.

y See Cicero, *De Amicitia*, 91 (25).

z See, e.g., the reference to "Roman ignorance" in Maurus Servius Honoratus (4th–5th century), *Commentary on the Aeneid of Virgil*, 8, 597.

all—that there is One in heaven who "resists the proud" and humbles the presumptuous.[a]

Therefore, after we had accomplished nothing by this disputation [in Leipzig] except greater confusion about the case in Rome, Karl von Miltitz came a third time, this time to the [Augustinian] fathers gathered for the chapter meeting of their order.[47] He asked their advice about how to resolve the case, which was now greatly disturbing and dangerous. Since there was no hope of proceeding against me by force (thanks to God's mercy!), some of their leaders were sent here to me. They requested that at least I show honor to the person of your Blessedness and in a humble letter plead that you and I are innocent. [They thought] that this matter was not yet completely hopeless as long as Leo X out of his innate goodness took a hand in it. Now, I have always offered and desired to keep the peace so that I might devote myself to quieter and more useful studies, since I have raged in this matter with such spirit in order that, by using great and forceful words and animus, I could restrain those whom I viewed as being no match for me at all. In this situation then, I not only freely yielded [to the delegation] but also accepted [the proposal] with joy and gratitude as a most welcomed kindness, provided that our hope could be realized.

[48] So, most Holy Father, I come and, even now, prostrate myself before you, begging, if possible, that you lay your hands on those flatterers and enemies of peace (who only pretend to want peace) and rein them in. In turn, let no one presume, Most Holy Father, that I will recant, unless such a person wants to envelop this case in even greater turmoil. Furthermore, I will permit no binding laws for interpreting the Word of God, since "the Word of God must not be bound" because it teaches freedom in all other matters.[b] Save for these two things, there is nothing that I could not or would not freely do or endure. I hate contentions. I will

---

47. This meeting of the heads of the German friaries of the Augustinian order met under the retiring vicar general, Johann von Staupitz (c. 1460–1524), in Eisleben on 28 August 1520, where von Miltitz also appeared. They sent a delegation to Wittenberg in early September. It consisted of von Staupitz, the new vicar general Wenceslaus Linck (1482–1547), and others.

48.   *3. A Closing Plea for Mercy*

---

a   See, e.g., 1 Pet. 5:5 and James 4:6.

b   2 Tim. 2:9, an indirect reference to the tract, *The Freedom of a Christian*, to which this letter became attached.

not provoke anyone at all. But, at the same time, I do not want to be provoked. But if I am provoked (with Christ as my teacher), I will not be at a loss for words. For, once this controversy has been brought before you and settled, Your Holiness could, with a short and simple word, command both parties to be silent and keep the peace, which is what I have always wanted to hear.

[Peroration: Advice for Pope Leo]

Consequently, My Father Leo, avoid listening to those sirens who turn you from being purely a human being into a demigod in order that you can command and decide whatever you wish. Do not let this happen; nor will you prevail in this way! You are a servant of servants and, more than all other human beings, in a most miserable and dangerous position. Do not let those deceive you who imagine that you are the lord of the world, who allow no one to be Christian outside of your authority and who babble on that you have power over heaven, hell, and purgatory.[49] They are your enemies and seek to destroy your soul, as Isaiah says, "O my people, those who call you blessed deceive you."[c] Those who place you above a council and the universal church err. Those who attribute to you alone the right to interpret Scripture err. For they seek to establish all manner of ungodliness in the Church under your name, and, alas, through them Satan has made great inroads among your predecessors.[d] In sum, believe none of those who exalt you but only those who humble you. For this is the judgment of God, who "has brought down the powerful from their thrones and lifted up the lowly."[e] Look at how different Christ is from his successors, although they still all want to be his vicars.[50] And I fear that most of them have been too literally his "vicars." For a person is a vicar only in the absence of a superior. But if the

49. Part of the original claims in the *95 Theses*. See above, pp. 35–37.

50. This technical term designates the pope as a substitute (vicarious) ruler of the church in Christ's visible absence.

c   Isa. 3:12 (Vulgate).
d   See Luther's *Address to the Christian Nobility* (1520), above, pp. 387–89.
e   Luke 1:52.

pope rules when Christ is absent and not present and dwelling in his heart, what is that but to be a Vicar of Christ? And then, what is the church other than a whole group of people without Christ? Truly, what is such a vicar except an Antichrist and idol? How much more correctly did the apostles call themselves servants of a present Christ than vicars of an absent Christ!

Perhaps I am presumptuous in attempting to teach such an exalted person, from whom all ought to be taught and (as your "plagues" boast)[51] from whom "the thrones of those who judge"[52] receive the [final] decree. But I emulate Saint Bernard in his book *On Consideration*, addressed to Pope Eugenius, which every pope should commit to memory.[f] I do this not from a desire to instruct you but from a sense of duty arising from pure and faithful solicitude that compels us to respect only the complete safety of our neighbors and that does not allow any consideration of their worthiness or unworthiness—being focused only on their dangers and particular situations. For since I know that Your Holiness is twisted and tossed about in Rome—that is, driven by unending dangers and surrounded by the highest seas—and that you are laboring on these things in miserable conditions such that you stand in need of even the smallest help from the least of the brothers, it did not seem foolish to me if for the moment I would forget your high majesty while fulfilling the duty of love. I do not want to flatter you in such a serious and dangerous situation. As far as that goes, if I am not understood to be your friend and most obedient servant, there is One who understands and judges.

[Introduction to the Tract][53]

In conclusion, so that I might not approach you, Holy Father, empty-handed, I offer this little tract, published under your name, in the prospect of an established peace and good hope. In it you can get a taste of the kinds of studies with

51. Luther's description of the pope's flatterers. See above, p. 477.

52. That is, the bishops.

53. Renaissance dedications typically ended with a brief description of the book to which they were attached.

---

f　See above, p. 479.

which I could and would occupy myself far more fruitfully, if only your godless flatterers permitted it now and before. It is a small thing with respect to its size, but (unless I am mistaken) it contains a summary of the whole Christian life, if you understand its meaning. Poor man that I am, I have nothing else to present to you. But then you do not need to be enriched by any other gift save a spiritual one. Therefore, I commend myself to your fatherly goodness. May the Lord Jesus preserve you forever! Amen.

Wittenberg, September 6, 1520.

ON CHRISTIAN FREEDOM

Introduction[g]

Many people view Christian faith as something easy, and quite a few people even count it as if it were related to the virtues.[54] They do this because they have not judged faith in light of any experience, nor have they ever tasted its great power.[h]

[Faith Is Learned through Tribulations][i]

This is because a person who has not tasted its spirit in the midst of trials and misfortune cannot possibly write well about faith or understand what has been written about it. But one who has had even a small taste of faith can never write, speak, reflect, or hear enough about it. As Christ says in John 4[:14], it is a "spring of water welling up to eternal life."

g   This subhead is not in sixteenth-century editions of the tract.
h   The same Latin word is translated here "virtues" or "power."
i   With few exceptions recorded in footnotes, all subtitles come from the second edition of the tract, printed in Basel by Adam Petri in 1521. See the introductory material, p. 468f, above.

54. In medieval moral theology, faith, hope, and love were the chief theological virtues (based on 1 Cor. 13:13). Over against this prevailing view, Luther understood faith relationally (experientially) as confidence or trust, arising in the midst of trials. He distinguished it from mere intellectual assent to doctrinal truths and thus opposed medieval theology, which derived its definition of faith from the basic Aristotelian distinction between "matter" and "form," interpreting the Latin version of Gal. 5:6 as "faith *formed* by love," meaning that faith by itself was insufficient (only the "material principle" of a saving disposition toward God), completed only by the "formal principle" of love for God.

55. For Luther, trials (*tentationes*; often denoted by the German word *Anfechtungen*, attacks or struggles) marked the Christian life of faith from beginning to end. Thus, Luther is not simply referring here to earlier struggles as an Augustinian friar concerned with God's righteousness and penitence but to his entire life as a believer. For an even earlier reflection on this notion, see his *Explanations of the Ninety-Five Theses*, thesis 15 (LW 31:125–30, esp. 129).

56. Luther probably had in mind both "fancy" humanist writers, such as Erasmus (in his *Handbook of the Christian Soldier*), and Scholastic theologians known for disputations, such as Gabriel Biel.

57. These two statements provide the basic themes of the entire tract, explicated below beginning on pp. 489 and 510, respectively.

Although I cannot boast of my own abundance of faith and I also know quite well how short my own supply is, nevertheless—given that I have been troubled by great and various trials[55]—I hope I can attain to at least a drop of faith. And I hope that I can talk about faith in a way that, if not more elegant, is certainly clearer than has been done in the past by the fancy writers and the subtle disputants alike, who have not even understood their own writings.[56]

The Main Themes[j]

In order to point out an easier way for common folk[k] (for I serve only them), I am proposing two themes[57] concerning the freedom and servitude of the spirit.

The Christian individual[l] is a completely free lord of all, subject to none.

The Christian individual is a completely dutiful servant[m] of all, subject to all.

Although these topics appear to contradict one another, nevertheless, if they can be found to be in agreement, they will serve our purposes beautifully. For both are from the Apostle Paul, when he says in 1 Cor. 9[:19], "For though I am free with respect to all, I have made myself a slave to all" and in Rom. 13[:8], "Owe nothing to anyone except to love one another." But "love" by its very nature is dutiful and serves the one who is loved. The same was true of Christ who,

---

j The word "themes" (*themata*) is a Greek loan word and a technical term in rhetoric and dialectics for the main topic or central proposition of a speech or an argument.

k Latin: *rudes*. This term can mean unlettered or uncultivated but here means the simple or common people, unfamiliar with the complexities of Scholastic theology. It is at this point that the German version begins. For further references to Luther's orientation toward the commoner, see his *Treatise on Good Works*, above, pp. 265f.

l Latin here and in the next line: *Christianus homo*.

m *Servus* can be translated either servant or slave but here is rendered servant to correspond with Luther's German version (*Knecht*). In the Pauline letters, the NRSV translates the Greek *doulos* as "slave").

although Lord of all, was nevertheless "born of a woman, born under the law"[n] and who was at the same time free and slave, that is, at the same time "in the form of God" and "in the form of a slave."[58, o]

Let us approach these two themes from a rather distant and unsophisticated starting point.[p] Every human being consists of two natures: a spiritual and a bodily one. According to the spiritual nature, which people label the soul, the human being is called a spiritual, inner, and new creature. According to the bodily nature, which people label the flesh, a human being is called the fleshly, outer, and old creature.[59] Paul writes about this in 2 Cor. 4[:16], "Even though our outer nature is wasting away, our inner nature is being renewed day by day." This distinction results in the fact that in the Scripture these contrary things are said about the same person, because these two "human beings" fight against each other in the very same human being, as in Gal. 5[:17], "For what the flesh desires is opposed to the spirit, and what the spirit desires is opposed to the flesh."[q]

[The Spiritual, New, and Inner Person] [60, r]

In looking at the inner person first, we grasp how someone may become righteous,[s] free, and truly Christian, that is, "a spiritual, new, and inner person."[t]

58. The basic themes of this tract first arose in Luther's *Two Kinds of Righteousness* from 1519 (LW 31:297–306, esp. 297), itself perhaps derived from a sermon on the appointed epistle lesson for Palm Sunday, Phil. 2:6-11.

59. By defining the whole human being according to these two aspects or natures, Luther is not simply taking over Platonic or other philosophical divisions between material and spiritual worlds. He often equated *soul* with the biblical term *heart*.

60. This begins the first main section of the tract on the first of the two themes introduced above. The second begins on p. 510.

---

n   An allusion to Gal. 4:4.

o   An allusion to Phil. 2:6-7.

p   *Altior* could mean distant, deeper, or ancient. Coupled with *crassior*, it seems to indicate either an old, crude example or one that seems far removed from the two stated themes.

q   In the Greek and Latin texts of Galatians, the word "spirit" can also refer to the Holy Spirit.

r   This subtitle was not in any sixteenth-century text.

s   Except where noted, the Latin words *iustus* and *iustitia* will be translated "righteous" and "righteousness," not "justice," which in current English usage denotes conformity to a legal principle.

t   An allusion to the wording in the preceding paragraph.

61. Luther often used the term *conscience* not simply as an ethical category but to denote the entire human being standing before the righteous God, as here.

62. This argument implies criticism of late medieval popular piety, which assumed that pilgrimages to see relics, fasting, and sacred acts performed by priests did affect the soul's standing before God. Luther's readers might also have been familiar with even harsher criticism of the late medieval priesthood by humanists and other pamphleteers. See the "appendix" below, pp. 531–38.

63. For Luther, the phrase "word of God" rarely meant simply the Bible but more generally God's oral, direct proclamation. Thus, here he modifies the phrase with the words (capitalized in the original) "Gospel of Christ." The German version, also written by Luther, has: ". . . except the holy Gospel, the word of God preached by Christ." Luther understood God's word not simply as informative but as powerful and creative, present

What Christian Freedom Does Not Consist In

It is evident that no external thing at all, whatever its name, has any part in producing Christian righteousness or freedom. Nor does it produce unrighteousness or servitude. This can be proven by a simple argument. How can it benefit the soul if the body is in good health—free and active, eating and drinking and doing what it pleases—when even the most ungodly slaves to complete wickedness may overflow in such things? On the other hand, how could poor health or captivity or hunger or thirst or any other external misfortune harm the soul, when even the godliest, purest, and freest consciences[61] are afflicted with such things? Not one of these things touches upon the freedom or servitude of the soul. Thus, it does not help the soul if the body wears the sacred robes set apart for priests or enters sacred places or performs sacred duties or prays, fasts, abstains from certain foods, or does absolutely any work connected with the body.[62] Righteousness and freedom of the soul will require something completely different, since the things just mentioned could easily be done by some ungodly person and since such efforts result only in producing hypocrites. On the other side, the soul is not harmed if the body wears street clothes, goes around in secular places, eats and drinks like everyone else, does not pray aloud, and fails to do all the things mentioned above that hypocrites could do.

The Word of God Is Necessary for the Soul

Moreover, so that we may exclude everything—even contemplation, meditation, and whatever else can be done by the soul's efforts—all of this has no benefit. One thing and one thing alone is necessary for the Christian life, righteousness, and freedom, and that is the most holy word of God, the Gospel of Christ.[63] As John 11[:25] states: "I am the Resurrection and the Life, whoever believes in me will never die." And John 8[:36]: "If the Son makes you free, you will be free indeed." And Matt. 4[:4]: "One does not live by bread alone but by every word that comes from the mouth of God." Therefore, we may consider it certain and firmly established, that the soul can lack everything except the word of God. Without it absolutely nothing else satisfies the soul. But when soul has the word, it is rich and needs nothing else, because the word of God is the word of life, truth, light, peace, righteousness, salvation, joy, freedom, wisdom, power, grace, glory, and every imaginable blessing.[64]

David in Psalm 119 [65]

This is why the prophet throughout Psalm 119 and in so many other places [in the Psalter] yearns and sighs with groans and cries for the word of God.

God's Cruelest Disaster

Again, there is no crueler disaster arising from God's wrath than when it sends "a famine of the hearing of his word," as stated in Amos 8[:11],[u] just as there is no greater grace than whenever God sends forth his word, as in Ps. 107[:20]. "He sent out his word and healed them and delivered them from their destruction." And Christ was not sent into the world for any other office than the word. Moreover, the apostles, bishops and the entire order of clerics[v] have been called and established only for the ministry of the word.

What the Word of God Is

You may ask, "What is this word and how should it be used, when there are so many words of God?" I respond as follows. Paul explains what this word is in Rom. 1[:1, 3]: "The gospel of God . . . concerning his Son," who was made flesh, suffered, rose, and was glorified through the Spirit, the Sanctifier.[w] Thus, to preach Christ means to feed, justify, free, and save the soul—provided a person believes the preaching. For faith

in creation (Genesis 1) and in the church's proclamation of the good news of Christ (whom John 1 calls the Word of God). Luther's insistence on the Word "alone" (*solum*) is the basis for later comments about faith alone.

64. Luther uses one of his favorite rhetorical devices, congeries (a heaping up of words), to emphasize the wide-ranging work of God's word.

65. Luther and most of his contemporaries assumed that King David, whom they often called a prophet because of the association of many psalms with Christ, wrote many if not all of the psalms. Luther wrote similar things about Psalm 119 in his 1539 preface to his German works (LW 34:279-88).

---

u   Luther's citation of Amos is a paraphrase.
v   Latin: *ordo clericorum*, that is, priests. Luther returns to this point later in the tract (p. 508f.).
w   Paraphrasing Rom. 1:3-4. "Sanctificator" here means the One who makes holy.

alone is the saving and efficacious use of the word of God. Rom. 10[:9] states: "If you confess with your heart that Jesus is Lord and believe in your heart that God raised him from the dead, you will be saved," and again [in v. 4]: "For Christ is the end of the law, so that there may be righteousness for everyone who believes." And Rom. 1[:17] states: "The one who is righteous will live by faith."

Faith Alone Justifies

For the word of God cannot be received or honored by any works but by faith alone.[66] Therefore, it is clear that the soul needs the word alone for life and righteousness, because if the soul could be justified by anything else, it would not need the word and, consequently, would not need faith. Indeed, this faith absolutely cannot exist in connection with works, that is to say, in connection with any presumption of yours to be justified at the same time by any works whatsoever. For this would be "to limp in two different opinions" to worship Baal[x] and to "kiss [my] hand," which, as Job says, "is a great iniquity."[y]

What Must Be Believed

Therefore, when you begin to believe,[67] you discover at the same time that everything in you is completely blameworthy, damnable sins, as Rom. 3[:23] states: "All have sinned and fall short of the glory of God." And Rom. 3[:10-12] says, "There is no one who is righteous," no one does good, "all have turned aside, altogether they have done worthless things."[z] By this knowledge you will realize that you need Christ, who suffered and rose again for you, in order that, believing in him, you may become another human being by this faith, because all your sins are forgiven and you are justified by another's merits, namely, by Christ's alone.

66. First in the spring of 1518 (e.g., in his *Sermon on Penance* [*Sermo de poenitentia*; WA 1:324, 15]), Luther used the Latin phrase "faith alone justifies" (*sola fide iustificet*) in print. By stressing faith *alone*, he rejected the common medieval stance, based upon the Aristotelian notion that because everything consisted of matter and form, faith and love together justified. (See above, p. 487, n. 54.) For Luther, faith itself was not a human work. Thus, he was also attacking the notion, championed by Gabriel Biel and other Nominalist theologians, that "to those who do what is in them God will not deny grace." This whole paragraph is only in the Latin version.

67. In the German version, Luther uses the phrases "to believe firmly" and "to trust." In Latin, he uses "to believe" (*credere*) and "faith" (*fides*). Already here Luther is moving from law (commands that reveal and condemn sin) to gospel (promises that provide faith in Christ), a central part of his theology. See below, p. 494.

x   An allusion to 1 Kgs. 18:21, Elijah's mocking of the priests of Baal.

y   Job 31:27, which contrasts worship of God to worship of gold, nature, or the self.

z   Reading with the Vulgate.

A Human Being Is Justified by No External Work

Because this faith can only rule the inner person, as Rom. 10[:10] says ("one believes with the heart and so is justified"), and because this faith alone justifies, it is clear that the inner person cannot be justified, freed, or saved by any external work or activity at all and that no works whatever have anything to do with the inner person. In the same way, on the other hand, the inner person becomes guilty and a condemned slave of sin only by ungodliness and unbelief of the heart and not by any external sin or work. It follows that the primary concern of each and every Christian ought to be that, by putting aside the supposition about works, they strengthen faith alone more and more and through that faith "grow . . . in knowledge" not of works but "of Christ Jesus," who suffered and rose again for them, as Peter in 2 Pet. 3[:18] teaches.[a] For no other work makes a Christian. Thus, when the Jews in John 6[:28] asked what they should do to perform the works of God, Christ dismissed their multitude of works, which he realized puffed them up, and prescribed one work for them, saying, "This is the work of God, that you believe in him whom he has sent," for "it is on him that God the Father has set his seal."[b]

Faith Is an Incomparable Treasure

Therefore, true faith in Christ is an incomparable treasure that includes with it complete salvation and protection from all evil, as it says in Mark 16[:16]: "The one who believes and is baptized will be saved; but the one who does not believe will be condemned." Isaiah contemplated this treasure and foretold it in chapter 10[:23, 22]: "The Lord will make an abbreviated and completed word upon earth," and "a

---

a   Literally: "In the last chapter of 1 Peter," leading most editors and translators to refer to 1 Peter 5:10. However, the preceding language comes from the last chapter of 2 Peter (3:18): "But grow in the grace and knowledge of our Lord and Savior Jesus Christ."

b   John 6:29, 27. See the *Treatise on Good Works*, above, p. 267.

completed abbreviation will overflow with righteousness." *c*
It is as if to say, "Faith, which is a compact and complete fulfillment of the law, will fill believers with such righteousness
that they will need nothing else for righteousness." So, too,
Paul says in Rom. 10[:10]: "For one believes with the heart
and so is justified."

Scripture Contains Commands and Promises*d*

You may be asking, however, how it comes about that faith
alone justifies and how it confers so many great treasures
without works, given that so many works, ceremonies,[68]
and laws are prescribed in the Scriptures. I answer this way.
Before all else, remember what has been said above, namely,
that faith alone without works justifies, frees, and saves.
We shall make this clearer in a moment. In the meantime,
it should be pointed out that the entire Scripture of God
is divided into two parts: commands and promises. Commands, to be sure, teach what is good, but what is taught is
not thereby done. For the commands show what we ought
to do but do not give the power to do it. They were instead
established for this: so that they may reveal individuals to
themselves. Through the commands they know their inability to do good, and they despair of their own powers. This
explains why commands are called and indeed are the *old
testament*.[69]

68. Here and in the appendix, Luther uses the word *ceremonies* for all types of religious rules and regulations, not just for liturgical rites.

69. Emphasis added. It would appear that in this context Luther, rather than referring strictly to the books of the Old and New Testaments, equates "old testament" with any part of the Bible that commands something and "new testament" for language that contains God's promises. For Luther's later reflections on the relation between the Old and New Testaments, see *How Christians Should Regard Moses* (1525) in LW 35:155–74.

---

c   Luther paraphrases v. 23 and then v. 22 of the Vulgate, adding
the term "word." The Vulgate reads: "An abbreviated completion
will overflow with righteousness. For the Lord God will make a
completion and an abbreviation of troubles in the midst of all the
earth." The NRSV states: "Destruction is decreed, overflowing with
righteousness. For the Lord God of hosts will make a full end, as
decreed, in all the earth." Here Luther treats this text, which refers to
a remnant of believing Israel that will survive Assyria's destruction,
allegorically.

d   Luther introduced this theme earlier. See p. 492.

All Commands Are Equally Impossible for Us [70]

For example, "you shall not covet"[71,e] is a command that convicts us all of being sinners, because no one can avoid coveting, no matter how hard we might struggle against it. Thus, in order to keep this commandment and not covet, individuals are forced to despair of themselves and to seek help elsewhere from someone else. As it says in Hos. [13:9]: "Destruction is your own, O Israel. Your help is only in me."[f] However, what occurs with this single commandment occurs in the same way with them all. For all of them are equally impossible for us.

The Law Must Be Satisfied

Now, when through the commands individuals have been made aware of their powerlessness and now become anxious about how to satisfy the law (since the law must be satisfied so that "not one letter, not one stroke of a letter, will pass away"[g]—otherwise every person would be condemned without hope), they are then humbled and reduced to nothing in their own eyes. They find nothing in themselves by which to be justified and saved. At this point, the second part of Scripture (God's promises, which announce God's glory) arrives and says: "If you want to fulfill the law, 'You shall not covet,' as the law demands, then look here! Believe in Christ, in whom grace, righteousness, peace, freedom, and all things are promised to you. If you believe, you will have these things; if you do not believe, you will lack them."

We Fulfill Everything through Faith

For what is impossible for you to fulfill using all the works of the law, which though great in number are useless, you will fulfill easily and quickly through faith. Because God the Father has made all things depend on faith, whoever has

70. Luther is contradicting Jerome (c. 347–420), who in debates with Augustine (354–430) insisted that commands could be fulfilled, though not without God's grace.

71. See the discussion of this commandment in Rom. 7:7-13. See Luther's similar explanation of the Romans passage in his 1522 preface to the book for his German translation of the New Testament (LW 35:376–77).

---

e   Exod. 20:17.

f   Luther cites the Vulgate, which mirrors the Greek and Syriac. Following the Hebrew, the NRSV has: "I will destroy you, O Israel; who can help you?"

g   Matt. 5:18.

faith has everything and whoever lacks faith has nothing. "For God has imprisoned all in unbelief, so that he may be merciful to all" (Rom. 11[:32]).[h] Thus, God's promises give what the law demands, so that everything may belong to God alone, both the commands and their fulfillment.

God Alone Commands and Fulfills[72]

God alone commands, and God alone fulfills. Therefore the promises of God pertain to and, indeed, are the *new* testament.[i]

The First Power of Faith

Now since these promises of God are holy, true, righteous, peaceful, and filled with total goodness, what happens is this: The soul that adheres to them with a firm faith is not simply united with them but fully swallowed up by them, so that it not only shares in them but also is saturated and intoxicated by their every power. For if Christ's touch healed, how much more will this tender touch in the spirit—or, better, this ingestion by the word—communicate to the soul all things that belong to the word. Therefore, by this means, through faith alone without works, the word of God justifies the soul and makes it holy, true, peaceful, and free, filled with every blessing and truly made a child of God, just as John 1[:12] says: "To all who . . . believe in his name, he gave power to become the children of God."

From these arguments it is easy to understand the source of faith's singular ability and why any good work—or all of them put together—cannot equal it at all. Why? Because no good work can cling to the word of God or even exist in the soul. Instead, faith alone and the word rule in it. For the word is of such a nature that the soul is formed by it. Just as heated iron glows like fire because of its union with fire, so it is clear that a Christian needs faith for everything and

72. This sentiment echoes Augustine's famous prayer in the *Confessions* X:29: "Give what you command, and command what you will."

---

h Luther cites the Vulgate. NRSV has "in disobedience."

i Emphasis added. See above, p. 494, n. 69.

will have no need of works to be justified. Now if works are unnecessary, then so is the law. If the law is unnecessary, then certainly such a person is free from the law. Moreover, it is true that "the law is not laid down for the righteous."^j So, this is the Christian freedom referred to above, namely, our faith, which does not cause us to be lazy and lead evil lives but instead makes the law and works unnecessary for the righteousness and salvation of the Christian.[73]

73. Here Luther summarizes the first major theme of this tract and hints at the second (p. 510).

The Second Power of Faith

Let this suffice for the first power of faith. Let us now look at the second. Faith functions also in the following way. It honors the one in whom it trusts^k with the most reverent and highest regard possible for this reason: Faith holds the one in whom it trusts to be truthful and deserving.

The Highest Honor

For no honor is equal to attributing truthfulness and righteousness to someone, which is how we honor the one in whom we trust. Could we ascribe to anyone anything greater than truthfulness, righteousness, and absolutely perfect goodness?

The Highest Contempt

Conversely, the greatest contempt is to suspect or to accuse someone publicly of being, in our opinion, a liar and wicked, which we do when we do not trust a person. So when the soul firmly believes the God who promises, it regards God as true and righteous. Nothing can show God greater respect!

---

j   1 Tim. 1:9, cited according to the Vulgate, which mirrors a literal translation of the Greek. NRSV has "for the innocent."

k   The phrase *credere in* (literally, "to believe in") in this paragraph is best rendered "to trust." See Luther's comments on the equivalent German phrase (*glauben an*) in his *A Short Form of the Ten Commandments, Creed and Lord's Prayer* (1520), later printed in his *Personal Prayer Book* (1522) in LW 43:24: "The second kind of faith means believing in God—not just that I believe that what is said about God is true, but that I put my trust in him."

This is the highest worship of God: To bestow on God truthfulness and righteousness and whatever else ought to be ascribed to the One in whom a person trusts. Here the soul submits itself to what God wishes; here it hallows God's name and allows itself to be treated according to God's good pleasure. This is because, clinging to God's promises, the soul does not doubt that God is true, righteous, and wise—the One who will do, arrange, and care for everything in the best possible way.

Perfect Obedience

Is not such a soul completely obedient to God in all things by this very faith? What commandment remains that such obedience has not completely fulfilled? What fulfillment is fuller than obedience in every situation?^{l} However, not works but faith alone offers this obedience.

Rebellion

Conversely, what greater rebellion against God, godlessness, and contempt of God is there than not to believe the One who promises? What is this but either to make God out a liar or to doubt that God is truthful? Or, to put it another way, is this not to ascribe truthfulness to oneself and falsehood and vanity to God? In so doing, is one not denying God and setting oneself up as an idol in one's very heart? Of what good are works done in this state of godlessness, even if they were angelic and apostolic works? Therefore, God rightly "imprisons everything under unbelief," not under anger or lust,^{m} so that people do not imagine that by chaste and gentle works of the law[74] they fulfill the law (granted that such things are civic and human virtues). Such people assume they will be saved, even though they are caught in

74. The opposite of anger and lust. See Luther's commentary on Gal. 5:22 in his *Commentary on Galatians* (1519) in LW 27:377–78, where he condemns works of the law.

---

l   Luther plays on the words for "fulfill," "fulfillment," and "fuller" (*impleverit, plenitudo, plenior*).

m   Referring to Rom. 11:32, cited above.

the sin of unbelief and must thus either seek mercy or be justly condemned.

God Honors Those Who Believe in Him

But when God sees that we ascribe truthfulness to him and by our heart's faith honor him as is his due, then in return God honors us, ascribing to us truthfulness and righteousness on account of this faith. For faith results in truthfulness and righteousness, giving to God his own.[75] Thus, in return God gives glory to our righteousness. For it is true and righteous that God is true and righteous, and to ascribe this to God and to confess it means being true and righteous.[n] As 1 Sam. 2[:30] states: "For the ones who honor me I will honor, and those who despise me shall be treated with contempt." As Paul says in Rom. 4[:3] that Abraham's faith "was reckoned to him as righteousness," because through it he fully gave God the glory. For the same reason, if we believe it will be reckoned to us as righteousness.

The Third Benefit of Faith: Union with the Bridegroom[76,o]

The third incomparable benefit[77] of faith is this: that it unites the soul with Christ, like a bride with a bridegroom. By this "mystery" (as Paul teaches)[p] Christ and the soul are made one flesh. For if they are one flesh and if a true marriage—indeed by far the most perfect marriage of all—is culminated between them (since human marriages are but

---

n   Given the standard definition of justice, *iustus* could be translated here "just" rather than "righteous."

o   Combining consecutive marginal notes from the 2d ed.

p   Luther uses here the term *sacramentum*, found in the Vulgate's translation of Eph. 5:32, applying what was said about the church to the soul. This translation of the Greek *mysterion* led eventually to the designation of certain rites in the church as sacraments (literally, in Latin, "oaths" or "vows" but also "mysteries"). First, in the 1522 German translation of the New Testament, Luther renders the phrase "secret" (*Geheimnis*), in line with the Greek, while adding a marginal comment noting the Latin and Greek words.

75. Throughout this discussion of faith's second power, Luther uses a standard definition of *iustitia* (righteousness or justice), proposed by Aristotle (384–322 BCE) and employed by Cicero and the Latin legal tradition, as "giving to each his [or her] own." Here, however, by attributing to God truth and righteousness (literally, "God's own"), the soul then receives them back from God as a divine gift. See also his preface to Romans in his translation of the New Testament (1522), in LW 35:371.

76. Luther borrows the marital image not only from Ephesians 5 and traditional Christian interpretations of the Song of Songs but more directly from Augustine's *Expositions on the Book of Psalms*, which Luther used in his lectures on the Psalms from 1513 to 1515. See, e.g., Augustine's comments on Ps. 38:3 (Vulgate: 37), par. 5 (English translation in NPNF ser. 1, 14 vols., 8:104), and Luther's glosses on the same psalm (WA 55/1:329). The union of the soul and Christ is also found in many medieval thinkers, including Bernard of Clairvaux and Johannes Tauler (c. 1300–1361).

77. In keeping with medieval usage, Luther can still use the word grace (*gratia*; here translated as "benefit") as a "bestowed power" and thus a synonym of the word *virtus*, the term for the first two "powers" of faith. By 1521 he would accept Erasmus's argument that in the Greek New Testament the word *charis* (traditionally translated *gratia*) means God's favor (*favor Dei*) or, as the Wittenberg reformers often rendered it, God's mercy (*misericordia Dei*). For

Luther's early, still critical comments on Erasmus's proposal, see the commentary on Galatians (1519) in LW 27:252; and for his acceptance of it two years later, see the tract *Against Latomus* (1521) in LW 32:226-28.

78. Luther uses this traditional language about the marriage of Christ and the soul to illustrate his understanding of justification by faith. Roman marriage law distinguished between property (what one owned) and possession (what one had full use of) and held that in marriage the property of the one spouse became the possession of the other and vice versa. Similarly, Luther argues here and in the ensuing paragraphs that what is Christ's own (grace, life, and salvation) becomes the soul's and what is the soul's own (sin, death, and damnation) becomes Christ's, all by the marriage of faith. Luther first published his thoughts on this "joyous exchange" (the phrase used in the German version of *The Freedom of a Christian*) in *Two Kinds of Righteousness* (1519) in LW 31:297-99, a forerunner to this tract, although he employed it earlier in the lecture hall, pulpit, and correspondence. For one example, see the letter to Georg Spenlein (1486-1563) from 8 April 1516 (LW 48:12-13).

79. Luther's description of the extended metaphor of Christ's battle against sin for his bride is reminiscent of chivalry.

weak shadows of this one), then it follows that they come to hold all things, good and bad, in common. Accordingly, the faithful soul can both assume as its own whatever Christ has and glory in it, and whatever is the soul's Christ claims for himself as his own.[78]

Consider These Invaluable Things!

Let us examine these things in detail to see how invaluable they are. Christ is full of grace, life, and salvation; the soul is full of sins, death, and damnation. Now let faith intervene and it will turn out that sins, death, and hell are Christ's, but grace, life, and salvation are the soul's. For if he is the groom, then he should simultaneously both accept the things belonging to the bride and impart to the bride those things that are his. For the one who gives his body and his very self to her, how does he not give his all? And the one who receives the body of the bride, how does he not take all that is hers?[q]

Love's Duel in Christ

This is truly the most delightful drama,[79,r] involving not only communion but also a saving war, victory, salvation, and redemption. For Christ is God and a human being in one and the same person, who does not and cannot sin, die, or be damned; and his righteousness, life, and salvation are unconquerable, eternal, and all-powerful. When, I say, such a person shares in common and, indeed, takes as his own the sins, death, and hell of the bride on account of the wedding ring of faith, and when he regards them as if they were his own and as if he himself had sinned—suffering, dying, and descending into hell—then, as he conquers them all and as sin, death, and hell cannot devour him, they are devoured by

q   Here, among other things, Luther echoes the language of 1 Cor. 7:4.
r   Latin: *spectaculum*, literally, "a piece of theater."

him in an astounding duel.[80] For his righteousness is superior to all sins, his life more powerful than death, and his salvation more invincible than hell.

The Wedding Ring of Faith for the Bride of Christ

So it happens that the faithful soul, through the wedding ring of its faith in Christ her bridegroom, is free from all sins, secure against death, protected from hell, and given the eternal righteousness, life, and salvation of her bridegroom, Christ. Thus, "he takes to himself a glorious bride without spot or wrinkle . . . making her clean by washing . . . in the word of life,"[s] that is, through faith in the word, life, righteousness, and salvation [of Christ]. As Hos. 2[:19] says, [the Lord] becomes engaged to her "in faith, in mercy and compassion, in righteousness, and judgment."[t]

The Majesty of the Wedding Garments

Who can even begin to appreciate this royal marriage? What can comprehend the riches of this glorious grace? Here, this rich, upstanding bridegroom, Christ, marries this poor, disloyal little prostitute, redeems her from all her evil and adorns her with all his goodness. For now it is impossible for her sins to destroy her, because they have been laid upon Christ and devoured by him. In Christ, her bridegroom, she has her righteousness, which she can enjoy as her very own property. And with confidence she can set this righteousness over against all of her sins and in opposition to death and hell and can say, "Sure, I have sinned, but my Christ, in whom I trust, has not sinned. All that is his is mine and all that is mine is his." As it says in the Song of Sol. [2:16]: "My beloved is mine, and I am his." This is what Paul says in

80. This image of Christ as victor, popular among many Greek fathers and Augustine, was overshadowed in medieval theology by other explanations. Luther, however, uses this notion throughout his career. For just two examples of many, see his hymn "A Mighty Fortress" or his commentary on Gal. 3:13 (1535) in LW 26:276–91.

---

s   A fairly close rendering of Eph. 5:27a and 26b, leaving out the words "church" and "water."

t   This citation matches the Vulgate: "And I will take you as my wife in righteousness and judgment and in mercy and in compassion, and I will take you as my wife in faith."

1 Cor. 15[:57]: "Thanks be to God, who gives us the victory through our Lord Jesus Christ." But this "victory" is over sin and death, as he notes in the previous verse [v. 56]: "The sting of death is sin, and the power of sin is the law."

Why Ascribe These Things Only to Faith?[u]

From the preceding, you may once again understand why the fulfillment of the law and justification without any works by faith alone may only be ascribed to faith. You observe that the first commandment, "You shall worship one God," is fulfilled by faith alone.[81]

True Worship of God

For even if you were nothing but good works from the soles of your feet to the top of your head, you would still not be righteous, worship God, or fulfill the first commandment, since God cannot be worshiped unless the glory of truth and of complete goodness is ascribed to him, as truly must be due him.

Faith Does Works[v]

But works cannot do this—only faith of the heart can. For not by working but by believing do we glorify God and confess that God is truthful. On this basis, faith alone is the righteousness of a Christian and the fulfilling of all the commandments, because the one who fulfills the first commandment easily fulfills all the works of the others. Now works, being inanimate, cannot glorify God, although they can be done to God's glory if faith is present.[82] At this juncture, however, we are not asking about the kinds of works that are to be done but about the person who does them, who glorifies God and who produces works. This faith of the

---

81. This reflects Luther's interpretation of the first commandment, already expressed earlier in 1520 in his *Treatise on Good Works* (see pp. 267–86) and later in his catechisms of 1529.

82. Luther here distinguishes works, the fruits of faith, which he labels inanimate, from faith itself, which is alive in the heart of the believer. Works for him are an effect of faith; faith is the cause.

---

u This section summarizes Luther's argument regarding the three powers of faith.

v This refers to the second power of faith. See above, p. 497.

heart is the source and substance of all of our righteousness. Thus, it is a blind and dangerous instruction that teaches works must fulfill the commandments, because the commandments must be fulfilled before all works and thus works follow this fulfillment, as we will hear.*w*

The Prerogatives of the Firstborn[83]

In order to examine more closely this grace that our inner person possesses in Christ, it must be realized that God in the Old Testament consecrated to himself all firstborn males. And this birthright was highly prized, giving power over all others with a double honor: priesthood and kingship.[84] The firstborn brother was a priest and ruler over all others. This figure foreshadowed Christ who, as the true and only firstborn of God the Father and of the Virgin Mary, was true king and priest but not according to the flesh and this world.

What Christ's Kingdom and Priesthood Consist In*x*

For his "kingdom is not from this world."*y* He rules over and consecrates heavenly and spiritual things, such as righteousness, truth, wisdom, peace, and salvation. Not that everything on earth and in hell is not subjected to him (otherwise, how could he protect and save us from them?), but his kingdom does not consist in nor is it derived from such things. Similarly, his priesthood does not consist in the external pomp of robes and gestures, as did that human priesthood of Aaron then and as our ecclesiastical priesthood does today. But his consists in spiritual things, through which, in an invisible, heavenly office, he intercedes for us before God, offers himself there, and does all the things that a priest ought to do.

83. Here Luther introduces a new argument. For the law of the primogeniture of priests, see Exod. 13:2. For the primogeniture of kings, see, e.g., the struggle of succession at the time of David's death in 1 Kings 1–2 (esp. 2:22). Luther, following the longstanding practice of the church, views these historical facts in the Old Testament as types or figures, pointing to Christ.

84. Throughout, the word *sacerdos* is translated "priest," a term used in the Old Testament for the official priests and in the New only for Christ or for all believers in him. The word *priest* in English (as in many other European languages) is derived from the Greek word *presbyteros* ("elder").

---

w See the second major theme on p. 510 below.

x Combining two marginal glosses (2d ed.).

y John 18:36.

The Priestly Office

This is how Paul describes him in Hebrews [7], using the figure of Melchizedek.[z] Not only does he pray and intercede for us, but he also teaches us inwardly in the spirit by the living instruction of his Spirit. These two things are properly speaking the offices of a priest that are prefigured by the visible prayers and sermons of human priests.

How Faithful Christians Ought to Be Understood as Priests and Kings[a]

Now, just as Christ by his birthright possessed these two ranks, so he imparts them to and shares them with every believer legally in accord with the marriage described above, where whatever are the bridegroom's belong to the bride. Hence, all of us who trust in Christ are all priests and kings in Christ, as 1 Pet. 2[:9] states: "You are a chosen race, an acquired people, a royal priesthood and a priestly kingdom, so that you may recount the powers of the one who called you from darkness into his marvelous light."[b] The nature of these two ranks is as follows.

The Spiritual Kingdom[c]

First, what pertains to kingship is this: through faith every Christian is exalted over all things and, by virtue of spiritual power, is absolutely lord of all things. Consequently, nothing at all can ever harm such a one to whom, indeed, all things are subject and forced to serve for salvation. Paul states this in Rom. 8[:28]: "We know that all things work together for

---

z   Based upon Genesis 14 and Ps. 110:4. The authorship of Hebrews was contested in the sixteenth century, so that on other occasions Luther admitted that Paul did not write this letter.

a   Combining two marginal glosses (2d ed.).

b   Here Luther follows the Vulgate, replacing "holy nation" with "priestly nation" and "announce" with "recount." Luther also uses this text in his *Address to the Christian Nobility* (p. 382).

c   Mg. (2d ed.), moved slightly to correspond to the text.

good for the elect."[d] He says the same thing in 1 Cor. 3[:21b-23]: "All things are yours, whether . . . life or death or the present or the future . . . and you belong to Christ."

Note!

Now, this does not establish that Christians possess and exercise some sort of secular[e] power over everything—ecclesiastical leaders far and wide are possessed by such madness—for this is something that belongs to kings, princes, and human beings on earth.[f] We see from our daily experience in life that we are subjected to all kinds of things, suffer many things, and even die. Indeed, the more Christian a person is, the more he or she is subject to evils, suffering, or death, as we see in Christ, the firstborn prince himself, and in all his holy brothers [and sisters].

This power, which "rules in the midst of enemies"[g] and is powerful "in the midst of oppression,"[h] is spiritual. This is nothing other than "power made perfect in weakness" so that in "all things . . . I may gain" salvation.[i] In this way, the cross and death are forced to serve me and to work together for salvation. This is a lofty, splendid high rank and a true, omnipotent power and a spiritual sovereignty, in which there is nothing so good or nothing so evil that cannot "work together for good,"[j] if only I believe. Still, because faith alone suffices for salvation, I do not need anything else except for faith exercising its power and sovereignty of freedom in these things. Look here! This is the immeasurable power and freedom of Christians.

---

d NRSV: "for those who love God." Reference to the elect comes in the following verse.

e The word *corporali*, translated "secular," is literally, "bodily" or "physical."

f Luther expanded this distinction in 1523 in *On Secular Authority* (LW 45:75–129).

g Ps. 110:2.

h An allusion to 2 Cor. 4:8 as rendered in Erasmus's Latin translation of the Greek.

i Allusions to 2 Cor. 12:9 and Phil. 3:9.

j Rom. 8:28.

We Are Priests Forever[k]

Not only are we the freest kings of all, but we are also priests forever. This is more excellent by far than kingship, because through the priesthood we are worthy to appear before God, to pray for others, and to teach one another the things that are of God. For these are the priestly duties that absolutely cannot be bestowed on anyone who does not believe. Christ obtained this priesthood for us, if we trust in him, so that as we are confreres, coheirs, corulers, so we are co-priests with him, daring to come with confidence into God's presence in the spirit of faith and cry, "Abba, Father,"[l] to pray for another and to do all the things that we see are done and prefigured by the visible and corporeal office of priests.

Only Evil Comes to Nonbelievers

But nothing serves persons who do not believe, nor does anything "work together for good."[m] Instead, such individuals are slaves of all things and give themselves over to evil, because they use everything wickedly for their own advantage and not to the glory of God. Thus, they are not priests but profane people. Their prayers become sin, nor do they appear in God's presence, because God does not listen to sinners. Who, therefore, can comprehend the height of this Christian rank, which through its regal power is lord of all things—death, life, sin, and the like—but through its priestly glory can do all things before God, because God does what the priest asks and desires? As it is written: "He fulfills the desire of all who fear him; he also hears their cry, and saves them."[n] A person certainly arrives at this glory not by works but by faith alone.

---

k Referring back to Ps. 110:4.

l Rom. 8:15.

m Rom. 8:28. Luther uses the singular ("a" person) throughout this paragraph.

n Ps. 145:19.

The Freedom of Christians[85]

From the foregoing, anyone can clearly see how the Christian is free from all things and is over all things, so that such a person requires no works at all to be righteous or saved. Instead, faith alone bestows all these things in abundance. Now, if someone were so foolish as to presume to be made righteous, free, saved, and Christian through any good work, then such one would immediately lose faith along with all other good things. This foolishness is beautifully illustrated in that fable where a dog runs along a stream holding a piece of real meat in his mouth. When, deceived by the reflection of the meat in the water, the dog tries to get it by opening its mouth and loses both the meat and the reflection.[86]

[A Digression on the Meaning of Priesthood][87]

At this point, you may ask, "If all people in the church are priests, by what name do we distinguish those we now call priests from the laity?" I respond that an injustice has been done to these words—"priest," "cleric," "a spiritual one," and "a churchman"—when they are transferred from all other Christians to those few who now are called by this faulty usage "churchmen."[88] For Holy Scripture does not distinguish at all among them, except that it calls "ministers," "servants" and "stewards" those who now are proudly labeled popes, bishops, and lords but who should be serving others with the ministry of the word in order to teach the faith of Christ and the freedom of the faithful. For, although it is true that we are all equally priests, nevertheless we cannot all serve and teach nor, even if we can, ought we all to do so publicly. As Paul states in 1 Cor. 4[:1]: "Let a person regard us as servants of Christ and dispensers of God's mysteries."*o*

85. This begins the conclusion to the first major theme, which Luther picks up again after the digression on priesthood and then applies it to preaching.

86. Luther filled his writings with allusions to classical sources, including *Aesop's Fables*, as here. His 1530 translation of these fables was published in 1557 (WA 50:432–60).

87. This subtitle was not in any sixteenth-century text. These two paragraphs form a digression from Luther's main argument, in order to discuss the proper meaning of "priest" (*sacerdos*). See also his discussion of what later became known as the "priesthood of all believers" in the *Address to the Christian Nobility* (pp. 382–84).

88. Although his main interest is in the use of the word *priest* (*sacerdos*), Luther employs other common terms for the ordained here: *cleros* ("cleric," a loan word into ecclesiastical Latin from the Greek, designating the clergy), *spiritualis* (a spiritual person [both priests and monks], as opposed to the laity, who live in the world) and *ecclesiasticus* ("ecclesiast," a church official [especially a teacher or preacher], but literally, "one who belongs to the church").

o Reading with the Vulgate.

What the Ministry of Churchmen Has Become

Against this, such "dispensing" has now turned into such a display of power and a terrible tyranny that no national or worldly political power can be compared to it. It is as if the laity were something other than Christians. As a result of this perversity, the knowledge of Christian grace, faith, freedom, and Christ has perished entirely, only to be replaced by an intolerable captivity to human works and laws. As the Lamentations of Jeremiah puts it, we have become slaves of the vilest possible people on earth, who abuse our misery in all baseness and degradation of their desire.*p*

How Christ Must Be Preached

To return to my main topic, I believe that it has become clear that it is not sufficient or even Christian if, as those who are the very best preachers today do, we only preach Christ's works, life, and words just as a kind of story or as historical exploits (which would be enough to know for an example of how to conduct our lives). Much worse is when there is complete silence about Christ and human laws, and the decrees of the fathers[89] are taught instead of Christ. Moreover, some even preach Christ and recite stories about him for this purpose: to play on human emotions either to arouse sympathy for him or to incite anger against the Jews.[90] This kind of thing is simply childish and womanish nonsense.[91] Preaching, however, ought to serve this goal: that faith in Christ is promoted. Then he is not simply "Christ" but "Christ for you and me," and what we say about him and call him affect us.[92] This faith is born and preserved by preaching why Christ came, what he brought and gave, and what are the needs and the fruit that his reception entail. This kind of preaching occurs where Christian freedom, which we gain from him and which makes us Christians all kings and priests, is rightly taught. In him we are lords of all, and we trust that whatever we might do is pleasing and acceptable in God's sight, as we said above.

89. Luther was probably thinking of canon law, the church rules from ancient and medieval teachers, popes, and councils that regulated the practice of penance, marriage, and all other aspects of church life.

90. For Luther's earlier criticism of this kind of preaching during Holy Week, see *A Meditation on Christ's Passion* (p. 169).

91. Luther assumes, as did most men of his time (following Aristotle among others), that the emotions of children and women are especially easily manipulated by such preaching.

92. Luther reflects this conviction in comments about Christ in his catechisms, where he speaks of Christ as "my Lord, who redeemed me."

p Perhaps an allusion to Lamentations 1 or to the entire book.

The Fruit of the Best Preaching[q]

What person's heart upon hearing these things would not rejoice from its very core and upon accepting such consolation would not melt[r] in love with Christ—something completely unattainable with laws and works? Who could possibly harm or frighten such a heart? If awareness of sin or dread of death overwhelms it, it is ready to hope in the Lord. It neither fears hearing about these evils nor is moved by them, until finally it despises its enemies.[s] For it believes that Christ's righteousness is its own and that its sin is now not its own but Christ's. More than that, the presence[t] of Christ's righteousness swallows up every sin. As noted above, this is a necessary consequence of faith in Christ. So the heart learns with the Apostle to scoff at death and sin and to say: "Where, O death, is your victory? Where, O death, is your sting? The sting of death is sin, and the power of sin is the law. But thanks be to God, who gives us the victory through our Lord Jesus Christ."[u] For death is swallowed up in victory—not only Christ's but ours—because through faith it becomes our victory and is in us and we are conquerors.

In a scene from the 1530 edition of the *Large Catechism* printed in Wittenberg, a preacher addresses a congregation from the pulpit, illustrating the petition in the Lord's Prayer, "Hallowed be your name."

q   Luther moves from what preaching is to its effects.

r   Literally, "become sweet."

s   Perhaps an allusion to Ps. 110:1.

t   Literally, "face."

u   1 Cor. 15:55-57.

Enough now has been said about the inner person, its freedom and its origin in the righteousness of faith. This inner person requires neither laws nor good works, which are harmful to it whenever someone presumes to be justified through them.

[The Outer Person]⁹³, ᵛ

Let us now turn to the second part, which concerns the outer person. Here we will respond to all those people who are offended by the word of faith and what has been said about it. They say, "If faith does all things and alone suffices for righteousness, why then are good works commanded? We will therefore be content with faith, take our ease and do no works." I respond, "Not so, you wicked people, not so!"⁹⁴ To be sure, this would be true if we were completely and perfectly inner, spiritual persons, which will not happen until the resurrection of the dead on the last day. As long as we live in the flesh, we are only beginning and advancing toward what will be perfected in the future life. The Apostle in Romans 8[:23] calls this the "first fruits of the Spirit," because in this life we will have received only a tenth but in the future life the fullness of the Spirit. So, this part of the essay pertains to what was said at the beginning: The Christian is a slave of all and subject to all.ʷ Insofar as a Christian is free, he or she does nothing; insofar as the Christian is a slave, he or she does all things. Now we shall see how this can happen.

To be sure, as I have said, the inner person is in the spirit fully and completely justified through faith. Such a one has what he or she ought to have, except of course that this very faith and its riches ought to increase day by day toward the future life. For now, however, this person remains in this

---

93. This begins the second main section of the tract on the second of the two themes introduced above (p. 489).

94. Luther is attacking moralistic opponents for pretending to make this argument as a way of destroying Christian freedom.

ᵛ   This subtitle was not in any sixteenth-century text. Instead, the marginal gloss in the second edition reads: "A question from those who do not understand Luther—or rather—what faith is."

ʷ   See above, p. 488.

mortal life on earth. In this life a person's own body must be ruled and be in relation with other human beings.

Where Works Begin [95]

Now here is where works begin. Here is not the time for leisure; here care must be taken to train the body by means of fasting, vigils, and other labors and to subdue it by the spirit.[96] In this way it may obey and be conformed to the inner person and faith, so that it may not rebel against or impede the inner person (as is its nature when not held in check).

The Single Concern of the Inner Person

For the inner person—conformed to God and created in the image of God through faith—is joyful and glad on account of Christ, in whom all good things have been conferred upon such a one. Because of this, that person has only one concern: to serve God joyfully, with boundless love and with no thought of earning anything. While acting this way, immediately the inner creature offends a contrary will in its own flesh, one that serves the world and tries seeking after what belongs to it. Because the spirit of faith cannot tolerate this at all, it attempts with joyful zeal to suppress and coerce the flesh. As Paul says in Rom. 7[:22-23]: "I delight in the law of God according to my inner person,ˣ but I see in my members another law fighting against the law of my mind and making me captive to the law of sin." In another place,ʸ he writes, "I punish my body and enslave it, so that after proclaiming to others I myself should not be disqualified." And in Gal. 5[:24] he states, "And those who belong to Christ Jesus have crucified the flesh with its passions and desires."[97]

95. Here begins the first part of the second major theme on discipline of the flesh and works in general. For the second part (on love of neighbor), see below, p. 519.

96. Luther alludes to common practices of the day designed to restrain the flesh.

97. Throughout this section, Luther uses the technical term *concupiscentia*, translated here "desire." Concupiscence was said by medieval theologians to be the "matter" of sin that remained after baptism. Without the "form" of the willing conscience willing a sinful act, it was not viewed as sin. Luther and Reformation theologians rejected the imposition of medieval Aristotelian categories and insisted that such desires were themselves already sin. Thus, already in the lectures on Romans (1515–1516), in LW 25:336, and throughout his career (e.g., in the commentary on Galatians [1535] in LW 26:232), Luther declared that the justified person was *simul iustus et peccator* (at the same time justified and sinner).

ˣ   Reading with the Vulgate.
ʸ   1 Cor. 9:27.

Under What Supposition Are Works to Be Done?

These works, however, ought not to be done under the supposition that through them a person is justified before God. For faith, which alone is righteousness before God, does not endure this false opinion but supposes [that works be done] only so that "the body may be enslaved" and may be purified from its evil "passions and desires" so that the eye may not turn again to these expunged desires.[z] Because the soul has been cleansed through faith and made to love God, at the same time it wants all things (in particular the body) to be cleansed, so that all things may love and praise God with it. As a result, the human creature cannot be idle because of the demands of its body, and, because of the body, it attempts to do many good things to bring it under control. Nevertheless, these works are not what justify someone before God. Instead, the person does them in compliance to God out of spontaneous love, considering nothing else than the divine favor to which the person wishes to comply most dutifully in all things.

How to Discipline the Body

For this reason, all individuals[a] can easily figure out for themselves the "measure or discretion" (as people call it)[98,b] to which they ought to discipline their bodies. For they may only fast, perform vigils, and labor to the extent that they see it to be necessary for suppressing the body's wantonness and desire. Those who presume to be justified by works, however, have no regard for extinguishing[c] desires but only for the works themselves. They suppose that if they do so many great works, then they will fare well and be made righteous—sometimes even injuring their minds and destroying or at least rendering useless what makes them human. Wanting

98. Here Luther uses traditional language in relation to the freedom of faith, allowing the individual believer, not the confessor, to determine how much to discipline the body. See already his *Treatise on Good Works*, above, p. 324.

---

z   Cf. 1 Cor. 9:27; Gal. 5:24; and 1 John 2:16.

a   In the singular in the original.

b   Latin: *mensura aut discretio*. This phrase is found in medieval books on virtues and vices and in medieval penitential manuals.

c   Latin: *mortificatio*.

to be justified and saved through works without faith is simply monstrous foolishness and ignorance of the Christian life and faith!

An Excellent Analogy

So that we may make it easier to understand what we have said, let us illustrate these things with some analogies. The works of Christian individuals,[d] who are justified and saved through their faith by the pure and gracious mercy of God, ought not be considered from any other perspective than would be the works of Adam and Eve and their children had they not sinned. This is talked about in Gen. 2[:15]: God "placed the man," whom he had formed, "in paradise . . . so that he might work and take care of it."[e] Now, God created Adam to be righteous, upright, and without sin, so that through his work and care he had no need to be justified or made upright. Rather, so that he would not become idle, the Lord gave him a job, namely, that he care for and watch over paradise. These were truly the freest works, done neither "to make [a person] acceptable to anyone"[99] (except to divine favor) nor to obtain righteousness, which Adam already had fully and which would have been inborn in all of us.

Faith Puts a Person Back in Paradise

It is the same way with works of believing individuals,[f] who through their faith are once again put back in paradise and recreated from scratch. They would not do works to become or to be righteous but in order not to be idle and "to work and watch over" their bodies. For them these works arise

In this engraving from a 1545 Leipzig publication of Luther's *Small Catechism*, God is shown marrying Adam and Eve.

99. Medieval theologians defined justifying grace as *gratia gratum faciens*, the grace that makes acceptable, namely, by infusing a disposition (*habitus*) of love (*charitas*) into the soul and thus moving the soul from a state of mortal sin into a state of grace. Such a person then did good works acceptable to God.

---

d Singular in the original text.

e Cited according to the Vulgate.

f In the singular throughout this paragraph in the original.

from the same freedom [as Adam's], done only in consideration of divine favor—except that we are not yet fully recreated with perfect faith and love, which ought to increase not through works but through themselves.

Another Comparison

Here is another analogy. When a consecrated bishop dedicates a church building, confirms children, or performs some other duty pertaining to his office, he is not consecrated into office by performing these very works. Far from it! Unless he had already been consecrated a bishop beforehand, all of these works would be worthless; they would instead be foolish, childish, and silly. So also individual Christians,[g] who are consecrated by their faith, do good works, but through them they are not made holy[h] or Christian. For this arises from faith alone; indeed, unless they believed and were Christian beforehand, all of their works would be worthless and would be truly ungodly and damnable sins.

Two Statements Worth Remembering

Therefore, these two sayings are true: "Good works do not make a person good, but a good person does good works," and "Evil[i] works do not make a person evil, but an evil person does evil works." Thus, a person's essence or character must be good before all works, and good works follow and proceed from a good person.[100]

A Comparison

As Christ also says, "A good tree cannot bear bad fruit, nor can a bad tree bear good fruit."[j] It is obvious that fruit do not bear a tree nor does a tree grow on fruit, but just the reverse: trees bear fruit and fruit grow on trees. Therefore, just as it is necessary that trees exist prior to their fruit and

100. This is against the notion in Aristotelian ethics, followed by medieval theologians, that a person becomes good by doing good.

---

g   In the singular throughout this paragraph in the original text.

h   The same adjective translated "consecrated" above.

i   In these paragraphs the Latin *malum* is translated either "evil" or "bad," depending on the context.

j   Matt. 7:18.

that fruit make trees neither good nor bad, but that, on the contrary, specific kinds of trees make specific kinds of fruit, so it is necessary that first the very character of a person be good or evil before doing any good or evil work and that a person's works do not make one evil or good but rather that a person does evil or good works.

Another Comparison

Similar things can be seen in construction. A good or bad house does not make a good or bad builder, but a good or bad builder makes a good or bad house. As a general rule, no work makes its kind of artisan, but an artisan makes a particular kind of work. This same reality obtains for the works of human beings. Whatever kind of person one is—either in faith or unbelief—that determines one's work: good if done in faith, evil if done in unbelief. But this may not be reversed: as if whatever the kind of work determines the kind of human being—either in faith or unbelief. For just as works do not make someone a believer,[k] so also they do not make a person righteous. On the contrary, just as faith makes someone a believer and righteous, so also it produces good works.

Faith Alone Justifies

Since, therefore, works do not justify anyone and a person must be righteous before doing something good, these things are absolutely clear: that faith alone—because of the sheer mercy of God through Christ [given] in his word—properly and completely justifies and saves a person; and that no law is necessary for a Christian's salvation, since through faith one is free from every law and does everything that is done spontaneously, out of sheer freedom. Such a person seeks nothing for a payment or for salvation—already being satisfied and saved by God's grace from one's faith—but seeks only what pleases God.

k   See above, p. 493.

Unbelievers Do Not Become Evil by Works

In the same way, no good work of an unbeliever contributes toward righteousness or salvation. On the other side, no evil work makes an unbeliever evil or damnable. Instead, unbelief, which makes an evil person and tree, does evil and damnable works. Thus, when someone is good or evil, this arises not from works but from faith or unbelief, as Sir. [10:14] says, "This is the beginning of sin, that a person falls away from God," that is, "does not believe." Paul states in Hebrews 11[:6]: "For whoever would approach God must believe." And Christ says the same thing: "Either make the tree good, and its fruit good; or make the tree bad and its fruit bad,"[l] as if he were saying, "Let whoever wants to have good fruit begin with the tree and plant a good one." Therefore, let whoever wants to do good things begin not with the doing but with the believing. For only faith makes a person good, and only unbelief makes someone evil.

Works Make a Human Being Good but Only in Human Eyes

To be sure, it is true that in the eyes of other human beings, works make a human being good or evil. But this happens the same way as when it is known or shown that someone is good or evil, as Christ says in Matt. 7[:20], "You will know them by their fruits." But all of this remains external and on the surface, which is just where many who presume to write and teach about "the good works by which we are justified"[101] are led astray.

The Source of Some Peoples' Error

Meanwhile, they do not even mention faith: going their false ways,[m] always leading astray, "progressing from bad to worse,"[n] "the blind leading the blind,"[o] wearying themselves

---

101. Luther has in mind especially Gabriel Biel (c. 1420–1495) and Luther's own opponents who followed Biel's argument that a person merited justifying grace. See Heiko A. Oberman, *Harvest of Medieval Theology: Gabriel Biel and Late Medieval Nominalism*, 3d ed. (Durham, NC: Labyrinth, 1983), 141, esp. n.66.

---

l   Matt. 12:23.

m   Echoing biblical condemnations, as in 2 Kgs. 8:18.

n   Paraphrasing 2 Tim. 3:13.

o   Matt. 15:14.

with many works and still never arriving at the true righteousness. Paul speaks about these people in 2 Tim. 3[:5, 7]: "Holding to the outward form of godliness but denying its power . . . who are always being instructed and can never arrive at knowledge of the truth."

Therefore, whoever does not want to fall into the same error with these blind people must look beyond works, laws, and teachings about works. More than that, one must focus on the person completely apart from works and on how such a one is justified. A person is justified and saved not by works or laws but by the Word of God (that is, by the promise of God's grace) and by faith. In this way, what remains firm is the glory of the divine majesty, which saves us who believe not by works of righteousness that we do but in accord with God's mercy through the word of his grace.

Rules for Understanding the Teachings of Many People Today

From all that has been said, it is easy to understand on what grounds good works must be rejected or accepted and by what rule everyone's current teachings about good works must be evaluated. For if works are coupled with righteousness and by that perverse Leviathan[102, p] and false persuasion take on such a character that you presume to be justified through them, then they become absolutely compulsory and extinguish freedom along with faith. By this kind of linkage, such works are no longer good but instead truly damnable. For they are not free, and they blaspheme against the grace of God, to whom alone belong justification and salvation through faith. What works are powerless to guarantee, they nevertheless pretend to do by this godless presumption and through this foolishness of ours, and thereby they intrude violently into the function of grace and its glory.

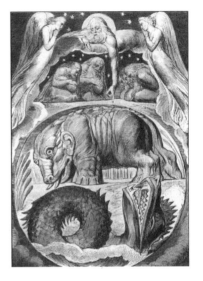

Leviathan and Behemoth.

102. As had medieval interpreters and even the Hebraist Johannes Reuchlin (1455–1522), Luther identifies Leviathan (a monster made up of a perverse mixture of parts) with the combination of sins or improper teachings prompted by the devil. See, e.g., the reference in his earliest lectures on the Psalms (1513–1515) in LW 10:273.

p See Job 41; Isa. 27:1; Pss. 74:14; 104:26; and Job 3:8.

The Basis of Luther's Teaching[q]

Therefore, we do not reject good works. On the contrary, we highly cherish and teach them. For we do not condemn them for their own sake but on account of this godless linkage and perverse opinion that try to seek righteousness [through them]. This makes them appear good on the surface when in reality they are not good. By such works people are deceived and, like ravenous wolves in sheep's clothing, they deceive [others].[r]

The Work of Leviathan

But this Leviathan and perverse opinion about works is impossible to overcome where genuine faith is lacking. These "work-saints" cannot get rid of this [monster] unless faith, its destroyer, comes and rules in the heart. Nature by itself cannot drive it out and, worse yet, cannot even recognize it but rather considers it the ground for the holiest of desires. In this situation, if (as godless teachers have done) custom invokes and strengthens this depravity of nature, it becomes an incurable evil that seduces and destroys countless people irreparably. Thus, while it is fine to preach and write about penitence, confession, and satisfaction,[103] nevertheless, they are without a doubt deceptive and diabolical teachings when placed here [with works] and not derived from faith as taught above.[104] For this is why Christ, like John [the Baptist], did not only say, "Repent,"[s] but added the word of faith, saying: "The kingdom of heaven has come near."[t]

Faith Ought to Be Awakened in Preaching

For we must preach not only one word of God but both, "bringing forth new and old from the treasure"[u]—both the

103. Here Luther is referring to the three parts of the sacrament of penance: contrition (sorrow for sin out of love of God), (private) confession, and (works of) satisfaction. For the first part he uses the more general term, *poenitentia*, which can refer either to the entire sacrament or to the sinner's penitence. For the role of penance in the origins of the Reformation, see above, pp. 13–16.

104. This reframes Luther's basic argument in the first four of the *95 Theses*. See above, p. 34f.

q   The second of several marginal glosses from the second edition referring to Luther in the third person. See above, p. 510, note *v*.

r   See Matt. 7:15.

s   In the Latin Vulgate, the text (*poenitentiam agite*) may be translated either "Do penance" or "Repent."

t   Matt. 4:17, also quoted in the *95 Theses*, thesis 1. See above, p. 34.

u   Matt. 13:52. In contrast, medieval commentators interpreted "old and new" as the Old and New Testaments. See above, p. 494, n. 94.

voice of the law and the word of grace. The voice of the law ought to be "brought forth" so that people may be terrified and led to a knowledge of their sins and thereby directed toward repentance[v] and a better basis for life. But the word must not stop here. For this would be only "to wound" and not "to bind up"; "to strike down" and not "to heal"; "to kill" and not "to make alive"; "to lead into hell" and not "to lead out"; "to humble" but not "to exalt."[w] Therefore, the word of grace and promised forgiveness ought also to be preached in order to instruct and awaken faith. Without this other word [of grace], law, contrition, penitence, and everything else are done and taught in vain.

The Origin of Repentance and Faith

To be sure, preachers of repentance and grace are still around, but they do not explain God's law and promise in light of their purpose and spirit, so that people can find out where repentance and grace come from. For repentance arises from God's law, but faith or grace come from the promise of God, as Rom. 10[:17] states: "So faith comes from what is heard, and what is heard comes through the word of Christ." It happens like this: A person, who has been humbled by the threats and fear of the divine law and led to self-knowledge, is consoled and raised up through faith in the divine promise. As Psalm 30[:6] says, "Weeping may linger for the night, but joy comes with the morning."

Concerning Works for the Neighbor[105]

Up to now we have spoken about works in general and, at the same time, about those specific things that a Christian must do to train his or her own body. Finally, we will discuss those things done for one's neighbor. For a human being does not live in this mortal body solely for himself or herself and work only on it but lives together with all other human

105. What follows constitutes a second major section of this part of the tract. For the first section (on discipline of the flesh), see above, p. 511.

---

v   Latin: *poenitentia*, a word that may be translated as "repentance," "penitence," or the "sacrament of penance."

w   A combination of Deut. 32:39; 1 Sam. 2:6-7; and Hos. 6:1.

106. Luther's references to Phil. 2 throughout the tract suggest its origins as a sermon on the epistle for Palm Sunday. See p. 489, n. 58.

107. "Afterward she [Wisdom] appeared on earth and lived with humankind." Already the ancient church associated references to Wisdom (here and in Prov. 8) with Christ. Luther accorded some authority to the Apocrypha, and his complete translation of the Bible into German, first published in 1534, always included the Apocrypha, although his introduction to Baruch in LW 35:349–50 is rather harsh.

beings on earth. Indeed, more to the point, each person lives only for others and not for himself or herself. The purpose of putting the body in subjection is so that it can serve others more genuinely and more freely. As Paul says in Rom. 14[:7-8], "We do not live to ourselves. If we live, we live to the Lord, and if we die, we die to the Lord." Thus, it can never happen that in this life a person is idle and without works toward one's neighbors. For it is necessary to speak, act, and live with other human beings, just as Christ was "made in human likeness and found in human form"[106],[x] and "lived with humankind," as Bar. 3[:37] says.[107]

Serving All People

Nevertheless, no one needs even one of these works to attain righteousness and salvation. For this reason, in all of one's works a person should in this context be shaped by and contemplate this thought alone: to serve and benefit others in everything that may be done, having nothing else in view except the need and advantage of the neighbor. So the Apostle commands that "we work with our hands so that we may give to those in need."[y] Although he could have said, "so that we may support ourselves," he said instead, "give to those in need."

Why the Body Must Be Taken Care Of

For, under these circumstances, it is also Christian to care for the body. At times when the body is healthy and fit, we can work and save money and thereby can protect and support those who are in need. In this way, the stronger members may serve the weaker[z] and we may be sons [and daughters] of God: one person caring and working for another, "bearing

---

x   Phil. 2:7, according to the Latin Vulgate.

y   Luther here paraphrases the Latin Vulgate of Eph. 4:28. The Vulgate reads: "Let [the former thief] labor by working with his hands, which is a good thing, so that he may have a source from which he might contribute to the one who suffers need."

z   Luther was combining images from Rom. 14 and 1 Cor. 8–9, 12.

one another's burdens and so fulfilling the law of Christ."[a] Look here! This is truly the Christian life; here truly "faith is effective through love."[108] That is, with joy and love [faith] reveals itself in work of freest servitude, as one person, abundantly filled with the completeness and richness of his or her own faith, serves another freely and willingly.

The Christian Life

Thus, after Paul had taught the Philippians how they were made rich through faith in Christ (in which faith they had obtained all things), he then teaches them by saying, "If then there is any encouragement in Christ, any consolation from love, any sharing in the Spirit, any compassion and sympathy, make my joy complete: be of the same mind, having the same love, being in full accord and of one mind. Do nothing from selfish ambition or conceit but in humility regard others as better than yourselves. Let each of you look not to your own interests but to the interests of others."[b] Here we see clearly that the Apostle places the life of Christians into this framework,[c] so that all of our works may be ordered toward the advantage of others. Since each and every person thus thrives through their own faith—so that all other works and the sum total of life flows out from that very faith—by these works each may serve and benefit the neighbor with willing benevolence. To this end, Paul introduces Christ as an example, stating: "Let the same mind be in you that was also in Christ Jesus, who, though he was in the form of God, did not regard himself to be equal to God, but emptied himself, taking the form of a servant, made in human likeness, and being found in human vesture . . . became obedient to the point of death."[d]

108. Luther's own rendering of Gal. 5:6. The Vulgate's "faith which works through love" (*fides per charitatem operatur*) led to the medieval insistence that love (*caritas*) provided the (Aristotelian) "form" for the material of faith. Luther not only uses the word *efficax* ("efficacious") but also, following Erasmus, *dilectio* ("ardent love") for *caritas*. See his discussion of this verse in the commentary on Galatians (1519) in LW 27:335–36.

---

a   Gal. 6:2.
b   Phil. 2:1-4. This precedes the biblical text on which the original sermon may have been based. See p. 489, n. 58.
c   Latin: *regula* (rule).
d   Phil. 2:5-8, according to the Vulgate.

109. The christological interpretation of Phil. 2 was standard from the time of the ancient church. Luther here is complaining that applying this verse only to the doctrine of Christ's two natures loses sight of its relation to the life of faith.

Perverters of Apostolic Teaching

To be sure, those who have completely misunderstood the apostolic vocabulary ("form of God," "form of a servant," "vesture," "human likeness") and have transferred it to the divine and human natures [of Christ] have obscured for us this most salutary word of the Apostle—even though Paul wanted to say the following.[109] Although Christ was filled with "the form of God" and abounded in all good things—so that he required no work or suffering in order to be righteous and saved (for he possessed all these things right from the very beginning)—nevertheless he was not puffed up by these things nor did he raise himself above us and arrogate to himself some kind of power over us, even though he could by rights have done so. But he acted contrary to this: living, working, suffering, and dying just like other humans, and in "vesture" and action he was nothing other than a human being, as if he lacked all of these things and possessed nothing of God's "forms." Yet he did all of this for our sake, in order to serve us and in order that all things that he had accomplished in the "form of a servant" might become ours.

Let the Christian Be Conformed to Christ

As Christ, their head, was rich and full through his faith, so each and every Christian ought to be content with this "form of God" obtained through faith, except that (as I have said) this very faith ought to increase until it is made perfect. For this faith is one's life, righteousness, and salvation: preserving and making each person acceptable and giving the Christian all things that Christ possesses, as stated above.[e] Paul also confirms this in Gal. 2[:20] when he says, "And the life I now live in the flesh I live by faith in the Son of God." Although individual Christians[f] are thereby free from all works, they should nevertheless once again "humble themselves" in this freedom, take on "the form of a servant," "be made in human form and found in human vesture," and serve, help, and do everything for their neighbor, just as they

e   See p. 499.

f   Singular in the original throughout this paragraph.

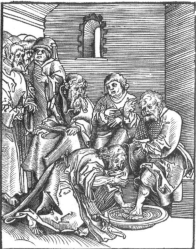

Jesus washing his disciples' feet contrasted with the pope's feet being kissed
from the Passion of Christ and Antichrist (1521). See also pp. 417–18.

see God has done and does with them through Christ. And
they should do this freely, having regard for nothing except
divine approval.

Christian Trust

Moreover, a Christian should think as follows: "Although
I am unworthy and condemned, in Christ my God devotes
to my insignificant person, without any merit and by sheer
gracious mercy, all the riches of righteousness and salvation,
so that I need absolutely nothing else further except faith,
which believes that it is so. Thus, to such a Father as this,
who overwhelms me with these his inestimable riches, why

should I not freely, joyfully, with a whole heart and willing eagerness do everything that I know is pleasing and acceptable to him? Therefore, I will give myself as a kind of Christ to my neighbor, just as Christ offered himself to me. I will do nothing in this life except what I see will be necessary, advantageous, and salutary for my neighbor, because through faith I am overflowing with all good things in Christ."

The Fruits of Faith (See, My Reader, How Worthily Luther Is Condemned!)[110]

Look at what love and joy in the Lord[g] flow from faith! Moreover, from love proceeds a joyful, gladsome, and free soul,[111] prepared for willing service to the neighbor, which takes no account of gratitude or ingratitude, praise or blame, profit or loss. For such a soul does not do this so that people may be obligated to it, nor does it distinguish between friends and enemies, nor does it anticipate thankfulness or ingratitude. Instead, it expends itself and what it has in a completely free and happy manner, whether squandering these things on the ungrateful or on the deserving. For as its Father also does—distributing everything to all people abundantly and freely and making "his sun to rise on the evil and on the good,"[h] so the son [or daughter] only does or suffers everything with spontaneous joy, as each person has through Christ been filled with delight in God, the lavish dispenser of all things.

Recognizing How Great the Things Given to Us Are

Therefore, you see that if we recognize those great and precious things that have been given to us, then, as Paul says, "love . . . is poured out in our hearts through the . . . Spirit."[i] By this love we are free, joyful, all-powerful workers and victors over all tribulations, servants of our neighbors and, nev-

110. The papal bull threatening excommunication, *Exsurge Domine*, condemned Luther for saying that the righteous sin in all their good works. See *Defense and Explanation of All the Articles* (1521) in LW 32:83–87.

111. Luther does not usually use this word to designate some more spiritual, less material part of the human being, but as a way of talking about the entire human creature standing before God. See p. 489, n. 59 above.

g   See Phil. 4:4.
h   Matt. 5:45.
i   Rom. 5:5.

ertheless, still lords of all.*j* But for all who do not recognize what has been given to them through Christ, Christ was born in vain, and such people carry on using works, never attaining a taste or sense of the things just described. Therefore, just as our neighbor has need and lacks what we have in abundance, so also we had need before God and lacked God's mercy. For this reason, as our heavenly Father supported us freely in Christ, so also we ought freely to support our neighbor with our body and its actions, and each person ought to become to the other a kind of Christ, so that we may be Christs to one another and be the same Christ in all, that is, truly Christians!

The Glory of the Christian Life

Therefore, who can comprehend the riches and glory of the Christian life? It can do all things and has all things and lacks nothing. It is lord of sin, death, and hell but, at the same time, is servant and obedient and beneficial to all.[112] And yet how terrible it is that in our day this life is unknown! It is neither preached about nor sought after.

Why We Are Called Christians

What is more, we are also completely ignorant of our very name, why we are Christians and bear that name. Without a doubt we are named after Christ—not absent from us but dwelling in us; in other words: provided that we believe in him and that, in turn and mutually, we are a second Christ to one another, doing for our neighbors as Christ does for us.*k* But nowadays, using human doctrines,*l* we are taught to seek nothing but merits, rewards, and the things that are ours, and we have made out of Christ nothing but a slave driver far harsher than Moses.[113], *m*

112. For this contrast, see p. 488f.

113. Luther, following John 1:17, often contrasted "Moses" to Christ as harsh lawgiver to gracious savior. He did not, however, think that there was no grace in the "books of Moses" (Genesis through Deuteronomy). See, e.g., *How Christians Should Regard Moses* (1525) in LW 35:161–74.

j See above, p. 488.
k See Matt. 7:12 and John 13:34.
l See Mark 7:7.
m Latin: *exactor.*

114. Although rejecting the notion that Mary should be worshiped, Luther often pointed to Mary as an example of faith. See his *Commentary on the Magnificat* (written at Wartburg and published in 1522) in LW 21:297–358 and his exposition of the Ave Maria (Hail, Mary) in the *Personal Prayer Book* (1522) in LW 43:39–41. The marginal gloss uses the equivalent of *theotokos*, "Divine God-bearer" (*diva Dei genitrix*).

115. In this section of his argument, Luther provides a series of biblical examples to prove his point.

116. Luther held that Mary had herself conceived Jesus of the Holy Spirit without sin. Thus, she had no need of any purifying sacrifice.

117. Luther uses here a medieval term for court judges, *iustitiarii*, which contains within it the Latin word for righteousness (*iustitia*).

118. Luther uses the term *Magister*, which means teachers in general but in medieval Latin more specifically designated those Scholastic "masters" of theology. Luther takes up Romans 14 on p. 534.

The Holy Mother of God as an Example of Faith[114]

The blessed Virgin provides a preeminent example[115] of this very faith, when (as is written in Luke 2[:22]) she was purified "according to the Law of Moses," as was the custom of all women. Although she was not bound by such a law and had no need of purification,[116] nevertheless, she subjected herself to the law out of free and voluntary love, doing just as other women did, so that she did not offend or disdain them. She was therefore not justified by this work, but as one already righteous, she did it freely and spontaneously. So also our works ought not be done for the purpose of being justified, since—already justified by faith—we ought to do all things freely and joyfully for the sake of others.

Paul Teaches Works

St. Paul also circumcised his disciple Timothy,*n* not because circumcision was necessary for righteousness but rather so that he would not offend or disdain the Jews who were weak in faith and who could not yet grasp faith's freedom. However, on the contrary, when in contempt of this freedom of faith they insisted upon circumcision as necessary for righteousness, he resisted and did not permit Titus to be circumcised (Gal. 2[:3]). For just as he did not want to offend or disdain any person's weakness in faith, yielding to their wishes as appropriate, so also he did not want the freedom of faith to be offended against or disdained by hardened "justices."[117] He took a middle course, sparing the weak as appropriate and always resisting the hardened, so that he might convert everyone to the freedom of faith. Our actions also ought to be done with the same devotion, so that we support the weak in faith (as Rom. 14[:1] teaches) but resist boldly the hardened "masters" of works, about which we will say more below.[118]

n   Acts 16:3.

The Example of Christ the Lord

Moreover, in Matt. 17[:24-27], when a tax payment was demanded from the disciples, Christ discussed with Peter whether or not a king's sons were exempt from paying taxes. But when Peter affirmed that they were exempt, Jesus nevertheless commanded him to go to the sea, saying [v. 27]: "However, so that we do not give offense to them, go to the sea and cast a hook; take the first fish that comes up; and when you open its mouth you will find a coin; take that and give it to them for you and me." This example beautifully supports our argument,[119] in that Christ refers to himself and his own as free sons of the king, who need nothing, and yet he willingly submits and pays the tax. As little as this deed was necessary or useful for righteousness or salvation, so all of his other works and those of his followers contribute nothing to righteousness, since all of these things are a result of righteousness and free, done only as an example and a service to others.

Let All the Religious Understand
and Let Luther Be Your Teacher*o*

The same thing goes for what Paul commands in Rom. 13[:1] and Titus 3[:1], saying, "Let" them "be subject to the governing authorities" and "be ready for every good work"—not that they may be justified through this (since they are already justified by faith) but so that through these things and in the freedom of the Spirit they may serve the authorities, among others, and may obey them out of willing, spontaneous love. The works of all clerical institutions,[120] monasteries, and priests should be of this kind, too. Thus, each would only do works of his own profession and walk of life,[121] in order to work not toward righteousness but, in the first place, toward the subjection of his own body as an example for the sake of others, who have need to discipline their own bodies, too. In the second place, they would

119. A *propositio* meant either the theme of a speech or the major premise of a logic syllogism.

120. Literally, "colleges," a designation for legally constituted groups of clergy supported by a foundation or cathedral for the purpose of performing certain religious observances.

121. Luther uses the Latin *status* here as a synonym for the German *stand*, "station in life" or "walk of life."

o Latin: *religiosi*, a technical term encompassing the ordained (priests and bishops) and those under a vow (monks, nuns, and friars).

also obey others and do their bidding out of spontaneous love. Nevertheless, here the utmost care must be taken, so that a false trust does not presume that such works justify, earn reward, or save—which is all from faith alone, as I have repeatedly said.

A True Christian's Knowledge

Therefore, whoever has this knowledge can easily and without danger manage those countless rules and commands of the pope, bishops, monasteries, churches, princes, and magistrates. Some foolish shepherds[p] insist that these things are all necessary for righteousness and salvation, calling them "commands of the church,"[122] although they are nothing of the kind. For a free Christian will say instead, "I will fast, pray, and do this or that because it is commanded by human beings—not because this is necessary for righteousness or salvation but because in this behavior I may conduct myself toward the pope, bishop, community, this or that magistrate, or my neighbor as an example. I will do or suffer all things, as Christ often did and suffered many things for me—none of which he needed for himself at all, having been "placed under the law" on my account, although he was not under the law.[q] And although tyrants may harm or use force [to effect compliance], it will still not do harm, as long as [what they commanded] was not against God."[123]

Distinguishing Good Shepherds from Evil Ones

From all these examples,[124, r] any person can derive firm judgment and reliable distinction among all works and laws and can recognize who are the blind, foolish shepherds and who are the true and good ones. For any work not directed toward the purpose of either disciplining the body

122. For example, this phrase occurs in Thomas Aquinas, *Summa Theologica* II/II q. 39 a. 1, ad 2 (a discussion of schism in the church), but it was more commonly used in moral theology, which listed five or six precepts of the church that must be followed. Lists might include receiving the Lord's Supper during the Easter season, following appointed fasts, supporting the church monetarily, obeying the church's marriage laws, hearing the Mass on Sundays and holy days, and going to private confession yearly.

123. This double attitude toward authority is reflected in Luther's letter to Pope Leo X, toward whom he tries to demonstrate both obedience and freedom (see above, p. 468). Later he applies this respect toward and limits of authority to secular authority as well. See *On Secular Authority* (1523) in LW 45:81–129.

124. There are four examples beginning with Mary.

---

p   Latin: *pastores.*

q   Some modern versions end the quotation here. Quotation marks were not employed in sixteenth-century printings. The reference is to Gal. 4:4-5.

r   Literally, "things."

or serving the neighbor (as long as the neighbor demands nothing against God) is neither good nor Christian. As a result, I greatly fear that nowadays few if any clerical institutions, monasteries, high altars,[125] or ecclesiastical offices are Christian, along with special fasts and prayers for certain saints. To repeat, I fear that in all of these things nothing is sought after except what has to do with us, because we think that through them our sins are cleansed and salvation is attained. In this way, Christian freedom is completely obliterated, because [this attitude] arises from ignorance of Christian faith and freedom.

Many completely blind shepherds zealously support such ignorance and suppression of freedom, while at the same time inciting and encouraging the people in their devotion by praising these things and inflating them with indulgences,[126] and yet never teaching faith at all.

Advice

Instead, I desire each of you to consider that if you really want to pray, fast, or establish a foundation in churches (as they say),[127] pay attention to whether you are doing it for the purpose of obtaining some temporal or eternal reward!

Be Concerned for Faith Alone

You may harm your faith, which alone offers you all things. For this reason, let faith be your sole concern, so that faith may be increased by exercising it either through works or suffering. Meanwhile, whatever you give, give freely and without reward, so that others may experience increase and reap benefits from you and what is yours. For in this way, you will be truly good and Christian. For what are your good works (which function most fully for bodily discipline) to you, when for yourself you are filled through your faith, in which God gives you all things?[s]

125. Latin: *altaria*. Luther is probably referring to altars reserved for saying Masses for the dead.

126. In late medieval piety and connected with the sacrament of penance, many works, such as special fasts, prayers, or pilgrimages, were made even more meritorious with the addition of specially crafted indulgences. These limited indulgences, designed to encourage a variety of works, differed in scope from the plenary "Peter's Indulgence," which Luther attacks in the *95 Theses*. See above, p. 15f.

127. Luther is referring to the practice of establishing monetary foundations so priests could recite perpetual Masses for one's deceased family members.

s   Luther uses the word *you* (singular: *tu*) five times in this sentence, including *pro te* ("for you").

128. Luther is alluding to the baptismal language of "taking off" and "putting on" found in Col. 3:1-17.

129. Luther reworks the "joyous exchange" (see above, p. 499f.) to describe relations between the believer and the neighbor.

130. This verb begins the concluding section of Luther's tract, similar to the peroration in good Latin rhetoric of the time. It summarizes the chief argument, introduced on p. 488.

131. The *Postilla moralis* of Nicholas of Lyra (1270–1349), provides a similar allegory, in that preachers ascend to the deity of Christ and descend "when they seek the need of the neighbor raised up for their love." For a different interpretation of this text by Luther, in sermons from 1538, see LW 22:200–211.

The Rule for "Brotherly Love"

Look here! This should be the rule: that the good things we have from God may flow from one person to the other and become common property. In this way each person may "put on" his [or her] neighbor[128] and conduct oneself toward him [or her] as if in the neighbor's place. These good things flowed and flow into us from Christ, who put us on and acted for us, as if he himself were what we are. They now flow from us into those who have need of them. Just as my faith and righteousness ought to be placed before God to cover and intercede for the neighbor's sins, which I take upon myself, so also I labor under and am subject to them as if they were my very own.[129] For this is what Christ did for us. For this is true love and the genuine rule of the Christian life. Now where there is true and genuine faith, there is true and genuine love. Hence, the Apostle in 1 Cor. 13[:5] attributes to love that "it does not seek its own."[t]

The Christian Lives in Christ and the Neighbor

Therefore, we conclude[130] that Christian individuals[u] do not live in themselves but in Christ and their neighbor, or else they are not Christian. They live in Christ through faith and in the neighbor through love. Through faith they are caught up beyond themselves into God; likewise through love they fall down beneath themselves into the neighbor—remaining nevertheless always in God and God's love, as Christ says in John 1[:51]: "Very truly I say to you, you will see the heavens opened and the angels of God ascending and descending upon the Son of Man."[131]

Let this suffice concerning that freedom, which, as you see, is spiritual and true, making our hearts free from all sin, laws, and commands, as Paul says in 1 Tim. 1[:9], "The law is not laid down for the righteous person."[v] This freedom is

---

t Following here the more literal Latin Vulgate.

u This is singular in the original throughout this paragraph.

v A literal rendering of the Latin Vulgate and the Greek text.

far above all other external freedoms, as high as heaven is above the earth. May Christ cause us to know and preserve this freedom! Amen.

[Appendix] [132] Against the Freedom of the Flesh[w]

Finally, this must be added because of those for whom nothing can be stated well enough that they cannot distort it by warped understanding—if they could even understand what is said here at all. There are so many people who, when they hear about this freedom of faith, immediately turn it into "an occasion for the flesh."[x] They imagine that straightaway all things are permitted for them, and they want to be free and seem Christian in no other way than by showing contempt and disdain for ceremonies,[y] traditions, and human laws. As if they were Christians precisely because they do not fast on the stated days or because they themselves eat meat while others fast[133] or they refrain from saying the customary prayers! They stick up their noses, make fun of human commands, and hold the other things that in fact pertain to the Christian religion in low esteem.

Against Trust in Works

These people are stubbornly resisted by those who strive for salvation solely by reverent observance of ceremonies—as if they might be saved because they fast on the appointed days or abstain from meat or pray certain prayers. They boast about the precepts of the church and the Fathers while not caring one wit about those things that concern our genuine faith. Both sides are plainly in error, because they are so confused and troubled about unnecessary and silly things while neglecting the more serious things that are necessary for salvation.

132. This marginal word is not in sixteenth-century editions, which simply put a larger space between the preceding and what follows. This appendix, found only in the Latin edition, deals with a persistent charge against Luther and his followers: that their understanding of Christian freedom resulted only in license to sin and, hence, fostered civil disobedience. Dealing with this issue also gives Luther opportunity to attack what he views as his opponents' legalism. Thus, each section, as the marginal notations from the second edition help make clear, deals with both sides of the problem. The Latin here is somewhat more complicated than the preceding, perhaps because of the absence of a German text.

133. In late medieval practice, people were to abstain from meat on certain days (especially Fridays) and seasons (especially Lent)—religious regulations enforced by local authorities. In 1523 in Zurich, eating of meat during Lent by a prominent printer led to the wholesale rejection of episcopal authority and the establishment of an important center for what became Reformed Christianity.

---

w   "Against the Freedom of the Flesh" is from the 2nd ed.

x   Gal. 5:13 according to the Vulgate and Greek text. NRSV: "an opportunity for self-indulgence."

y   For Luther's use of this word throughout this section, see above, p. 494, n. 68.

How much more correct is the Apostle Paul, who teaches taking the middle way and condemns both sides completely when he says, "Those who eat must not despise those who abstain, and those who abstain must not pass judgment on those who eat."[z] You see here that those who neglect or despise ceremonies—not out of a sense of piety but rather out of sheer contempt—are upbraided, since Paul teaches not to condemn, for "knowledge puffs them up."[a] On the other hand, he teaches those other, obstinate people not to judge the former group. For neither side cares about the "love that builds up" the neighbor.[b] Therefore, Scripture must be listened to, which teaches that we "will turn aside neither to the right nor to the left"[c] but will follow "the acceptable righteousness of the Lord that gladdens the heart."[d] For just as no one is righteous by preserving or being a slave to the works and rites of ceremonies, so also no one is deemed righteous by simply omitting and condemning them.

For we are not free from works through faith in Christ but from conjectures about works, that is, from the foolish presumption of justification acquired through works. For faith redeems, makes right, and guards our consciences, so that we realize that righteousness is not in works—although works can and should not be lacking. For example, we cannot exist without food and drink and all the other works of this mortal body, and yet our righteousness is not built upon them but upon faith. Still these things must not be condemned or omitted. Thus, in this world we are bound by the necessities of this bodily life, but we are not righteous because of them. Christ said, "My kingdom is not from this world . . . not from here," but he did not say, "My kingdom is not here in this world."[e] Paul also says, "For though we walk

---

z   Rom. 14:3.
a   Paraphrasing 1 Cor. 8:1.
b   Paraphrasing 1 Cor. 8:1.
c   Paraphrasing Deut. 2:27 and 28:14.
d   Paraphrasing Ps. 19:8.
e   John 18:36.

in the flesh, we do not war according to the flesh."[f] And in Gal. 2[:20] he says, "The life I now live in the flesh I live by faith in the Son of God." Thus, the necessities of life and the need to control the body cause us to act and live and exist with works and ceremonies. Nevertheless, we are righteous not through these things but through faith in the Son of God. For this reason, the same middle way is set out for each Christian, who must also keep in mind these two types of people.

How to Deal with the Stubborn

On the one hand, the Christian encounters the stubborn and obstinate ceremonialists. Like deaf adders,[g] they do not want to hear freedom's truth, but instead they boast about their ceremonies as the means of justification, imperiously commanding and insisting on them quite apart from faith. The Jews of old, who did not want to understand anything about how to behave properly, were like this.[134] Against these people one ought to resist, do the opposite, and boldly offend them, so that they do not mislead many others as well by this ungodly opinion. In their presence it is appropriate to eat meat, to break fasts, and for the freedom of faith to do other things that they take for the greatest of sins. It must be said of them, "Let them alone; they are blind guides of the blind."[h] In line with this, Paul did not want Titus to be circumcised when some demanded it,[i] and Christ defended the apostles because they wanted [to pluck] grain on the Sabbath and in many other instances.[j]

134. As what follows makes clear, Luther had in mind conflicts between Jesus and the Pharisees over keeping the law. See, e.g., Mark 2:1–3:6.

f   2 Cor. 10:3, using the more literal rendering of the Greek, which matches the Latin Vulgate.

g   Ps. 58:4 (see also Mic. 7:16-17).

h   Matt. 15:14.

i   Gal. 2:3.

j   Matt. 12:1-8.

135. A reference to Luther's Roman opponents, especially the priests and bishops.

Regarding the Common Folk

On the other hand, the Christian encounters the simple, un-educated, ignorant, and (as Paul calls them) weak in faith, who cannot yet understand this freedom of faith, even if they want to. Care must be taken not to offend these people but to defer to their weakness until they are more fully instructed. For fasts and other things that they think are necessary must be kept to avoid causing them to fall—not because their actions or thoughts are motivated by deep-seated wickedness but only because they are weak in faith. For love, which seeks to harm no one but only to serve all, demands it. After all, they are weak not by their own fault but by that of their shepherds,[135] who have taken them captive and wickedly beaten them using the snares and rods of their traditions, from which they should have been freed and healed with the teaching of faith and freedom! As the Apostle teaches in [1 Cor. 8:13],[k] "I will never eat meat, so that I may not cause one of them to fall." And he says elsewhere, "I know and am persuaded by the Lord Jesus that nothing is unclean . . . but to anyone who thinks it is unclean it is unclean . . . [and] it is evil for that person who eats to give offense."[l]

Concerning Laws and the Lawgivers

Therefore, although those master teachers of traditions must be boldly resisted and the papal laws, by which they plunder God's people, must be sharply criticized, nevertheless one must refrain from injuring the frightened masses—which those ungodly tyrants hold captive with these very laws—until they may be set free from them. Thus, fight vigorously against the wolves but *for* the sheep and not, in the same breath, against the sheep. Each of you may do this by inveighing against the laws and the lawgivers while at the same time guarding the weak from being offended, until

---

k   The original text refers to Romans 14, the passage Luther cites next.

l   Rom. 14:14, 20, where Luther cites the Vulgate, which provides a more literal rendering of the Greek.

they themselves recognize this tyranny and understand their own freedom. If you desire to exercise your freedom, do it in secret, as Paul says in Rom. 14[:22], "The faith that you have, have for yourself before God." [m] But be careful not to exercise [faith's freedom] before the weak. Contrariwise, before tyrants and stubborn people you may exercise that freedom with contempt and without ever letting up at all. Then they, too, will understand that they are ungodly, that their laws contribute nothing to righteousness, and that, frankly, they did not even have the right to enact them.

For the Young and Untrained

Thus, it is clear that in this life one cannot live without ceremonies and works. Indeed, hotheaded and untrained adolescents need to be held back and guarded by such restraints. Moreover, individual Christians must discipline their bodies with such efforts. The servant of Christ [n] must be wise and faithful, so that he may so rule and teach Christ's people about all these things, so that their conscience and faith are not offended. Otherwise, an opinion or "root of bitterness" may arise in them "and through it many become defiled," as Paul warns in Heb. [12:15].[136] That is to say, "so that, in the absence of faith, they begin to be defiled by the opinion about works, as if they were justified through them." This happens quite easily and defiles many people. Unless faith is constantly inculcated at the same time, it is impossible to avoid the situation where (faith having been silenced) human regulations alone are taught. This has happened today through the pestilent, ungodly, soul-destroying, traditions of our popes and the opinions of our theologians.[137] With an infinite number of souls being dragged to hell by these snares, you can recognize Antichrist.[138]

136. In the sixteenth century, biblical interpreters debated whether Paul wrote Hebrews. Luther was of a divided mind on the subject but here supports the traditional viewpoint.

137. See above, *Address to the Christian Nobility*, p. 430.

138. Luther uses the widespread depiction of the devil, who at the end of time binds the souls of the damned around the neck and leads them into hell. By this stage of the Reformation, Luther was convinced that the Antichrist ruled in Rome and was associated with the institution of the Roman papacy. See, e.g., *On the Papacy in Rome against the Most Celebrated Romanist in Leipzig* (1520), in LW 39:49–104.

---

m Following Luther's citation of the Vulgate, which renders the Greek more literally.

n Latin: *minister Christi*, Luther's favorite designation for the public minister.

Danger in Ceremonies

In conclusion, just as riches endanger poverty; business dealings, honesty; honors, humility; banquets, abstinence; or pleasures, chastity; so also ceremonies endanger the righteousness of faith. Solomon asks, "Can fire be carried in the bosom without burning one's clothes?"[o] And yet, as with riches, business dealings, honors, pleasures, and feasts, so also one must take part in ceremonies—that is, in dangers. To say this as strongly as possible:[p] Just as infant boys need to be attentively caressed at a young woman's bosom, in order that they may not perish (even though as adults it endangers salvation for them to be consorting with young women), so also hotheaded, untrained youth need to be restrained and disciplined by the iron bars of ceremonies, so that their unrestrained heart may not go blindly into corruption. And yet it would be the death of them if they insisted on imagining that justification came from them. Instead, they should be taught that they have been imprisoned in this way not to be righteous or to merit something but so that they would be kept from evil and might more easily be instructed in the righteousness of faith. For, unless their impulsiveness be put in check, they would not put up with such instruction.

The Place for Ceremonies

Thus, ceremonies are to have the same place in the Christian life as a builder's construction plans or an artisan's instructions. They are not prepared to be the substance and lasting part of a building but because without them nothing can be built or made. For they are set aside once the structure is finished. Here you can see that they are not being despised but rather are especially required. What is being despised is a [false] opinion about them: because no one imagines that plans are the real and permanent structure. Who would be so silly that they would care for nothing in life other than

---

o   Prov. 6:27.

p   Latin: *immo*, an adversative much beloved by Luther, who used it to introduce radical or even contrary ideas from what had just been stated. It is similar to the archaic "forsooth" or "nay, verily."

plans that they had most lavishly, carefully, and stubbornly[q] prepared while never thinking about the structure itself and only being pleased with and boasting about their work in making plans and such vain first steps? Would not everybody have pity on such insanity and judge that something great could have been built by this wasted expense? In the same way, we do not despise ceremonies or works but rather especially require them. However, we despise the [false] opinion about works, so that a person may not imagine that they are true righteousness, as hypocrites do. They waste their whole life by tying their life to works, and yet they never arrive at the goal for which works are done. As the Apostle says, they "are always being instructed and can never arrive at knowledge of the truth."[r] For it seems that they want to build and to prepare themselves and yet never actually build anything. So they remain with "the outward form of godliness and do not" attain "its power."[s]

On Hyper-Religious[t] People

All the while these people are pleased with their efforts and dare to judge everyone else whom they do not see glowing with a similar display of works. Instead, had they been filled with faith, by properly using God's gifts (rather than vainly wasting and abusing them) they could have brought about great things for their salvation and the salvation of others. But human nature and natural reason (as they call it)[139] are naturally hyper-religious and, whenever some laws and works are proposed, promptly jump to the conclusion that justification may be attained through them. Added to this, reason is trained and strengthened in this very point of view by the practice of all earthly lawgivers. Therefore, it

139. This term went back to Cicero and was a central concept in Roman law.

---

q   Latin: *pertinacissime*. In this context, Luther means "meticulously," but he is using the same word that he had already used to describe "*stubborn* ceremonialists."

r   2 Tim. 3:7.

s   2 Tim. 3:5.

t   Here and below *superstitiosus* (here translated "hyper-religious") means fixed on one's own unreasonable ideas about religion.

is impossible that by its own powers [reason] may free itself from servitude to this view of works and come into the necessary knowledge of faith's freedom. For this reason, prayer is needed, so that the Lord may "draw us" and make us "*theo-didaktos*," that is, "taught by God."[u] Moreover, as he promised, he will "write the law in our hearts."[v] Otherwise, it is all over for us. For unless God teaches this wisdom hidden in mystery[w] inwardly, [human] nature, because it is offended and regards it as foolish, can only condemn it and judge it to be heretical.[x] What we observe happened to the prophets and Apostles, those godless and blind pontiffs and their flatterers are now doing to me and people like me. In the end, "may God be merciful to us . . . and cause his face to shine upon us, so that we may know his way on earth, among all nations the saving power of the one"[y] who is blessed forever. Amen.

---

u Luther is quoting John 6:44-45, mixing the Latin and Greek text.

v Jer. 31:33.

w See Col. 1:26.

x See 1 Cor. 1:23.

y A close paraphrase of Ps. 67:1-2.

Image Credits

Index of Scriptural References

NEW TESTAMENT

Index of Names

Index of Works
by Martin Luther

Index of Subjects